Finally, a Political Party for the Majority:

The Ameritorians

Lawrence W. Judd

Ameritorian Press
Chicago, Illinois

ISBN 978-0-692-86429-6

To patriots who are underemployed, underpaid, out of work, overworked, or just discouraged by decades of unnecessary economic, technological and military decline in the United States.

TABLE OF CONTENTS

A note from the author i
Preface iii

Part 1: **The Case for a Third Party**

Chapter 1. The Majority Doesn't Like Free Trade and Why 1
Chapter 2. The Washington Consensus 10
Chapter 3. The Media Oligopoly is a Dysfunctional Echo Chamber for the Two Parties and the Special Interests That Both Parties Serve. 13
Chapter 4. The Heritage of the Mount Rushmore Presidents: Prosperity and Strength 28
Chapter 5. Why the Theory of Free Trade Is Scientifically and Logically Invalid 38
Chapter 6. Who and What The Money Power is 62
Chapter 7. The Descent of America: A Story of Weak Presidents and Misguided Priorities 84
Chapter 8. Comparative Advantage is a Bunch of Bananas, Protectionism is a Bushel of Apples. 124
Chapter 9. Don't Be Fooled: Those *Demopublican* Trade Deficits Are Killing Us. 132
Chapter 10. How the Republicans and Democrats Made America the World's Largest Debtor Nation: The Twenty Trillion Dollar National Debt 140
Chapter 11. Recounting The Myths of Free Trade 160

Chapter 12. So... Now What? 167

Part 2: The Building of the Ameritorian Party

Chapter 13. The Who, What, When, Where, and How of Restoring America - and A Bit More On Why We Must Do So 181

Part 3: A Mistake We Must Never Repeat

Chapter 14. How Bush and Cheney *untruthed* us into Iraq 197

Part 4: The Final Chapter

Chapter 15. Why the Ameritorians Are Needed More Than Ever 237

Afterword 244

Short Glossary of Economics Related Terms 245

Index 248

Endnotes 255

A note from the author

This book was conceived long before Donald Trump and Bernie Sanders became candidates for President. Research for the book began in 2010 and continued until the date of publication. Writing began in 2012. A basic manuscript, sans endnotes, was finished in 2014. Additional chapters and endnotes were added in 2015. I anticipated when Barack Obama was elected President that America's trade policy would be a big issue in the 2016 presidential election. I was right about that, but the book was not ready for publication before Donald Trump and Bernie Sanders, who both made trade reform centerpiece issues, began their campaigns.

I decided to wait out the election, find out who the winner was, (Trump or Clinton), and revise the book as needed. I saw no need to edit most of the chapters in this book after the election, but I did add a chapter, (Ch. 15), that discusses the policy prescriptions of Trump and Sanders and the ramifications of their outspoken and welcome criticisms of America's trade policy. Hillary Clinton is also discussed there.

Although Trump made some very good points about the failures of America's trade policy, I considered him a dangerous choice for the office of President from the start. The national debt is probably going to mushroom under Trump; His ideas about how to retire the national debt are deeply flawed. Trump fails to understand the actual mechanics of international trade theory, policy and reality. He is, literally, a bull in *the* China shop. His crude threat of a forty-five percent tariff on Chinese imports "or else," was (and is) a laughable lie. His post election threat of placing a thirty-five percent tariff on American firms that move production offshore, (presumably without placing similar tariffs on all foreign competing firms), was even more laughable. We do need tariffs, but they *must be a permanent tool and always a ready part of America's trade defense,* which must be carefully designed and administered.

We cannot go on following the free trade paradigm which the Republicans and Democrats (and even Trump himself if you believe his own words), still believe in. We do need trade, and we cannot become isolationist. However, we cannot have truly "free" trade even if China agrees to stop its currency manipulation. All this is explained in detail within. Far more is needed to fix America's problems than more tax cuts which primarily benefit the rich and bellicose threats of high tariffs from Donald Trump. Trump seems as doomed to failure over the long haul as were his post WWII predecessors, both Democratic and Republican.

I was very thankful that Sanders was not chosen by Democrats as their nominee. Though I believe that various social, educational and aid programs are needed, socialism, (state mandated collectivized ownership of the means of production), is quite simply unacceptable.

Please make frequent excursions into the endnotes which accompany the text as you read this book. A great deal of corroborative and useful additional information and sources are available in them. For those of you that have not taken a high school or college course in economics, or who need a bit of a refresher, a short glossary of relevant economics related terms is provided within.

Since I am asking you to join me in helping to form the Ameritorian Party you need to know a few things about me. I provided some background about myself in the preface which follows.

Preface

I was born in 1956, during the period of what was arguably the height of American prestige, power, and prosperity as a nation. I was 10 years old in 1967, when anti-miscegenation laws were banned by the Supreme Court in Loving v. Virginia. Today, although extremely serious problems in race relations and racial disparity continue, the biggest problem facing America is the economy. We need to create economic prosperity and real opportunity for all citizens, no matter their race, creed or other circumstances. In order to do that, we absolutely must lead in technology and manufacturing instead of following. We cannot remain a powerful military force unless we do. America is already behind China in emerging technologies that are absolutely vital to our national security.

For a good portion of my life, I identified with the Democrats. As a four year old, I watched JFK give a speech, and I was moved by it. That speech affected my later interest in social and political thought. I also remember being moved when I saw portions of Martin Luther King's "I Have A Dream" speech, though I was a very young child at the time.

Though I was twelve years old when he died, my Dad influenced my political thinking more than any other person on Earth. He was a kind man who spent a lot of time doing volunteer work. He became a Catholic deacon, and I was proud to watch him do Gospel readings every so often on Sundays. I idolized my Dad. Part of the reason I felt so proud of him was that he had fought in WWII. My Dad served as a Tech Sergeant in the 8th Air Force. He flew at least thirty-five missions on B-17's.

Dad's moral instruction and kindness continued to inspire and protect me after his death. I had known a good and happy home, and my soul had become strong thanks to him. To my mother too I owe deep and equal thanks. She passed away peacefully in 2016, and I will always miss her.

When I was a very young child, my Dad told me about how millions of Americans had gone to Europe to fight Hitler and the Germans, who had invaded and occupied large portions of Europe. Dad explained to me the difference between the American system and Hitler's fascist hell. He told me that day about the *Constitution of the United States* and how it meant that America was ruled by laws and not by evil dictators like Hitler. We were not and never would be a nation where torture was used to extract confessions he told me, but a land of justice and freedom. America was a place where the police were public servants, not the barbaric guard dogs of a police state, or the secret soldiers of organized crime. I was very young, but my Dad's talk left an impression which affected me from that day forward.

Though I majored in political science before I went to law school, I never had any interest in running for office after I finished law school. I saw the two political parties as corrupt, run by clout, controlled by money and intellectually limited. I was already deeply concerned about our newly developed trade deficit and the loss of high value jobs when I began college in 1974. But I knew there was nothing I could do to change things because economists and politicians were all preaching the gospel of free trade. I would have written this book over thirty years ago, but I had to wait for the economy to nearly collapse, for a handful of good economists to wake up to the falsity of free trade doctrine, and for the public in general to begin to wake up. Today, a plurality of Americans have had it with our crazy economic policies, but no change has yet come. Even today, the vast majority of voters are horribly uninformed about trade theory, and unfortunately, they too often believe the free trade myth that the corporate media and the political establishment feeds them.

President Trump has promised to make America great again, but his positions on other issues, such as his view that global warming is a hoax, that tax cuts are needed for very wealthy people, and that the use of torture should be expanded, completely turn me off. Trump has no plans to unite America around a well designed set of policies that *a large majority of voters will support.* Trump after all won election through the Electoral College. Hillary Clinton won the popular vote. The country will remain polarized and gridlocked under Trump. To the extent that Trump and his Republican majority are able to achieve extremist goals, such as gutting the Environmental Protection Agency, and slashing taxes on the rich, it is likely that a wave of disgruntled and alienated middle and lower income voters will sweep Trump out of office, and elect another liberal globalist like Obama in 2020. The pattern of gyrating between left and right has been digging America deeper and deeper into a hole for decades. Neither party gets things *just right*. The Democrats and Republicans have been so bad at governing the nation that we can no longer allow them to run things. We need to form a new political party that operates under different rules and truly serves the public interest 24/7.

The legacy of failures by the two parties described on the back cover of this book, (the second page of the ebook version), could be expanded to fill an entire book after this one. In fact, a semester college course called "The Failures of American Government,"would not provide enough time for even the best students to do more than scratch the surface on the subject of governmental dysfunction and failure. America's highest elective offices are filled with people who are either intellectually or morally (or both) unfit to serve. So please forgive me for referring to the parties derisively, and interchangeably, as "republocrats" or "demopublicans" throughout this book. The names of the parties are combined because both parties promote myths about free trade, and both serve special interests and in some ways, even foreign interests over the national interest. The two parties are so pathetically inadequate that it is imperative we get rid of their power monopoly or we won't survive as a great and prosperous nation. We might not even survive as a nation at all if we continue along the path we are on.

Another failed institution in our society is the media. We should never have gone to war in Iraq in 2003, and we never would have except for the fact that the media pushed Bush administration lies about weapons of mass destruction in Iraq as gospel truth.

In the chapters of this book I lay out an indictment of our government leaders, the press, and the doctrine of free trade they have been pushing on us for the last fifty plus years. Free Trade has been denounced by some truly brilliant economists, historians and others. They are men and women who know their subject. Their arguments are persuasive. I believe that most people already agree that our trade agreements with other nations have in many cases worked a great deal more harm on Americans than good. We simply can't go on like we have. Those of us who know that must band together against our "*money power*" rulers, and create a real democracy that serves the public, not simply the wealthy and powerful. We can do it! Have confidence in your own ability to help America escape from the "Demopublican" political prison crafted by the two parties, the big corporations, Wall Street, and the media monopoly.

There is a crisis of quality in government because of the pervasiveness of nepotism, cronyism, greed, and moral corruption in the two political parties, and in the greater economy as well. The parties have been corrupted in part by the wealth concentration that has been brought about by the big banks, billionaires and corporations that together constitute *the money power*. Most politicians today are mediocrities who have risen to power by virtue of the money handed them by the *money power*, and by plain old lying. They spin false narratives that sound good in theory but don't hold water in the real world. Mediocrity has crept into areas of the academic community too, where "group think" has been maintained by the enormous influence of establishment elites from both the left and the right. Truth, free expression and common sense frequently take a back seat to political and economic dogma and myth.

The media has become so concentrated in ownership it is today nothing more than an echo chamber for the two party debate. Debate in the media is severely limited in scope for reasons of political expediency and private interest. Meaningful discussions of our enormous trade deficits and the even larger deficits in free trade theory are strictly avoided by our corporate anointed press censors. They parrot the party lines of Democrats and Republicans, who in turn march to the drum beat of Wall Street and the one percent on economic issues. The Democrats sat idly by while union membership declined from thirty five percent of employed people (in the mid 1950's) to about seven percent today, yet Democrats claim to carry the banner for working Americans!

Americans are getting poorer fast. The middle class is shrinking. We are failing to stay ahead, let alone stay even in critical technologies. Our competitiveness is rapidly declining across the board. Things will only get worse; In this book I will prove that to your satisfaction, and hopefully, convince you to join me at once in forming a new political party that will restore broad based prosperity to America. Nothing will change unless a great many people get involved, so please read on, and start thinking about what you can do for your country.

1

The Majority Doesn't Like Free Trade And Why

At the core of my belief that Americans must dispose of two party rule, and unite around the commonly held opinions of the real majority in this country, is the servile way the Republocrats have shoved unfair free trade policies down our throats for over fifty years. Why have our opinions hardened on trade?

Americans are inundated with stories about closing factories, Chinese imports, outsourcing and low wages and high underemployment. The term "Rust Belt," is known to just about everybody, and has been for more than four decades. During those decades, many indicia of national economic health have declined. For example, America had the highest wages and standard of living in the world when I was a boy. By 2011, the United Nations Human Development Report listed the United States as twenty-third on the inequality-adjusted Human Development Index, behind Ireland, Italy, Israel, Canada, Spain, Czech Republic, and Slovenia, to name a few.[1] The US lost an average of fifty thousand manufacturing jobs per month between 2001 and 2011,[2] and over forty two thousand factories closed permanently during the same period.[3] According to an Economic Policy Institute report, Bureau of Labor statistics establish that every billion dollar increase in our trade deficit costs an average of fifteen thousand American jobs.[4]

Even more disconcerting to the better informed public than the unemployment rate is the decline in the civilian labor participation rate. Figure 1.1 graphs the sharp and continuing decline in the male employment participation rate from the "good old days," of my youth to the twenty first century era of widespread underemployment, declining wages, income inequality, crumbling infrastructure, huge trade deficits and the gargantuan national debt. *The problem is not limited to males however*. Despite the entry of women into the workforce in ever increasing numbers for decades, as of February 9, 2012, according to an article on SFGate (a website associated with the San Francisco Chronicle), 88 million working age Americans did not have a job, and the percentage of people participating in the work force dropped to 63.7 percent, the lowest since May, 1983.[5] By August of 2012 the percentage of people participating in the work force dropped to 63.5 percent.[6] By September, 2014 the rate had dropped to 62.7 percent, a thirty seven year high in percentage terms with about 92.8 million Americans able to work but not employed.[7] Despite what Obama and the media claim about low unemployment, the employment participation rate had dipped even lower by the end of 2015, when it stood at 62.6 percent.[8]

Clearly public concern about the changes wrought by free trade is not without a basis. A large percentage of Americans are concerned about free trade, and a majority believe, (correctly) it is harmful to America. A poll conducted for NBC and the Wall Street Journal in September

Figure 1.1

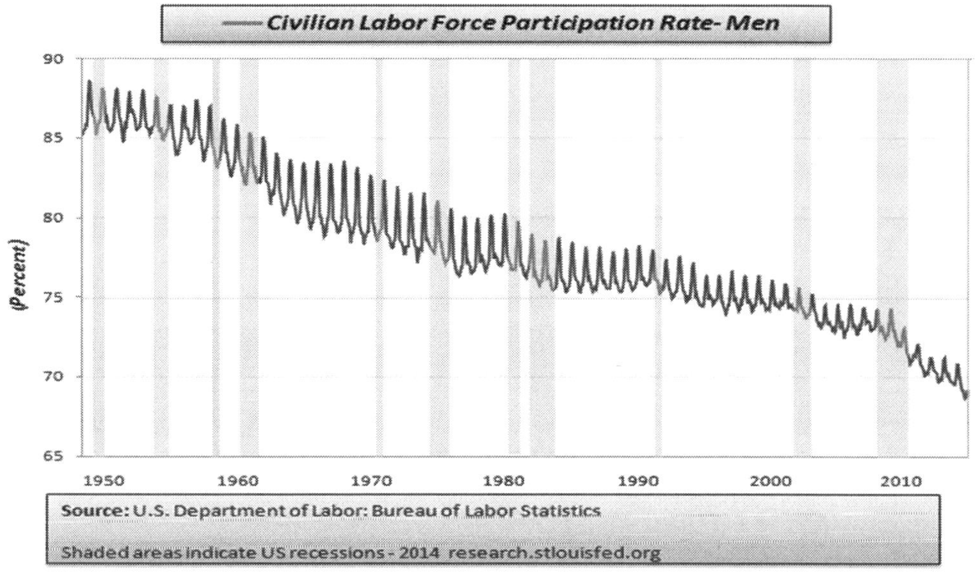

2010 showed that 53% of Americans believed free trade agreements to be harmful to America.[9] In a February, 2012 Gallop poll, 53% of Americans polled thought China is the leading economic power in the world today, making 2012 the second consecutive year in history Americans saw China as the world's greatest economy. This contrasts with the year 2000, when only 10% of Americans saw China as dominant.[10] In 2014, a poll conducted by North Star Opinion Research and the Mellman Group found that 69% of voters believe that outsourcing is the reason why manufacturing jobs are scarce.[11] You don't have to look hard to find trade related bad news statistics cited in the main stream media. The bad news about trade sometimes gets through to us from the media, but control of the media has become so monopolized that the mainstream media uniformly gives the silent treatment to economists who have been sounding the alarm about free trade for years. Following is a small random sampling of just eleven articles and highlights from them obtained from an internet search. I had to revise the articles listed below a year after I wrote the first draft of this chapter with the advent of the presidential campaigns of Donald Trump and Bernie Sanders. These reports cover a period from October 2, 2010 through March 9, 2016:

1 *Why Trump Gets Traction From Trade*, Huffington Post, April 19, 2011. Dave Johnson writes why Donald Trump attracted interest early in the run up to the Republican primaries by

talking about the trade deficit with China and our resultant job losses. Dave cites a poll by the Alliance for American Manufacturing which finds that 86% of voters want Washington to focus on manufacturing and that 63% feel that working people are forgotten while banks and Wall street get bailouts. The same poll finds that a strong majority believe manufacturing is more central to our economic strength than the high tech, knowledge, or financial service industries. Dave argues that Americans are sick of factories being packed up and shipped to places where people and the environment are exploited.[12]

#2. *U.S. Trade Deficit Widens in May*, CNN Money, July 12, 2011. By Annalyn Censky. This article reports the deepest monthly trade deficit since October 2008: $50.2 billion, exceeding the April estimate by $6.6 billion.[13]

#3 *Americans Sour on Trade*, The Wall Street Journal, October 2, 2010. A report by Sara Murray and Douglas Belkin highlights many negative impressions Americans hold about trade blaming the rising hostility to the lack of an economic recovery and high unemployment. A recent poll is cited in which 83% of blue collar workers, and an even higher 95% of professionals and managers blame outsourcing of manufacturing to foreign countries with lower wages as a reason the economy continues to struggle.[14]

#4 *U.S. To Share Cautionary Tale of Trade Secret Theft With Chinese Official*, The New York Times, February 14, 2012. This article by Jonathan Weisman reported about then Senator John Kerry's plan to raise the issue of Chinese theft of trade secrets of western companies with China's next leader, Xi Jinping. Kerry had decided to take that action after a wind energy business in Kerry's home state of Massachusetts was driven out of business. The Chinese paid one of the employees of the wind energy company to steal proprietary computer technology from his employer. The article describes an avalanche of such claims by western companies, and highlights the common practice of China that requires foreign firms to turn over their proprietary technology as a condition of doing business in China. The Chinese then build factories using the technology so obtained, and enter the market as direct competitors.[15]

#5. *Focus Shifts from China's currency to its other trade policies*. Los Angeles Times, February 14, 2012. By Don Lee and David Person. This article reports that as China's currency increases in value, currency manipulation by the Chinese, a favorite target and traditionally, the singular target of free trade advocates, is losing its punch as a scapegoat for our huge trade imbalance with China. James Bacchus, a former Florida congressman and chairman of the appellate body of the world trade organization is quoted: "The singular focus by the the U.S. (on the Chinese currency) has been misplaced. President Obama is quoted saying the Chinese should follow "the same rules of the road as everybody else."[16] I will add that the "everybody else" Obama is referring to, almost without exception, does follow the same rules as China, it's multifaceted protectionism for them, and free trade for us.

#6. *Trade Official Urges Action In China*. February 29, 2012, Associated Press. Jim Abrams reported that Ron Kirk, then the current top U.S. Trade official in the Obama administration, had asked Congress to restore a punitive trade sanction after a tariff the Obama administration imposed on low grade Chinese tires in 2009, was declared invalid by a federal appeals court.[17]

#7. *Intelligence Community Fears U.S. Manufacturing Decline*. Forbes. February 14, 2011 By

Loren Thompson. This story states that since 2001 "China has mounted the biggest challenge to the U.S. manufacturing ever seen, threatening producers of steel, chemicals, glass, paper, drugs and any number of other items with prices they cannot match. Not coincidentally, the United States has lost an average of 50,000 manufacturing jobs every month during the same period." According to this Forbes story, "China has been rapidly eroding the industrial foundations of American economic power." The industrial decline is so marked that the Director of National Intelligence has ordered a National Intelligence Estimate on the threat posed to our national security. It was discovered way back in 2007 that the U.S. only had one steel plant left that could make steel strong enough for military uses, and that plant has already been taken over by European steel maker Arcelor Mittal. The "arsenal of democracy," it would seem has become a rusted relic, or as stated in the Forbes article "a fragile affair."[18]

#8. *Huffpollster: Opinions On Trade Don't Divide Along The Usual Party Lines*. June 12, 2015. Huffington Post. Article by Mark Blumenthal, Ariel Edwards-Levy and Janie Velencia. This story reports that 63 percent of repondents to a CBS News and New York Times poll agreed with the statement that "trade restrictions are necessary to protect domestic industries."[19]

#9. *McConnell Warns That Trade Deal Can't Pass Congress Before 2016 Elections*. December 10, 2015. Washington Post. Paul Kane and David Nakamura report that since granting President Obama fast track authority to negotiate the Trans-Pacific Partnership (TPP) trade agreement in June, Congress has become more wary of voter backlash. Mitch McConnell says legislators won't pass the agreement before the 2016 election.[20]

#10. *How The Presidential Election Could Endanger Obama's Big Trade Deal*. January 27, 2016. Huffington Post reporter Dan Marans writes that the Obama administration is telling legislators that Donald Trump's candidacy makes passage of the TPP before the end of 2016 urgent. Marans also points out that Hillary Clinton, who has always been an ardent supporter of free trade, has told voters she does not support passage of the TPP. Socialist Bernie Sanders is also against it.[21]

#11. *Free Trade Loses Political Favor*. March 9, 2016. A Wall Street Journal article written by Bob Davis tells WSJ readers news many of them don't want to hear but already know: More and more Republican and Democratic voters are turned off by free trade agreements. The rising tide of negative opinion against free trade has stalled progress in Congress towards passing the Trans Pacific Partnership trade agreement. The 2016 primaries are seen as slowing passage of the TPP.

The same negative trade news that appears in print sometimes gets reported by the broadcast media. Occasionally, people see reports regarding large American trade deficits, budget deficits, and the national debt on televison and hear them on the radio. The constant stream of bad news is one reason people have soured on free trade. There are hundreds of economics related blogs that report the cons of our trade policy. Let me share one bad news bulletin I received from "The Economic Collapse," a blog run by lawyer Michael Snyder. Mr. Snyder's comments are picked up and reported by blogs all over the internet, as was this one:

55 Interesting Facts about the U.S. Economy in 2012 by Michael Snyder.[22]

#1 As you read this, there are more than 6 million mortgages in the United States that are overdue.

#2 In January, U.S. home prices were the lowest that they have been in more than a decade.

#3 In Florida right now, some drivers are paying nearly 6 dollars for a gallon of gas.

#4 On average, you could buy about 10 gallons of gas for an hour of work back in the mid-90s. Today, the average hour of work will get you less than 6 gallons of gas.

#5 Sadly, 43 percent of all American families spend more than they earn each year.

#6 According to Gallup, the unemployment rate was at 8.3% in mid-January but rose to 9.0% in mid-February.

#7 The percentage of working age Americans that have jobs is not increasing. The employment to population ratio has stayed very steady (hovering between 58% and 59%) since the beginning of 2010.

#8 If you gathered together all of the workers that are "officially" unemployed in the United States into one nation, they would constitute the 68th largest country in the entire world.

#9 When Barack Obama first took office, the number of "long-term unemployed workers" in the United States was approximately 2.6 million. Today, that number is sitting at 5.6 million.

#10 The average duration of unemployment in the United States is hovering close to an all-time record high.

#11 According to Reuters, approximately 23.7 million American workers are either unemployed or underemployed right now.

#12 There are about 88 million working age Americans that are not employed and that are not looking for employment. That is an all-time record high.

#13 According to CareerBuilder, only 23 percent of American companies plan to hire more employees in 2012.

#14 Back in the year 2000, about 20 percent of all jobs in America were manufacturing jobs. Today, about 5 percent of all jobs in America are manufacturing jobs.

#15 The United States has lost an average of approximately 50,000 manufacturing jobs a month since China joined the World Trade Organization in 2001.

#16 Amazingly, more than 56,000 manufacturing facilities in the United States have been shut down since 2001.

#17 According to author Paul Osterman, about 20 percent of all U.S. adults are currently working jobs that pay poverty-level wages.

#18 During the Obama administration, worker health insurance costs have risen by 23 percent.

#19 An all-time record 49.9 million Americans do not have any health insurance at all at this point, and the percentage of Americans covered by employer-based health plans has fallen for 11 years in a row.

#20 According to the New York Times, approximately 100 million Americans are either living in poverty or in "the fretful zone just above it."

#21 In the United States today, corporate profits are at an all-time high. The percentage of Americans that are living in "extreme poverty" is also at an all-time high according to the U.S. Census Bureau.

#22 In the United States today, the wealthiest one percent of all Americans have a greater net worth than the bottom 90 percent combined.

#23 The poorest 50 percent of all Americans now collectively own just 2.5% of all the wealth in the United States.

#24 The number of children living in poverty in the state of California has increased by 30 percent since 2007.

#25 According to the National Center for Children in Poverty, 36.4% of all children that live in Philadelphia are living in poverty, 40.1% of all children that live in Atlanta are living in poverty, 52.6% of all children that live in Cleveland are living in poverty and 53.6% of all children that live in Detroit are living in poverty.

#26 Since Barack Obama entered the White House, the number of Americans on food stamps has increased from 32 million to 46 million.

#27 As the economy has slowed down, so has the number of marriages. According to a Pew Research Center analysis, only 51 percent of all Americans that are at least 18 years old are currently married. Back in 1960, 72 percent of all U.S. adults were married.

#28 In 1984, the median net worth of households led by someone 65 or older was 10 times larger than the median net worth of households led by someone 35 or younger. Today, the median net worth of households led by someone 65 or older is 47 times larger than the median net worth of households led by someone 35 or younger.

#29 If you can believe it, 37 percent of all U.S. households that are led by someone under the age of 35 have a net worth of zero or less than zero.

#30 After adjusting for inflation, U.S. college students are borrowing about twice as much money as they did a decade ago.

#31 According to the Student Loan Debt Clock, total student loan debt in the United States will surpass the 1 trillion dollar mark at some point in 2012. If you went out right now and starting spending one dollar every single second, it would take you more than 31,000 years to spend one trillion dollars.

#32 Today, 46% of all Americans carry a credit card balance from month to month.

#33 Incredibly, one out of every seven Americans has at least 10 credit cards.

#34 The average interest rate on a credit card that is carrying a balance is now up to 13.10 percent.

#35 Of the U.S. households that do have credit card debt, the average amount of credit card debt is an astounding $15,799.

#36 Overall, Americans are carrying a grand total of $798 billion in credit card debt. If you were alive when Jesus was born and you spent a million dollars every single day since then, you still would not have spent $798 billion by now.

#37 It may be hard to believe, but the truth is that consumer debt in America has increased by a whopping 1700% since 1971.

#38 At this point, about 70 percent of all auto purchases in the United States involve an auto loan.

#39 In the United States today, 45 percent of all auto loans are made to subprime borrowers.

#40 Mortgage debt as a percentage of GDP has more than tripled since 1955.

#41 According to a recent study conducted by the BlackRock Investment Institute, the ratio of household debt to personal income in the United States is now 154 percent.

#42 To get the same purchasing power that you got out of $20.00 back in 1970 you would have to have more than $116 today.

#43 When Barack Obama first took office, an ounce of gold was going for about $850. Today an ounce of gold costs more than $1700 an ounce.

#44 The number of Americans that are not paying federal incomes taxes is at an all-time high.

#45 A staggering 48.5% of all Americans live in a household that receives some form of government benefits. Back in 1983, that number was below 30 percent.

#46 The amount of money that the federal government gives directly to Americans has increased by 32 percent since Barack Obama entered the White House.

#47 During 2012, the U.S. government must roll over nearly 3 trillion dollars of old debt.

#48 The U.S. debt to GDP ratio has now reached 101 percent.

#49 At the moment, the U.S. national debt is sitting at a grand total of $15,419,800,222,325.15.

#50 The U.S. national debt is now more than 22 times larger than it was when Jimmy Carter became president.

#51 During the Obama administration, the U.S. government has accumulated more debt than it did from the time that George Washington took office to the time that Bill Clinton took office.

#52 If the federal government began right at this moment to repay the U.S. national debt at a rate of one dollar per second, it would take over 440,000 years to pay off the national debt.

#53 If Bill Gates gave every single penny of his fortune to the U.S. government, it would only cover the U.S. budget deficit for about 15 days.

#54 Right now, the U.S. national debt is increasing by about 150 million dollars every single hour.

#55 Spending by the federal government accounted for about 2 percent of GDP back in 1800. It accounted for 23.8 percent in 2011, and according to former U.S. Comptroller General David M. Walker, it will account for 36.8 percent of GDP by 2040.

Mr. Snyder's daily posts usually have a similar tone to *55 Interesting Facts about the U.S. Economy in 2012* which was published at his website, (*theeconomiccollapseblog.com)* and emailed to his hundreds of thousands of subscribers. Snyder's posts are communicated to millions of others via other websites. The September 5, 2016 post at his *The Economic Collapse* web site was titled *From An Industrial Economy To A Paper Economy – The Stunning Decline Of Manufacturing In America.* Here is just the first paragraph:

> Why does it seem like almost everything is made in China these days? Yesterday I was looking at some pencils that we had laying around the house and I noticed that they had been manufactured in China. I remarked to my wife that it was such a shame that they don't make pencils in the United States anymore. At another point during the day, I turned over my television remote and I noticed that it also had "Made In China" engraved on it. It is still Labor Day as I write this article, and so I think that it is quite appropriate to write about our transition from an industrial economy to a paper economy today. Since the year 2000, the United States has lost five million manufacturing jobs even though our population has grown substantially since that time. Manufacturing in America is in a state of stunning decline, our economic infrastructure is being absolutely gutted, and our formerly great manufacturing cities are in an advanced state of decay. We consume far more wealth than we produce, and the only way that we are able to do this is by taking on massive amounts of debt. But is our debt-based paper economy sustainable in the long run? [23]

Anybody who wants to can find dozens of websites that attack free trade as a dire threat to America. There is a constant stream of negative fact and opinion flowing at the public that is washing away their confidence in the "Washington Consensus" that free trade is good for America. Even so, Democrats, Republicans, and most economists have been telling people for decades that free trade is good because it allows consumers and producers to make purchases at lower prices. That is an assumption not a conclusion, and it is false. Free trade is hurting the vast majority of Americans.[24] Despite the fact that media support for free trade has been obsequious for decades, a majority of Americans now correctly believe that free trade agreements are harmful to America.[25]

I believe most Americans, who now view free trade agreements with suspicion and out right hostility, have largely been motivated by the failure of the economy to truly bounce back since the financial crisis of 2008. However, for a very select few, which does not include the vast majority of journalists, TV and radio pundits, Hollywood elites, and politicians from the lowest to highest office in the land, there is a far more powerful reason to conclude that free trade is harmful to America. The reason is that the economic theory underlying free trade has been exposed by leading economists in recent years to be invalid. As will be explained in later chapters of this book, free trade theory is based on deductive reasoning, and some of the underlying axioms that are required by the theory to be true are in fact false. In addition, the theory behind free trade is incomplete; For one thing, it largely ignores how countries can use protectionist methods to outperform and surpass their open market competitors. For another, it ignores vitally important productivity growth factors that are central to improving living standards. Economists today are forced to admit that since adopting free trade as a policy, America has declined from once unchallenged economic supremacy to our current status as the world's largest debtor nation with typical American auto workers earning less than half what their counterparts in Germany make.[26]

In addition to the barrage of media reports concerning trade, there are numerous books that have been written in the last ten years that carefully detail the failings of international trade theory. I doubt even one percent of American's have heard of any of those books. However, I will introduce you to some of those books and to some of our best and brightest economists who are leading the charge on free trade doctrine, which continues to be a core component of what remains of the "Washington Consensus" on economic policy.

Well you say, so what? Didn't most of our politicians, like Rick Santorum, Mitt Romney, and President Obama talk tough on trade during the 2012 election campaign?[27] In 2016, didn't Donald Trump make a campaign promise of placing a 45% "tax" on China?[28] Also in 2016, both Hillary Clinton and Bernie Sanders announced they were not in favor of the proposed Trans-Pacific Partnership.[29] Since some of our politicians seem to be turning against free trade in favor of "fair trade" and getting "tough" with countries like China do we really still need a third party? If we can only get all the other countries to play fair, the gigantic benefits of free trade will immediately begin flowing and our economy will be reborn; The country will have a bright future and grand prospects for a new American century. Isn't that right? We certainly don't need a new political party to fix things do we? The short answer is *Yes We Do*! The long answer is provided in the remainder of this book. Politicians are as "whorrible" as ever. We must fix *our* country *ourselves*. You know that Uncle Sam poster the military once used that says "We Want You." I have news for you, that guy is pointing his finger in your direction right now. It is *imperative* that *you* answer the call!

Later chapters of this book review how our national economic policies and practices and the theoretical justifications for them have changed over the years. The theory upon which free trade is based is critically analyzed, and its mathematical and logical defects are explained in plain and simple language. The problems of the media are also explored. Finally, the necessity of building a new political party is discussed. The next chapter explains what economists and pundits are referring to when they talk about the Washington Consensus concerning international trade.

2

The Washington Consensus

Economists and pundits often comment in some way about the "Washington Consensus" without providing a definition of what it means, leaving the general reader and economists themselves to infer the meaning from the context or search elsewhere for a definition. In his book, *The Betrayal of American Prosperity: Free Market Delusions, America's Decline, and How We Must Compete in the Post-Dollar Era*, Clyde Prestowitz, head of the Economic Strategy Institute, described the Washington Consensus as a set of economic policy rules and guidelines originally designed to help Latin American countries cope with economic and financial crises during the nineteen eighties. The term *Washington Consensus* "eventually came to signify a broad set of market-oriented--even market fundamentalist--policies deemed essential for economic success anywhere and everywhere." Thus the term was an "amalgamation of free market and free trade theory."[30] The path to riches for all countries, according to the Washington Consensus, meshed well with, (but did not necessarily include), the ideas of Reaganomics, and "trickle down," which are terms more familiar to most people. The "formula" for the Washington Consensus, as described by Prestowitz, "included the principles of deregulation, privatization, rule of law, transparency, primacy of market forces, free trade, fiscal discipline, promotion of inward foreign direct investment, (for developing countries), competitive exchange rates (preferably floating exchange rates), and democratization."[31]

Economist John Williamson coined the term "Washington Consensus" to refer to "what most people in Washington at the time believed Latin America ought to be undertaking as of 1989." Williamson gave a speech at the Center for Strategic Studies called "Did the Washington Consensus Fail?" In the outline for the speech, which was given on November 6, 2002, Williamson blamed the failure of Latin American countries to think about potential crises when they implemented the Washington Consensus as an "ideology," or "thought economizing device," rather than as a general set of policy guidelines.[32] Following the major interventions undertaken by central governments and central banks following the worldwide financial crisis of 2008, the effects of which linger still, Gordon Brown, former prime minister of Great Britain voiced the conclusion that the Washington Consensus was "over."[33] Early in 2006, two years before the 2008 crisis, noted economist Dani Rodrik wrote an article entitled "Goodbye Washington Consensus, Hello Washington Confusion." In that article, Rodrik, a Harvard

Professor, wrote that nobody really believes in the Washington Consensus anymore. The real question he said, was; What will replace it?[34]

Despite those pessimistic statements about the Washington Consensus, John Williamson denied in an April, 2009, Washington Post interview that the Washington Consensus was dead with respect to the ten policy elements he had delineated as parts of it in 1989. Williamson complained that others who had used the expression, most notably the well known economist, Joseph Stiglitz, had "foisted" an expanded meaning on the expression, turning it into a "neoliberal tract." Williamson agreed that when used with the expanded meaning as a "neoliberal tract," the Washington Consensus was dead. Williamson did not define what he meant by "neoliberal track."[35]

Whatever it means, since Williamson's vaunted policy guidelines included "trade liberalization," as a policy imperative, I cannot agree with anybody who says the consensus is presently dead in Washington.[36] Williamson wrote a paper with the title "A Short History Of The Washington Consensus" for an economic conference in Barcelona which was held on September 24-25, 2004. In that paper, Williamson mentioned some areas of economic thought where there was no consensus, but he maintained that trade liberalization was controversial only with respect to: "how fast trade should be liberalized."[37]

I find that conclusion by Williamson true with respect to economic policymakers who were influential in Washington. It seems questionable with respect to other trade experts working both inside and outside the beltway given how many books and articles by well known economists or leading politicians had been written by 2004 which were highly critical of the benefits of free trade. In addition to the books and articles, a number of political candidates who were opposed to free trade had gained widespread public support; Ross Perot ran for President in 1992 on an anti free trade platform. Patrick Buchanan ran similar campaigns in 1992 and 1996. Economist Ravi Batra wrote "The Myth of Free Trade The Pooring of America" published in 1993.[38] Then congressman, now U.S. Senator Sherrod Brown wrote "Myths of Free Trade: Why American Trade Policy Has Failed" which was published in 2004.[39] Brown, a Democrat, opposed President Clinton on NAFTA, which was passed by the fairly close vote of 234-200, on November 17, 1993, in the House of Representatives.[40]

In "Goodbye Washington Consensus, Hello Washington Confusion," Dani Rodrik cited the World Bank report "The World Bank's Economic Growth in the 1990s: Learning from a Decade of Reform" (2005) to show how far economic leaders from around the world had come from the original Washington Consensus. Rodrik wrote "There are no confident assertions here of what works and what doesn't—and no blueprints for policy makers to adopt."[41] The emphasis is on the need for humility, for policy diversity, for selective and modest reforms, and for experimentation." Rodrik quotes Gobind Nankani, the World Bank vice-president who wrote the preface to the report "...there is no unique universal set of rules.... we need to get away from formulae and the search for elusive 'best practices'..."[42]

Nankani's recommendation sounds like something the developmental economist Erik S. Reinert advises we do. Reinert is a "heterodox economist" who has written a great deal about the history and dynamics of economic development. He is the chairman and founder of "The Other Canon Foundation." Reinert, who was born in Oslo, has an MBA from Harvard and a Ph.D in economics from Cornell. In addition to his invaluable contributions to the field of economics, he founded a leading firm in the automotive paint industry. Reinert and various others have given us an alternative approach to think about in place of the beleaguered Washington Consensus. Reinert wrote *How Rich Countries Got Rich and Why Poor Countries Stay Poor*, published in 2007,[43] one year before Ha Joon Chang's book *Bad Samaritans: The Myth of Free Trade And The Secret History of Capitalism* came out.[44] Chang earlier authored "Kicking Away The Ladder" (2003),[45] which argues as does *Bad Samaritans* and Reinert's book that free trade does not inevitably work for rich nations, and, that developing countries have frequently been kept poor because of pressure from world trade organizations and rich nations to adopt free trade policies.

Economist Clyde Prestowitz, a former trade official and advisor to the Reagan administration added the best seller *The Betrayal of American Prosperity: Free Market Delusions, America's Decline, and How We Must Compete in the Post-Dollar Era* in 2010,[46] and economist, Ian Fletcher also in 2010, gave us *Free Trade Doesn't Work What Should Replace It and Why*.[47] We shall delve into the advice the non consensus economists have given us in this book. Their work, and those of other economic and financial experts who have scrutinized Wall Street's failings, taken collectively, constitute a powerful refutation of what Washington has done to our country for decades. They provide us with an ample intellectual foundation for a new political party which fixes what is broken in our economic system. We cover the details of economic history and theory in detail in chapters four through eleven of this book. For now, lets move on to another of our shared concerns: the news media.

3

The news media is a dysfunctional echo chamber for the two parties, and the special interests that both parties serve.

Where does one begin in criticizing the media? The answer is anywhere and everywhere, but many if not most of the problems the media suffers from stem from the concentration of media ownership in too few hands. Berkeley journalism professor and emeritus dean Ben Bagdikian made famous the words "media monopoly" with the publication of his 1983 book *The Media Monopoly*.[48] At that time, just fifty corporations controlled most of the media businesses in America

By the start of the year 2001, six editions of Bagdikian's book had been published. In 2004, Bagdikian reported in *The New Media Monopoly* that only five conglomerates owned nearly every media company in America, including but not limited to magazines, newspapers, radio stations, TV stations, TV networks, cable networks, and book publishers. The Walt Disney Company, Time Warner, Viacom, News Corp., and Betelsmann made up what Bagdikian called "The Big Five." Bagdikian bemoaned the cartel like operations of the five media giants, pointing to their tendency to enter into joint venture agreements, work together to dominate government policy concerning them, and employ interlocking directorships. The media giants, according to Bagdikian, "manufacture a social and political world" and "their concentrated influence" exerts "cultural and political forces reminiscent of the royal decrees of monarchs rejected by the revolutionists of 1776."[49] Bagdikian convincingly painted a picture of a media system which has been bought and paid for by the money power to report the news in ways consistent with the interests of Wall Street.[50]

It seems clear that the "concentrated influence" exercised over public opinion and knowledge by the media oligopoly has not been lessened by the growth of the internet. The idea that the internet has restored journalistic freedom and integrity is absurd. People using desktop computers, tend to get news quickly from sources such as the Huffington Post on AOL, or other big name news media. Many people go to the digital version of their favorite newspapers, magazines, TV stations or network shows for their news. News apps for smartphones and tablets must be downloaded from app stores controlled by the manufacturers of such devices; The news apps of leading media companies completely dominate the news app offerings at both Apple and Google. The media oligopoly has a choke hold on the public's access to truth, and it limits the nature and scope of public debate more effectively than a dictatorship can. People know when they are living in a dictatorship, and they naturally distrust the news handed out by a state controlled press. In our two party tyranny, people don't realize just how completely the issues discussed in the media are censored to please corporate interests, advertisers, media owners, and the two party elites.

During my writing of this book I benefitted from reading the books and articles of some of journalism's finest academicians, and the work of other scholars concerned with the problems of media dysfunction. The work of Robert W. McChesney was most helpful. McChesney is a Research Professor of Communication at the University of Illinois, and one of the nation's foremost experts on the media. McChesney described eight myths which protect a "corporate - insider hegemony over media policy debates," in his book, *The Problem of the Media, U.S. Communication Politics in the 21st Century.*[51] I summarize the *myths* McChesney brilliantly wrote about as follows:

McChesney's Media Myths

1. The media merely reports the news as is, so the media does not shape the news.

2. The small number of companies that control almost all of the media today result from a free market, and the free market is the best protection for a free flow of ideals, so the system of concentrated ownership we have today is a result of, and consistent with, the intentions of America's founding fathers.

3. Government policies concerning the media in the United States are fully debated in the media, and adequate attention is given by the media to the full spectrum of public opinion and to the public interest where media policy is concerned.

4. The large media companies provide the highest quality of journalism possible. The high journalistic standards of the large media companies are consistent with the need that voters have to make informed choices. This allows representative democracy to function properly.

5. The news media has a left wing bias, but no right wing bias.

6. The presence of a free market assures that the media supplies the people with what they want, just as in any free market.

7. The technologies employed by a particular media (such as newspapers or television to name two), may limit the scope of media coverage, but taken as a whole, and including the internet, media coverage is robust and whole.

8. The media is as good as it can ever be.

McChesney's book was focused on the structure and history of the media itself, so he did not analyze specific instances of corporate - insider influence over the direction and scope of the media's coverage of the issues which are of greatest concern to this book. Further research was needed with respect to the way the media covers international trade policy, foreign policy, and climate change. I discovered a large body of scholarly work that supports the conclusion summarized in the title to this chapter: *The news media is a dysfunctional echo chamber for the two parties, and the special interests that both parties serve.* The evidence follows below in three sections.

Slanted Coverage of Trade Issues

Before writing this book it was my opinion that the media slants news and commentary involving trade issues to encourage the belief that free trade is a proven theory, that it is inevitably beneficial to the United States, and that it is beneficial to a majority of American citizens. McChesney did not deal specifically with media coverage of trade issues in his book. To test my opinion, I did a search for academic work on the subject of media bias on international trade issues. I immediately found a December, 2006 article in the academic journal Presidential Studies Quarterly by David M. Rankin: "Featuring the President as Free Trader: Television News Coverage of U.S. Trade Politics." Rankin is the current Chair of the Political Science Department at the State University of New York at Fredonia. He coauthored *Winning the White House 2008*, and he has published numerous other scholarly works.[52]

What do you think Rankin found? Well, lets review what he did. With the help of student assistants, Lexis-Nexis, and news abstracts compiled in a Vanderbilt University archive, he found and analyzed the content of 1,310 televised reports concerning trade issues broadcast on the evening news by ABC World News Tonight, CBS Evening News, NBC Nightly News, and CNN Headline News. The period reviewed was the years 1988-2002, which apparently accounts in part for the failure to include other leading cable networks like FOX and MSNBC. You should read his article for all the details - but his conclusion was clear. Rankin found that the media consistently fixates on the President as a lasting symbol that free trade is a good thing. Rankin also found that when free trade is prominent in the news, the President and the White House get significantly more attention from news media than those who are opposed to free trade. Other media analysts have made similar findings and Rankin mentions some of them in his article. Rankin also quoted a passage from an article by Melissa Michelson:

> as the (NAFTA) vote approached, coverage became friendlier, including anti-Perot stories, and the Clinton campaign for support....Overall, the media's focus changed from how the pact would affect American workers and jobs to a personal battle between the President and his opponents (especially Perot), with the attendant horse race and vote-counting coverage....This shift in media attention probably helped the administration win public support for NAFTA following the Gore-Perot debate.[53]

My experience goes back quite a way, and I have been tuned into the trade issue since I was just a teenager, age 15, in 1972. I have never seen an economist who is an opponent of free trade allowed to debate an economist who is a supporter of free trade on television in all that time. I have seen a great amount of obviously slanted and outrageously false reporting in favor of free trade. The kind of journalism practiced by the American media on the subject of free trade justifies in no small way the use of the word "myth" in the titles and text of the many books which detail how America is declining because of its gargantuan trade imbalance.

One form of media trickery I have seen employed for decades by reporters and commentators is their use of a totally discredited pseudo theory about the cause of the Great Depression known to economists as the Smoot-Hawley Myth. I am appalled by what passes for fair and accurate reporting when it comes to the issue of free trade. The Smoot-Hawley Myth is a knee jerk response for pundits and talking heads throughout the media oligopoly - from cable news shows to right and left wing talk radio and print media. It would be nice to see a Rankin style analysis of the Smoot-Hawley Myth.

The Smoot-Hawley Myth is an utterly absurd argument that somehow an increase in the tariff rate for about one third of America's imports in 1930, (which constituted but a tiny percentage of America's GDP), either caused the Great Depression or greatly worsened it. Senator Reed Smoot, the Senate Finance Committee Chairman at the time and Congressman Willis Hawley, the House Ways and Means Committee Chairman, were the sponsors of the law which raised the tariff rate.

Nobody in their right mind and properly educated in the field of economics, could ever, in good faith, actually believe the Smoot-Hawley Myth! It's nothing more than an article of political spin, and surely most of the people who have advanced it have known it was utter nonsense. The myth has never been accepted by leading economic theorists, and both the founders and leading voices of Keynesianism and Monetarism have rejected it.[54] Only crackpots, partisan pundits, and spin doctors profess to believe it. Despite the fact that the vast majority of economists reject the Smoot-Hawley Myth, media monopoly pundits frequently rely on it to justify free trade. Those same pundits never permit any economists who disagree with the Smoot-Hawley myth to speak about or debate the subject! The propagation of the Smoot-Hawley Myth by the corporate media is perhaps the greatest example of how the news is slanted to control public opinion and government policy.

I was never a victim of the myth myself. I learned in grade school, learned again in high school, and learned again in college that the Great Depression was caused by a series of stock market crashes in 1929 which sucked the capital out of the economy. The resulting loss of demand and unemployment was not dealt with effectively until surges in demand, production and technology coinciding with World War II, and FDR's New Deal efforts to stimulate employment, restored prosperity. In the postwar period, American prosperity continued until the Washington Consensus policy of free trade began doing serious damage to the economy of the United States.[55]

We will review historical reality in chapter four, which covers America's rise to become the world's greatest economic power, possessing the highest gross national output and the highest per capita income on Earth. The simple fact is that the United States had a protectionist economic policy throughout history, beginning with Alexander Hamilton and George Washington and not ending until the post WWII period.[56] In the post war environment, America fell victim to the free trade mentality and began the process of completely and at times unilaterally removing protectionism, assuring our slowly accelerating national decay ever since.[57]

In 1929, American prosperity and America's seemingly unstoppable economic progress was given a body blow by the same improperly regulated institution that bedeviled us again with the financial crisis of 2008, that being of course Wall Street! Wall Street and their banker buddies who ran the Federal Reserve Board helped cause the Great Depression, and back then, automatic bailouts and the "too big to fail" approach to bank regulation did not apply.[58] [59]

The absurdity of the Smoot-Hawley Myth is illustrated by Figures 3.1 and 3.2, which are graphs of U.S. GDP, total trade, and total exports as a percentage of GDP, before, during and after the depression era.[60] As you can see from Figure 3.1, total trade, (the value of all export sales less the cost of all imports), was lower than one billion dollars per annum in 1929, and total trade as a component of GDP hardly changed at all during the Great Depression. This data obviously indicates that the Smoot-Hawley tariff had no part in causing the Great Depression or even exacerbating it to any significant extent. If exports had constituted a significant percentage of gross domestic product before the Great Depression, then the tiny net change in total trade during the Great Depression might be misleading, as the role exports played in powering the economy might be hidden by looking only at total trade

Figure 3.1

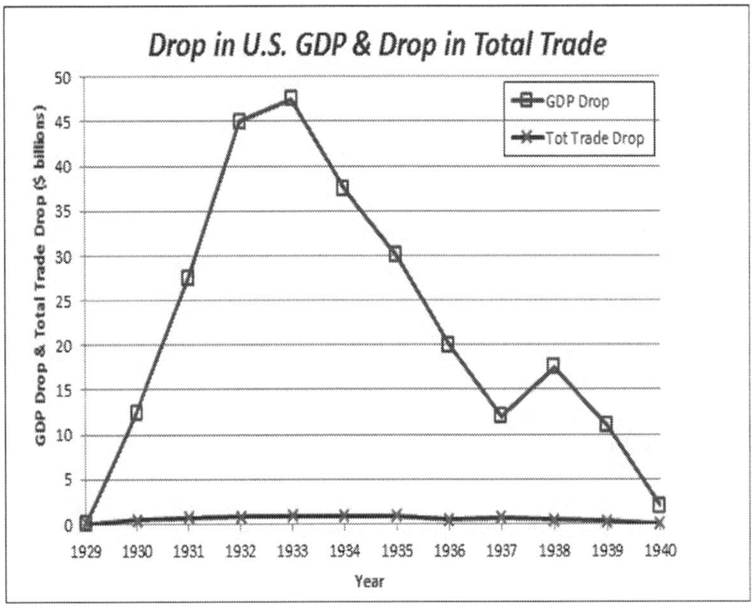

Graph adapted from Robert E. Powell, Ph.D., *Smoot Hawley Fiction*. Total Trade equals exports minus imports. Used with permission. Retrieved from http://www.exponentialimprovement.com/cms/smoot.shtml#1

However, exports were less than one percent of the value of gross domestic product between 1929 and 1941. Imports were even less. Yet America's gross domestic product dropped by about forty seven percent between 1929 and 1934![61] How could it be that a tariff on imports caused such a large drop in America's gross domestic product? It simply couldn't be. The Smoot-Hawley myth is utterly preposterous. As explained in detail in later chapters, America was a protectionist economy from the beginning. A policy of protecting "infant industries,"[62] using tariffs on manufactured imports originating with Alexander Hamilton was wholeheartedly embraced by George Washington and beloved by Abraham Lincoln. The judicious use of tariffs to foster national development remained a national policy until after free trade was adopted as

Figure 3.2 Exports as a percentage of U.S. GDP 1929 to 1941

Graph adapted from Robert E. Powell, Ph.D., *Smoot Hawley Fiction*. Used with permission. Dr. Powell. Retrieved from http://www.exponentialimprovement.com /cms/smoot.shtml#1

the mantra of FDR, and soon thereafter, the Republican party. In the postwar era, America considered itself too big to fail, and American leaders figured free trade would allow its mighty corporations to penetrate foreign markets without creating gigantic American trade deficits. America's leaders were wrong, and responsibility for what is arguably the greatest economic blunder in human history can be traced back to FDR's Secretary of State, Cordell Hull. Those that have followed him have established a most vexatious tradition of putting the permanent interests of the American majority behind the transient interests of Wall Street and the upper level managements of transnational corporations.

The media has been criticized again and again by press watchdogs for failing to cover economic news fully, truthfully, and fairly. For instance, a report by media watchdog group Media Matters criticized the media for acting almost as a cheerleader for the Tea Party when it got started, but when the Occupy Wall Street protests began, the media made scant mention of the protests.[63] Not until a noisy protest march across the Brooklyn Bridge caused huge traffic jams and lead to the arrest of some seven-hundred demonstrators, did coverage of the Occupy Wall Street movement begin to pickup.[64] No such noisy demonstration was needed by the Tea Party, which attracted coverage ab initio, and very favorable coverage at that.[65] Yet a poll by Princeton Survey Research Associates International in October, 2011, showed that 59% of adult American's "agreed or mostly agreed" with the Occupy protestors.[66] Interestingly, a September, 2011 CNN/ORC poll showed that only 28 percent of Americans held favorable views of the tea party, while 53 percent of Americans thought poorly of the tea party.[67] It would seem that since Americans preferred the goals, (however ambiguous), of the Occupy movement to the Tea Party by a wide margin, the media was more responsive to its own biases and preferences than those of the public when it made the decision to ignore the Occupy protestors early on.

The point of this chapter is to adduce evidence that the media is a dysfunctional echo chamber for the two parties and the special interests they serve. The evidence so far shows that both parties favor free trade, and opponents of free trade get less coverage, and less than fair coverage in the media.[68] The evidence also shows that the Occupy Wall Street movement and the Tea Party movement were treated differently by the media, with the Tea Party getting the more positive treatment early on.

Slanted Coverage of Global Warming

Another policy area where mistakes bring large and nasty consequences is global warming.[69] The tentacles of industry reach deep into the media monopoly, and those tentacles have put the squeeze on the flow of accurate information about the science of global warming to the public. Misinformation campaigns by spin tanks and climate contrarians, and scant coverage in daily newspapers and television news have allowed public opinion to remain uninformed and divided on global warming. The myth of a monolithic left tilting media is never more obvious than when one looks at how effectively the media has ignored and downplayed the seriousness of global warming.

There is no dearth of academic studies concerning the media's culpability for and complicity with fossil fuel fired efforts at preventing Americans from learning the plain truth about global warming. It's not a matter of opinion. It's a scientific reality. Global warming is occurring and it is caused by the massive industrialization that has taken place as a result of technological progress since the industrial revolution and even before then. There is practically universal agreement among climate scientists that global warming is taking place, and that it is caused by human activities which increase the volume of greenhouse gases in the atmosphere.[70]

The aforesaid consensus within science seems absolutely clear and incontrovertible, and NASA seems to agree.[71] At least one of NASA's website contains statements from numerous scientific bodies that agree with the consensus opinion. Among those prestigious associations are the following: The American Association For the Advancement of Science, the American Chemical Society, the American Geophysical Union, the American Medical Association, the American Meteorological Society, the American Physical Society and The Geological Society of America. Nonetheless, aided by the media, climate skeptics have succeeded in creating the appearance of scientific controversy where there is none.[72]

The laudable work of Maxwell T. Boykoff, Ph.D., and Jules Boykoff, Ph.D., is very instructive on the subject of corporate - insider control of the direction and scope of the public policy debate on climate change. Maxwell T. Boykoff has a Ph.D in Environmental Studies and he is a Senior Visiting Research Associate for the Environmental Change Institute at the University of Oxford. He is also an Assistant Professor for the Cooperative Institute for Research in Environmental Sciences at the University of Colorado-Boulder. Jules Boykoff, Ph.D., is an Associate Professor and Chair of the Politics and Government Department at Pacific University. Jules Boykoff's books and articles include studies of U.S. politics, mass-media politics, and the methods employed by the media and political parties to suppress dissenting opinion. The two Boykoffs have written extensively on how the media manipulates public awareness away from the scientific certainty that climate change is caused by human action. They co-authored an academic journal article titled "Climate Change and Journalistic Norms: A Case Study of U.S. Mass-Media Coverage," in *Geoforum*, (2007).[73]

A significant and growing volume of academic work by highly reputable scholars examines the role that the political and business sides of media ownership play in controlling and slanting news reports to please owners and their advertisers. The Boykoff and Boykoff article cited above acknowledges the role that monied interests play in censoring the media, but it is focused on describing and analyzing the "*journalistic norms*" followed by reporters and pundits that lead to incomplete and distorted press coverage of global warming.[74] Media distortions have prevented the development of a public consensus about the reality of global warming that is consistent with the scientific consensus. So it is valuable to review and analyze those norms in order to understand why the media has become an echo chamber for the two parties and the special interests they serve.

In the words of the Boykoffs, "Climate change is one of the most serious risks of the twenty-first century. Nevertheless, the prospect of...concerted action by the United States is dim. Former President Bush's ties to carbon based industry were commonly cited reasons for the U.S.'s persistent unwillingness to follow...a reduction program. however, a more subtle factor that helps explain US inaction also exists: journalists...professional norms."[75]

Building on the work of other scholars, Boykoff and Boykoff tested a particularly insightful model for understanding our dysfunctional press - by analyzing the content of news reports regarding global warming over the seventeen year period from 1988 to 2004. The Boykoff and Boykoff article describes three "*first order*" journalistic norms; *personalization*, *dramatization* and *novelty*.[76] There are also two "*second order*" norms; "*authority order bias*" and "*balance*."[77] Personalization is "the tendency to downplay the big social, economic, or political picture in favor of the human trials tragedies and triumphs that sit at the surface of events."[78] Examples of personalization can be found in the press coverage regarding the passage of NAFTA. As the vote on passage of the bill approached, the focus of reporters shifted from looking at the merits of the bill to focusing on the foibles and clashes of the personalities involved, and the horse race for votes.[79]

Dramatization is where the press creates “news dramas,”[80] emphasizing “crisis over continuity, the present over the past or future, conflicts,”[81] and downplaying “complex policy formation , the workings of government institutions, and the bases of power behind central characters”[82] “Dramatized news tends to eschew significant and more comprehensive analysis of the enduring problems, in favor of covering the spectacular machinations that occur at the surface of events.”[83] The Boykoff and Boykoff article points out that the lack of drama in an event can lead to “blocking out...news that does not hold an immediate sense of excitement or controversy.”[84] The last first order journalistic norm, “novelty,”[85] is the tendency of the press to treat stories that are fresh and new as more press worthy than stale material. “As Stockings and Leonard put it”[86] ‘It ain’t news unless its new’- quoted the Boykoff and Boykoff article.[87]

The first order journalistic norms are first in order because they deal with “what is news” in addition to affecting the content of media reports about events that are deemed newsworthy. There are two “second order” journalistic norms: “authority-order” and “balance.”[88] These second order norms are initiated and informed by the first order norms that decide what news is reported. The authority-order journalistic norm is a bias journalists show in favor of consulting with primarily government officials, business leaders, and other establishment figures that tend toward assuring the public that “order, safety and security will soon be restored.”[89] This journalistic tendency accents the “desirability of social order”[90] and “the need for national leadership in maintaining that order.”[91] Journalists display a tendency to look to and support the views of governmental and business elites with an eye toward maintaining social order. The second of the two second order journalistic norms, “balance”[92] is “often seen as a synecdoche for objectivity,”[93] since objectivity was dropped as a term from the ethics code for journalism promulgated by the Society of Professional Journalists.

The journalistic norm of *balance* is based on the ethical duty of reporters to “present the views of legitimate spokespersons of the conflicting sides in any significant dispute, and provide both sides with roughly equal attention.”[94] As wonderful as the *balance* norm sounds, Boykoff and Boykoff point out that the second order norm of balance combined with the first order norm of personalization leads to the scenario of “dueling scientists.”[95] Thus a leading scientist presenting the consensus view among scientists is frequently (and falsely), presented as just one side in a heated scientific debate. One can add the scenario of high powered (or formerly high powered) politicians like George W. Bush dueling with scientists. Thus, the balance norm has helped create a false impression of a hot scientific debate and great uncertainty about anthropomorphic climate change, obfuscating the overwhelming world wide scientific consensus on the subject.

Boykoff and Boykoff’s study used the methodology of “content analysis”[96] to get some data on the role journalistic norms have played in defining the scope and content of global warming coverage in the press. They used standard research methods to cull a representative sampling of global warming stories from media reports made between 1988 and 2004, a seventeen year period.[97] You may recall that 1988 was a year that saw a drought and a heat wave throughout much of the United States. The heat and drought that year stimulated commentary by experts and politicians about global warming, and press reports concerning global warming. Because the extreme weather and four other global warming related events took place that year, Boykoff and Boykoff chose 1988 as the starting year for their research project.[98] The other four events were: 1) leading climate scientist James Hansen told Congress that anthropomorphic global warming is a "critical problem in need of immediate action."[99] 2) Margaret Thatcher made a similar comment when she said "we may have unwittingly begun a massive experiment with the system of the planet itself."[100] 3) The IPCC or Intergovernmental Panel on Climate Change was formed by the UN, and 4) The WMO or World Meteorological Organization sponsored an international symposium concerning the atmosphere in Toronto.[101]

The Boykoffs analyzed a random selection from a base of 4887 news articles published in the New York Times, Washington Post, Los Angeles Times, and the Wall Street Journal. Also analyzed was a random selection of televised news reports concerning global warming broadcast on ABC World News Tonight, CBS Evening News, and NBC Nightly News. Each news report analyzed was coded as to whether it exhibited evidence of the five journalistic norms under study. They found that the amount of news reports about global warming rose substantially in years 1990, 1992, 1997, 2001-2002, and 2004. Three factors, 1) unusual weather, 2) political controversy or commentary about global warming, and 3) scientific developments were found to interact together to account for the increased amount of coverage given climate change by journalists in those years.[102] The final conclusion that the Boykoffs came to is hardly unsurprising. In their words, "Cultural factors like first and second order journalistic norms go a long way in explaining why climate change, as an environmental issue, has struggled to attain fair and accurate attention from U.S. newspaper and televison news media."[103] They give examples of how journalistic norms have obscured the practical scientific consensus which exists.[104]

One of the more laughable manifestations of the journalistic norms of drama, novelty and balance mentioned in the Boykoff and Boykoff article is a story published by the Washington Post titled *Primary Ingredient of Acid Rain May Counteract Greenhouse Effect*. The Post article quoted a leading climate "contrarian" who talked about the potential of placing new fossil fuel powered generating facilities on the eastern extremes of land masses to fight global warming. The theory behind that idea being that while they lingered in the atmosphere sulfates from the plants would reduce the warming effects of carbon dioxide, after which the sulfates would be deposited harmlessly in the oceans with the rain.[105]

The idea that you can fight a pollution source that causes both global warming and ocean acidification, with a pollution source that causes acid rain, ignores the fact that the acidification of the world's oceans is already at dangerously high levels; It is a serious environmental problem in and of itself.[106] Carbon dioxide is the leading cause of ocean acidification as well as being the leading greenhouse gas. If burning fossil fuels has gotten us where we are, burning more of them as the solution is patently absurd.

You can read more about the threat of global warming and the politics and spin which surrounds it in the book *The Hockey Stick And The Climate Wars* by Michael E. Mann.[107] Another superb book which tells the truth about global warming and the very real near term threat it poses is *Storms Of My Grandchildren The Truth About The Coming Climate Catastrophe And Our Last Chance to Save Humanity* by James Hansen. Hansen is a leading American scientist on the subject.[108]

An example of the personalization norm in action occurred in a March, 1990 NBC Nightly News segment where the arguments of a relatively tiny platoon of climate contrarians was given the same credence as the overwhelming full army of scientists by Tom Brokaw when he stated "for all the alarm about global warming, there's a major new study questioning whether it is happening...certain to trigger *even more debate* over whether temperatures in fact are on the rise on planet Earth."[109]

What did Brokaw mean when he said "even more" debate? There was and is remarkably consistent agreement among climate scientists that global warming is occurring and that it is caused by human activities. Brokaw's report created an illusion of balance by personalizing global warming, and describing as a debate the difference in viewpoint between a tiny number of climate contrarians and the nearly unanimous body of climate scientists who maintain that global warming is caused by humanity. For the latter overwhelming majority, the debate is long over. To his credit, Tom Brokaw has since become an influential voice for restoring the atmospheric balance before it is too late.[110] But problems with the media continue. The journalistic norms investigated by Boykoff and Boykoff and other experts have been a hindrance to getting the truth out to the public time after time after time.

More recent studies echo the findings of Boykoff and Boykoff. In *Media, Politics and Climate Change: Towards a New Research Agenda*, an article published in Sociology Compass, Professor Allison Anderson provides an overview on research which concerns how the media reports on climate change.[111] She finds that social scientists who study the media utilize three complimentary approaches: The political economy approach, (think how money influences the media), the structuralist (think the Boykoffs and the role of journalistic norms), and the culturalist approach, which involves the broader influence of prevailing political and social thought and practice on how the media conceptualizes issues.[112]

Professor Anderson provides a revealing look into the heart of the media's problem with telling the plain truth. She reviews the work of numerous scholars on the subject, noting that research by several academicians has shown "how powerful industry groups, special interest lobbies and PR companies in the United States have manipulated claims and exploited the news media."[113] Anderson also cites the book by Pulitzer Prize winning journalist Ross Gelbspan, *Boiling Point*[114] indicating that Gelbspan found strong ties between the oil companies Mobile and Exxon and the American Enterprise Institute plus other "climate sceptic think tanks."[115] Anderson cites other work by Gelbspan which found that an industry interest group with fifty four members called Global Climate Coalition has, since 1989, been spending vast amounts on PR and lobbyists in order to undermine the scientific consensus on global warming and influence public opinion on the subject.[116]

Other examples provided by Anderson confirmed the fact that Exxon Mobile has paid millions of dollars to various think tanks that work to challenge the science of global warming, and change public opinion on the subject.[117] Anderson's article also identifies a study that found that 92 percent of 141 books written in English that express skepticism on the subject of environment issues, were tied in some way to similar think tanks that are run by conservatives. The same study identified fifty think tanks that concern themselves with environmental issues, and found that ninety percent of them express skepticism via their websites and published works about environmentalist causes. Not surprisingly, every one of eight such organizations located in the United States was found to be skeptical of the scientific consensus on climate change.[118] The study's authors concluded that a major goal of climate change think tanks is to "manufacture uncertainty."[119]

Anderson also cited a newspaper report which revealed that a think tank funded by Exxon Mobile offered a bounty of $10,000 to economists or scientists who produced research papers which challenged the conclusions contained in a report issued by the Intergovernmental Panel on Climate Change.[120] "The Intergovernmental Panel on Climate Change (IPCC) is the leading international body for the assessment of climate change. "It was established by the United Nations Environment Programme (UNEP) and the World Meteorological Organization (WMO) in 1988 to provide the world with a clear scientific view on the current state of knowledge in climate change and its potential environmental and socio-economic impacts."[121]

It's understandable and perhaps to be expected that research done by think tanks funded by big corporations would find its way into the news media. However, the problem of corporate - insider influence on the direction and scope of public policy debates goes well beyond the act of funding research by friendly experts. Perhaps the most glaring example of deliberate press censorship with respect to global warming was described in a January 8, 2013 report by Media Matters for America.[122] Media Matters is an internet not for profit organization "dedicated to comprehensively monitoring, analyzing and correcting conservative misinformation" which is distributed via the news media.[123] The Media Matters report, which concerns global warming coverage on Sunday television news talk shows, convincingly shows that Sunday news talk shows like *Meet the Press* display a startling lack of journalistic balance on the subject of climate change. In my view, the Sunday news programs have been little more than propaganda instruments of the climate contrarian industry and big energy companies when it comes to the subject of global warming.

I was already aware of how unbalanced those shows tend to be, but the Media Matters study just blew me away: In four years, between January 1, 2009 and December 31, 2012 none of the Sunday news talk shows, including the two heavyweights *Meet the Press* and *Face the Nation*, ever quoted, interviewed, or had on as a guest a climatologist or other scientist competent to opine as an expert on global warming. Of the guests who discussed climate change on the Sunday shows, fifty four percent were media personalities and thirty one percent were politicians. Not even one scientist was allowed to tell the public of the scientific consensus that global warming is anthropomorphic and a grave threat to the world which requires immediate action! *Not even one!*

I told you previously of my opinion that economists who wish to present the case against free trade are never allowed to speak on such shows, but the Media Matters study went beyond mere opinion. The scientific methodology used by media matters provided great credence to the belief that the media is little more than an echo chamber for the powerful monied interests and the politicians who serve them. Another fact Media Matters uncovered was that during 2012, not a single politician who is a Democrat was quoted or allowed to speak on a Sunday news talk show such as Meet the Press or Face the Nation on the subject of global warming.

So, they shut out Democrats and climatologists, allowing only Republicans and media figures to talk about global warming. That's not all. The same January 8, 2013 Media Matters article reports other disturbing facts. Despite the occurrence in 2012 of Hurricane Sandy, unprecedented shrinkage of Arctic sea ice, unheard of melting of surface ice in Greenland and record setting heat, huge wildfires and a drought of historic proportions in the western United States, the broadcast media showed little interest in informing the public about relevant climate change findings that year. In fact the dismal lack of responsible reporting by broadcasters continued a four year trend.[124] In 2012, CBS Evening News covered climate change more than any other network. CBS News provided viewers with a total of only 22 minutes of climate change coverage *during the entire year*! NBC Nightly News covered climate change the least of any network, with a total of just 17 minutes coverage.[125]

A recent article by the media watchdog group known by the acronym FAIR, which stands for Fairness and Accuracy In Reporting, contains some corroborating evidence for the view that the news media has a tendency to avoid talk of global warming when commenting on extreme weather. A January 13, 2013 report by Jim Naureckas which has the caption: *Ignoring Climate Change When It Stares You in the Face*. provides an example of how broadcast news shows avoid the subject of global warming.[126]

Naureckas wrote that news anchor Lester Holt started out the January 12, 2013, NBC Nightly News with this comment: "Strange winter" "Why is it so cold where it should be warm, and so warm where it should be cold? What is going on with all this extreme weather." Holt's questions were answered by the Weather Channel's Greg Postel, whose report was introduced by NBC correspondent Kristen Dahlgren. Postel said: "A very strong dip in the jet stream has placed itself over the western part of the country and that's allowed some cold air from Canada to move southward."[127]

Postel's meteorological jargon did not touch on the question that every informed viewer was thinking, that being: Is it related to global warming? Naureckas went beyond Postel's not very informative reply to Holt, providing the following scientific facts from the blog ClimateSight:

> The jet stream isn't straight...it's rather wavy in the north-south direction, with peaks and troughs... Sometimes a large peak or trough will hang around for weeks on end, held in place by certain air pressure patterns. This phenomenon is known as "blocking," and is often associated with extreme weather...
>
> As climate change adds more energy to the atmosphere it would be naive to expect all the wind currents to stay exactly the same. Predicting changes is a complicated business, but a recent study by Jennifer Francis and Stephen Vavrus made headway on the polar jet stream. Using North American and North Atlantic atmospheric re-analyses ... from 1979-2010, they found Arctic amplification--the faster rate at which the Arctic warms, compared to the rest of the world--makes the jet stream slower and wavier. As a result, blocking events become more likely.[128]

Instead of presenting the existing scientific research which connects the dots between the scientific consensus about global warming and the extreme weather they were reporting on, Holt,

Postel and Dahlgren ducked the subject of climate change. Dahlgren ended the report with the simple minded comment: "Talk about upside-down weather."[129]

Naureckas concluded his article criticizing the NBC news and Postel by saying: "Let's talk, rather, about journalists who are failing to [report] acknowledged global climate changes when they're staring them in the face."[130]

Slanted Coverage of The War in Iraq

Following the attacks on the World Trade Center and the Pentagon on September 11, 2001, everybody wanted to go after the perpetrators. If that meant attacking the Taliban and going after Bin Laden in Afghanistan, most of us thought the same thing: *Bring it on!* Unfortunately, for so many of our soldiers and their families, and for thousands upon thousands of innocent people abroad, we also went to war with Iraq. Bush and Cheney decided to start a war with Iraq despite the fact that Iraq that had nothing whatsoever to do with 9/11. The later point is made in detail with extensive references in chapter fourteen.

The administration campaign to get America into a war with Iraq was, in my opinion, conducted by people who wantonly, recklessly, and at times intentionally, used fabricated documents, fabricated testimony and plain old lies to support the argument that Saddam Hussein had stores of weapons of mass destruction - and the means and intent to use those weapons on America. Bush and Cheney constantly tried to link Iraq with Al Qaeda's attacks on 9/11, despite there being clear evidence to the contrary. Admittedly, highly informed people and newshounds got enough information out of mainstream media sources to know that the Bush administration's case for making war on Iraq was all hogwash. Nevertheless, the media frequently acted as an echo chamber for the falsehoods which emanated from the Bush-Cheney White House. The result was a tragedy of lives wasted, and a fiscal disaster of unparalleled scope. If you don't already think as I do, I strongly recommend that you read some books about Iraq.

Perhaps the best book about the Iraq war is *Hubris: The Inside Story of Spin, Scandal, and the Selling of the Iraq War*, by Michael Isikoff and David Corn.[131] Another good read is *Fiasco The American Military Adventure in Iraq*, by Thomas E. Ricks.[132] Another is *So Wrong for So Long, How the Press, The Pundits - And The President - Failed On Iraq*, by Greg Mitchell.[133]

Another interesting book about the tragedy in Iraq is *Anatomy of Deceit How the Bush Administration Used the Media to Sell the Iraq War and Out a Spy* by Marcy Wheeler.[134] The Spy referred to is of course Valerie Plame. Bush's former press secretary, Scott McClellan, wrote a book concerning the Bush administration's propaganda campaign to get us into a war with Iraq. The book is reviewed in a Washington Post article which has the caption *Ex-Press Aid Writes That Bush Mislead U.S. on Iraq*.[135] There are too many more good reads about the Iraq War to list them all here.

Chapter fourteen provides a discussion of some of the fabrications, prevarications and PR trickery that was used to get America into that costly and senseless conflict. If you don't agree that America was duped into war by falsehoods and propaganda, chapter fourteen may help convince you.

This chapter has touched on the three broad subject areas the media covers which most significantly impact the ability of voters to vote rationally, namely the economy, the environment, and national defense. In all three areas there are glaring failures, and those failures occur because the media is often not watching out for the public interest, but instead acting almost as a lapdog to advertisers and those in power. The media is not doing the job the framers intended for it. Ownership of the media is so concentrated, that Ashley Lutz was able to write an article for *Business Insider* in 2012 bearing the caption *These 6 Corporations Control 90% Of The Media In America.*[136] What was once called "the free press" is now referred to as "the media monopoly,"[137] and "the corporate media,"[138] in common parlance.

Chapter six moves from the question of if and how the *money power* influences and controls the media discussion on trade, and other issues of concern to this book, to describe who and what *the money power* is. In the next chapter, we return to the early days of American democracy, to understand what policies the founding fathers adopted on related issues they faced.

Please keep this in mind as you read the rest of this book: By honestly describing the damage done by *monied interests* to American prosperity and democracy in this book, I am in no way attempting to undermine the principles of liberty and free enterprise that America was founded upon. *I am trying to preserve and protect freedom and America's democratic intuitions from corrupting influences and practices*. My main purpose is to help restore American prosperity.

4

The Heritage of the Mount Rushmore Presidents: Prosperity and Strength

The purpose of this book is to create a new political party and change America. But this book is not so much about change as it is about restoration. Most Americans don't know the names of the Presidents whose faces adorn Mount Rushmore.[139] Those men were builders and leaders all. I happen to believe in what they stood for: freedom, justice, opportunity, and another thing once mentioned in speeches by politicians: *progress.* American sociologist Robert Nisbet wrote extensively about the appeal of progress and the different ideas people have had about it throughout history. In 1979, Nisbet wrote "Idea of Progress: A Bibliographical Essay" in which he described the view of progress held be early Americans:

> Few places in the eighteenth century displayed a stronger belief in the philosophy of progress than did the American colonies and, then, the new, infant republic. Henry Steele Commager, in his recent *The Empire of Reason*, gives a good deal of stress to this; so does Edward McNall Burns in his *The American Idea of Mission*. Thomas Jefferson, in 1824, two years before his death, marveling at the progress already to be seen on earth and all that he had seen in his 81 years of life, writes: "And where this progress will stop no one can say. Barbarism has, in the meantime, been receding before the steady step of amelioration, and will in time, I trust, disappear from the earth." The sometimes dour John Adams, in the Preface to his *Defense of the Constitutions of Government of the United States*, writes of "the regular course of progressive improvement" in the arts and sciences, and goes so far as to declare that "The institutions now made in America will not wholly wear out for thousands of years." Benjamin Franklin, in a letter to his friend Joseph Priestley in 1780, writes: "It is impossible to imagine the Height to which may be carried, in a thousand years, the Power of Man over Matter." Such sentiments were commonplace in the America of the Founding Fathers.[140]

Thomas Jefferson marveled at the pace of progress during his lifetime. Ben Franklin and John Adams fairly swooned over the march of progress in early America. George Washington, whose likeness decorates the Mt. Rushmore memorial along with Jefferson's, was as concerned about fostering progress in America as any of our other founding fathers. Washington made Alexander Hamilton the nation's first Treasury Secretary and adopted Hamilton's scheme to use protectionism in the form of tariffs on foreign manufactures, and direct subsidies to domestic manufacturers, to bring progress to America as rapidly as possible.[141]

Washington saw the need for a strong manufacturing base in America as absolutely imperative. He was a vocal advocate of buying American and he practiced what he preached. Though the well off men of his day favored expensive European clothes, Washington made a point of wearing a new American made suit for his inauguration. He once said he hoped "it will not be a great while, before it will be unfashionable for a gentleman to appear in any other dress."[142] To George Washington, the interests of working Americans and the encouragement of manufacturing were of paramount concern, both to him personally and to the national interest. He made a pledge to a leading manufacturing association of his day "to demonstrate the sincerity of my opinion...by...giving decided preference to the produce and fabrics of America, whensoever it may be done without involving unreasonable expenses, or very great inconveniences."[143] True to his word, President Washington signed America's first tariff law on July 4, 1789 for "the encouragement and protection of manufactures."[144]

Washington recognized that Hamilton's call for even higher import duties than the average 8.5 percent rate imposed by the 1789 tariff would have to wait. During Washington's presidency, a national political schism that would remain throughout the decades leading up to the civil war developed. The nascent manufacturing interests in the north faced off against the agrarian slave holders of the south on the issue of protectionism. Consequently tariffs did not rise appreciably until the War of 1812 with Great Britain. After the war began, surging patriotism and wider recognition that the lack of sufficient manufacturing constituted a profound military disadvantage lead to acceptance on the part of powerful southern leaders that a protectionist policy was needed.[145] Congress then quickly increased tariffs to an average of 25 percent.[146] After 1816, a system of medium high to very high tariffs remained in force for most all of the years that followed until the end of World War II.[147]

Peering from the world famous mountain in South Dakota along with the likenesses of Washington and Jefferson is the face of another of our greatest Presidents: Abe Lincoln. Following the example of Washington, later Jefferson, and also Presidents such as Madison, Monroe, John Adams, and his son John Quincy Adams, Abraham Lincoln was a dyed in the wool protectionist.[148] Thanks in large part to Lincoln the average tariff on dutiable imports remained between forty and fifty percent during his tenure as President.[149] The system of protectionism employed by the United States transformed America into the world's greatest industrial powerhouse in the decades before America's critical triumphs in the world wars of the twentieth century.[150] Protectionism no doubt greatly aided America's triumph in both conflicts.

The only other American President honored at Mount Rushmore is Theodore Roosevelt. In addition to railing against the corporate trusts and robber barons of his day, Teddy Roosevelt was a staunch believer in the necessity of nurturing the growth and strength of American production and income through protectionism. His party's 1904 platform read: "Protection, which guards and develops our industries, is a cardinal policy of the Republican Party. The measure of protection should always at least equal the difference in the cost of production at home and abroad."[151]

Teddy Roosevelt would have no use for the billionaire financed think-tank-economist-spin-doctors we have today. He said: "The question of what tariff is best for our people is primarily one of expediency, to be determined not on abstract academic grounds, but in the light of experience." Roosevelt also said that the lesson of experience was not that "we could afford...to follow those professional counselors who have confined themselves to study in the closet; for the actual working of the tariff has emphatically contradicted their theories."[152] Teddy Roosevelt had plenty of experience to draw upon. While he was President, Roosevelt said "These forty odd years have been the most prosperous this nation has ever see; more prosperous years than any other nation has ever seen." He added that "Every class of our people has benefitted by the protective tariff.[153]

Considering the horrible blunders by our inept leaders in connection with Vietnam, Iraq, Katrina, the superfund toxic waste scandal, the savings and loan RTC debacle, and the derivatives/bad mortgage bubble burst economic collapse of 2008, these other words of Teddy Roosevelt come to mind: "*...thank God I am not a free trader. In this country pernicious indulgence in the doctrine of free trade seems inevitably to produce fatty degeneration of the moral fibre.*"[154] Those words were indeed prophetic: Since my youth, I have witnessed the systematic destruction of American prosperity by the servile politicians of the one percent who go by the names Democrat and Republican, and by the media monopoly which echoes them in the delivery of myth and misinformation on a daily basis to the American people. There is plenty of fatty degeneration in the moral fibre of our politicians and journalists these days and the effects of free trade have been a pernicious cause of their moral decline.

How could it be that the greatest presidents in history, the ones who are honored at Mount Rushmore, all chose to use protectionism to make America safe and prosperous? Why isn't there a free trader up there? In actual fact, Thomas Jefferson did initially feel that America should remain primarily an agricultural country and trade with Europe for manufactured goods. When Jefferson was elected president in 1801, he switched from Hamilton's scheme of protectionism to agrarianism. Jefferson came to realize that switching policies had been a mistake. By the end of the War of 1812, a number of developments persuaded Jefferson to reject free trade.[155] Jefferson realized that British manufacturers had been dumping products below cost in the American market which had prevented American manufacturers from developing. Jefferson also realized that the lack of manufacturing compromised American security and helped precipitate the War of 1812. Jefferson feared that America would not survive the disadvantages of a free trade economy and so Jefferson did a complete turn about. He then told the nation "manufactures are now as necessary to our independence as to our comfort."[156] He advised people to "keep pace with me in purchasing nothing foreign where an equivalent of domestic fabric can be obtained without regard to a difference of price."[157] By 1816, America had an average tariff of 35 percent,[158] with tariffs of 30 percent on iron imports and tariffs of 25 percent on major textiles.[159] By 1820 the average tariff rose to 40 percent.[160]

Our fifth and another great president was James Monroe. In 1822 Monroe said "whatever may be the abstract doctrine in favor of unrestricted commerce, that doctrine rests on two conditions--international peace and general reciprocity--which have never occurred and cannot be expected."[161] In 1824, Monroe signed a tariff bill into law which included duties on items never before subject to the tariff.[162] In 1828, while John Quincy Adams was President, even higher tariffs on foreign dutiable goods were enacted by Congress. The average tariff skyrocketed to

61.7 percent!![163] Adam's successor, President Andrew Jackson, also felt that a high protective tariff was best. Jackson said "It is time we should become a little more Americanized, and instead of feeding the paupers and laborers of Europe, feed our own, or else in a short time...we shall all be paupers ourselves."[164]

So it was that the policy of protectionism became entrenched after 1816 until the close of World War II.[165] The new policy of free trade slowly transformed America from the late sixties on into the largest debtor nation on Earth.[166] The still declining America of today suffers from the largest trade deficits in the world thanks to its one-way free trade policy.[167]

The foregoing quotes from some of our greatest leaders in history prove both that *they understood the theory of free trade,* and that - *they rejected it for pragmatic reasons.* They rejected free trade because the wanted to keep America on the path to progress, peace and prosperity. They knew that free trade would bring dependence on imports, reduce technological advancement, lower wages and weaken America's military in both absolute and relative terms. They would surely have foreseen, (as I did as a boy), America's rapid decline after free trade became the policy of the republicrats; They would have warned us sternly not to let it happen. But they were patriots all, and not merely *self seekers* and *servants of the money power.*

Protectionism brings Progress: The Rise of Britain, then America

It was during the age of American protectionism, roughly between 1790 and 1955 that America became a superpower. How did it come about? For one thing, the former colonists knew the history of America's "mother country," Great Britain. There are a whole host of myths that Demopublicans propagate through their lapdog - echo chamber - media monopoly, and one of them is the idea that first Britain, and then America, became rich countries through open markets and free trade policies. Nothing could be further from the truth."[168] That fact is well known to economists, but they, money powered politicians and media mouthpieces love to pretend otherwise. World famous University of Cambridge economist Ha Joon Chang has written the true history. England had a generally backward economy and was overshadowed by the more advanced nations of Belgium and the Netherlands until the Tudor Monarchs used *industrial espionage* and *protectionist methods* to develop England's wool manufacturing industry, which was Europe's high tech industry at the time."[169]

Chang points out in his writings on the subject that England's wool industry would not have become the world leader but for protectionism. England's protectionism provided its high tech wool industry with the earnings needed to finance the massive import of raw materials and food that helped bring about the Industrial Revolution.[170] Chang's 2008 book *Bad Samaritans The Myth of Free Trade and the Secret History of Capitalism* did not change my life long held view about the damage being done to America by free trade. But Chang's book, along with a small avalanche of similar academic work by other good economists, did help convince me that Americans could finally be persuaded that the Republicans and Democrats have abjectly failed to govern America competently.

Our founding fathers were no doubt well aware of the powerfully positive influence that the zealously protectionist Robert Walpole had on the progress of the British economy. The city of Walpole, Massachusetts was named for him at its founding in 1724.[171] Walpole became the defacto Prime Minister of Great Britain in 1721 and he did not leave that position until 1742. He believed that the public was best served by a policy of government promotion of manufacturing exports. In the year he became prime minister Walpole helped get protectionist laws passed that imposed significantly higher tariffs on imported manufactured goods. The legislation Walpole helped usher in also created subsidies for exports, and regulations to control and maintain the high quality of British manufactures, particularly textiles, so that the reputation of British exports would not be damaged by shoddy producers. Walpole's protectionist polices had their intended effect and Britain became the leading manufacturing country in the world. Protectionism remained in place, and Britain remained at the top of the world economically *and militarily* for more than a century after Walpole.[172] "In 1820, Britain's average tariff rate on manufacturing imports was 45-55%, compared to 6-8% in the Low Countries, 8-12% in Germany and Switzerland, and around 20% in France."[173]

If you have studied economics or history you know that Britain did not remain the richest and most productive industrial power. Britain's decline can be traced to two key factors: The first is that America rejected the free trade theory of the famous economists David Ricardo and Adam Smith. The second is that Britain, at the height of its superiority as an industrial power, embraced free trade as a way to open up foreign markets to its high quality goods. The British believed their vast industrial machine was too far ahead for foreigners to ever catch up. Thus they believed free trade would allow England to sell even more of the high value added manufactured goods that its wealth and military supremacy were built on. The British hoped that the lower prices they could offer world markets would keep other countries from developing competitive industries and so remain low income nations built around supplying raw materials and agricultural goods.[174]

What the British failed to realize is that they lived in a very large world teaming with resources and enterprising people who wanted to be on top. It's true of course that a segment of the political elite in colonial America (whose wealth was based on agricultural production or the supplying of raw materials), wanted to continue as an economic vassal state to England. To our good fortune, our greatest and most influential leaders, most notably the four presidents honored at Mt. Rushmore, sought a better future for the American people. They wanted to compete with Britain, and to do so they needed to keep the low cost and high tech British goods out of the United States market.[175] Because they did so, our country was first to the atomic bomb and first to the moon. Had the free traders had their way, America would probably have been conquered early in its history or during the world wars of the last century. It was weak government regulation over the "money power," not Smoot-Hawley or any other tariff which caused the Great Depression.[176] It was in large part the Great Depression that allowed fascism to take root in Germany.[177] Therefore, weak government regulation over the "money power," helped bring about the rise of Nazism and World War II. Of course, many other factors also played a causative role in Hitler's rise to power.

In addition to helping America win the War of 1812, our protectionist policies kept the Union together during the Civil War and allowed for the abolition of slavery in the United States. The industrial North spent over $2.3 billion dollars on military expenditures during the Civil War. The Confederates spent much less than half that, about $1 billion. That's largely because the South's share of both the U.S. population and the U.S. GDP was less than one third of the total before the war. The South relied on low value added agriculture while the North encouraged high value manufacturing by placing high tariffs on imports - despite Southern opposition. The South began the Civil War with about 20,600 factories which generated revenue of $155 million. The North had about 100,500 factories which generated about ten times more in revenue - an estimated $1.5 billion. In 1860, the North produced 32 times the number of firearms produced by the South. The North also kept possession of the entire U.S. Navy, which successfully blockaded the rebel South, cutting it off from its weapons suppliers while preventing it from selling its agriculture products, most notably slave made cotton. Putting it simply, the South was out spent, out gunned, and out of existence as a separate "country" in short order.[178] Unquestionably, the high tariffs on manufactured imports which remained in place for most of the period between 1816 and 1945 played a decisive role in helping bring about America's triumph in the Civil War and both world wars.

In our own day, the financial crisis which began in 2007 took place despite America's vaunted free trade policy. Inadequate regulation of banking by government of course played a leading role in causing the crisis, but America's free trade policy is also thought by good economists to have played a role in causing it. Currency manipulation by the Chinese to prop up the dollar is seen as having helped inflate the mortgage bubble,[179] while falling American wages caused by job outsourcing helped deflate it.[180]

I believe that *but for* the protectionist policies followed by the Mt. Rushmore Presidents, (assuming that Hitler would still have risen to lead Germany), Nazi rockets would have been to the first to the moon where Nazi *Kosmonaute* would have planted the Nazi Swastika. NASA would never even have come into existence. Thanks to tariffs on foreign manufactures, my description of what might have been is rhetorical only. There is nothing rhetorical however about the fact that protectionism was crucial to America's progress and security from its inception. So called "free" trade has clearly been the main cause of America's decline.

The American System of Manufacturing

There was another factor that eventually led Thomas Jefferson to decide protectionism was a good policy. That factor came into being when Jefferson learned about a plan by a Frenchman named Honore Blanc to manufacture standardized parts for muskets. Unfortunately for Blanc, he subsequently lost military financing for his planned musket factory as the result of two events; The first was the death of Blanc's patron, French General Jean Baptiste Vaquette de Gribeauval. General Gribeauval is given credit for being the first notable and leading proponent of the idea of building guns with interchangeable parts. The second event that helped ruin Blanc's chances of building a musket factory was the occurrence beginning in 1789 of the French Revolution.

After becoming discouraged because of the rejection of his ideas by French businessmen following the events of 1789, Blanc discussed the possibility of taking his idea to the United

States with Jefferson. Previously Jefferson had been so impressed with Blanc's idea that in 1785 Jefferson had written to the U.S. Secretary of War about it. Jefferson had realized that fledgling American industry and America's military would benefit if Blanc's idea could be developed further.

Although Blanc never cut a deal with the Americans, the famous American inventor Eli Whitney independently began lobbying the government to support the development of interchangeable parts.[181] President Washington became aware of the concept and he supported it.[182] The War Department tasked the federal armories that had been established at Springfield, Massachusetts and Harper's Ferry, (now a part of West Virginia) with the job of helping create guns with interchangeable parts. Eli Whitney, the famous inventor of the cotton gin who is also recognized as having promoted the idea of interchangeable parts, was given contracts to produce muskets for the United States, but it is unclear what innovations involving interchangeable parts Whitney actually produced.[183]

By the 1820's, the development of machine tools had begun to eliminate the need for specialized labor to do the time consuming work of "fitting" parts together. Standardized (interchangeable) parts permitted the separation of manufacturing parts from the assembly of finished products, lowering labor costs and eventually lead to the adoption of assembly line production.[184] The great strides in engineering made under the "American System" also led to a revolution in the methods of business organization and management. By 1854, an English machine tool maker named Joseph Whitworth visited the U.S. to learn from the upstart protectionist Americans.[185] He described what he had seen as follows:

> The laboring classes are comparatively few in number, but this is counterbalanced by, and indeed, may be one of the causes of the eagerness by which they call in the use of machinery in almost every department of industry. Wherever it can be applied as a substitute for manual labor, it is universally and willingly resorted to ....It is this condition of the labor market, and this eager resort to machinery wherever it can be applied, to which, under the guidance of superior education and intelligence, the remarkable prosperity of the United States is due."[186]

The fact that Whitworth was correct was not in dispute. It was simple logic that wealth was being created by using machines to increase productivity. Though there were fewer workers needed, those who were employed enjoyed greater prosperity. The nation was benefitted by increased demand, increased tax revenue, greater manufacturing capacity, greater engineering capability, and greater military might. That none of these benefits would have been realized had cheaper British exports not been subject to a substantial tariff gets at the very essence of what is wrong with free trade.

The very famous statesman Henry Clay made first use of the phrase "American System" to describe the protectionist trade strategy and the manufacturing and technical practices it encouraged to assure the military strength, independence and progress of the American nation.[187] Clay, a Kentuckian, served as a Senator, a Congressman, three terms as Speaker of the House, and four years as Secretary of State.[188] He also organized the Whig party and played a role in helping keep the United States from breaking apart with the brokering of the Missouri Compromise of 1820 and the Compromise of 1850.[189]

In 1957, a Senatorial committee chaired by John F. Kennedy tasked with picking the initial five members for a "Senatorial Hall of Fame" (four more have been added since 2004), chose Henry Clay as one of them.[190] Clay was a leading proponent of protectionism in Congress. Over a three day period in 1832, Clay debated the merits of the American System with the spokesman for the southern cotton growers in the Senate. Domestic manufacturing was seen as a threat by the great plantation owners to their monopoly on power in the South. They wanted no tariffs on goods made by Great Britain. Clay's remarks go on for about 31 pages in the Register of Debates in Congress. Most of the observations that Clay made in 1832 are still true today. Consider this remark by Clay during the 1832 debate:

> When gentlemen have succeeded in their design of an immediate or gradual destruction of the American System, what is their substitute? Free trade! Free trade! The call for free trade, is as unavailing as the cry of a spoiled child, in its nurse's arms, for the moon or the stars that glitter in the firmament of heaven. It never has existed; it never will exist. Trade implies at least two parties. To be free, it should be fair, equal, and reciprocal. But if we throw our ports wide open to the admission of foreign productions, free of all duty, what ports, of any other foreign nation, shall we find open to the free admission of our surplus produce? We may break down all barriers to free trade on our part, but the work will not be complete until foreign powers shall have removed theirs. There would be freedom on one side, and restrictions, prohibitions, and exclusions, on the other. The bolts, and the bars, and the chains, of all other nations will remain undisturbed.[191]

So, I ask you: Is any part of what Clay said above untrue today? Our record setting trade imbalance in 2006 reached 811.5 billion dollars![192] One explanation for why America has lost so many jobs, and produces so few good jobs in the modern era of "free" trade is that it's *not* free, it's *fixed* trade. America is getting screwed by the protectionist practices of its trading partners.[193]

Later chapters in this book discusse how foreign ownership of real estate and businesses located in America just continues to increase. Our once great industries are in decline or already gone. GM went bankrupt and the "great" spokesman for free trade, George Bush II, violated all his free market principles to bail out the auto industry.[194] Let's hear more of what Mr. Clay had to say:

> Gentlemen deceive themselves. It is not free trade that they are recommending to your acceptance. It is, in effect, the British colonial system that we are invited to adopt; and, if their policy prevail, it will lead substantially to the recolonization of these states, under the commercial dominion of Great Britain.[195]

It certainly seems that we could substitute the word China for Britain in the above comment by Mr. Clay, and we would have a statement that is pertinent to the future course the Demopublicans have charted for us. Of course, not all foreign investment is a bad thing, but when such investment is in the wrong direction close to two thirds of the time and results from gigantic American trade deficits, it is not a healthy thing.[196]

As for what Clay meant by the commercial domination by great Britain there is little doubt. We have already touched on the history of British protectionism, and it is well documented; After Britain thought its manufacturing industries had progressed so far ahead that they could stifle all competition, and after America embraced protectionism, Britain adopted free trade and replaced protectionism as a policy. It was an attempt to pry open the American market to Britain's manufactured goods and monopolize it. Had American leaders fallen for the trap the nascent American industrial complex would have been destroyed before it became a threat to British economic domination.[197] Clay said this:

> ..But I have said that the system nominally called "free trade," so earnestly and eloquently recommended to our adoption, is a mere revival of the British colonial system, forced upon us by Great Britain during the existence of our colonial vassalage. The whole system is fully explained and illustrated in a work published as far back as the year 1750, titled 'The trade and navigation of Great Britain considered by Joshua Gee,' with extracts from which I have been furnished by the diligent researches of a friend. It will be seen from these, that the South Carolina policy now, is identical with the long-cherished policy of Great Britain, which remains the same as it was when the thirteen colonies were part of the British empire.[198]

Clay then recites the writing of Joshua Glee as follows:

> '1. That manufactures, in the American colonies, should be discouraged or prohibited. Great Britain, with its dependencies, is doubtless as well able to subsist within itself as any nation in Europe. We have an enterprising people, fit for all the arts of peace and war. We have provisions in abundance, and those of the best sort, and are able to raise sufficient for double the number of inhabitants. We have the very best materials for clothing, and want nothing, either for use or even for luxury, but what we have at home, or might have from our colonies: so that we might make such an intercourse of trade among ourselves, or between us and them, as would maintain a vast navigation. But we ought always to keep a watchful eye over our colonies, to restrain them from setting up any of the manufactures which are carried on in Britain; and any such attempts should be crushed in the beginning: for if they are suffered to grow up to maturity, it will be difficult to suppress them...
>
> ...Our colonies are much in the same state Ireland was in, when they began the woollen manufactory, and, as their numbers increased, will fall upon manufactures for clothing themselves, if due care be not taken to find employment for them in raising such productions as may enable them to furnish themselves with all their necessaries from us.'[199]

After quoting the above passages from Glee, Clay spoke on:

> Then it was the object of this British economist to adapt the means or wealth of the colonists to the supply required by their necessities, and to make the mother country the only source of that supply. Now it seems the policy is only so far to be reversed, that we must continue to import necessaries from Great Britain, in order to enable her to purchase raw cotton from us.[200]

One can easily see why Henry Clay was such a successful politician and also why America's

Presidents from the inception of the nation to the mid twentieth century were usually in favor of using protectionism to insure progress. Clay made another remark in that 1832 debate that is still relevant today. One of the arguments free traders always made in Clay's day was that foreign products were cheaper and better. Clay disputed that. He pointed out that over a seven year period prior to his speech, prices on products protected by tariffs had actually fallen. He noted that "*under the operation of the American System, the objects which it protects and fosters are brought to the consumer at cheaper prices than they commanded prior to its introduction, or than they would command if it did not exist*."[201]

One thing free trade theory cannot measure, and what free trade economists hate to discuss are the technological spin offs, new inventions and engineering advances that are lost when imports are allowed to destroy domestic industries and jobs.[202] Although free trade economists make an effort to *cherry pick measure* job losses from free trade,[203] they never measure the loss of jobs in new and improved domestic industries that would have been developed but for the technology devastating impact of free trade.[204] Those losses from free trade are unquestionably huge, but they are completely ignored. Also not measured by economists is the economic value of military *capability and strength losses* caused by free trade, yet the nations's security infrastructure has enormous economic value. When you consider the fact that free trade is actually *fixed* trade, because countries such as China, Japan and Germany are all still using protectionist measures, the losses are even greater. The history of our rise during the period of protectionism and our subsequent decline since free trade was instituted supplies a ton of experiential data as to the merits of free trade theory, as does the experience of many other countries. All of it leads to the conclusion that our unilaterally free trade with low wage protectionist countries like China, and higher wage protectionist countries like Germany and Japan, is sinking America in much the same way that America sank Britain in the nineteenth and early twentieth centuries. But we do not need to proceed on the basis of experience alone. Free trade theory is not only broken in practice. It is broken in theory as well, a fact which is discussed in the next chapter.[205]

5

Why the Theory of Free Trade Is Scientifically and Logically Invalid

From the inception of the idea of free trade it has almost always been presented to the public by its boosters as a theory of economic science,[206] rooted in a sublime mathematical proof that defies all criticism.[207] Nothing could be further from the truth. Free trade theory is mathematically invalid. It has also been proved by experience to have been a disaster for most Americans and for America as a country.

In 1776, the famous economist Adam Smith published his almost equally famous book, *An Inquiry into the Nature and Causes of the Wealth of Nations.*[208] Smith's theory of free trade's benefits was rooted in his conception of "absolute advantage." George Washington had every opportunity to read and digest Smith's book. If you did not know it already, you know from reading the last chapter that George Washington took the side of Alexander Hamilton and rejected Adam Smith's endorsement of free trade.

The advent of the idea of *comparative advantage* postulated by David Ricardo in his 1817 book *On the Principles of Political Economy and Taxation*,[209] did away with Smith's notion that countries would produce those goods in which they had an absolute advantage. The theory of comparative advantage, to the extent it is true, (which it is not when it is used to go beyond its limited axioms), proves mathematically that Smith's theory of absolute advantage is untrue.[210] As for the theory of comparative advantage, Henry Clay was of the opinion (as noted in the last chapter), that Britain began advocating free trade only after mercantilism became impossible owing to the fact that America had become both independent and protectionist. Clay argued successfully that free trade was really just a strategy adopted by Britain to keep America a backwater nation that was forced to buy British.

Clay made his comments in 1832, fifteen years after Ricardo published his ideas about comparative advantage. Clay had more to say against free trade, and his words were prophetic of the beating over that modern research has given to Ricardo's theory. It is a theory which has taken on more complexity and new forms but which remains as illogical as ever when applied to the real world. Clay said:

> I pass, with pleasure, ...to...general propositions which cover the entire ground of debate. The first is, that, under the operation of the American System, the objects which it protects and fosters are brought to the consumer at cheaper prices than

> they commanded prior to its introduction, or than they would command if it did not exist. If that be true, ought not the country to be contented and satisfied with the system...? And is the fact not indisputable, that all essential objects of consumption, affected by the tariff, are cheaper and better, since the act of 1824, than they were for several years prior to that law? I appeal, for its truth, to common observation and to all practical men. I appeal to the farmer of the country, whether he does not purchase, on better terms, his iron, salt, brown sugar, cotton goods, and woollens, for his laboring people. And I ask the cotton planter if he has not been better and more cheaply supplied with his cotton bagging...[211]

In the above quote Henry Clay made the point that a rapid succession of innovations and inventions relating to a broad swath of different types of products was increasing productivity and decreasing prices better under protectionism over a seven year period than America could have obtained by importing manufactured goods from Britain during that same period. What Clay called the "American System" we might call "industrial policy" today. Lets go back and consider what Whitworth, (in 1854), said was the explanation for American prosperity:

> The laboring classes are comparatively few in number, but this is counterbalanced by, and indeed, may be one of the causes of the eagerness by which they call in the use of machinery in almost every department of industry. Wherever it can be applied as a substitute for manual labor, it is universally and willingly resorted to....It is this condition of the labor market, and this eager resort to machinery wherever it can be applied, to which, under the guidance of superior education and intelligence, the remarkable prosperity of the United States is due."[212]

The more you learn about the dangers of shifting manufacturing out of America to wherever wages are cheapest, the more you will see that free trade is an inane idea and a suicidal strategy. Now lets turn to the main concept free trade economists rely on.

The Incomplete and Fanciful Idea of Comparative Advantage

For a general to go into war with a strategic overview as primitive and incomplete as the idea of comparative advantage provides economic policy makers, he would have to ignore all the technical advantages of his enemy. He would have to ignore his enemies superior weapons, such as tanks, artillery, warships, missiles, drones, jet fighters, advanced radar systems, command and control systems, hyperspeed weapons, and weapons of mass destruction. His unsound military mind would rely solely on a simple arithmetic comparison between the number of soldiers each army had. That is what free trade theory does.

Free trade theory completely ignores what trade does to a countries technological and military capacities both in absolute terms and vis a vis its trading partners. But ignoring losses does not make them go away. Spin off technologies that are lost because of cheap foreign labor are lost for good. Also lost are all other positive "externalities" that would have benefitted other domestic industries, and also benefitted the country's military capabilities both in absolute and relative terms. Those losses are compounded by a process of "reverberation." Innovations in one industry spread to other industries generating other innovations that bounce back to and improve the original innovation. Reverberation is a poor word for the process, because echos fade. Innovation which results in one industry could and does lead to an ever growing cascade of progress which is unlimited in time and scope. It is true that most great innovations eventually spread out over the Earth, but before they reach foreign shores subsequent innovation in the country of origination has nearly always taken place - if that is a protectionist country. If not, uh oh! Thus, nations that start out behind will remain behind forever unless they can devise strategies to steal the thunder from their superior competitors. Can you discount the value of invention to progress? Nations rise and fall depending upon whether they recognize or lose sight of the value of invention and its chief progenitor, which is the ever evolving process of creating wealth by adding value to raw materials using labor and capital.

How then is it that our government went astray and continues to weaken and impoverish the nation as a whole? Why does our nation accept a gargantuan national debt which must grow inexorably because of our enormous yearly trade deficit? Why does our nation accept ever declining wages, the slow but sure devaluation of the dollar, ever lowering participation in the work force, and the growing military threat posed to us and our allies because our share of the world's manufacturing and GDP keeps declining? A factor in the continuing failure of our national government to get trade policy right is the seductive simplicity of the false idea of comparative advantage. But a bigger factor lies in the rise of the new "money power," which some experts suggest has achieved monopolistic control over the media and undue influence over the minds of our people.[213] We look first however at Ricardo's comparative advantage model.

Riccardo's theory that free trade is beneficial to every country is based on a simple comparison between two countries, each of which produces the same two goods. In my example below, the two countries America (U.S.A.) and China produce both guns and butter.[214]

We assume, (like Ricardo did), the following things to make our model work:

(1) We assume only two countries, only two goods, and the same two goods produced in each country.

(2) We assume that maximizing total world production for the trading period is our goal.

(3) We assume zero Transportation/Transaction Costs.

(4) Factor Mobility/Immobility - we assume that labor, and capital are absolutely mobile within each country and absolutely immobile between countries.

(5) Full employment - We assume full employment in each country.

The production rate for each country is as follows:

(good produced)	(units produced)	(man hours needed per unit per country)	
		U.S.A.	China
Guns	10,000	8	10
Butter	1 ton	4	8

Suppose further that each country has 2,000 hours of labor. Finally, suppose that each country devotes half of its labor resource to each good. Then the production in each country is as follows:

U.S.A

1000 hrs./(8 h rs./10,000 Guns) = 1,250,000.00 Guns
1000 hrs./(4 hrs./Ton of Butter) = 250 Tons of Butter

China

1000 hrs./(10 hrs./10,000 Guns) = 1,000,000.00 Guns

1000 hrs./(8 hrs./Ton of Butter) = 125 Tons of Butter

Thus, world production is 2,250,000.00 Guns and 375 Tons of Butter. Notice that the U.S.A. has an "absolute advantage" in both goods. Clearly, the U.S.A. is more efficient than China in the production of both guns and butter. For every 25 guns produced by the U.S.A., China can produce only 20 guns with the same amount of man hours. Similarly, for every ton of butter produced by the U.S.A., China can produce only one half ton of butter with the same amount of man hours. Notice that although the U.S.A has an absolute advantage in making both goods, China's productivity lags behind the U.S.A. more in butter production than in gun production. China is only half as productive as the U.S.A. at making butter, but it is eighty percent as productive as the U.S.A at making guns. In order to increase total world production to its maximum what needs to be done? Well, if the U.S.A put all of its labor into the production of butter where it enjoys the greatest "absolute advantage," then we would have 2000 hrs./(4 hrs./Ton of Butter) = 500 Tons of Butter. If China puts all its labor into gun production we would have 2,000,000.00 guns. However, in order to maintain the previous level of world production of guns (2,250,000.00 guns), it is necessary for the U.S.A. to produce at least 250,000 guns. Thus, the U.S.A must allocate 200 hours to gun production to produce 250,000 guns. This would leave 1800 hours for America to produce butter. Our final tally then is 2,000,000.00 guns from China (its entire output), 250,000.00 guns from the U.S.A., and 450 tons of butter from the U.S.A. The world realizes a benefit of an additional 75 tons of butter from free trade in this simplistic model.

That's it, we are done. David Ricardo came up with the theory in October of 1816 as an improvement on the ideas of Adam Smith concerning free trade. There is nothing more to know about comparative advantage. You have just seen the whole theory. All economists have done in the last two centuries is extend the two-country, two-goods model to larger number of goods or a larger number of countries but not both.[215] The essence of the theory is the same.

The popular appeal of comparative advantage theory is based on the principles of arithmetic, i.e. addition, subtraction, multiplication, and division. All arithmetic follows the rules of inference, which is to say, it's deductive logic. When ordinary people learn about the theory in school they are blown away by the arithmetic. The assumptions seem ridiculous to the average student (the assumptions are ridiculous), but the math is crystal clear. Not only that, the reason for the assumptions is frequently not clear to the average student. In terms of logic, the theory of comparative advantage is a deduction based up *axioms*. Every time a student is taught the theory he must memorize the assumptions underlying it to get a good grade on his test. For a deduction to be true, its axioms must all be true, or its an invalid deduction. If you postulate that even one of the axioms to a deduction is false, the whole deduction is rendered *logically invalid*. You only need to read the assumptions specified in any explanation of what comparative advantage is to know that the theory is illogical. It is illogical because as a deductive argument its axioms must be true and those axioms are not even close to being true. Modern economists like Ha-Joon Chang, Clyde Prestowitz, and Ian Fletcher have written easily understandable books trying to warn the general public that free trade theory is a false doctrine. Each of them exposes the absurdity of the underlying *logical axioms* that *must be true* for the theory to be a valid deduction.

The assumptions underlying the idea of comparative advantage all have to do with the idea that individual countries are "endowed" with certain "factors." These endowments can be thought of in the same way as say an individual person's endowments. A beautiful woman with a degree in drama and enormous talent as an actor will find work as an actor sooner than a man who has no neither experience as an actor, nor the natural abilities required to become one.

There is no way on this earth that either the woman with beauty and talent or the man with neither talent nor looks can ever exchange their comparative advantages with respect to acting is there? But countries can and do change their comparative advantages in order to increase their national wealth. A poor country can overtake and pass a rich country using protectionist methods. No rational country wants to be consigned to poverty because economists tell it that its comparative advantage lies in a single industry, such as *growing bananas*. Countries adopt industrial policies and almost inevitably resort to protectionist strategies in order to change their comparative advantages and move into high value wealth producing industries. They do this by inducing investment in new domestic industries and by acquiring the advanced technology they need from other countries.[216]

Let's consider each of the assumptions without which the idea of comparative advantage falls apart, to see if any of them are true. Here is the list again:

(2) We assume that maximizing total world production for the trading period is our goal.

(3) We assume zero Transportation/Transaction Costs.

(4) Factor Mobility/Immobility - we assume that labor, and capital are absolutely mobile within each country and absolutely immobile between countries.

(5) Full employment - We assume full employment in each country.

I have omitted the first axiom because that is one that says there are only two countries and two products. The arithmetic still holds when the equations are adjusted to accommodate more countries or products, but the theory remains in even its most advanced formulations to be invalid. Assumption (2) is clearly not true. Countries adopt strategies for the future just as individuals do. Just as an individual will sacrifice his current income in order to get an education and earn a better living in the future, countries will lower the value of their currencies or adopt other protectionist schemes in order to nurture, development and maintain industries they covet for reasons of future wealth maximization and military power.[217] Assumption (3) is also false. Though economists have made attempts to incorporate certain trade costs into free trade theory, the cost of increased pollution, increased energy consumption, and other non financial transaction costs is never zero. Efforts to measure these costs and include them in the theory are problematic at best. The fourth assumption (4) is utterly false and its falsity obliterates the theory of comparative advantage.[218] The underlying factors that change and define a nation's comparative advantage can be moved rapidly between countries. In the case of technology and money, comparative advantage can move across national borders at close to the speed of light. You better believe that the transference of tens of thousands of American factories and all the technology used in them to China and other low wage countries has altered the comparative advantages of both China and the United States. Assumption (5) is required to be true because if employment falls, wages will fall and that affects comparative advantage. Nevertheless, Assumption (5) is obviously false in the real world.

The assumptions underlying the theory of comparative advantage are necessary because if you remove them then the idea that comparative advantage is relatively unchanging and fixed by cultural, geographical and other factors breaks down. Comparative advantages between countries can then change quickly enough so that the arithmetic contained in the theory does not add up.

In truth, the idea of comparative advantage is largely obsolete in the modern world. The presence of cheap labor and dangerously lax pollution control laws in less developed countries is what determines their "comparative advantage" in getting the high value added manufacturing, engineering and managerial jobs that multinational corporations create. The idea of comparative advantage can be thought of as a *mirage*, as soon as you look at it up close it *disappears before your very eyes*.[219] The fact that a country's human resources (HR) are a significant element in a country's "comparative advantage" is admitted by most if not all economists. Recently I asked the Chairman of the College of Economics and Business at a major university this question:

> Do you believe that the assumption of factor immobility is of central importance to the idea of comparative advantage as described by Riccardo?

The answer I received did not surprise me:

> Factor mobility or lack thereof is critical in explaining comparative advantage. We can see where HR moving from country to country has changed comparative

advantage with the brain drain from various countries to the US, but that is in an area where a few can make a huge difference. For commodities, moving HR around is not very practical and not allowed. The US will let in a few talented individuals but we like to build walls to keep out the masses, so importing several ...million workers so we can assemble iphones does not make sense.[220]

HR or human resources, known more traditionally as *labor and management* constitute two of the factors of production. The other two factors are *capital and land.* Capital includes all the machinery, tools, buildings and processes employed to create goods. Thus the value of capital is in part dependent on the technology used to create, maintain and control it. It is common for economists to lump in management with capital leaving a total of three factors of production.

Not mentioned in the answer the economics department chairman provided me is the significance of capital movements and technology transfers between countries. That did not surprise me, because capital and technology move freely from the United States to competitor countries. That is why free trade has ruined America's comparative advantage in manufacturing. Now America is forced to compete largely on the cost of labor because any technology created in the U.S.A. can be sent abroad with few exceptions. That is also why American wages keep falling and good American jobs keep disappearing.

Even before the advent of modern high speed communications, banking, and transportation systems, the theory of comparative advantage was justifiably laughed at by American leaders like Henry Clay who saw it for what it was, a ruse by Britain to dupe the United States and prevent its rise.

The HO Model

I was convinced free trade was bad policy long before I went to college in 1974, took a course in International Economics, and learned about the Heckscher-Ohlin model. After obtaining an A in that course I still believed that free trade was basically just a way for American companies to get rid of unions, hire slave like labor overseas, circumvent pollution controls, indulge in unfair labor practices and avoid fair and reasonable taxation. To me, the building up of our giant industrial base had been the result of generations of hard work, bitter struggle, and all too frequent wars. To pack it up and ship it to the Mexican maquiladora area, sweatshops in Indonesia, and hell holes elsewhere was counter to what I believed in. Although the outsourcing by America based businesses was bad, even worse was the Demopublican decision to provide open markets to other countries (such as Japan and Germany), despite the fact those countries were still practicing protectionism against us. I predicted a dismal future: the decline of manufacturing, falling wages, increasing divorce rates, fewer marriages, more crime. more violence, more poverty and military decline. I watched our trade deficits, (we had our first in modern history in 1973), grow and grow to their present gynormous size. I was never against trade, I was just in favor of being smart about it.

Obviously, Henry Clay and his generation of leaders had a look at Ricardo's theory of comparative advantage and rejected it. They knew it was in the national interest for America to develop a manufacturing base second to none. They were not willing to rely on random chance, i.e. a free market, to develop one. After all, a simple minded theory based on two goods in two countries based on false assumptions is not sufficient to overcome the belief that dominating manufacturing is the surest path to continuing prosperity and security for any great nation. For small countries with special endowments, (think oil and natural gas in Qatar for example), relying on a small basket of production items for export can perhaps be a reasonable policy. For large nations like America, only high mass production offers a way to achieve high mass consumption. The more we dominate manufacturing the richer we can be. It's just that simple.

In the effort to further illuminate the way trade between nations takes place, in the early part of the nineteenth century Swedish economists Eli Heckscher and Bertil Ohlin came up with a new model. Ricardo's concept of comparative advantage simply assumes that there are differences in efficiency between countries in producing goods. Heckscher and Ohlin looked at the situation in terms of two easily distinguished factors used to make all products, labor and capital. They reasoned that a countries relative abundance of labor and capital would determine the relative prices of its goods. Thus, a more capital intensive country would tend toward making capital goods, and a more labor intensive country would tend toward making labor intensive goods. The Heckscher – Ohlin theory, known as the HO Theorem or HO Model.[221] Their theory makes certain assumptions which are:

1. There are two nations (Nation 1 and Nation 2), two commodities (commodity x and commodity y), and two factors of production (labor and capital).
2. Both nations use the same technology in production
3. Commodity x is labor intensive, and commodity y is capital intensive in both nations.
4. Both commodities are produced under constant returns to scale in both nations.
5. There is incomplete specialization in production in both nations.
6. Tastes are equal in both nations.
7. There is perfect competition in both commodities and factor markets in both nations.
8. There is perfect factor mobility within each nation but no international factor mobility.
9. There are no transportation costs, tariffs, or other obstructions to the free flow of international trade.
10. All resources are fully employed in both nations.
11. International trade between the two nations is balanced.

For the model to be mathematically valid, each and every one of the above eleven assumptions has to be true, and of course you can tell from reading them that they are not all true in the real world. Let us assume country 1, China is a labor abundant country. Country 2, America is a capital abundant country. K stands for capital and L stands for labor. P stands for price. Remember from Assumption 3 above that commodity x is labor intensive, and commodity y is capital intensive in both nations. If you have trouble with the next few lines that's ok. Don't stop reading the book! I summarize what economists say about the validity of the HO model just past this exposition. Here's the math in the simplest terms possible:

1. America is capital abundant and China is labor abundant thus,

America China

$$\frac{K}{L} > \frac{K}{L}$$

2. In both countries commodity y is capital intensive and commodity x is labor intensive,

$$\frac{K(y)}{L(y)} > \frac{K(x)}{L(x)}$$

3. Because of the principle that the greater abundance of a factor, (all other factors being equal) leads to a lower price for the commodity which is intensive in that factor, the consequence is:

America China

$$\frac{P(x)}{P(y)} < \frac{P(x)}{P(y)}$$

Just from the simple formulation above you can see that the HO model predicts that a capital intensive country should specialize in capital intensive goods, leaving labor intensive countries stuck with producing labor intensive goods. This conclusion seems counter intuitive to us now, but that is because we all know that capital flows to wherever labor is cheaper and regulations are fewer and weaker in a race to the bottom for wages, the environment, and the middle class. Well you ask, what of it, has HO been tested to see if it works? The answer is yes and to a great extent.

A study was conducted by economist Wassily W. Leontief in 1954 which found that the United States, which at the time was a very capital intensive country, was actually exporting more labor intensive goods. This contradiction of the HO model is known as the "Leontief paradox." Subsequent attempts to solve the paradox and save the theory have all failed.[222] The free traders had to jettison the theory I was taught in college and fall back on the two century old nonsense of comparative advantage.

That perhaps explains why economist Douglas Irwin, a professor of economics at Dartmouth College does not mention Eli Heckscher or Bertil Ohlin anywhere in his book: *Free Trade Under Fire.*[223] Irwin does mention comparative advantage of course. He uses it to try to show that free trade maximizes national wealth. He also makes reference to criticism of the theory along the lines I have presented here, writing this:

> Critics of free trade sometimes insist that the theory of comparative advantage is obsolete because Ricardo did not consider capital mobility or technology transfer between countries. But modern economists have altered many of the assumptions underlying Ricardo's analysis, and the main result--that international exchange remains mutually advantageous--remains intact *[224]

Professor Irwin's claim that the comparative advantage theory remains intact is supported by a footnote comment which reads as follows:

> *(fn 9) In fact, the United States is a large free trade area with labor and capital mobility and transferable technology across regions. Yet despite lower wages in the south for much of the late nineteenth and early twentieth centuries, high-wage regions of the country did not suffer from a "race to the bottom," and the South did not get rich at the expense of the north, but rather a slow process of convergence to higher incomes occurred across regions. See McLean and Mitchener 1999.[225]

That argument is unpersuasive. After the civil war, the owners of northern armament producers, steel mills, railroad manufacturers, and other factories that could be used for war production did not all rush on down to the deep south to take advantage of cheaper labor - assuming there was any. It is logical to conclude that most all northern leaders were protectionist (and defensive concerning the possibility of another future civil war) in outlook. Subsequent to the civil war northern business leaders did not change their opinions about protectionism until the mid twentieth century. The South was slow to shed its agricultural tradition for cultural and political reasons as well. We know what happened after that. We got the "rustbelt phenomenon." The South did eventually lure a great number of factories from the North because of the anti-union sentiment that took hold of middle America in the decades following WWII. Free trade and union busting became the policy of the Republican establishment, and with that policy the rust began to form. Below is an excerpt from the Wikipedia article "Rustbelt:"

> The **Rust Belt** is the informal description for a postindustrial region straddling the Northeastern and the East North Central States, referring to economic decline, population loss and urban decay due to the shrinking of its once powerful industrial sector. The term gained popularity in the United States in the 1980s. The Rust Belt begins in central New York and traverses to the west through Pennsylvania, West Virginia, Ohio, Indiana, and the Lower Peninsula of Michigan ending in northern Illinois and eastern Wisconsin Previously it was known as the industrial heartland of America. However, industry has been declining in the region since the mid-20th century due to a variety of economic factors, such as the transfer of manufacturing to the Southeast, increased automation, the decline of the US steel and coal industries, globalization and internationalization. While some cities and towns have managed to adapt by shifting focus towards services, others have not fared as well, witnessing rising poverty and declining populations.[226]

Supposedly, according to Irwin, capital mobility and technology transfer did not take place between the North and the South in America to any great extent, so free trade actually is advantageous for all nations. Irwin's conclusion does not jibe with common recollection. The common wisdom is that industries moved from the northern industrial states to the sun belt to escape unions. Economic research shows that the common wisdom is correct.[227]

It goes without saying of course, that firms can make goods cheaper if their labor and pollution control costs go down. That is not a justification for slave wages, horrible working conditions, and grossly inadequate environmental protections. It also does not provide a good reason for Americans to accept the loss of the benefits of a large technologically diverse manufacturing base, which generates the positive externalities and the value added production which is necessary to achieve ever higher mass consumption, higher wages, improving GDP vis-à-vis other nations, and enhanced military security.

Because of the shortcomings of free trade in theory, and negative experience with free trade in practice, economists are writing more and more books attacking the theory. They have come up with some fascinating new theoretical insights which cast a dark and deepening shadow on the theory that free trade is good. The truth is that the supporters of free trade have been forced to admit that the theory of free trade is logically invalid. Even Doug Irwin admitted it in his book *Free Trade Under Fire* when he wrote:

> It is sometimes said that free trade is right in theory but wrong in practice. Actually, the opposite is true. Any clever graduate student in economics can quickly come up with half a dozen reasons why free trade fails as a theoretical proposition. Yet in practice, the economic benefits of trade and the costs of protection are tangible.[228]

Thank you Professor for admitting that. All free trade proponents have left is cherry picked experiential data to support a theory that is logically invalid. That is a huge admission by Dr. Irwin, but it's true. Yes, we theoretically can get lower prices over a short term period hiring foreign slave wage workers toiling long hours in toxic sweatshops; but how do we pay for their goods? What happens to our *national prosperity* and our *military security* as other nations take away more and more of our high value added manufacturing jobs where productivity and wage gains are highest over time? The answer is we get lower and lower relative wages, we get pushed into service industries with little potential for productivity growth, and, our military becomes both absolutely and relatively weaker and weaker over time. Do we actually save a few pennies on consumer goods or do the vendors in fact gobble up the entire profit from off shoring? I had the same opinion of free trade in college forty years ago that I have today, but times have changed. Times are harder for most Americans. College graduates frequently can't find jobs, and the pool of good jobs just keeps shrinking. The economic statistics are generally bad and the future looks bleak for Americans.[229]

Are you asking for the meat? What concrete proof do I have that free trade is wrecking (and has to a great extent already wrecked), Yankee ingenuity and American manufacturing? A recent study by the Massachusetts Institute of Technology was reported about in the Manufacturing and Technology News Blog (Sept. 25, 2013, Vol. 20 No. 13). The headline reads: *MIT: With Loss of Manufacturing The U.S. Innovation Engine Is No Longer Working.*[230] There are reams of data showing that America is declining because of free trade, but it is hard to measure the value of the positive externalities domestic industries produce in terms of productivity increases, new product development, and enhancements to our military security and general national welfare.[231]

Precisely because it is difficult to measure the value of future inventions and innovations of every sort that domestic industry provides, free traders simply ignore them at *our* peril. In other words, *America's free trade polcy ignores the loss of future progress in order to take advantage of cheap labor now.* Our trade policy also ignores the energy wasted and the pollution created transporting raw materials and finished products back and forth all over the world to get to the spot and back where labor is cheapest.

The MIT study supports every criticism I have made. Capital and technology transfers and the loss of manufacturing is destroying America. The article in Manufacturing and Technology News by Richard A. McCormack summarizes the MIT research as follows:

> The loss of so much manufacturing capacity from the United States over the past decade has had a negative impact on the country's ability to innovate, long considered to be the nation's greatest economic and sociological strength, according to a two-year study from the Massachusetts Institute of Technology. The United States no longer has the industrial "ecosystem" necessary to bring new ideas to market. Finance, equipment, suppliers and manufacturers are not available in the United States to make prototypes and scale up commercial production of innovative ideas and products. This holds true for high-tech start-ups, the best small- and medium-sized manufacturing companies, and U.S.-based multinational corporations. "Serious basic weaknesses in the industry ecosystem are prevalent," according to MIT's Production in the Innovation Economy (PIE) study in a book published on Sept. 20 (2013) titled Making in America: From Innovation to Market.[232]

I doubt that McCormack's conclusions come as any surprise to anybody reading this book, including free traders. Free traders have obviously known all along that excoriating our manufacturing base with imports and off shoring would reduce America's ingenuity and inventiveness, lower wages, destroy jobs by the millions and concentrate wealth in fewer and fewer hands. Who pushes free trade harder than big corporations, Wall Street investment bankers, their political and media lackeys and their economists? Where do economists get jobs outside of banks, spin tanks, and large multinational corporations and private colleges which rely on endowments financed by right and left wing fat cats? Government and public universities employ also many economists, and *government is run by Republicans and Democrats who favor free trade.*

Donald Trump is a recently come exception to the rule - but I predicted a Republican pivot on free trade way back in the late mid seventies! Yes! I. Saw. It. Coming. I knew that free trade was being used as a tool to destroy the union movement. I also knew it was being used as a way to bludgeon environmental protection laws over the long haul. In 2016, Donald Trump suckered the whole working class with his call to make America great again. It's true. Trump is going to bring back manufacturing - but at what cost? Surely the Republicans will attempt to achieve all their long terms goals. *They were all in on the generation old scheme of free trade*! They knew all along that free trade would never work over the long term. As of this writing, Trump has just hired his team of billionaires to cut taxes to the bone on the wealthy and corporations and hollow out or simply gut the Environmental Protection Agency. But that's not all they will do. They will eviscerate the laws that protect that natural inalienable right of ordinary working people to bargain collectively for decent working conditions, hours, pay and benefit. Do you remember when everybody at least got a decent pension for working all their lives for peanuts? Free trade was *deliberately used to take all that away*. Trump - and the reasons ***I want him out of office in four years***, are discussed further in Chapter 15.

Prior to Trump, the last thing establishment politicians wanted was for economists employed by government to make waves about free trade. You all know the difference between your personal lawyer and the corporate lawyer your lawyer is fighting on your behalf. How many individuals hire economists to represent them in the economy? Maybe we should get some of those. It's a fact that greed and prejudice against unions and working people helps explain why a theory as bankrupt and stupid as free trade has been allowed to vanquish the American economy and people. I have waited forty years for the proof to emerge; It has emerged, and more proof will continue to emerge until the system is changed.

(*The rest of this chapter was written before any presidential campaigns for the 2016 election had commenced. Trump's election obviously has changed the polical landscape, but for the reasons elucidated above and in later chapters, I am convinced that the need for a new political party has never been greater. Please read on with that in mind.*)

The revelations made in the 2013 book by MIT, *Making in America: From Innovation to Market* will never get significant press coverage. If the book is ever mentioned on shows like 'Meet the Press," its findings will be written off as just a natural development as the world draws closer together through a globalized economy that helps foster peace and fair sharing of the wealth. The MIT study will be buried by the media because the media monopoly misinformation machine does the bidding of the money power; The money power is not yet ready to stop milking slave wage workers toiling in sweatshop conditions the world over.

McCormack's article about the MIT study included the results of an interview with Martin Schmidt, an MIT Professor, Associate Provost and Director of the Task Force on Production in the Innovation Economy. Let's review Professor Schmidt's credentials: "His teaching and research is in the areas of micro and nanofabrication of sensors, actuators, and electronic devices, microelectromechanical systems (MEMS), design of micromechanical sensors and actuators, and micro/nanofabrication technology. He is the co-author of more than 80 journal publications and 120 peer-reviewed conference proceedings. His is also an inventor on more than 30 issued US Patents. More than 25 students have completed their PhD degrees under his supervision." Professor Schmidt "is a recipient of the National Science Foundation Presidential Young Investigator Award and an honorary doctorate from the Technical University of Denmark. He was elected as a fellow of the IEEE in 2004 for contributions to design and fabrication of microelectromechanical systems. He has received the Ruth and Joel Spira Teaching Award and the Eta Kappa Nu Teaching Award at MIT. In addition to his academic pursuits, he is active in consulting with industry in the commercialization of technology." He is a "co-founder or co-inventor of the core technology of six companies that are commercializing MEMS-enabled products."[233]

McCormack asked Professor Schmidt whether the main finding of the MIT research - that the loss of manufacturing has resulted in the degradation of the America's innovative capacity - is well understood in this country. In reply, Schmidt stated in part as follows:

> We worked as hard as we could with rigorous, quantitative research to get to the bottom of understanding the importance of the linkage of a production ecosystem to innovation. Our conclusion is that they are terribly important. We can talk about jobs and national security, but if this is a nation that views its ability to innovate as a core strength, then we need to pay attention to manufacturing.
>
> Professor Schmidt was also asked by McCormack about the opinions of free trade economists who claim that manufacturing losses from free trade are not a concern:
>
> "Q: Over the years, I have heard many organizations like the Cato Institute and economists such as [Columbia University professor] Jagdish Bhagwati argue emphatically and successfully that the United States does not need manufacturing. Given what the PIE researchers have concluded, do you think we've heard the end of that argument?"

Schmidt's reply was this:

> Well, I hope so. I hope that our work and other people's work provide a real quantitative grounding for this discussion. The surveys we have done, the interviews we undertook and the benchmarking of other nations relative to China and Germany provide some fairly compelling arguments as to why a domestic production ecosystem is really important. The PIE study provides some historical perspective on why we are where we are today, namely the erosion of the vertically integrated firms associated with the push of the capital markets to make firms more efficient in their use of capital. That has had consequences. The PIE results provide a fairly comprehensive picture of not only what has happened, but what the consequences of that are. Then it provides a roadmap for what we ought to be doing: moving forward to strengthen this important ecosystem in terms of maintaining our innovative advantage.

The sequence of questions and answers that followed in McCormack's interview with Professor Schmidt is illuminating with regard to the positive externalities sucked away by free trade:

> Q: You said your quantitative research indicates the consequences of the hollowing out of the U.S. industrial ecosystem. What are they?
>
> Schmidt: As we focused on the start-ups and the Main Street firms, we found that their ability to innovate in new products was constrained by the inability to access this rich ecosystem. Or, said in a different way, when we looked at the firms that were successful versus ones that were less so, one of the key differentiators was whether or not they lived in a rich ecosystem for the work that they did. The consequence of not having that ecosystem is constraining our ability to innovate

and it slows things down. We saw lots of examples where the development time for new products is lengthened by the lack of access to production capabilities in a [product] development sense. While industry has figured out how to network a complex global supply chain, we don't have an effective means to use that supply chain in [new product] development.

Q: Do you think there is a direct correlation between what has happened with the hollowing out of the American manufacturing sector and the country's current economic doldrums, the jobless recovery and the Great Recession, since, as PIE notes, once the industrial base was lost, so too was the capacity to innovate and create good jobs and new industries?

Schmidt: Well I'm not an economist.

Q: I prefer that you not be an economist to answer that question, since most economists don't care.

Schmidt: We had 6 million manufacturing jobs that have been lost in the last decade and some people argue that they are never coming back and others argue that shale gas and rising costs of labor in China are all going to lead to a reshoring of manufacturing capability. I don't feel there is any good quantitative analysis of that, but our historic growth has been based on leveraging our innovation. If our ability to innovate is under threat, then our growth as a nation is also under threat. That is the way I view it.

At times, we look to singular industries and declare that if they can outsource production and be successful, then we shouldn't worry about this. So a lot of attention gets paid to consumer electronics -- and Apple being the greatest icon of that -- where you have firms that can innovate in new products but don't manufacture any of the products under their own roof -- and in many instances manufacture those products in other parts of the world. But while that is true, it is an anomaly -- a function of the standardization of the manufacturing processes for the core technologies that feed into consumer electronics. We don't see that standardization in other areas. The semiconductor industry is the epitome of that ability to standardize on a manufacturing process and then share that manufacturing process [globally] through the foundry mechanics. We just haven't seen that model work in other industries. If we focus on the consumer electronics industry as the example of why we don't need manufacturing to support innovation, then we are overlooking some enormously important areas and we are reaching the wrong conclusions.

Q: Most economists and policymakers are convinced that the United States remains the innovation engine of the world, but without manufacturing is that really the case? Is this a myth that has to be overcome?

Schmidt: Yes. Clearly we continue to innovate in software and services to some extent, but in the manufacture of real products it's a constraint. One of the things I would highlight in the PIE work is with the Main Street firms that doubled revenue and increased headcount between 2004 and 2008. When you look at those companies and ask what was the key to success, there were a few common denominators. Some had to do with having really innovative leaders who would look broadly at their core capabilities that they had and seek opportunities to deploy and pivot those capabilities in other markets. But a firm in Massachusetts that is really excellent at making and welding [storage] tanks isn't going to be realizing that opportunity to branch into new markets if they are not sitting next to innovators coming out of MIT who need that capability in a... new [technology] area. That startup from MIT might be able to find that tank manufacturer in some other place in the world, but that will slow them down, and they will be competitively disadvantaged. It's also a lost opportunity for, in this case, Massachusetts, to have had this enterprise really accelerated. If you have that capability nearby you are going to use it.

One of the things we overlook is that we have startups coming out of places like MIT and they garner the resources necessary to do what they want to do. But we argue that it takes them longer to do it when they can't access a local ecosystem. But what is completely overlooked is the idea that if they had that local ecosystem, they strengthen those firms through partnerships. There are spillover effects from innovations.

Q: The PIE research on the start-up companies from MIT that make physical products found that none of them could scale-up to commercial production in the United States. Was that a frightening finding?

Schmidt: We found that a large fraction of them were venture backed and when they got to the point of demonstrating a functional prototype and ramping production on their unique capability, the established sources of venture capital were challenged to support the last round of investment. One of the common sources of capital in that last round was foreign investment, which might have been coming from Singapore, Russia or China. Quite frequently, those investments carry with them a commitment to do something in the region where that investment is coming from. The invention and the scale-up is occurring here but you don't capture that production capability, which then feeds innovation of the next generation of products.

Q: One of the phrases I see in the report is that the loss of the U.S. industrial ecosystem has "alarm bells ringing in the halls of MIT." Do you see things changing for your students?

Schmidt: The national dialogue is healthy. A lot of people are talking about it and a lot of people are concerned. We have the ear of Washington in a bipartisan sense. Everyone appreciates the importance of this. But you need to focus on this at the regional level. MIT has a great partnership with the Commonwealth of Massachusetts as well as with local players. Each region needs to come together and make this a priority. So with the federal focus and the regional energy level there are lots of reasons to be optimistic because of the discussion and the thoughtful processes that people are going through.

> Q: Having covered Washington for 30 years, I know that to do anything requires legislation -- an authorization and appropriation. But the capacity for new legislation is not working at the moment. Congress is completely distracted. There are only a few on Capitol Hill who understand these issues, and fewer who propose legislation addressing them.
>
> Schmidt: We've had some very good engagements with the Deputy Secretary of Commerce Patrick Gallagher, but I'm not in Washington, so I can't comment on the state of function or dysfunction there. But we can make a difference at the regional level and maybe that is what should drive the change.[234]

Dr. Schmidt can try to make changes from within the establishment that has been kicking away the ladder of opportunity from millions of Americans while hitting the taxpayers up for cash to bail out too big to fail banks, mismanaged auto companies and defense contractors whose political lackeys moan about the cost of social programs for the poor. It is clear however that nothing significant will be done to repair the manufacturing ecosystem in America unless the American public takes action.

What we need is a whole new political party which will bring about a whole new economic and political order in this country. The free trade hogwash sold by the Republocrats never existed as a dominant policy in the United States until after World War II.[235] As a result of free trade we saw our first trade deficit in modern history in 1973, and America has been in decline ever since. The anti-free-traders are the ones standing up for traditional American values and beliefs, not the Tea Partiers, the other Republicans or the Democrats with but few exceptions.

It would be beneficial if researchers would make an estimate of the cost the United States has paid and will in the future pay because of the loss of technologically advanced American industries to foreign nations whose competitive advantage currently resides in slave level wages, grossly inadequate pollution laws and deplorable working conditions. We need to know how much energy is wasted so that greedy firms can offshore production ten thousand miles away from the consumers who buy their products at no or very slight savings in price. We do know that Henry Clay made the common sense argument that prices to consumers actually fall faster (and wages rise), when technology is constantly being improved to increase profits. Let's return to his argument about that:

> I pass, with pleasure, ...to...general propositions which cover the entire ground of debate. The first is, that, under the operation of the American System, the objects which it protects and fosters are brought to the consumer at cheaper prices than they commanded prior to its introduction, or than they would command if it did not exist. If that be true, ought not the country to be contented and satisfied with the system...? And is the fact not indisputable, that all essential objects of consumption, affected by the tariff, are cheaper and better, since the act of 1824, than they were for several years prior to that law? I appeal, for its truth, to common observation and to all practical men. I appeal to the farmer of the

> country, whether he does not purchase, on better terms, his iron, salt, brown sugar, cotton goods, and woollens, for his laboring people. And I ask the cotton planter if he has not been better and more cheaply supplied with his cotton bagging...[236]

Clay could not have gotten away with making that argument if it was not true when he made it. It remains the truth now as the MIT study helps show. It remains impossible to know exactly how the magic of the spin off synergies of the "production ecosystem' as Schmidt called it, or the "American System" as Clay called it, will play out in every instance, but inevitably those synergies produce lower prices, new technologies, new products, higher productivity, higher wages and more government revenue with lower tax rates because of rising incomes. Free trade on the other hand produces a race to the bottom, allowing greed driven corporations to sidestep centuries of moral and economic progress and ignore centuries of hard effort by the families of workers who created the industrial revolution with their sweat and defended democracy with their blood. Free trade is the ultimate betrayal of the prosperity that so many millions gave their lives for, hoping that their children would get their fair share. Free trade is a *moral outrage* as well as *economic suicide* for America and we must end it.

The Manufacturing Ecosystem is the Key to National Growth and Prosperity

Free trader economists generally plead the fifth when it comes to explaining economic growth. They can't explain growth because all their two dimensional model provides them with is a blurry one time snapshot of comparative advantage between two countries.[237] It's just a fleeting picture of the ever changing world taken at one moment in time. Their theory does not tell them why nations have comparative advantage or how nations can improve their advantages. The whole subject of competition between nations, and the rise and fall of nations is not their concern. They will say that it's better to shed a domestic industry, (even though that industry enjoys a significant technological advantage in making something), because another nation with lower labor costs (and higher energy use and dreadful working conditions), can make the same product for less money.

Free trade economists ignore where technical efficiency, energy efficiency and worker productivity comes from; They also ignore how those efficiencies can be improved over time. They ignore where inventions come from. They ignore where innovation comes from. Wearing blinders with respect to the *Whys* and *Hows* of technological development, (which is an obvious factor in economic growth), they claim growth is maximized when nations specialize in producing things they have a "comparative advantage" in.

If free trade theory were true, it would mean that countries that grow richer would display a pattern of shedding industries as they focus on building those products in which they hold a comparative advantage. Research has shown that the reverse is true. As nations grow richer their economies are generally becoming more diversified and more focused on manufacturing.[238] This is an important clue that comparative advantage is not static, and that a nation's economic growth is based on increasing its absolute advantages in science, technology and manufacturing.

More diversity brings more and better positive externalities or spinoffs. Concentrating production over a narrow band of technological skill sets deflates both the potential for and the realization of economic growth. This point is driven home persuasively by the economists whose books I have already mentioned and in many more books and academic studies.[239] The MIT study we discussed above is part of a long line of research and developmental methodology. One expert who has studied economic growth extensively is Erik Reinert. Erik S. Reinert is a professor of Technology Governance and Development Strategies at Tallinn University of Technology, Estonia, and a Senior Research Fellow at NORISS, the Norwegian Institute of Strategic Studies, in Oslo. He also organized and is the current chairman of the Other Canon Foundation. "His research interests and publications focus on the theory of uneven development, the history of economic thought and policy, and the role of the state in the process of economic development. As a consultant, his emphasis is on industrial and economic policy, the preconditions and management of innovations, and the relations between financial and production capital."[240]

After I became convinced that economists had finally begun to reject free trade theory in sufficient numbers to permit a successful political attack on the money power's domination of American economic policy, I began research for this book. It was then that I learned about Professor Reinert's work, He, along with Ha Joon Chang, Ian Fletcher, Clyde Prestowitz and others have provided us with the evidence needed to destroy the free trade paradigm, and perhaps just in time to save America from free trade suicide.

Professor Reinert has written a number of books and dozens upon dozens of articles on the history of economic development and strategies for economic growth. After I read two of his books, *How Rich Countries Got Rich ...and Why Poor Countries Stay Poor*, and *The Origins of Development Economics How Schools of Economic Thought Have Addressed Development* (coauthored with Jomo KS), I emailed Professor Reinert. I told him I felt like Moses and his people must have felt after trudging through the desert for forty years before reaching the promised land. It had literally been forty years since America's first trade deficit in 1973 when I contacted Dr. Reinert.

The great economists like Erik are modern day "Moses" who have worked for much of their lives to lead people in a different direction. It is a direction which is not really new at all but timeless and tested over many centuries of economic change and upheaval. Nations rise or fall depending on whether they follow the truths discerned by Erik and his contemporaries in the field of development economics. China knows this. Japan knows this. Germany knows this. America however does not get it, and America is being ruined from within by the money concentrating - prosperity ruining - catechism of greed sold by Wall Street and the one percenters. From his acknowledgments at the beginning of *How Rich Countries got Rich and ...Why Poor Countries Stay Poor* you quickly learn something about why Reinert has discarded free trade theory:

> Most ideas in this book are very old, and my biggest debt is to a large number of economic thinkers and policymakers who over the last 500 years successfully created wealth rather than reallocated it. I first came in contact with this group in 1974-6 when my wife worked at as a librarian at the Kress Library of Harvard

> Business School. This library specialized in economic theory before 1850, thus maintaining an accessible gene bank of their ideas...
>
> Other than from the ancients, inspiration came from Tom Davis, who taught economic history and development, and inspired the idea of differentiating economic activities, from Boston Consulting Group and their approach to measured human learning and experience, and from Jaroslav Vanek, formerly of the Hecksher-Ohlin-Vanek theorem in international trade, who had come to understand how welfare destroying international trade could be under given circumstances. His thorough deconstruction of conventional international trade theory confirmed why I had always found it counter-intuitive.[241]

Elsewhere in his book Reinert explains his view of what lies at "at the heart of successful development." He "argues that what enlightenment economists called 'emulation' rather than 'comparative advantage' and 'free trade' lies at the heart of economic growth."[242]

> In this context emulation means imitating in order to equal or excel. If the tribe across the river has taken the step from the Stone Age to the Bronze Age, your tribe is faced with the choice of either sticking to its comparative advantage in the Stone age or trying to emulate the neighboring tribe into the Bronze Age. Before David Ricardo there was little doubt that emulation would be the best strategy, and historically the most important contribution of Ricardo's trade theory was that, for the first time, it made colonialism morally defensible.[243]

When you take the time to consider the parallels between the findings of the MIT study and Reinert's description of the concept of technological "emulation," the theory of comparative advantage is seen for its obvious shortcomings. One can see that the march of technology throughout time has been a driving force behind economic development. The comparative advantage model ignores the question of how technology advances and what brings technological supremacy and a higher standard of living to a nation. Another factor it ignores is the will of people that there be progress and better standards of living over time for themselves and their children. The theory of comparative advantage lacks necessary ingredients and is only half-baked. What it lacks in theory it makes up for in potency as a political and economic bludgeon to halt the advance of worker's rights, lower wages, and circumvent environmental law. It has destroyed millions of good American jobs and severely damaged the ecosystem of innovation in America, taking a heavy toll on knowledge workers and the middle class in addition to laborers. Free Trade is a long term losing proposition for America, and it has been kept in place because of its wealth concentrating effects. The wealth holders, some of whom are foreign nations, corporations and individuals, keep free trade in place by buying politicians and political parties, funding spin tanks, spending billions on advertising and PR campaigns, and monopolizing the media. I refer to them collectively as "*the money power*," a term which is discussed in chapter six.

Economics writer Ian Fletcher had this to say about "ladder externalities"[244] in his book *Free Trade Doesn't Work What Should Replace It and Why*:

> But, if specialization according to comparative advantage isn't the key to growth,

> what is? ...Lets start with the common observation that real-world economic growth often seems to involve a virtuous cycle, in which the upgrading of one industry causes others to upgrade and so on. This has been seen time and again in nation after nation, industry after industry. For example, as one industry becomes a more sophisticated consumer of inputs, it may demand that its supplier industries become more sophisticated. Conversely, it may enable its downstream industries to increase the sophistication of their outputs. This process then ripples through the economy and repeats.
>
> Crucially some industries are better at starting this process (or keeping it going if it has already started) than others. And the free market, and *thus free trade*, won't optimize this process automatically Why? Because the value of an industry for the *next* step in industrial growth is often an externality, from the point of view of today. ...externalities occur when the profits of an industry do not reflect its full economic value. In this case, this means that the industry's present owners will not see profits that reflect its long term ability to help the economy upgrade or break into other industries. As a result, the industry will remain underdeveloped, relative to its long term value to the national economy, and the free market will *not* give the optimal answer for how much of this industry the economy should contain.[245]

Fletcher establishes in his book that nations and private business are well aware that industries often act as catalysts for developing other industries and that some industries are more strategic than others. Thus, economic growth is seen to be path dependent:

> To grow an economy must continually break into new industries. But to do this, it needs strong *existing* positions in the right industries. So a national economy that does not get on the right path (and stay on it) risks being sidelined into industries that lead nowhere in the long run...[246]
>
> Path dependence applies to economies at all levels of development, not just those starting to industrialize. Infant-industry protection is, of course, one of the best known cases for protectionism and industrial policy. (It is often the one case grudgingly conceded even by free traders.) But it is, in fact, only the most obvious case of the more general phenomenon of the path dependence of economic growth. Infant industries are merely the first rungs of the ladder.[247]

Fletcher also notes that industries that offer increasing returns are better catalysts for growth than those that offer decreasing returns. You will recall that increasing returns are present in industries where as output is increased, cost per unit produced is reduced. These are known as economies of scale. Fletcher points out that industries that have increasing returns tend to absorb capital more profitably than those that don't:

> Industries which exhibit increasing returns do so mainly because they can absorb endlessly rising capital investment. Not all industries can: buying another $1,000,000.00 worth of tractors for a coffee plantation that already has them won't increase the plantations productivity very much . Neither will buying every

> lawyer at a law firm another desk. But putting another $1,000,000.00 into production machinery in an automobile or semi-conductor plant will do a lot...[248]
>
> Why are some industries so good at absorbing capital? One big reason is that they are susceptible to innovation , and R & D is a big capital absorber. This activates a virtuous cycle in which innovation absorbs capital then repays it by raising profitability, generating more capital and repeating the cycle...[249]
>
> Having a lot of increasing returns industries is really the only way to be a developed economy. This is, in fact, the fundamental purely economic difference between the First and Third Worlds: the former is full of such industries, the latter is not. As a result, examining why some industries exhibit increasing returns and some do not can tell us a lot about why some economies grow and some do not. And how free trade can easily lead an economy astray.[250]

Ian Fletcher makes the case convincingly that dominating high value manufacturing is key to a large nation's wealth. When you consider that eighty percent of Americans today are poor for at least part of their lives, it's not hard to understand that our economy will never bounce back on its own from its free trade caused decline.[251] We are in real trouble; free trade has made us the world's largest debtor nation yet the *money power's* grip on American minds via the media monopoly misinformation machine has never been tighter. A small number of people control most of the American media system and a recent study of transnational corporations showed that a relatively small group of companies, most of which are banks, possess inordinate power over the world economic system.[252] Most Americans have absolutely no idea what is happening. Those of us who do must work together to stop the subversion of democracy and the impoverishment of America by the *money power*.

New Trade Theory

If you thought I was finished debunking the comparative advantage model of international trade you were wrong. You have to know about how "New Trade Theory" has pummeled the stuffings out of the idea of comparative advantage too. Let me introduce you to Clyde Prestowitz. Clyde did a masterful job of exposing just how destructive the Washington Consensus on free trade is in his book *The Betrayal of American Prosperity Free Market Delusion, America's Decline, and How We Must Compete in the Post Dollar Era*. Here is his bio from the Economic Strategy Institute website:

> Clyde Prestowitz is founder and President of the Economic Strategy Institute. His leadership has propelled ESI into an important role in the public policy process, influencing and often defining the terms of the debate in the areas of international trade policy, economic competitiveness, and the effects of globalization...Prior to founding ESI, Mr. Prestowitz served as counselor to the Secretary of Commerce in the Reagan Administration. There, he led many U.S. trade and investment negotiations with Japan, China, Latin America, and Europe. Before joining the Commerce Department, he was a senior businessman in the

United States, Europe, Japan, and throughout Asia and Latin America. He has served as vice chairman of the President's Committee on Trade and Investment in the Pacific and sits on the Intel Policy Advisory Board and the U.S. Export-Import Bank Advisory Board.

> Clyde Prestowitz regularly writes for leading publications, including the New York Times, the Washington Post, Fortune, and Foreign Affairs. He is the author of the best-selling book on U.S.-Japan relations, Trading Places, and co-author and editor of several other books on international trade and business strategy including Asia After the Miracle; Powernomics; Bit by Bit; The New North American Trade Order; Rogue Nation; and Three Billion New Capitalists. His latest book, The Betrayal of American Prosperity: Free Market Delusions, America's Decline, and How We Must Compete in the Post-Dollar Era, addresses how we can restore our economic leadership and excellence.
>
> Mr. Prestowitz has a B.A. with honors from Swarthmore College; an M.A. in East-West Policies and Economics from the East-West Center of the University of Hawaii; and an M.B.A. from the Wharton Graduate School of Business. He also studied at Keio University in Tokyo. He is fluent in Japanese, Dutch, German, and French.[253]

Here is a quote about New Trade Theory from Dr. Prestowitz's book:

> Of course, the disjuncture between theory and reality increasingly gave rise to various critiques of simple free-trade theory. The first of these were aimed at the ...assumptions underlying the theory. But this criticism then led to an analysis of possible new trade structures in which the trading partners might be as much adversaries as partners. Beyond this, some critics noted that the morphing of trade into the broader phenomenon of globalization had really obviated the conventional trade concepts and that none other than Ricardo himself had anticipated this possibility. Finally, analysts from the real world of economic development came to explain that the ultimate logic of conventional theory can actually lead to disastrous results...
>
> It was in the late 1970s and early 1980s that several young economists like Paul Krugman, Laura Tyson, James Brander, Barbara Spencer, and Joseph Stiglitz began to wonder whether the assumptions of simple free-trade theory were too much at odd with reality...[254]

Prestowitz explains in his book (which you should read) how Krugman "altered the conventional trade model so that rather than assuming away economies of scale, it incorporated them as a major element of the equation." Krugman "shook the foundations of orthodoxy." "Krugman and others "pointed out that contrary to" comparative advantage "theory," "government intervention" could "be in the national interest" if conditions warranted it.[255]

Following on the heels of Krugman in the early 1990s came "the former IBM chief scientist and Sloan Foundation president Ralph Gomory and the eminent economist William Baumol."[256] Gomory and Baumol developed models which included the element of increasing returns incorporated by Krugman, but also as well the variables of fast occurring technological changes and swift changes in productivity. Another innovation by Gomory and Baumol was to incorporate very large numbers of products and countries so as to truly reflect what happens in the real world.[257]

New trade theory knocks the conventional idea that everybody wins by maximizing comparative advantage out the window. In Prestowitz's words:

> Instead, they found that there are many possible trading patterns, of which some are optimal for one party, and others for other parties but none is optimal for all parties at all times at once. In other words, rather than always being win-win, trade is often adversarial or zero sum--my gain is your loss.[258]

You now know that when you see, hear and read in the media that free trade is based upon a sound theory that it is always a win-win proposition that you are not getting the full story. Both the comparative advantage theory and the Hecksher Olin theory of free trade are logically invalid. Whether free trade is advantageous or not depends upon the circumstances of the nation involved in it.

Good economists learn from history how trading patterns build nations, empires and civilizations and also destroy them. Science and the technology of manufacturing is responsible for our enjoyment of a high mass consumption society, and notions to the contrary are dangerous and destructive to society. You may have come to see by now that whether your political affinity is with Democrats or Republicans, (or Trump) you have been mislead. Both parties have an agenda to serve private interests and agendas rather than the public interest. Together they have caused our huge trade imbalance, and caused the United States to become a debtor nation with a growing national debt which is now close to twenty trillion dollars and growing.

Though Republicans blame the people who have been thrown out of work and made destitute by free trade for our national debt, blaming the poor is wrong. You will learn in the coming chapters of this book that our mountain of accumulated trade deficit IOU's has been responsible for a large portion of the national debt. The senseless war in Iraq also caused the national debt to rise appreciably. In the next chapter we consider the nature and extent that monied interests control the media and the election process, how they limit free speech, and how they propagate myth and misinformation to maintain their monopoly of power over the American people.

6

Who and What the Money Power Is

Is it any secret that monied interests attempt to influence government at every level to get what they want? Clearly it is not a secret to the average voter. Everybody knows that billionaires, multimillionaires, big corporations and labor unions as well try to elect officeholders that will make, interpret and administer the law in a manner which they believe is beneficial to their interests. So the "money power" in one sense of the phrase might be considered the collective set of actors that use their vast financial worth to control the political process as best they can.

Many people don't think of labor unions as being a part of the money power. After all, unions are aligned against the corporate world which seeks to restrict or eliminate unions. Unions have shrunk from a peak membership of around thirty five percent of the work force in 1954 to about eleven percent today.[259] A portion of that decline is shown in Figure 6.1, which also shows how the share of national income received by the middle class has declined alongside the decline in union membership. Unlike the private sector unions, public sector unions grew rapidly after 1960, and in many cases, helped government employees secure better wages and better (some say excessive) benefits and pensions. Though unionized jobs in manufacturing have steadily declined for four decades largely due to imports and off shoring, state and local governments increased employment from 4 million workers in 1950 to 16.6 million workers by 2009.[260] In 2010 there were 8.4 million unionized government workers all told.[261] In 2013, nearly half of all union members worked for the government.[262]

Public sector unions came along after private sector unions to seek better wages, benefits, and pensions. They often represent politically powerful individuals and groups such as public administrators, police, prosecutors, fire fighters and teachers. Because public workers are frequently involved in patronage style work to elect public officials, and because government work frequently cannot be outsourced overseas to low wage countries, public sector unions have done better than private sector unions for decades. However free trade caused economic decline has spread from the private sector to every level of government. In states and localities which are awash in red ink, public unions are facing strong efforts to reduce their benefits and pensions. My home state of Illinois is a prime example.[263] Obviously however, no matter what their particular circumstances, working people and public employees are generally not considered "rich," Overall, though unions do still play a role politically, we have seen their influence undergo remarkable decline over the last sixty years as the number of unionized workers in America declined by about two thirds despite enormous population growth.[264]

Figure 6.1

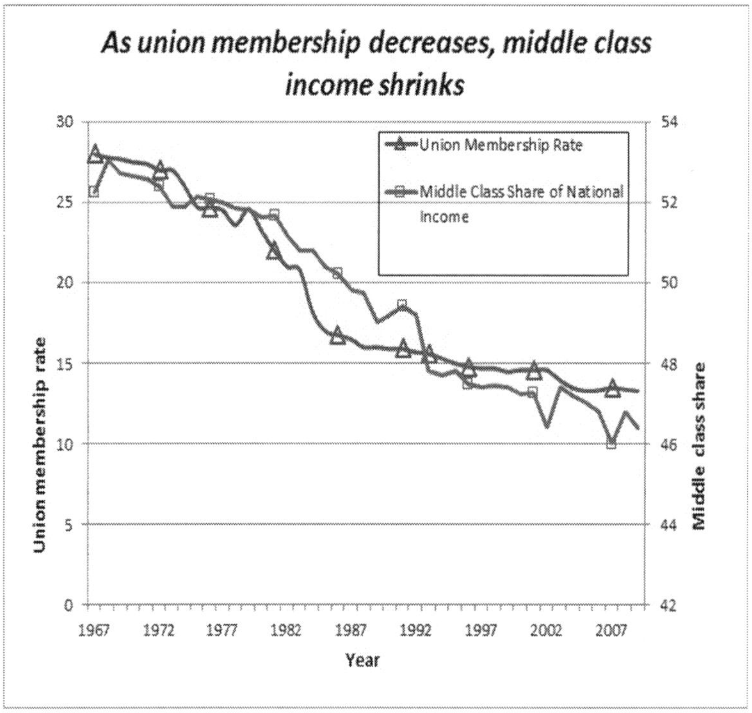

Graph adapted from David Madland, Ph.D. and Karla Walter, *Center For American Progress*. Used with permission. Retrieved from http://thinkprogress.org/economy//2011/01/20/173738/report-incomes

When I refer to the "money power" I therefore mean very large income (for profit) corporations and industries that have a huge stake in government policies, for example, the oil, gas and coal industries, large utilities like phone and electric companies, the financial sector, (which includes banks, Wall Street and the insurance industry) the aerospace industry, the auto industry, railroads and rail manufacturers, the media, the high tech sector, the gambling industry, agribusiness, miscellaneous big business and politically active private individuals with vast personal fortunes such as the Koch brothers.[265] Because foreign owned firms and individuals now operate a large number of businesses and have vast investments in the United States it is necessary to take note of their money power conceptually, though the nature and extent of foreign influence over our politicians is not well understood.[266] Taken collectively the individuals and firms that constitute *the money power* strongly support free trade, and they obviously have a pervasive influence on and financial involvement with the six conglomerates that own ninety percent of U.S. media outlets. The money power clearly has substantial influence over public policy. Two brilliant Americans experts on how American political polices are formed, Professor Benjamin Page at Stanford and Professor Martin Gilens at Northwestern University recently conducted a careful analysis of how government policy is formed. Their conclusion is not surprising:

> The central point that emerges from our research is that economic elites and organized groups representing business interests have substantial independent impacts on U.S. government policy, while mass-based interest groups and average citizens have little or no independent influence... [267]

We all know that we have little or no influence over government policy. I sure don't. I am not the son of a free trade loving Bush, Daley, Kennedy, Gore, Pelosi or any of a thousand other family clans that rule America through inherited clout. It's not a new idea that *the money power* is in charge. President Rutherford B. Hayes made a comment in 1887 that is as timely today as it was then:

> ...it is time for the public to hear that the giant evil and danger in this country, the danger which transcends all others, is the vast wealth owned or controlled by a few persons. Money is power. In Congress, in state legislatures, in city councils, in the courts, in the political conventions, in the press, in the pulpit, in the circles of the educated and the talented, its influence is growing greater and greater. Excessive wealth in the hands of the few means extreme poverty, ignorance, vice, and wretchedness as the lot of the many.[268]

It's not possible to exactly quantify the extent of *the money power* influence, but we do know that wealth in America is very concentrated. As shown in Figure 6.2, five percent of Americans own seventy two percent of the fiscal wealth of the United States.

As can be seen in Figure 6.2, the bottom eighty percent of Americans own only five percent of the financial wealth owned by all Americans. Collectively, that same eighty percent owns only eleven percent of the total net worth of private assets in the United States. One can reasonably suspect that the forty seven percent of Americans who don't pay income taxes - the ones that Mitt Romney famously commented about - own only a bare sliver of the 5 percent of the financial assets held by the lower eighty percent of Americans.

Figure 6.1 above, (not too mention our gargantuan trade deficits and national debt), shows something is wrong with our political system today. The two parties produce mediocre political candidates, ineffective policies and horrid results. One of the most weak minded comments I ever heard a politician say was what Romney said about the nearly half of our people who don't pay income taxes. If you don't recall the comment Romney made on September 17, 2012, here it is:

> There are 47 percent of the people who will vote for the president no matter what. All right, there are 47 percent who are with him, who are dependent upon government, who believe that they are victims, who believe that government has a responsibility to care for them, who believe that they are entitled to health care, to food, to housing, to you name it. That's an entitlement. And the government should give it to them. And they will vote for

> this president no matter what. And I mean, the president starts off with 48, 49, 48—he starts off with a huge number. These are people who pay no income tax. Forty-seven percent of Americans pay no income tax. So our message of low taxes doesn't connect. And he'll be out there talking about tax cuts for the rich. I mean that's what they sell every four years. And so my job is not to worry about those people—I'll never convince them that they should take personal responsibility and care for their lives.[269]

Figure 6.2

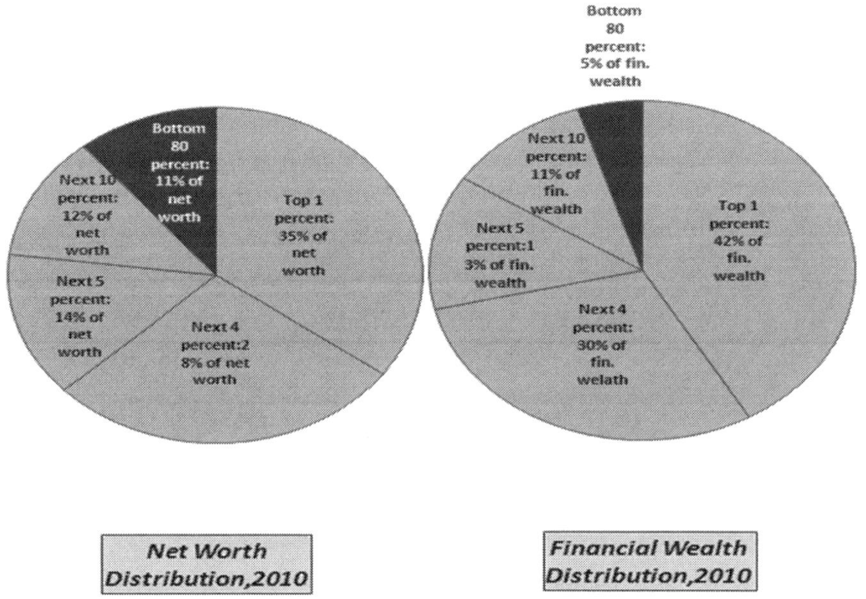

Graph adapted from Dr. G William Domhoff, Ph.D., Wealth Income and Power. *Who Rules America?* Used With Permission. Retrieved from http:// www2.ucsc.edu/whorulesamerica/power/wealth.html

I don't believe that the eighty percent of people who are struggling along with only five percent of America's financial wealth are losers and dead beats who don't "take personal responsibility and care for their lives." It is the changes in economic policy that have been orchestrated by *the money power* since World War II that I blame for America's declining fortunes, not the American people. Bad leadership is what is dragging us down. Following our non leaders blindly are the millions of knee jerk ideologues (*sheeple* is a good term for such voters), who parrot whatever their party leaders say, but a majority of us have had it with both parties. I was very pleased in October of 2013 when a Gallup poll found that sixty percent of Americans perceive the need for a third political party to represent them.[270] I say hallelujah to that! I've been waiting decades for this inevitable moment to come.

So far this chapter has not told you much you don't already know. We need to take a brief look at the development of *the money power* in America. We also need to look at some cutting edge research on what constitutes the money power today. Who pulls the strings of the media? Who is running the dog and pony show in Washington from behind the scenes? Why does the media slant certain issues in favor of *the money power*?

The subject of the money power's influence has been written about for as long as America has been a nation, and of course, even long before then. Ever since the United States was formed, uncommon virtue has battled uncommon greed in defense of our democratic values. Noted historians Steve Fraser and Gary Gerstle make this point in the introduction to their book *Ruling America: A History of Wealth and Power in a Democracy*:

> It is virtually impossible to make sense of any of the great epochs in American political history or of the grander chronicle of democracy in America without coming face to face with "Tories," "moneycrats," "the Monster Bank," the slaveocracy," "robber barons," "plutocrats," "the money trust," "economic royalists," "the Establishment," the "power elite," or the "military-industrial complex."[271]

But there is a key difference between our own epoch of economic decline, wealth concentration and broken American dreams and the previous gilded ages in America. When most of the money demeaning expressions quoted above were coined, America was still on the ascent economically and internationally, despite the periodic recessions and depressions brought on by irresponsible money power. America's great victory in World War II and its fantastic achievement in landing men on the moon were decades in the future. The invidious doctrine of free trade was a dark genie still trapped in the *American System* bottle that had been fashioned and preserved by the Mount Rushmore Presidents. Labor remained on the rise because improving manufacturing technologies made the productivity gains which now elude us plentiful. In past periods of financial trouble, recovery was certain and wages were destined to resume rising as manufacturing productivity grew, driven by government policy, demographic changes and market forces. Our recent financial crisis is different than those in the past. Our huge trade deficits are stalling a recovery despite the huge Wall Street bail out.[272] Free trade has caused American manufacturing industries to fail in droves and jobs have been lost by the millions.[273] The replacement of manufacturing industries by financial industries as the dominant component of the money power seems to have made a return to prosperity and climbing wages impossible. In Figure 6.3, a significant transformation in the make up of the money power can be seen.

Figure 6.3 shows that in 1948, manufacturing industries obtained sixty percent of all corporate profits while the financial sector lived off less than ten percent of corporate profits. Wall Street's share peaked at forty percent of all corporate profits in 2002, while manufacturing industries dropped to under ten percent in 2008. It is abundantly clear that Wall Street money has been growing as a component of the "money power" while domestic manufacturing has declined. For decades the decline in manufacturing has been ignored. Manufacturing has been viewed as some unimportant, naturally dying sector of the domestic economy as a new global economy that enriches all takes shape. Although free traders love to argue that new manufacturing technologies rather than imports and outsourcing have eliminated most manufacturing jobs, that argument is a red herring. The vast majority of jobs have been lost because so many factories have been closed and the jobs they provided, (along with the equipment and technology they used), have been shipped overseas.[274]

Money power politicians always used to say that America was becoming a service industry nation as part of "globalization," which they said was good, because free trade benefits all nations.[275] You know from reading chapter five that free trade does not necessarily benefit all nations. It has in fact been a disaster for our nation.[276] Not only did we lose millions of existing manufacturing jobs, we also lost the many new jobs that would have been created by the positive externalities, (spinoffs), associated with lost jobs and industries, as was discussed in the preceding chapter.

Figure 6.3 Red line is Manufacturing Firms / Blue line is Financial Firms

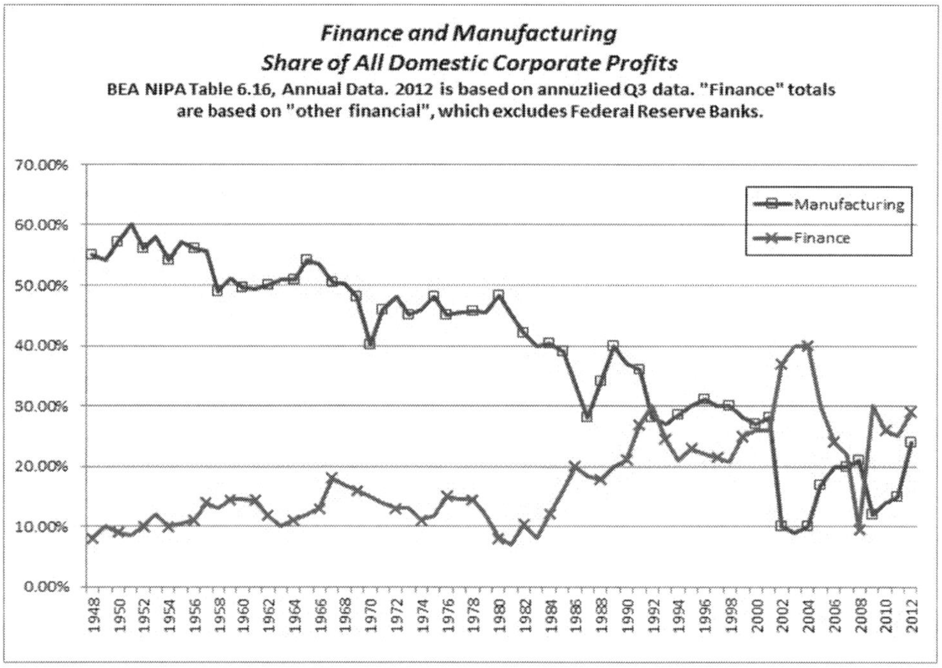

Graph adapted from *The Atlantic* from Weissmann, Jordan. March 5, 2013. "How Wall Street Devoured Corporate America." March 5, 2013. Used with permission. Retrieved from http://www.theatlantic.com/business/archive/2013/03/how-wall-street-devoured-corporate-america/273732/

We have even lost previously acquired manufacturing technology that took centuries to develop as the engineers and scientists who were formerly employed in now lost industries have moved into other work or died off. So, where are the service sector jobs that globalization and free trade were supposedly creating as Americans pursued their "comparative advantage" in service work?

The natural place to look to for evidence of new jobs would be in the industry where profits grew by leaps and bounds while domestic manufacturing plummeted and real wages declined. Figure 6.4 compares the long term changes in employment between manufacturing industries and the financial industry. Low and behold, despite the fact that the financial sector's share of American corporate profits rose from ten percent in 1948 to forty percent in 2002, employment in that sector was basically flat in percentage terms. Less than five percent of Americans worked for financial firms in 1948 and less than five percent of Americans work for financial firms today. Working Americans lost their jobs by the millions but banks and Wall Street were not hiring them into the *make believe service economy of the future*. The same old service economy just kept getting a larger share of the corporate profits because the most important component of the economy; *manufacturing*, was being *systematically destroyed by the money power*.[277] So much for the argument that free trade benefits all. Free trade benefits *the money power*.

Figure 6.4

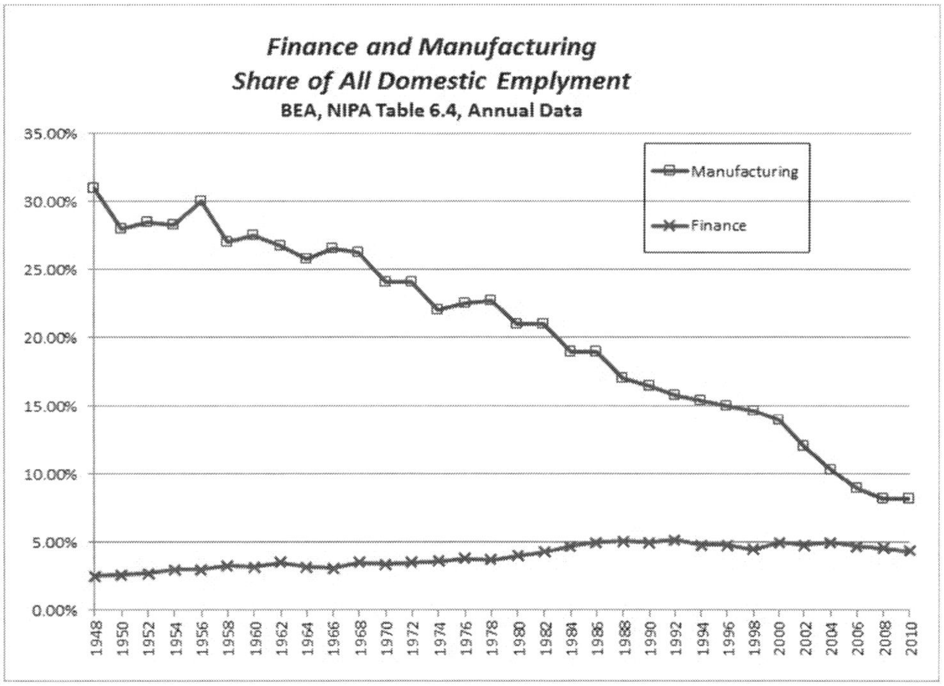

Graph adapted from *The Atlantic* from Weissmann, Jordan. March 5, 2013. "How Wall Street Devoured Corporate America." March 5, 2013. Used with permission. Retrieved from http://www.theatlantic.com/business/archive/2013/03/how-wall-street-devoured-corporate-america/273732/

That much of the "money power' today is held by Wall Street is not considered a dubious proposition. After all, why is the Occupy Wall Street movement named as it is? Ralph Nader was interviewed by Free Speech TV's Amy Goodman and Aaron Mate about the inordinate power of the monied interests on the Democracy Now News Hour in June, 2013. This is their account of what Nader said:

> Describing the United States as an 'advanced Third World country,' longtime consumer advocate and former presidential candidate Ralph Nader calls for a new mass movement to challenge the power corporations have in Washington. 'It is not too extreme to call our system of government now 'American fascism.' It's the control of government by big business, which Franklin Delano Roosevelt defined in 1938 as fascism,' Nader says. 'We have the lowest minimum wage in the Western world. We have the greatest amount of consumer debt. We have the highest child poverty, the highest adult poverty, huge underemployment, a crumbling public works — but huge multi-billionaires and hugely profitable corporations. I say to the American people: What's your breaking point? When are you going to stop making excuses for yourself? When are you going to stop exaggerating these powers when you know you have the power in this country if you organize it? [278]

As I have told you repeatedly I do not like either party. I would not vote for Ralph Nader either. Nader goes too far in describing America as a fascist state. Nader seems to believe that we could fix everything if we just raised taxes high enough to fund every new social program that Nader and other globalist liberals dream up. It is my belief that we must adopt industrial and trade policies that will bring prosperity while combating pollution and global warming, but we cannot encourage an attitude of dependancy and entitlement among disadvantaged citizens. We must teach the value of work, and the idea that work is a moral duty for those able to work. We must discourage people from having children until they have the maturity and economic wherewithal to raise them. We do not want to buy votes by promising undeserved entitlements to undeserving people. On the other hand, we must go to battle for programs that are needed to help the poor, particularly blameless children. It's a question of where to draw the line, and how to dissuade irresponsible behavior. Ralph Nader is however absolutely spot on when he tells us that corporations are running the government but that we the people have the power to change things in this country if we only organize to do so.

Kevin Phillips, has been a political and economic commentator for three decades producing a series of highly laudable books. Here is the dust jacket description of his book *Wealth and Democracy*:

> In Wealth and Democracy Kevin Phillips charts the ongoing saga of great wealth - how it has been accumulated, its shifting sources, and its ups and down over more than two centuries. He explores how the rich and politically powerful have frequently worked together to create or perpetuate privilege, often at the expense of the national interest and usually at the expense of the middle and lower classes.
>
> With intriguing chapters on history and bold analysis of present-day America,

Phillips illuminates the dangerous politics that go with excessive concentration of wealth...He exposes the subtle corruption spawned by a money culture and financial power, evident in economic philosophy, tax favoritism, and selective bailouts in the name of free enterprise, economic stimulus, and national security.

> Finally, Wealth and Democracy turns to the history of Britain and other leading world economic powers to examine the symptoms that signaled their declines - speculative finance, mounting international debt, record wealth, income polarization, and disgruntled politics - signs that we recognize in America at the start of the twenty-first century. In a time of national crisis, Phillips worries that the growing parallels suggest the tide may be turning for us all.[279]

Considering the fact that *Wealth and Democracy* was first published back in 2002, it may seem surprising to you that Phillips was writing about "selective bailouts," and "speculative finance"[280] because the financial crisis of 2008 did not take place for another six years. The truth is that the antecedents of that collapse were present in the economy for a long time and good government would have eliminated the threat of a crisis long before it took place.[281]

A superb source of information about the bailout is the book *13 Bankers: The Wall Street Takeover And The Next Financial Meltdown* written by MIT Professor Simon Johnson and businessman James Kwak. They trace the evolution of the banking oligarchy which nearly capsized the American economy in 2008, and which continues to exercise unbridled influence over government policy:

> Even after the ruinous financial crisis of 2008, America is still beset by the depredations of an oligarchy that is now bigger, more profitable, and more resistant to regulation than ever. Anchored by six megabanks - Bank of America, J.P. Morgan Chase, Citigroup, Wells Fargo, Goldman Sachs, and Morgan Stanley - which together control assets amounting, astonishingly, to more than 60 percent of the country's gross domestic product, these financial institutions, (now more emphatically 'too big to fail') continue to hold the global economy hostage, threatening yet another financial meltdown with their excessive risk-taking and toxic 'business as usual' practices.[282]

In their 2013 book, *Dollarocracy: How The Money-and-Media Election Complex Is Destroying America*, John Nichols and Robert McChesney describe what *the money power* is and how it works. Here is the publisher's synopsis:

> U.S. Elections have never been perfect, but America is now hurtling toward a point where the electoral process itself ceases to function as a means for citizens to effectively control leaders and to guide government policies. In *Dollarocracy*, two leading media experts - journalist John Nichols and academic Robert McChesney - examine the forces that have sapped elections of their meaning and stolen America's democratic potential: the pay-to-play billionaires and the politicians who do their bidding, the corporations that have been freed to buy elections and the activist judges who advance their agenda, and the media conglomerates that blow off journalism while raking in billions airing

intellectually and morally reprehensible advertising.

The unprecedented tidal wave of unaccountable money flooding the electoral system makes a mockery of political equality in the voting booth. The determination of media companies to cash in on that mockery, especially by selling ad time at a premium to campaigns - when they should instead be exposing and opposing - completes a vicious circle. What has emerged, argue Nichols and McChesney, is a "money and media election complex." This complex is built on a set of commercial and institutional relationships connecting wealthy donors, corporations, lobbyists, politicians, coin-operated "think tanks" beltway pundits, and now super-Pacs. These relationships are not just eviscerating democratic elections, they are benefitting from that evisceration.[283]

The Legacy of the *Powell Memo*

McChesney and Nichols follow liberal convention in tracing back the development of the modern complex of relationships connecting "wealthy donors, corporations, lobbyists, politicians, coin-operated "think tanks" beltway pundits, and now super-Pacs" to a political memorandum written by corporate tobacco attorney Lewis Powell at the request of a U.S. Chamber of Commerce official in 1971.[284] Most commentators agree that Powell's memo and his work as an associate justice of the U.S. Supreme Court, have been a powerful influence on the course that the money and media election complex has taken since then.[285] Powell was born in 1907 in Suffolk, Virginia. He was a partner for more than twenty five years at a large Virginia law firm known as Hunton, Williams, Gay, Powell and Gibson, He practiced primarily as a representative of the Tobacco Institute and various tobacco companies and in the areas of railway litigation law and mergers and acquisition. He was a board member of the tobacco giant Phillip Morris between 1964 and his appointment in 1971 to the Supreme Court by President Nixon.[286] At the time of his appointment by Nixon, Powell was on the boards of eleven corporations.[287]

The Tobacco Institute which Lewis Powell represented was a trade association created by cigarette manufacturers in 1958, and funded by the industry in proportion to each company's sales. The Tobacco Institute worked in tandem with the Tobacco Industry Research Committee and its successor, the Council for Tobacco Research. Their work involved creating junk science and arguments that painted smoking as both pleasant and safe. The Tobacco Institute put out good PR about tobacco. It also attacked scientific studies that put tobacco use in bad light, casting doubt as best it could on the proposition that smoking is harmful to human health.[288] The Tobacco Institute assembled information on peoples opinions and attitudes about smoking and it conducted intense lobbying while the tobacco industry plied legislators with campaign contributions and honorariums.[289] It put together a very successful record of preventing any significant regulation of tobacco products by government for decades.[290] Ironically in 1998, within just a few months of Powell's death, the Tobacco Master Settlement Agreement between the four largest tobacco manufacturers and forty six states that had sued to recover for expenses caused by smoking related illnesses was signed; In addition to requiring large reimbursements to the states by the tobacco industry, it was stipulated in the agreement that the Tobacco Institute and other tobacco groups that Powell had served and benefitted would be dissolved.[291] Authors Nichols and McChesney say this about Powell in their book *Dollarocracy*:

> In 1971, after his tobacco industry clients had been banished from the all powerful arena of TV advertising, where it had been profoundly easy to create a new generation of tobacco addicts, Powell pondered the political moment where the commercial interests of big business could be so thoroughly upended by regulators. He took two extraordinary steps. One was very public. the other was very private. Together, they would define the politics and policy-making of America and provide the set of circumstances that led us to write this book.[292]

The "very private" step Nichols and McChesney refer to was Powell's August 23, 1971 memo to his friend Eugene Sydnor, a director of the U.S. Chamber of Commerce. The memo was finished just two months before President Nixon nominated Powell to the Supreme Court.[293] The "very public" step taken by Powell was to accept Nixon's nomination.[294] Powell's memo can be found on the internet. It has been commented on widely. Various sources describe the memo in the terms used by Charles Cray, Cray is the director of the Center For Corporate Policy, "a non-profit, non-partisan public interest organization working to curb corporate abuses and make corporations publicly accountable."[295] Cray is also the co-author of *The People's Business: Controlling Corporations and Restoring Democracy.*[296] Cray has called the memo "a corporate blueprint to dominate democracy."[297] From *Dollarocracy*:

> Powell's memo was written in secret and delivered to his friend Eugene Snydor, Jr., a former Virginia legislator who chaired the education committee of the U.S. Chamber of Commerce. Snydor would circulate the memorandum, titled 'Attack on the American Free Enterprise System,' among the chamber's leadership immediately, as befit the sense of urgency underpinning a document that opened with a warning: 'The American economic system is under broad attack' by consumer activists, environmentalists, civil rights campaigns, and labor unions engaged in a frontal assault...on our government , our system of justice, and the free enterprise system.'[298]

Powell's memo[299] comes across as a right wing diatribe filled with excessive, paranoid and undocumented charges. Here is a sample of Powell's nebulous accusations:

> But what now concerns us is quite new in the history of America. We are not dealing with sporadic or isolated attacks from a relatively few extremists or even from the minority socialist cadre. Rather, the assault on the enterprise system is broadly based and consistently pursued. It is gaining momentum and converts.
>
> **Sources of the Attack**

> The sources are varied and diffused. They include, not unexpectedly, the Communists, New Leftists and other revolutionaries who would destroy the entire system, both political and economic. These extremists of the left are far more numerous, better financed, and increasingly are more welcomed and encouraged by other elements of society, than ever before in our history. But they remain a small minority, and are not yet the principal cause for concern. The most disquieting voices joining the chorus of criticism come from perfectly respectable elements of society: from the college campus, the pulpit, the media, the intellectual and literary journals, the arts and sciences, and from politicians. In most of these groups the movement against the system is participated in only by minorities. Yet, these often are the most articulate, the most vocal, the most prolific in their writing and speaking. Moreover, much of the media-for varying motives and in varying degrees-either voluntarily accords unique publicity to these "attackers," or at least allows them to exploit the media for their purposes. This is especially true of television, which now plays such a predominant role in shaping the thinking, attitudes and emotions of our people.
>
> One of the bewildering paradoxes of our time is the extent to which the enterprise system tolerates, if not participates in, its own destruction. The campuses from which much of the criticism emanates are supported by (I) tax funds generated largely from American business, and (ii) contributions from capital funds controlled or generated by American business. The boards of trustees of our universities overwhelmingly are composed of men and women who are leaders in the system. Most of the media, including the national TV systems, are owned and theoretically controlled by corporations which depend upon profits, and the enterprise system to survive.

Powell does identify a few individuals by name, but in doing so he makes his claim of a "frontal assault' and 'broad attack" on the free enterprise system sound even more laughable. Here are two examples:

> Perhaps the single most effective antagonist of American business is Ralph Nader, who — thanks largely to the media — has become a legend in his own time and an idol of millions of Americans. A recent article in Fortune speaks of Nader as follows:
>
> "The passion that rules in him — and he is a passionate man — is aimed at smashing utterly the target of his hatred, which is corporate power. He thinks, and says quite bluntly, that a great many corporate executives belong in prison — for defrauding the consumer with shoddy merchandise, poisoning the food supply with chemical additives, and willfully manufacturing unsafe products that will maim or kill the buyer. He emphasizes that he is not talking just about 'fly-by-night hucksters' but the top management of blue chip business."
>
> A frontal assault was made on our government, our system of justice, and the free enterprise system by Yale Professor Charles Reich in his widely publicized book: "The Greening of America," published last winter.

So, Ralph Nader, the guy who wrote "Unsafe at Any Speed," was *"the most effective attacker"* on the free enterprise system. Here is a partial wikipedia entry on Nader's book:

> Unsafe at Any Speed: The Designed-In Dangers of the American Automobile by Ralph Nader, published in 1965, is a book accusing car manufacturers of resistance to the introduction of safety features, like seat belts, and their general reluctance to spend money on improving safety. It was a pioneering work, openly polemical but containing substantial references and material from industry insiders. It made Nader a household name.[300]

I can see why Ralph Nader would be seen as enemy number one by a tobacco industry lawyer who knew his industry was covering up data regarding the health risks from smoking which include a lot more illnesses than just lung cancer and heart disease. Are we to believe that Powell, who both represented the Tobacco Institute and was on the board of Phillip Morris, did not know about the cover up, nor about the toxic additives like ammonia that were being added to cigarettes to make them even more addictive? That practice went on for decades before the industry got caught doing it.[301] I figure Powell not only knew, he probably laughed, (while counting all his money), about how successful he and his clients/partners were in getting away with it.

Building on his paranoid polemic about a broad based attack on free enterprise, Powell described in his memo a plan for a broad based counter-attack against the alleged dangerous elements in society, which included Ralph Nader, author Charles Reich, attorney William Kuntsler and among a few others, college students from Yale and every other major university, about which he had this to say:

> Yale, like every other major college is graduating scores of bright young men who are practitioners of 'the politics of despair' These young men despise the American political and economic system....(their) minds seem to be wholly closed. They live, not by rational discussion, but by mindless slogans.[302]

Charles A. Reich (born 1928) is an American legal and social scholar as well as writer who was a Professor at Yale Law School. In 1970 his book about the 1960's counterculture and youth movement, "The Greening of America" was published. The book made it onto the New York Times best seller list. As a law student, Reich was editor-in-chief of the Yale Law Journal. He was also a law clerk for U.S. Supreme Court Justice Hugo Black during the 1953-1954 term of the court. Prior to teaching at Yale, Reich worked for some big Washington, D.C. law firms representing *corporations*. Reich apparently is a bit of a lefty and he is gay.[303]

I'm sorry but I'm not seeing the threat that was posed to free enterprise by Reich. It is likely that over ninety nine percent of Americans don't recall anything about Reich because they never heard his name mentioned in their lives. Powell was being a *crafty tobacco lawyer* demonizing fine Americans and stirring the 'pot" to run cover for a *raise the money power plan* that is described in detail in his memo. Maybe Powell picked Yale students to describe as irrational followers of mindless slogans because Reich was there leading them astray. I won't make money betting on it, but it does give me a hearty laugh thinking about it.

William Kuntsler's famous career as a civil rights and criminal defense attorney does not need to be reviewed here any more than Nader's did. He supplied many high profile criminal defendants with the due process that is every defendant's legal right. Before attending Yale Law school and graduating with honors he served in the Army during World II in the Pacific theater, attaining the rank of Major, and winning the bronze star. He was a self described radical at a time when it was radical for a black citizen to drink from a white's only drinking fountain. He was never the judge or the jury; Others decided the facts and the law, not Kuntsler. He just served his client's zealously as was his legal duty. He was hated by some for defending accused terrorists, but somebody has to do that and it is a noble undertaking. Kuntsler also defended innocent people and blacks who were arrested merely for exercising their constitutional rights.[304] In no way was Kuntsler or anything he ever did a significant threat to "free enterprise." To the contrary, his work helped maintain the system of ordered liberty and blind justice that is at the heart of the American way. Powell just used the dislike many conservative businessmen felt for Kuntsler the same way he used their dislike for Nader and Reich: to persuade them to embrace his plan.

What did happen during the 1960's was *never a significant threat to free enterprise*. There were sit ins, demonstrations, some radical groups and some serious crimes that caused loss of life including bombings and bank robberies. Those events, the civil rights movement and the Vietnam war protests are what shifted Americans toward the political right and to the election of Richard Nixon, who promised he would end the Vietnam war. That shift to the right was well under way when Powell wrote his memo, and free enterprise was never in the slightest danger during the prosperous years of the sixties.

Nonetheless, to combat the supposed boogeymen - Nader, Reich, Kuntsler and all those mindless but bright, leftist slogan spouting Yale students, (in Powell's view, not mine), Powell came up with what his critics call his "corporate blueprint to dominate democracy."[305] Let's review the main points of his plan in his own words:

> The first essential - a prerequisite to any effective action - is for businessmen to confront this problem as a primary responsibility of corporate management. The overriding first need is for businessmen to recognize that the ultimate issue may be survival of what we call the free enterprise system, and all that this means for the strength and prosperity of America and the freedom of our people.[306]

Let's stop right here to examine the above paragraph. As you know, this book was written by *me* to convince *you* to join me in creating a new political party in America. Whose ideas form the backbone of my beliefs about what brings about progress and prosperity? Let me remind you; that would be the *Mount Rushmore Presidents,* George Washington, Thomas Jefferson, Abraham Lincoln and Teddy Roosevelt. It is my fervent desire to protect the free enterprise system in America. Our greatest presidents all knew that too many English imports would *impoverish* and *destroy* America. They adopted the *American System*, and that system of *government industrial policy in concert with free enterprise* is what built our nation into an industrial superpower with the might and wealth to win World War II.

It was not until *greedy corporations attacked the American Way* with free trade that America began its decline to our current deplorable and ever worsening condition. But this overrated Powell, *an apologist and propagandist for the tobacco industry merchants of death,* like his modern ilk, would have you believe otherwise. He would argue, like modern right wing spin tank policy wonks do, that America was built on free trade. *It was not*. Industrial policy is not socialism as right wing alarmists constantly decry it to be. Industrial policycan refer simply to the traditional time tested *American System*. Don't allow yourself to become deluded into believing otherwise from listening to the silver tongued devils who serve the money power.

Now, back to the discussion of the Powell plan to stop the consumer and environmental advocate Ralph Nader and the other *imaginary monsters* in Powell's mind:

> If our system is to survive, top management must be equally concerned with protecting and preserving the system itself. This involves far more than an increased emphasis on "public relations" or "government affairs" - two areas in which corporations long have invested substantial sums. A significant step by individual corporations could well be the designation of an executive vice president (ranking with other executive VP's) whose responsibility is to counter - on the broadest front - the attack on the enterprise system. The public relations department could be one of the foundations assigned to this executive, but his responsibilities should encompass some of the types of activities referred to subsequently in this memorandum. his budget and staff should be adequate to the task.[307]

Lets take a moment to consider what Powell is saying. Powell clearly states that corporations should be *as concerned* about controlling (he calls it protecting and preserving) the (political and economic) system *as they are about profits*. He is saying that corporations, which are *artificial legal entities created by the state to enhance economic development,* should now take it upon themselves to take sides in the political debate, ignoring the opinions of the "little people" like their own employees, and engage in politics on a massive scale to gain control of the way people think. This massive intrusion into the political discourse of the country is really meant to benefit the wealth and income of the corporate elite and screw everybody else. If the big cheeses in the corporations decide that their taxes should be low and that they should be able to ship all their factories overseas and fire all their American employees that's their absolute right under the free enterprise system according to Powell.

Powell was wrong. Under the American System created by the Mount Rushmore Presidents, the government could and did take measures that had enormous impact on keeping manufacturing and jobs in America to benefit Americans. Corporations were never meant to run America via a closely controlled media monopoly and a system of corporate advertising propaganda that is so huge today that it boggles the mind. *The reason that corporations are allowed to exist by states is to benefit the economy*. Free enterprise and the private interest has never been above the state and the public interest. The interests of the state in clean air and water, in public safety, and in the very lives and well being of the people is utterly transcendent over self-serving corporations whose activities frequently come into conflict with the public good. Yet today, the right wing in America is preaching a gospel that considers total mind control by corporations over the country - *Dollarocracy* - as Nichols and McChesney term it, a God given and absolute inalienable right.

Now for the Orwellian sounding elements of Powell's list of imperative corporate tactics to control things. This is quoted directly from Powell's initially secret memo:

> The national television networks should be monitored in the same way textbooks should be kept under constant surveillance. This applies not merely to so called educational (such as the "Selling of the Pentagon"), but to the daily "news analysis" which so often includes the most insidious type of criticism of the enterprise system. Whether this criticism results from hostility or economic ignorance, the result is the gradual erosion of confidence in "business" and free enterprise. This monitoring, to be effective, would require constant examination of the texts of adequate samples of programs. Complaints - to the media and to the Federal Communications Commission - should be made promptly and strongly when programs are unfair or inaccurate. Equal time should be demanded when appropriate. Effort should be made to see that the forum - type programs (the Today Show. Meet the Press, etc.) afford at least as much opportunity for supporters of the American system to participate as these programs do for those who attack it.[308]

Considering some of the facts mentioned in Chapter Three, Powell's plan to monitor and control the media succeeded beyond his wildest expectations. For instance, of the guests who discussed climate change on the Sunday news shows *Meet the Press* and *Face the Nation* over the four year period between 2008 and 2012, fifty four percent were media personalities and thirty one percent were politicians. Not even one scientist was allowed on either program to discuss climate change. You may have noticed in the foregoing quote how Powell appropriated the term "American System" from Henry Clay and Abraham Lincoln and turned its meaning inside out. The term was historically used to identify the system of industrial policy adopted by the federal government and followed until the post WWII period.[309] Ever the scheming tobacco lawyer, Powell used the words "American system" to argue that government efforts to protect and foster American industry by limiting free trade, policing polluters, or reigning in out of control speculation by too big to fail banks is somehow both novel and un-American. Powell even went so far in his memo, (like many right wing politicians do today), as to imply that the Mount Rushmore Presidents who had constructed and maintained the original American System were socialists. Powell wrote:

> There seems to be little awareness that the only alternatives to free enterprise are varying degrees of bureaucratic regulation of individual freedom — ranging from that under moderate socialism to the iron heel of the leftist or rightist dictatorship.[310]

That's sounds just like what free traders say when the subject of industrial policy protectionist strategies are discussed today. Never mind that it was George Washington who, on the advice of Alexander Hamilton, adopted an interventionist strategy when it came to supporting American manufacturing and encouraging innovation. Washington imposed tariffs and his successors imposed even higher tariffs on imports, subsidized private research and development efforts, and directly funded research to benefit manufacturing industries.[311] Republicans and democrats for the most part try to deny this history even today as our national economy remains in peril because of their inane policies.[312]

Powell went on in his memo, recommending that corporations and the Chamber of Commerce employ and underwrite a "faculty of scholars" to spread the gospel of free enterprise, (free of government oversight or regulation in the public interest that is), Here is more of what he wrote:

> Other Media
>
> Radio and the press are also important, and every available means should be employed to challenge and refute unfair attacks, as well as to present the affirmative case through these media.[313]

Judging from the above advice to use "every available means" to control radio broadcasting so as to prevent attacks while presenting the "affirmative case" of corporations, Powell would be ecstatic to learn that by 2004 Ben Bagdikian could write this in his book *The New Media Monopoly*:

> It is not simply a random artifact in media politics that three of the largest broadcast outlets insistently promote bombastic far-right political positions. Murdoch's Fox radio and television have almost unwavering right-wing commentators. The two largest radio groups, Clear Channel and Cumulus, whose holdings dwarf the rest of radio, are committed to a daily flood of far-right propagandistic programming along with their automated music.[314]

Powell's vision of corporate surveillance and expanded influence over the media was not limited to school textbooks, TV and Radio. He goes on in his memo to discuss other means by which a political mantra pleasing to a tobacco industry superlawyer like him could be injected into American culture:

> The Scholarly Journals
>
> It is especially important for the Chamber's "faculty of scholars" to publish. One of the keys to the success of the liberal and leftist faculty members has been their passion for "publication" and "lecturing." A similar passion must exist among the Chamber's scholars.
>
> Incentives might be devised to induce more "publishing" by independent scholars who do believe in the system.
>
> There should be a fairly steady flow of scholarly articles presented to a broad spectrum of magazines and periodicals — ranging from the popular magazines (Life, Look, Reader's Digest, etc.) to the more intellectual ones (Atlantic, Harper's, Saturday Review, New York, [sic] etc.) and to the various professional journals.
>
> Books, Paperbacks and Pamphlets The news stands — at airports, drugstores, and elsewhere — are filled with paperbacks and pamphlets advocating everything from revolution to erotic free love. One finds almost no attractive, well-written paperbacks or pamphlets on "our side." It will be difficult to compete with an Eldridge Cleaver or even a Charles Reich for reader attention, but unless the effort is made — on a large enough scale and with appropriate imagination to assure some success — this opportunity for educating the public will be irretrievably

> lost. Paid Advertisements Business pays hundreds of millions of dollars to the media for advertisements. Most of this supports specific products; much of it supports institutional image making; and some fraction of it does support the system. But the latter has been more or less tangential, and rarely part of a sustained, major effort to inform and enlighten the American people.
>
> If American business devoted only 10% of its total annual advertising budget to this overall purpose, it would be a statesman-like expenditure.
>
> The Neglected Political Arena.
>
> In the final analysis, the payoff — short-of revolution — is what government does. Business has been the favorite whipping-boy of many politicians for many years. But the measure of how far this has gone is perhaps best found in the anti-business views now being expressed by several leading candidates for President of the United States.[315]

Before looking further into how Powell's memo has borne fruit for *the money power* over the decades since it was written, consider also his desire that the Chamber oversee your child's education in a far more invasive manner than simply keeping their textbooks "under constant surveillance:"

> Balancing of Faculties
>
> Perhaps the most fundamental problem is the imbalance of many faculties. Correcting this is indeed a long-range and difficult project. Yet, it should be undertaken as a part of an overall program. This would mean the urging of the need for faculty balance upon university administrators and boards of trustees.
>
> The methods to be employed require careful thought, and the obvious pitfalls must be avoided. Improper pressure would be counterproductive. But the basic concepts of balance, fairness and truth are difficult to resist, if properly presented to boards of trustees, by writing and speaking, and by appeals to alumni associations and groups. This is a long road and not one for the fainthearted. But if pursued with integrity and conviction it could lead to a strengthening of both academic freedom on the campus and of the values which have made America the most productive of all societies.
>
> Graduate Schools of Business
>
> The Chamber should enjoy a particular rapport with the increasingly influential graduate schools of business. Much that has been suggested above applies to such schools. Should not the Chamber also request specific courses in such schools dealing with the entire scope of the problem addressed by this memorandum? This is now essential training for the executives of the future.
>
> Secondary Education
>
> While the first priority should be at the college level, the trends mentioned above are increasingly evidenced in the high schools. Action programs, tailored to the

> high schools and similar to those mentioned, should be considered. The implementation thereof could become a major program for local chambers of commerce, although the control and direction — especially the quality control — should be retained by the National Chamber.
>
> What Can Be Done About the Public?
>
> Reaching the campus and the secondary schools is vital for the long-term. Reaching the public generally may be more important for the shorter term. The first essential is to establish the staffs of eminent scholars, writers and speakers, who will do the thinking, the analysis, the writing and the speaking. It will also be essential to have staff personnel who are thoroughly familiar with the media, and how most effectively to communicate with the public.[316]

Nichols and McChesney trace the development of what they call "Vast Right-Wing Networks With Corporate Clout" back to the Powell Memo in their book *Dollarocracy*.[317] They report that the U.S. Chamber of Commerce tripled its budget over the six year period following Powell's memo as an "infrastructure of procorporate think tanks and advocacy groups" was built up.[318]

Kimberly Phillips-Fein is a historian of American history specializing in modern American politics. She teaches courses in American political, business, and labor history at the of New York University. Fein received a B.A. in History from the University of Chicago and her Ph.D. in American History from Columbia University. Her 2009 book, *Invisible Hands: The Making of the Conservative Movement from the New Deal to Reagan*, sheds a great deal of light on the development of right wing political groups and institutions following publication of the Powell memo. Fein described how conservative tycoons such as John Olin, Joseph Coors, Fred Koch, and Richard Mello Scaife helped push the post Powell Memo right wing agenda.[319] Charlie Cray linked some of the same *money power* activists with the organizations they helped found:

> Powell's Memo is widely credited for having helped catalyze a new business activist movement with numerous conservative family and corporations (e.g. Coors, Olin, Bradley, Scaife, Koch and others) thereafter creating and sustaining powerful new voices to help push the corporate agenda, including the Business Roundtable (1972), the American Legislative Exchange Council (ALEC - 1973), Heritage Foundation (1973), the Cato Institute (1977), the Manhattan Institute (1978), Citizens for a Sound Economy (1984 - now Americans for Prosperity), Accuracy in Academe (1985), and others.[320]

It seems to me very unlikely that Fein, Nichols and McChesney and many other commentators with similar views are wrong about the fact that Powell's memo was very influential both within the Chamber of Commerce and with other leading elements of what we might call the conservative money power. Powell himself counseled the Chamber of Commerce to move immediately to implement his plan for the construction of a nationwide corporate propaganda machine. It was one which was obviously to be of unparalleled size and scope:

> ...one should not postpone more direct political action, while awaiting the gradual change in public opinion to be effected through education and information. Business must learn...political power is necessary...such power must be

> assiduously ...cultivated; and that when necessary, it must be used aggressively and with determination — without embarrassment and without the reluctance which has been so characteristic of American business.[321]

It is clear that an event of major historical significance - a seminal event in American history - took place with the writing of Powell's secret memo. Powell's memo went public in 1973 when the famous syndicated columnist Jack Anderson got a hold of it and wrote about it in his column.[322] By then, Powell had been confirmed by the Senate as Nixon's choice to fill the vacancy of Hugo Black and Powell had been sitting on the bench for over a year. He had been confirmed by a vote of 89 to 1.[323] Such is the *power of money*. Powell remained on the bench until 1987.

It cannot be denied that the changes wrought in the U.S. Chamber of Commerce and the development of a large network of highly influential conservative think tanks and right wing political action organizations combined with vastly expanded corporate lobbying since Powell wrote his memo have profoundly affected our national economic policies over the last forty plus years. Powell also had a profound impact on the Supreme Court. The Supreme Court's rulings have allowed the growth of the money and media election complex which Nichols and McChesney decry in their book Dollarocracy.[324]

The absurd myth that free trade is the historical pillar of America prosperity could not have been spread so far and wide had the government done its job and prevented a handful of billionaires and corporations with interlocking directorships from monopolizing the media. Freedom of the press does not prevent the application of anti-trust and freedom of information laws to media corporations. The wealth concentrating - middle class hollowing - conservative agenda is now served slavishly by both political parties. The *money power* runs both parties. Consider what journalist Bill Moyers had to say to the crowd at the reform group Public Citizen's 40th Gala in October, 2011:

> During the prairie revolt that swept the Great Plains a century after the Constitution was ratified, the populist orator Mary Elizabeth Lease exclaimed: "Wall Street owns the country...Our laws are the output of a system which clothes rascals in robes and honesty in rags. The [political] parties lie to us and the political speakers mislead us...Money rules." That was 1890. Those agrarian populists boiled over with anger that corporations, banks, and government were ganging up to deprive every day people of their livelihood. She should see us now. John Boehner calls on the bankers, holds out his cup, and offers them total obeisance from the House majority if only they fill it. That's now the norm, and they get away with it. GOP once again means Guardians of Privilege.
>
> Barack Obama criticizes bankers as "fat cats", then invites them to dine at a pricey New York restaurant where the tasting menu runs to $195 a person. That's now the norm, and they get away with it. The President has raised more money from banks, hedge funds, and private equity managers than any Republican candidate, including Mitt Romney. Inch by inch he has conceded ground to them while espousing populist rhetoric that his very actions betray. Let's name this for what it is: Democratic deviancy defined further downward. Our politicians are

little more than money launderers in the trafficking of power and policy – fewer than six degrees of separation from the spirit and tactics of Tony Soprano.[325]

I agree with Mr. Moyers. In my opinion, the Democratic Party has turned into a stooge for Wall Street.

Looking into the structure of the organized money power, I discovered a list of over 802 conservative organizations, (648 in the U.S.), that employ two thousand, two hundred conservative policy experts.[326] Not counted on the list of experts are many thousands more that are employed in academia. lobbying firms, by the media, or just fly solo writing spin which is rewarded by corporate payments and favor. It is impossible to go into detail on all those organizations in this chapter. It would be more difficult than counting the loopholes in the federal tax code. One of the standout right wing organizations in terms of money and influence is the U.S. Chamber of Commerce. It's hardly surprising since the chamber is the flagship lobbying organization for big business in the United States. It was only natural that Powell prepared his infamous memo for the Chamber in the first place. The chamber was ranked first in dollars spent on lobbying in 2012 and for every of the ten prior years for which I collected data.[327]

The U.S. Chamber of Commerce celebrated its one hundredth birthday in April of 2012. It was the brain child of business leaders who feared the developing union movement and wanted a union of their own. President Taft, a Republican, endorsed the idea of an organization which would represent business interests. Taft organized a conference held in Washington at which the U.S. Chamber of Commerce was created. The Chamber is by far the largest lobbying organization in the United States. Its expenditures in 2012 amounted to $136,300,000.00, dwarfing spending by the second runner up, the National Assn. of Realtors who spent $41,464,580, that year.[328] About half of the money the Chamber of Commerce spent in 2008 came from just 45 anonymous donors.[329] In 2009 over half of the chambers money came from the American Health Insurance Providers (AHIP), a lobbying group consisting of the five largest health insurance companies.[330] In comparison to the Chambers spending, the nations's two biggest labor unions, the AFL-CIO and the Service Employees International Union together spent under $6 million in 2012.[331]

McChesney and Nichols in their book *Dollarocracy* provide an illuminating discussion of the growth of lobbying efforts by industry and the specialized spin tanks that have proliferated since Powell wrote his memo. They also describe the revolving door that our whorrible (my word for them), politicians take between elected and appointed government office and jobs as lobbyists for the very industries they were charged with governing or regulating:

> Powell argued that corporate America needed to forcefully enter and dominate the political process - a crucial idea the chamber and its members embraced. In 1971, according to David Vogel, only 175 U.S. corporations had registered lobbyists in Washington DC. A decade later, there were 2,500....In the late 1960's, there were about 100 corporate public affairs offices in Washington; by 1978 , there were more than 500.
>
> ...Suddenly Washington and especially Capitol Hill were crawling with tens of thousands of very- well paid representatives of industry trade associations and

specific corporations or the lobbying firms that served them.

> Where did corporate America find talented people who could greatly influence members of Congress and maneuver effectively around regulatory agencies? Former government employees - regulatory agency personnel and congressional aides and the like - provided a tried and true supply of labor, and there was a longstanding tradition of the "revolving door" already in place... Where better to find people who could influence Congress than Congress itself" In the early 1970's, 3 percent of retiring members became lobbyists; that quickly changed, and by 2012 the figure had grown to the fifty percent range.[332]

Lobbyist jobs for ex-legislators pay in the six to seven figure range and that's just for a starting salary. Lucrative employment can also be had by former legislators and White house officials on the boards and in the executive offices of the largest multinational corporations. They also obtain windfall salaries working for foreign countries whose economic betterment comes at grievous expense to American workers and taxpayers. As one astute observer has noted "The dirty little secret of American politics is that for most politicians, getting elected is just not that important - what matters most is post-election employment."[333]

For more information about the "money and media complex' and the media conglomerates that blow off journalism while raking in billions airing intellectually and morally reprehensible advertising" I recommend you read *Dollarocracy* from cover to cover.

What concerns me the most about the money power of Wall Street and big corporations is the way they have dominated both the Democrats and the Republicans when it comes to our failed international trade policies. The money power dominates media coverage of international trade, casting free trade in a positive light while squelching dissenting view points almost entirely as was discussed in Chapter Three.

Fairness and Accuracy in Reporting or FAIR, is a national media watchdog organization that has been analyzing and reporting on bias in the media for nearly thirty years. They work "to invigorate the First Amendment by advocating for greater diversity in the press and by scrutinizing media practices that marginalize public interest, minority and dissenting viewpoints."[334] They "expose neglected news stories and defend working journalists when they are muzzled."[335] FAIR advocates structural reform which includes breaking up the dominant media conglomerates and creating more diverse public broadcasting which operates independently from political and economic influences.[336] FAIR published a report of a study which found that journalists have more right wing tilt on economic issues than the general public. On the issue of the North American Free Trade Agreement, the bias of journalists was found to be the most pronounced.[337]

Obviously the average American did not wake up one day in 1945 and decide with his neighbors that America should dismantle the system of protectionism that the Mount Rushmore Presidents had put in place for the preceding 145 years. The move to free trade was largely brought about by the nation's political and economic elites without conferring with the general public. The next chapter looks into the reasons why and how free trade was adopted and slowly put into place, leading to the deplorable condition of our economy today.

7

The Descent of America: A Story of Weak Presidents, An Ineffectual Congress, And Misguided Priorities

Nobody knew it at the time, but the pooring of America's working class and the hollowing out of America's middle class began way back in 1934 when Franklin Delano Roosevelt became President. Don't get me wrong, I think FDR was one of our greatest presidents and he deserves his stellar reputation for leading America out of the Great Depression and to victory over Nazism and Japan in World War II. He was a wonderful man and a strong leader who united the country in a time of grave danger. Nevertheless, one of FDR's policy decisions created a condition that, left unchecked, brought about the eventual decline of America to the conditions we are suffering from today. That ill fated decision was FDR's acquiescence to a recommendation by his newly appointed Secretary of State, Cordell Hull, that the administration back House Resolution 8687, which was a proposed amendment to the Tariff Act of 1930. The amendment was sold to Congress by Hull and his collaborators as a means to expand exports, and it granted the president temporary authority for a three year period to raise or lower tariffs as much as fifty percent from the levels set in 1930.[338]

The first generation of American economic leaders had of course felt anger towards Britain in part for its policy of mercantilism.[339] Americans were prevented by the self-serving mercantilism of their mother country from engaging in high value manufacturing industries. Britain wanted to make money off its colonies, not compete with them. Once independence was achieved, America quickly resorted to a protectionist system of its own to keep English products out, and to develop a manufacturing technology that was superior to that of Britain.[340] A dichotomy existed from the beginning between the industrializing north and the southern agrarian slave states. It was factory versus plantation politics. Lacking an industrial sector to compete with that of Britain the southern elites saw no value in tariffs designed to nurture the productivity of the industrial north.[341] It was not until free trade was implemented in the mid to late twentieth century that northern industrial firms, reeling from foreign competition, began shifting industry to the Sunbelt to take advantage of the lower wages and anti-union sentiment there.[342]

So it was that southern politicians like Cordell Hull tended to continue the tradition of favoring free trade when the Great Depression hit home. Cordell Hull was born in Tennessee in the sixth year following the Civil War. Hull's early dislike of the *America System* favored by the Mount Rushmore Presidents is therefore, unremarkable. What is remarkable is the extent to which Hull influenced history. Kenneth W. Dam, a Max Pam Professor Emeritus of American and Foreign Law wrote about Hull:

> In his instructive Memoirs, Hull explained that before he came to Washington he had 'breathed in the fire of great tariff battles—but they were battles fought on the home grounds that high tariffs or low tariffs were good or bad for the United States as a purely domestic matter. There was little or no thought of their effect on other countries.'[343]

According to Hull, the fire he had breathed, which had its origin in the southern slave state dislike for the *American System,* was later transformed. While serving as a congressman during World War I, Hull proposed that at wars end an international conference should be held to examine and change "trade methods, practices, and policies which in their effects are calculated to create destructive international controversies…."[344] Hull later wrote in his memoirs:

> I saw that you could not separate the idea of commerce from the idea of war and peace. You could not have serious war anywhere in the world and expect commerce to go on as before. And I saw that wars were often caused by economic rivalry. I thereupon came to believe that if we could increase commercial exchanges among nations over lowered trade and tariff barriers and remove international obstacles to trade, we would go a long way toward eliminating war itself.[345]

Hull gave a radio address to the nation on May 18, 1941, over six months before the Japanese attacked Pearl Harbor, outlying a plan to create a system of free trade for the world - as soon as the axis powers were defeated.[346]

But in 1934, when Hull was pressing for passage of House Resolution 8687, he had portrayed the resolution to give the executive branch control of tariffs as an emergency response to conditions of panic.[347] In his must read book, *Opening America's Market U.S. Foreign Trade Policy since 1776*, Alfred E. Eckes, Jr., wrote this about Hull's approach:

> On Capitol Hill, secretary Hull portrayed the plan as 'an emergency measure to deal with emergency conditions.' He emphasized that the 'entire policy of this bill would rest upon trade relationships which would be *mutually and equally profitable* both to our own and other countries....'[348]
>
> In requesting this unusual delegation of authority from Congress, which after all had constitutional responsibility for regulating commerce...the administration emphasized what was to become known as the 'no injury concept.' As President Roosevelt stated in his transmittal message: 'The successful building up of trade *without injury to American producers* depends upon a cautious and gradual evolution of plans...*no sound and important American interest will be injuriously disturbed.*[349]

Nonetheless, Hull and his allies in the Department of State secretly avowed to usurp congressional authority to regulate tariffs permanently.[350] How much of this stemmed from a utopian desire to bring about world peace as opposed to Hull's southern upbringing amid "the fires" of the north-south struggle over free trade?

Whatever the answer, it is laughable to suggest that world peace has been brought about by free trade.[351] Since the end of World War II, peace between the great powers has been maintained by the arsenal of nuclear weapons held by the United States, Russia, and China. The official gospel of peace for both sides in the cold war was called Mutual Assured Destruction. Mutual Assured Destruction, (MAD), is the name for the military strategy of deterrence whereby a nation maintains the ability to launch a massive nuclear counter attack even after it has been the victim of a preemptive nuclear attack. Since the end of the cold war, the unilateral de-industrialization of the United States caused by its enormous trade deficits has resulted in the accelerating militarization of China and poses an ever growing threat to peace.[352]

In addition to being harshly criticized in recent years for keeping poor nations poor;[353] free trade is seen as the great leveler of the working class and middle class in rich countries.[354] It is a form of economic heroin that has totalitarian China hooked on exports to pay for increasing militarization. China is not learning how to achieve self sustaining economic growth and equitable wealth distribution.[355] That is the kind of growth America achieved unilaterally under the American System. Thus, free trade should be seen as an outmoded theory that endangers the peace because it weakens democracy, strengthens totalitarianism, concentrates wealth in fewer and fewer hands and worsens global warming and arguably, other forms of pollution.[356] It is generally accepted as fact that excessive wealth concentration and high poverty levels helped lead to the development of fascism versus socialism conflicts in Italy and Germany prior to World War II.[357] Aided by the *money power*, fascism won out in both countries, leading directly to the holocaust and the bloodiest war of all time. Unsurprisingly, a recent study involving twenty-eight countries confirmed that right wing extremist parties became more popular as the Great Depression wore on.[358]

Cordell Hull never lived to see the level of annihilation his legacy of one-way free trade would bring to American workers and their families. He died at the height of American power and prosperity in 1955, one year before I was born. Hull sounded as though he meant well; His rhetoric was high sounding, but the rhetoric of the free traders today is not so rosy. Their silver tongued speeches promising more and more have changed to disquieting predictions of less and less. The descriptions of free trade loving economists in the 60's 70's and 80's of an America transforming from a grimy industrial powerhouse into a better paid and shiny new "knowledge economy" has quietly morphed into the one sold by Tyler Cohen. Libertarian (read laissez faire and free trade), economist Cohen is the author of two recent books whose texts tell a much less optimistic tale of America's recent past and future. The two books are: *The Great Stagnation: How America Ate All The Fruit of Modern History, Got Sick and Will Eventually Feel Better* and *Average is Over, Powering America Beyond The Age of the Great Stagnation*. Cohen's vision of the American future is one where a tiny aristocracy lords it over a vast majority who can afford nothing more than mini-sized houses and apartments that are so cramped current housing codes designed to deter shantytowns will have to be changed to permit them[359] The money power politicians and pundits have gone from praising the industriousness and productivity of American workers during the golden age of the *American System*, to insulting large voting blocs including the unemployed and underemployed for having poor entrepreneurial skills in the Tea Bag Party economy that America has today.[360]

Perhaps if Cordell Hull were alive today he would be shocked to see what has happened to America since he schemed to replace the relative transparency and accountability of Congressional tariff making with that of unelected and highly secretive trade officials whose identities were not known to the public or even Congress.[361]

Hulls method was to satisfy the legal requirements of House Resolution 8687 by creating two public "dummy" committees the "Executive Committee on Commercial Policy" and a "Committee for Reciprocal Information." The former was purportedly responsible for general tariff policy supervision. The latter was to receive petitions and take testimony on proposed tariff reductions.[362] But Hull created a third committee that actually decided trade policy and he kept Congress in the dark about it. This sham was described by trade historian Eckes, who wrote that:

> The real power, however, would be lodged in the Committee on Trade Agreements (CTA), a group of technicians from the State Department and other agencies who coordinated trade strategy and supervised negotiations....the members of this committee operated secretly and anonymously. Indeed, for over twenty years State declined to reveal the identities of these technicians to Congress.[363]

I have not found any evidence to suggest that even FDR, the then sitting President of the United States, fully understood the implications of what the secretive and deceitful Hull was up to. Hull sure kept Congress out of the loop. Who were these men who absconded with the most vital power Congress was entrusted with by the framers of the Constitution? Who stole away the economic value of democracy itself from the American people? Who carried out the plan to beat down the American labor movement and place American workers into competition with foreign wage slaves? It was and remains a competition that American workers can but rarely win. International trade is a fixed competition that America continues to lose, and lose badly.[364]

The majority of the CTA members were recently hired economists who lacked any significant experience in the real world of business and trade. They were free trade ideologues. Eckes described their mindset:

> With a mandate from Hull and little daily supervision, these economic theorists turned with delight to the...task of reducing trade barriers... Members of the Committee on Trade Agreements held that the 'primary objective' of the RTAP 'is to reduce trade barriers rather than to drive a sharp bargain.' Their policy 'permitted a greater increase in imports than in exports...'[365]
>
> Discussions in CTA...did not consider whether the long-term national interest required maintaining a balanced and healthy industrial base as insurance against a future challenge to U.S. security interests. Instead members evaluated issues on the basis of English classical economic theory...Assuming that competitive advantages reflected basic resource endowments and remained unchanging over time, the State Department planners focused on... the specialization of production. Implicit, too, was their assumption that industries inefficient in the 1930's would

> continue to lag behind foreign competitors, and that export-competitive industries - like automobiles - would retain a comparative advantage in the future...With the United States running a strong merchandise trade surplus, they attached no urgency to considering how U.S. government policies might encourage emerging industries with export-competing potential.[366]

The economists on the CTA failed to understand that America had passed England in manufacturing technology only because America became protectionist, while England adopted free trade as a gambit (which failed) to open up America's market to English manufactures. When the Brits lowered their tariffs unilaterally, America flooded England with American made products, but Americans bought little in exchange from English producers.[367] With the help of Demopublicans, China and other countries are doing the same thing to America today with enormous success.

Even in the middle of the Great Depression the ideology driven star chamber economists of the CTA took their sledgehammers and began to swing blindly at the great engine of prosperity that the American System had created. Right after the passage of House Resolution 8687, Belgian trade negotiators went to Washington. Mindful of Roosevelt's no injury pledge, the Belgians did not expect a one way windfall to be handed to them by the Americans. To their delight the Belgians left Washington with a treasure trove of tariff cuts on Belgian steel, construction materials, and textiles. The inexperienced free trade ideologues secretly running trade matters for the State Department gave away the store. Historian Alfred E. Eckes, Jr., described it this way:

> ...Hull's subordinates 'ran wild,' with maximum allowable offers on building materials, steel, and textiles. Protests from affected domestic injuries ultimately forced the White House to intervene and withdraw some of the more extreme concessions, and for a time it seemed that the state Department might lose control over trade policy.[368]
>
> In retrospect, this...agreement...proved a harbinger of the generous approach the State Department would take through the Reciprocal Trade Agreements Program. ...Despite the generous tariff reductions, the Belgians were permitted to retain quotas and to depreciate their currency (by 28 percent), which they did before the trade agreement took effect, essentially nullifying their concessions to America and giving their exports additional stimulus.[369]

Eckes provided another example of the unilateral trade giveaways made by Hull's secret committee members. In 1936, a few months after concluding a reciprocal trade agreement with the U.S. which was lopsided in its favor, Switzerland turned around and devalued Swiss currency by thirty percentage points. Thereafter American watch making companies complained to the State Department about huge losses. It also became clear that Swiss watch makers were evading payment of the tariff that remained in effect. The Swiss companies were shipping the watches in a partially disassembled state and then adding the remaining parts (jewels) after the watches cleared customs. The Swiss also erected non tariff trade barriers to American watches. By 1938, Swiss exports to America were nearly two and a half times greater than imports from America. Despite all that, the State Department turned a blind eye to American losses and a deaf ear to the complaints of American business.[370]

The Swiss incident highlights one of the reasons America has sacrificed jobs and industry time and again, that being to improve diplomatic relations with a country. In the case of Switzerland the reasons for that are obvious. Before and during World War II the United States military and intelligence system benefitted from maintaining friendly relations with Switzerland. Judicious use of trade concessions was helpful to international relations. Nonetheless, unilateral free trade is a formula for national destruction when it is based on the misguided belief held by overly zealous economists that even one-way free trade maximizes national wealth.[371]

In 1937, when the three year grant of tariff negotiation authority to the executive branch granted under House Resolution 8687 was set to expire, Hull easily obtained a three year extension of the power from Congress. On the second time around Hull told Congress that executive control of trade policy via reciprocal trade agreement making would give the United States "a powerful instrument of economic appeasement and stability...to strengthen the foundations of world peace."[372] With Hitler and Mussolini on the march and World War II fast approaching, Congress agreed to Hull's request. From that point on, the Regional Trade Agreement Program under Hull became more a tool of American foreign policy than a means of expanding American exports or developing the American economy.[373] In 1938, a British-American trade agreement was signed which accomplished a major reduction in the U.S. tariff across hundreds of items. America was the disadvantaged party to the agreement but Anglo-American solidarity was on display as a threat to the Axis powers.[374] Another give away trade treaty was made with Turkey in 1939 to counter the growing entreaties and influence of the fascist states in the region. America also concluded lopsided trade agreements favoring Mexico and the Latin American countries of Venezuela, Peru, Uruguay and Argentina between 1939 and the end of 1942. These trade agreements were made to counter Nazi efforts to gain a toehold in South and Central America. Favorable trade pacts were also handed out to Cuba and Canada as a strategy to maintain a Western Hemisphere free of Nazi interference with America's interests. Iceland received similar treatment from the State Department in 1943, and Iran obtained a package of trade concession "goodies" that same year.[375]

Cordell Hull retired from the his job as Secretary of State after the 1944 election because of failing health. FDR died in April, 1945 about a month before Germany surrendered. FDR never had a chance to review how trade policy should proceed in the post war period, but it is not at all doubtful that he would have continued to follow his wartime approach, and for good reason. Germany, France, England., Italy and Japan had been subjected to extensive wartime destruction and their economies were in ruins after the war. America's economy was greatly improved. War time planning, construction of new factories, and a rush of technical innovations, plus the free acquisition of British and German technologies during and at the end of the war put America way out in front of the rest of the world.

President Truman continued FDR's trade policy with the view that foreign policy considerations had precedence over the concerns of domestic corporations regarding foreign competitors. So did the Presidents who followed Truman. Truman stated his view this way:

> 'Our industry dominates world markets....American labor can now produce so much more than low-priced foreign labor in a given days work that our workingmen need no longer fear, as they were justified in fearing in the past, the

competition of foreign workers.'[376]

America had become so strong by the end of World War II that I do not see any permanent harm in unilaterally lowering tariffs to aid Europe and Japan after the war. It made sense to spend some of our wealth helping the world recover from the war. It aided in the struggle against communism, as did the Marshall Plan. It was also *morally right.* Unfortunately, American economists have made the dubious concept of comparative advantage into a sacred cow, and economics has become a fundamentalist religion of comparative advantage and the unregulated free market. Free trade loving economists are more spin doctor than scientist. Greed and self interest often blinds people to what is right and fair, and in the best interests of the public, the nation, and the world as a whole. Economists often find jobs working for large corporations, banks, insurance companies, right wing think tanks and other organizations that benefit from keeping the wages of working people low. The influence of the *money power* on the field of economics should not be discounted; We should not forget the unseen apparatus built up in the wake of the Powell memo that to this day is "balancing the faculties," "reaching the campus and secondary schools," "monitoring...the national television networks," "in the same way textbooks" are "kept under constant surveillance," and doing the other Orwellian things that tobacco lawyer and Supreme Court Justice Powell recommended.[377] Chapter 12 contains further discussion about economists and why they act and think as they do.

President Eisenhower, who had served as the Supreme Allied Commander during the WWII, saw it as imperative that the threat of communist expansion be contained.[378] The famous "domino theory" that communism would march through western Europe and Asia if the Soviets were not stopped dominated the thoughts of policy leaders in America during the cold war era. Because of the desire of American leadership to maintain strong capitalist economies in Europe and Asia, America pursued a policy of deliberately encouraging imported goods. Free trade economists had free reign to lower America tariffs unilaterally. It was official government policy.[379] Eckes described the throw caution-to-the-winds exuberance which marked this period in history:

> Public officials seemed to have complete confidence in America's ability to lead during the 1940's and 1950's. At a time when imports of goods and services were less than 4 percent of gross national product, they spoke and acted as if American manufacturing would remain permanently strong, efficient, and invulnerable to foreign competition. A 1953 report, prepared by President Harry S. Truman's Public Advisory Board for Mutual Security, even called for the United States to eliminate 'unnecessary' tariffs on industries producing automobiles, machinery, and consumer electronics like radios and television. These industries are so 'highly developed and very efficient' that 'this country has nothing to fear.' The report also identified pottery products, flatware, textiles, and apparel, and sundry items with duties of 25 percent or more. It called for tariff reductions to open the way for a 'substantial increase in imports.'[380]
>
> ...Out of the Marshall Plan era of helping troubled neighbors emerged a pattern of tolerance for discrimination against American exports. U.S. officials proudly embraced a policy of 'trade, not aid,' implying that foreign nations should earn their way. Trade in goods would substitute successfully for direct income

> transfers and so promote effective recovery. To facilitate this process, the United States chose to ignore discrimination against U.S. exports and investments. In fact, the 'trade not aid' policy had its origins in London, not Washington. The British Foreign Office considered it 'a most successful slogan for winning public acceptance of the need for more imports' in the United States.[381]

President Kennedy gave a speech in May, 1962, promising great gains from more free trade as the result of congressional passage of his Trade Expansion Act. Kennedy predicted that American workers would benefit enormously as other nations began to lower tariffs and open their markets to American production.[382] But during the ten year period after 1950, America's share of industrial country exports had been reduced from thirty-two percent to twenty-eight percent.[383] America was still riding the wave of post war prosperity when Kennedy took office, but trouble was brewing for the future economy. In 1959, President Eisenhower had noticed: He became concerned about the balance of payments in the years following a bilateral international trade agreement with Japan in 1955. Eisenhower, (who was known by the popular nickname Ike), did an about face of sorts telling his trade advisors with regard to negotiation of a trade pact with the European Economic Community (EEC):

> It seems to me we ought to put our own current balance of payments situation very strongly before the conferees and make unmistakably clear that we have gotten into this situation through generous and liberal assistance and trading policies. Now it is time for them to do their share, and a failure on their part to do so would bring into question our basic relationships and attitudes toward these problems.[384]

I give credit to Ike. As an experienced military leader he had the ability to think strategically. He likely understood that America was being made into a patsy. Perhaps it was not a coincidence that Eisenhower sent the memo containing his aforesaid message on the 19th anniversary of the attack on Pearl Harbor, December 7, 1960. But Eisenhower's time was up. One month and thirteen days later he was out of office, replaced by JFK.

Kennedy sought and obtained from Congress "greater flexibility and tariff reducing authority" than had been given to the executive branch "in the history of the trade agreements program."[385] Kennedy, like the other four post WWII democratic presidents who followed him, (Johnson, Carter, Clinton and Obama), pursued the policy of allowing ever more imports despite the lack of reciprocity in cutting tariffs and other protectionist mechanisms by our trading "partners." By 1973, America's share of the total exports by industrial countries fell to twenty percent. That year also marked the occasion of the first American trade deficit since 1893, when a bank panic had lead to a depression.[386]

Following the "Kennedy Round" of trade concessions bipartisan anger welled up in Congress.[387] The steel, chemical and textile industries were up in arms. To placate the negatively affected industries and labor groups the House or Representatives passed a non binding resolution, H.R. 478, in September of 1967. The resolution granted President Johnson discretion to roll back the tariff reductions that threatened to savage American business interests and jobs. The measure passed by a vote of 340 to 29. One angry labor leader denounced the Kennedy Round, complaining about the fact that American jobs were being lost to foreign workers being paid between 12 and 26 cents per hour.[388] President Johnson had in fact been warned by the highly prominent economist John Kenneth Galbraith in March, 1964, that America faced being "screwed" by the Kennedy Round tariff cut giveaway. Galbraith's prediction came true without Lyndon Johnson having taking any effective action, despite his new authority to restore the tariffs granted to him by Congress. Starting in 1968, the tariff cuts took effect incrementally over a five year period, ending in 1973, when America suffered its first trade deficit in eighty years.[389] The *American System* (of protectionism) which had been used so successfully to turn the United States into the greatest military and industrial power in the world, now lay in ruins. The pernicious effects of America's unbalanced trade policy had begun to eat away at America's financial health. Come March of 1973, the American dollar had lost nineteen percent of its value.[390]

After Johnson's departure the Nixon administration blamed the trade deficit in part on the Vietnam War, which they correctly concluded was inflationary as it was ramping up demand and the Japanese among others were only too happy to supply that demand. Nixon's economists also blamed lagging productivity gains for the loss in American competitiveness.[391] You will recall how Henry Clay persuasively argued that the American System tariffs nurtured productivity growth, arguing that prices for American goods had, over a seven year period following the imposition of a tariff, declined to less than the price of similar British goods.[392] The reason for the price declines was that American research and development expenditures had increased worker productivity and allowed for the lower prices. Don't forget too that sometimes tariff money was used to directly subsidize innovation and productivity increases by private industry under the American System.[393] Is it surprising that American firms, faced with elimination of the protective tariff structure and stinging competition from foreign firms chose to cut back on R&D? They had also begun moving to the Sun Belt, and later they began dismantling factories and shipping them overseas. The process of off shoring factories continues to this day.[394]

Nixon's economists also tried to blame increasing oil prices for the trade deficit.[395] That argument was true in part, rising energy costs did contribute to the overall balance of payments deficit, but merchandise trade had also gone into deficit. Nixon's economists made whatever excuses they needed to; Nothing could change the fact that Nixon had gone to China in 1972. He wanted "peace with honor" in Vietnam to fulfill his campaign promise to the American people. His bargaining chip with China was of course trade. Nixon always focused his energy on foreign policy. Like his post war predecessors, Nixon saw trade as a means for advancing his foreign policy objectives, which also included his desire to obtain Russia's co-operation in ending the Vietnam conflict.[396] Nixon placed great emphasis as well on finding a way to bring peace to the Middle East. However his decision to supply arms to Israel during the 1973 Yom Kippur War led to the Arab oil embargo six days later.[397] Nixon had his hands full dealing with foreign policy and he was not much interested in the complexities of international trade policy. Nixon was of course not completely indifferent to trade patterns; Imports were increasing rapidly and both industry and labor groups were howling for relief throughout his presidency.[398]

In fact, Nixon's presidency was mired in economic problems. The vast expenditures on the Vietnam war and the tab for Johnson's great society program had helped create an inflation problem. Rising imports undoubtedly contributed to extensive job losses.[399] Unemployment reached 6.1% by August, 1971. Nixon resorted to wage and price controls in 1971. He also imposed a temporary ten percent surcharge on imports in 1971 and ended the convertibility of dollars into gold, allowing the currency to float.[400] The occurrence of continuing high unemployment and inflation was once thought to be mutually exclusive, but "stagflation," plagued the economy during Nixon's presidency. The reality is that America's policy of one way free trade had much to do with the bad economy during the Nixon years. The age of falling wages, fewer good jobs, and declining manufacturing and labor union participation had begun. I lived right through that age. I saw televison set manufacturing and the textile industry get wiped out. I watched the steel industry and machine tools industry decline and Detroit get swamped by imports. Many industries which generate the critical positive externalities needed for productivity growth, a good innovation ecosystem, and good jobs were damaged or destroyed.[401] The critical year was 1973, when we experienced our first trade deficit in eighty years. The handwriting was on the wall, and back in "73, we still had a chance to rebuild the *American System* without seeing the middle class hollowed out.

The breakdown of the gold standard was also a clear sign that our trade policy needed an overhaul. Why was "Tricky Dick" Nixon (who was induced to resign by the Watergate scandal), forced to abandon the international system which had been a source of American pride and influence? The Bretton Woods system of fixed exchange rates created in 1944 was designed in large part by Henry Dexter White, who was the chief international economist at the U.S. Treasury.[402] With the world's largest economy, which had enjoyed a trade surplus since 1894, the United States had a large stock of gold which represented a portion of its savings from international trade. There had been deficiencies in the system for fixing international exchange rates prior to World War II, when every major trading nation had currency backed by gold. According to economist Ben Bernanke, a past chairmen of the Federal Reserve Board, the Great Depression was caused in part by the structurally flawed gold standard in use before the war. When the banking crisis in 1931 occurred it helped cause an international run on gold. As individuals and institutions turned in currencies for gold worldwide it created a contraction in the money supply and resultant steep drops in demand and production. Countries began to leave the gold standard; By 1936 the gold based exchange system had collapsed.[403]

In 1944, at a conference held at the Washington Hotel in Bretton Woods, the allied countries agreed on a post war system where all currencies would be pegged to the dollar. The dollar alone would be convertible to gold at the fixed rate of $35.00 an once. All other currencies would be pegged to the dollar. Stability would be maintained in the world economy by the strength of the dollar. It was believed that whatever negative economic conditions developed after Bretton Woods could no longer be snowballed by fear into an international gold run and money contraction. The participants from the forty four nations that attended the Bretton Woods conference had every reason to believe that the American economy would remain strong and that America would remain a creditor nation.[404] Nobody in their right mind would believe that the Americans would not only finance the restoration of their former enemies after the war, but also carve up large chunks of their own precious economy, and, hand them out to both friend and foe alike in the years following the war. That however is *exactly* what America ended up doing.

By the time Richard Nixon showed up on the scene promising "peace with honor" and "law and order,"[405] America's power, influence, safety, security, and happiness in general was on the decline. The unpleasant developments in America were bringing smiles elsewhere. Between 1950 and 1969, Germany and Japan had fully recovered but their protectionist economic policies remained in place to gobble up American prosperity. Between 1950 and 1969 America's share of world output fell from 35 percent to 27 percent.[406] America's share of world exports fell from 32 percent in 1950 to 20 percent in 1973.[407] Large sectors of American enterprise had been or were being eliminated.[408] Between September, 1967 and March 1968, the value of America's gold stock plunged by 18 percent.[409] The dollar was depreciating. West Germany dumped the Bretton Woods system in May of 1971 and the Deutsche Mark soared in value against the dollar. The German economy improved over the next three months. The weakening dollar prompted France to trade in $191 million for gold that same year. Then in August, 1971 Switzerland too pulled the plug on Bretton Woods. Nixon had no choice. By Executive Order 11615 he ended the convertibility of dollars into gold [410]

Nixon resigned from office in disgrace because of Watergate. His visit to China is heralded by some as a great achievement in foreign policy. However, Nixon's China policy is seen by others as a failed one. Nixon had three goals in going to China. His primary objective was to obtain Chinese agreement to a cease fire in Vietnam. He sought a truce in some ways similar to the onc Truman had achieved in Korea. The second purpose of Nixon's trip was to reduce the international influence of the Soviet Union by developing normalized diplomatic relations with Red China. Finally Nixon wanted to settle the conflict between America and mainland China over Taiwan. Arguably, Nixon failed to achieve all three goals. Saigon was overrun by North Vietnam just two years after the Paris Peace Accords; Nixon's Vietnamization strategy of withdrawing American troops while helping South Vietnam develop a self sufficient military was a complete failure. Secondly, the collapse of the USSR can be seen as the inevitable outcome of the failure of its centrally planned economy. The Russians provided vital assistance to North Vietnam throughout the war, and Nixon's thawing of relations with China did nothing to stop it.[411] Finally it is no secret that China's meteoric rise as an economic power is powered by America's economic decline.[412] China's trade surplus with the United States increased by ten times between 2004 and 2009 despite the financial crisis that began in 2007. China's trade surplus with America was over $315 billion in 2012.[413] In 2013, China surpassed the United States as the world's largest trading nation.[414] China's surplus from international trade, and its acquisition of foreign technologies from factories placed in China is enabling a massive military buildup by China at sea and on its borders.[415] Taiwan and the American naval forces that help defend it have never faced a greater threat. China is also using its growing military might to intimidate Japan and India over disputed territories.[416]

Nixon, (like his successors) sacrificed America's future economic and military strength by effectively ignoring the trade deficits which began during his presidency. At a moment in history when economic decline could have been reversed, Nixon went to China. In China, Nixon used the promise of opening up trade as a bargaining chip without any coherent plan to strengthen the American economy and improve America's standing in the international economic community. But the public had become unhappy with unilateral free trade. Nixon wisely acknowledged publicly that import competition was hurting American industry and he supported a 1974 revision of the Trade Act escape clause which substituted a scheme of helping industries adjust to the new reality of foreign competition. However the 1974 change eliminated a president's blanket authority to nullify tariff concessions.[417]

The coping mechanisms provided for by the amended escape clause allowed a five year period during which affected industries could obtain tariff protection, quotas, or adjustment assistance. The reason for this change in the escape clause was that no relief had ever been provided under the former escape clause except for the remedy of nullifying tariff concessions. The former escape clause was agreed to so that Congress went along with the setting of trade policy by the executive branch. Nullifying tariff concessions had however been looked upon with extreme disfavor by the State Department, which was preoccupied with maintaining favorable foreign relations. Nixon can indeed be given some credit for reducing some of the losses suffered by business and labor during his stay in office. During his time in office Nixon gave escape clause relief in seven out of the nine cases that went before him.[418] The fact remains however that Nixon believed free trade was a good thing. He ignored the fact that even technologically and environmentally superior American manufacturing methods frequently cannot compete with slave wage foreign production. Recent research has shown that America no longer has a good innovation ecosystem because of the loss of a myriad of growth and development enhancing positive externalities that were formerly provided by now lost domestic industries.[419] Nixon shares the blame. He should have known better. I was only twelve at the time, but I had already become concerned because I knew that imports were putting people out of work and hurting America's technological progress.

Nixon's embrace of a "Southern Strategy" to break up the New Deal coalition put together by FDR did however cause a divided America to turn away from the failed efforts of liberal Democrats; The American pie was shrinking because of unilateral free trade and Americans were feeling more and more pain caused by misguided government policies.[420]

Gerald Ford became Vice President after Nixon's first Vice President, Spiro Agnew, resigned following an investigation by the office of the U.S. Attorney for his home state of Maryland. Agnew was charged with taking bribes which totaled in excess of one hundred thousand dollars. His wrongdoing was alleged to have taken place while he served as Vice President, earlier when Agnew served as Governor of Maryland and earlier still when Agnew was the Baltimore County Executive. Agnew's resignation from the Vice Presidency was required as part of a plea deal entered into between Agnew and the prosecution in his criminal case.[421]

Ford assumed the office of President when Nixon resigned on August 9, 1974. As President, Ford inherited the problem of economic "stagflation" that had plagued Nixon's reign. Ford's presidency is reviewed on a website operated by the Miller Center at the University of Virginia:

> ...the public's (and Congress's) goodwill towards Ford quickly dissipated when the new President pardoned Nixon a mere month into his tenure. Ford certainly believed that the pardon would help the nation, as well as his own presidency, move forward. He also understood that most Americans wanted Nixon punished. But Ford miscalculated. Instead of further salving the wound of Watergate, Ford re-opened it. The howls of protest from both politicians and the public—including questions about a "deal" between the former and current Presidents—greatly

damaged Ford's popularity and ended his honeymoon.

> Ford emerged from this maelstrom to achieve a mixed record. In domestic affairs, the Ford administration failed to remedy the nation's dire economic problems, although by 1976 the economy had begun to recover from the previous year's recession. In Ford's defense, rising unemployment, soaring inflation, and the energy crisis, in addition to the nation's longer-term economic decline, were complex and interrelated challenges that confounded the era's most prestigious economists.[422]

I was not "confounded" by our nations decline back in 1976, though I knew then that the "era's most prestigious economists" *claimed* to be. I knew that the flood of imports and growing trade deficit were creating a rustbelt across America's industrial heartland which represented a grave danger to the future of the middle class. It was abundantly clear.

After he assumed the presidency Ford did nothing worth mentioning to address America's long term economic decline. He rejected providing import quotas in five of six cases in which the U.S. International Trade Commission had found that unfair trading practices against American businesses warranted escape clause relief. Ford gave relief in just one case, which involved specialty steel products simply because he had *no choice*. Congress was determined in that instance that the steel industry should be granted relief.[423] There was a trade deficit in 1976 and America has had a trade deficit every year since.[424] Real hourly wages earned by workers (as Figures 7.1 and 7.2 below show), all but flatlined, while the top ten percent of wage earners gobbled up a large preponderance of the increase in household income in the decades after Ford left office. It was of course foreseeable that placing our workers in direct competition with low paid foreign workers would constrain American wages and force the relocation of production overseas.

I will never forget laughing when Ford made the following unbelievable statement during a 1976 debate with Jimmy Carter: "There is no Soviet domination of Eastern Europe and there never will be under a Ford administration." The debate moderator gave Ford a chance to correct his statement saying to him: I'm sorry, what? ... did I understand you to say, sir, that the Russians are not using Eastern Europe as their own sphere of influence in occupying most of the countries there and making sure with their troops that it's a communist zone?" Ford replied that he did not believe that the Romanians, Yugoslavians and Poles considered themselves to be under Soviet domination.[425] It was gaffe that Ford would never live down. Ford lost his bid to win election to the Presidency on his own lack of merit. He left the White House the only man in history who served as both President and Vice President without winning an election for either office.

From Plains, Georgia, came a very fine man to serve as Commander in Chief: James Earl Carter. Nearly everyone knows of his legacy of service with the Carter Center, Habitat For Humanity and other noble causes following his presidency. Carter is an intelligent man. He attended the Naval Academy, graduating in the top ten percent of his class. He later took graduate courses in reactor technology and nuclear physics at Union College in preparation for his service in the nuclear submarine program.[426] Born in 1924 and being a product of southern culture who was raised on a farm, it is no surprise that Carter believed that free trade would somehow benefit America. But he admitted that the trade deficits he inherited from the Ford administration were a problem, stating in his 1978 State of the Union Address that:

> We still have serious problems on which all of us must work together. Our trade deficit is too large. Inflation is still too high, and too many Americans still do not have a job... Economic success at home is also the key to success in our international economic policy. An effective energy program, strong investment and productivity, and controlled inflation will... [improve] our trade balance and balance it, and it will help to protect the integrity of the dollar overseas. By working closely with our friends abroad, we can promote the economic health of the whole world, with fair and balanced agreements lowering the barriers to trade. Despite the inevitable pressures that build up when the world economy suffers from high unemployment, we must firmly resist the demands for self-defeating protectionism. But free trade must also be fair trade. And I am determined to protect American industry and American workers against foreign trade practices which are unfair or illegal.[427]

Figure 7.1

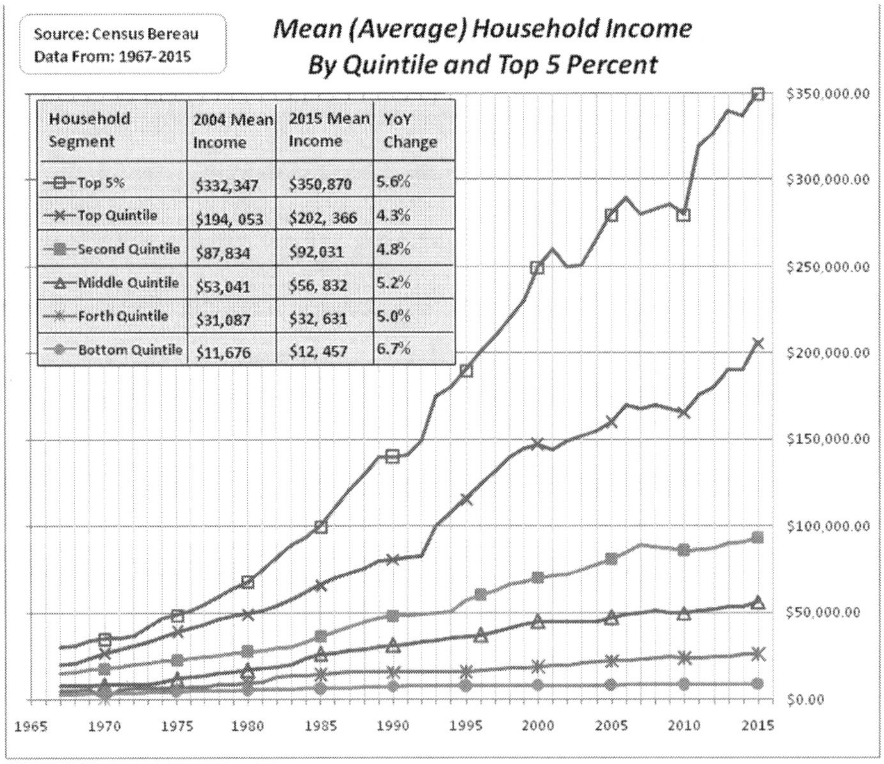

Graph adapted from Dr. Doug Short, Ph.D., "U.S. Household Incomes: A 47-Year Perspective." September 17, 2015. *Advisors Perspectives.* Used With Permission. Retrieved from http://www.advisorperspectives.com/dshort/updates/Household-Income-Distribution.php

Figure 7.2

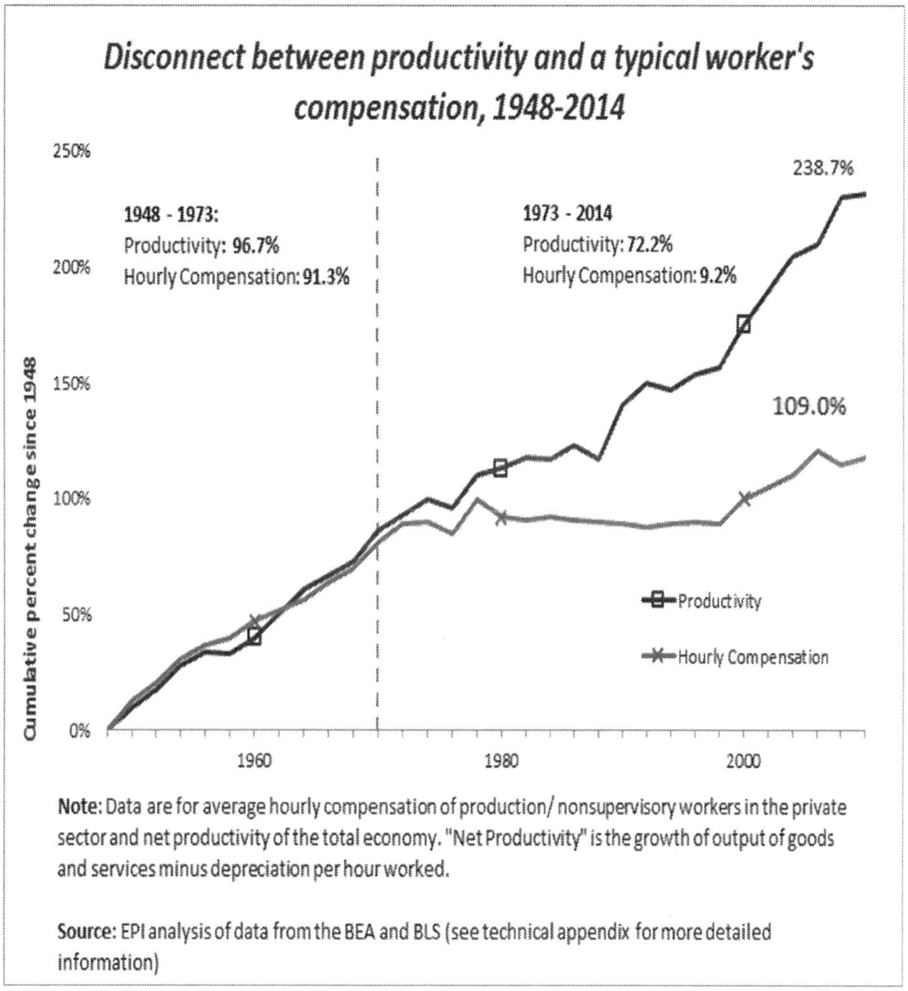

Graph adapted from Josh Bivens and Lawrence Mishel. September 2, 2015. Understanding the Historic Divergence Between Productivity and a Typical Worker's Pay: Why It Matters and Why It's Real. *Economic Policy Institute*. Used With Permission. Retrieved from http://www. epi.org/publication/understanding-the-historic-divergence- between-productivity-and-a-typical-workers-pay-why-it-matters-and-why-its-real/

Let's go over what Carter said. In the middle of the quote above it states "*working closely with our friends abroad we can promote the economic health of the whole world...*" What friends were those? The nations we fought in WWII continue to use protectionist methods against us to this day. Clearly, President Carter had no plan to achieve "fair trade." He said what he said to placate people who were upset about the trade deficit. More revealing is that Carter said "*we must firmly resist the demands for self-defeating protectionism.*" I don't think Jimmy knew much about the subject of protectionism. He was probably unfamiliar with what Cordell Hull did to dismantle the system that the Mount Rushmore Presidents, (and in fact most Presidents) had used with unqualified success to create American prosperity and military strength prior to WWII.

Jimmy also talked about "*the inevitable pressures that build up when the world economy suffers from high unemployment..*" That phrase makes it sound as though world unemployment was worsening America's unemployment. In reality, the reduction in our own trade barriers coupled with the continuance of protectionism in other nations had already lead to *very low unemployment* in Japan and other countries. We were having economic trouble in large part *because of free trade*. Our loss was Japan's and those other nations' gain.

Faced with "stagflation" which began with Nixon and America's new pattern of trade deficits, Carter focused on the oil price increases caused by the OPEC (Organization of Petroleum Exporting Countries), cartel as the leading cause of the weak economy during his administration. As a way to deal with the energy crisis which threatened the economy, Carter called for a reduction in the speed limit on interstate highways and the voluntary setting of thermostats lower in the cold months and higher in the warm months to reduce the cost of heating and cooling the nation's homes and offices. Carter like Ford, failed to truly acknowledge that America's give-it-all-away trade policy was a root cause of the nation's long term economic decline. A quotation from historian Alfred Eckes Jr. reveals why both Ford and Carter simply ignored the balance of payments deficits caused by America's one-way free trade:

> During the Ford and Carter years, archival evidence shows that foreign policy considerations continued to affect the president's evaluation of escape clause recommendations. The Ford and Carter Administrations rejected trade remedy petitions from U.S. industries to avoid unsettling allies and disrupting multilateral negotiations during the Tokyo round GATT talks.[428]

Eckes described a similar episode that took place in the Carter years. In 1978 Carter had to decide whether to protect copper manufacturers from import competition that the International Trade Commission deemed to be advisable. The former chairman of the Democratic Party, Robert Strauss, serving in the Carter administration as a special trade representative, advised President Carter to approve temporary protection for the copper industry. Strauss argued the move would help pacify congressional trade hawks who were seeking to restore the commerce clause authority granted to Congress and stem the red ink caused by the now permanent trade deficits. Carter was fully aware that job losses and plant closings in the Arizona copper industry would surely result but he allowed the copper imports to continue. Carter took the advice of the State Department and his National Security Council: "They warned that import restrictions would damage relations with Canada, Peru, Chile, Zambia, and other copper exporters."[429]

Carter's decision may have been motivated by foreign policy considerations instead of economic concerns, but it is noteworthy for workers and environmentalists who think the Democratic Party is on their side. Carter's copper policy had a dramatic and negative outcome. By 1981, copper prices had fallen by almost fifty percent resulting in huge losses and the lay off of about half of Arizona's copper workers. About 16,000 jobs were lost. That's not all. Faced with competition from foreign producers (who are not required to pay the costs of environmental protection), the Chairman of Phelps Dodge, a major American copper producer at the time, desperately tried to get concessions from the remaining workers because the company was losing money. In 1983, Munroe offered a deal to workers that would link their wages to the price of copper. Instead of accepting the financial uncertainties of accepting wages tied to the price of copper the union called a strike. Monroe responded by hiring replacement workers.

Injunctions were quickly issued by local government limiting picketing and demonstrations at the mine. Name calling and verbal threats were exchanged between the union workers and their "scab' replacements. Within days union striking workers found themselves subject to arrest. The state government moved with alacrity and used overwhelming force against the striking workers. The military power of the state was brought in to intimidate and defeat the strikers. A force of 751 national guardsmen and state troopers using tanks, helicopters, and other military vehicles arrived to disperse the striking miners. The strike did not officially end until 1986, but in the interim the *new replacement workers voted almost unanimously to decertify the unions involved.* The National Labor Relations Board denied all appeals brought to halt decertification.[430] Twelve years later, a Chicago attorney named Jonathan Rosenblum wrote the book, *Copper Crucible: How The Arizona Miners' Strike Of 1983 Recast Labor-Management Relations In America.*[431]

As a Democrat, Carter was supposed to be a friend of working people, but *he undermined the labor movement and conservation at home to aid foreign copper producers who showed little regard for the environment.* His inability to aid the domestic copper mining and smelting industry, and at the same time induce it through *industrial policy measures* to be a responsible partner in preserving the environment was a critical failure of leadership. If Carter had agreed to the industry request for import restraints, the strife and dislocation caused by the 1983 strike would never have taken place. Copper prices rose soon afterwards and import protection could have been ended, while pollution abatement methods *could have been permanently improved.*

The failure of both Democrats and Republicans to expand the economy, restore prosperity and bring about rapidly improving environmental conditions is inexcusable.

Carter faced a difficult election for a second term. He had failed miserably in his attempts to gain the release of the fifty two hostages who were prisoners of Iran for 444 days following their capture by the Iranian Revolutionary Guard. Carter's failed diplomacy lead to a risky rescue mission to Iran which was aborted because of the mechanical failure of two helicopters used for the mission. Following the order to abort the mission, eight American service men involved in the rescue attempt were killed as the result of a collision between a helicopter and a C130 transport plane.[432] Carter's economic policies had failed as well and he was no match for Ronald Reagan's Hollywood cachet, patriotic tough talk, and promises of big tax cuts to fix the economy and restore fairness. Nevertheless, the polls showed that the election would be competitive. The election was however not even close. It turned into a blow out in favor of Reagan.[433] Writing about the election in 2009, a former Newsweek and Associated Press Reporter named Robert Parry tells about a discussion on CBS concerning why Reagan won so handily:

> After this year's death of longtime CBS anchor Walter Cronkite, one of our readers was examining Cronkite archival footage and was surprised to find a clip of Cronkite leading a discussion of CBS correspondents on Election Night 1980

about why Reagan had won a landslide after the pre-election polls had shown a much closer race.

> Correspondent Leslie Stahl noted how the coincidence of the first anniversary of the Iran hostage-taking falling on Election Day had forced Americans to relive the year-long humiliation and thus they turned to Reagan, a perceived hard-liner who would confront American adversaries.
>
> That comment reminded Cronkite of an earlier interview he had done with Henry Kissinger who, Cronkite said, was "suggesting tonight that he thinks that Reagan being in the White House will help get [the hostages] back and he bets they'll get back shortly after the Inaugural. Well, that's still some time. That means that Henry Kissinger must be thinking in terms of long negotiations in order to put the package together."
>
> As it turned out, of course, Kissinger's prediction was right on the money. Immediately after Reagan was inaugurated on Jan. 20, 1981, the hostages were freed and Reagan basked in the perception that his tough-guy persona had done the trick.[434]

After conducting extensive interviews, Parry, an investigative journalist, summed up the evidence:

> The accumulated evidence – including government documents and statements from some two dozen witnesses – now points to a conclusion that the Reagan campaign did develop covert contacts with Iranian officials and that those dealings did undermine Carter's efforts. The hostages were freed after Reagan's was sworn in as President on Jan. 20, 1981.
>
> An October Surprise conclusion that the Republicans were guilty of a political dirty trick bordering on treason also puts into a more sinister light those crystal balls of GOP operatives who foresaw the hostages returning only after Reagan got into office.
>
> On Sept. 16, 1980, ... Iran's acting foreign minister Sadegh Ghotbzadeh spoke publicly about Republican interference. 'Reagan, supported by Kissinger and others, has no intention of resolving the problem,' Ghotbzadeh said. 'They will do everything in their power to block it.'[435]

The list of individuals who claimed that Iranian officials did make a deal with representatives of the Reagan campaign not to release the Iranian hostages until after the 1980 election includes some highly notable individuals. They include Abulhassan Bani-Sadr, the former Iranian President, Yitzhak Shamir, the former Israeli Prime Minister, Gary Sick, an expert on the Middle East and Iran who served on the staff of the National Security Council under Presidents Ford, Carter, and Reagan and Barbara Honegger, a former Reagan/Bush campaign and White House staffer.[436] As for Robert Parry, his credentials as a journalist are impressive. He received the prestigious George Polk Award for investigative reporting. He is best known for his coverage of the Iran Contra scandal and the CIA cocaine trafficking scandal of 1985.[437]

Both the Senate and the House held investigations into the question of whether Reagan campaign made a secret deal with the Iranians not to release the hostages until after the presidential election of 1980. The House and Senate committees issued reports on their findings in 1992 and 1993 respectively. Both found the evidence did not establish that a deal had taken place.[438] Not convinced, journalist Parry continued investigating the allegations against the Reagan camp and he eventually concluded that some very significant evidence had not been considered by either the House or the Senate. Among the neglected evidence was a report received by the investigating House committee from the Russian government which concerned intelligence Russia had regarding the matter.[439] The Russian report clearly states that Reagan's lieutenants did meet repeatedly with the Iranians in effort to keep the hostages locked up in Iran until after the election.[440] The republicans had feared that if Carter succeeded in getting the hostages released just before the election, giving the voters what the republicans called an *October Surprise,* Carter's approval rating would skyrocket and Carter would win the election.[441] Parry's conclusion supports the view of Carter's Persian Gulf expert Gary Sick, who wrote the book *October Surprise: America's Hostages in Iran and the Election of Ronald Reagan.*[442] As you would expect, pundits on the right lambast the view that the Reagan campaign committed such an act of treachery.[443]

I don't know for sure what happened. I report about the *October Surprise* in this chapter because I lived through the *January Surprise,*[444] and I strongly suspected at the time that Reagan's side had secretly negotiated with the Iranians. I have not seen anything since then that convinces me otherwise. The release of the hostages at the moment that Reagan completed the oath of office seemed like something fictional; like something that could only take place in a Hollywood movie. It seemed like a staged PR event rather than a bona fide display of weakness and fear by the Iranians. I simply do not believe that Iranian leaders were so terrified of Reagan that they released the hostages without obtaining anything in return at the moment Reagan took office. The idea is laughably absurd. In any event, the Reagan administration is known to have entered into an illegal arms deal with the Iranians which was exposed during the investigation of the Iran Contra *arms for hostages* scandal.[445]

Reagan's term as president is heralded by the political right as a time when America came roaring back economically.[446] The truth is otherwise. It was none other than George H. W. Bush who coined the phrase "Voodoo Economics," to describe Reagan's economic strategy.[447] It was none other than Reagan's Director of the Office of Management and Budget, David Stockman, who resigned in protest over Reagan's policy of combining giant tax cuts for the rich with increased spending,[448] leading to a three trillion dollar national debt. Reagan created an artificial prosperity fueled by his enormous budget deficits. George W. Bush copied Reagan's strategy of borrowing wildly while granting tax cuts to the rich. Stockman wrote a bitter memoir explaining why he quit the Reagan administration: *The Triumph of Politics Why the Reagan Revolution Failed.*[449] I don't agree that the Reagan revolution failed, I would say that it succeeded: It is America that is failing...under a mountain of debt while real incomes and employment prospects continue to falter for most Americans. Reagan's tax cuts for the rich lead to Bush's tax cuts for the rich. The combined budget deficits of those two presidents account for the lion's share of our $19 trillion national debt.[450]

Stockman wrote another book in 2013: *The Great Deformation: The Corruption of Capitalism in America*. The book was foreshadowed by a 2010 article he wrote for the New York Times entitled "Four Deformations of the Apocalypse." It is instructive to quote from Stockman's article:

> ...the new catechism, as practiced by Republican policymakers for decades now, has amounted to little more than money printing and deficit finance — vulgar Keynesianism robed in the ideological vestments of the prosperous classes.
>
> This approach has not simply made a mockery of traditional party ideals. It has also led to the serial financial bubbles and Wall Street depredations that have crippled our economy. More specifically, the new policy doctrines have caused four great deformations of the national economy, and modern Republicans have turned a blind eye to each one.[451]

The very first of Stockman's "deformations" is the cumulative effect of our trade deficits since Nixon's term. In Stockman's words, we "have lived beyond our means as a nation for nearly 40 years, our cumulative current-account deficit - the combined shortfall on our trade in goods, services and income - has reached nearly $8 trillion. That's borrowed prosperity on an epic scale."[452] Stockman's second claimed deformation is the explosion in the national debt. He points out a number of salient historical facts that support his claim. Those include the fact that the national debt was only 40 percent of America's GDP in 1970, a mere $425 billion. That's peanuts compared to the $20 trillion debt we are facing these days and almost equal to America's entire gross domestic product. Stockman rightly blames the Reagan tax cuts and the belief among Republicans that deficits are not a problem if they are a consequence of tax cuts.[453]

Stockman's third deformation concerns the "too big to fail" banks which brought us the financial crisis of 2007-2008, and which continue to threaten economic stability. He blames the abolition of regulations restricting speculation and leveraging and the growth in the cumulative value of finance companies and investment banks from half a trillion dollar in 1970, to sixty times that amount, ($30 trillion), by the early fall of 2008. Stockman convincingly argues that the multi-trillion dollar interconnected financial corporations of todays business world owe their existence not to free market capitalism, but to federally guaranteed deposits and the free flow of low to no interest funds from the Fed and ultimately the public to cover their reckless risk taking.[454]

The fourth deformation Stockman describes is, in essence, the general decline of America's economy. Stockman points to specific historical facts to support his thesis. He points to the massive loss of jobs which has resulted from free trade. For instance, in the ten years before Stockman wrote his article America lost eleven million good paying jobs in manufacturing and service industries. He also points to the growing wealth disparity caused by the ever increasing share of the national wealth that the top one percent of Americans are grabbing for themselves.[455]

Stockman's deformations seem more like three to me, the first and fourth relate to the decline in our economy which has resulted from our free trade free fall. The second is the growth in the national debt, a big chunk of which is caused by our trade deficits. The third has to do with the change in the banking system from one of staid domestic investment in the 1950s, to one of wild gambling on derivatives, and, globalized banking that aids in tearing down American manufacturing in search of overseas profits.[456] Stockman thus agrees with the prevailing view among academic financial experts that the financial crisis of 2007-2008 was caused by too much deregulation, too much consolidation, and the resultant mentality of bailing out "too big to fail" investment houses with taxpayer money.[457] Whether there are three horsemen or four, America clearly remains in a financial crisis and in a long term economic decline. The positive numbers coming out of Wall Street at the time of this writing are bringing little comfort to the majority of Americans who own no stock. Things have not changed since Michael Snyder wrote this in November, 2013:

> ...things have never been better for the top 0.01 percent of ultra-wealthy Americans that have got millions of dollars invested in the stock market. But for most of the rest of the country, things are very hard right now. At this point, more than102 million working age Americans do not have a job, and 40 percent of those that are actually working earn less than $20,000 a year in wages. If we actually are experiencing an "economic recovery", then why is the federal government spending nearly a trillion dollars a year on welfare? And that does not even include entitlement programs such as Social Security and Medicare. We live in a nation where poverty is exploding and the middle class is shrinking with each passing day. But nothing is ever going to get fixed if we all stick our heads in the sand and pretend that everything is "just fine."[458]
>
> In October, the U.S. labor force participation rate fell from 63.2 percent to 62.8 percent. It is now the lowest that it has been since 1978. ...the labor force participation rate has been steadily declining since the year 2000. How can the economy be "healthy" if the percentage of Americans that are participating in the labor force is continually declining?
>
> If the labor force participation rate was still at the same level it was at when Barack Obama was elected in 2008, the official unemployment rate would be about 11 percent right now.
>
> ...Right now, there are more than 11 million Americans that are considered to be "officially unemployed", and there are more than 91 million Americans that are not employed and that are considered to be "not in the labor force". When you add those two numbers together, the total is more than 102 million. Overall, the number of working age Americans that do not have a job has increased by about 27 million since the year 2000. But aren't things getting better? After all, the mainstream media is full of headlines about how "good" the jobs numbers for October were. Sadly, the truth is that the mainstream media is not being straight with the American people.
>
> In this day and age, it is absolutely imperative that people start thinking for themselves. Just because the media tells you that something is true does not mean that it actually is. If unemployment was actually going down, the percentage of the working age population that has a job should actually be going up...that is

simply not the case.[459]

Most of the damage that has been inflicted on the American economy because of the removal of the time tested *American System* of tariff protection did not begin until after the start of the Kennedy Round of tariff concessions.[460] Eckes wrote about the vilification of Smoot-Hawley by the presidents. He wrote this regarding President Johnson:

> Concerned about a protectionist backlash following the Kennedy Round, President Lyndon Johnson, directed his staff to draft a speech emphasizing that 'this is no time for high tariff walls or Smoot-Hawley.' A few days later, while signing a trade proclamation, Johnson asked what 'captain of industry or...union leader...is eager to return to the days of Smoot-Hawley? For the world of high tariffs...was also the world of...deep depressions, rampant unemployment.'[461]

I wrote about the Smoot-Hawley Myth in chapter three. It is an obvious fact that the Smoot-Hawley tariff neither caused nor significantly altered the course of the Great Depression. The two most influential economists of the last 75 years, the founder of Keynesianism, John Maynard Keynes, and the founder of Monetarism, Milton Friedman, agreed that *the Smoot-Hawley Tariff did not cause the Great Depression*. Former Fed chairmen Ben Bernanke agrees, and so does popular trade theorist Paul Krugman.[462] Ben Bernanke only mentioned the Smoot-Hawley tariff once in his famous 320 page treatise published in 2004, *Essays on the Great Depression*. This is all he said about it:

> ...the direct evidence for a disruptive effect of trade restrictions is weak: in particular, the Smoot-Hawley Tariff of 1930 primarily affected imports of agricultural goods and finished manufacturers, not intermediates (Eichengreen, 1986). Indeed, because of the worldwide glut of raw materials and commodities, the real prices of most important intermediaries (inclusive of tariffs) fell during the Depression.[463]

In *Essays on the Great Depression,* Bernanke mentioned economist (Barry) Eichengreen not once, but *ninety one times*. According to Brian Domitrovic writing in Forbes, "Ben Bernanke's views of Eichengreen's work have been uniformly laudatory over the years."[464] Eichengreen wrote about the Smoot-Hawley Tariff in 1986. He concluded that "...the direct macroeconomic effect of the tariff is likely to have been expansionary."[465]

The reality of the Smoot-Hawley Myth is summed up by Alfred Eckes, Jr. at the end of his brilliant 39 page refutation of the myth in *Opening America's Market U.S. Foreign Trade Policy since 1776*:

> There is no persuasive documentation that the Smoot-Hawley Tariff precipitated the stock market crash. Nor is there compelling evidence that it exacerbated the Great Depression. Foreign governments and private interests did seek to influence the US tariff revision process, but few of these communications constituted formal diplomatic protests. Contrary to the conventional wisdom, Smoot-Hawley produced little retaliation or discrimination against American exports. The fury of the global depression, not the irritation of American tariff changes, forced foreign government to restrict trade and currency flows, and to concentrate on domestic

> economic recovery. Nor does the archival evidence confirm claims that the 1930 tariff contributed significantly to the breakdown of international peace and the coming of World War II.
>
> That the legend of Smoot-Hawley endures and continues to influence trade policy debate is a tribute to the public relation skills of partisans and ideologues with agendas. They successfully transformed a molehill into a mountain.[466]

Despite the obviousness that Smoot-Hawley had nothing to do with causing or significantly worsening the Great Depression, postwar president's from Eisenhower to Reagan lied to the American people about the tariff. They kept the Smoot-Hawley myth alive to avoid public controversy over their one-way trade give-aways. In so doing, they were also covering up the true history of America's progress and prosperity under the *American System,* which used tariffs and other measures to protect and nurture important industries.[467]

Ronald Reagan was either a liar or a pathetically uniformed featherweight on the subject of economics (I say both), when he said "the Smoot-Hawley tariff act, helped plunge this nation and the world into a decade of depression and despair" during an August 31, 1985 "radio address to the nation on free and fair trade."[468] In his book on trade history, Eckes served up other laughably inaccurate comments about Smoot-Hawley by President Reagan:

> During the 1980s President Ronald Reagan regularly assailed the mistakes of 1930. 'The Smoot- Hawley tariff helped bring on the Great Depression,' he said in November, 1987. On another occasion he asserted that 'the Smoot-Hawley tariff...made it virtually impossible for anyone to sell anything in America, and...spread the Great Depression around the world.' In other remarks, Reagan chided Smoot and Hawley for coauthoring the bill that 'brought about the collapse of the world trading system...[469]

Wrapping himself up in a rhetorical American flag and using his acting skills to full effect Reagan could say those absurd things and the media would lap it up uncritically.[470] Reagan's first term mirrored the trade policy preferences of Nixon, Ford and Carter. Trade concessions were used as a carrot to serve foreign policy objectives. Trade protection via the escape clause was served up occasionally as a carrot to congress, the concerned public and politically potent industry.[471]

In one instance, Reagan approved escape clause relief for motorcycle maker Harley Davidson following an investigation by the International Trade Commission. The requisite finding that motorcycle imports were threatening serious injury to the domestic injury was made. Granted a five year period of tariff protection Harley invested in improving its product and production methods. The company raced back into the black and was able to decline further tariff relief before the five year period elapsed. Reagan scored political points with Harley riders everywhere and he was able to enthusiastically proclaim that "Like America, Harley is back and standing tall...You...at Harley Davidson are living proof that our laws are working."[472] But were they really? The isolated instance of relief granted to Harley probably was the most effective use of the escape clause in its entire history.[473] But Reagan was a big believer in unregulated markets, trickle down economics and cutting taxes on the rich.[474] Reagan's dislike for "interfering" government got the better of the escape clause during his second term. Reagan appointed two free trade ideologues to the Commission in 1984 and 1985, Susan Liebeler and Anne Brunsdale. Reportedly both women had an apparent disagreement with the protectionist purpose of the escape clause and they refused to ever grant relief under it.[475] Liebeler was a corporate lawyer and law professor. Reagan tried to appoint her to the U.S. Court of Appeals in 1987, but Democrats in the Senate refused to confirm her. According to one source she did not get confirmed because of temperament issues.[476] Brunsdale had a masters degree in comparative government from Yale, and was a free trade ideologue.[477] According to trade historian Eckes, the escape clause was declared to be "a dead statute" by one senator within a few years after the arrival of Liebeler and Brunsdale.[478] For Eckes, 1985 was the "turning point:" when Reagan refused to give escape clause protection for non rubber footwear:

> ...At high levels of the administration a perception had emerged that section 201 of the Trade Act was a protectionist law. In his public statement, the president noted that the quotas proposed to limit shoe imports 'could invite retaliation.' He warned of a 'trade war, a war we fought in 1930 with the infamous Smoot-Hawley tariffs and lost. Stating that the United States 'must live according to our principles' and ensure that the world trading system remains open, free, and, above all, fair,' Reagan signaled a determination not to provide remedies...[479]

I heard Reagan give that speech and when he stated that the "United States must live according to *our* principles," I knew he actually meant the principles of *his* administration. Reagan was certainly not talking about the principles underlying the *American System* that gave America the greatest economy in the world, and, provided the manufacturing capacity that won World War II. Reagan was not talking about the principles of the Mount Rushmore Presidents. Our nations father, George Washington, rejected free trade. Protectionism became the "cornerstone" of national economic policy thereafter.[480] Lincoln said "Give us a protective tariff, and we will have the greatest nation on earth."[481] Reagan was talking about the period beginning in the sixties when imports began flooding into the United States and America began its inevitable decline because of one-way free trade.[482] The Reagan administration made the escape clause in the Trade Act a dead statute. Relief has rarely been given since Reagan left office.[483]

Trade historian Eckes ends his book with an epilogue that includes his observations that both George H.W. Bush and Bill Clinton were fervent believers in free trade.[484] Bush I and Clinton both permitted the loss of industry, increased outsourcing, declining wages and falling economic participation rates. The economy was stagnant under Bush I, but Clinton came in with an aggressive effort to lower spending, eliminate the budget deficits and pay down the national debt. Stock prices climbed under Clinton, buoyed in part by the Wall Street's enthusiastic approval of Clinton's budgetary surplus.[485] Clinton's policies allowed America to temporarily enjoy an illusion of recovery and prosperity based on the real estate and derivatives "bubble economy" that was in the famous words of Alan Greenspan, powered by "irrational exuberance."[486] Wall Street was also pleased with Clinton's refusal to back laws reversing the relaxation of New Deal era regulations that had hampered Wall Street's ability to make high risk gambles in the derivatives market.[487] This enthusiasm occurred despite the fact that Clinton had succeeded in raising taxes on upper income Americans.[488] But Clinton's prudent combination of raising taxes and cutting spending was only one third of the formula needed to fix the economy over the long term. Two other elements were needed. The first was a concerted effort to eliminate the gigantic trade deficits which represented the loss of millions of jobs and the loss of the invaluable positive externalities that lost industries had once contributed to America's production ecosystem. The second needed element, the absence of which represented as glaring a failure as the first, was recognition of the fact that reliance on high risk derivatives trading involving the securitization of junk mortgages to power the economy was reckless and irrational. The idea that America could prosper on a *service economy* which produced mainly *junk jobs* while *too big to fail banks* using the government as their *free insurance policy* was known by financial experts to be dangerous one. Clinton just did not get it.[489]

Democrats like Clinton are especially good at "feeling the pain"[490] of increasingly poor Americans at election time, but once they get into office they act as though they are the leaders of the free *trade* world. They focus on expanding international trade no matter what the cost to the United States. Democrats just sat around while the union movement was all but eviscerated over a forty year period. It's hard to fathom what drives Democrat politicians besides the desire to please the Wall Street fat cats who finance them and placate the public interest groups that support them.[491] Republicans support free trade for an easy to understand reason. That reason can be summed up in one word, "greed." The leading proponents of free trade justify everything from child labor to lax environmental laws based on the argument that without the foreign investments that produce those conditions, developing countries would be even worse off.[492] They used similar arguments in earlier times to fight the passage of child labor laws and environmental protection regulations in the United States.

Alfred E. Eckes, Jr. wrote about Clinton's duplicity, (my word), concerning free trade in the epilogue to his book, *America's Opening America's Market U.S. Foreign Trade Policy since 1776,* Eckes' narrative describes a Clinton who expressed concern to the electorate about the failures of America's trade policy prior to his election. After he was elected, his trade representative, Mickey Cantor, echoed Clinton's concern, noting that trade concessions had regularly been granted to achieve foreign policy objectives. Kantor said American policymakers had "failed to enforce our laws at home or open markets abroad."[493] Clinton said that America's trade policies had produced "higher unemployment and lower wages for some of our people...."[494] Clinton also said of the problems caused by trade policy: "This is a powerful testament to the painful difficulty of trying to maintain a high-wage economy where production is mobile and can quickly fly to a place with low wages."[495] Perhaps without realizing it, Clinton had admitted that one of the essential axioms to the Riccardo's theory of comparative advantage, the one that says that there is zero factor mobility between countries, is totally untrue. Clinton was describing the *race to the bottom*, for wage rates in developed countries that free trade represents. He did not provide the solution, but there is only one, and that is good industrial policy. There are some Democrats who understand that gigantic trade deficits have caused the loss of American prosperity.[496] Eckes' history confirms that Clinton was not one of them. He likens Clinton's beliefs to those of Cordell Hull.[497]

True to his misguided globalist principles no matter what the cost to America, Clinton embarked on his plan to pass the North American Free Trade Agreement, (NAFTA), and implement the

Uruguay Round of GATT. Opposition by organized labor to NAFTA was fierce, so Clinton engaged in a vote buying scheme, providing unwilling legislators with whatever pork it took to get their votes. The estimates of the cost to the treasury for Clinton's payoffs in pork run as high as $50 billion.[498] At the signing ceremony for NAFTA, Clinton made a speech telling Americans that NAFTA was an agreement that would help lessen the damage that free trade had been doing:

> Ours is now an era in which commerce is global and in which money, management, technology are highly mobile. For the last 20 years, in all the wealthy countries of the world, because of changes in the global environment, because of the growth of technology, because of increasing competition, the middle class...has been under severe stress. Most Americans are working harder for less. They are vulnerable to the fear tactics and the averseness to change that is behind much of the opposition to NAFTA.
>
> ...I believe that NAFTA will create 200,000 American jobs in the first 2 years of its effect. I believe if you look at the trends--and President Bush and I were talking about it this morning--starting about the time he was elected President, over one-third of our economic growth and in some years over one half of our net new jobs came directly from exports. And on average, those exports-related jobs paid much higher than jobs that had no connection to exports. I believe that NAFTA will create a million jobs in the first 5 years of its impact. And I believe that that is many more jobs than will be lost, as inevitably some will be, as always happens when you open up the mix to a new range of competition.[499]

Clinton had found a new way to sell free trade claiming that NAFTA would expand exports by 200,000 jobs in two years and one million jobs in five years. Clinton did not make mention of job losses from imports that would occur under NAFTA, it seemed as though he was promising a *net benefit* to Americans. It's been over twenty years since NAFTA was passed, so let's look at the record. NAFTA has not panned out. These are the words of the advocacy group, *Public Citizen*:

> The small U.S. trade surplus with Mexico pre-NAFTA turned into a massive new trade deficit. The pre-NAFTA U.S. trade deficit with Canada expanded greatly. Overall, the inflation-adjusted U.S. trade deficit with Canada of $29.1 billion and the $2.5 billion surplus with Mexico in 1993 (the year before NAFTA took effect) turned into a combined NAFTA trade deficit of $181 billion by 2012.1 The Economic Policy Institute (EPI) estimated that the NAFTA deficit had eliminated about one million net American jobs by 2004. Meanwhile, U.S. food processors moved to Mexico to take advantage of low wages and food imports soared. U.S. beef imports from Mexico and Canada, for example, have risen 130 percent since NAFTA took effect, and today U.S. consumption of "NAFTA" beef tops $1.3 billion annually. The export of subsidized U.S. corn did increase, displacing over one million Mexican *campesino* farmers. Their desperate migration pushed down wages in Mexico's border maquiladora factory zone and contributed to a doubling of Mexican immigration to the United States.
>
> The U.S. public's view of NAFTA has intensified from broad opposition to

> overwhelming opposition to NAFTA-style trade deals. According to a 2012 Angus Reid Public Opinion poll, 53 percent of Americans believe the United States should "do whatever is necessary" to "renegotiate" or "leave" NAFTA, while only 15 percent believe the United States should "continue to be a member of NAFTA." Rejection of the trade deal is the predominant stance of Democrats, Republicans and independents alike.[500]

Predictably, the NAFTA trade deal turned out to be an almost unmitigated disaster. The industries of high wage developed countries simply cannot compete with the low wages of poor countries. Free trade is a race to the bottom for wages, working conditions, and environmental protections. Free trade has brought the United States less technological diversity, the takeover of many iconic American companies and much real estate by foreign interests, a vastly increased national debt, and national decline.

The Uruguay Round which began in 1986 ended in 1994 during the administration of Bill Clinton. Before its passage it too was vigorously opposed by labor. Concern over yet another round of unilateral trade concessions was not limited to the working class. *Fortune Magazine* wondered "Will there be enough jobs to go around?"[501] *Business Week* noted that "global competition is dragging down pay for...workers - widening the gulf between rich and poor."[502] Even the staid bastion of money power support for free trade, *The Economist* agreed that workers were "right to be worried," and predicted that "occupations higher up the earnings ladder" would "also feel the force."[503] As usual the protestations of workers and the concerns of academics and a minority of business leaders were brushed aside by the overwhelming influence of the money power and its controlled media and political establishment. In their rush to grease the profit wheels for transnational corporations the American negotiators once again weakly conceded that European and Asian protectionist structures would be left largely in tact, while America made more concessions.[504] In 1995, the highly controversial World Trade Organization was created replacing the less structured intergovernmental mechanism which had functioned under the General Agreement on Tariffs and Trade dating back to 1947. Subsequently in 2001, the next, Doha Round of international trade negotiations orchestrated under the WTO began.

With the creation of the World Trade Organization, dispute resolution panels composed of WTO officials, not independent jurists were given final say on unfair trade disputes. Losing member nations could no longer veto panel findings, and the WTO agreement provisions were made superior to and took precedence over the laws, regulations and administrative proceedings of all member states. Losing parties to WTO disputes face substantial penalties for noncompliance with WTO judgments.[505] In his book, *The Betrayal of American Prosperity: Free Market Delusions, America's Decline, and How We Must Compete in the Post-Dollar Era*, Clyde Prestowitz wrote this about the new structure of international trade:

> Finally in 1994, the Uruguay Round of GATT negotiations concluded by turning the GATT into the World Trade Organization (WTO), the final realization, after forty-odd years, of the International Trade Organization (ITO) that had been rejected in 1952 because of overwhelming opposition in the U.S. Senate. Institutionally, substantively, and structurally the WTO revolutionized both the concept and the administration of the world economy. Of the two key new

> elements, the most important was compulsory dispute settlement - a term that sounds like bureaucratese, but is a requirement that essentially cut the United States off at the knees and made the WTO perhaps the most powerful international governing body.[506]

The trade deficits grew before and after the Uruguay Round as reported by Prestowitz:

> ...the Japanese continued to gnaw away at U.S. industry while their own market remained mostly closed. It became clear that Chrysler was destined to be replaced by Honda as number 3 in the U.S. auto market. Under its ambitious CEO Jack Welch, General Electric acquired RCA in 1986 and Welch promised that it would 'be able to compete successfully with anyone, anywhere, in every market we serve.' By 1988, however, Welch decided RCA couldn't compete with anyone and sold it to France's Thompson SA. (Woodrow Wilson must have twirled in his grave.) As a symbol of the decline of American competitiveness, this was powerful indeed. But it was soon topped by Mitsubishi Estate Corp.'s acquisition of New York's Rockefeller Center. And that was just the start. Soon the Japanese owned the famed Pebble Beach and virtually all the hotels in Waikiki... While Japanese were free to buy those trophy properties in America , Americans would not have been allowed to make similar acquisitions in Japan.[507]

For Republocrats, America and Americans are no longer the most important concern. It is now a global economy and U.S. based tycoons are free to seek the country with the lowest wages on Earth to locate their manufacturing in. Those tycoons and their campaign contributions are what matters most to American politicians. The voters are controlled by the media which in turn is controlled by the cash that monied interests lavish on elections.

The mind set of successful Democratic party candidates, like that of successful Republican candidates, is controlled by the billions of dollars Wall Street and union busting transnational corporations pour into political races.[508] The media's corporate mandated slant against fair trade and its lapdog reporting concerning the interests of its *money power* owners and advertisers is a powerful lever of control over the political and economic systems.[509] Candidates from either party who understand how to fix America simply don't stand a chance of winning the presidency because of the money powered media. Voters just don't have the time or the inclination to read a dozen or so solid texts on economic theory and economic history. The *money power* knows it and its most favored political servants and the media blatantly lie about the true history of trade. They also conceal the dynamic new ideas in trade theory and academic studies, like the one by MIT that is discussed in chapter five.[510]

America gives away the store. The truth is that other countries only buy things from America that they cannot produce themselves. They use America to get trade surpluses, and grow their economies. Because other countries choose to purchase American made goods only as a last resort, the threat of "trade wars" that free traders always warn us about is a hollow one.[511]

This topic is discussed in greater deal in Chapter 8, but for now just consider this: The total value of all U.S. imports in 2013 was $2.744 trillion.[512] The current rule of thumb on job losses from imports is from 9000 to 15,000 lost jobs per billion dollars of imports.[513] Thus, making the products we currently import at home could produce a hypothetical maximum of 41,160,000 jobs, not counting any growth externalities produced by restoring domestic production to such a massive extent. At the end of 2013, the unemployment rate was less than 11 million. The total number employed was 139 million. Another 68 million people in the U.S. were of working age but not employed or seeking employment. Many of the people who are not seeking employment have simply given up on finding a job worth having, so the *real* unemployment rate is much higher[514] The point is that restoring lost industries by junking our one-way free trade laws and following the methods of the American System could possibly wipe out unemployment, reverse the declining fortunes of the middle class and restore America's "production ecosystem."

Obviously we do not want to end all imports, but we must make international trade serve our national interest, as *we* define that interest. We can rebuild our manufacturing base and regain our lost prosperity despite what demopublicans say. We do not need to become isolationist and our involvement in World War I, the League of Nations, World War II and the United Nations before the age of unfair trade deficits was hardly isolationist. Strengthening our country's economic structure will strengthen the dollar and give America greater leeway in foreign affairs. We do not need to fall under the economic and military domination of China, and be forced to sell the ownership of even our most vital defense industries to make good on the trillions of IOU dollars sitting in the treasure chests of the protectionist countries. The *American System* worked well for over a century. Free trade has failed for decades.

As the final version of this chapter was being written, Donald Trump was just weeks away from taking office as President. I was pleased by Trump's selection of Peter Navarro, (a noted expert on the failures of America's trade policy whose work is discussed herein), to serve as Director of the White House National Trade Council. The "White House National Trade Council" is a newly minted title/position which was created by Donald Trump on December 21, 2016 as President - Elect.

As I have noted previously, I am in general agreement, (with exceptions), with the *tone* of Mr. Trump's statements about the failures of a our national trade policy. I also liked the sound of his campaign slogan: *Make America Great Again*. That however, is where Trump and I part company. It is clear that Trump rode the same wave of discontent and frustration with America's trade policy that helped power Bernie Sander's campaign; Yet, the two men are polar opposites politically. Trump is a right wing billionaire hell bent on cutting taxes on the rich despite the fact that America is twenty trillion dollars in debt. Trump has appointed Climate Contrarians to be Secretary of State, Secretary of Energy, and head of Environmental Protection Agency. Let me make this clear: *Climate Contrarians have no place in the Ameritorian Party movement!*

I am also completely opposed to the socialist idea of state ownership, (including state mandated employee ownership), of the means of production. Thus, I am opposed to socialism and to many of the ideas which have been expressed by Bernie Sanders, who calls himself a "Democratic Socialist." That is why I went ahead with the publication of this book despite the election of Donald Trump. Our national trade policy does needs fixing, but we must fight tooth and nail to remove Trump from office in 2020 and roll back any stupid mistakes he makes as President.
Continued free trade will destroy the United States but Trump is unacceptable as President. The solution is clear. We simply must form a new political party and drive both Trump and the free

trader Democrats and Republicans from office using our collective power as voters. We already constitute an electoral majority.[515] Let's organize a new political party and save our country!
Returning to the subject of this chapter after a rather lengthy digression brings us to the blunder wonder presidency of George W. Bush. Bush II is also discussed in Chapter 10, which concerns the national debt, and in Chapter 14, which is about the War in Iraq. George W. Bush was a big believer in free trade. I'm not sure whether Bush is familiar enough with American history to *even know* what the *American System* followed by the Mount Rushmore Presidents was. Bush expanded the area covered by NAFTA when he entered into the Dominican Republic-Central America Free Trade Agreement, known as CAFTA-DR.[516]

The countries CAFTA-DR includes are not industrial power houses. America's trade balance with CAFTA-DR signatory nations has swung from negative to positive and back again since CAFTA-DR was adopted.[517] In both 2013 and 2012, America's trade deficit with CAFTA-DR countries, (Dominican Republic, Costa Rica, El Salvador, Guatemala, Honduras, and Nicaragua), was under a billion dollars.[518] What is noteworthy about CAFTA is that organizations of U.S. citizens from Central America, including the Salvadoran American National Network, vigorously opposed passage of the trade agreement. Before its passage opponents raised concerns about the provision in CAFTA that would allow pharmaceutical manufacturers to keep test data from the development phase of new drugs confidential. In America such data must be made public so that generic manufacturers can produce equivalent drugs at low cost.[519] After passage of CAFTA-DR opposition to it in Central America continued. On December 8, 2008, a report was issued by the Stop CAFTA Coalition asking then incoming President Obama to draft a new agreement. Stop CAFTA had conducted a three year study on the effects of CAFTA and claimed the evidence showed that poverty and unemployment were increasing because of it.[520] President Obama never lifted a finger to modify the provisions of CAFTA-DR.[521]

Although a welling up of patriotism among Americans following 9/11 increased Bush's approval rating to the ninety percent range, his popularity fell quickly owing to his weakness as a leader. Figure 7.3 graphs the steady descent in Bush's approval rating which rose noticeably on 9/11, again at the start of the Iraq war, and once more when Saddam was apprehended. As Americans realized that Bush's claims about WMDs in Iraq were false they considered the terrible toll paid in human casualties plus the financial costs from Bush's unnecessary war. Bush's approval rating sank. As the financial crisis of 2007/2008 progressed Bush's approval rating fell to a low of ***nineteen percent*** in one poll.[522]

In 2004, when Bush still enjoyed a public approval rating of nearly fifty percent, a survey conducted by George Mason University of 415 historians foreshadowed Bush's later fall from favor with the public. Eighty-one percent of the historians, (338 of those polled), judged Bush's presidency as a failure. However, seven of the historians who judged Bush's presidency a success wrote comments that it was the best *since Clinton.* Another historian who voted in Bush's favor said his presidency was the best since Millard Fillmore. Fillmore is considered one of the worst presidents in history. The votes of the eight historians who only pretended that Bush's presidency had been a success should be counted as no votes. Thus, Bush got an approval rating of 16.3 percent from historians. If you still think that is too high *you are right*. Two more historians who gave Bush the thumbs up wrote that Bush had been remarkably successful at pursuing *disastrous policies*.[523]

Figure 7.3

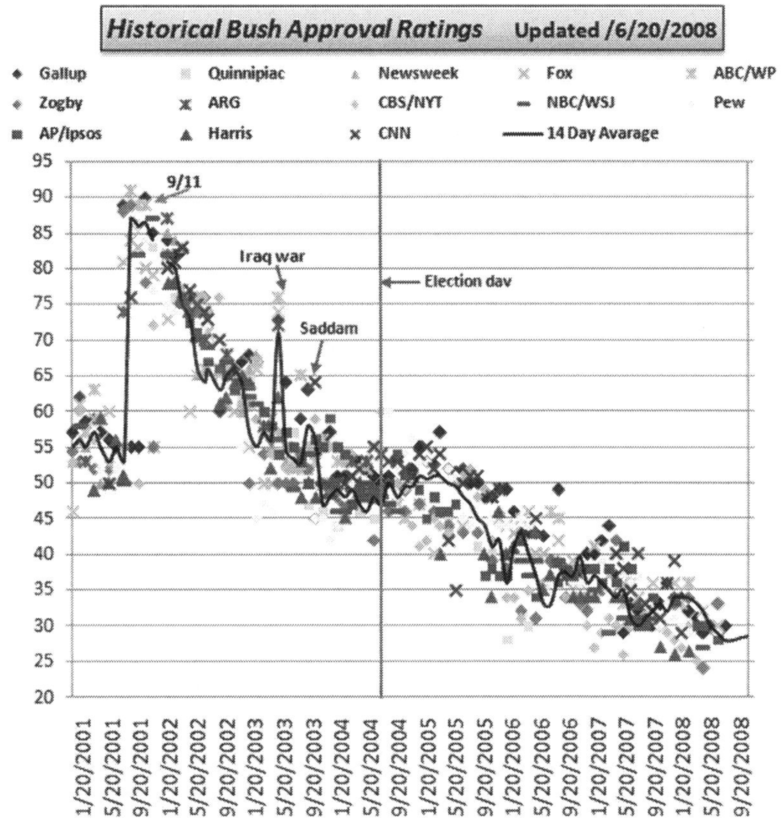

Graph adapted from data collected and charted by Dr. Steven Ruggles, Ph.D., Regents Professor of History and Population Studies. University of Minnesota. Retrieved from http://users.hist.umn.edu/~ruggles/Approval.htm Used With Permission.

Four years later, in 2008, George Mason University conducted another informal survey of historians asking them to rate the presidency of George W. Bush as a success of failure. In the second poll, *ninety-eight percent* of the 109 historians who responded to the survey voted the Bush presidency a failure![524] If you want, take a "laugh break" now and watch an old segment of *Great Moments In Presidential Speeches* on *YouTube*.

Let's turn now to the Obama Administration. On November 20, 2013, President Obama's approval rating was down to 37% according to a CBS News poll. Obama's approval rating had reached a low point.[525] Obama remained an unpopular president on June 23, 2014 when CBS news reported his approval rating stood at only forty percent.[526] As of October 1, 2014, only a quarter of Americans thought the country was heading in the right direction according to a Rasmussen poll.[527] Even fewer citizens, *only fifteen percent,* approved of the way Congress was doing its job as of July, 15, 2014, according to a Gallup poll.[528] An NBC News article published on October 10, 2013 reported that sixty percent of those surveyed in an NBC/WSJ poll favored the firing of every member of Congress. The same NBC article highlighted voter dissatisfaction with the economy as a reason for the public's dismal view of the politicians in Congress.[529]

The economy of the rich had to some extent rebounded in America under the quantitative easing policy favored by Obama when the aforesaid polls were taken, but unsurprisingly, voters remained unhappy with the government.[530] Obama's choice for Chair of the Federal Reserve Board, Janet Yellen, continued the policies of the George W. Bush and former Fed Chair, Ben Bernanke. Those polices had of course come under fire from many who said the Fed's policy of quantitative easing was designed to help Wall Street not Main Street.[531] At least one of those critics previously worked in high level management at the Federal Reserve Board himself. Andrew Huszar managed the $1.25 trillion Mortgage Backed Securities (MBS) Purchase Program conducted out of the Federal Reserve Bank of New York, (FRBNY), for "QE1." QE1 is a moniker for the first round of quantitative easing conducted by the Fed between 2008 and 2010. There have been three rounds of "QE" so far.[532] Huszar publicly apologized for his role in the QE program. Huszar wrote his apology in an Op-Ed to the Wall Street Journal:

> I can only say: I'm sorry, America. As a former Federal Reserve official, I was responsible for executing the centerpiece program of the Fed's first plunge into the bond-buying experiment known as quantitative easing. The central bank continues to spin QE as a tool for helping Main Street. But I've come to recognize the program for what it really is: the greatest backdoor Wall Street bailout of all time.[533]

Huszar told it like it is, but unfortunately the Wall Street Journal refused to permit me to quote from Huzar's analysis at greater length without paying them for it. I'm not one to pay to hear an apology. Huzar's admission and apology above is a part of history in and of itself, and so I could at least quote that. Huzar pointed out in his article that the Federal Reserve Board's policy of quantitative easing gave the too big to fail banks of Wall Street their greatest profits of all time in 2009, and the record profits continued up until Huzar's article was published. All the while, Main Street was suffering and the American economy remained sluggish.

Huzar agreed with the German minister of finance, Wolfgang Schäuble that conducting a second round of QE was "clueless." Huzar decided after the Fed announced a new round of buying Wall Street's garbage bonds that the Fed was placing Wall Street's interests above the national interest. Huzar mentioned the fact that a financial expert at Pimco, which is a major player in the stock market, had calculated that the Fed had spent $4 trillion on Wall Street's junk assets to produce only a $40 billion rise in US gross domestic profit. Huzar concluded that by propping up Wall Street with trillions of dollars the Fed was allowing the federal government to ignore the unsoundness of the US economy.[534] For the most part I agree with Huszar, but I will add that the unsoundness of the American economy is caused only in part by poor government oversight over Wall Street. The underlying cause of America's unsound economy is clearly *free trade*.

Separate and apart from quantitative easing was the Fed's policy of keeping interest rates extremely low during Obama's presidency. The Dow Jones Industrial made it over 18,000 in 2015 and those of us with nest eggs were pleased things were not worse. Obama is a crazy free trader who says more trade deals like NAFTA will restore prosperity.[535] Does he really believe that? I can understand why hedge fund managers and corporate fat cats claim that. They get rich out of transferring middle class jobs to China. But free trade has hollowed out the middle class, brought crushing poverty to hard working people, and beat down America's once strong "production ecosystem." How much more evidence do you need of that? Don't worry I have much more in store for you in this book if you have not yet seen the light.

Obama's only real strategy for helping Main Street (other than encouraging the Fed to keep interest rates low) was *deficit spending* and more *free trade agreements*. The report card is in on the performance of Obama's 2011 trade agreement with South Korea. Obama gets an "F." Obama promised a major win for American workers from increased exports, and his administration promised approximately 70,000 new jobs but not even one new job has materialized. Instead, exports to South Korea fell by $3.5 billion in 2012, representing a decline of 8.3 percent.[536] Within two years from the date the South Korean trade agreement was put in effect, imports from South Korea surged by 9.8 percent, a $5.6 billion increase! Our trade deficit with South Korea grew astronomically by a factor of 59.6%, costing the American economy an estimated 60,000 jobs.[537] Thus we lost almost as many jobs as President Obama said we would gain. It sure seems like Obama knew, and most certainly Obama should have known, that his trade deal with South Korea would cost many American jobs.

Obama was advised via an April 7, 2011 article written by Robert E. Scott of the Economic Policy Institute (EPI) that Colombia did not deserve passage of a pending trade agreement because 2800 trade unionists had been murdered there since 1986, and Scott also estimated a loss of 55,000 jobs if the agreement was entered into.[538] Colombia "ardently" desired a free trade agreement, and withholding one was the only leverage America had to stop the murderous violence against unions.[539] Obama had in fact stated during his 2008 campaign that a trade agreement with Colombia "would make a mockery of the very labor protections that we've insisted be included in these kinds of agreements."[540] After the election Obama changed his mind, despite the pleas of desperate human rights activists, labor lawyers, and unions from both Colombia and the United States. Obama decided the trade agreement coveted by Colombia would be best for both sides. On May 31, 2013, a report headlined *The Horrific Costs of the US-Colombia Trade Agreement* appeared in The Nation online edition. Reporters Micheal Norby and Brian Fitzpartrick cited fact after fact justifying the earlier warnings to Obama, who might have prevented the escalation in the violence against workers which took place after the trade agreement was passed.[541] The trade agreement was passed by Congress in October, 2011, but it did not take effect until May 12, 2012.

The Census Bureau reports that in 2013 the United States posted a $3.234 billion trade deficit in goods with Colombia.[542] Scott's estimate of jobs lost has not as yet been proven correct. In fact, Colombia had developed a small trade deficit with the United States as of October, 2014.[543]

Experts blamed Columbia's poor infrastructure and high transportation costs for causing the unexpected trade deficit.[544] Colombia's finance minister, Mauricio Cárdenas remains confident that Colombia's actions to lower the value of the Colombian peso combined with government plans for remedying the infrastructure problem will lead to greatly increased exports from Colombia to the United States.[545] Colombia's currency has already reached the exchange rate that the Colombian government targeted for it against the dollar, but its manufacturing sector has not enjoyed the hoped for surge in exports.[546] Colombia may in the foreseeable future make sufficient progress through currency manipulation, reducing costs, and improving infrastructure to restore and greatly enlarge its trade surplus with the United States. I would hate to see Colombia become another example of a developing country that is severely harmed by free trade. Manufacturers in Colombia were complaining about being harmed by cheap imports at the time of this writing.[547] Instead of nurturing Columbia's high value added industries, free trade may undermine and eventually destroy them. The destructive effect that free trade often has on poor countries is discussed further in chapter eight.

The latest name in the "giant sucking sound" business is the Trans Pacific Partnership, or TPP. It's a proposed agreement that so far includes twelve countries, (The U.S., Japan, Vietnam, Malaysia, Singapore, Mexico, Peru, Chile, New Zealand, Australia, Canada, and Brunei), and many more have expressed interest in joining.[548] There are so many negative media stories about this budding trade agreement that the public may rally against it. I clicked on the hyperlink I obtained from a google search that read "Trans Pacific Partnership - Huffington Post and found not one story but a grouping of 101 articles about the TPP at the Huffington Post Politics blog. The vast majority of the stories carried headlines that were negative about the trade deal. The last article on the list had a title which made it clear that the author was extremely pro free trade so I read that story first. It turned out to be written by the President and CEO of the Consumer Electronics Association, (CEA), Gary Shapiro.[549]

America used to be a leading manufacturer of televison sets, radios, and stereo equipment, but we make very few of those products anymore.[550] You might suppose that the largest member organizations in the CEA (which you might also assume are manufacturers), are either foreign owned or have outsourced at least ninety percent of their jobs or input purchases overseas. That's not the case. CEA membership rules allow retail sellers like Walmart to join, along with their advertising firms, public relations firms, and law firms. In fact, the Chairman of the CEA as of June, 2012 was Randy Fry. Fry is the President and co-founder of Fry's Electronics, a large retailer of consumer electronics. The CEA is very concerned about its member stores, so the support of the CEA for free trade is not surprising. I know that stores make higher profits selling the cheaper stuff we get from places like China, but we as consumers don't get much of a benefit, if any on price, and I have already explained why. Not only that, the large number of Americans who work in retail today are getting smaller and smaller slices of the economic pie just as our remaining manufacturing workers are.[551]

As I was writing this chapter trade experts and reporters were wondering if the TPP will be passed by Congress. Usually the media piles on the free trade band wagon as soon as the vote on passage gets close. The coverage of the Trans Pacific Partnership has been more critical than on past trade deals. Some critics charge the TPP encroaches on state sovereignty in order to further the interests of transnational corporations.[552] Others are concerned because the agreement fails to contain measures to curtail the use of currency manipulation as a means of protectionism.[553] Still others object to the inclusion of provisions similar to SOPA and PIPA, two proposed laws that were defeated because of the hue and cry raised by public interest groups opposed to internet censorship.[554] As of this writing, sixty percent of U.S. Senators had signed a letter demanding that the Obama administration include a provision in the TPP limiting currency manipulation.[555] In addition, 151 Democratic members of the House and 25 Republican members had gone on record as opposed to granting Obama fast track authority to pass the TPP in its present form.[556]

Part of the reason that TPP may be defeated lies in the fact that the agreement was drafted in secret and even Congress was kept in the dark about its terms.[557] The top corporate interests had full access to the agreement and the Obama administration seems to have crafted the agreement to benefit trans national corporations, but not American workers.[558] On November 13, 2013 WikiLeaks published the full text of the Intellectual Property rights chapter of the TPP.[559] Having the TPP outed by the same vehicle that gave us the Snowden revelations about NSA spying was not good for TPP's image with Congress or the public.

Robert E. Scott, the economist from the Economic Policy Institute who wrote with prescience that Obama should nix the Columbia trade agreement wrote another story with similar advice regarding the TPP: "*No Jobs From Trade Pacts:The Trans-Pacific Partnership Could Be Much Worse than the Over-Hyped Korea Deal*."[560] In that article Scott recounts the bad news from the South Korea Free Trade Agreement and discusses the likely outcomes from both the TPP and the lesser known Transatlantic Trade Investment Partnership or TTIP. Scott points to a "preponderance of evidence" that free trade agreements "and other trade deals do not work as expected, and have been harmful to the overall U.S. economy and to manufacturing in particular." Scott also notes that government estimates of the impact of Free Trade Agreements (FTA's) fail to predict the extent and negative effect of the outsourcing that occurs because of them. Scott notes how outsourcing to Mexico almost tripled within ten years of NAFTA's passage. According to Scott, more than half of China's exports in 2011 were produced by foreign owned firms or joint ventures which included foreign owned firms. Scott warns that outsourcing may be expected to similarly increase the trade deficits that are expected under the TPP and the TTIP.[561]

You can read more about Dr. Scott's backround at the EPI website.[562] Dr. Scott earned his Doctorate in Economics from the University of California at Berkeley after obtaining a Bachelor of Science Degree in Engineering from Washington University in St. Louis.[563]

In contrast to Dr. Scott, who has written numerous scholarly articles on the subject of trade agreements and free trade, President Obama has written one such article, a 2005 letter to the editor. Obama wrote that letter to the Chicago Tribune when he was the junior U.S. Senator from Illinois. The President's lack of understanding (or outright dishonesty), concerning trade theory can be assessed from his own words:

> Globalization is not someone's political agenda. It is a technological revolution that is fundamentally changing the world's economy, producing winners and losers along the way. The question is not whether we can stop it, but how we respond to it. It's not whether we should protect our workers from competition,

> but what we can do to fully enable them to compete against workers all over the world.
>
> So far, America has not effectively answered these questions and American workers are suffering as a result. I meet these workers all across Illinois, workers whose jobs moved to Mexico or China and are now competing with their own children for jobs that pay 7 bucks an hour. In town meetings and union halls, I've tried to tell these workers the truth--that these jobs aren't coming back, that globalization is here to stay and that they will have to train more and learn more to get the new jobs of tomorrow.
>
> But when they wonder how they will get this training and this education, when they ask what they will do about their health-care bills and their lower wages and the general sense of financial insecurity that seems to grow with each passing day, I cannot look them in the eyes and tell them that their government is doing a single thing about these problems.[564]

Let's deconstruct what Obama said. First we will consider the phrase *Globalization...is a technological revolution.* That statement cannot be found in any learned treatise on this planet unless it is an analysis of Obama's 2005 letter to the editor. So this book may be the only other writing on this Earth that has that phrase in it. If you don't believe me try doing an internet search right now. Globalization is not a technological revolution. It is true that nearly instantaneous global communications, the internet and advances in transportation and other technologies have advanced globalization of commercial activity, free trade remains an economic and political policy choice and globalization has not brought about a technological revolution in the United States. Globalization has in fact retarded the growth of technology in the United States as was shown by the MIT Study that was written about by Richard McCormack in his paper *MIT: With Loss Of Manufacturing The U.S. Innovation Engine Is No Longer Working.*[565]

President Obama is a silver tongued orator and skillful writer. He took the well used phrases "Globalization and Technology" and "The Technology Revolution." and he made himself the whole new phrase *Globalization is a Technological Revolution.*[566]

That verbal transformation by the President set up his next sentence. He had established the rhetorical illusion that globalization i.e. free trade is somehow a manifestation of the natural progression of science and technology. Obama's semantic maneuver is an example of what I said free traders always do, (in the first paragraph of chapter three), which I will now repeat:

> *From the inception of the idea of free trade it has almost always been presented to the public by its boosters as a theory of economic science, rooted in a sublime mathematical proof that defies all criticism. Nothing could be further from the truth. Free trade theory is mathematically invalid. It has been proved by experience to have been a disaster for most Americans and for America as a country.*

With the wave of his literary hand Obama had magically removed all the evidence of human hardship, relative technological and military decline, and growing national indebtedness from consideration. He did so in addressing a question which can be stated as follows: *Has free trade harmed American interests more than it has helped them and should it therefore be replaced by a different system of international trade*? Obama made that question irrelevant without offering a single iota of proof that free trade has not in fact brought more harm to America than good.

Having established with his initial axiom that free trade and globalization have become as immutable as gravity, then Senator Obama proceeded to declare the consequence:

> *The question is not whether we can stop it, but how we respond to it. It's not whether we should protect our workers from competition....*[567]

In all of Obama's comment he offers not a single example of how America or Americans have benefitted from globalization. Most of what he wrote is an evocative description of the financial hardship and emotional turmoil Americans have endured because of free trade. Obama ended his letter to the Chicago Sun Times with an ominous observation that portended his later transformation by the media into the image of a messiah of *Yes We Can* change:

> *I cannot look them in the eyes and tell them that their government is doing a single thing about these problems.*[568]

President Obama also mentioned the need for education to prepare American workers for the *"jobs of tomorrow."*[569] What jobs are those? Service jobs right? What kind? Where are they? It's been forty years Mr. President!! Where are the jobs of tomorrow???? Unless trade policy is reformed they are not coming to America until American wages, benefits, and working conditions are lousy enough to entice corporations to return to America. The *jobs of tomorrow* don't seem worth waiting for Mr. Obama. We want the *jobs of today* without delay. To the Republocrats I offer these words from Shakespeare about waiting for tomorro

> To-morrow, and to-morrow, and to-morrow,
>
> Creeps in this petty pace from day to day,
>
> To the last syllable of recorded time;
>
> And all our yesterdays have lighted fools
>
> The way to dusty death.
>
> Macbeth Act 5, scene 5, 19–23[570]

The bottom line is this: Obama has done his job to enrich the money power.

Obama did not mention anything about the 192 year old theory of "comparative advantage," in his statement about globalization, but that is the theory that conservative economists still use to justify free trade agreements.[571] A book published in 1988 by the publishing arm of the prestigious National Academy of Sciences provides a window into the minds and objectives of neoliberals like Obama who see free trade as inevitably beneficial, particularly to the world's poor. The book is called *Globalization of Technology: International Perspectives*.[572]

Here is a quote from second chapter which concerns the restructuring of the global economy sought by the authors:

> The world needs much more material growth; the world population has reached 5

> billion and will increase to 8 billion in 2050 before it stabilizes at something under 10 billion. The increase will take place almost entirely in the Third World. A quarter of the world's population now inhabits today's industrialized countries, but this proportion will fall to less than 20 percent in 50 years. The inhabitants of industrialized countries already consume three-quarters of the world's energy and mineral resources. It is difficult to imagine that disparity on this scale can continue far into the next century. It is essential for world society that the existing gap between North and South be narrowed. This narrowing should be seen not only as a moral obligation for prosperous nations but also as in their own long-term interest.[573]

In the above passage there is no mention of *comparative advantage*. There is a declaration of concern (which I find laudable and wholly agree with), for the world's poor. We are told by the authors that "*it is essential for world society that the existing gap between North and South be narrowed.*" But what about the comparative advantage rationale for free trade whereby it is argued that both rich efficient countries and their poor inefficient trading partners benefit from it? With regard to that concept, the book makes a remarkable admission meant for the specialized eyes of globalist planners, not downtrodden American workers. The overview to the book states as follows:

> The rapid rate of innovation and the dynamics of technology flows mean that comparative advantage is short-lived....Rapid technological innovation and the proliferation of transnational organizations are driving the formation of a global economy that sometimes conflicts with nationalistic concerns about maintaining comparative advantage and competitiveness.[574]

The statement in the quote above that comparative advantage is *short-lived* is of course an admission that it flows with the same speed that capital and technology flow, rendering the idea of comparative advantage laughably inane as a justification for free trade. But comparative advantage can only flow via the "proliferation of transnational organizations" when governments allow it to. The neoliberals like Obama are obviously arguing that "nationalistic concerns about maintaining comparative advantage and competitiveness" are in conflict with their plans for global economic equality.

I disagree significantly with the quoted authors of *Globalization of Technology.* I believe that bringing about the desired narrowing in the wealth gap between North and South should not come from lowering the American standard of living for most Americans. Forcing American workers into the unemployment and underemployment lines and lowering the share that eighty percent of Americans take from the national GDP has not brought about the change needed by the economies of the third world. People are mired in poverty there, as here, owing to the greed of corrupt *money power* government. One perfect example of that greed is the way Mexican maquiladoras workers have been kept in poverty for over four decades.[575] The evidence that free trade has brought poverty instead of plenty to many developing countries is impossible to refute. But that is a subject for the next and later chapters.

When Obama's current term ends our last two presidents, one from each party, will have left office as losers, doomed by their limited vison and weak servility to the money power. From the past, our greatest leaders call out to us to rid ourselves of the failed weaklings who are tearing the muscle and spine from our national economy. George Washington and Abraham Lincoln are to Obama and Bush II what two iron bars are to a couple of bread sticks. Washington knew the importance of a diversified self-sustaining industrial base (second to none) to the national prosperity and defense. He eschewed giving "equivalents for nominal factors" to other trading nations only to be "reproached with ingratitude for not giving more." He also knew the dangers of allowing foreign control of American production, cautioning Americans about the "insidious wiles of foreign influence."[576] Eckes tells of Washington's long lasting *American System*, knowledge of which remains hidden from most Americans today:

> A century later Washington's basic approach remained the cornerstone of American commercial policy. In a farewell address presented in December 1892, President Benjamin Harrison celebrated the protective system as a 'mighty instrument' for the development of our national wealth and a most powerful agency in protecting the homes of our workingmen from the invasion of want.' Like other gilded age Republicans, Harrison worried that trade liberalization would bring wage reductions and distress for American working people and their families: 'A general process of wage reduction cannot be contemplated by any patriotic citizen without the gravest apprehension. It may be...possible for the American manufacturer to compete successfully with his foreign rival in many branches of production without the defense of protective duties if the pay rolls are equalized; but...the distress our working people when it is attained ...is not pleasant to contemplate.[577]

Truer words could not be spoken today and the lines on the graphs of American productivity, wages, home ownership, individual debt, national debt, trade deficits, job losses, poverty rates, marriage rates, work force participation rate, and self reported happiness prove the wretched truth of the matter. Obama admitted it when he said: *I cannot look them in the eyes and tell them that their government is doing a single thing about these problems.*[578]

So we end this brief polemical but factual account of America's postwar decline with one last bit of historical fact, an observation made by former Louisiana Senator Russell Long. Russell Long was the son of the famous American political leader, Huey Long**Error! Bookmark not defined.**. Known by the nickname "Kingfish," Huey Long was an outspoken populist politician who became the governor of Louisiana and later served as a U.S. Senator from that state. He was vilified by the money power for his public works programs and taxes on the rich during the depression. The elder Long also generated dislike because he was a dictatorial political boss who required state government workers to fork over a percentage of their earnings to his campaign war chest. A campaign war chest owned by Long actually existed in the form of a small metal lock box famously known as the "deduct box." Notwithstanding any shortcomings in his character or policies, Long was a brilliant orator and very insightful about how to win elections. He understood the needs and feelings of working people.[579]

Russell Long inherited his father's genius for politics. He had a long and storied career in the Senate serving as the chairman of the Senate Finance Committee from 1966 to 1981. The junior Long was not the firebrand that his father had been and he was well liked in the business community. Ronald W. Reagan described him as a "legend ... one of the most skillful legislators, compromisers and legislative strategists in history."[580] He was once described as the "the fourth branch of government" by the Wall Street Journal.[581]

In 1976, Long made a prediction to Henry Kissinger. It was a prediction which accounts for why this chapter and more generally this book was written and what it is intended to accomplish. It is the light at the end of a rhetorical and literal tunnel of despair.

> *...if we trade away American jobs and farmer's incomes for some vague concept of a 'new international order,' the American people will demand from their elected representatives a new order of their own, which puts their jobs, their security, and their incomes above the priorities of those who dealt them a bad deal.*[582]

I say to that, *Amen*. Getting rid of Trump and his gang of money power climate contrarians - along with traditional *free trade supporting* Democrats and Republicans - is the job at hand. *Let's be about our work.*

8

Free Trade is a Bunch of Bananas; Protectionism is a Bushel of Apples.

Economists Ha Joon Chang and Erik S. Reinert, both have written books which tell the hidden history of international trade. Reinert wrote *How Rich Countries Got Rich...and Why Poor Countries Stay Poor.*[583] Chang wrote *Bad Samaritans: The Myth of Free Trade and the Secret History of Capitalism.*[584] There is no doubt about what both men tell us; Almost all rich countries used protectionism to become wealthy.[585] America and Britain both used protectionism to get rich. When Britain resorted to free trade as a means to open America's market, it accelerated the rise of America and brought about the decline of Britain.[586] Britain's gambit with free trade failed because American Presidents, following the lead of Washington and Hamilton, recognized the trap which free trade with Britain represented. America rejected free trade and developed a trade surplus with Britain by placing high tariffs on British goods, subsidizing research and development, and copying and improving British manufacturing technology.[587]

Poor countries stay poor for a variety of reasons, but one reason given by both Chang and Reinert is this: Driven by pressure from rich countries to adopt free trade, poor countries have eschewed protectionism and specialized in producing agricultural commodities and raw materials following the free trade logic of comparative advantage.[588] So the phrase, "bunch of bananas," in the title to this chapter refers in one sense to the banana republics and other low wage nations of the Americas, Asia and Africa that have been exploited by outsiders (and/or corrupt insiders), for their natural resources. Such nations have been prevented from developing effective strategies to grow high value manufacturing industries and achieve national prosperity.

The phrase "bushel of apples" in the title to this chapter refers in one sense to the creativity and profitability of Apple Computer, and more broadly to the high value added, technology driven manufacturing industries that America used to have in great abundance. By employing protectionism, America was once the place where everything was being invented or reinvented, from radio and TV to microwave ovens, computers, stereos, machine tools, printed circuit boards, and all the other products of modern technology.[589]

One of the narratives in Ha Joon Chang's aforesaid book is hilarious: Chang tells how writer and journalist Thomas Friedman was struck by inspiration while riding a Japanese bullet train to

Tokyo following a visit to a Lexus car factory. Seeing the advanced robotic technology on display at the Lexus factory had left Friedman feeling a sense of wonder. Then while riding the train home Friedman read a news story concerning the latest troubles in the Middle East. Friedman was inspired by the news story to made an ideational connection between Lexus and an olive tree. Lexus represented to Friedman a symbol of the advancement in technology brought about by free trade and globalization. The olive tree symbolized to Friedman traditional Middle East culture, provincialism and conflict. The contrast between the Lexus and the Olive Tree represented to Friedman the difference between countries seeking to prosper from "modernizing, streamlining and privatizing" and those mired in old traditions, backward thinking and regional antagonisms.[590]

Friedman wrote a best selling book following his epiphany on the subject of globalization to which he gave the title *The Lexus and the Olive Tree*.[591] In that book, Friedman insisted that in order to achieve Lexus style prosperity the olive tree nations must don a "golden straightjacket" of economic policies.[592] The policies Friedman recommended mirror the neoliberal Washington Consensus polices which are described in chapter two of this book. One such principle espoused by Friedman was "eliminating and lowering tariffs on imported goods."[593] That's why Chang's account of Friedman's use of the Lexus name as a symbol of the alleged prosperity that results from free trade made me laugh; Equating Lexus with free trade is simply absurd. Chang described in detail how Japan "kicked" American car manufacturers out of the Japanese market and kept them out while Japan subsidized its domestic auto industry after WWII.[594]

Japan's Ministry of International Trade and Industry (MITI) has used industrial policy to build up Japan and beat American competitors for decades. Toyota owns the Lexus brand. Chang concluded that if the Japanese government had decided to wear Friedman's "Golden Straightjacket" in 1958, Toyota would today either no longer exist or be the "junior partner" of a "western car manufacturer." In fact, claimed Chang, "the same would have been true for the entire Japanese economy."[595] Chang's book makes it clear to any literate reader that the view of globalization Friedman presented in his book is laughable nonsense.

Eckes' account of America's trade history confirms that Japan followed the protectionist route while feeding off of American trade concessions:

> Japan made few concessions of its own...Perhaps learning from the experience of nineteenth-century America, wily bureaucrats in the Japanese Ministry of International Trade and Industry (MITI) knew how to gain export opportunities without yielding the home market. In effect, they dined at the world trade buffet but declined to share the bill.[596]

The same holds true for other countries that enjoy high GDP. The strategy of the large and successful manufacturing countries is to use protectionism, pay lip service to free trade, and take advantage of America's trade giveaways. For instance, Germany has the largest GDP in Europe and it had a protectionist industrial policy throughout most of its history. It continues to employ protectionist measures today.[597] Germany was a larger exporter than China until 2008.[598] Germany employs a higher percentage of its work force in manufacturing than America does[599] and Germany pays its workers wages which average over twenty percent higher than the wages Americans get.[600] German auto workers fare even better, earning more than double what

American auto workers are paid.[601] In fact thirteen European countries pay their workers more than Americans are paid.[602]

European Union countries resort to various non tariff methods to protect home industries. These include voluntary import restraints, discretionary enforcement of anti-dumping laws, and the use of value added taxes or VAT. Value added taxes are imposed at each step in the process used in making goods, from the sale of raw materials to the assembly of finished products. VAT taxes on exported goods are rebated to manufacturers, placing competing American products at a cost disadvantage which can be as high as thirty percent.[603]

China is as notorious as Japan for using protectionism. Currency manipulation by China is estimated to reduce the cost of its imports to America by as much as forty percent. China's protectionist strategy employs many other tools. Theses include keeping wages low, subsidies, permitting widespread manufacture of counterfeit "knock offs" encouraging foreign direct investment, (FDI), imposing technology sharing requirements on foreign firms, and neglecting health, safety and the environment.[604]

Sitting on the other side of the world from me, Ha Joon Chang lived through the unimaginably rapid economic rise of South Korea while I watched prosperity wither and die for tens of millions of Americans. Though our experiences were completely different, I shared Chang's perspective on why our respective homelands fared as they did. As a boy in the late sixties I saw America begin its decline when Japanese steel, automobile and electronics imports stormed the American economy and helped to create the American rust belt. What I saw was the product of Japan's protectionist industrial policy combined with America's open market - free market policy.

It's no secret to the American people. Free trade has forced American industries out of business and the pensions my parents generation took for granted have been phased out in favor of 401k retirement plans.[605] The trouble with those, (aside from stock market instability), is that people who are forced to work for peanuts *don't have money for retirement savings*. Even the money power media monopoly finds it prudent to report on the story of growing poverty and desperation among seniors. A report in *Forbes*, (March 20, 2013), headlined *The Greatest Retirement Crisis In American History* tells some depressing facts: for one, independent experts calculate the nestegg sitting in the 401k plan of the average sixty-five year old lucky enough to have one is twenty-five thousand dollars. Good luck making it to age sixty-six people! Another statistic is even more dire; Only one third of people in the work force have a 401k![606] That statistic does not include the millions more who don't even have a job.

As a boy growing up in South Korea, Ha Joon Chang was in the exact opposite situation (not because he was a genius), of the one I was in. In 1961, when I was five, South Korea's per capita income was eighty-two dollars. The Korean War had destroyed most of South Korea's railways and about half of its factories. Imperial Japan had ruled Korea between 1910 and 1945 and during the Japanese occupation the literacy rate in Korea was only twenty-two percent.[607] Following the WWII, as the result of the cold war conflict between the U.S. and the U.S.S.R., separate zones of control above and below the 38th parallel had been created. In 1948, a U.N. supervised election led to the division of North Korea and South Korea as separate states.[608] During the 1950s, South Korea's economic situation was considered to be almost hopeless by the

United States Agency for International Development; Korea's main exports were tungsten, fish and other primary commodities.[609]

South Korea's economic situation may have seemed hopeless to the free trade minded Americans, but it did not seem so hopeless to the far-sighted industrial policy planners and entrepreneurs that ran South Korea.[610] During the period between 1963 and 2008 the purchasing power of South Koreans grew by fourteen times. It took Britain over two centuries, and America a century and a half to accomplish similar growth.[611] Today, South Korea is at the top of its game. Samsung, the South Korean electronics leviathan outsold all of its competitors in the smart phone market *combined* in the third quarter of 2013.[612] Yet Samsung began as a humble exporter of fish vegetables and fruit in 1938.[613] How did Samsung, L.G. Electronics, Hyundai, Kia, and a host of other large South Korean companies become so successful that Ha Joon Chang could boast about being "a citizen of one of the wealthier if not the wealthiest countries in the world" in 2008?[614] Chang tells how South Korea's economic *bushel of apples* was harvested in his book.[615]

By closely consulting with the industries it sought to foster growth in, South Korea's government formulated an always evolving national plan for economic development. Tariffs, subsidies and other forms of protection were used to nurture South Korean firms. The South Korean government owned the banking system outright; Thus, insuring that funds flowed to industries that were strategically important in the creation of positive technological externalities and a productive production ecosystem was never a problem for South Korea.[616] The South Korean government was *flexible and pragmatic*, not *ideologically rigid* when it came to spawning new high value industries. Thus, the South Koreans were not hesitant to resort to the use of state-owned enterprises (SOEs), when private enterprise was not getting the job done. Short term-short sighted economics was avoided. If private sector industries were backward and dysfunctional, the South Korean government would obtain control of them, restructure them, and *most often, sell them back to the private sector*. The South Korean government held tight control over foreign exchange, insuring that the surplus from its exports was used to import machinery and other inputs that would help South Korea raise productivity, foster inventiveness and generate wealth. The South Koreans also closely regulated FDI, encouraging it in sectors where it was desired to help boost South Korea's production ecosystem, and banning it where it was considered dangerous to South Korea's development plan.[617]

As Ha Joon Chang, Clyde Prestowitz, Ian Fletcher, Erik Reinert and many other economists have noted, South Korea's phenomenal success could be discounted by free trade ideologues as a fluke, except for the fact that South Korea's use of protectionism was not unusual; Nearly all rich countries got rich through protectionism.[618] Our founding fathers for the most part knew it, and they knew that free trade was in part a trap laid by Britain to capture the American market and stop America's rise.[619] The idea that free trade is a trap set by rich countries to exploit poor countries is discussed by Ha-Joon Chang.[620] Chang notes, as did our early political leaders, the timeless observation (and implicit warning) of the German economist Friedrich List, who said:

> Any nation which by means of protective duties and restrictions on navigation has raised her manufacturing power and her navigation to such a degree of development that no other nation can sustain free competition with her, can do

> nothing wiser than to throw away these ladders of her greatness, to preach to other nations the benefits of free trade, and to declare in penitent tones that she has hitherto wandered in the paths of error, and has now for the first time succeeded in discovering the truth.[621]

South Korea, (2013 est. pop. 50 million), is a member of a group of four economies known as the Asian Tigers. The others, in order of population, are Taiwan, (2014 est. pop. 23.4 million), Hong Kong (2014 est. pop. 7.23 million) and Singapore with an estimated population in 2012 of 5.31 million.[622] These four countries are called tigers, and surely not just because they all enjoyed rapid industrialization and income growth between the 1960s and the 1990s. Undoubtedly they are thought of as tigers because all but one aggressively employed industrial policy to induce economic growth. Taiwan, the second most populous of the group adopted a strategy that, like South Korea's, eschewed neoliberal free trade ideology, and was on the hunt for high value exports. Taiwan differed from South Korea in that it was slightly less restrictive of foreign investment but it made greater use of SOE.[623] Singapore aggressively used subsidies to entice foreign investment and it was very aggressive in the use of SOE's. Singapore also invested heavily in infrastructure projects and education projects that were tailored to industries it considered strategic to the success of its development plan.[624] Only the city of Hong Kong had a laissez faire attitude toward economic development. Hong Kong's role as a trading center between Britain and Asia accounts for its nonchalance about trade. Wealth from international trade accrued naturally to Honk Kong because it served as an economic pivot point between the continents.[625]

Arguing against Germany adopting the free trade and laissez-faire policy that the British began advocating after Britain had achieved manufacturing superiority, Friedrich List pointed out that the British had used protectionism to achieve their superiority:

> Had the English left everything to itself—'Laissez faire, laissez aller', as the popular economical school recommends—the [German] merchants of the Steelyard would be still carrying on their trade in London, the Belgians would be still manufacturing cloth for the English, England would have still continued to be the sheep-farm of the Hansards, just as Portugal became the vineyard of England, and has remained so till our days, owing to the stratagem of a cunning diplomatist. Indeed, it is more than probable that without her [highly protectionist] commercial policy England would never have attained to such a large measure of municipal and individual freedom as she now possesses, for such freedom is the daughter of industry and wealth.[626]

List was an extremely influential economist and political thinker. He was born in Germany in 1789,[627] but he emigrated to the United States in 1825.[628] List published a pamphlet in 1827 to which he gave the title *Outlines of a New System of Political Economy.* The pamphlet contained List's arguments in favor of the use of protectionism.[629] In 1841 List published a four volume book containing a much fuller exposition of his ideas. List's book bore the title *The National System of Political Economy*.[630]

List's ideas were seminal to the development of the German historical school of economics, which held that the study of economic development patterns in history and empirical analysis of economic policy as effective or ineffective in creating growth are of paramount importance in economics. Rigid ideological principles based upon mathematical theorems, such as Ricardo's idea of comparative advantage were rejected as overly simplified and based upon false assumptions.[631] There were parallel schools of thought among English and American economists.[632] Obviously List's ideas continue to have great currency with the governments of the fastest growing economies of the present.[633] List is also given credit as providing an ideational foundation for European unity and he is seen as providing the theoretical basis for the European Economic Community.[634]

Post WWII presidents from Truman on may have been aware of List's advice, but they felt pressured to cement alliances with nations all over the globe to counter the threat posed by communism. In addition, America's postwar presidents believed that America was just too big to fail. Japan, South Korea, the other "Asian Tigers" and the Europeans were well aware of America's overconfidence in the benefits of free trade and America's fear of "falling dominos."[635] To their credit, those countries took full advantage of America to better themselves. The resulting competition facing American business was so great that U.S. industries previously thought to be too big to fail were lost; Profits fell in others and Wall Street became the most profitable sector in the economy.[636] Wall Street and the corporate elite became addicted to cheap labor, and CEO's saw the relocation of American factories to foreign locations to be an absolute political, economic and God given right.[637] Pride in country, a desire to give back, and recognition of a responsibility to create good jobs at home became obsolete ideas for those in the ranks of top management.[638] American workers were now citizens of a world economy, and left to fend for themselves as best they could in the new world order. Globalism replaced patriotism, and this change has been trumpeted to the public by the media monopoly and money powered politicians ever since.

A new era of wealth concentration which has been compared with the gilded age of the late nineteenth century began in America and it remains today.[639] But the current age is more gilded than any before it. *There is greater wealth disparity in America today than in any other nation or civilization that has ever existed in all of recorded history.*[640] Roman slaves and medieval serfs were closer in wealth to their owners and feudal lords than today's hourly wage workers are to their corporate masters.[641] America's efforts to foster a global system of free trade has become an engine of growth for a handful of other countries and an instrument of decline for America.

The only real "golden straightjacket" involving free trade is the one worn by Republocrat legislators and presidents, whose hands are tied by the gold that the money power lavishes on them and their political campaigns. The politicians and the media have relied on cherry picked data, juggled statistics and economic fables like the Smoot-Hawley myth to keep the public in line.[642] America is on a downward trajectory which can only be reversed by a new political party which is independent of the money power and able to outflank the media monopoly.

Having considered how most well off countries used protectionism to grow rich, the next question to consider is this: What has free trade and the Washington Consensus done to lift the blight in poor countries over the last sixty years? Christian Aid is an agency operated by forty churches in Britain and Ireland dedicated to fighting and ending poverty in the low income nations of the world. In 2005, Christian Aid published "The Economics of Failure: The Real

Cost of 'Free' Trade for Poor Countries" a nine page briefing paper which summarizes the results of an econometric analysis of trade data from thirty two countries done by Dr. Egore Kraev Ph.D.[643] Kraev's research is reported more fully in the paper "Estimating GDP Effects Of Trade Liberalisation On Developing Countries."[644]

Christian Aid wanted to find out what would have happened in the poor countries included in Kraev's study if they had not been induced by the World Bank, the International Monetary Fund, the WTO and G8 lending countries into liberalizing trade and opening their markets. Kraev's research shows that free trade has been a bad trip for Africa and the nations in Latin America and Asia that were included in the study. The Christian Aid briefing paper summarized the results this way:

> Trade liberalisation has cost sub-Saharan Africa US$272 billion over the past 20 years. Had they not been forced to liberalise as the price of aid, loans and debt relief, sub-Saharan African countries would have had enough extra income to wipe out their debts and have sufficient left over to pay for every child to be vaccinated and go to school. Two decades of liberalisation has cost sub-Saharan Africa roughly what it has received in aid. Effectively, this aid did no more than compensate African countries for the losses they sustained by meeting the conditions that were attached to the aid they received. And these losses dwarf the US $40 billion worth of debt relief agreed to at the recent meeting of G7 finance ministers. If new aid and debt relief comes with strings attached that require countries to liberalise trade, it may well do more harm than good. When they meet at Gleneagles, G8 leaders must agree to stop demanding harmful conditions as the price of aid and debt relief.[645]

Economist Ian Fletcher has written about the alarming trend of middle income and even rich nations being turned into poor nations because of free trade, citing the data analysis of an economist at Erasmus University.[646] Fletcher reported that 16 out 19 non-Western nations looked at had declined from rich status to non-rich status after adopting free trade policies. Twenty out of twenty two nations that were considered to be "upper-middle-income" declined to lower income categories after adopting free trade. Most of the countries in the third from the top income category declined as well.[647] The author of the study opined: "We seem to inhabit a downwardly mobile world..." and "by 2000 most countries were either rich or poor, in contrast to the 1960 when most nations were in middle income groups."[648]

The reason for this decline is obvious and it is part of the explanation of why free trade is a bunch of bananas; When free trade is adopted as a policy by poor and middle income countries the developing industrial sectors in those countries that are not yet competitive in the world market get killed off by imports. Agriculture that is not yet efficient can also fall victim to free trade.[649] Fletcher goes into great detail in his book about the harm done by free trade and the benefits of protective industrial policy and its use historically by America, Britain, China, Japan, Germany, and other nations great and small. I suggest again that you read his book, and the books by Ha Joon Chang and Erik Reinert that are mentioned in the beginning of this chapter.

Back in 1973, I knew that economists would eventually wake up and tell the truth about free trade and protective industrial policy. I began this book with the belief that Americans have finally suffered enough pain. Society is waking up to the fact that changing our trade policy is imperative, but the national interest will continue to suffer whenever it is in conflict with the money power's short term interests. The money power's policy is to concentrate wealth in its own hands by outsourcing jobs and building production facilities overseas in low wage countries. Consumers benefit very little in the short run and they are harmed terribly in the long run. In order to pursue their goals, Wall Street and much of corporate America find it necessary to maintain a controlled media, manipulate public opinion, and dominate political spending and the two party system. America's production ecosystem and its ability to create new and better jobs has been substantially damaged as a result.

Donald Trump rode the wave of America's discontent with free trade and was selected to become the President of the United States by the Electoral College. Nonetheless, Hillary Clinton received 2.9 million more votes than Trump. Most Americans distrust Trump and many fear him for very good reason. Trump plans to cut taxes on the rich substantially, and to pay for those tax cuts by gutting vitally important federal agencies. It would be absolute lunacy for Trump to impose large tariffs on foreign manufactures all at once in a misguided effort to eliminate America's giant trade deficits and defray the costs of his tax cuts. Tariffs should be imposed *gradually* to offset the economic edge China and other countries have because of low wages, lax environmental laws. currency manipulation, and various other protectionist methods. In the short term, granting tax cuts to the wealthy people who caused America's gigantic trade deficits is unfair and unworkable without sacrificing the public interest in clean air, clean water, safe streets, and national security. Fouling the air and water, and increasing wealth disparity and the public debt to pay for tax cuts will not make America great again.

Things will only improve when Americans such as *you* who recognize the harm free trade does, but who also recognize the harm Donald Trump is going to do, become organized in a new political party.

9

Don't Be Fooled: Those Trade Deficits Are Killing Us

If you read the preceding pages in this book you already know that successive large trade deficits occurring over decades cause massive job losses, lower wages for workers, a hollowing out of the middle class and the loss of manufacturing and technological competitiveness. With lower wages and a weaker production ecosystem one would expect that our GDP is significantly lower than it would have been had America stayed with the American System of industrial policy. In 2006, the Economic Strategy Institute (ESI) calculated that our GDP was losing a minimum of one percent per anum because of the trade deficits. This was well before America's record setting trade deficit of $731.2 billion in 2007, which represents the loss of between 6,580,800 to 10,968,000 jobs.[650] The ESI calculation was given during testimony before the U.S.-China Economic and Security Review Commission. Here is the relevant portion from the Commission hearings:

> ...growing trade deficits with China and other Asian economies have shifted U.S. employment from import-competing and export industries to non tradable service producing activities. Import-competing and export industries create about 50 percent more value added per employee, and spend more than three times as much R&D per dollar of value added, than the private business sector as a whole. By reducing investments in R&D, an econometric model constructed for the Economic Strategy Institute* indicates the overvalued dollar and resulting trade deficits are reducing U.S. economic growth by at least one percentage point a year - or about 25 percent of potential GDP growth. China accounts for about half of this lost growth.
>
> Importantly, this one percentage point of growth has not been lost for just one year. The trade deficit has been taxing growth for most of the last two decades, and the cumulative consequences are enormous. Had...large trade deficits not robbed this growth, U.S. GDP would likely be at least 10 percent greater and perhaps 20 percent greater, than it is today. GDP and tax revenues would be higher, and other things remaining the same, the federal budget deficit would be smaller.[651]

According to the ESI figures, but for our cumulative trade deficits the GDP in 2006 would have been as much as twenty percent larger. Obviously, an increase in GDP of even half that magnitude would have been enough to moderate or eliminate our persistent problem of high unemployment and underemployment and raise the living standard of the American people. Although money power pundits point to the decline in the unemployment rate as proof that prosperity has been restored in America, it can't be forgotten that most new jobs are for low pay and part time work.[652] It was less than two years after the ESI estimate of the GDP loss from free trade was made that the financial crisis of 2008 struck. It was a meltdown caused largely by the large scale securitization of junk mortgages given to people who could not afford to pay them.[653] Might avoiding the lower wages and loss in GDP caused by free trade have made all the difference in averting the financial catastrophe of 2008, the effects of which continue? The answer to that question is that years of economy destroying free trade was a necessary prerequisite to the 2008 financial crisis.[654]

Zealous free traders argue that our large and continuing trade deficits are no problem. Despite the fact of continuing high unemployment, the melting away of American manufacturing, shrinking wages, the fact that the financial sector gobbles up more profits than any other - and the fact that America's competitiveness has declined to a dangerous low point - to the free trade lovers, everything is rosy. In 2011, the Director of the Herbert A. Stiefel Center For Trade Policy Studies at the Cato Institute, Daniel Griswold, wrote an article telling politicians not to worry about trade deficits.[655] His argument goes something like this: First, trade deficits tend to rise during periods when American manufacturing is increasing and stock prices are up, showing that trade deficits don't hurt the stock market or manufacturing.[656] Second, during periods of rising trade deficits employment has grown, but during periods of falling trade deficits employment has fallen.[657] Third, since 1980, America's GDP has grown 3.6 times faster during periods of rising trade deficits than it has during periods of falling trade deficits.[658] Griswold concludes that the described patterns accompanying periods of rising and falling trade deficits show that regularly produced estimates by the Economic Policy Institute, (EPI), of job losses from trade deficits are wrong; The EPI econometric model is therefore flawed according to Griswold.[659]

It does not take an economist to see through Griswold's argument, though economists do know better than most people that when the economy booms for whatever reason - be it the business cycle, a financial bubble, increased spending, an expansion of the money supply, or rapid technological advancement - people tend to spend more on consumer goods generally. Domestic sales tend to rise during boom periods but *so do imports*. This fact does not rebut the EPI model to the slightest degree. As imports slowly take away market share from domestic producers, jobs must be lost. These job losses accumulate as does the loss to GDP reported by the EPI. At least Griswold has the honesty to admit in his article that economic commentators on the monthly trade deficit figures reported by the Commerce Department *uniformly disagree with his view of trade deficits*.[660]

Griswold claims that the dollars lost to trade deficits return to America to purchase treasury bills corporate stock and bonds, real estate and to increase bank deposits. He calls this use of trade dollars foreign investment.[661] How could any argument be more laughable than Griswold's? Trade deficits are one of the main factors that cause our national debt to grow and grow. Foreign governments holding dollars generally don't want to buy American products. This is particularly true of China. The Chinese use a hefty portion of their trade surplus with the U.S. to purchase IOU's in the form of bonds sold by the U.S. Treasury. This adds to the national debt, which is nearing $20 trillion. Simply paying the interest on the debt cost 13.9 cents out of every dollar of federal individual income tax Americans paid in 2013. That was nearly seven times more than was spent on education and more than half of what was spent from those tax dollars on the military budget.[662]

The countries holding dollars are also buying up control of American owned corporations and real estate and that is giving them more and more control over American business and the U.S. government.[663] For instance, the Chinese announced plans in September, 2013, to acquire America's leading pork producer, Smithfield Foods, for $5 billion. The Chinese are known to be after proprietary genetics and production technology controlled by Smithfield, and many experts suspect that the Chinese intend to cut corners on food safety to wring higher profits out of the American consumer. Smithfield is known for requiring that strict food safety policies and practices be followed by its suppliers, so there is plenty of room for slippage in Smithfield's food safety practices once China takes control of the company.[664] Speaking of pigs, (no pun intended), the Chinese dumped at least 16,000 diseased hog carcasses into Huangpu River and its tributaries in the spring of 2013. The Huangpu is the source of Shanghai's drinking water.[665] Is it wise for us to give the Chinese control of our food supply, our businesses and our pay to play politicians, and also let China buy up our advanced technologies which they can turn to military use?

The media has been filled with stories of foreign takeovers of iconic American properties and businesses for years. Examples include the Japanese purchase of New York's famous Rockefeller Center in 1989,[666] Sony's purchase of Columbia Pictures that same year,[667] the Belgian purchase of Anheuser-Busch (makers of Budweiser beer), in 2008,[668] and the purchase of the Chrysler Building in 2008 by Abu Dhabi.[669] German automaker Daimler-Benz had already taken a controlling interest in Chrysler corporation in 1998.[670] Other famous American brands that are now under foreign ownership include Good Humor Ice Cream, Ben & Jerry's ice cream, Alka Seltzer, Hellmann's mayonnaise, IBM ThinkPad, 7-Eleven, Gerber baby food, Twin Popsicle, Sunglass Hut, Purina dog and cat chow, Firestone Tires, Trader Joes, Vaseline Petroleum Jelly, Citgo Gas, French's Mustard, Frigidaire, AMC Theaters, and Dial soap.[671] Other once famous brands such as Zenith Electronics and RCA are gone forever and now largely forgotten because of imports.[672] In 2014, newspapers and blogs were filled with stories about massive real estate purchases by Chinese interests.[673]

In 2006, an attempt was made by the United Arab Emirates, (UAE), to buy the port management leases at twenty two seaports in the United States. The proposed purchase included ports with large cargo operations in New York, Camden, New Jersey; Philadelphia, Baltimore, Miami, Portland, Maine; Boston, Davisville, Rhode Island; Newark, Camden, New Jersey; Wilmington, Delaware; three locations in Virginia at Newport News, Norfolk, and Portsmouth, and nine locations along the Gulf of Mexico at the Texas cities of Beaumont, Port Arthur, Galveston, Houston, Freeport, and Corpus Christi, and the city of New Orleans and the Port of Lake Charles, Louisiana.[674]

Coast Guard intelligence officials had raised security concerns about the deal but the Committee on Foreign Investment in the United States (an interagency group chaired by the Secretary of the

Treasury, and including the United States Trade Representative, the Secretary of Commerce and the Secretary of State among others), approved the takeover of the national ports by the UAE state owned enterprise, DP World.[675] President Bush emphatically supported the deal.[676] Owing to concerns about Arab terrorists smuggling WMD or other unwanted cargo or people into the country, Congress balked. Senator Schumer of New York and other Senators demanded a more thorough review of the proposal as well. The press would probably have largely ignored the transaction but for the political opposition which took hold in the legislative branch. To quell growing bipartisan disapproval of the deal, DP World hired former Senator and Republican presidential candidate Bob Dole to lobby Congress. Paid to play Dole failed to convince the House Appropriations Committee to allow the UAE takeover to go through, and the committee members voted 62-2 to block the deal. Facing majority opposition in both Congress and the Senate, and overwhelming opposition by the general public, DP World judiciously decided to end the takeover bid on March 9, 2006.[677]

I must note that, true to form, media outlets understated the number of ports involved in the deal. It was widely reported throughout the months long controversy over the agreement that only six ports were involved, thus understating the magnitude of whatever threat may have existed.[678] Both the New York Times and the Washington Post continued to report that only six ports were involved right up to the date that DP World pulled out of the deal.[679] The reason for the omission appears to have been that the media had relied on a one page fact sheet handed out by the Department of Homeland Security which contained the error.[680]

Even more disconcerting than the well publicized buyouts of big Americans companies and real estate holdings by foreigners is the rapidly escalating percentage share of ownership of U.S. based companies that foreign states and companies hold. In 2005, foreign interests owned 13.9% of all companies operating in the United States! That was double the percentage held by foreign powers in 1996. In 1971, foreign ownership of companies located in America was only 1.3 percent.[681] But things are worse now and soon to be much worse. A 2011 study found that foreign ownership of companies in America was estimated to be 18 percent in 2007, 22 percent in 2010, and projected to be 51 percent by 2033! The same study also found that as of 2011, foreigners already owned $8 trillion more worth of American businesses than all Americans combined owned in foreign businesses located anywhere in the world.[682]

It is ridiculous to maintain that the takeover of American businesses, intellectual property and real estate by foreign interests has had the net effect of increasing employment, wages or the general welfare of the majority of citizens of the United States. As economist Ian Fletcher points out in his book, *Free Trade Doesn't Work: What Should Replace It and Why*, the U.S. is no longer creating any new jobs, (net of jobs lost to foreign competition), in manufacturing or service industries that are subject to import competition. It is a complete myth that the United States is transitioning to higher tech jobs and away from low skilled jobs. There are no new net "jobs of tomorrow" to use President Obama's phrase being created in America. The official government statistics on trade prove it. Net new jobs are only being created for service workers like bartenders, hotel clerks, dishwashers, and parking lot attendants.[683] The problem is not just that American companies and their trade secrets are being snatched up by foreign protectionist powers like China, Japan, South Korea and Germany: American firms are shipping good jobs overseas with greater success than they have in exporting their products. For instance, IBM now employs more people in India than in America.[684] A survey of executives who are alumni of the Harvard Business School released in September of 2014 found that fifty percent of the respondents favored outsourcing jobs over hiring employees. Forty percent of the executives favored hiring part time help instead of full time workers. Statistics like that would be impossible were it not for our "whorrible" politicians who grease the wheels of the Wall Street steamroller of greed that is destroying America's future

The result of so much American made technology being snapped up by protected foreign competition - via outright purchase of American businesses and also via technology sharing requirements imposed on American firms that outsource jobs and production - is that future innovations, natural resources, land, and profit flows are lost forever. Americans end up owning less, getting paid less and owing more because of large trade deficits and the related problem of outsourcing.[685] It won't be long before foreigners own a majority of the businesses operating in our country. Undoubtedly, it will be too late to free ourselves from foreign domination once the foreigners are running our media and providing most of the campaign contributions to our two faced politicians. It's almost too late to take back our country now, but we've got to try.

President Trump has clearly resolved to try and reverse America's giant trade deficits. But Trump talks like he is going to give corporate polluters carte blanc to foul America's air and water like they used to in the 1960's before the passage of Clean Air and Water Acts and the creation of the Environmental Protection Agency in 1970. American corporations left the U.S. in order to evade absolutely essentially pollution control laws, vital workplace safety regulations, child labor laws, and workers rights in general. Now that the union movement has been largely eliminated and Democratic politicians like Hillary Clinton are owned by the corporate elite, *the money power,* which *Donald Trump is part and parcel of*, may finally do something to shore up the American economy. But *the money power* is no more concerned about the health, safety and financial security of working Americans than it ever was. Republican politicians and think tanks have been zealous supporters of free trade for over half a century. So have the Democrats. It is highly unlikely that either Republicans, (including Trump), or Democrats will bring back the millions of jobs that have been lost.

In fact, the myths of free trade are still being spouted by Trump, the Republicans, and the Democrats. They are only interested in getting other countries to stop using protectionist methods such as currency manipulation. Both political parties continue to sell the idea that if only free trade can be made "fair," the supposed "win -win" equation of comparative advantage theory still holds true. As discussed extensively in Chapter 5, and elsewhere of this book, *free trade theory is invalid and illogical.*

The argument that giant trade deficits *create more net jobs* is so pathetically weak that free traders always fall back to the defense that *things are cheaper* and that makes the loss of so many good jobs and so much tax revenue acceptable. This second argument proves to be just as illusory, circular, and inapposite with factual reality as the ones Griswold made about trade deficits producing domestic growth. Ian Fletcher points out that there is no data that proves that the savings to consumers from buying imports is greater than the losses resulting from not making goods domestically.[686] Furthermore, there is also no theoretical guarantee that the savings to consumers from buying imports is greater than the wages lost by not making goods domestically.[687] In truth, prices may not fall at all, and often don't when American firms migrate overseas.

Think about it. When American firms move their production overseas they are looking to increase their profit. If they give their cost savings back to the consumer in the form of lower prices their sales may not expand enough to justify the give back. This is particularly true when an entire industry migrates overseas and that is what generally happens because each firm in the industry is forced to lower their costs just to stay in business. So the prices stay put, industry sales stay about even, and the company management makes more money. If the public realized the gain from lower labor costs how would the companies that move overseas pay the enormous cost of closing old factories, firing all their workers, and rebuilding new factories overseas? When you go to the store to buy a stereo, a TV, home or office furniture, office equipment, a car, an iPhone, or anything else are you seeing what seems like a low price or does it seem more expensive than it ought to be considering that it was made by dollar an hour wage slaves? You can't blame the unions or workers for the high prices we pay today because the unions have nearly been destroyed and wages have been declining as a share of the national income for decades.

Another cost consumers must pay because of trade deficits may be deferred but it can't be eliminated. That is the cost of currency devaluation. As more and more dollars circulate in foreign hands because of trade deficits the natural tendency is for the value of the dollar to decline. When it happens devaluation results in higher prices for foreign goods, higher prices for domestic goods made with foreign raw materials and other foreign inputs, and much greater expenses for foreign travel.[688]

In the long run, of course, there is no doubt that our chronically gigantic trade deficits will result in catastrophe. America cannot keep selling treasury notes and selling off its businesses and real estate forever to pay for trade deficits that total well over half a trillion dollars each year.[689] America has already suffered a grievous loss to its production ecosystem.[690] Its manufacturing sector continues to decline.[691] Good jobs are harder and harder to find.[692] America is the world's largest debtor nation.[693] As of January 1, 2015 the U.S. had the lowest participation rate of men in the economy, (68.7 percent), since records began to be kept.[694] Millions of American men and women have given up hope of ever getting married and having children because they simply cannot afford them.[695] Each year less of America is owned by Americans and that process won't be reversed unless free trade is stopped.

Obama unsuccessfully sought to increase exports.[696] There is no reason to believe that exports will increase to any appreciable extent no matter what Democrats or their Republican antagonists do. Obama's *big idea* was the creation of a "National Network for Manufacturing Innovation," (NNMI), i.e. technology hubs.[697] That idea is laughable while free trade is national policy: If it remains cheaper to employ Chinese workers then no matter what new technology is created with government subsidies the Chinese will soon get it when new plants that use the new technology are constructed overseas by domestic firms. Remember, *the Chinese government gets the complete plans and all the technology used in every new plant constructed in China.*[698] The use of subsidies to stimulate the development of manufacturing and technology was part of the

American System beginning with President Washington, but obviously if the new technology brought about by NNMI is allowed to slip into foreign hands, *and it will be*, it will hasten America's decline at the taxpayers expense .

Our largest trading partners are not stupid enough to permit massive trade deficits. They pretend to play the free trade game, but use protectionism to make our jobs and our technology their jobs and their technology.[699] The figures are appalling. In 2012, America had a trade deficit of $315 billion with China, $116 billion with the European Union, $76.4 billion with Japan, $61.6 billion with Mexico, $31.4 billion with Canada, and $16.6 billion with South Korea. Our net trade deficit with all countries in 2012 was $730.6 billion.[700]

Economists who say that getting rid of our huge trade deficits will only produce a couple million jobs are lying through their teeth. Economists who say that automation has arrived and that's why manufacturing has dropped to only about ten percent of the GDP are lying too. They have no data to back them up. The facts are clearly inapposite. For instance, between January 1, 2001 and the end of 2010 the United States lost 56,190 factories. We continue to lose an average of over fifteen factories every day.[701]

We have obviously lost factories because production has been moved overseas. We have in fact lost whole industries to free trade. For example, outsourcing not automation was responsible for the loss of our textile factories; In fact, automation has helped restore some good jobs to Americans in that industry according to an article published in 2013 in the New York Times.[702] In 2011, 97.8 percent of our imports from China were for manufactured goods. Virtually all of those manufactured goods were made with cheap Chinese labor and were of a type formerly manufactured, (or formerly manufactured in greater amounts), in the United States.[703] Trade deficits caused by outsourcing and imports from foreign businesses have transformed America from an economic powerhouse with low unemployment and good jobs to a deeply indebted nation with fewer good jobs and an exploding poverty rate.[704] After years of intellectually and morally bankrupt leadership by the Republicans and Democrats we are in deep trouble.

I remember predicting a terrible outcome from free trade when I was in college in 1975. The citizens of what was once the world's largest creditor nation were being forced into competition with overseas low wage workers. It was a competition they could never win. I knew that the pain that began on the factory floor would spread to the middle class. I knew that decent jobs would become hard to come by. The money power and their politicians knew it as well. They made suckers out of the public using their total control over the media to create the illusion of democratic debate when there was little to no meaningful debate taking place.[705] Their propaganda machine is still in operation. The same lies are being told. Thankfully, because of the work of a few good people in the economics field, the theoretical basis of free trade's destructive effect on our country has now been made clear to more Americans. Now that distinguished and authoritative academicians of the highest intellectual and moral caliber have rejected the idea that free trade always works, the public's abiding dislike for free trade can no longer be dismissed as ignorance.

Can you continue to tolerate the phony baloney philosophy of the free trader Republicans and Democrats? People want good jobs, not to live off welfare. Democrats generally claim that there are always gains from free trade and that all we have to do is tax the rich and redistribute the wealth to the losers from trade.[706] That's nonsense because as we have seen, the theory behind free trade is deductively invalid and proven by experience and scientific examination to be false.

In addition, transfer payments will not reduce our trade deficits by one cent. Such payments would probably increase our economy destroying trade deficits because the recipients of the transfer payments would be able to buy more imports. The idea of using transfer payments to make up for a lack of good jobs is un-American and unworkable. We must restore American prosperity by restoring the *American Way* that Washington, Lincoln and other great Presidents defined and followed.

The Republicans told us the big lie for decades that more tax cuts for the rich combined with free trade would bring growth. *Where are the jobs*? In China mostly, that's where. On December 1, 2013, the Chinese launched a rocket carrying a lunar rover to the moon.[707] Our own space program is in tatters thanks to trade with China.[708] Until Trump came along, we got to choose between promises of more free trade,"trickle down," and "voodoo economics" from Republicans or more free trade, higher taxes and new social programs galore to pay for the mounting armies of free trade impoverished people from the Democrats. That was not a choice worth having was it?

Now we have President Trump selling the same snake oil nonsense that giant tax cuts for the rich will keep jobs in America and even bring them back from overseas. Admittedly, Trump may accomplish some good *using tariffs*, but the price we will have to pay in the form of increased pollution, unchecked climate change, mounting federal debt, lowered opportunity for education, loss of worker rights, increasing intolerance, loss of privacy rights, and other costs too numerous to mention here makes re-electing Trump an unacceptable option.

For the morally upright, intelligent and fully informed American, neither the Democratic Party nor Republican Party is acceptable as a first choice when we vote. We want a new political party to emerge which has as its central objective the elimination of trade deficits, the elimination of our national debt, the restoration of the middle class, the maintenance of American prosperity and security, the protection of the environment and public health, the continued extension of educational opportunity to the poor and the protection of social security from privatization schemes. The wolves have entered the hen house, and we must evict them in 2020.

Those of us who are like minded must work together to repair our trading system and our government. Part II of this book contains a plan for us to do just that. The damage done by our trade deficits is discussed further in the next chapter, which explains how our nearly $20 trillion national debt came into being.

10

How the Republicans and Democrats Made America the World's Largest Debtor Nation: The Twenty Trillion Dollar National Debt

One of the things important about history is to remember the true history.

- George W. Bush, Washington, D.C., June 6, 2008

My "pan plays" down an unprecedented amount of our national debt.

- George W. Bush, speech regarding the budget, Feb. 27, 2001

As we peer into society's future, we -- you and I, and our government -- must avoid the impulse to live only for today, plundering, for our own ease and convenience, the precious resources of tomorrow. We cannot mortgage the material assets of our grandchildren without risking the loss also of their political and spiritual heritage. We want democracy to survive for all generations to come, not to become the insolvent phantom of tomorrow.

- Dwight D. Eisenhower, Farewell Address, January 17, 1961

In case you are wondering, Bush actually did say "pan plays" as quoted above, but that's discussed later in this chapter so let's move on. The national debt was $17, 249, 692, 000,000.00 when I began to write this sentence. The debt increased by about five million dollars by the time this next sentence was finished![709] This chapter ends with a report of how much the national debt increased while the chapter was being written - and that's before any editing was done.

Figure 10.1 shows how the debt has grown from a relatively small amount *after* World War II to mind boggling size today. As shown in Figure 10.1, the national debt began to slowly inch up after 1968, when Richard Nixon was elected. After 1980, when Ronald Reagan became President, the debt curve increases rapidly, giving the appearance of exponential growth.

Of course part of the national debt is caused by our trade deficits which have continued in an unbroken chain since 1976. As of January 1, 2015, our cumulative trade deficit with all other countries stood at about $13 trillion.[710] At the start of 2014, foreign governments and investors owned about $5.6 trillion of America's national debt, which stood at about $17.2 trillion.[711] That was roughly thirty-two percent of the total U.S. national debt at the time. Thus, our trade deficits were the outright cause of about one third of our national debt. At the end of 2013, China owned $1.3 trillion of our debt, followed by Japan at $1.2 trillion. Other Asian countries owned about $1 trillion in total. European countries owned roughly $1 trillion as well. Much of the rest was owned by oil exporting nations.[712]

From this data it appears that at the start of 2014, other countries held well less than half of their trade surpluses with the U.S. in treasury notes. Therefore, the lion's share of the dollars other countries obtain from their surplus exports to the U.S. are used to buy ownership in America corporations, real estate, and other assets such as financial assets other than government bonds.[713]

Figure 10.1

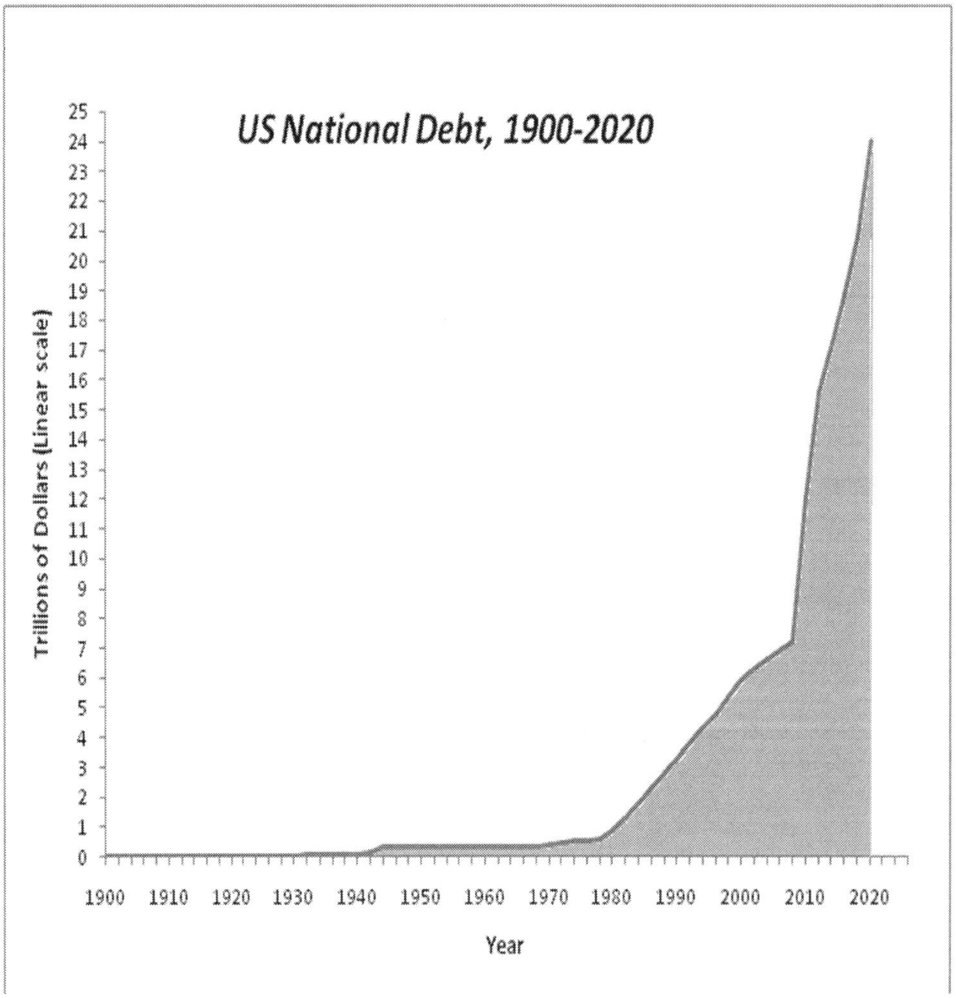

Graph adaped from informational chart found at Futuretimeline.net and based on data collected by the US Department of Commerce and the Congressional Budget Office.

It might seem that because one third of our national debt is directly caused by trade deficits, about two thirds of our national debt is caused by an imbalance between tax revenues and government spending. But is that really all there is to it? The answer is a resounding no! Trade deficits are indirectly responsible for more of our national debt in two ways: First, trade deficits cause increased government expenditures to pay for the social costs of declining wages. Second, the lower wages caused by free trade mean lower tax revenues. Over the long run free trade eliminates good jobs and important industries, reduces innovation, and transfers capital and technology from our economy to foreign economies. Free trade means that good jobs are replaced by lower paying service jobs, or no jobs at all. Thus, free trade is a significant driver of increased government spending to pay for unemployment benefits, food stamps, public aid, and a host of other social costs.[714]

Jobs lost to free trade represent the loss of taxable income to the states as well.; As explained in the preceding chapter, the Economic Strategy Institute measured the loss to our GDP from free trade to be as much as twenty percent for the period from 1995 to 2005.[715] We had thirty-one other trade deficit years between 1971 through the end of 2015 that were not included in the ESI estimate. We can guestimate that the total loss to our GDP might average as much as twenty percent for each of the ten year periods not included in the ESI estimate, so as of 2014, our GDP might well have been significantly more than twice as large as it was but for our trade deficits. Don't forget too that we used to run *trade surpluses* every year when the *American System* of industrial policy was in use, but the ESI model only looked at the *cost of trade deficits*. The ESI model failed to measure the effect of the lost *trade surpluses*. This means that the total cost of free trade may have reduced our GDP to much less than half of what it would have been on an annual basis by the end of 2014. We would most likely not have any national debt at all today - even with the Reagan-Bush tax cuts - but for free trade!

It's all true! Without free trade the civilian participation rate would be much higher and the unemployment rate would be much lower. It is highly unlikely that cities like Detroit and Camden would be bankrupt, and America would not have a rust belt. The financial crisis of 2008 would never have occurred and undoubtedly, America would not have crumbling infrastructure and a disappearing middle class. This chapter examines how free trade and other factors caused our national debt to rise

A picture is sometimes *worth a thousand words*, and If you look at Figure 10.1, you can see the accusing finger of history points directly at *Ronald Reagan* as the chief culprit in the rise of our national debt. The national debt starts its rapid escalation during Reagan's two terms as President. Republicans used to stand for balanced budgets and they also used to believe in the *American System* of industrial policy. By lowering taxes without cutting spending, (and permitting unilateral free trade), President Reagan created a time paradox fit for *Dr. Who* to solve. If you ever watched the British Sci fi TV show *Dr Who*, you know what can happen from a time paradox: The universe gets destroyed unless the paradox is resolved. *Dr. Who*, (an extraterrestrial time traveler), has always managed to avoid time paradoxes, but Ronald Reagan created a financial time paradox meant to eventually destroy the New Deal programs he despised, in particular, Social Security. To do it, Reagan used all the acting skills his career in

Hollywood gave him.

Reagan's role in creating our national debt monster was foundational. During his tenure as President he passed high spending budgets that tripled the size of the national debt but he also cut the highest marginal federal income tax rate from seventy percent to twenty-eight percent.[716] Peacetime Republican presidents prior to Reagan had always sought to lower the national debt and balance budgets if possible. Reagan's increases in federal spending were largely to pay for a military buildup. The buildup included plans for an expensive space based defense from nuclear missile attack formally known as the Strategic Defense Initiative but better known by its nickname "Star Wars." Another feature was Reagan's never achieved plan to increase the size of the Navy to 600 ships. Another was the production of the MX mobile nuclear missile. By the time he left office Reagan had increased the military budget by a whopping forty three percent more than it had been raised at the height of the Vietnam War.[717]

Reagan took office after years of stagflation under President's Nixon, Ford and Carter.[718] If it were not for the syphoning affect that *growing trade deficits* had *before, during and after Reagan's term*, his high deficit spending might have boosted the economy permanently; Deficit spending during, prior to, and after WWII helped to end the Great Depression and ignite a period of economic prosperity after the war ended.[719] Reagan's unprecedented peace time budget deficits had to produce some positive economic results - at least over the short term - and they did. Though unemployment remained high during Reagan's years in office, it eventually fell to 5.5 percent in his final year as President.[720]

Reagan's budget deficits and tax cuts had a purpose in addition to stimulating the economy and improving military capabilities; Reagan made this other purpose clear when he answered criticism that had been leveled at him for seeking large tax cuts before equally large spending cuts could be obtained. He spoke to the nation in a televised address on February 5, 1981:

> Over the past decades we've talked of curtailing government spending so that we can then lower the tax burden. Sometimes we've even taken a run at doing that. But there were always those who told us that taxes couldn't be cut until spending was reduced. Well, you know, we can lecture our children about extravagance until we run out of voice and breath. Or we can cure their extravagance by simply reducing their allowance.[721]

Reagan's strategy of cutting taxes to force spending cuts came to be known as "Starve the Beast." The phrase caught on after a 1985 Wall Street Journal article by Paul Blustein quoted an unnamed administration official who used it.[722]

Though President Reagan wanted to starve the spending beast, he also wanted to *shift the tax burden from the rich to the poor and middle class*. Reagan got other *federal taxes raised eleven times, in order to offset his large tax cut to the very rich*. Here is a partial list of the tax hike laws Reagan ushered through Congress, which *increased tax revenues by about half the amount the Reagan tax cut gave to the rich*: the Tax Equity and Fiscal Responsibility Act of 1982, the Highway Revenue Act of 1982, the Social Security Amendments of 1983, the Railroad Retirement Revenue Act of 1983, the Deficit Reduction Act of 1984, the Consolidated Omnibus Budget Reconciliation Act of 1985, the Omnibus Budget Reconciliation Act of 1986, the

Superfund Amendments and Reauthorization Act of 1986, and the Omnibus Budget Reconciliation Act of 1987.[723] The net effect of Reagan's tax hikes was of course regressive, meaning that the poor paid a higher percentage of their income for those taxes than did the rich.[724]

I respect Reagan's honesty in sharing with the public his starve the beast strategy to rein in spending. But I find fault with Reagan for lying to the American people when he asked for an increase in the social security tax. I have to give credit to Professor Emeritus Dr. Allen W. Smith, PhD formerly of the Eastern Illinois University Economics Department for writing a book on the subject. Smith is the author of *Ronald Reagan and the Great Social Security Heist*: *How Reagan Gave Birth to The Looting of Social Security.*[725] Smith's writing caused me to remember back to 1983, when I listened to Reagan and initially felt grateful to him for making the social security trust fund solvent for my generation. I quickly realized back at the time that it was all a lie. Reagan *could not dupe me because of my background in economics and political science*, but *he did succeed in duping millions of Americans who believed his high sounding rhetoric*. Let's hear from Professor Smith on the subject:

> It is so ironic that many people, today, still believe that Ronald Reagan came galloping up on a great white horse to sound the alarm that Social Security was in deep financial trouble. He then allegedly figured out a solution to the problem and rammed his legislative proposal through Congress in a three-month period. On April 20, 1983, the signing ceremony for the new legislation took place with great fanfare. Below are some of Reagan's remarks at the signing ceremony.
>
> 'This bill demonstrates for all time our nation's ironclad commitment to social security. It assures the elderly that America will always keep the promises made in troubled times a half a century ago. It assures those who are still working that they, too, have a pact with the future. From this day forward, they have our pledge that they will get their fair share of benefits when they retire…'
>
> 'Today, all of us can look each other square in the eye and say, "We kept our promises." We promised that we would protect the financial integrity of social security. We have. We promised that we would protect beneficiaries against any loss in current benefits. We have. And we promised to attend to the needs of those still working, not only those Americans nearing retirement but young people just entering the labor force. And we've done that, too…'[726]

But Reagan was telling bald faced lies. Here is more from Smith:

> President Reagan and his advisors knew, from the very beginning, that the government would soon face a severe cash shortage. Budget Director, David Stockman, had deliberately rigged the computer at the Office of Management and Budget to generate bogus revenue forecasts in an effort to convince Congress to enact Reagan's unaffordable proposed tax cuts. When Stockman first fed the data from Reagan's economic proposals into the computer, he was shocked. The computer forecast that, if Reagan's proposals were enacted into law, massive budget deficits would loom ahead for as far as the eye could see.

> Reagan needed a new source of revenue to replace the revenue lost as a result of his unaffordable income tax cuts. He wasn't about to rescind any of his income-tax cuts, but he had another idea. What about raising the payroll tax, and then channeling the new revenue to the general fund, from where it could be spent for other purposes? An increase in Social Security taxes would be easier to enact than a hike in income tax rates, and it would leave his income tax cuts undisturbed. Reagan's first step in implementing his strategy was to write to Congressional leaders. His first letter, dated May 21, 1981 included the following:
>
> As you know, the Social Security System is teetering on the edge of bankruptcy…in the decades ahead its unfunded obligations could run well into the trillions. Unless we in government are willing to act, a sword of Damocles will soon hang over the welfare of millions of our citizens.[727]

With that evidence we can conclude that at least some of the Congressional leaders may have been unaware that Reagan planned to use the incoming social security tax receipts as general revenue to help lessen the increase in the national debt caused by his tax cut for the rich. Reagan wrote another letter adduced by Professor Smith to show that Reagan was lying to Congress, (or providing cover to them), as well lying to the American people. In that letter, dated July 18, 1981, Reagan wrote this to Congressional leaders:

> The highest priority of my Administration is restoring the integrity of the Social Security System. Those 35 million Americans who depend on Social Security expect and are entitled to prompt bipartisan action to resolve the current financial problem.[728]

As a result of Reagan's appeals, Congress felt obliged to insure the safety of social security. Reagan's social security tax hike was passed. Passage of the bill was never in doubt. Social Security has long been known as the third rail of politics. That is why efforts to get rid of social security have always come in the form of proposals to "privatize" it. But had Reagan really intended to rescue social security from a status "teetering on the edge of bankruptcy?" Had he instead intended to create a paradox that could be used to destroy social security when the national debt grew to untamable dimensions? Reagan's attitude toward social programs, including social security, was no secret. Smith summarized them this way:

> Reagan had never been a friend of Social Security. He was a hardliner when it came to all government social programs. He called unemployment insurance 'a prepaid vacation plan for freeloaders.' He said the progressive income tax was 'a brainchild of Karl Marx.' And, he called welfare recipients 'a faceless mass waiting for handouts.' Reagan referred to Social Security as a 'welfare program' and, during the 1976 Republican Presidential Primary, Reagan proposed making Social Security voluntary, which would have essentially destroyed the program... He had always wanted the program eliminated, or at least privatized.[729]

Sure enough, Reagan intended all along to starve the social security beast and use the revenues generated by the new social security tax to help pay the cost of his tax cut for the rich:

> The public was led to believe that the surplus money would be saved and invested

> in marketable U.S. Treasury Bonds, which could later be resold to raise cash with which to pay benefits to the boomers. But that didn't happen. The money was all deposited directly into the general fund and used for non-Social Security purposes. Reagan spent every dime of the surplus Social Security revenue, which came in during his presidency, on general government operations. His successor, George H.W. Bush, used the surplus money as a giant slush fund, and both Bill Clinton and George W. Bush looted and spent all of the Social Security surplus revenue that flowed in during their presidencies. So we can't blame the whole problem on Reagan. Reagan was the one who figured out a way to use Social Security money as general revenue, and his successors just followed his example.[730]

These days of course, billionaire Warren Buffet admits he pays a lower effective tax rate than his secretary. President Trump refused to release his tax returns before his election, but the last time his returns were released publicly they showed he paid no income tax at all.[731] The Congressional Research Service reported in 2012 that about a quarter of all millionaires pay lower taxes, (percentage wise), than people in the middle class.[732] Obviously, the rich have the money to pay tax experts to manipulate their assets and incomes in order to avoid taxes.

Today the spread between the rich and the middle class is greater than at any time in the past.[733] Income inequality in America has been rising since the seventies and it is higher than at any time since 1928, well before the start of the Great Depression.[734] Reagan's statements that he needed to raise taxes for social security to protect it for the future generations were a fraud upon the American people. His real purpose was to raise taxes on the poor while he cut them on the rich. Reagan's long term goal was to starve social security of funds and raise the national debt in order that the social security program would be destroyed. Reagan's budgets nearly tripled the national debt, raising it to $2.8 trillion from $998 billion.[735] We will explore the cumulative effect of Reagan's tax cut on the national debt since he left office later in this chapter, after we review what effects subsequent Presidents have had on the size of the national debt. Note that for each President, the amounts they borrowed from social security revenues to use as general revenue are added to their yearly budget deficits in order to correctly measure how much they added to the national debt.

Reagan's successor, President George H. W. Bush, (Bush I) had one term in office. Poor economic conditions under his administration led to Clinton's famous campaign slogan "It's the Economy Stupid."[736] Bush I was run out of office because the economy was back in recession.[737] Reagan's so called "supply side economics," which was largely "demand side economics" because of his gigantic budget deficits, had failed. The so called Reagan recovery hyped by the media monopoly had been a mirage. It vaporized once the funds Reagan borrowed, (stole is a better word), from social security had been spent on an increased military budget. Adding to Bush's defeat was his famous broken promise of "Read My Lips: No New Taxes." Bush made the pledge at the 1988 Republican National Convention and it was a popular sound byte that was often repeated in the broadcast and print media. Here is what Bush said in his acceptance speech for the nomination:

> And I'm the one who will not raise taxes. My opponent now says he'll raise them

> as a last resort, or a third resort. But when a politician talks like that, you know that's one resort he'll be checking into. My opponent won't rule out raising taxes. But I will. And the Congress will push me to raise taxes and I'll say no. And they'll push, and I'll say no, and they'll push again, and I'll say, to them, '**Read my lips: no new taxes**.' [emphasis added][738]

Bush was probably lying when he made his promise of no new taxes. I conclude that because Bush is the man who invented the phrase "voodoo economics" to describe Ronald Reagan's economic policy proposals when Bush was campaigning against Reagan in 1980 for the Republican presidential nomination. Years later, Bush denied inventing or even using the words "voodoo economics" to describe Reagan's economic proposals. I think Bush was lying then too, because Bush was caught on tape when he stated that Reagan's plans amounted to "voodoo economics."[739]

Bush probably never actually believed that Ronald Reagan had brought lasting prosperity to the economy as Republicans then and long after claimed. Did Bush really have no idea that free trade was sapping America's economy of its jobs and competitive edge? Reagan's *cut taxes but spend more debt machine*, though still in operation while Bush was in office, was no match for the free trade produced rust belt decline that the media and government tried to ignore and explain away as the price of progress. The economy was declining and mandatory social spending was increasing. That is what happens when you impoverish your working class, hollow out your middle class, and send your technology and factories overseas. You pay increased social costs.

The rich had a tax cut so they were profiting from both much lower taxes *and* wage annihilating free trade. Other fiscal pressures Bush Sr. faced paled in comparison with the lack of balance between Reagan's tax cut and his spending on military programs like "Star Wars." For instance, the cost of the Savings and Loan Crisis, (another example of bad Republocrat government), amounted to about $525 billion by 1993, the year Bush left office.[740] Operation Desert Storm, the war to liberate Kuwait, cost approximately $61 billion, but coalition member states reimbursed the United States $54 billion of that amount.[741] The tax revenue resulting from the Omnibus Budget Reconciliation Act of 1990, (the legislation that broke Bush's no new tax promise), offset Bush's deficit spending by about $82 billion.[742] That was nowhere near enough to get the tax "beast" off the starvation diet that Reagan had put it on. In his one term, Bush I added $1.554 trillion to the national debt, a whopping increase of fifty four percent.[743]

Now it's time to look at President Bill Clinton's claim that he produced budget surpluses in his second term. As shown in Figure 10.2, Clinton's claim is, *in a limited sense*, correct. Figure 10.2 shows that Clinton produced budget surpluses in 1998, 1999, 2000 and 2001. Clinton is entitled to count 2001, the first year of Bush's first term, (budget wise), because Bush could not affect changes to the budget after he took office until the start of a new fiscal year.[744] Clinton has claimed that he produced a budget surplus of $600 billion.[745] According to figures supplied by the Congressional Budget Office, Clinton had a total surplus between 1998 and 2001 of about $560 billion.[746] But Clinton had budget deficits between 1994 and 1997, so he cannot claim an actual cumulative budget surplus for all his years in office of more than about $69 billion.[747] However, Clinton and all other presidents since Reagan *failed to hold Social Security receipts in trust and spent all the money that should have been set aside for future retirees*. Clinton's budget surplus claim is based on the bald-faced lie that the intergovernmental promissory notes that the treasury gave the social security administration to pay for Clinton's spending of social security tax receipts was the same as cash in the bank. Subtracting the revenue from the social security tax that Clinton spent, and then counted again in his budget surpluses, *turns his claimed $600 billion surplus into a cumulative budget deficit*. Clinton's cumulative addition to the national debt from all his years in office actually totals $1.396 trillion, a thirty-two percent increase![748]

Figure 10.2

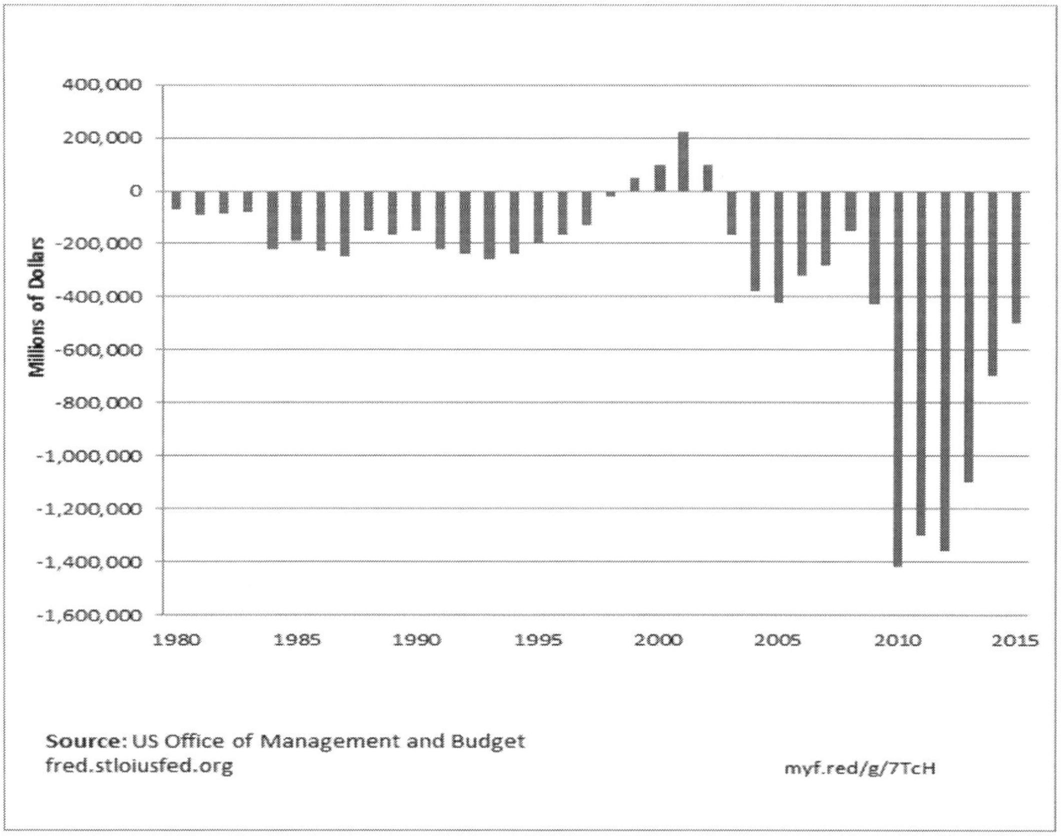

Bill Clinton can be given some credit nevertheless for moving in the right direction in part. He cut out many unnecessary military expenditures and Clinton also made a laudable effort to reduce unhealthy dependency on government handouts with his workfare program.[749] Also, the stock market was in a bull market during Clinton's two terms in office in part because Clinton was trying to balance government spending with income.[750] But Clinton ignored advice from financial experts to expand the federal regulations governing Wall Street to deal with derivatives trading.[751] The Clinton administration was *undoubtedly aware of the danger from unregulated derivatives trading*; The dangerous financial bubble brought about by securitization of high risk mortgages and the sale of junk mortgage based derivatives was adding to the Wall Street and housing booms. When major losses were incurred by Orange County and other large investors in 1994 - because of bad investments in derivatives - Congress responded with a major investigation. Several bills were introduced to regulate the derivatives market.[752] The reform effort went nowhere because of Clinton; Clinton had close ties and financial backing from Wall Street. The derivatives financial bubble was probably seen by Clinton as a golden goose that should be left alone. Clinton *obeyed his money power masters and he opposed reform legislation to stop Wall Street's wild and reckless gambling on derivatives*; All efforts in Congress to enact needed regulatory reform of derivatives trading ceased by the end of 1994.[753]

Clinton can be seen, (like Reagan), as helping to create a temporary mirage of prosperity which lacked substance and permanence.[754] Clinton should have focused on America's growing trade deficits, but he was effectively blind to the problems caused by free trade because of his neoliberal education, his liberal globalist perspective and perhaps - because of the cold hard cash and support his campaign was getting from free trade loving Wall Street.[755] Half of the ten year period, (1995-2000), included in the ESI Econometric Model of GDP losses from free trade, (discussed in this and the last chapter), took place while Clinton was president.[756] It is therefore reasonable to conclude that the gross domestic product during Clinton's years in office would have grown significantly larger if only Clinton had come up with a good workable plan to eliminate our trade deficits gradually. Instead, Clinton guided the North American Free Trade Agreement to passage, handing out an estimated $50 billion in pork to legislators to buy their votes for the bill.[757] After it became law, NAFTA turned America's $1.7 billion trade surplus with Mexico into a $61.4 billion trade deficit by 2012, and NAFTA has caused an estimated net loss of over one million American jobs.[758]

After Clinton came President George W. Bush. Al Gore won the popular vote 50,999,897 to 50,456,002,[759] but the Republican dominated Supreme Court of the United States overturned a Florida Supreme Court ruling which had ordered an election recount.[760] Bush ended up winning in Florida by an unbelievably thin margin of 537 votes.[761] When and if our third party emerges to take on the free traders, our party must fight tooth and nail to insure that every bona fide vote counts and every fraudulent vote is thrown out! We must modernize and make uniform the procedures for recounts from state to state. The law should favor recounts where *election fraud* or *faulty vote counting methods* may have changed the election outcome, but every effort must be made to get the correct vote count the first time around.

This chapter starts off with a couple *"Bushisms."* Bushisms are statements made by George W, Bush, (Bush II) that are so poorly worded or mispronounced, that they make people laugh.[762] The first Bushism quoted was made during an interview when Bush was trying to justify the war in Iraq; The interview took place in 2008, long after the truth had come out about the lack of pre-war evidence that Iraq possessed WMD, supported al qaeda, or had anything whatsoever to do with 9/11.[763] Bush made the second quoted comment during an address to Congress about his budget plan for the year 2002, in which he called for a huge income tax cut.[764] Bush had meant to say "My plan pays down our national debt..." The inanity in what Bush said was not in the his laughably bungled language; It was in his laughably absurd assurances to Congress and the American people that tax revenues would rise, and spending would fall, because of the growth that Bush's proposed new tax cuts would bring to the economy.

You may believe, (not unreasonably), that the wars in Iraq and Afghanistan were the principle cause of the giant increase in the national debt during the two terms Bush II was President, but they were not. By the time Bush left office, the first Bush tax cut passed in 2001, combined with the second Bush tax cut passed in 2003, had cost the treasury $1.7 trillion in revenue.[765] The total cost for wars in Iraq and Afghanistan between 2001 and 2008 was $800 billion.[766]

A study estimating the increase in economic activity from the Bush tax cut of 2001 published by the Brookings Institution in 2002, indicated that though some growth to GDP would accrue because of the tax cut, other economic factors caused by the tax cut would cause a net shrinkage to the economy. The study found that the GDP would lose .3 percent over a ten year period because of the tax cut. The study looked at the effects of the Economic Growth and Tax Relief Reconciliation Act of 2001, which the studies authors refer to as EGTRRA:

> EGTRRA has complex effects on economic growth. Lower tax rates will raise incentives for people to work, acquire human capital, save, and invest, but EGTRRA has relatively small effects on marginal tax rates. Treasury data show that a surprisingly large share of households receive no reduction in marginal tax rates, including 72 percent of those who file tax returns and 64 percent of all filers who actually pay positive amounts of income tax. As a result, effective marginal tax rates fall by just two to three percentage points for wages, interest, dividends, and sole proprietorship income.
>
> These changes will create relatively small increases in after-tax wages. Using research estimates of the sensitivity of hours worked to after-tax wages, we estimate that by 2011, EGTRRA will induce people to work about 0.5 percent more hours than they otherwise would have. Lower taxes and incentives for education are also likely to raise the amount of education and training that workers obtain. These effects are difficult to estimate, but using a variety of published studies, we estimate that these items will be about 0.2 percent higher in 2011 due to the tax cut.
>
> EGTRRA will affect private saving by raising the after-tax rate of return, shifting the distribution of income toward higher-income households, who tend to save more, providing new retirement and education incentives, and repealing the estate tax. Our reading of the evidence from economic research suggests these changes will raise private saving by about 0.5 percent of GDP by 2011.
>
> Taken together, the increases in labor supply, education, and private saving induced by the tax cut tax incentives will raise the size of the economy by about 1 percent by 2011. But improved tax incentives are only part of the story. EGTRRA

> is a set of tax incentives financed by reductions in public saving. The full effects on economic growth include the impact of higher deficits (lower surpluses).
>
> EGTRRA will reduce government saving by about 1.6 percent of GDP through 2011. This reduction is substantially larger than the induced increase in private saving noted above. As a result, national (the sum of public and private) saving will fall. Estimates suggest that about one-third of the decline in national saving will be offset by increased capital inflows from other countries. The net effect of the rise in private saving, the decline in public saving, and the increase in capital inflows will be to reduce the amount of financing available for new investment in the United States. We find that the resulting decline in the amount of physical capital (e.g., machines, structures, etc.) is sufficiently large that, despite the results of improved tax incentives, the overall net effect of EGTRRA will be to slightly reduce GDP by about 0.3 percent after ten years.[767]

Many other assessments of the Bush tax cuts since have been negative as well. This brings to mind another comment made by President George W. Bush on January 12, 2009: *In terms of the economy, look, I inherited a recession, I am ending on a recession.*[768]

President Bush gave as his reason for the tax cuts the need to get the economy out of recession. His explanation as to why he wanted tax cuts may have been something he sincerely believed, but I doubt that's true. An article by Henry Blodget for Business Insider headlined *Bombshell: New Study Destroys Theory That Tax Cuts Spur Growth* reported that tax cuts for the rich don't work as alleged:

> Do tax cuts really spur growth? The answer appears to be "no."According to a new study by the Congressional Research Service (non-partisan), there's no evidence that tax cuts spur growth. In fact, although correlation is not causation, when you compare economic growth in periods with declining tax rates versus periods with high tax rates, there seems to be evidence that tax cuts might hurt growth.[769]

The study by the Congressional Research Service referred to by Blodget is *Taxes and the Economy: An Economic Analysis of the Top Tax Rates Since 1945*. The study was published on September 14, 2012.[770] Other studies report similar findings. Another study completed in 2012 using different methods was the subject of a New York Times Economix commentary by economists Laura Tyson and Owen Zidar. They reported this finding:

> ...there is no link between income tax cuts for the top 5 percent and subsequent job creation. (We also examined the relationship between tax cuts for the top 10 percent and subsequent job creation and found the same result.)[771]

The findings of both studies are consistent with the predictions made by the Brooking Institution that the Bush tax cuts would reduce GDP by .03 percent after ten years. Think about it. When government spends money for virtually anything it is creating an economic stimulus. Government purchases many technologically advanced products and invests billions in basic research, engineering, transportation infrastructure, military technology and a host of other things that spin off benefits for the consumer economy. Why would tax cuts for the rich do much to grow our economy? The rich buy foreign luxury cars, wear expensive foreign made clothes, take expense trips overseas, buy multimillion dollar villas all over the world and invest in foreign factories. They can afford those things without tax cuts. With tax cuts they have even more money to invest in growing overseas economies. The rich frequently consider America a bad place for investment unless they are opening up a store to sell us foreign made products. After all, we don't allow child labor or unregulated pollution, and we don't allow employers complete freedom to set wages or discriminate in hiring. Tax cuts for the rich don't appear to help our economy per se, but they do have one definite negative effect - income inequality. This comes from a working paper published in May, 2013, by the National Bureau of Economic Research:

> The top 1 percent income share has more than doubled in the United States over the last thirty years.. While other English speaking countries have also experienced sharp increases in the top 1 percent income share, many high-income countries such as Japan, France, or Germany have seen much less increase in top income shares. Hence, the explanation cannot rely solely on forces common to advanced countries, such as the impact of new technologies and globalization on the supply and demand for skills. We highlight four main factors. The first is the impact of tax policy... Top tax rates have moved in the opposite direction from top income shares. The effects of top rate cuts can operate in conjunction with other mechanisms. The second factor is indeed a richer view of the labor market...top rate cuts may lead managerial energies to be diverted to increasing their remuneration at the expense of enterprise growth and employment. The third factor is capital income. Overall, private wealth (relative to income) has followed a U-shaped path over time.... The fourth, little investigated, element is the correlation between earned income and capital income, which has substantially increased in recent decades in the United States.[772]

The dollar amount of the national debt more than doubled during the presidency of George W. Bush. Here is the breakdown on his addition to the national debt: 2009 + $1.632 trillion, 2008 + $1.017 trillion, 2007 + $501 billion, 2006 + $574 billion, 2005 + $554 billion, 2004 + $596 billion, 2003 + $555 billion, 2002 + $421 billion.[773] That's comes to a grand total of $5.849 trillion.[774] In effect, Bush borrowed the full cost of his two tax cuts and the wars in both Iraq and Afghanistan, plus another $3.349 trillion!

President Obama's first budget was prepared for fiscal year 2010 with the national debt standing at $11.910 trillion.[775] During his next five years as president, the national debt rose an estimated $5.914 trillion, to $17,824 trillion on September 30, 2014, the last day of the 2014 fiscal year.[776] Congress passed the Economic Stimulus Act (ESA) in February, 2009 with Obama's approval, and so $253 billion of debt incurred during fiscal 2009 to pay for the ESA must be added to Obama's debt total.[777] That brings the total addition to the national debt attributable to Obama as of September 30, 2014 to $6.167 trillion. By February 16, 2015, the national debt had climbed to $18.122 trillion,[778] and Obama's contribution to the national debt stood at $6.469 trillion. Obama was thus responsible for increasing the national debt by over 55 percent with over 23 months and slightly under fifty percent of the time remaining in Obama's second term as President.

Are you still unsure why spending and tax revenues have gotten so out of whack over time and made the national debt so large? It can be seen from looking at figure 10.3 that, but for the continuing effects of the Reagan and Bush tax cuts on the revenue, and the deficit spending by Reagan and Bush, there would have been a relatively small national debt by 2008. The chart in figure 10.4 shows the effect of the Reagan tax cut and deficit spending which was continued by Bush I, and then another even more steep rise in the size of the national debt under Bush II. Figure 10.4 also shows that President Clinton's deficit reduction efforts helped to slow the rise of the debt.[779]

Figure 10.3

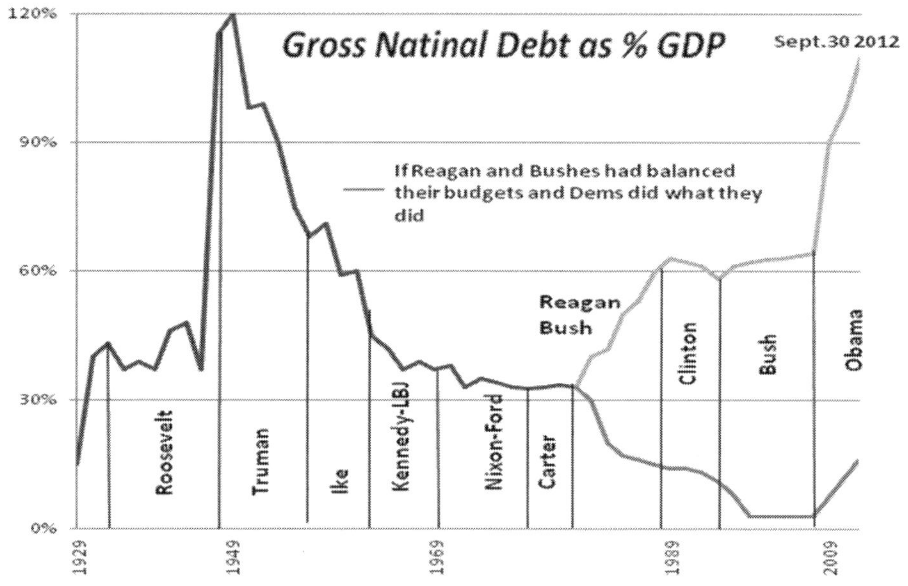

Graph adapted from Dr. Steven Stoft, Ph.D., *ZFacts* (Used With Permission) Retrieved from http://zfacts.com/

Clinton deserves a lot of credit for raising taxes moderately and cutting spending in an effort to rein in the *starve the beast* debt monster that Reagan deliberately gave birth to. Under Bush II's combination of high military spending and large tax cuts for the rich, everything Clinton managed to do to put the governments financial house in order was erased. However, since financial experts blame the Clinton administration as well as George W. Bush for the financial crisis of 2007, and since Clinton was as much a free trader as Reagan and the Bushes, there's plenty of blame to go around between the Republicans and Democrats for the mess we are in today.[780]

Figure 10.5 illustrates some of the leading causes of the national debt. The effect of Bush era tax cuts on the aggregate debt is shown to grow over time. The cost of the wars in Iraq and Afghanistan are shown to be a much smaller component of the debt than the Bush era tax cuts.

The cost of tax cuts unbalanced by spending cuts can clearly be seen to grow over time. Figure 10.5 attempts to illustrate the leading role that the Bush era income tax cuts played in increasing the public debt to its present enormity. The cost of the wars in Iraq and Afghanistan are dwarfed by the cost of Bush tax cuts.

Figure 10.4

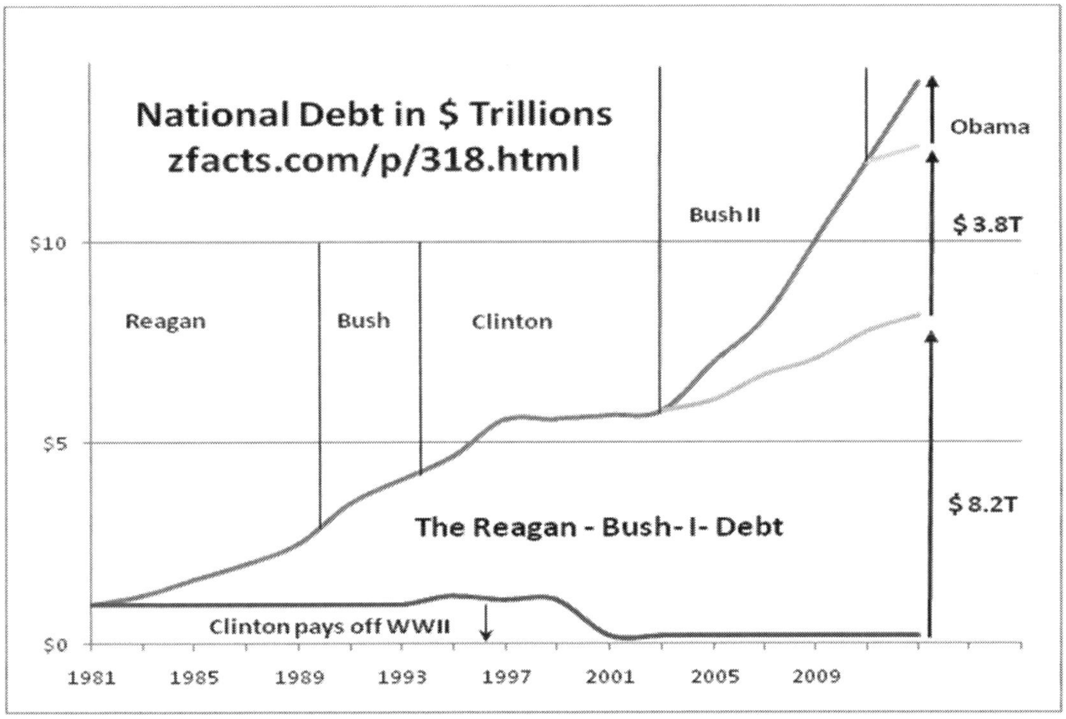

Graph adapted from Dr. Steven Stoft, Ph.D., *ZFacts* (Used With Permission) Retrieved from http://zfacts.com/p/gross-national -debt.html

Figure 10.5 fails to place a label on the gray (bottom) portion of the national debt. Roughly two thirds of the grey area in Figure 10.5 can be attributed to Reagan's huge income tax cut for the rich and his deficit spending.

During his two terms in office, Reagan succeeded in getting the highest marginal federal income tax rate reduced from 70 percent to only 28 percent.[781] Bill Clinton later got the highest marginal rate raised to 39.6 percent.[782] When Bush II got into office he got the highest marginal rate kicked back down to 35 percent.[783] Figure 10.5 blames the entire amount of the national debt caused by lowering the highest marginal income tax rate from 70 percent to 35 percent, (after Clinton's changes), on President George W. Bush. It must be pointed out that the cumulative effect of Ronald Reagan's tax cuts can only be fully and fairly measured by including the effect of the lowered marginal income rates Reagan brought about for all succeeding administrations. That would presently include all the lost revenue during the Clinton, (from 70 to 39.6 percent) and the George W. Bush and Barak Obama, (from 70 percent to 35 percent) administrations. If that was done in Figure 10.5, *the area attributable to Ronald Reagan would cover well more than half of the national debt*. That is the amount of the current national debt that Ronald Reagan is truly responsible for.

Figure 10.5

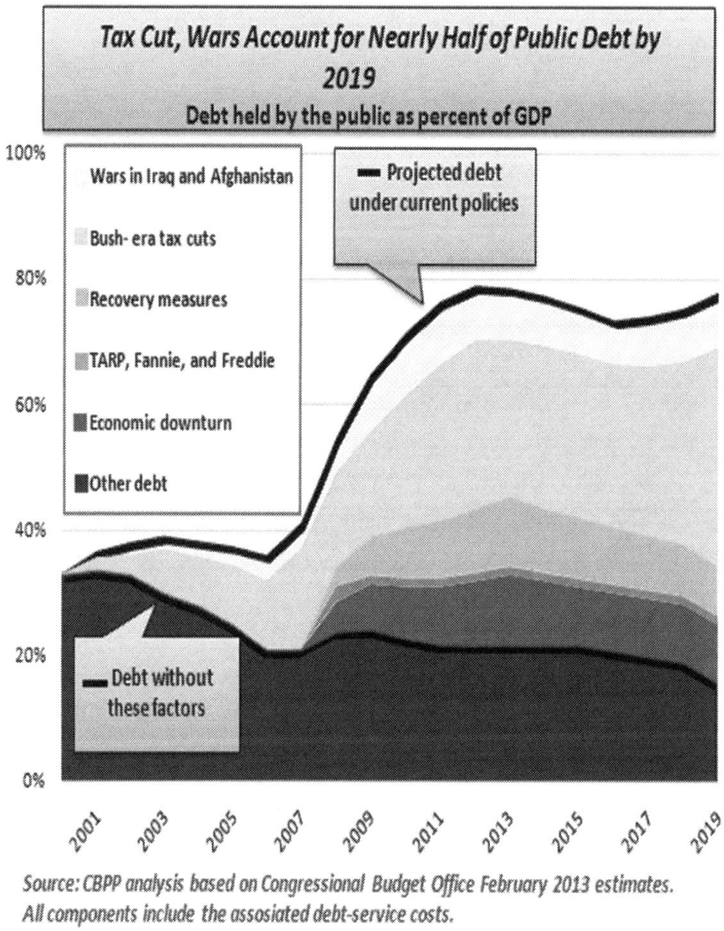

Graph adapted from data chart from the *Center On Budget Priorities*. (Used With Permission.) Retrieved from http://www.cbpp.org/blog/whats-driving-projected-debt

George H. W. Bush broke his famous read my lips pledge and he *raised taxes in the aggregate without raising or lowering the federal income tax one iota* as President. So it is clear, *Ronald Reagan should be seen as the chief culprit behind our ever growing national debt, and history will surely judge him so.*

Historically, American Presidents sought to balance the budget *but that all changed with Ronald Reagan.* Reagan wanted an end to big government and an end to the New Deal reforms like social security, that most Americans believe in.[784] Reagan pushed through a tax cut for the very rich that was guaranteed to grow the national debt.[785] He hiked taxes on social security but spent all the money taken in from social security taxes to partially defray the cost of his tax cut and his costly military build up.[786] Reagan was a handsome and charismatic man who made great sounding speeches, but *his actions were often at odds with his rhetoric.*[787] The charges made against him by his budget director, David Stockman,[788] and his later Vice President George H. W. Bush, that *his budget policies amounted to voodoo economics* were all true.[789]

Clinton deserves credit for trying to balance his budgets. Nonetheless Clinton should have imposed needed reforms on Wall Street. Additionally, Clinton *should have recognized that free trade was gutting America's production ecosystem.* Clinton should have resolving to end trade deficits and stop the loss of critical American technology to China and other foreign nations. We would not be in the mess we are in today if Clinton had done his job right. Assuming the Presidents following Clinton continued the policies that Clinton should have followed. Our GDP would be much larger today and we would have the best wages, best jobs, and best standard of living on Earth. *That is what America once enjoyed thanks to the Mount Rushmore Presidents - and that is what America has lost because of free trade and government by and for Wall Street.*

Part II of this book contains a plan for people to unite under the banner of a new political party whose central purpose is to displace the Demopublicans and bring down the free trade paradigm. In the United States, the male participation rate in the economy declined from 86 percent in 1956 to 68.7 percent in 2015.[790] Also, by 2015, only 44 percent of U.S. adults worked over thirty hours a week.[791] The middle and working classes have been in economic decline since the late sixties. America's decline has been going on for a very long time. Today we are faced with an unacceptable future. We must act decisively to end free trade once and for all, and move to a modernized version of the *American System* used by our forefathers to create a huge middle class and general prosperity. If we do not do so we are on a trajectory which guarantees the continued decline of the middle class, lower and lower real wages for most Americans, the takeover of over half of domestic corporations by foreigners by 2033, and by implication, effective control of our government by foreign powers.[792] According to one study, unemployment may rise to 35 percent within the same period.[793]

Mainstream economists have finally woken up to the fact that wealth concentration impedes economic recovery and economic growth. The growing agreement on that fact was described by Chistopher S. Rugaber of the Associated Press in a story (dated 12/17/13), carried by the Huffington Post: *Income Inequality Is Hurting The Economy, 3 Dozen Economists Say.* The byline on the accompanying video report was *Gap Between Richest Americans And Everybody Else Is Causing Big Problems.*[794]

Although Donald Trump is now the President, he is continuing the Republocrat tradition of dividing and polarizing the American people. Our country keeps jerking back and forth between the Republican Party and the Democratic Party. There are dangerous and completely unnecessary divisions between North and South, East and West, and the urban and rural parts of our country. The Republicans, including Trump, are scientific illiterates who are determined to roll back air and water pollution laws, completely ignore the reality of global warming and give industry free reign to smog up the whole country and pour toxins into our water supplies.

In addition to his misguided effort to gut environmental protection laws, Trump wants to cut the income tax on the rich even more. It's nuts. Although restructuring the tax system to aid our exports and reduce imports is desirable, Trump's plan is deeply flawed. Republicans serve corporations and the rich exclusively. Although Trump recognizes the damage that Republican backed free trade has done to the United States, he too will help the rich, hurt the poor and do damage to the middle class.

The Democrats are no more acceptable than the Republicans. They are wedded to a moonbeam free trade - open border - globalist vision that has brought about the rapid decline of the United States. They keep saying it's not true, but we know that it is true. Do you want to see the adoption of socialist income redistribution policies and the proliferation of *pay for no work* schemes to redress the destructive wealth and jobs imbalance in our society? Don't you want to promote individual effort, hard work, and a sense of responsibility among our citizens? The answer is obvious. We must rebuild our middle class and working class and create general prosperity by producing new jobs via *real economic growth*, not by *unaffordable* spending programs and *unaffordable* welfare plans. But, we must also do things fairly, and the rich must pay their fair share.

To accomplish our goals we must emulate the *nation building* policies of the founding fathers while discarding the *Ayn Rand Godless selfism* of free trade economists like Alan Greenspan. Continued free trade will inexorably drag every worker in America down closer and closer to the lower wage levels of China, *and lead to the socialist takeover of the United States*. It is quite possible that a bloody civil war will eventually occur. Perhaps we are seeing the antecedents of such a conflict in the infantile internecine conflict that takes place among dumb policy Democrats and dumb policy Republicans every day in Congress.

The Democrats seem to me to be destined to go the socialist route if Wall Street ever loses controlling influence over the Democratic candidates they help nominate with their money. That may seem incredible to you, but in 2012, a Rasmussen poll found that 45 percent of Democrats already have a favorable opinion of socialism![795] A Gallup poll taken early in 2010 found even more Democrats, 53 percent of them, that favor socialism.[796] More shocking are the results of a 2011 Pew Research Center poll which found that 49 percent of young people between the ages of 18 and 29 view socialism positively. That was larger than the percentage of 18 - 29 year olds who viewed capitalism favorably![797]

This book was written in large part to benefit the young men and women of America who need jobs and careers now, not in some decades distant fictional future when the "new jobs of tomorrow," finally materialize.[798] Irresponsible demopublican government has for decades failed to adopt wise national economic policies and as a result, our inalienable economic rights are under attack by socialists. The extremists on the right and the left have endangered the bedrock principle that neither freedom nor justice can exist without the other. Although Bernie Sanders is right to attack free trade, he goes far beyond the pale in his calls to expropriate private property. For example, Sanders has said that "in the long run, major industries in this...nation should be publicly owned and controlled by the workers themselves.[799] Sanders would strip men and women of their dream of happiness and their inalienable right to pursue it. Under Sanders, government would not just control the people, it would own them. No government can legitimately exist that would do such a thing.

Republican politicians are on the opposite extreme from Sanders. With few exceptions they sell the myth that America was built on the principles of free trade and laissez faire economics. Some of them try to link their political ideology with religious ideology. For example, George W. Bush told Americans he was a believer in Christ and a "compassionate conservative."[800 801] Ronald Reagan similarly proclaimed his faith, and he maintained close ties with the Christian right throughout his presidency.[802] However, my personal view is that the axiomatic basis of modern conservatism is much closer in structure to Ayn Rand's philosophy, which is known to its followers as "objectivism," than it is to the teachings of Jesus Christ.[803] Rand was an atheist who taught people that "selfishness is a virtue,"[804] and "altruism is shameful."[805] Former Fed Chairman Alan Greenspan was one of Rand's leading disciples.[806] Greenspan once said that he "was intellectually limited until he met her."[807] Other prominent republicans who have publicly praised Rand include recent republican presidential aspirants Paul Ryan, and Rand Paul.[808] Yet another of Rand's self described "admirers" was Ronald Reagan.[809]

I aim to help as many rank and file Republicans escape from the objectivist train to nowhere as I possibly can. I know that many Republicans think much like I do on the subject of free trade. Ross Perot, Pat Buchanan and Donald Trump are just the three leading examples of modern era Republicans who have come to reject the noxious doctrine of free trade. There are of millions of others, and undoubtedly tens of millions more who, if they knew the true economic history of the United States, would also reject free trade. I bet that well under five percent of all voters, be they Republican, Democratic or Independent, even know that Abe Lincoln, the first Republican elected President, was strongly opposed to free trade.[810]

Donald Trump's high poll numbers and both his and Bernie Sander's outspoken opposition to free trade came as no surprise to me as 2016 approached. You will recall that as a boy in the 1970's I was opposed to free trade. I resolved to do whatever I could to reverse the policy all those years ago. It hardly surprised me that by 2016, large cracks caused by widespread public opposition to free trade had formed at the very foundations of both parties. I had been waiting for that to happen for over forty years. Free Trade was suddenly being fired on by Sanders and Trump and I had been working on this book for a few years. My book had always been a mission impossible type undertaking. Now it seemed to one of my friends that my book was too late; He asked me, "Larry are you going to bother to finish your book? Your ship has sailed"

I quickly pointed out that Donald Trump's proposal to suddenly slap a 45 percent tariff, (Trump called it a tax), on China is unworkable nonsense. I told my friend that talking tough on trade has helped Trump, but he obviously does not have a handle on how trade policy needs to be reformed. Rome was not built in a day, I said, and fixing our economy will require careful planning, extensive diplomacy and top tier management. Trump seems to me to be too bombastic, too impulsive and too uniformed to make a good president. In any case, his proposal to cut the top income tax rate for the wealthiest Americans to only 15 percent was and is patently absurd in the light of our national debt, which is now just under $20 trillion.

However, although the Reagan-Bush tax cuts were originally designed to starve the social security "beast," I see no reason why the Reagan-Bush income tax cuts will need to be rolled back *if we make the needed change to a sound industrial policy which produces trade surpluses instead of massive trade deficits, and which restores a healthy production ecosystem and technostructure in America.* I must admit though - *I personally would have no problem with raising taxes on the very rich if the need arises.* Nevertheless, I think the experts who are selected to create and manage the implementation of the Ameritorian Party trade policy should try their best not to rely on any income tax increases. I am adamantly opposed to raising income taxes on the middle class. Also, we absolutely must preserve social security despite the decades old desire of the Republicans to destroy it.

If change is not brought about soon, a bleak outcome will be had by rich and poor alike in America. Already China is leading the United States in patents. When I was a boy America was the world's largest steel producer but now China produces about nine times more steal that the United States.[811] So it goes with a host of economic indicators. If GDP is adjusted for actual purchasing power, (purchase power parity in economics terminology), China passed the United States in gross domestic product in 2014.[812] Given that this development has taken place not from healthy wage growth within China, but from China sucking the bone marrow of America's production ecosystem dry, China's economic and military rise is a dangerous development for America and the American people.[813]

The *one percent* will have much more to fear from Democrats than just increases in the minimum wage if they are able to stop America's economic comeback under a modernized trade policy. We are all in danger of coming under the control of a socialist government because of *money power* greed gone wild. For the sake of all Americans, rich and poor, I wish that the Republicans and the Tea Party would wake up to that fact. However, that does not seem to be happening. The vital interests of the American majority have gone unrepresented in Washington D.C. for decades. Good citizens like you and me must form our own political party in America, and our party must roll back the power of the "one percent" and act in the best interests of the nation as a whole.

As for the Democrats, there are tens of millions of them who are as sick and tired of country wrecking free trade as I am. Where are the good jobs? *Where are the good jobs*? You know where they are as well as I do. Too many jobs are overseas. Imports could be made more cheaply here in America if we maintained a technological lead over our foreign rivals, and doing so is a matter of national security and it ought to be a national priority. Clearly we need to follow the same path to greatness that our founding fathers did. Only by doing so can we arrest our national decline and avoid economic disaster and far worse.

11

Recounting The Myths Of Free Trade

In writing this book I relied on the knowledge and opinions of some top economists and business experts who label the theory of free trade in their writings as a myth. Many of those experts have identified and itemized individual fallacies which underlie the theory as specific myths. It is useful to catalogue the myths mentioned by these leading critics of free trade in their writings. This is not an attempt to identify every negative consequence of free trade that economists and others have identified, such as income inequality, falling wages, loss of industry, loss of military advantage, decreased GDP, increased national debt, higher unemployment, lower economic participation rates, weaker currency valuation, falling national influence on the international community, and the loss of positive externalities related to technical development, innovation, and productivity.

This is instead an attempt to carefully specify each of the unfounded and false notions that economists, politicians and media people frequently rely on in arguing that free trade maximizes wealth for the majority of Americans. I did not attempt to identify any such myths myself, I merely collected the insights contained in the body of works I have cited in this book. Many of the myths listed in this chapter are described by more than one author, and I have not attempted to link each myth enunciated herein to the person or persons who originated it, or those who first identified the underlying fallacy and described it specifically as a myth.

Experts who are not included in this attempt to summarize the myths of free trade but whose valuable writings raise or mention issues concerning free trade, or arguments against free trade, include economic history writers such as Kevin Phillips and Alfred Eckes, Jr, and the authors of books and articles which discuss industrial policy solutions. The later group includes Hans W. Gottinger and Mattheus F. A. Goosen who edited *Strategies of Economic Growth and Catch Up: Industrial Policies and Management*, Mario Cimoli, Giovanni Dosi, and Jospeh Stiglitz, who edited *Industrial Policy and Development: The Political Economy of Capabilities Accumulation* and Michelle Nash-Hoff, who authored *Can Manufacturing Be Saved? Why We Should and How We Can.*[814] Finally the writings of politicians, journalists and others regarding free trade, no matter how caustic, are generally not included because they are not economists or business experts. The sole exception to the politician-author category is the book written by Sherod

Brown, former Congressman and current Senator from the State of Ohio, who wrote *Why American Trade Policy Has Failed; Myths of Free Trade.*[815] Brown's book is included because his writing contains a convenient list of seven myths that serve as an ideational reference point for comparing the findings of the top economists who stand out as the most vociferously and publicly opposed to our current trade paradigm. I have also included the writings of free trade critic Ian Fletcher, whose course work at Columbia and the University of Chicago helped to hone his ability to understand and describe trade theory far better than any economist who sells the snake oil theory of comparative advantage. None other than George C. Lodge, describes Ian's book *Free Trade Doesn't Work What Should Replace It and Why* as a "powerful and refreshing critique of some cherished assumptions held by mainstream economists. It is uniformly insightful, often brilliant, and remarkably readable. Obama's team should read it - and soon."[816] Lodge is a Professor Emeritus at the Harvard Business School and author of *Globalization In The Age of Interdependence.*

No inference should be made that the specific books reviewed in the making of the list of myths described in this chapter are the only or even the best books written on the subject of the failure of the free trade model. All of the books included on the list were prepared for the general reader in order to influence public opinion on international trade. Any representations made with respect to the content of the books have not been cleared with their authors, who might find fault with the analysis presented in this chapter. That being established, the books are as follows: 1) *Bad Samaritans The Myth of Free Trade And The Secret History of Capitalism* by Ha Joon Chang, 2) *Why American Trade Policy Has Failed; Myths of Free Trade* by Sherrod Brown, 3) *The Betrayal of American Prosperity: Free Market Delusions, America's Decline, and How We Must Compete in the Post-Dollar Era* by Clyde Prestowitz, 4) *Free Trade Doesn't Work What Should Replace It and Why by Ian Fletcher*, 5) *The Myth of Free Trade: The Pooring of America* by Ravi Batra, *6) Death by China Confronting the Dragon - A Global Call To Action*, by Peter Navarro and Gene Autry, and finally *7) How Rich Countries Got Rich ...and Why Poor Countries Stay Poor* by Erik S. Reinert.[817] In addition to the books mentioned, some other sources which delineate the myths of free trade, or preach them as gospel have been incorporated herein and referenced in the endnotes. Taken together the above sources point to a total of seventeen leading myths about free trade:

Myth 1: Trade Deficits Are Helpful And Can Be Sustained Forever.

Myth 2: Free Trade Is Sustainable Indefinitely By All Countries.

Myth 3: Free Trade Benefits More Americans Than It Hurts.

Myth 4: The Desirability Of Free Trade Is A Settled Question On Which All Good Economists Agree.

Myth 5: Free Trade Does Not Lead To Inequality.

Myth 6: The Only Cost of Free Trade Is Temporary Unemployment And Better Jobs Are Soon Created For Those Out of Work.

Myth 7: America Was Founded To Permit Free Trade And End Protectionism.

Myth 8: Government Can't Pick Winners and Losers Better Than The Free Market.

Myth 9: Free Trade Is A Win For Every Country.

Myth 10: Free Trade Has Increased The Size of the American Economy.

Myth 11: Free Trade Promotes Peace And Stability.

Myth 12: Free Trade Is Transforming The United States Into A Knowledge Economy With the Jobs of the Future.

Myth 13: Free Trade Exports Democratic Values Turning Totalitarian States Into Democracies.

Myth 14: If We Make Free Trade Fair Trade By Ending Other Countries Protectionist Policies The Theoretical Benefits Of Trade Will Finally Be Realized.

Myth 15: Dumping By Other Countries Is Not Harmful To The U.S. Because We Get Lower Prices.

Myth 16: America Keeps The High Tech Industries And Exports The Low Tech Industries: This Makes America Stronger And Richer.

Myth 17: The Smoot-Hawley Tariff Caused Or Worsened The Great Depression And That Experience Must Never Be Repeated.

Most of the enumerated myths were dispelled earlier in the pages of this book. Chapter 9 deals specifically with the fallacy filled argument underlying Myth 1 that trade deficits are not only not harmful but actually beneficial. Chapters 1, 4, 5, 8, and 9, together refute Myths 2, 3, 4, 5, 6, 9, 10, 14, and 16. Chapters 1, 4, 5, and 8, support the arguments presented in Chapter 9 with respect to the specific harm done to our nation by trade deficits. The Smoot-Hawley Myth, (Myth 17) is described and demolished in Chapters 3 and 7. The seventh myth on the list, that America was founded to permit free trade and end protectionism, is inapposite with all historical evidence and this is made abundantly clear by the discussion in Chapters 4 and 7. Myth 8 is inconsistent with evidence presented in Chapters 4 and 8.

Myth 13 states that *Free Trade Exports Democratic Values Turning Totalitarian States Into Democracies*. This myth is discussed by Senator Sherrod Brown in his book *Why American Trade Policy Has Failed; Myths of Free Trade.* Brown devotes forty pages to the subject in Chapter 5 of his book which bears the title: "Myth 5: Free Trade Will Bring Democracy, Human Rights, and Freedom to Authoritarian Nations." Chapter 5 is the longest chapter in Brown's book. Brown begins his chapter with a quote from a Chinese human rights activist, Wei Jingshen, who said

> "U.S. Companies always look the other way when China breaks the rules... Our greatest adversary on human rights is American business..."[818]

Jingshen's statement gets at the very essence of what free trade is really all about. It is not being used to re-balance factory production world wide to take advantage of the unique comparative advantages countries have so as to maximize the wealth of people everywhere. Free trade is simply a hunt by big corporations for the places with the lowest wages, weakest environmental laws, lack of collective bargaining rights, and authoritarian governments that can suppress workers in their efforts to achieve better working conditions and fair wages. In reality, free trade encourages and underwrites authoritarian government quite often. Brown gives many examples, including Chile under the repressive dictator General Augusto Pinochet...the democratically elected government was overthrown with the help of the CIA.[819] Brown also writes about other Latin American countries, and Myanmar (formerly Burma), as places where free trade and despotic government have existed side by side for many decades.[820]

Indonesia had relatively free trade under the brutal dictatorship of President Suharto, who ruled the country for thirty-one years until he was toppled by the 1997 Asian Financial Crisis. Indonesia's free trade policies increased national wealth and reduced poverty, but it was the popping of a free-market-free-trade financial bubble, and the failure of the International Monetary Fund's efforts to stabilize the Indonesian economy, that led to a popular revolt against Suharto and the beginnings of democracy in Indonesia.[821] Reform efforts in Indonesia resulted in the passage of four significant constitutional amendments between October, 1999 and August, 2002, and the democratization process since then has been quite successful.[822]

Today Indonesia enjoys a healthy growth rate, realizing a six percent rise in GDP in 2013.[823] It has adopted an industrial policy following the examples of the other great Asian economies. Indonesia makes extensive use of SOE (state owned enterprise), a practice that began with the Dutch and continued after Indonesia became independent in 1949.[824] Today the development of Indonesia is being shepherded by its government, which has created the "Indonesia Economic Masterplan 2011-2025." The plan has three main elements: (1) developing six Indonesia economic corridors, by establishing centers of development within every corridor and developing industry clusters and special economic zones based on advanced commodities resources; (2) strengthening national connectivity, which includes intra and inter connectivity of centres development, intra-islands (corridors), and international trade, and (3) national science and technology acceleration to support the development of the main program.[825]

There are of course other countries where democracy can be shown to have been fostered because democratic values were encouraged by rising affluence generated by trade surpluses with the United States.[826] The lesson to be learned from that is that rising affluence empowers people.[827] That's because *money is power.* Market economies that are regulated by wisely considered government industrial policies designed to promote rapid technological progress and high mass consumption through high value added high mass production tend to spread affluence, create a large middle class, and move in the direction of democracy.[828] The countries under authoritarian rule where actual free trade is practiced have not seen democratic reform come about. Countries that have gone from autocracy to or towards democracy, such as South Korea and Indonesia, have used rational protectionist industrial policies to produce economy expanding trade surpluses and to nurture high value industries. Pure free trade however, clearly enriches *the money power* but lowers wages, producing stagnation and growing poverty, as was discussed in chapters 8 and 9.

Although the workers who get new factory jobs brought by foreign investment in developing countries are obviously benefitting from foreign trade, the pattern followed by many governments is to work with foreign investors to keep wages and benefits down. A perfect example of this is the maquiladora factories that pump out manufactured goods along Mexico's border with the United States. Typical maquiladora workers in 2010 made about $7.50 a day. The workers frequently live in dirt floor shacks without running water, and with maybe one incandescent bulb haning from the ceiling for lighting. The Mexican government works to hold their people in these wretched conditions, ostensibly to insure that Mexican worker's don't lose their jobs to people living in other, even poorer countries, who will work for even less.[829] Mexico of course, has never attempted to compete with the United States by imposing tariffs or using other methods to keep out foreign production and build up an industrial base.[830] Studies show that the North American Free Trade Agreement has hurt workers in both countries, but enriched corporations.[831] The maquiladora system has been in place for four decades in Mexico, but the workers in the approximately three thousand maquiladora plants have not been allowed to unionize or join the middle class.[832]

It's no secret as Senator Sherrod Brown writes in *Why American Trade Policy Has Failed; Myths of Free Trade,* that the U.S. Government has often been on the side of dictatorship in Latin America, largely in order to help bankers and big corporations profit using cheap non-unionized labor.[833] The famous words of America's most highly decorated marine until the Iraq War, Brigadier General, Smedley Butler, who wrote *War is a Racket*, (published in1935), come to mind:

> I spent thirty - three years and four months in active military service as a member of this country's most agile military force, the Marine Corps. I served in all commissioned ranks from Second Lieutenant to Major-General. And during that period, I spent most of my time being a high class muscle- man for Big Business, for Wall Street and for the Bankers. In short, I was a racketeer, a gangster for capitalism.
>
> I suspected I was just part of a racket at the time. Now I am sure of it. Like all the members of the military profession, I never had a thought of my own until I left the service. My mental faculies remained in suspended animation while I obeyed the orders of higher-ups. This is typical with everyone in the military service.
>
> I helped make Mexico, especially Tampico, safe for American oil interests in 1914. I helped make Haiti and Cuba a decent place for the National City Bank boys to collect revenues in... I helped purify Nicaragua for the international banking house of Brown Brothers in 1909-1912. I brought light to the Dominican Republic for American sugar interests in 1916. In China I helped to see to it that Standard Oil went its way unmolested.[834]

More recent examples of U.S. intervention in Latin America include the 1954 Guatemalan coup d'état,[835] the 1964 Brazilian coup d'état,[836] the 1973 Chilean coup d'état[837] and President Reagan's support of the Nicaraguan Contras.[838] The point of course is *not that free enterprise is bad*; It is that there is no causal link between a country following the Washington Consensus on *free trade* and the development of democracy in Latin America, or anywhere else.

Myth 15 states that dumping by other countries is not harmful to the U.S. because we get lower prices. The free trader economists here, as they do everywhere, focus on one thing. Is the price to consumers lower right now - this minute? If the price is lower, the free traders say take the deal and be happy about it.[839] The free traders do the same *snapshot analysis* of the effects of predatory dumping by foreign corporations, and SOE operating from the protected harbor of a protectionist economy, as they do for free trade in general.[840] The long term costs caused by the loss of industries that are economically, technologically, and/or militarily vital to America's growth and security are completely ignored.[841] No effort is made to consider the value of lost positive externalities from lost industries. No inventory is made of the damage meted out by dumping to our nation's production ecosystem, job base, or military capabilities.[842]

The cultural, political and economic forces which fight to maintain the free trade paradigm have caused a hollowing out the middle class, impoverished the working class, and transformed America into a service economy kept on life support by desperate out of control borrowing, wasteful and poorly conceived public spending and bailouts for too big to fail banks and corporations.[843] Despite the obvious wisdom of preventing the destruction of competitive and vital domestic industries by predatory foreign pricing, the free trade myth machine has had great success in duping our Congress of money-powered sheep into allowing the overturning of traditional antidumping protections.[844]

Trade economist Lawrence Chimerline has had a long and brilliant career in international business. Currently serving as an international business consultant, Dr. Chimerline was the Managing Director and the Chief Economist of the Economic Strategy Institute from 1993-2000, He served as the Senior Economic Advisor to DRI/McGraw Hill from 1992-1994. He was also Chairman and CEO of the WEFA Group (Wharton Econometric Forecasting Associates) from 1987-1990. Before that, Dr. Chimerline served eight years (1979-1987), as Chairman, CEO and Chief Economist of Chase Econometrics. His prior position was as the Manager of U.S. Economic Research and Forecasting at IBM for fourteen years from 1965 to 1979. Chimerline worked with the noted trade expert Greg Mastel, international economics consultant Adam Szamosszegi, and the highly accomplished trade lawyer John Magnus to study the pernicious effects of dumping and the value of the anti-dumping provisions and remedies adopted by the United States to protect American industry and jobs. They published a ninety-two page report of their study titled *Strong Trade Laws As The Foundation of a Sound American Trade Policy Enforcing the Rules*. In the introductory paragraphs the four trade experts wrote about the need for the study and its scope:

> Dumping is subject to more debate as some have argued that dumped goods should simply be considered as "bargains." This perspective fails to recognize that dumped sales over any significant period are a clear sign of a deep distortion in the market. Inevitably, repeated dumping can be traced back to companies operating in a sanctuary market – a home market closed to imports in which high prices can be charged, a state-run economy, or one of a variety of related trade barriers. These distortions harm efficient producers..., and – ultimately – damage

> the entire economy. The specific costs of dumping and subsidies are also usually underestimated.[845]

The fact that dumping is frequently orchestrated by foreign governments to permanently snatch away vital manufacturing and defense related industries from the United States was also documented in the *Enforcing The Rules* study:

> For example, one of the cases mentioned above, involves past and continuing instances of the dumping and subsidization of semiconductor imports. In this case, there is clear evidence that the dumping and subsidization was part of an explicit policy by Japanese semiconductor companies and the Japanese government, and later their counterparts in South Korea to gain a dominant position in semiconductor production. Economic analyses often assume that resources can shift without cost from one sector to another; in this view, a semiconductor plant that is closed due to dumping one year can easily re-open the next year when the dumping is halted. In the real world, this is obviously not the case. The losses in human and financial capital are often irreplaceable, or at least would take years to rebuild. Additionally, the benefits of continuing semiconductor production to serve as an incubator of the next generation of technology are considerable. Without a manufacturing facility in place, it can be very difficult to spring into the new generation of semiconductor technology and the input technologies will be less likely to be based in the United States if the primary consumers are overseas. These competitive impacts are particularly acute in the high technology industry, but there are parallels in traditional manufacturing.[846]

Professor Alfred E. Eckes, the former Chairman of the U.S. International Trade Commission did a good job of summing up in his book *Opening America's Market U.S. Foreign Trade Policy since 1776,* how predatory dumping has harmed or destroyed American industries, and forced the closing of plants that made or helped to make semiconductors, facsimile machines, televisions, radios, photocopy machines, various other industrial, scientific and consumer electronics products, clothing, cars, ships, watches,, machine tools, and a myriad of other products.[847]

Dumping is a predatory practice of our protectionist trading partners which is frequently a threat to national security and national well-being.[848] It must be combated. Arguing that dumping is good for us because it lowers prices is like telling a seven year old that he can eat ice cream every night for dinner. By consuming the here and now benefit of dumping we have been losing out on much of what high value added manufacturing offers us over the long run - just as a seven year old would be losing out on the benefits of good nutrition if he were allowed to eat ice cream every night for dinner. Thankfully, parents are never so stupid. Unfortunately, too many economists are, as our Mount Rushmore Presidents, George Washington, Abraham Lincoln, Thomas Jefferson and Teddy Roosevelt would be happy to tell you if they were alive today.

12

So... Now What?

Good Economic Policy Does Not Require Good Economists.
- Cambridge Economist Ha Joon Chang

Dr. Ha Joon Chang, you will recall, wrote *Bad Samaritans: The Myth Of Free Trade And The Secret History of Capitalism.*[849] Chang also wrote *23 Things They Don't Tell You About Capitalism.*[850] Thing 23 is Chang's quote at the beginning of this chapter.[851] I was thrilled when I first learned that Dr. Chang had written *Bad Samaritans* and I was also thrilled to find that other economists - some very good ones - were finally waking up to the fact that free trade theory is illogical, unscientific, and untrue. The greed of the "bad Samaritans" is often what blinds them to the harm that free trade causes, but economists like Chang are sounding the alarm, and helping to wake up the general public to economic reality.

Ebenezer Scrooge, the literary archetype of greed was taught the lesson that selfishness can be very self-destructive. His creator, Charles Dicken's *A Christmas Carol*, has warmed the hearts and minds of children and adults everywhere since 1843 when it was first published. A historical account which can be found at various online sites describes how Scrooge got his name. According to those sources, Dickens came up with the name Scrooge while walking past a grave marker in Edinburgh. The marker bore the inscription "Ebenezer Lennox Scroggie," a known relative of Adam Smith, the famous author of *The Wealth of Nations*. Supposedly, Dickens misread the marker in the fading light as stating that Scroggie was a "mean man." The actual wording used on the marker, according to the same sources, was "meal man" a concise way of stating that Scroggie had been in the business of supplying whiskey made from corn meal. Other sources indicate that the name Scrooge came from the old English verb *scrouge,* which means to press upon or squeeze.[852]

I was unable to find any historical writings by Dickens or any of his contemporaries which verifies the former explanation of how Scrooge came to be named. But even if Scroggie was not actually a relative of famed economist Adam Smith, the reason a tall tale drawing a connection between the two of them came into being is not hard to discern. The character of Scrooge was meant to be a stand in for greedy and coldly calculating bankers, brokers and money men of every stripe. Wall Street bankers and brokers are what most of us think of when we think of greed. Another familiar literary example of greed personified is Mr. Potter, the mean hearted banker in the 1946 film *It's A Wonderful Life.*[853] A more recent fictional incarnation of Scrooge that everybody has heard of is Gordon Gecko, the greed monger broker played by Michael Douglas in the 1987 movie *Wall Street* and the 2010 sequel *Wall Street Never Sleeps.*[854] In 2013, *The Wolf of Wall Street,*[855] starring Leonardo DiCaprio as a crooked, substance abusing and whore loving Wall Street broker, received an Oscar nomination as Best Picture.

Many bankers are economists, and many if not most economists are employed by financial firms and large corporations.[856] Is it any wonder that we associate economists with a selfish notion of what self-interest means? Selfishness is part of the gospel of economists. Economic analyses are generally built on the assumption that human beings have "purely self-regarding preferences."[857]

Two of the greatest conservative economists of the last century fit the mold. Former Federal Reserve Board Chair Alan Greenspan was a zealous follower of Ayn Rand's "selfishness is a virtue," philosophy.[858] Milton Friedman, the Noble Prize winning economist who taught at the University of Chicago and famously founded *supply side economics* has been described, and not unfairly, as "an economist version of Ayn Rand."[859] Nothing better illustrates Friedman's monochromatic view of life than the beginning to his 1962 book *Capitalism and Freedom*:

> In a much quoted passage in his inaugural address, President Kennedy said, 'Ask not what your country can do for you—ask what you can do for your country.' It is a striking sign of the temper of our times that the controversy about this passage centered on its origin and not on its content. Neither half of the statement expresses a relation between the citizen and his government that is worthy of the ideals of free men in a free society. The paternalistic 'what your country can do for you' implies that the government is the patron, the citizen the ward, a view that is at odds with the free man's belief in his own responsibility for his own destiny. The organismic, 'what you can do for your country' implies that the government is the master or the deity, the citizen, the servant or the votary. To the free man, the country is the collection of individuals who compose it, not something over and above them. He is proud of a common heritage and loyal to common traditions. But he regards government as a means, an instrumentality, neither a grantor of favors and gifts, nor a master or god to be blindly worshiped and served.[860]

The way I see it, in Friedman's perspective, like Rand's, it is not only government that should not be "served," it is the human collective i.e. the *nation itself* which *should not be served.* The words "public servant" have no meaning to both elected and unelected government office holders and employees who share the Friedman view of life. The rest of us are mere instrumentalities - means to the betterment of those who possess the ability and or capital to make good use of both our talents and the tax dollars that we pay. There's not much room in the Friedman/Rand view of human life for the valiant infantryman who goes above and beyond the call of duty to save the lives of his comrades. To those who believe that selfishness is a virtue, the soldier who sacrifices his life for his country is just a sucker.

Notice how Friedman totally misinterprets what Kennedy was saying in the first part of his timeless call to citizens to patriotically serve their country and not just themselves. When Kennedy advises people to *ask not what your country can do for you*, he was not focused on welfare recipients and disabled people. He was talking about the high and mighty movers and shakers in society that finagle lucrative government contracts and from corrupt politicians and bureaucrats. He was talking about the self aggrandizing politicians who see government as their personal piggy bank. He was talking as well about the complex of lawyers, accountants, and other experts who oil the gears of corrupt government. Kennedy was not attacking freedom or capitalism. He was pleading with Americans to use their freedom responsibly and to have big hearts and big minds. Kennedy was standing up for the moral values that are the very foundation of a successful free society.

Friedman also butchered the meaning of the second part of Kennedy's most famous utterance. When Kennedy said *ask what you can do for your country*, he was telling people to develop their individual talents, skills, services and products to best serve the economy, and thus, themselves. Kennedy was advising Americans that they had to hone their abilities, set realistic educational and career goals, and work hard to better themselves without expecting government to do those things for them. Kennedy was telling people that by working hard and making wise choices people would be doing their best for themselves *and* their society.

To Friedman, America was not a *nation,* it was just a collection of individuals; Government was not instituted to promote the *general* welfare and to secure the *blessings* of liberty to *our* posterity as the preamble to the Constitution of the United States says it is. To Friedman, the words *our* and *general* must be ignored. It's every woman, man and child for their own self. Government in Friedman's mind was the means by which *the few* enjoy freedom unfettered by the needs of *the many.* I guess Spock had it wrong when he sacrificed his own life in *The Wrath of Khan* to save the crew of the starship *Enterprise*. Spock's famous last words to Captain Kirk, "the needs of the many outweigh" were interrupted and completed by Kirk: "the needs of the few" With his last breath, Spock replied "or the one."[861]

The Randbots[862] felt the need to correct Spock. *The Objective Standard,* an online journal which was founded to advance Ayn Rand's selfist philosophy of *objectivism* carried an article in 2013 headlined *Spock's Illogic: "The Needs of the Many Outweigh the Needs of the Few."*[863] The author of the article claims that Spock was being logical when he sacrificed his life - but only because he was going to die anyway.[864] But who knows, perhaps Spock could have ordered somebody else to do the heroic deed or Spock could have escaped in a space shuttle. The latter option is the one that the selfist Dr. Zachary Smith from *Lost in Space* would have chosen.[865] Personally, I think the needs of the many do outweigh the greedy desires of the few to grab more and more wealth *at the expense of America's vital military - industrial - technical complex* and the vast majority of Americans. Most Americans think as I do. It's time we use our vote power to counteract Wall Street money power *together via a brand new political party built on merit principles* .

Both contemporary research and new and old quotes by and about economists confirm the stereotype that their hearts are a bit more chilly than the those of the average citizen. In one study, the survey responses of Israeli college students who were majoring in economics were compared to those of students majoring in math, law, business administration and philosophy. It was found that when faced with the dilemma of firing half of a hypothetical company's employees or keeping them, (the company was already profitable but firing half the workers would have increased profits), the econ majors were over three times more likely to fire the workers than the philosophy and math majors were. The economics students were nearly twice as likely to fire the workers than the law students were. The budding economists were even more likely than the MBA students to fire the workers - by a factor of one-third.[866] The same percentage results for economics students were obtained in a second study done using the same survey questions on graduate students in economics at Harvard University.[867] Note that the hypothetical company involved was operating in a temporary recession after which firing the employees might not have improved profits. Also, there was no penalty to the students for assuming that firing employees would create a greater loss to the company long term than the diminution in profits during a temporary recession. Nonetheless, the economics students choose to assume in greater numbers that the company would be better off by maximizing profits in the short run. Long term thinking is also lacking in real world economists who measure the benefits of free trade using "snapshot" "right now" analyses of comparative advantage, ignoring, among other things, the substantial but intangible future costs associated with lost positive externalities.[868]

In another study, sociologists Gerald Marwell and Ruth E. Ames conducted a series of experiments designed in part to investigate the "free rider" tendencies of different groups of people under different conditions. The subjects in the study were told that they were being given tokens that they could invest in two "exchanges." One exchange was designated "private" and the return for each token invested was fixed. The other exchange was designated "public" and the return for each token invested was contingent upon the total amount of tokens invested in the public exchange by every participant. Participants also received a second guaranteed return from the public exchange that was not based on the tokens, if any, they had personally invested in the public exchange; This "group payout" was based on the total tokens paid in to the public exchange without regard to which participants had invested them. Every participant in the experiment received an equal share of the group payout from the public exchange even if they contributed no tokens to the public exchange. Thus participants could "free ride" on other people's investments in the public exchange and invest all their tokens in the private exchange for a fixed-rate risk-free pay out. The public exchange payout could be as low as zero to all participants unless a significant number of tokens were invested with the public exchange by the participants as a whole. If a sufficient amount was invested in the public exchange by the participants as a whole, the total payout to participants who had invested in the public exchange at a high enough percentage would be greater than that of those who invested more in the private exchange.

So basically, if enough people chose to trust others not to "free ride" and to invest enough in the public exchange themselves, people who invested more in the public exchange would do better than those who chose to do more free riding. Conversely, if a large majority chose to be free riders then the public exchange investors would come away with nothing from the public exchange. The results of the study were fascinating. Only one group of individuals differed markedly from the mean with respect to free riding. *Graduate students in economics were far more likely to free ride.* They contributed about half as much to the public exchange, (twenty percent vs. forty one percent), as all other types of students who participated in the experiments.[869] One might summarize this result as *it takes one to know one*. Graduate economics students were far more inclined to expect people to be selfish than every other student group tested. Perhaps that's because *economists are inclined to be more selfish than other people*.

Numerous other studies confirm and round out the results of the two studies reported above. Economist John R. Carter and Michael D. Irons did a study in 1991, which found that *economics students are naturally different than other people*. Economics students who participated in the study displayed a tendency to approach problems in a "rational, self interested way" rather than view problems from a perspective of maximizing fairness and sharing. Carter and Irons also found that economics students are born that way and do not become that way as a result of their training in economics.[870]

Economist Robert H. Frank along with psychologists Thomas Gilovich and Dennis T. Regan did a study, (in 1993), which sought to answer the question: "Does studying economics inhibit cooperation." The *economics professors they studied were less likely to make charitable donations than professors in any of the four broad fields of study they looked at*, including (in addition to economics), social sciences, math, computer science and engineering. They also found that economists tended toward being less cooperative and more inclined to being free riders.[871]

Yet another study, this one by German Economists Bjorn Frank and Gunther G. Schulze, was done to answer the question "*Does Economics Make Citizens More Corrupt*? Frank and Schulze designed an experiment which involved letting students decide whether to accept a bribe for recommending a plumber. They found that among all academic disciplines they looked at, *economics students were "significantly more corrupt than others*." They also found that the greater corruptibility of economics students was due to "self-selection," rather than "indoctrination." There are quite a few more studies like the ones discussed above.[872]

More insight on the nature of economists has been offered by authors, celebrities, dignitaries and assorted news makers throughout modern history. Here is a collection of quotes from a few such notables:

> *Economics is extremely useful as a form of employment for economists.*
>
> - Economist John Kenneth Galbraith
>
> *If economists could manage to get themselves thought of as humble, competent people on a level with dentists, that would be splendid.*
>
> - Economist John Maynard Keynes
>
> *English majors understand human nature better than economists do.*
>
> - Jane Smiley
>
> *Economists treat economics as if it is a pure science divorced from the facts of life. The result of this false accountancy is a willful confusion under cover of which industry wreaks its havoc scot-free and ignores the environmental cost.*

- Vivienne Westwood

Years ago, I noticed one thing about economics, and that is that economists didn't get anything right.

- Nassim Nicholas Taleb

Many economists are great believers in the idea that everything in nature is competitive and that we should set up a society which is competitive to reflect that. Anyone who cannot keep up, well, too bad.

- Frans de Waal

If all the economists were laid end to end, they'd never reach a conclusion.

- George Bernard Shaw

If all the economists in the world were laid end to end, it wouldn't be a bad thing.

- Peter Lynch

When better business decisions are made, economists won't make them.

- Herbert Prochnow

An economist is an expert who will know tomorrow why the things he predicted yesterday didn't happen today.

- Laurence J. Peter

Economist should be spelled echonomist, because they all repeat each other.

- Jarod Kintz

The use of mathematics has brought *rigor* to economics. Unfortunately, it has also brought *mortis*.

- Attributed to Robert Heilbroner

The First Law of Economists: For every economist, there exists an equal and opposite economist.

The Second Law of Economists: They're both wrong.

- David Wildasin

The purpose of studying economics is not to acquire a set of ready-made answers to economic questions, but to learn how to avoid being deceived by economists.

- Joan Violet Robinson

When an economist says the evidence is "mixed," he or she means that theory says one thing and data says the opposite.

- Attributed to Richard Thaler [873]

Hopefully you got a few chuckles from reading the quotations about economists in this chapter. The most important quote is the one by Ha Joon Chang which states *Good Economic Policy*

Does Not Require Good Economists. Chang's conclusion that good economists are *not* required to run good economic policies is solidly based on historical fact. The economic bureaucrats that have been most successful are usually not economists. Chang points out that for the most part, lawyers ran the protectionist trade and industrial policies of Japan, and South Korea during their miracle growth years. In Taiwan and China, engineers and scientists have been running economic policy, so engineers and scientists are the economic miracle workers in those countries, not economists.[874]

Chang's point is that since free trade theory is unsound, the best and brightest economists - to the extent they parrot the free trade theory they learned in the classroom - are the worst people we could pick to plan and implement a comeback strategy for the American economy. In the narrative below Chang lays the blame for 2008 and other financial crises on economists:

> ...Economists are not some innocent technicians who did a decent job within the narrow confines of their expertise until they were collectively wrong-footed by a once-in-a-century disaster that no one could have predicted.
>
> Over the last three decades, economists played an important role in creating the conditions of the 2008 crisis (and dozens of smaller financial crises that came before it since the early 1980's, such as the 1982 Third World debt crisis, the 1995 Mexican peso crisis, the 1997 Asian crisis and the 1998 Russian crisis) by providing theoretical justifications for financial deregulation and the unrestrained pursuit of short-term profits. More broadly, they advanced theories that justified the policies that have led to slower growth, higher inequality, heightened job insecurity and more frequent financial crises that have dogged the world in the last three decades...On top of that, they pushed for policies that weakened the prospects for long-term development in developing countries... In rich countries, these economists encouraged people to overestimate the power of new technologies..., made people's lives more and more unstable..., made them ignore the loss of national control over the economy..., and rendered them complacent about de-industrialization... Moreover, they supplied arguments that insist that all those economic outcomes that many people find objectionable in this world - such as rising inequality..., sky-high executive salaries..., or extreme poverty in poor countries..., - are really inevitable, given (selfish and rational) human nature and the need to reward people according to their productive contributions.
>
> In other words, economics has been worse than irrelevant. Economics, as it has been practiced in the last three decades, has been harmful for most people.[875]

Dr. Chang knows what he is talking about. So do other opponents of free trade, such as Clyde Prestowitz, Erik Reinert and Ian Fletcher, to name a few.

Economists are not just wrong about free trade. Many of them profess to believe that by lowering taxes on the rich our economic problems will just go away. A number of websites have even published articles which report that Milton Friedman was one of those who thought cutting taxes was a panacea. Web sites such as *Business Insider*, The "Becker-Friedman Institute at the University of Chicago", *Wikiquote,* and *TaxFoundation*, to name a few, report that Milton

Friedman once said

> "I am in favor of cutting taxes under any circumstance and for any excuse, for any reason, whenever it's possible."[876]

The foregoing statement allegedly made by Friedman is absurd, since it is always possible for lawmakers to cut taxes. I doubt Friedman actually said anything so stupid. I could not find any proof that Friedman actually said it. The quote does serve to illustrate the attitude many conservatives have these days: After running up our national debt to over $20 trillion, *Republicans are still demanding tax cuts for the rich*!

I do believe however, that we will eventually be able to reduce the costs of many of the social programs we have today without much political opposition - if we go back to following a manufacturing and technology enhancing industrial policy - before it is *too late*. It is clear that relying on quantitative easing and artificially low interest rates to propel a recovery on Wall Street has not restored prosperity on Main Street. We simply must take on the problem of our huge trade deficits and the resultant deterioration in our "production ecosystem," and we must do so soon.

The data bears out that when the unemployment rate declines, the number of those who drop out of the work force increases.[877] In order to reduce the need for social spending we must first greatly increase the number of good jobs our country produces. We must raise our growth rate using the methods of the Mount Rushmore Presidents, modified to suit modern conditions. Tech companies that manufacture everything overseas will be supplanted by their Asian competitors in time. They have been permitted to manufacture in China so that China can obtain all of their proprietary technologies and manufacturing secrets.[878] Likewise, companies like GE that are supposedly creating the "jobs of tomorrow" building high tech products domestically are required by China to form joint ventures with Chinese firms and share their technology with them in order to secure large Chinese orders for their goods. American firms go along with these Chinese requirements rationalizing that "half a loaf" is better than none.[879]

Like the other Asian nations on industrial policy "miracle grow," China has no intention of permanently opening its markets to anyone. China is using its huge trade surplus to buy up big American companies, and they won't let Americans sell in China unless the Chinese reap a huge trade surplus. Consider Apple Computer as it is presently constituted. Apple is essentially a Chinese firm already. Almost all of the 70 million iPhones, 30 million iPads and 59 million other products Apple sold in 2012 were manufactured in China or elsewhere in Asia. According to a story in the *New York Times, Apple's management has decided that foreign workers are better skilled, more diligent and more flexible than American workers*.[880]

Apple executives expect our boys to get killed protecting the "homeland," but they simply do not care if our veterans find jobs or happiness. That is obvious. We are the ones who care, and like America's founding fathers, who marched the British mercantilists out of this country, we must - by lawful democratic action - restore the rules they followed and make the economy function the way that the founders intended - to build up America for Americans.

For change to come each of us must realize our personal responsibility to help create a better future for America than the plutocrats of Wall Street have planned for it. I have written this book because it was my duty to America to do so. But obviously I can't achieve anything alone. It is up to each one of us to do whatever we can, but we won't get anything accomplished working alone. *We must work together.*

One economist who realizes that free trade is killing our economy is Paul Craig Roberts. Dr. Roberts was an Assistant Secretary of the Treasury in the Reagan administration. He is recognized as a contributor to the development of supply side economics and Reaganomics. At one time Dr. Roberts worked for the right wing Cato Institute, which zealously promotes free trade. Paul also worked as a writer and editor for the free trade loving Wall Street Journal, plus Scripps Howard News Service and Business Week.[881] Judging from those credentials, one would expect that Paul sees free trade as some kind of panacea like most Republicans do, but he doesn't. Paul Craig Roberts has a very independent mind and he is not afraid to speak his mind. For instance, Paul recognized early on that the Iraq War was based on lies and he called for the impeachment of George W. Bush back in 2005.[882] Paul is not blind to the damage free trade is doing to us. His book, *The Failure of Laissez-Faire Capitalism and the Economic Erosion of the West*, published in 2013, tells it like it is with respect to how corporations and Wall Street have outsourced jobs and destroyed consumer income while wrecking the environment needlessly.[883] In February of 2014, Paul wrote an article aimed at "junk economists" who rationalize away the decline of American manufacturing as harmless. His remarks in that article and his book confirm the harm done by Wall Street's economic model. Thanks to Dr. Robert's generosity and his earnest desire to inform the public, I was granted permission to quote the following excerpt from his article, *How Junk Economists Help The Rich Impoverish The Working Class*:

> ...Business Week published an article, "Factory Jobs Are Gone. Get Over It," by Charles Kenny... Kenny expresses the view of establishment economists, such as Brookings Institute economist Justin Wolfers who wants to know "What's with the political fetish for manufacturing? Are factories really so awesome?"
>
> "Not really," Kenny says. Citing Eric Fisher of the Cleveland Federal Reserve Bank, Kenny reports that wages rise most rapidly in those states that most quickly abandon manufacturing. Kenny cites Gary Hufbauer, once an academic colleague of mine now at the Peterson Institute, who claims that the 2009 tariffs applied to Chinese tire imports cost US consumers $1 billion in higher prices and 3,731 lost retail jobs. Note the precision of the jobs loss, right down to the last 31.
>
> In support of the argument that Americans are better off without manufacturing jobs, Kenny cites MIT and Harvard academic economists to the effect that there is no evidence that manufacturing tends to cluster, thus disputing the view that there are economies from manufacturers tending to congregate in the same areas where they benefit from an experienced work force and established supply chains.
>
> Perhaps the MIT and Harvard economists did their study after US manufacturing centers became shells of their former selves and Detroit lost 25% of its population, Gary Indiana lost 22% of its population, Flint Michigan lost 18% of its population, Cleveland lost 17% of its population, and St Louis lost 20% of its population. If the economists' studies were done after manufacturing had departed, they would not find manufacturing concentrated in locations where it

formerly flourished. MIT and Harvard economists might find this an idea too large to comprehend.

Kenny's answer to the displaced manufacturing workers is–you guessed it–jobs training. He cites MIT economist David Autor who thinks the problem is the federal government only spends $1 on retraining for every $400 that it spends on supporting displaced workers.

These arguments are so absurd as to be mindless. Let's examine them. What jobs are the displaced manufacturing workers to be trained for? Why, service jobs, of course. Kenny actually thinks that "service industries–hotels, hospitals, media, and accounting–have taken up the slack." (I don't know where he gets media and accounting from; scant sign of such jobs are found in the payroll jobs reports.) Moreover, service jobs have certainly not taken up the slack as the rising rate of long-term unemployment and declining labor force participation rate prove.

Nontradable service sector jobs such as hotel maids, hospital orderlies, retail clerks, waitresses and bartenders are low productivity, low value-added jobs that cannot pay incomes comparable to manufacturing jobs. The long term decline in real median family income relates to the movement offshore of manufacturing jobs and tradable professional service jobs, such as software engineering, IT, research and design.

Moreover, domestic service jobs do not produce exportable goods and services. A country without manufactures has little with which to earn foreign exchange in order to pay for its imports of its shoes, clothing, manufactured goods, high-technology products, Apple computers, and increasingly food. Therefore, that country's trade deficit widens as each year it owes more and more to foreigners.

A country whose best known products are fraudulent and toxic financial instruments and GMO foods that no one wants cannot pay for its imports except by signing over its existing assets. The foreigners buy up US assets with their trade surpluses. Consequently, income from rents, interest, dividends, capital gains, and profits leave US pockets for foreign pockets. It is a safe bet that Hufbauer did not include any of these costs, or maybe even the loss of US tire workers' wages and tire manufacturers' profits, when he concluded that trying to save US tire manufacturing jobs cost more than it was worth.

Eric Fisher's argument that the highest wage growth is found in areas where higher productivity manufacturing jobs are most rapidly replaced with lower productivity domestic service jobs is beyond absurd. (Possibly Fisher did not say this; I'm taking Kenny's word for it.) It has always been a foundation of labor economics that workers are paid the value of their contribution to output. Manufacturing employees working with technology embodied in plant and equipment produce more value per man hour than maids changing sheets and bartenders mixing drinks.

In my book, The Failure of Laissez Faire Capitalism And Economic Dissolution

> Of The West (2013), I point out the obvious mistakes in "studies" by Matthew Slaughter, a former member of the President's Council of Economic Advisors, and Harvard professor Michael Porter. These academic economists conclude on the basis of extraordinary errors and ignorance of empirical facts, that jobs offshoring is good for Americans. They were able to reach this conclusion despite the absence of any visibility of this good, and they hold to this absurd conclusion despite the inability of a "recovery" (or lack of one) that is 4.5 years old to get off the ground and get employment back up to where it was six years ago. They hold to their "education is the answer" solution despite the growing percentage of university graduates who cannot find employment.
>
> Michael Hudson is certainly correct to call economists purveyors of "junk economics." Indeed, I wonder if economists even have junk value. But they are well paid by Wall Street and the offshoring corporations.
>
> Kenny and junk economists speak of the decline of US manufacturing jobs as if they are not being offshored to countries where labor is cheap but replaced by automation. No doubt there has been automation, and more ways of replacing humans with machines will be found. But if Manufacturing jobs are things of the past, why is China's sudden and rapid rise to economic power accompanied by 100 million manufacturing jobs? Apple computers are not made in China by robots. If robots are making Apple computers, it would be just as cheap to make the computers in the US. The Chinese manufacturing workforce is almost the size of the entire US work force.
>
> Economic development has always been about acquiring the capital, technology, business knowledge, and trained workforce to make valuable things that can be sold at home and abroad. US capital and technology are being located abroad, and the trained domestic workforce is disappearing from disuse and abandonment. The US is falling out of the ranks of the industrialized countries and is on the path to becoming an undeveloped economy.[884]

Economist Paul Craig Roberts makes perfect sense about America's need for a diverse and technologically advanced industrial base. He has impressive conservative credentials. He obtained a B.A. in economics from Georgia Institute of Technology and later got his Ph.D. in economics at the University of Virginia. After that Roberts studied further in economics at the University of California, Berkeley and at Merton College, Oxford University.[885] He wrote the Kemp-Roth Tax cut bill while working as economic counsel to Congressman Jack Kemp. Dr. Roberts also served as economic counsel to conservative Orrin Hatch. In addition, Roberts played a major role in bringing about bipartisan agreement on supply side economics and Reaganomics when Reagan was president.[886]

In 1982, Roberts resigned from his position as an assistant secretary of Labor to accept the honor of becoming the first William E. Simon Chair for Economic Policy at the Center for Strategic and International Studies at Georgetown University.[887] He left the chairmanship in 1993 to write *The Supply-Side Revolution: An Insider's Account of Policymaking in Washington*, which was published in 1984.[888] Some of his other books on economics include *How the Economy Was*

Lost: The War of the Worlds, (2010), *Meltdown: Inside the Soviet Economy,* (1990), *The Capitalist Revolution in Latin America,* (with Karen LaFollette Araujo and Peter Bauer) (1997), *Alienation and the Soviet Economy: The Collapse of the Socialist Era*, (with Aaron Wildavsky) (1999), *Marx's Theory of Exchange, Alienation, and Crisis* (1973).

Ha Joon Chang begins the conclusion to his book *23 Things They Don't Tell You About Capitalism*, by saying "The daunting task ahead of us is to completely rebuild the world economy."[889] I agree with Dr. Chang, but as Americans we must recognize what our politicians refuse to see: that we have a special duty as Americans to our country and to our fellow Americans. We must adopt policies that will give America the most advanced manufacturing infrastructure and the best products and production methods on Earth - while making American wages the highest on Earth. *We must at the same time reform our environmental and energy policies to avert disastrous climate change.*

Acting alone we are powerless to change anything. None us have the ability as individuals to bring about the needed changes no matter who we are. We all must act together by forming a new political party. Up until now, political campaigns to reform our trade policy have been lead by people who wanted to become the President. The most famous two, (before 2015), being Ross Perot and Pat Buchanan. Walter Mondale showed some concern about the economy when he campaigned for President in 1984 against Ronald Reagan. Mondale talked about the need for re-industrializing America during his campaign. Reagan's runaway deficit spending and oversized military buildup during his first term, combined with tax cuts for the rich, (which caused a nearly three-fold $3 trillion increase in the national debt), had however put some temporary steam into the American economy. Mondale had served as Carter's Vice President, and Carter's economic polices had failed. It was Mondale's destiny to lose in a landslide.

Another Presidential aspirant who made some noises about "fair trade" during his two campaigns for the Democratic nomination was Dick Gephardt.[890] It is unknown to me what if anything Gephardt would have done to fix the economy, but since leaving the Senate in 2005 he has been a consultant to Goldman Sachs, and a lobbyist for Boeing. Gephardt has also been extensively involved with the pharmaceutical industry and health insurance companies. As such, Gephardt is now regarded as a sell out to anti-union forces by many. One of the stories confirming that view appeared in the October 19, 2009 edition of *The Nation*. That story about Gephardt was written by Sebastian Jones and carried the title: *Dick Gephardt's Spectacular Sellout / As a politician he was a champion of progressive reform. Now he lobbies for its enemies.*[891]

In any case, until Trump and Sanders became candidates, individuals trying to run for president on an anti free trade platform have never received sufficient support from within the Democratic and Republican parties to even come close to winning. Instead of taking the time to build mass support at the grassroots level via the slow and careful building of a new political party, both Perot and Buchanan tried to capitalize on widespread public discontent to achieve personal victory and power *overnight*. Both men had no chance of winning in part because the money-powered media monopoly did not have to contend with an *established new political party which enjoyed an existing base of support among the public and existing seats in Congress*. Despite getting over eight million votes in 1992, Ross Perot was successfully *shut out of the presidential debates by the media monopoly just four years later* because he was just a loner against a rigged system. Despite the millions he was able to spend on paid advertising, Perot never had a chance of winning because he lacked the power of a strong national political party to back his campaign, and because he had no experience as an elected official.

Buchanan ran as candidate for the Republican nomination for President in 1992 and 1996, and in 2000 he ran as the Reform Party candidate. Buchanan's strong views on various issues were out of sync with public opinion and that probably hurt him more with voters than his opinions about trade policy. Given the strong support free trade had among republican politicians and voters at that time, it is difficult to conceive how Buchanan could ever have won the Republican nomination for President. In 2000, as candidate for the Reform Party, Buchanan, like Perot, had never held elective office. He faced the same disadvantages that Perot had with the media and Buchanan had far less money for his campaign than the self-financed Perot. Buchanan never had a chance of winning and he garnered less than one half of a percent of the popular vote in the 2000 election.

In 2016, just as I had expected, free trade became a huge issue in the presidential election. Admittedly, I like that President Trump talks tough on trade. Nonetheless, Trump has a very unscientific view of global warming and no plan to integrate his trade policy with a far reaching strategy to deal effectively with the problem of global warming. America can and must profit from the new industries and jobs that reducing emissions, (while at the same time ramping up American manufacturing), will create. It seems clear as well that *Trump's plan to cut taxes on the rich is mostly a bad idea*. Some restructuring of business taxation could prove very beneficial to America's trade balance, but I leave that particular issue to future discussion at the Ameritorian Party website: AmeritorianParty.org. Please don't get get our official website confused with "AmeritorianParty.com" which, (at the time of this writing) is an unused domain name which appears to have been created by a "cybersquatter" or webcrawler used for cybersquatting. See Chapter 15 of this book for further discussion of Trump, Bernie Sanders and Hillary Clinton.

After all these years of long term general economic decline punctuated by short periods of financial bubble - smoke and mirrors prosperity, we desperately need real change. We don't need the kind of "change" that is all talk. That's the kind we get from free-trader Wall Street suck-ups like Obama.[892] Polling results suggest that a landslide majority of the American people are open to the idea of joining a new political party and helping to bring about permanent prosperity.[893] *Americans know that more tax cuts won't fix the economy*.[894] Americans also know that cutting social security would be the worst thing we could do.[895] Privatizing social security would probably turn out to be a form of mass murder. It could literally cause the deaths of millions of Americans who have little else to depend on as their old age and retirement draws closer and closer.

We know that many of the elected officials from the Tea Party would gut social security in a heartbeat if they could get away with it.[896] It is also true that the majority of Tea Party politicians, like the majority of Republican politicians, faithfully support free trade principles.[897] But a significant majority of Tea Party *voters* (not elected officials), see free trade as harmful to America.[898] *The public simply does not have anywhere to turn for good leadership*. The Rasmussen Tracking Poll reported on April 27, 2015, that President Obama had a Presidential

Index Approval Rating of negative fifteen percentage points,[899] and most U.S. voters simply do not approve of either party.[900] Obama's approval rating rebounded somewhat in 2016, but much of his increased popularity resulted from widespread fear and loathing of Donald Trump. Trump lost the popular vote *by nearly three million votes*! A new political party formed around a core of policy positions and operational principles that appeal to a solid majority of Americans is urgently needed to bring about a stable, well functioning and efficient federal government.

The pages of history point an accusatory finger at the Democrats and Republicans. There is no uncertainty about the answer to the question posed in the title to this chapter: America's best and probably only hope of restoring general prosperity and national leadership in manufacturing and technology is this: *Americans will form a new political party which will take on the problem of broken government.* The questions are: How will a third party come about? How should it be organized? What policy positions besides opposing free trade should it take? How can it win, and what can you do to help? Part II of this book provides some answers to those questions.

13

The Who, What, When, Where, and How of Restoring American - and A Bit More On Why We Must Do It.

The answer to *who not* is clear. There is no doubt that the two party tyranny which rules over us is made far less competent and far more insufferable by the ubiquitousness of nepotism in every facet of government and politics. Adam Bellow, son of accomplished author Saul Bellow is the author of a book called *In Praise of Nepotism: A Natural History*.[901] The book is a treasure trove of history on the subject of the unfair and unhealthy advantage that family clout and connections play in the governmental process. The text of the book is 511 pages.

Bellow recognizes the negative consequences that flow from nepotism, such as favoritism, incompetence, and corruption in government. Nevertheless, he makes arguments in favor of nepotism, pointing out as one example that children born into political dynasties have early learning experiences and family influence that allows them to hit the ground running for office at a very young age.[902] Bellow concludes that leaders who gain their positions aided by nepotism but who then fail to measure up to expectations are "mercilessly hounded from the stage."[903] I don't agree. Whether people with family clout are good or mediocre at their work is often immaterial to their successful trip to the top. That is especially true in politics, where it matters most.

Adam Bellow is honest in admitting that he lacked an appropriate academic background to write a book about the history and dynamics of nepotism through the ages.[904] His father Saul Bellow's accomplishments and fame as a literary genius undoubtedly provided Adam with an advantage in getting an entry level job in the publishing business, getting promotions, and in getting his book about nepotism published. Adam admits to it in his book with respect to how he got his first job and why his book was deemed worthy of publication.[905] There certainly was no nepotism caused harm with respect to the publication of Adam's book. Adam writes well and his book is very informative and useful. Merit should never be disadvantaged and *raw* talent is by definition *inherited.* But after that point Adam and I separate. Merit is all too often buried alive because parents frequently succeed in bequeathing political office to their mediocre sons and daughters. The public interest routinely suffers from the practice. In the worst cases, lives are needlessly lost or ruined, because of poor decision making by weak leaders who owe their election to office to nepotism. Bellows himself gives numerous examples of how government employment follows family lines, or results from them.[906]

Bellows excuses what he considers to be the downside of nepotism because of the advantages to society which he sees in it. He expresses his general view in the introduction to his book, where he claims that nepotism is all but indispensable for three reasons. The first one is that "nepotistic concern" is the driving force in the capitalist system. The second is that meritocracy without person to person connections is "inhumane." The third reason has to do with the idea that nepotism is a "moral relationship" by which important bonds between generations are maintained. Bellow concludes that nepotism feels good and that it works for both society and individuals [907]

It's not hard to pick apart Bellow's defense of nepotism when it comes to nepotism in government. Nepotism is defined in Merriam Webster online dictionary as:

> the unfair practice by a powerful person of giving jobs and other favors to relatives[908]

The foregoing definition is over broad so let's modify it and limit it:

> the practice by powerful people of helping relatives to obtain important government jobs or positions as elected officials - even when it would be strongly in the public interest for much more well qualified candidates to be placed in the government jobs and positions as elected officials.

The latter definition might be further refined but it is sufficient for this discussion. Government should be concerned with the pursuit of the public interest. Private business is a different matter. Individual citizens can be relied on to prevent incompetents from controlling or inheriting control of their private businesses. They can do with their businesses as they please and the market system will eventually correct their mistakes for them - unless of course a government run by corrupt "nepocrats" favors inefficient monopolies run by relatives and cronies of government officials. Where nepotism is concerned, government is a different matter entirely. There is only one government, it is not part of a market place that effectively gets rid of inefficient producers, nor can it be. In our two party government, if both parties go bad, (and they have), we are in big trouble! Government is a matter of life and death decisions affecting the public. The career advantages children acquire from their parents can be especially dangerous when it comes to holding high public office.

Can we allow ourselves to end up in a senseless and costly war because of out of control nepotism - even to the point of allowing entrenched political nepotism to elevate a dangerous incompetent into the position of U.S. President? A mistake like that could cost us trillions of dollars and cost the lives or health and happiness of tens of thousands of our soldiers. That kind of nepotism does not feel good to any sensible person. It's no laughing matter.

We can fight that kind of nepotism and avoid misguided wars, needless poverty, needless financial meltdowns, and many other problems by doing so. *Where government is concerned, we want to stamp out much of the nepotism and promote the truly best and brightest*. The very idea of modern democracy was born because of the repeated failures of governments run by greedy and blundering monarchs, who *inherited power regardless of their merit*. Today we have a government that is desperately in need of fixing in large part due to nepotism.[909] Nepotism in government is generally bad news.

We don't presently have political parties that are run according to merit system principles, but creating one should be our goal. That is the kind of political party that would feel good to true patriots, but not to the money power flunkies who talk red, white and blue, but who really work for green, i.e. *money*. Where family comes first over the public interest, is it any surprise that money can buy public policy? Either the public interest is the only interest to be served by government, or it is *not even a close second*.

Nepotism is the fount of favoritism and corruption. A favor done is a favor owed. "*We don't want nobody nobody sent*," is a old quote attributed to a machine politician from Chicago.[910] That old saying is a reminder that in many places, government or political party hires are rarely made without the thought of either a favor owed or a favor rewarded. That is especially true in my hometown. Former Illinois Governor Rod Blagovich, who owed his political rise to his father in law, a powerful Chicago politician, is sitting in federal prison right now for a crime akin to trying to sell an appointment to the U.S. Senate.[911] In Illinois, politics is routinely described as pay to play.[912]

Politics as practiced in Chicago, (and let's face it, it's the same almost everywhere), was described by Chicago's first black mayor, Harold Washington, (in office 1983 -1987), in terms that I think perfectly describe the Democratic and Republican parties generally:

> In this business, you get what you take. In this business, nobody does anything for anybody for nothing. In this business, you only get what you pay for, and, in this business, you may not get all you pay for. But one thing is sure in hell, that unless you are politically involved up to here, you are gonna be one of the used, and not one of the users.[913]

Perhaps inadvertently, Mayor Washington admitted that we the voters are the *used* and politicians are the *users*.

Chicago is a place where family connections are largely determinative of political success.[914] An anonymous commentator who created a word for places where nepotism is rampant in politics used my home state of Illinois as an example of it:

> Nepocracy:
>
> 1. Nepotism plus hypocrisy masquerading as Democracy. 2. Any political system where politicians are closely related to other politicians by blood or marriage. *The election of Nepocrats in Illinois, such Lisa Madigan, Richard Daley, Todd Stroger, Emil Jones, Jr and Dan Lipinski, to name but a few, makes Illinois a functioning Nepocracy.*[915]

The same can be said about many other places in America.[916]

The point of this discussion is not to make passage of an anti-nepotism law a hot button issue of a new political party. The point is to let you the reader know that if you share the desire for a government that is *run in pursuit of the public interest*, you are the kind of person that should consider joining me in an effort to build one.

I don't care who your parents are and nobody else should. If you are reading this book because you already dislike what free trade is doing to the American economy and the American people, then the answer to *who* is *you*.

My purpose in writing this book was to communicate with people who think like me. According to polls there are already more Americans who see free trade as harmful than there are either Republicans or Democrats.[917] Those of us who understand that free trade has undermined America's economic, technological and military strength are the majority of the electorate right now. If you already see free trade as the main culprit for America's declining economic prospects then you don't have to sit and take it anymore. You can fight back. You don't need *family connections* or *family money*. All you need is to be of adult age, be an American citizen, and have the means to access the internet and send and receive emails. You don't need money. You just need to care and be an honest person.

Of course, as I have already written, although President Donald Trump appears to understand that free trade is not working for America, he simply does not understand that there are other urgent matters that can no longer be ignored by government. Global warming is one of them. Our enormous national debt is another. Trump's plan to cut taxes on the super rich will worsen the national debt. There simply is no valid reason to cut the marginal rates on wealthy people any further.

A new party can be built from scratch. If *you* don't take action, *America will continue to decline*. In order for a large society such as the USA to enjoy high mass consumption it must have high mass production. It must have a low unemployment rate and a high civilian participation rate. America is losing the high value jobs that manufacturing and engineering businesses create. The Chinese have targeted our major industries for takeover.[918] They have lured multinational corporations into their country in order to obtain their proprietary technologies and to transform America into a weak foe which cannot compete on the world stage. China's military is growing ever stronger. Our government is deep in debt. Our military expenditures are being paid for with borrowed funds. Our trade deficits each year are staggering. Until Trump came on the scene, the people who ran the Republican and Democratic parties kept pushing free trade as the answer. If you recognize how bad free trade is - and how unfit Trump is, your country needs you. You must also understand that the socialist wealth redistribution schemes of Bernie Sanders and the many democrats who think like him are not the answer to our problems.

The question is: How many of us are there? Are there enough of us to achieve the goal of changing American trade policy permanently? Even if you don't have the time to participate in politics or get out the vote, the *who* must include *you*. I am looking for Americans from every walk of life who want to end the harm free trade is doing to America. No matter what you do, you can help change things. Every economist who recognizes that free trade is not worth its cost can be part of the *who*. So can every scientist, engineer, lawyer, doctor, and soldier. We especially need people with advanced degrees from every field of academia who understand and reject free trade theory. But every citizen who has the sense to know how harmful free trade has been is both welcome and *desperately needed*. Are you a mom who wants her son to find a decent job, find a wife and have some kids some day? Do you worry there will not be a good job for your son? Come and join the party. Are you an expert in election law and political campaigning who despises our free trade agreements? Come and join the party! Are you a teacher whose pension is in danger of being ripped off now that you are ready to retire? We need you! Our party and our methods will create not millions of jobs, but tens of millions of good, high-paying jobs. We will eventually be able to lower taxes because of the wealth we create. Our policies will create wealth just as the policies of the Mount Rushmore Presidents created wealth.

I am here to make sure that *the public interest is the boss*. If you are looking for power, stay away. People who seek power and wealth from politics will be weeded out. If you become an elected official, like a soldier *you will serve. Never will you rule*! *Our master is the public interest. You must accept that or stay away*! Considerations of merit will determine who we select to be candidates. Does this sound good to you? Do you believe government should be run by merit principles and not as a family or personal business?

I have picked the name for a new party after giving it a lot of thought. *Ameritorian* is a portmanteau that combines the two central values that should animate our new party. The first thing we value is *America* and the *collective interest of the American people*. We reject any notion that the public interest in maximizing national prosperity, national wages and national power has become obsolete in the age of globalism. This does not mean that we don't care about and seek to be good neighbors to all the people of the world, it simply means that *we are a nation* and we will look to create the greatest national prosperity fairly possible. Our forefathers and foremothers did that. We will use the methods of the founding fathers and mothers and those that followed them to assure that Americans prosper and are happy as individuals to the greatest extent possible. Poverty and joblessness would be a rare phenomenon in America but for the destructive effects of free trade and bad government. In the past, before free trade took hold, jobs were plentiful and wages were far more fair in America. *Free trade is anathema to fairness and to economic justice. Free trade is detrimental to our national technological development and military security.*

The second thing we value is merit. A bonafide and fully functioning merit system should guide our party in choosing candidates for political office. The policies we follow shall be chosen for their merit in accomplishing our goal to serve the public interest. What better name for our party than *The Ameritorian Party*? There will always be efforts made to subvert our party and make it serve private interests. We will fight those efforts and expel those who make them. We will create mechanisms and protocols that allow us to police the party and keep it free of corruption.

Before we get to *how* we will organize our new party we must decide *what* policies we will pursue. What should this new party designed to serve the public interest stand for? *In order to serve the larger public interest in national prosperity and security, we must be willing to overlook differences of opinion we have with others who join our party*. Given that our main concern is the restoration of national prosperity and national *progress*, we should accept the fact that differences we have on social policies and other matters will ultimately be decided by the voters in the districts in which we field candidates. In cases where we disagree, the overwhelming imperatives of *repairing our trade policy*, *creating a truly prosperous economy*, *dealing with global warming*, making sure that *government is run in the public interest*, making sure that *the criminal justice system is efficient and fair*, and *insuring the safety of the nation*, must never be compromised or sacrificed.

We need to undercut the support Democrats get from working and poor Americans, and we have every reason to believe we can do that. Many if not most rank and file Democrats are tired of our unfair trade laws. We must also draw support from the Republican base; Many Republicans are patriots first, and they know that the decline of American manufacturing and industry is causing material harm to the economy and to national security. Our candidates at the local level should focus on trade and economic policy, and they must agree with the national platform on those issues.

That being said, we must be careful to avoid selecting candidates who say anything which is misleading or untrue about their personal opinions on issues. We must have mechanisms in place to insure that our candidates have the right moral and intellectual stuff to hold political office. I envision our new party using methods that are somewhat similar to the methods businesses use to find and retain high level executives according to their merit. Each state has different laws on party organization and election procedures, and an integrated system between the local state and national levels will have to be created and maintained.

We all must work together, and respect the differences of opinion which exist between different groups within the party. If you are pro life and you are opposed to gay marriage, we need you in the party. If you are pro choice and favor gay marriage, we need you in the party. My opinions on those subjects are irrelevant to the job at hand. The economy is a basket case in so far as working people and the middle class are concerned. The stock market might even collapse again and another financial crisis greater than ever may descend upon us in the near future.[919]

The economic well being of America hangs on the machinations of greedy self absorbed Wall Street traders and a myriad of international economic forces, instead of on a sound high value production ecosystem in the United States. Not long ago, the American corporate icon, *Motorola,* was absorbed by the Chinese state controlled computer manufacturer *Lenovo.* Along with their $3 billion purchase the Chinese acquired about 2000 high tech patents that will help them compete with Samsung and other smart phone makers.[920] Lenovo was already the largest personal computer maker on Earth.[921] So much for the myth of America leading in high tech while the low wage nations take our “low tech and unimportant” manufacturing jobs. China intends to take everything from us, and they are doing it. Our wages are falling, and theirs are rising.[922] That is the inevitable consequence of free trade.

There is a website now in existence, (AmeritorianParty.org), where you can go and learn more about how to join the Ameritorian Party. Please don’t get get our official website confused with “AmeritorianParty.com” which, (at the time of this writing) is an unused domain name which appears to have been created by a “cybersquatter” or webcrawler used for cybersquatting. How many do I seek to join me as an equal partner in saving America? *twenty million in the first year!* That’s how many. I know that seems impossible and I don’t care. Ignore what others may think as I do. Be among the first to join. Do you want America to be “great again” to use Donald’s Trumps slogan? If so, you must join. Nobody is going to be able to fix America unless a majority of members of Congress are solidly behind the idea. America is in trouble, and *you must make yourself a part of the solution.* It's almost too late now. We narrowly avoided a financial collapse in 2008 and General Motors - once the largest corporation in the world - went bankrupt and only survived because of a government rescue effort. The same is true for some of America's largest banks - but they continue to gamble recklessly in the derivatives market.[923] The entire economy continues to need a rescue effort. Economist Clyde Prestowitiz wrote an opinion piece about President Obama's State of the Union Message in 2014 which bears repeating. Clyde was very kind in granting me permission to share his sage counsel in this book:

> In his State of the Union message, President Obama suggested apprenticeships, tax reductions on new investments, and building new infrastructure as ways to increase jobs and reduce inequality in America. But he said virtually nothing about what is probably the single biggest cause of lost jobs and stagnating earnings for all but the richest of America's citizens: the U.S. current account deficit, which includes the trade deficit. Although the Federal Reserve Bank says we're in the midst of a recovery, and the official unemployment rate has fallen below 7%, the economy is far from being out of the woods. That official rate — technically known as U-3 — doesn't begin to tell the real story. It is only one of six unemployment measures kept by the U.S. government and counts all those who say they are unemployed and looking for work. But it does not include those discouraged unemployed workers who have given up looking for a job or those who would like to work full time but are only able to find part-time work. The rate that includes all those people — U-6 — is about 13%. Granted, that is below the 17% of 2010, but it is still far above the 8% of 2007, as we navigate what is being called a recovery — albeit an abnormally slow one.
>
> Perhaps even more disturbing is the dramatic increase in the gap between the incomes of the wealthiest 5% of Americans and the rest. Virtually all of the benefit of the present "recovery" is going to those in the top income brackets. As far as the rest are concerned, it's still the Great Recession. Since 1973, the wealthiest 1% of Americans' share of GDP has risen from about 7.7% to more than 19%. Meanwhile, the inflation-adjusted earnings of the median American household have been essentially unchanged. As this was happening, the U.S. trade deficit rose from virtually nothing in the early 1970s to about $540 billion in 2012. Take advanced technology goods as an example. Here the trade deficit over the last decade has accumulated to more than $500 billion, and this is the area in which the United States is supposed to be the world leader. The Information Technology and Innovation Foundation has estimated that more than 60% of the 5.7 million U.S. manufacturing jobs lost over the last decade were because of rising imports of manufactured goods. The Peterson Institute of International Economics estimates that 39% of the increase in U.S. income inequality is because of this imbalanced trade.
>
> Yet Washington keeps negotiating so-called free-trade agreements that seem to open the U.S. market while leaving others relatively closed. A major reason for

this is the classic economists' argument that the generally lower consumer prices that may arise from imports will exceed the more limited wage losses that may occur in a few specific industries, and therefore, on balance, free trade will always and everywhere be a win-win arrangement. In other words, despite the millions of jobs lost as a result of the rising U.S. trade imbalance, the overall U.S. economy is supposed to be better off today than 10 years ago because of lower prices for consumers. The argument is that the wage losses occur only in a limited number of industries, while the lower prices are available to the entire population.

This simplistic analysis is incomplete and wrong. Its key assumption is that the economy is at full employment. In such a situation, workers who lost jobs in a few industries would lose wages only for a limited period until they found new jobs at the same wages as the old jobs. Thus there would be no overall downward pressure on wages and only limited and temporary wage losses for a relatively small part of the labor force, while the whole population would be benefiting from lower consumer prices. Well, it is clear now, after a long and deep recession, that the economy is not always at full employment and that even if workers find new jobs, the pay is often lower than at their old jobs. Indeed, most of the jobs created in the last year have been in low-wage industries such as retailing and food service. This means that there is overall downward pressure on wages from the loss of jobs to imports, and that the losses might well outweigh the gains for consumers. Indeed, the average American has not seen much in the way of real income gains over the last 40 years as the trade deficit has mounted.

Moreover, it's clear that those gains that have been achieved have gone overwhelmingly to the very tiny, richest percent of the population. Statistically, it may look as if the GDP has risen. But the country is not really better off if all the gains have gone only to the top half of 1% of the citizens. As former IBM chief scientist and former Sloan Foundation President Ralph Gomory and former American Economics Assn. President William Baumol noted in their groundbreaking book, "Global Trade and Conflicting National Interests," free trade is not always a win-win proposition. It can be win-win under some circumstances, but it can also be a losing proposition under other circumstances. For the United States, the latter has too often been the case.

In the past, the president has called for the doubling of exports. He would have done better Tuesday night simply to call for balancing U.S. trade, which by creating 5 million jobs would bring America to full employment and greater equality.[924]

Clyde Prestowitz knows what the problem is with our economy. He has been doing everything he can to wake up the policymakers in Washington for over thirty years. But most of our elected officials only listen to their Wall Street campaign contributors and other special interests. They don't care about American workers and middle class people except to play them as suckers. I truly believe that - don't you? Clyde and other economists who care about America have been writing books for years trying to warn the nation - but the media has always refused to give critics of free trade fair and accurate coverage.[925]

My own reaction to the then President's 2014 speech was that it was taken as an opportunity by the President to do damage control regarding his declining approval ratings. I felt he presented only those facts and opinions regarding the State of the Union which were beneficial to him, leaving out any real mention of the economic disaster that we were living through at that juncture in history. He was for instance, silent about his grossly unpopular and highly feared plans with regard to gaining passage of the Trans Pacific Partnership trade agreement. He said nothing of the terms of that agreement. Obama made brief mention of a plan to fund some new technology centers to help American companies innovate. It represented a major admission that free trade does not work, and that intervention in the economy was an absolute must. Sadly, the type of technological progress former President Obama sought to foster, would have been transferred to foreign hands and used in foreign factories almost as soon as it was developed. It thus represented little more than a taxpayer giveaway to transnational corporations, Wall Street fat cats and foreign countries, lead by China.

Obama also mentioned Apple's Inc's contributions to a fund to aid schools in his 2014 State of the Union Address, but Apple transfers its newly developed jobs and technology overseas, and maintains only a tiny fraction of the workers it employs, all in non-manufacturing facilities, in the United States.[926] The former President steered clear of any mention that most of the jobs he took credit for creating were for part time work, and for low pay dead-end full time work.[927] He also was silent about the fact that, but for a decrease in the civilian participation rate in the workforce, the unemployment rate would not have declined at all.[928]

I do agreed with some of the general comments made by then President Obama, such as his exhortation that America can do more to help women achieve opportunity and income equality. I also agreed with the former President's assertion that global warming is a proven threat which must be dealt with by government policy. Unfortunately, Obama did not offer a specific assessment of the immediacy and level of that threat, nor of any specific solution. On the aforesaid subjects, and others, the President 's remarks were nebulous and designed not to inform and educate, but to win support from his base. As a public relations speech, I gave the President's comments a C+. As a State of the Union address, I give his effort a grade of D as I do the entire political establishment of the United States. I am being generous in doing so, because in truth, the Demopublicans have largely failed America since the 1960's.

The media is just as bad, especially when it sugar coats foreign takeovers of American corporations, and tries to make the free trade poison pill seem like a super-powered multivitamin for the economy. For example, the ever right-wing free-trade pushing Chicago Tribune carried a story in 2014 headlined *After 2 Decades in Illinois, Chinese Trailblazer Looks To New Challenge: Head of Elgin-based Wanxiang America boosts outreach to developing markets overseas.*[929] Kathy Bergen, author of the story, writes with glowing approval about the rise of Wanxiang America Corporation. Twenty years ago the company's Chinese owner, Pin Ni, started buying up small American auto parts manufacturers that were failing as foreign car makers took over more and more of the American market. In 2013, Wanxiang acquired the high tech battery maker *A123 Systems* which will help Wanxiang make inroads into the electric car market, and build cars in China for export back to the United States. This is a "long held goal" of

Wanxiang corporation.[930] Is it any surprise that in April of 2012, China's State Council announced a plan to produce 500,000 alternative energy vehicles, including all electric vehicles, plug-in hybrids and fuel-cell vehicles by 2015, and two million electric vehicles per annum by 2020? [931] Chinese companies arc ultimately under the control of the Chinese totalitarian state, no matter what corporate charters and bylaws may have written on them. China's takeover of America corporations is a strategically well planned part of its industrial and military policy.[932]

America's state and local politicians fall all over themselves begging for foreign investment without ever thinking or caring about the ramifications for the growth and success of competing American firms. They think we are living in a global economy, but we are simply being taken over by global predators. The politicians point with pride to their accomplishments in luring foreign firms to their states and localities, but they never do the math and realize that those firms are mostly seeking American technology and access to the American market for their products that are produced predominantly overseas. The media is only too happy to accept advertising dollars from these foreign firms, and to do public relations stories for them disguised as news reporting.

Once foreign firms take over American companies they rarely use American facilities to supply products to their homelands, though they sometimes make use of domestic parts suppliers. However the profits from those factories, and more importantly any new technology generated by the foreign businesses that own them are no longer in American hands. America is made poorer and less secure as a result. It has become common for foreign companies to buy American companies for the marketing advantages of a famous domestic brand name, but to then shift production of the famous brand overseas.[933]

If there was some kind of balance between what Americans sell to overseas markets, and what they buy from foreign sources - so that we did not have less and less high value industry located in the United States, the investments made in America by foreign companies might not be so bad overall for the American people. However our trading partners almost always protect their home markets from our production.[934] The critical mistake American leaders make is in failing to recognize that large and continuing trade deficits are destructive to an economy.

Michael Stumo, CEO of the Coalition for a Prosperous America has worked ceaselessly to help educate legislators about the harm that large trade deficits are doing to the United States. In 2014 he pubicly commented on the inability of government officials to recognize that harm:

> A core problem of our trade policy is that officials refuse to acknowledge that the balance of trade matters. Have you ever… I mean ever… heard a trade official talk about the balance of trade? It's the elephant in the room. You'd think they'd make an offhand remark about it somewhere… sometime. But the focused aversion of their eyes is really astounding.
>
> So the theme here is balance of trade matters for growth. The volume/level of trade – focused upon by USTR – is a misguided cover up for trade deficits. The "net" matters and the "gross" is a smokescreen. The thing is, a lot of people believe in their hearts that the volume of trade matters. Not because they have an intellectual basis for the belief, but because the Very Smart People in Washington

> simply repeat it a lot.
>
> In this week's e-newsletter from the Office of the U.S. Trade Representative, we find another example.
>
> 'Increased trade in environmental goods is an important part of President Obama's Climate Change Action Plan, a key objective of U.S. leadership in global trade policy, and a potential driver of job growth here at home. This new effort will build on the United States' work with Asia-Pacific partners to make renewable and clean energy technologies cheaper and more accessible for everyone," Ambassador Froman said. "This effort among like-minded WTO partners will also help to maintain momentum in Geneva for the kinds of fresh, credible approaches to trade negotiation and results that led to success at Bali last year.'
>
> The consequence of their ignorance is the destruction of American families, communities and industries that our forefathers and ancestors built.[935]

Mike and the CPA did a great job in helping to prevent the passage of the Trans Pacific Partnership Agreement before Obama left office. In 2014, Bill Reinsch, President of the National Foreign Trade Council, had predicted victory for the transnational corporations stating: "I think we can get there. The business community is at its best when there is an actual tangible bill for them to lobby for, and that's what we have now. People will step up."[936]

Reinsch was wrong about the TPP, but he was right about the power of big business. Under both Democrats and Republicans, money power lobbyists have been able to get most of what they want. In the process, they have kept large numbers of Americans from getting decent paying jobs and a decent life. Do you remember Obama's nebulous PR slogan "*Yes We Can*." What *can-do* did Obama demonstrate in fixing the economy? So many national and international indicators remain bad that pervasive fear of another economic downturn and even a major stock market crash are still with us.[937] Michael Snyder of the economic collapse blog wrote on February 2, 2014 about the state of the Union from the viewpoint of the average American:

> ...the middle class in America is dying. According to a report out...from the Corporation for Enterprise Development, nearly half of Americans are living in a state of 'persistent economic insecurity,' that makes it 'difficult to look beyond immediate needs and plan for a more secure future.' That same report also found that 56 percent of all Americans now have 'subprime credit'. We are a nation that is losing our independence and sinking into poverty. Right now, 49.2 percent of all Americans are receiving benefits from at least one government program, and the U.S. government has spent an astounding 3.7 trillion dollars on welfare programs over the past five years.[938]

In that same blog post Michael Snyder wrote about how "the death of the middle class is manifesting itself is in the death of shopping malls all over America."[939] Snyder reports that Howard Davidowitz an investment banking advisor and consultant to the retail industry has opined that up to half of all shopping malls in America will be forced to close over the next fifteen or twenty years due to adverse economic conditions.[940]

In other words, if free trade continues things are going to keep getting worse for the next twenty years and beyond. How could they not get worse? In a fully global economy where nearly all the top wage manufacturing economies use protectionism, *except the United States*, and where there is nothing to stop American based companies from moving their operations to low wage countries - with lax labor laws and few pollution regulations, *why would anybody expect America's economy to improve for the majority*? Only a minority of Americans have profited from free trade; *The middle class has been shrinking for half a century.*[941] Can it be mere coincidence that poverty has increased and the middle class has declined ever since the nation building system the Mount Rushmore presidents gave us - the *American System of Manufactures* - was destroyed in the years following World War II?

In light of economic reality, are you going to stand for more Republicans who say that if we cut taxes for the rich, the rich will produce more good jobs for workers? Get real - Republican Party policy has always been to cut taxes, export good jobs to low wage countries and cut wages here too. *Do you believe that Donald Trump has sparked a change of opinion by the average Republican politician about the merits of free trade*? Clearly, Trump has not. Donald Trump is a bizarre anomaly among Republicans on the issue of free trade - but only on that issue. Of course Republicans in Congress prefer having Trump as president to any Democrat; Trump has said he wants to abolish or limit environmental protection and pollution control laws. Trump wants to cut taxes on the rich. Trump also seems hostile to the laws that protect labor unions. Those are positions nearly every Republican favors. But, what chance is there that Republicans in general will permanently reject the false doctrine of free trade and really make America great again for everybody - and not just themselves?

Please join the Ameritorian Party organizing drive right now! The website address is AmeritorianParty.Org. *Please don't get get our official website confused with "AmeritorianParty.com" which, (at the time of this writing) is an unused domain name which appears to have been created by a "cybersquatter" or webcrawler used for cybersquatting.* Lets get moving towards repairing our government - *our way - right away*. Once the sign up threshold is reached, supporters will be contacted if they have requested to be contacted. You don't have to volunteer or send us an email if all you want to do is show support for our cause - just let us know by clicking on the easy to find icon provided for that purpose at our website.

I hope that every single American who would like to see the Ameritorian Party become a legally organized reality in every state, will access our website and let us know they support us. It is critical that we get a large show of support from millions and millions of people. If we can get that, it will be easy to find good candidates and build a party organization to support them. Remember, we are not going to be a party of one man like Ross Perot and his "Reform Party" was - and Donald Trump is now. *We are not going to have candidates who are unfit to hold high office*. We must build our party up from the local level, fielding candidates to the all important body that has the power to change national trade policy; That is the Congress of the United States. Individual state governments can do nothing about free trade. Governors are forced to their knees begging for foreign jobs - and they are forced to give unfair tax cuts to powerful corporations that employ people in their states - or watch their state's jobs leave for China. Corporations end up leaving America anyway, after all is saidd and done.

If you are coming up with any reason not to log on and visit the Ameritorian website, AmeritorianParty.Org, (remember it's not AmeritorianParty.com), - even though you agree with me about free trade and global warming - you will be doing material harm to the future of the United States and yourself and your loved ones. For every person who thinks their support is not needed there are 100,000 more people thinking the same thought. *Don't think like that!* America needs *you!* Just by having read this far in the book you are a special American. You care about our country. You are a Patriot! *America needs you in this desperate hour.*

At this point you may be thinking: "Ok, I know free trade is hurting America - but what exactly is the Ameritorian Party going to do to fix it?" Here is the answer: Now that this book has been published, the next step is contingent on how many people read this book and what the readers of this book do. Unless enough citizens confirm their interest in joining the ranks of the Ameritorian Party by going to the Ameritorian website, (AmeritorianParty.org), and being counted, nothing further will be done. America will continue on its downward path. As founder of the party, I plan on doing (or have already begun doing) the following things:

1. Recruiting members for the Ameritorian Party Economic Council. I have of course already identified a number of highly qualified economists who have written persuasively on the problems caused by free trade. I want to put together committees of American economists, scientists, engineers and other experts who will formulate plans for a new American trade policy. Policy formulations shall include a plan for eliminating American trade deficits and insuring a trade surplus. Such plans will probably include the use of tariffs on imported goods. Tariffs will be implemented gradually and incrementally so as to avoid sudden adverse effects on the national and international economies. The full range of industrial policy measures which have been used by America and other countries to achieve economic growth and technological advancement in the past shall be considered by the committee in working out two successive four year plans to achieve growth targets for employment, wage growth and enhancement of the manufacturing ecosystem. An underlying goal of making America the pre-eminent technical leader in manufacturing and technology in general will be adopted. A corollary goal will be to increase average wages and median and mean income in the United States, while reducing the poverty rate, and in consequence, welfare expenditures. The long term goal is to restore American wages and jobs, making them and keeping them *the best on Earth.* Long term tax reduction which is both conducive to economic growth and *the complete elimination of the national debt,* will also be included goals of any policy proposals the council makes. Policy will be turned into reality.

2. Recruit members for the Ameritorian Party Special Committee on Global Warming and Environmental Protection. Leading experts on climatology, natural science, environmental protection, energy production, transportation, engineering, agriculture, food processing, military planning and other fields, will be brought together to create two successive four year plans designed to reduce emissions and meet a goal of avoiding climate changes that are predicted to have drastic

consequences for society during the next 30 years and beyond. The committee will be asked to formulate a long term plan for achieving a sustainable near zero emission rate for residential, industrial and government pollution sources in the United States and world wide. The Special Committee on Global Warming will work jointly with the Ameritorian Party Economic Council to insure that economic goals and pollution control goals are jointly considered and jointly created. In order for America and the rest of the world to avert a catastrophe caused by global warming, *government planning simply must take place and a workable plan must be put in place and carried out.* America's defense can no longer be left to the helter skelter efforts and unscientific lame brain policies produced by laissez faire economics and kook politicians.

3. Recruit members for the Ameritorian Party Council on Press Fairness and Accuracy. In chapter three of this book, the failures of the media oligopoly to fully report the facts about global warming and free trade were discussed. Because of the influence of extreme and non-traditional laissez faire thinking over the last several decades, the government has permitted an oligopolistic media system which is under the control of a few large corporations to come into existence. This structure, commonly referred to by media experts as the *media monopoly,* censors the news and circumscribes the debate that takes place on televison, on radio, and in print in the United States. By using traditional methods of anti-trust regulation and enforcement, we can stop the media misinformation machine from brain washing the public in the future. Creative thinking by select experts in journalism and anti-trust law can help the Ameritorian Party design effective measures that will force the media system to reliably inform the public of the full truth and permit meaningful and full debate on important issues.

4. Recruit members for the Ameritorian Party Organization Committee. This committee will be composed of experts in business, political, and military organization and structure. The committee's function will be to recommend operational structure for the Ameritorian Party at the national, state and local levels. Its guiding principles will be designed to insure that public policy is formed by the party *only to serve the public interest.* Expert panels and expert committees of the party will be formed and operated with the input and assistance of the organization committee.

Using America's best academic experts to help us form policy at the national party level will be one of the best weapons we have, to prevent *the money power* from continuing to buy control of government at the local and state levels. The Ameritorian Party will have a unique structure which is totally unlike what the Democrats and Republicans have. For instance, the Democratic National Committee (DNC) is composed of the chairs and vice chairs of the state Democratic parties. There are no central policy committees staffed and chaired by academic experts. The main function of the DNC is to raise money for Presidential candidates. It has no ethics enforcement rules. It has no rules on nepotism in politics. The DNC is composed of political spin doctors and donation seekers, not scientists and intellectual leaders. The DNC does not help form well thought out government policies. Its main purpose is to collect money. The Republicans are no better than the Democrats.

I wrote this book so that patriotic true blue believers in democracy - people who want to see middle class prosperity restored in America - could band together and change the political status quo forever. We will set our party policy at the national level with policy committees that do for our party what the Joint Chiefs of Staff do for the United States Armed Services. Our policy committees won't operate as dictators, but they will formulate well thought out policy positions and they will work with state parties to help them with their individual policy and operational needs. This structure will go a long way toward protecting the party from the undue influence that campaign contributions buy from the Republocrats. The revolutionary organizational structure adopted by the Ameritorian Party will make it extremely difficult for corporate and other special interests to put Ameritorian Party candidates on retainers, (like they do with Republicans and Democrats), paid regularly in the form of campaign donations.

Thus far I have only named a few of the committees that will be formed to help guide our party in policy formation. Getting meritorious academic leadership for the party committees is not going to be a problem, if only - *you* - help too. The problem we face is the same problem faced by America's founders. It is the problem of attracting and mobilizing a body of citizens to join the cause and contribute their time and talent to the fight we face.

> *Whatever America hopes to bring to pass in the world must first come to pass in the heart of America.*
>
> - President Dwight D. Eisenhower

For well over ten years now, economists have been coming forth at home and abroad to criticize America's suicidal strategy of free trade in a protectionist world. Where do the citizens of America stand on the issue today? Opinion polls support the notion that Americans are sick and tired of national economic decline. A majority of our citizens see free trade agreements as harmful.[942] A large majority hope that a third political party will emerge to represent their interests - instead of serving the interests of the money power.[943] Our last two presidents, (ignoring the current one), one a Republican, the other a Democrat, initially obtained high approval ratings by promising change and prosperity. The Republican, (George W. Bush), delivered a senseless war in Iraq (based on fabricated evidence), and an economic collapse. He understandably lost his support from Americans. Then came the Democrat, (Barak Obama), with promises of *change* and boasts of *Yes We Can.* In late 2016, Barack Obama was president of few real accomplishments. He remained surrounded by Wall Street advisors whose bad advice he followed like a puppy on a leash. Less than a year and a half earlier, (before Trump's candidacy helped boost Obama's popularity), 40 percent of Americans strongly disapproved of Obama and only 27 percent of Americans thought America was headed in the right direction.[944]

President Trump is a suitor that only a very desperate nation could have elected President. He lost the poplar election by millions of votes for obvious reasons. People are just sick to death of living in a rut that keeps getting dug deeper with each election. Millions of them held their nose as they voted for Trump. Millions more did the same when they voted for Clinton. Yes, Trump makes perfect sense when he decries our huge trade deficits. His campaign theme "Make

America Great Again," was right on! But, is Trump himself "great," in the sense of an Abe Lincoln or a George Washington? Obviously, that's simply not the case.

Just by stopping by the website and indicating a thumbs up you can help give impetus to the creation of a new political order in America, one that is attuned to and pursues the public interest. You can become a driving force in the new party. You can help bring back America's prosperity and pride. It will be a prosperity that is based on real income growth and low unemployment. It will be a pride that is based on real accomplishment, not on money powered - media manufactured myth and rhetorical illusion. These are troubled times and both men and women must come forth now to right the thousand wrongs that are dragging America down. Many aspects of American law and policy need examination and reform. Bring your expertise and ideas on subjects as diverse as automation, constitutional reform, genetic engineering, internet surveillance and privacy law, zero emissions technology and everything in between to the party! Together, we will win the lasting loyalty and support of the American people. Together, we will build a new and lasting American majority party which bring peace, prosperity, and a safe, healthy environment to America and the entire world.

The recently created official website, AmeritorianParty.Org, contains contact information. Amazingly, although I reserved the domain names Ameritorian.com, Ameritorian.net and Ameritorian.org way back in 2012, a cybersquatter apparently got wind of the formation of the Ameritorian Party movement and obtained control of the domain name "AmeritorianParty.com in early 2016. Legal action against the owner of that domain name is pending, and the individual(s) associated with it have no connection, past or present, with the Ameritorian Party movement.

Where are our men of abilities? Why do they not come forth to save their country?

- George Washington

Please act now and join the Ameritorian Party movement. America's future depends on *you.* More information and articles which supplement this book can be found at our website, *AmeritorianParty.org*. Your ideas, suggestions and participation are needed.

The next chapter of this book discusses the war in Iraq. It was a blunder of unprecedented magnitude and it was the fault of both political parties and the media. I knew all along that there was no WMD in Iraq. I knew that Saddam Hussein had nothing to do with the September 11, 2001, attack on the World Trade Center. I knew also that Saddam, as a secular and oppressive dictator, was in conflict with the goals of Al Qaeda. Many other Americans knew what I knew. The march to war followed a trail of deceptions by Bush administration officials that was infuriating to me each step of the way. Any review of the failures and breakdowns of American government under the ever gridlocked and bickering republicans and democrats must include discussion of that infamous conflict.

14

How Bush and Cheney untruthed us into Iraq

The CIA gave us bad intelligence.
- George W. Bush, July 11, 2003

The administration used intelligence not to inform decision-making but to justify a decision already made. It went to war without requesting – and evidently without being influenced by – any strategic-level intelligence assessments on any aspect of Iraq.
- Paul Pillar, February 11, 2006, former high ranking CIA officer

Perhaps the best book about the Iraq war I've read is *Hubris: The Inside Story of Spin, Scandal, and the Selling of the Iraq War*, by Michael Isikoff and David Corn.[945] Another good read was *Fiasco The American Military Adventure in Iraq*, by Thomas E. Ricks.[946] A third book about Iraq I found worth reading was *So Wrong for So Long, How the Press, The Pundits-And The President-Failed On Iraq*, by Greg Mitchell.[947] Still another was *Curveball: Spies, Lies, And The Con Man Who Caused A War* by Bob Drogan.[948] Another I liked was *Anatomy of Deceit: How the Bush Administration Used the Media to Sell the Iraq War and Out a Spy* by Marcy Wheeler.[949] The Spy referred to in the last title is of course Valerie Plame, the former CIA operative who was outed by Robert D. Novak in his Washington Post column. There are of many more good books about the war in Iraq and the Bush administration personnel that helped bring it about.

One thing that all the aforementioned books[950] have in common is that they confirm two facts I knew all along: Saddam Hussein's program to build nuclear weapons had been found out about and destroyed before 1997,[951] and Saddam Hussein had absolutely nothing to do with the September 11, 2001 attack at the World Trade Center.[952] I knew those two facts to be true in part because after operation Desert Storm, I read and watched media reports which detailed how weapons inspectors and sometimes the Iraqi's themselves had combed through Iraq and had found and incapacitated, removed or destroyed all the components of Saddam's nuclear weapons program plus the vast majority of his other WMD.[953] I also read, heard or saw many reports in the media which questioned the idea that Saddam was linked to 9/11 and Al Qaeda.[954]

I knew it also because Iraq was subjected to crippling economic sanctions and it was subjected to American fighter jet patrols and overflights which shot down as ordered any Iraqi aircraft which violated the no fly zones imposed as part of the cease fire conditions forced on Iraq after Desert Storm.[955] Saddam was boxed in by the world's most powerful military force and he had absolutely no realistic way of attacking the United States with WMD.[956] Had he successfully done so his capital city and it's entire population could have been incinerated with a hydrogen bomb within minutes. That outcome would have been very unlikely as the result of a chemical attack by Saddam, but he would have been faced with an immediate attack and inevitable conquest by superior Americans forces if he used WMD on America. If Saddam attacked America he would have been removed from power and Saddam well knew it after having had his military forces blasted out of Kuwait during Desert Storm. Saddam's government desperately denied the presence of WMD in Iraq right up until the moment Bush broke a negotiated cease fire agreement and launched his unprovoked war on Iraq. It was obvious to me that the Iraqi government would have done anything to avoid another confrontation with and inevitable defeat by superior American military forces. I felt absolute clarity - utter certainty - from the moment Bush began linking Saddam Hussein with Bin Laden and 9/11 - that America was being deceived, not by Saddam Hussein, but by America's own President and his administration.

So the idea that Saddam Hussein could have or would have attacked the United States with nuclear weapons, chemical weapons or biological weapons was sheer nonsense all along. The idea that he would launch any attack on the United States was patently absurd. He had nothing to gain from such an attack. He was a secular dictator not a religious fanatic hell bent on spreading Islam into every American home that hosts a Christmas tree or a menorah during the holidays.[957] If you want the true story about Iraq, read the book *Hubris* and/or watch the MSNBC documentaries *Hubris* and *Why We Did It.*[958]

This chapter recounts some of the most ridiculous assertions made by Bush and his administration during the run up to the war and the search for WMD. It shows how baseless those assertions were known to be when they were made. The material in this chapter may provide the reader with a good laugh at times, just as watching President Bush often had viewers in fits of laughter watching *Great Moments in Presidential Speeches* on the David Letterman show.[959] As long as we don't forget about the needless deaths, the mindless violence, the ruinous expense, the horrible aftermath in Iraq and the rest of the Middle East, and the incalculable physical and emotional loss the Bush Administration brought about, it's okay for us laugh at Bush and Cheney. Absurdity makes us laugh. Laughter is a coping mechanism that has helped people survive terrible misfortune and suffering through the ages.

As for our brave troops, we will forever mourn the loss of so many of our beloved soldiers and the debilitating injuries so many of them must endure for the rest of their lives. There were excesses in Iraq, but the use of torture and the other disgusting violations of the Geneva convention which Bush, Cheney and lawyers like *John Yoo* arguably helped make happen in Iraq and Afghanistan, were not the fault of our fighting men and women.[960] We citizens, including our soldiers, past and present, must band together to prevent demopublicans from ever putting our solders and the populations of other nations in harm's way needlessly again. America should be governed by minds with *merit* and *moral character.* The Republocrats are not filling the bill.

It is beyond the scope of this book to go into at length the reasons why neoconservative foreign policy "experts" in the Bush administration believed, (long before 9/11 ever happened), that attacking Iraq was necessary. Explanations and theories about that can be found in the books and other materials referenced in this chapter, and elsewhere. The most important thing to know about Iraq is that the evidence of WMD and the claim of a connection between Saddam and 911 was the result of fabrication. The flimsy evidence which was put forth in favor of attacking Iraq was controverted by the best experts in American government, and it was utterly lacking in credibility.

The Axis of Spiel: Perle, Wolfowitz and Feith

Before covering the absurd claims and statements that George W. Bush, Dick Cheney and Colin Powell made trying to convince us and the world that Iraq was an imminent threat, it is desirable to briefly review some of the opinions and actions of the three powerful foreign policy experts close to or part of the Bush administration who perhaps most vehemently argued the case for war against Iraq.

Referring to Richard Perle, Paul Wolfowitz and Douglas Feith collectively as the *Axis of Spiel* is ofcourse a play on the words of President Bush's famous *Axis of Evil* speech.[961] Quite simply, "spiel" is the best word in the English language I can think of to describe the absurd overblown arguments and specious evidence that came out of the Pentagon's Office of Special Plans run by Feith, and from Wolfowitz and Perle as foreign policy officials in the Bush Administration.[962] The personal and professional connections between Perle, Wolfowitz and Feith and their similar opinions and shared goals concerning Iraq also warrant referring to the three men as an axis. The phrase *Axis of Spiel* is then just a humorous reference to the three men, and nothing more. To make that point even more clear, one need only consider the fact that *Jewish Americans were, as a group, more opposed to going to war with Iraq than the American public at large was before the war began.*[963] Furthermore, Gallop opinion polls taken between January 1, 2005 and February 23, 2007 indicate that Jewish Americans as a group remained more likely to oppose the Iraq war than American Catholics, American Protestants, and Americans who are not affiliated with a religion.[964]

It ought be noted too that it is not anti-Semitic to question whether any patriotic feelings or ideologies that Perle, Wolfowitz or Feith may have had concerning Israel might have influenced their opinions and recommendations about Iraq; Many respectable commentators have discussed the issue of dual loyalty, (loyalty to more than one country), and its influence on American foreign policies, practices and concerns.[965]

The first of the three, Richard Perle, was the Chairman of the Defense Policy Board Advisory Committee under President Bush from 2001 to March 26, 2003. Perle resigned under fire as chairman, but he remained as a member of the commission until February, 2004.[966] The Defense Policy Board Advisory Committee is organized as a group of private "experts" that advise the Defense Department.[967] Numerous advisory boards composed of private citizens exist to "assist" federal agencies to do their work pursuant the Federal Advisory Committee Act of 1972.[968]

Perle came under fire in March, 2003 because his responsibility as Chair of the Defense Policy Board was seen as conflicting with his financial interest in *Trireme Partners*. Seymour Hersh, an investigative reporter who gained fame and won a Pulitzer Prize for discovering and exposing the facts about the My Lai Massacre, wrote a story published in *The New Yorker* one week after American bombs began falling on Iraq. Hersh revealed that Perle was a managing partner of Trireme Partners.[969] Trireme Partners was an investment firm specializing in companies offering products, services and technology needed for homeland security and military defense. It was registered as a Delaware corporation just a month and three weeks after the September 11th attack on the World Trade Center.[970] A representative of Trireme once boasted in a letter to a prominent potential investor from Saudia Arabia of Richard Perle's close association with then Secretary of Defense, Donald Rumsfeld.

In his role as Chairmen of the Defense Policy Board, Perle was subject to U.S. law governing the conduct of federal employees, and that law bars federal employees from accepting gain from outside business interests which is connected with their work for the federal government.[971] Perle was not a stranger to scandalous news reports about his financial dealings before Hersh wrote about Perle's connection with Trireme Partners. In 1982, while an Assistant Secretary of Defense, Perle had written a memo to the Secretary of the Army requesting that an Israeli arms manufacturer called Soltam be considered for contracts to supply mortars to the Army. The New York Times subsequently investigated whether Perle had violated the conflict of interest provisions of federal law because he had worked as a consultant for Soltam less than one year before he wrote his memo recommending Soltam to the Army. Perle also had received a $50,000.00 payment which originated with Soltam but was paid to Perle by a second company after Perle became an Assistant Secretary of Defense. Perle told the New York Times that the payment he got from Soltam was for work he had done before he became an Assistant Secretary of Defense.[972] On top of all that, after leaving his Defense Department job in 1987, Perle went back to work for Soltam.[973]

It's easy to understand why Perle's failure to recuse himself from making recommendations on behalf of Soltam, so soon after he left a job in which he had earned still payable funds from Soltam, received criticism. Perle said of the matter that, "the ultimate issue, of course, was a question of procurement, and I am not a procurement officer."[974]

Between 1969 and 1980, Perle was employed by U.S. Senator Henry Martin "Scoop" Jackson.[975] In 1970, Perle was heard by FBI agents discussing classified information he was not authorized to divulge with Israeli officials via a secret wiretap the FBI had at the Israeli embassy. Perle was not prosecuted.[976] In 1978, Admiral Stansfield Turner, then director of the Central Intelligence Agency, asked Jackson to fire Perle because Perle had publicly disclosed classified information he had obtained from a CIA source earlier that year. Perle was able to keep his job with Jackson.[977] Perle again found himself in a bit of a pickle when, during the Senate hearings held to confirm Perle as an assistant secretary of defense, Perle designated Stephen Bryen as someone he would seek as his deputy assistant secretary of defense. The FBI had investigated Bryen for giving Israel classified documents in 1978. An online article written by Stephen Green posted by *Counterpunch*, carrying the title *Neo-Cons, Israel and the Bush Administration,* has the skinny on Stephen Bryen:

In April of 1979, Deputy Assistant Attorney General Robert Keuch recommended in writing that Bryen, then a staff member of the Senate Foreign Relations Committee, undergo a grand jury hearing to establish the basis for a prosecution for espionage. John Davitt, then Chief of the Justice Department's Internal Security Division, concurred.

The evidence was strong. Bryen had been overheard in the Madison Hotel Coffee Shop, offering classified documents to an official of the Israeli Embassy in the presence of the director of AIPAC, the American-Israel Public Affairs Committee. It was later determined that the Embassy official was Zvi Rafiah, the Mossad station chief in Washington. Bryen refused to be poly-graphed by the FBI on the purpose and details of the meeting; whereas the person who'd witnessed it agreed to be poly-graphed and passed the test.

The Bureau also had testimony from a second person, a staff member of the Foreign Relations Committee, that she had witnessed Bryen in his Senate office with Rafiah, discussing classified documents that were spread out on a table in front of an open safe in which the documents were supposed to be secured. Not long after this second witness came forward, Bryen's fingerprints were found on classified documents he'd stated in writing to the FBI he'd never had in his possession....the ones he'd allegedly offered to Rafiah.

Nevertheless, following the refusal of the Senate Foreign Relations Committee to grant access by Justice Department officials to files which were key to the investigation, Keuch's recommendation for a grand jury hearing, and ultimately the investigation itself, were shut down. This decision, taken by Philip Heymann, Chief of Justice's Criminal Division, was a bitter disappointment to Davitt and to Joel Lisker, the lead investigator on the case, as expressed to this writer. A complicating factor in the outcome was that Heymann was a former schoolmate and fellow U.S. Supreme Court Clerk of Bryen's attorney, Nathan Lewin.

Bryen was asked to resign from his Foreign Relations Committee post shortly before the investigation was concluded in late 1979. For the following year and a half, he served as Executive Director of the Jewish Institute for National Security Affairs (JINSA), and provided consulting services to AIPAC.

In April, 1981, the FBI received an application by the Defense Department for a Top Secret security clearance for Dr. Bryen . Richard Perle, who had just been nominated as Assistant Secretary of Defense for International Security Policy, was proposing Bryen as his Deputy Assistant Secretary! Within six months, with Perle pushing hard, Bryen received both Top Secret-SCI (sensitive compartmented information) and Top Secret-"NATO/COSMIC" clearances.

The Bryen investigation became in fact the most contentious issue in Perle's own confirmation hearings in July, 1981. Under aggressive questioning from Sen. Jeremiah Denton, Perle held his ground: "I consider Dr. Bryen to be an individual of impeccable integrity....I have the highest confidence in [his] loyalty, patriotism and character."

Several years later in early 1988, Israel was in the final stages of development of a prototype of its ground based "Arrow" anti-ballistic missile. One element the program lacked was "klystrons", small microwave amplifiers which are critical components in the missile's high frequency, radar-based target acquisition system which locks on to in-coming missiles. In 1988, klystrons were among the most advanced developments in American weapons research, and their export was of course strictly proscribed.

The DOD office involved in control of defense technology exports was the Defense Technology Security Administration (DTSA) within Richard Perle's ISP office. The Director (and founder) of DTSA was Perle's Deputy, Dr. Stephen Bryen. In May of 1988, Bryen sent a standard form to Richard Levine, a Navy tech transfer official, informing him of intent to approve a license for Varian Associates, Inc. of Beverly, Massachusetts to export to Israel four klystrons. This was done without the usual consultations with the tech transfer officials of the Army and Air Force, or ISA (International Security Affairs) or DSAA (Defense Security Assistance Agency.

The answer from Levine was "no". He opposed granting the license, and asked for a meeting on the matter of the appropriate (above listed) offices. At the meeting, all of the officials present opposed the license. Bryen responded by suggesting that he go back to the Israelis to ask why these particular items were needed for their defense. Later, after the Israeli Government came back with what one DOD staffer described as "a little bullshit answer", Bryen simply notified the meeting attendees that an acceptable answer had been received, the license granted, and the klystrons released.

By now, however, the dogs were awake. Then Assistant Secretary of Defense for ISA, (and now Deputy Secretary of State) Richard Armitage sent Dr. Bryen a letter stating that the State Department (which issues the export licenses) should be informed of DOD's "uniformly negative" reaction to the export of klystrons to Israel. Bryen did as instructed , and the license was withdrawn.

In July, Varian Associates became the first U.S. corporation formally precluded from contracting with the Defense Department. Two senior colleague in DOD who wish to remain anonymous have confirmed that this attempt by Bryen to obtain klystrons for his friends was not unusual, and was in fact "standard operating procedure" for him, recalling numerous instances when U.S. companies were denied licenses to export sensitive technology, only to learn later that Israeli companies subsequently exported similar (U.S. derived) weapons and technology to the intended customers/governments.[978]

That Perle favored regime change in Iraq long before 911 is indisputable. In 1996, Perle was one of the authors of a report prepared by the Institute for Advanced Strategic & Political Studies, an Israeli think tank with a branch in Washington D.C. The report, *A Clean Break: A New Strategy for Securing the Realm,* advocated an aggressive Middle East policy which included as a goal the removal of Saddam Hussein from power in Iraq. The report was prepared for the leader of Israeli Likud party, Benjamin Netanyahu.[979] In addition, on January 26, 1998, Perle along with ten other neocon members of the *Project For a New American Century* posted a public letter to President Bill Clinton calling on the President to overthrow Saddam Hussein.[980]

Next in line in the *Axis of Spiel* is Paul Wolfowitz. He speaks six languages. His father was a brilliant mathematician and Paul is brilliant as well.[981] So what? What good is it to have genius policymakers if they sell half-baked conclusions and help lead America into senseless wars based on fabricated evidence?[982] We need government *in the public interest.* Wolfowitz and Richard Perle are very old friends. They worked together on the staff of Senator Scoop Jackson starting in 1968.[983] As a member of the neocon *Project For a New American Century,* Wolfowitz joined Perle in putting his signature on a public letter to President Bill Clinton delivered in 1998, calling on the President to overthrow Saddam Hussein.[984] President George W. Bush made Wolfowitz a Deputy Secretary of Defense, (2001-2005), reporting to Donald Rumsfeld.[985]

Wolfowitz told San Francisco Chronicle reporter Robert Collier in February, 2002, that the September 11th attack was "a wake up call and that if we take proper advantage of this opportunity to prevent the future terrorist use of weapons of mass destruction that it will have been an extremely valuable wake up call.[986] At a meeting of the National Security Council held on the day of the 9/11 attack, Secretary of Defense Donald Rumsfeld asked "Why shouldn't we go against Iraq, not just al-Qaeda?"[987] Wolfowitz, who was in attendance at the meeting said that Saddam's government was a "brittle, oppressive regime that might break easily—it was doable,"[988] In addition to being Bush II's Secretary of Defense, Donald Rumsfeld was also a member of the neocon group *Project For a New American Century.*[989] So was Vice President Dick Cheney.[990] Like Wolfowitz and Perle, Rumsfeld had signed the 1998 letter sent to President Clinton demanding regime change in Iraq.[991]

Also in attendance at the meetings held by the National Security Council on 9/11 was the chief counter terrorism expert on the National Security Council, Richard Alan Clarke. In his book, *Against All Enemies: Inside America's War On Terrorism*, Clarke tells of feeling sick when he realized while attending meetings at White House on 9/11 that Rumsfeld and Wolfowitz were going to take advantage of the attack on the World Trade Center by Al Qaeda to promote war on Iraq.[992]

At this point the reader who is not already familiar with subject of this chapter can begin to see that the false pronouncements later made by Bush and Cheney linking Saddam Hussein with the attack on the World Trade Center, and the comments they made alleging Saddam had WMD and was going to use it were part of a deliberate strategy of deception by the Bush administration.[993]

In 1992, while serving as Undersecretary of Defense for Policy, Paul Wolfowitz had his assistants produce the Defense Planning Guidance policy memo of 1992. The memo, dated February 18, 1992, was leaked to the New York Times the month after it was written.[994] The leak caused an uproar. The excerpts from the memo below are some of the more controversial statements in it:

> Our first objective is to prevent the re-emergence of a new rival, either on the

> territory of the former Soviet Union or elsewhere, that poses a threat on the order of that posed formerly by the Soviet Union. This is a dominant consideration underlying the new regional defense strategy and requires that we endeavor to prevent any hostile power from dominating a region whose resources would, under consolidated control, be sufficient to generate global power.
>
> There are three additional aspects to this objective: First the U.S. must show the leadership necessary to establish and protect a new order that holds the promise of convincing potential competitors that they need not aspire to a greater role or pursue a more aggressive posture to protect their legitimate interests. In non-defense areas, we must account sufficiently for the interests of the advanced industrial nations to discourage them from challenging our leadership or seeking to overturn the established political and economic order. We must maintain the mechanism for deterring potential competitors from even aspiring to a larger regional or global role.[995]

Professor Andrew J. Bacevich made a public comment to Wolfowitz about his Defense Planning Guidance Paper in a letter to Harper's that was published in the March, 2013 edition:

> I refer here to the famous (or infamous) Defense Planning Guidance of 1992, drafted in the aftermath of Operation Desert Storm by the Pentagon policy shop you then directed. Before this classified document was fully vetted by the White House, it was leaked to the New York Times, which made it front-page news. *The draft DPG announced that it had become the "first objective" of U.S. policy "to prevent the re-emergence of a new rival." With an eye toward "deterring potential competitors from even aspiring to a larger regional or global role," the United States would maintain unquestioned military superiority and, if necessary, employ force unilaterally. As window dressing, allies might be nice, but the United States no longer considered them necessary.* (emphasis added)
>
> Unfortunately, you and the team assigned to draft the DPG had miscalculated the administration's support for your thinking. This was not the moment to be unfurling grandiose ambitions expressed in indelicate language. In the ensuing hue and cry, President George H. W. Bush disavowed the document. Your reputation took a hit. But you were undeterred....
>
> You immediately saw the events of 9/11 as a second and more promising opening to assert U.S. supremacy. When riding high a decade earlier, many Americans had thought it either unseemly or unnecessary to lord it over others. Now, with the populace angry and frightened, the idea was likely to prove an easier sell. Although none of the hijackers were Iraqi, within days of 9/11 you were promoting military action against Iraq. Critics have chalked this up to your supposed obsession with Saddam. The criticism is misplaced. The scale of your ambitions was vastly greater.
>
> In an instant, you grasped that the attacks provided a fresh opportunity and Iraq offered a made-to-order venue. 'We cannot wait to act until the threat is

> imminent,' you said in 2002. Toppling Saddam Hussein would validate the alternative to waiting. In Iraq the United States would demonstrate the efficacy of preventive war.
>
> So ...the Bush Doctrine was largely your handiwork. The urgency of invading Iraq stemmed from the need to validate that doctrine before the window of opportunity closed. What made it necessary to act immediately was not Saddam's purported WMD program. It was not his nearly nonexistent links to Al Qaeda. It was certainly not the way he abused his own people. No, what drove events was the imperative of claiming for the United States prerogatives allowed no other nation.[996]

Bacevich is a retired U.S. Army Colonel who served in Vietnam during 1970-1971. He graduated from West Point in 1969. After his service in Vietnam, Bacevich went on to serve with the U.S. Army in Germany, the United States and the Persian Gulf. In 2007, his only son, also named Andrew, was killed in action in Iraq while serving as a first lieutenant assigned to the 3rd Battalion, 8th U.S. Cavalry Regiment, 1st Cavalry Division.[997]

I imagine that the elder Bacevich accomplished more as a U.S. Army colonel than most of us do in our whole lives, but he has made as great or greater a contribution to national security since his retirement from the military. Colonel Bacevich obtained an MA in History (1977) and a PhD (1982) from Princeton University in American Diplomatic History. He has had fellowships with the Kroc Institute for International Peace Studies, the University of Notre Dame, The American Academy in Berlin, The Paul H. Nitze School of Advanced International Studies at Johns Hopkins University and The John F. Kennedy School of Government at Harvard University. He is the former Director of the International Relations Department at Boston University, and is currently a Professor Emeritus of History and International Relations there.[998]

Professor Bacevich's writing is brilliant. He combines the depth of scholarly knowledge and ability that one expects from a person of his academic background with the invaluable experience of a career soldier who has attained high rank. His worthy books include among others *Breach of Trust: How Americans Failed Their Soldiers and Their Country* (2013). *Washington Rules: America's Path to Permanent War* (2010); *The Limits of Power: The End of American Exceptionalism* (2008); *The Long War: A New History of US National Security Policy since World War II* (2007) (editor); *The New American Militarism: How Americans Are Seduced by War* (2005); and *American Empire: The Realities and Consequences of U. S. Diplomacy* (2002).[999]

I really don't know the truth of the matter, but it is clear that Wolfowitz's desire to remove Saddam from Iraq was not inspired by fear that Iraq possessed or was developing weapons of mass destruction. It's also clear that the Defense Planning Guidance of 1992, otherwise known as the "Wolfowitz Doctrine" was viewed by many experts at the time as an over reaching and deeply flawed plan to inhibit the development of other nations.[1000]

The last member of the *Axis of Spiel* is Douglas Feith. Feith is the son of a now deceased wealthy industrialist named Dalck Feith. The elder Feith escaped from the Nazis during WWII to join the British and later the American merchant marine. In the 1930's, Dalck was a member of a right wing Zionist group called Betar. He settled in Philadelphia after arriving in the United States.[1001]

Douglas Feith matriculated at Harvard University and in 1978 he obtained a law degree from Georgetown.[1002] While at Harvard, Feith was a student of Professor Richard Pipes, a historian of Russian history.[1003] Pipes and Feith had much in common. As a boy, Pipes lived in Warsaw during the Nazi occupation. Pipes and his family, who were Jewish, escaped from the Nazi's in 1939 and settled in America. During the 1970's Professor Pipes was an advisor to Senator Scoop Jackson.[1004] During that time period Douglas Feith had occasion to make the acquaintance of Senator Jackson and his assistants, Richard Perle and Paul Wolfowitz. In 1975, Feith joined the staff of Senator Jackson.[1005] In 1981, Feith was employed by the National Security Agency as a Middle East Specialist to work with his former Harvard professor, Dr. Richard Pipes.[1006]

In 1982, Feith left the National Security Agency to become Special Counsel to Assistant Secretary of Defense Richard Perle. In 1984, then Secretary of Defense Caspar Weinberger gave Feith a promotion to Deputy Assistant Secretary of Defense for Negotiations Policy.[1007] In 1986, Feith left his Pentagon job and joined with Washington attorney Marc Zell to create a law firm that did lobbying for Israel, Turkey, Bosnia, Lockheed Martin, Northrup Grumman and other clients.[1008] In 1988, Marc Zell, an avid Zionist, moved to Israel with his family. The Zells lived in an Israeli settlement on the West Bank called Alon Shvut, which was and remains an illegal settlement under U.N. resolutions. Zell provided legal representation to and lobbied on behalf of West Bank settlement groups after his relocation to Israel.[1009] The professional relationship between Feith and Zell lived on through a professional and business alliance the two men maintained. In 1999, Feith and Zell redesigned their work arrangement and named their joint business arrangement the Fandz International Law Group. The word "Fandz"comes from the initials "F" for Feith and "Z" for Zell, which are united by the conjuctive, "and."[1010]

Feith like Perle has in the past raised Washington eyebrows with his professional dealings.[1011] For instance, after Feith formed the legal services firm Fandz International Law Group with Zell, Feith was nominated to become the Under Secretary of Defense for Policy by President George W. Bush. While serving as the Under Secretary of Defense for Policy, Feith was given responsibility for overseeing various reconstruction related matters in Iraq. At the same time that Feith was influencing reconstruction policy in Iraq, the website for Fandz International Law Group had a statement on it that the firm had "established a task force dealing with issues and opportunities relating to the recently ended war with Iraq....and is assisting regional construction and logistics firms to collaborate with contractors from the United States and other coalition countries in implementing infrastructure and other reconstruction projects in Iraq."[1012] That Feith may have had an impermissible conflict of interest while he was both responsible for helping set reconstruction policy and involved with Fandz seems possible.[1013] Feith was however never prosecuted for any of his dealings relating to Fandz.

During the period Perle, Wolfowitz and later Feith worked for Senator Scoop Jackson, Richard Pipes was a leading critic of detente with the Soviet Union.[1014] In May, 1976, a presidential election year, Pipes chaired a CIA group known as "Team B" which independently produced a National Intelligence Estimate (NIE) on the Soviet Union for comparison with the NIE produced by the regular CIA Soviet analysts, who were referred to as "Team A."[1015]

President Ford who was running for a second term had asked Pipes to chair Team B. The Team

B report indicated that the regular NIE produced by the CIA had underestimated Soviet military power and had also failed to determine the true extent of the strategic threats posed by the Soviets. Soon after Jimmy Carter was elected, (aided by the public's reaction to Watergate and Ford's pardon of Nixon), the Team B report was leaked to the press, but not at Carter's behest.[1016]

Prior to the completion of the Team B report, President Ford's Secretary of Defense, Donald Rumsfeld, had made speeches claiming that the Russians were quietly building weapons in violation of the detente and that the Russians possibly had a plan to attack the United States. At the time, Paul Wolfowitz, who served as an advisor to Team B, was in general agreement with Rumsfeld as to the threat posed by the Soviet Union.[1017] This piece of history was largely forgotten about by the public and the media during the run up to the Iraq War when Rumsfeld and Wolfowitz both sounded false alarms about secretly held weapons of mass destruction held by Saddam Hussein.[1018]

The Team B report contained the highly questionably finding that the Soviet Union was not operating under the belief that a nuclear attack by the USSR against the United States would result in mutual assured destruction. In other words, Wolfowitz and Pipes were trying to sell the idea that Russia's leaders thought they could win a nuclear war with the United States despite the thousands of nuclear weapons that the United Sates kept trained on Russia at all times, day and night.[1019] This conclusion was, understandably, harshly criticized as were the Team B conclusions about the types and quantities of weapons systems the Soviets were building, and the capacities of the Soviet economy to build such weapons. Ray Cline, a past CIA Deputy Director and leading CIA analyst at the time said the Team B report was a product of a "kangaroo court of outside critics all picked from one point of view."[1020] Then CIA Director and future President George H. W. Bush opined that the use of the Team B approach had placed "in motion a process that lends itself to manipulation for purposes other than estimative accuracy."[1021]

The use of the Team B approach was part of the inspiration for what later happened to junk the quality and reliability of the CIA's intelligence estimates prior to and during the Iraq war.[1022] That brings us to Douglas Feith's prominent role in cobbling together bits of evidence that the CIA and State Department had previously discredited in an effort to establish links between terror groups and countries alleged to be sponsoring them. The data collected by Feith and other investigators was used to support untrue statements that Rumsfeld, Cheney, Bush and Colin Powell made about an Iraqi - 9/11 - Al Qaeda nexus. Soon after September 11, 2001, Feith set up a secret Pentagon intelligence unit named the Policy Counter Terrorism Evaluation Group or PCTEG. The group was tasked with gathering together whatever bits of raw intelligence data they could find linking terrorist groups with state sponsorship. Feith assigned another Jewish neocon named David Wurmser to do the work of the group, along with F. Michael Maloof.

Maloof was an old Pentagon employee with close ties to Perle.[1023] Wurmser was a coauthor with Feith and Perle among others of *A Clean Break: A New Strategy for Securing the Realm,* the policy paper which had been prepared in 1996 for Benjamin Netanyahu and the Likud party.[1024] The Policy Counter Terrorism Evaluation Group did its work in a 225 foot square foot room in the Pentagon.[1025] Its "evaluation" work, done as a kind of mini Team B, was really just a game of connect the dots between bits of raw and often discredited intelligence. The object of the game was to draw an intelligence picture which could be used by the White House to justify a war on Iraq.

Feith provided Wurmsler and Maloof with computer access to classified CIA, DIA, and other intelligence agency data, along with software to help evaluate it. Wurmsler and Maloof covered the walls of their cramped work room with butcher paper and created a giant chart of interconnected data on it. Evidence sources found to be lacking credibility together with evidence sources positively determined to be false by seasoned intelligence agency analysts outside the tiny PCTEG group were included in the huge jumble of information that the two man crew collected.[1026] The job of PCTEG it seems, was not to find the truth, but to fashion the implements for a propaganda campaign justifying war.[1027]

On his wall charts, Maloof integrated highly dubious information supplied to him by Ahmad Chalabi and the Iraqi National Congress, (INC), with the suspect evidence PCTEG obtained from intelligence agency computer records. Chalabi had met Paul Wolfowitz and Richard Perle in 1985 and the three men were closely linked with other neocons, including Douglas Feith, for years before the 9/11 attacks.[1028] An ambitious Iraqi born businessman and politico, Chalabi, who was on the executive council of INC, aspired to take power in Iraq. He had been militating for the U.S. to invade Iraq even before 1992 when INC was formed.[1029] But INC was not formed by Iraqi expatriates like Chalabi independently. The Iraqi National Congress was financed by the U.S. government. President H. W. Bush had directed the CIA to bring about the conditions for regime change in Iraq in May of 1991. The INC was largely a creation of the CIA pursuant to the Bush directive. The name Iraqi National Congress is said to have been coined by a PR firm with CIA connections named the Rendon Group. INC received millions of dollars in secret from the CIA before 1998, in which year the group openly received $8 million in public funding following passage of the Iraqi Liberation Act during Clinton's presidency.[1030] In November of 2000, Congress increased the amount paid to INC to $18 million, and Chalabi's group used the funds to channel payments to Iraqi "defectors" who told tall tales concerning WMD and Iraq to American intelligence and the media.[1031] After 9/11 Chalabi's accomplices also gave phony accounts which suggested a connection between Iraq and Al Qaeda, terrorism, and the attack of 9/11 on the WTC.[1032] Little if any of the information Chalabi and the INC supplied PCTEG and its successor policy group, the Office of Special Plans, ultimately proved to be reliable. Nonetheless, much of the most important seeming intelligence cherry picked by Feith's crew and added to their wall charts came from INC supplied sources.[1033]

The upper levels of the Bush administration were well aware of what was going on at PCTEG and they took interest in PCTEG's growing web of unproven fragments of evidence while PCTEG's final report was still a work in progress. Cheney had a Jewish Neocon foreign policy aide named Samantha Ravich who visited the Pentagon office which housed the PCTEG wall charts, took notes on the teams progress, and reported back to Cheney's Chief of Staff, Irving Lewis "Scooter" Libby. On one occasion, Wolfowitz, who has an incredible mind for details, reportedly spent forty five minutes studying the wall charts.[1034]

Wurmser and Maloof assembled their mass of implausible or obviously false evidence into a neat looking slide show, Their 154 slide presentation was given the title *Understanding the Strategic Threat of Terror Networks and their Sponsors.*[1035] Before PCTEG could complete a detailed report for use by the White House to argue the case for war, Maloof was forced out of the CIA. In December of 2001, Maloof lost his security clearance and was removed from his job because of his alleged unauthorized contacts with a person he had met while on a trip to a former USSR territory.[1036] By January of 2002, Wurmser had also left PCTEG to work at the State Department. Feith added Chris Carney and Christina Shelton to his team as replacements. On January 22, 2002 Deputy Secretary of Defense Paul Wolfowitz wrote a memo to Feith which complained about the policy counterterroism evaluation group's failure to pull "together intelligence... links between Iraq and Al Qaida."[1037]

Feith's new crew assembled their credibility lacking evidence into a new presentation by the summer of 2002 which they named *Assessing the Relationship between Iraq and al Qaida.* On September 16, 2002, their report was presented to Scooter Libby (Vice President Cheney's Chief of Staff), and Deputy National Security Advisor Stephen Hadley. The title of the slickly done report was deceptive because Feith's researhers had failed to include contradictory evidence obtained and contradictory analysis done by the CIA, DIA, State Department and other employees of federal agencies.[1038]

Feith himself told Hadley that September that PCTEG had uncovered patterns that had escaped detection by the CIA and the rest of the U.S intelligence community. Feith also claimed that Saddam Hussein had a more expansive relationship with al-Qaeda and Osama bin Laden than any of the U.S. intelligence agencies had uncovered.[1039] It was a "conclusion" of the PCTEG group that the September 11, 2001 attack on the world Trade center resulted from "..a complex operation carried out by al-Qaeda - but assisted by the Hizbollah Shiites, financed by the Saudi royals, and sponsored by the secular Baathists of Baghdad."[1040] This conclusion was at odds with the majority view at the CIA, DIA and the State Department, which was that there was insufficient evidence to conclude that Saddam Hussein had anything to do with 911, or that he was supporting or directing al-Qaeda.[1041]

Douglas Feith was never cited for any ethical or criminal violations with respect to his work as a Pentagon employee, but an official investigation did find his office used insufficient procedures in collecting and reporting evidence that was used to promote the case for war in Iraq to the American people and Congress.[1042] The Inspector General for the Department of Defense found that Feith and his group deliberately ignored the consensus within the intelligence community that there was no causal link between Iraq and al-Qaeda, or Iraq and the September 11, 2001 attacks on the World Trade Center and the Pentagon. Feith's office was found to have used an inappropriate approach to evaluating data and of making inaccurate reports to White House officials.[1043]

Well before he provided PCTEG's junk evidence to White House staffers Libby and Hadley, Feith was involved in post war planning. During the summer of 2002, Feith was given approval by the White House to hire additional staffers. His workload was growing as the Bush Administration angled its way towards war in Iraq.[1044] William Luti was made Deputy Under Secretary of Defense to assist Feith with his new staff, which became part of a group known as the *Office of Special Plans* or OSP.[1045] The work produced by the OSP included *inter-alia* two briefing papers. The first was titled *Pros and Cons of Provisional Government.* The document laid out an adumbrative strategy for how Iraq would be governed following invasion by United

States forces. The second briefing paper dealt with the subject of *Iraqi Opposition Strategy.*[1046] The reason for naming the new office for post war planning that Feith was put in charge of the "Office of Special Plans," is likely related to the history of other "special plans" groups within the military.

Dr. Jeff Richelson, PhD is a well known expert on intelligence agencies both domestic and international. At the time of this writing Richelson was a senior fellow of the National Security Archive. He had written at least thirteen books on subjects involving intelligence agency structure and operations and a large number of academic articles on related topics.[1047] In February, 2014, Dr. Richelson posted online National Security Archive Electronic Briefing Book No. 456, The book is captioned *Special Plans and Double Meanings: Controversies over Deception, Intelligence, and Policy Counterterrorism*. Richelson edited the book, which explains in some detail how and when the term *Special Plans* has been used by the Pentagon:

> the term "Special Plans" has been a euphemism for deception since World War II, and for 'perception management' (which included deception and 'truth projection') since at least the mid-1970s. And during the George W. Bush administration the term apparently had a dual use — as a traditional euphemism (for perception management) as well as a temporary title for planning with regard to Iraq, Iran, and counterterrorism.1048

Richelson provides some examples of when "*Special Plans*" have been used for deception in the past that seem to shed light on why the Pentagon used the oblique phrase *Office of Special Plans...* to describe Feith's new office's terror "evaluation" and war planning activities. One of Richelson's examples dates back to WWII: General Omar Bradley organized a *Special Plans* unit to "prepare and implement deception and cover plans for all United States forces in the United Kingdom."1049 Most readers are no doubt familiar with the massive campaign of deception that was orchestrated by Allied Commanders to deceive Hitler and the German High Command as to where the location for the D-Day landings would be.1050

A *Special Plans Branch* within the Joint Staff's Special Operation Division was used for "perception management," of the Iranian government, Ayotallah Khomeini and the terrorists holding the American hostages following the seizure of the U.S. Embassy in Tehran in November, 1979. Deception was taken to a higher level during the Reagan administration when a *Defense Special Plans Office* (DSPO) that would assist with the "US strategic deception program" was proposed. The DSPO was *reportedly* dissolved for lack of funding. Nevertheless, Richelson provides documentary evidence of the continued existence during the Reagan years of the Special Plans Branch in the Joint Staff Special Operations Division, plus another Special Plans Branch organized within the Human Resources Division of the Defense Intelligence Agency. These branches both had to do with "perception management."1051

Another fact worth noting - concerning the Axis of Spiel - is that Scooter Libby and Paul Wolfowitz had known each other for decades before Libby, in 2001, became an aide to the Vice President. Libby was a student of Wolfowitz at Yale,[1052] and Libby has stated that Wolfowitz was "one of his favorite professors."[1053] The feeling was mutual. Wolfowitz became a mentor to Libby and helped guide his rise to the elite ranks of the Republican Party. In 1981, when Wolfowitz was Director of Policy Planning at the State Department he put Libby on his Policy

Planning Staff. Wolfowitz became the Assistant Secretary of State for East Asian and Pacific Affairs in 1982, and he then made Libby the Director of Special Projects for the Bureau. In 1992, while serving as Deputy Undersecretary of Defense for Policy under Wolfowitz, Libby assisted Wolfowitz in the preparation of the highly controversial Defense Planning Guidance paper containing the Wolfowitz Doctrine which was leaked to the New York Times.[1054]

One year after 9/11, Libby, Wolfowitz, Perle and Donald Rumsfeld all had not a one year old, but a four year old or older desire to oust Saddam Hussein by force.[1055] Nearly ten years before the September 11, 2001 terrorist attacks, President George H. W. Bush had signed a directive to the CIA to create the conditions for regime change in Iraq.[1056] Additionally, on May 6, 2013, MSNBC aired the documentary *Why We Did It* , which presents documents and testimony which support the conclusion that before he became President, George W. Bush wanted to oust Saddam Hussein.[1057]

The Sham Evidence of WMD and an Iraqi Connection to 911 and Al-Qaeda

On January 28, 2003, President Bush delivered his State of The Union Address. In it, Bush made a sixteen word statement that voiced a conclusion that his speech writers had been warned against making by the CIA on four previous occasions.[1058] His statement was designed to move public opinion to support his still secret plan to invade Iraq. His words were:

> The British government has learned that Saddam Hussein recently sought significant quantities of uranium from Africa.[1059]

In truth, Iraq had not recently sought to acquire uranium from Africa or anywhere else. The idea that Iraq had obtained or attempted to obtain uranium ore had been investigated by a series of U.S. and foreign intelligence officials who found no credible evidence to support it.[1060] There were two bits of evidence involved. The first was the fact that in February of 1999, Iraq's envoy, Wissam al-Zahawie, had visited Niger and three other African countries. The official reason for Zahawie's trip, never shown to be untrue, was to encourage African leaders to reestablish commercial relations with Iraq.[1061] Iraq had been subject to sanctions since 1991 following the successful conclusion of Operation Desert Storm to liberate Kuwait. As many as one million people had died in Iraq, most of them children, because of the sanctions.[1062] Zahawie's trip was an understandable effort by Iraq to circumvent the U.N. sanctions, which had been brutally harmful to the Iraqi people.[1063] By 1996, to mitigate the harm to the Iraqi people, the U.N. had created an oil for food and medicine exception to the sanctions in the face of mounting criticism of the sanctions on humanitarian grounds.[1064]

The second piece of evidence Bush relied on were forged documents that were made with blank forms that had most likely been stolen from the Niger Embassy in Italy on New Years Day, 2001. On that date official Niger government stationary, letterheads and an official stamp were known to have been stolen from the embassy. The theft had been reported in Italian papers. Later an Italian known to have had dealings with the Italian spy agency SISMI named Rocco Martino peddled documents that bore official Nigerian government letterhead, and bore the mark of an official Nigerian government stamp, to the French government. The documents Martino sold contained details regarding an agreement for the sale of 500 tons of uranium yellowcake, by

Nigeria to Iraq. Uranium yellowcake can be processed into the enriched uranium needed to make a nuclear bomb. Martino has since said he obtained the documents from a female Italian spy who worked for the Nigerian embassy. He has also said that SISMI asked him to sell the documents to western intelligence agencies without tipping off those agencies that SISMI had asked them to do it.[1065]

The French government quickly determined that the Niger documents Martino wanted to sell them were fakes. A French consortium had complete control of Niger's uranium yellow cake output, and it would have been impossible for a sale of 500 tons of yellow cake, (equal to one sixth of Niger's entire annual production), to have been sold without having been noticed by French authorities. Unsurprisingly, the French paid Martino only a tiny fraction of the $100,000 he was asking for the documents.[1066]

Clearly the Italian authorities (who deny having used Martino as an agent), did obtain copies of the Niger Documents shortly after 911. They then notified American and British intelligence of the existence of the documents. American Intelligence then contacted French Intelligence for information about any yellowcake sales that might have taken place between Niger and Iraq. The French advised the Americans that the documents were fakes, but only after sending a special team to Niger to double check their original conclusion that the documents were indeed fraudulent. The CIA station chief in Paris sent numerous reports to CIA headquarters confirming that the Niger documents were forgeries as well. The U.S. Ambassador to Niger checked with the head of the French controlled consortium in Niger, and cabled Washington on November 20, 2001 that she too, had been assured that no yellowcake had been sold to Iraq.[1067]

Earlier, in mid-October of 2001, copies of the Niger documents had been sent to the State Department. State Department analyst Simon Dodge and others determined that the documents were most likely fakes. They also had found an impossible seeming agreement among the Niger papers of a "rogue state alliance" between Iraq, Iran and Islamic terrorist groups.[1068]

In February, 2002, the CIA sent former Ambassador Joe Wilson to Niger to investigate whether the Niger documents might be authentic. Joe Wilson had served in Niger as a member of the foreign service early in his career and he had extensive knowledge of the uranium industry there. After interviewing dozens of Niger officials and others, Wilson reported back to the CIA that it was highly doubtful that the yellowcake transaction between Iraq and Niger ever took place.[1069]

In all there were fifteen material anomalies from which it could be established with virtual certainty that the Niger documents were fakes. One suspicious item was the fact that the signature of a Niger minister who had been out of office for a decade was on one of the documents. Another was that the 1965 Constitution of Niger had been revised in 1999, but the documents wrongly indicated the Constitution of 1965 as the authority for the transaction described in the documents. One of documents referred to a future event as having happened in the past. Other mistakes involved the format and letterhead of one or more of the documents. The International Atomic Energy Commission determined with finality that the documents were fakes well before the war began.[1070]

President Bush thus had no concrete evidence to support his charge that Saddam had sought uranium, but he portrayed Iraq as a growing threat, stating:

> If Saddam Hussein does not fully disarm, for the safety of our people and for the peace of the world, we will lead a coalition to disarm him.[1071]

Bush sought to add to his credibility, by drawing upon the credibility that Colin Powell had amassed from years of almost always favorable, and frequently gushing, treatment by the media. Bush knew that Powell had the reputation of being a careful and logical thinker, and for being honest.[1072] Bush thus announced that Powell would provide detailed evidence of the allegedly grave threat posed by the regime of Saddam Hussein, stating:

> The United States will ask the U.N. Security Council to convene on February the fifth to consider the facts of Iraq's ongoing defiance of the world. Secretary of State Powell will present information and intelligence about Iraqi's--Iraq's illegal weapons programs, its attempts to hide those weapons from inspectors and its links to terrorist groups.[1073]

Colin Powell's subsequent speech to the United Nations represented the culmination of the Bush Administrations drive toward war in Iraq, which began the moment that Bush became President.[1074] The allegations made by Colin Powell on February 5, 2003, to the United Nations Assembly, set out with considerable detail the Bush Administration's claim that a preemptive war was needed against Iraq, to protect the United States from Iraqi WMD,[1075]

Let's begin with the most convincing reason offered by Powell which, *if true*, justified a preemptive war against Iraq. That is the assertion he made that Iraq was working with al-Qaeda, leaving open the possibility that Saddam had helped orchestrate the September 11th attack on the World Trade Center. Here is an excerpt from Powell's speech at the point where he first mentions "al-Qaida:"

> But what I want to bring to your attention today is the potentially much more sinister nexus between Iraq and the al-Qaida terrorist network, a nexus that combines classic terrorist organizations and modern methods of murder. Iraq today harbors a deadly terrorist network headed by Abu Musab al-Zarqawi an associate and collaborator of Usama bin Laden and his al-Qaida lieutenants.[1076]

Powell had waited until nearly the end of his speech to imply that Iraq was working with al-Qaeda. Before considering Powell's comments regarding Zarqawi, it is very helpful to know something about him. Born Ahmed Fadhil Nazar al-Khalaylah, Zarqawi came into the world in late October, 1966 and grew up in Zarqa, Jordan. Zarqa is about thirteen miles from Jordan's capital of Amman. At some point in adulthood Zarqawi changed his name to Abu Musab al-Zarqawi. al-Zarqawi means "one from Zarqa." Abu Musab means "Musab's father."[1077] Musab means strong, capable, and like a bull.[1078]

Zarqawi is said to have been unruly and combative as a youth and a street thug who was arrested on many occasions. He came from a poor family, and as a boy he spent much of his time playing street soccer. He was also a high school dropout who wore tattoos and drank heavily. In the 1980's, Zarqawi's street thug lifestyle landed him in prison on a sexual assault charge. It was while he was in jail that Zarqawi got religion, and he became serious about Islam. So it was that at age twenty three, Zarqawi went to Afghanistan to aid the mujahideen fighting the Soviet occupation there. He is reported to have met Osama Bin Laden after arriving in Afghanistan just after the war ended. Zarqawi went back to Jordan with the desire of overthrowing the Hashemite monarchy of King Hussein, one of America's best friends in the Mideast. Zarqawi was imprisoned in Jordan in 1992, after a cache of arms and explosives was found in his residence there.[1079]

Seven years later, Zarqawi fled Jordan after a scheme he was involved in to blow up the Radisson Hotel in Amman was foiled. He headed to Peshawar, Pakistan, where he again met with Osama Bin Laden.[1080] Bin Laden is said by Jordanian government sources to have given Zarqawi $200,000.00 to build a terrorist training camp for his group of about 150 Jordanian militants who called themselves Jund al-Sham. Jund al-Sham means "Soldiers of the Levant" in Arabic. Their training camp was located near Herat, Pakistan. The camp trained its recruits in guerrilla style fighting techniques, the use explosives, sabotage, and chemical weapons.[1081] Other sources report that Zarqawi set up the group Jama'at al-Tawhid wal-Jihad in 1999 at the same camp.[1082] Zarqawi went to the Kurdish region of northern Iraq between mid 2002 and early 2003 and began working with a Salafist Islamic insurgent group known as Ansar al-Islam which was opposed to the secular government of Saddam Hussein.[1083] Whether it was before or after he left Afghanistan, Zarqawi is generally believed to have founded the group called Jama'at al-Tawhid wal-Jihad, which means "The Organization of Monotheism and Jihad" Jama'at al-Tawhid wal-Jihad is one of the groups which formed the Islamic State.[1084]

Ansar-al Islam means "Partisans of Islam."[1085] Saddam Hussein knew Ansar-al Islam as a threat to his regime because the group wished to create an Islamic state in Iraq, and that would result in Saddam being deposed.[1086] Zarqawi was attracted to Ansar and its leader Mullah Krekar, because in addition to wanting to overthrow King Hussein in Jordan to establish an Islamic state, Zarqawi and his band wished to drive American military forces out of the Islamic world. They also wished to destroy Israel and restore Palestine.[1087]

With that background knowledge of who Zarqawi was (he was killed by US forces in 2006), lets return to Powell's words at the UN. The quotation from his speech which follows is a bit lengthy, but it contains the allegations within the speech that purport to establish a working relationship between Saddam Hussein or his lieutenants, Zarqawi and al-Qaeda:

> ...the Zarqawi network helped establish another poison and explosive training center camp, and this camp is located in northeastern Iraq...The network is teaching its operatives how to produce ricin and other poisons. Let me remind you how ricin works. Less than a pinch -- imagine a pinch of salt -- less than a pinch of ricin, eating just this amount in your food, would cause shock, followed by circulatory failure. Death comes within 72 hours and there is no antidote. There is no cure. It is fatal. Those helping to run this camp are Zarqawi lieutenants operating in northern Kurdish areas outside Saddam Hussein's controlled Iraq.[1088]
>
> But ***Baghdad has an agent in the most senior levels of the radical organization Ansar al-Islam that controls this corner of Iraq.*** [emphasis added] In 2000, this agent offered al-Qaida safe haven in the region. After we swept al-Qaida from Afghanistan, some of those members accepted this safe haven. They remain there today...[1089]

Iraqi officials deny accusations of ties with al-Qaida. These denials are simply not credible. Last year, an al-Qaida associate bragged that the situation in Iraq was "good," that Baghdad could be transited quickly.

We are not surprised that Iraq is harboring Zarqawi and his subordinates. This understanding builds on decades-long experience with respect to ties between Iraq and al-Qaida. Going back to the early and mid-1990s when bin Laden was based in Sudan, ***an al-Qaida source tells us that Saddam and bin Laden reached an understanding that al-Qaida would no longer support activities against Baghdad***. [emphasis added] Early al-Qaida ties were forged by secret high-level intelligence service contacts with al-Qaida, secret Iraqi intelligence high-level contacts with al-Qaida. ***We know members of both organizations met repeatedly and have met at least eight times at very senior levels since the early 1990s***. [emphasis added] In 1996, ***a foreign security service tells us that bin Laden met with a senior Iraqi intelligence official in Khartoum and later met the director of the Iraqi intelligence service***.[1090] [emphasis added]

Saddam became more interested as he saw al-Qaida's appalling attacks. ***A detained al-Qaida member tells us that Saddam was more willing to assist al-Qaida after the 1998 bombings of our embassies in Kenya and Tanzania***. [emphasis added] Saddam was also impressed by al-Qaida's attacks on the USS Cole in Yemen in October 2000. Iraqis continue to visit bin Laden in his new home in Afghanistan. A senior defector, one of Saddam's former intelligence chiefs in Europe, says Saddam sent his agents to Afghanistan sometime in the mid-1990s to provide training to al-Qaida members on document forgery. From the late 1990s until 2001, the Iraqi Embassy in Pakistan played the role of liaison to the al-Qaida organization.[1091]

...Al-Qaida continues to have a deep interest in acquiring weapons of mass destruction. As with the story of Zarqawi and his network, ***I can trace the story of a senior terrorist operative telling how Iraq provided training in these weapons to al-Qaida***. [emphasis added] Fortunately, this operative is now detained and he has told his story. I will relate it to you now as he, himself, described it.

This senior al-Qaida terrorist was responsible for one of al-Qaida's training camps in Afghanistan. His information comes firsthand from his personal involvement at senior levels of al-Qaida. He says bin Laden and his top deputy in Afghanistan, deceased al-Qaida leader Muhammad Atif, did not believe that al-Qaida labs in Afghanistan were capable enough to manufacture these chemical or biological agents. They needed to go somewhere else. They had to look outside of Afghanistan for help.

Where did they go? Where did they look? They went to Iraq. The support that this detainee describes included Iraq offering chemical or biological weapons training for two al-Qaida associates beginning in December 2000. He says that a militant known as Abdallah al-Iraqi had been sent to Iraq several times between 1997 and 2000 for help in acquiring poisons and gasses. Abdallah al-Iraqi characterized the relationship he forged with Iraqi officials as successful.[1092]

Powell stated (see the highlighted areas of the quotes from his UN speech above) that the only evidence the U.S. had of an al-Qaeda - Saddam working relationship came from "an al Qaida source," "a foreign security service," "a detained al-Qaida member," and a "a senior terrorist operative responsible for one of al-Qaida's training camps in Afghanistan." Referring to Saddam's regime and al-Qaeda Powell also said "we know members of both organizations met repeatedly and have met at least eight times at very senior levels since the early 1990s."[1093]

It is very easy to debunk the myth fashioned by the Bush Administration operatives who scared America into the Iraq War, when it comes to the false claims made about WMD in Iraq. Everything in Powell's speech about WMD was just so much hogwash.[1094] The assertions relating to WMD in Powell's address to the UN were known to CIA, DIA, State Department and military analysts to lack credibility at the time Powell spoke in February, 2003.[1095] The conclusion that defense establishment experts and analysts knew beforehand that Powell's claims about a working relationship between al-Qaeda and Iraq was also hogwash is also inescapable.[1096]

Powell tried to lessen the potential harm to his reputation from making a speech calling for war based on specious evidence by asking his trusted aid, Lawrence Wilkerson, to go over the rough draft for the UN speech that Powell had been given by Dick Cheney. Powell wanted Wilkerson to delete any incredulous assertions that had been put into the speech by its author, Scooter Libby. When Wilkerson went through the speech he quickly realized that the speech was fatally flawed.[1097]

Much of the information in Libby's draft had already been discredited by intelligence agency analysts.[1098] Wilkerson reviewed the speech with George Tenet, then the Director of the CIA, and four other Pentagon employees. He simply could not verify the statements put in the speech by Libby when he referred to the source documents that were being provided to him by his panel of assistants. After six hours he had only been able to approve about two pages of the text. He threw the speech to the table and said "This isn't going to cut it...."[1099] Then Tenet suggested that they could write a new speech using the National Intelligence Estimate (NIE) that had been shown to certain high level Senators to gain their approval of going to war.[1100] Libby's draft was trashed and a new draft was hacked out which removed the most absurd and already disproved assertions that Libby had perhaps taken in part from Feith's web of false evidence. However, the final draft contained conclusions that the experts of the State Department's Bureau of Intelligence and Research did not believe. As Secretary of State, Colin Powell went before the United Nations to give evidence which he knew his own experts did not believe.[1101] I knew it too, and I mocked and parodied Powell as a liar while watching him give his speech during a meal at a crowded restaurant - drawing uproarious laugher from the crowd of patrons who were listening to me.

As Paul Pillar, the CIA's national intelligence officer for the Near East and South Asia later put it, analysts had consistently felt "a strong wind" blowing in the direction of war from the Commander in Chief and the White House.[1102] They, much like Powell, were induced by the political wind to include discredited and unscientific conclusions about nuclear, biological and chemical WMD in the NIE, and to rely on highly questionable sources in finding there had been cooperation between al-Qaeda, Zarqawi and Saddam's regime.[1103] There were unusually strong dissents about the questionable items in the NIE by some of the best of the analysts and experts involved, but Powell relied on the questionable conclusions in the NIE.[1104]

After the war, the Senate Select Intelligence Committee held hearings to determine why the pre-war intelligence had been so wrong. In 2006, the committee produced a report titled *Postwar Findings about Iraq's WMD Programs and Links To Terrorism And How they Compare with Prewar Assessments.*[1105] That report states many conclusions. With respect to Colin Powell's claim that "members of" al-Qaeda and Saddam's regime "met repeatedly and" [had] "met at least eight times at very senior levels since the early 1990s," the Senate Select Intelligence Committee found as follows:

> ...**Postwar findings have identified only one meeting between representatives of al-Qa'ida and Saddam Hussein's regime reported in prewar intelligence assessments. Postwar findings have identified two occasions not reported prior to the war, in which Saddam Hussein rebuffed meeting requests from an al-Qa'ida operative. The Intelligence Community has not found any other evidence of meetings between al-Qa'ida and Iraq.**[1106]
>
> Postwar information indicates there were three instances in which al-Qa'ida communicated with representatives of Saddam's regime, one of which have been identified by the Intelligence Community prior to the war. All of the contacts were initiated by al-Qa'ida. Debriefings and captured regime documents show that the Intelligence Community accurately assessed that Iraqi intelligence officer Faruq Hijazi met with bin Laden in 1995 in Sudan. Debriefings of Hijazi indicate that, prior to the meeting, Saddam directed Hijazi to 'only listen' and not negotiate or promise anything to bin Laden. At the meeting, bin Laden requested an office in Iraq, military training for his followers, Chinese sea mines and the broadcast of speeches from an anti-Saudi cleric. Hijazi told debriefers that Saddam immediately rejected bin Laden's request for the office, mines and training, but considered broadcasting the speeches. Postwar information does not indicate whether Iraq actually broadcasted the speeches. Postwar debriefings also indicate that al-Qa'ida operative Abu Hafs al-Mauritani traveled to Iraq in 1998 and 2002 seeking a meeting with Saddam Hussein. Saddam refused to meet Abu Hafs on both occasions and directed that he should leave the country because he could "cause a problem" for Iraq.[1107]

In that same 2006 report from the Senate Select Committee on Intelligence, a conclusion from an earlier 2004 investigation by the committee regarding prewar intelligence was summarized as follows:

SSCI July 2004 Report Conclusion - Contacts

> The Senate Intelligence Committee concluded that the CIA "reasonably assessed that there were likely several instances of contacts between the Iraq and al-Qa'ida throughout the 1990s, but that these contacts did not add up to established formal relationship."[1108]

With respect to Powell's claim to the UN of contacts between Zarqawi, who was living in northern Kurdish controlled Iraq and working with Ansar al-Islam, and Iraq's regime, the committee report states as follows:

> In its July 2002 Special Analysis, the DIA focused on contacts between al-Qa'ida and Iraq by examining the activities of Ansar al-Islam a radical Islamic organization based in Kurdish-controlled northern Iraq. The DIA said that 'Baghdad may have an indirect tie to al-Qa'ida through the militant Islamic Kurdish group Ansar al-Islam' but noted various reports alleging regime complicity with this troublesome organization, 'each also has flaws that undermine confidence in the reporting.' The DIA said that al-Qa'ida 'has proven ties to Ansar al-Islam' but noted there were no indications of an Iraqi government role in these activities.[1109]

Ultimately of course, there was no evidence credibly linking Iraq and al-Qaida as working partners either before the Iraq war, or after it. If there was such evidence, the Senate Select Committee on Intelligence would have noted it. When Colin Powell made his speech he did not fully understand what he was talking about with respect to claimed links between Iraq and Al-Qaida or between Saddam's regime and Zarqawi. His trusted aid, Lawrence Wilkerson later came forward and said that on February 1, 2003, Powell was ready to delete every assertion about Saddam's links to al-Qaeda from his speech. Wilkerson said he agreed with Powell "that what we had was bull___t." But then in the space of one hour the Director of the CIA, George Tenet and his deputy, John McLaughlin convinced Powell that a high level al-Qaeda operative, whose name Tenet would not reveal, had made a statement during interrogation that there were indeed substantial contacts between al-Qaeda and Iraq. Tenet told Powell that the operative had stated that Iraq had helped to train al-Qaeda terrorists in the use of biological and chemical WMD.[1110]

Experts I have talked to have told me it will take years of FOIA requests to unravel all the delusive evidence that was used by Bush and Cheney's crew at the CIA, in serving up the bogus NIE, and other questionable evidence that Powell and Wilkerson relied on in drafting Powell's remarks to the UN. Some of it came from credibility lacking stories that Chalabi and other INC Iraqi expatriates told, in order to encourage America to go to war with Saddam.[1111] There is also evidence of an even more troubling source for the falsehoods that were spoken by Powell about a nexus between Saddam's regime and al-Qaeda, and it came from Wilkerson. Wilkerson has told reporters he believed that Ibn al-Shaykh al-Libi, was the al-Qaeda operative that Tenet was referring to when he convinced Powell to keep the Zarqawi material in his UN speech.[1112]

In 2006, the Senate Select Intelligence Committee concluded that Ibn al-Shaykh al-Libi was lying about an Iraq - al-Qaeda nexus in order to avoid torture, and that the CIA should have known it at the time:

> Postwar findings support the DIA February 2002 assessment that Ibn al-Shaykh al-Libi was likely intentionally misleading his debriefers when he said that Iraq provided two al-Qa'ida associates with chemical and biological weapons (CBW) training in 2000... Postwar findings do not support the CIA's assessment that his

> reporting was credible... No postwar information has been found that indicates CBW training occurred and the detainee who provided the key prewar reporting about this training recanted his claims after the war... CIA's January 2003 version of Iraqi Support for Terrorism described al-Libi's reporting for CBW training "credible", but noted that the individuals who traveled to Iraq for CBW training had not returned, so al-Libi was not in position to know if the training had taken place... In January 2004, al-Libi recanted his allegations about CBW training and many of his other claims about Iraq's links to al Qa'ida. He told debriefers that, to the best of his knowledge, al-Qa'ida never sent any individuals into Iraq for any kind of support in chemical or biological weapons. Al-libi told debriefers that he fabricated information while in U.S. custody to receive better treatment and in response to threats of being transferred to a foreign intelligence service which he believed would torture him... He said that later, while he was being debriefed by a (REDACTED) foreign intelligence service, he fabricated more information in response to physical abuse and threats of torture. The foreign government service denies using any pressure during al-Libi's interrogation. In February 2004, the CIA reissued the debriefing reports from al-Libi to note that he had recanted information. A CIA officer explained that while CIA believes al-Libi fabricated information, the CIA cannot determine whether, or what portions of, the original statements or the later recants are true of false.[1113]

The important revelations from the Senate finding include the fact that the Defense Intelligence Agency had decided in February, 2002, one year before Colin Powell spoke at the UN, that Ibn al-Shaykh al-Libi was lying. The DIA report language makes it quite clear that Ibn al-Shaykh al-Libi could not be believed. On February 22, 2002 the DIA had issued a *Defense Intelligence Terrorism Summary* which stated:

> This is the first report from Ibn al-Shaykh al-Libi [al-Libi] in which he claims Iraq assisted al-Qa'ida's CBRN efforts. However, he lacks specific details on the Iraqi's involvement, the CBRN materials associated with the assistance, and the location where the training occurred. It is possible he does not know any further details; it is more likely this individual is intentionally misleading the debriefers. Ibn al-Shaykh al-Libi has been undergoing debriefs for several weeks and may be describing scenarios to the debriefers that he knows will retain their interest. Saddam's regime is intensely secular and is wary of Islamic revolutionary movements. Moreover, Baghdad is unlikely to provide assistance to a group it cannot control.[1114]

Just six days later the Defense Intelligence Agency issued yet another type of report, a *DIA Special Analysis* touching on the laughable idea that the Iraqi military was helping train Islamic fundamentalists, (all of whom wanted to depose Saddam Hussein), in the use of weapons of mass destruction. The later analysis paper drew a similar conclusion as the first:

> Iraq has been repeatedly accused of aiding al-Qa'ida's chemical and biological acquisition efforts. Despite recent information from a senior al-Qa'ida trainer currently in custody, all-source intelligence has not confirmed Iraq's involvement.

> Iraq is unlikely to have provided bin Laden any useful CB knowledge or assistance.[1115]

The DIA again cautioned against believing al-Libi again, in July, 2002.[1116]

After having properly decided to delete every assertion about Saddam's links to al-Qaeda from his draft speech, there was no good reason for Colin Powell to then rely on the single unnamed witness that CIA Director George Tenet and Tenet's deputy John McLaughlin told Powell about at the last minute. More to the point, Powell claimed in his speech that there was more evidence than just one unnamed witness to justify his claims of cooperation between al-Qa'ida and Saddam Hussein, but that must have been the evidence that Powell had previously found to be such "bull___t" he was willing to throw it all out.[1117] Powell also knew or should have known of the three or more DIA reports which came out well before his speech that found al-Libi to be unbelievable. It certainly seems that Powell knew as he gave his speech, which was delivered in a remarkably polished, well rehearsed and persuasive manner, that there was every possibility that much of what he was saying would later be proved to be untrue.[1118]

Powell had already removed a truly absurd "Atta in Prague" allegation from his speech despite the fact that both Bush and Cheney had made strong public statements claiming they knew that Mohammad Atta, a ringleader of the 9/11 attack, had worked with Iraqi intelligence, having met an Iraqi intelligence officer in Prague.[1119] The Atta in Prague allegation was utterly false and based on Feith's nonsensical web of intelligence data that had already been proved unreliable.[1120] Powell also knew every word he said to the UN about Iraq having WMD might later blow up in his face and trash his reputation. His Chief of Staff, Lawrence Wilkerson has said this about the day Congress authorized Bush to attack Iraq:

> Powell walked into my office and without so much as a fare-thee-well, he walked over to the window and he said, "I wonder what'll happen when we put 500,000 troops into Iraq and comb the country from one end to the other and find nothing?" And he turned around and walked back in his office. And I—I wrote that down on my calendar—as close for—to verbatim as I could, because I thought that was a profound statement coming from the secretary of state, former chairman of the joint chiefs of staff.[1121]

Wilkerson has also admitted that Powell was unsure whether the assertions he made in his UN address were true when he made them.[1122] It has been alleged that in addition to speaking from culpable ignorance, Powell knowingly misrepresented the meaning of some audio transmissions that had been intercepted by U.S. intelligence in Iraq. Towards the beginning of his speech, Powell played audio recordings which contained conversations between Iraqi soldiers about UN inspections for WMD. Powell also used overhead projections containing what was supposed to be verbatim transcripts of the audio recordings. The overhead text contained terms that were not in the intercepts, and so did Powell's English translation of what had been said by the Iraqis.[1123] According to Bob Woodward's book *Plan of Attack*,[1124] and Jonathan Schwartz's article *Lie After Lie After Lie: What Colin Powell Knew Ten Years Ago Today and What He Said,*[1125] Powell's description of what the Iraqi's said turned the audio recording evidence inside out; Conversations which tended to support the premise that Iraqi had not violated UN resolutions were converted by Powell's subtly deceptive translation to show that the Iraq had failed to abide the UN resolutions.[1126]

In the transcript segment below the words in italics were creations of Powell and cannot be heard on the recorded audio:

> POWELL reading from the transcript: "Lt. Colonel: They're inspecting the ammunition you have, yes."
>
> "Colonel: Yes."
>
> "Lt. Colonel: For the possibility there are forbidden ammo."
>
> " Lt. Colonel: For the possibility there is by chance forbidden ammo?"
>
> "Colonel: Yes."
>
> "Lt. Colonel: And we sent you a message *yesterday to clean out all of the areas*, the scrap areas, the abandoned areas. *Make sure there is nothing there*."

The guilt suggesting words "clean all of the areas" and "make sure there is nothing there" were never spoken by the Iraqi soldiers. Those phrases were made up in order to transform an innocent conversation into an incriminating one.[1127]

Here is what the Iraqi's actually said:

> "Lt. Colonel: They are inspecting the ammunition you have.
>
> "Colonel: Yes.
>
> "Lt. Col: For the possibility there are forbidden ammo.
>
> "Colonel: Yes?
>
> "Lt. Colonel: For the possibility there is by chance, forbidden ammo.
>
> "Colonel: Yes.
>
> "Lt. Colonel: And we sent you a message to inspect the scrap areas and the abandoned areas.
>
> "Colonel: Yes."[1128]

According to Powell, what the Iraq's were talking about doing was "all part of a system of hiding things and moving things out of the way and making sure they have left nothing behind."[1129] But no weapons of mass destruction were ever found after the war in Iraq began,[1130] and as you will see in the "assertions and reality" section of this chapter below, there was no other reliable evidence before the war of WMD in Iraq. It was easy for me to conclude that Powell was attempting to mislead the nations of the world in order to justify an unnecessary war.

From the forgoing tiny segment of what might have been a much longer and more easily understood conversation, it is impossible to conclude that the Iraqi regime had any stockpiles of chemical, biological or nuclear WMD which might have been used on the United States. Iraq did have deployable chemical weapons at one time, and Iraq was working on developing a nuclear weapon before their defeat in the first gulf war. After the Desert Storm, the war to liberate Kuwait, Iraq had agreed to eliminate their nuclear program, to allow unfettered inspections, and to eliminate certain missile systems. Their nuclear materials were found by weapons inspectors and completely destroyed.[1131] No reliable evidence has ever been unearthed that indicates Iraq's nuclear program was restarted after it was ended.[1132]

It is likely that the commanding officer who spoke in the recorded conversation wanted to make sure that the unused portions of the ammunition storage facilities were safe, and that any obstructions or debris that might cause injury to the inspectors in the scrap areas and abandoned areas were removed and the area cleaned up. Under normal operating conditions, scrap and abandoned areas of Iraqi ammunition storage facilities would not be areas where important VIPs and foreigners would visit. Any competent commanding officer would want to make sure his career did not go down the drain because his neglect caused an injury to an important visitor from the UN. This fact would be true anywhere, but especially so in a country ruled by a despot with a reputation for brutality.[1133]

Both Woodward and Schwartz checked the official State Department transcript of the audio recordings and Schwartz also checked with an Iraqi who could personally translate the recordings in Arabic. It is quite troubling that after Journalism Professor Emeritus Gilbert Cranberg of the University of Iowa confirmed the existence of a discrepancy between what the two Iraqi's said, and what Powell said they had said,[1134] that the State Department quickly and quietly removed the transcript containing the correct translation from its website.[1135] The correct version is however still available at archive.org.[1136]

The rest of the fairy tale that Powell told the UN is similar to what Bush, Cheney and Rumsfeld and other Bush administration figures told the American people during the run up to the Iraq War, which fact brings us to the final section of this chapter.

Assertions and Reality: False Statements of Bush, Cheney, Rumsfeld and Powell

Immediately after 911, long before Powell's address to the UN, the misinformation had begun to flow out of the mouths of Bush and Cheney. Below is a short list of some of the false assertions they made, together with the actual facts that they knew or should have known at the time they made their statements.

Assertions regarding: *Atta in Prague*

12/09/01 Stated by Cheney on Meet the Press:

> Well, what we now have that's developed since you and I last talked, Tim, of course, was that report that's been pretty well confirmed, that he [Atta] did go to Prague and he did meet with a senior official of the Iraqi intelligence service in Czechoslovakia last April, several months before the attack.[1137]

09/08/02 Stated by Cheney on Meet the Press:

> We've seen in connection with the hijackers, of course, Mohamed Atta, who was the lead hijacker, did apparently travel to Prague on a number of occasions. And on at least one occasion, we have reporting that places him in Prague with a senior Iraqi intelligence official a few months before the attack on the World Trade Center.[1138]

09/14/03 Stated by Cheney on Meet the Press:

> With respect to 9/11, of course, we've had the story that's been public out there. The Czechs alleged that Mohamed Atta, the lead attacker, met in Prague with a senior Iraqi intelligence official five months before the attack, but we've never been able to develop anymore of that yet either in terms of confirming it or discrediting it. We just don't know.[1139]

The Actual Reality regarding: *Atta in Prague*

The CIA and the FBI had already conducted a thorough investigation and had discredited the Atta in Prague evidence before Cheney made his initial claim about Atta in December, 2001. No new evidence was ever adduced to change the conclusions reached by the CIA and the FBI. The evidence that Atta may have met with an Iraqi intelligence agent originated with the Czech intelligence service. The Czechs had received a report from a Middle Eastern man who had seen Atta's picture in the paper after the 9/11 attack. The man thought he recalled having seen someone who may have been Atta on April 9, 2001 at 11:00 o'clock in the morning outside the Iraqi embassy in Prague. The Czech source thought that when he saw Atta he was talking to Ahmed Khalil Ibrahim Samir al-Ani outside the embassy. Al-Ani was the station chief for Iraqi intelligence in Prague at the time. The Czechs also sent a photo of a Middle Eastern looking man to American intelligence. The photo had been taken in close proximity to the Iraqi embassy on the same date that the witness thought he might have seen Atta with Al-Ani. Both the FBI and CIA carefully analyzed the photo and concluded that the person who had been photographed was probably not Atta.[1140] Isikoff and Corn reported in their book *Hubris* that an American counter terrorism expert who had examined the photo personally said that "we knew right away that's not Atta."[1141] Moreover, the FBI investigated and found no evidence that Atta, had traveled to Prague in April of 2001 when his meeting with Al-Ani might have occurred. Atta's cell phone was used in Florida on the date he was supposed to be in Prague. Al-Ani was not even in Prague at the time he was allegedly meeting with Atta.[1142] The 911 Commission found that the available evidence did not support the original Czech report of an Atta - Ani meeting.[1143]

When FBI agent Mark Rossini, who had seen the photo and knew it was clearly not Atta, saw Cheney claim on Meet The Press that it had "been pretty well confirmed that he [Atta] did go to Prague and he did meet with a senior official of the Iraqi intelligence service in Czechoslovakia last April,"[1144] Rossini "actually threw something at the television because" he "couldn't believe what" he had "just heard."[1145] Rossini, who was assigned to work with the CIA investigating Atta later made the following statement in the Hubris video on MSNBC:

> Mohammed Atta was a sleight guy ... barely 5'5 or 5'6, and skinny. The guy in the photograph was muscular, thick, and had a neck like the size of two of my necks. And I thought, "that's not Mohammed Atta in the photograph!" But I sent it to the lab anyway, knowing that would put it to rest.[1146]

The Atta in Prague allegation is similar to the phony yellowcake sale by Niger to Iraq allegation that was based on stolen official documents that were used to create phony evidence using forgery. We clearly have a situation where *somebody* may have been creating false evidence that would help push America into a war that the *Bush* administration wanted very badly. Why would somebody tell the Czech police they thought they recalled having seen a person they did not know, and had never even seen before, based upon having seen a newspaper photo five months later? How many people could remember seeing a stranger's face even five weeks after the fact, let alone five months after the fact? The person who made the report to the Czech authorities may have been seeking attention and a sense of self-importance. That individual may also have been lying as a willing tool of those who needed fabricated evidence to justify the Iraq war. The man who sold the Niger documents to French authorities, Rocco Martino, and or others who were involved in that caper may also have been used willfully as tools by those who wanted war in Iraq.

Assertions regarding: *Iraqi Stockpiles of Chemical and Biological Weapons of Mass Destruction*

8/26/2002, stated by Dick Cheney at the National VFW meeting in Nashville:

> The Iraqi regime has in fact been very busy enhancing its capabilities in the field of chemical and biological agents...
>
> Simply stated, there is no doubt that Saddam Hussein now has weapons of mass destruction. There is no doubt he is amassing them to use against our friends, against our allies, and against us. And there is no doubt that his aggressive regional ambitions will lead him into future confrontations with his neighbors -- confrontations that will involve both the weapons he has today, and the ones he will continue to develop with his oil wealth.[1147]

9/12/2002 stated by George W. Bush at the United Nations:

> Right now, Iraq is expanding and improving facilities that were used for the production of biological weapons.[1148]

09/18/2002, stated by Donald Rumsfeld, Secretary of Defense before Congress:

> We do know that the Iraqi regime has chemical and biological weapons. His regime has amassed large, clandestine stockpiles of chemical weapons -- including VX, sarin, cyclosarin and mustard gas. ... His regime has amassed large, clandestine stockpiles of biological weapons—including anthrax and botulism toxin, and possibly smallpox."[1149]

10/5/2002, stated by George W. Bush in a radio address:

> Iraq has stockpiled biological and chemical weapons, and is rebuilding the facilities used to make more of those weapons...We have sources that tell us that Saddam Hussein recently authorized Iraqi field commanders to use chemical weapons -- the very weapons the dictator tells us he does not have.[1150]

10/7/2002, stated by George W. Bush in speech at Cincinnati Union Terminal:

> The Iraqi regime . . . possesses and produces chemical and biological weapons... We know that the regime has produced thousands of tons of chemical agents, including mustard gas, sarin nerve gas, VX nerve gas...
>
> We've also discovered through intelligence that Iraq has a growing fleet of manned and unmanned aerial vehicles that could be used to disperse chemical or biological weapons across broad areas. We're concerned that Iraq is exploring ways of using these UAVS for missions targeting the United States.[1151]

01/28/2003, stated by George W. Bush during State of the Union Address:

> Our intelligence officials estimate that Saddam Hussein had the materials to produce as much as 500 tons of sarin, mustard and VX nerve agent.[1152]

02/05/2003, stated by Colin Powell at the United Nations:

> Numerous human sources tell us that the Iraqis are moving...weapons of mass destruction, to keep them from being found by inspectors. While we were here in this Council chamber debating Resolution 1441 last fall, we know from sources that a missile brigade outside Baghdad was dispersing rocket launchers and warheads containing biological warfare agent to various locations, distributing them to various locations in western Iraq.[1153]
>
> Most of the launchers and warheads had been hidden in large groves of palm trees and were to be moved every one to four weeks to escape detection. We also have satellite photos that indicate that banned materials have recently been moved from a number of Iraqi weapons of mass destruction facilities.[1154]
>
> Let me say a word about satellite images before I show a couple. The photos that I am about to show you are sometimes hard for the average person to interpret, hard for me. The painstaking work of photo analysis takes experts with years and years of experience, poring for hours and hours over light tables. But as I show you these images, I will try to capture and explain what they mean, what they indicate, to our imagery specialists.[1155] [Following this point in his address Powell launched into a long discussion of satellite photos and the WMD they allegedly showed.]
>
> ...We have first-hand descriptions of biological weapons factories on wheels and on rails.The trucks and train cars are easily moved and are designed to evade detection by inspectors. In a matter of months, they can produce a quantity of biological poison equal to the entire amount that Iraq claimed to have produced in the years prior to the Gulf War.[1156]

03/17/2003, stated by George W. Bush

> Intelligence gathered by this and other governments leaves no doubt that the Iraq regime continues to possess and conceal some of the most lethal weapons ever devised.[1157]

The Actual Reality regarding: *Iraqi Stockpiles of Chemical and Biological Weapons of Mass Destruction*

Before 9/11 the highly professional agents of the Counterproliferation Division (CPD) of the Directorate of Operations at the Central Intelligence Agency had the job of seeking intelligence on foreign WMD development efforts worldwide.[1158] The CPD also did planning and developed covert methods for thwarting efforts by other countries to obtain WMD.[1159] CPD contained a unit known as the Joint Task Force on Iraq (JTFI) which was created out of a smaller "Iraq unit" in the summer before 9/11.[1160] The higher ups at the CIA greatly increased the staff and resources of the JTFI after 9/11. JTFI also came under extreme pressure to provide evidence of WMD programs in Iraq. By the spring of 2002, JTFI was in a frenzy to find a WMD smoking gun in Iraq. JTFI found dozens of reliable new sources among Iraqi scientists and weapons experts, but JTFI learned nothing from those scientists and weapons experts to suggest Iraq had or was attempting to create WMD.[1161]

What JTFI did find was that as the talk by Bush Administration officials about the threat posed by Saddam became more urgent sounding and the drums of war at the White House began beating faster JTFI began to become inundated with Iraqi self described “defectors,” who showed up at CIA offices looking for cash in return for telling what they knew.[1162] These “defectors” told incredible stories of WMD, but one story after another from these dubious witnesses proved to be false. The JTFI officers came to realize that the Iraqi’s who came their way with phony stories of WMD were sent by the Iraqi National Congress.[1163] The INC was a CIA front organization paid for with funds appropriated by Congress to help obtain regime change in Iraq.[1164] The absurdity of the claims by the INC plants was sometimes glaringly obvious, but Feith and his henchmen dutifully strung together the shards of discredited evidentiary bits and pieces to sculpt the image of a mad cap Saddam sitting astride a gigantic stockpile of WMD.[1165]

Colin Powell had serious doubts all along about the truth of the allegations he made about WMD programs run by Iraq to the United Nations.[1166] He knew that the White House had subjected the intelligence agencies to unrelenting pressure to find evidence of WMD in Iraq.[1167] Powell’s Chief of Staff, Larry Wilkerson had tossed out Scooter Libby’s entire proffered draft for Powell’s U.N. speech, because it was filled with unreliable evidence from sources such as the Iraqi National Congress, which had been laundered by Feith’s crew at the Pentagon.[1168] Powell himself was subsequently working on the speech when he looked at Libby’s subsequent draft of a section for the speech on terrorism. He told Wilkerson: “I’m not reading this. This is crazy.”[1169] Powell also had reason to doubt the reliability of the final draft of his speech, which was based largely on an October, 2002, National Intelligence Estimate (NIE) which bore the title: *Iraq’s Continuing Programs for Weapons of Mass Destruction.*[1170]

A little more than a year after the war began it was clear there were was no WMD to be found in Iraq. The NIE which Powell had uncritically relied on was quickly discovered by the Senate to have been based on worthless sources and unreliable analysis.[1171] There were analysts and experts in the government who had desperately tried to get the truth out, but the Commander in Chief was easily able to ram his desired conclusions through an Intelligence Community that had become hardly more than a propaganda machine for administration lies to the American people.[1172] The media monopoly dutifully reported White House propaganda as fact checked “fair and accurate,” truth.[1173] The first and most general conclusion contained in the report of the Senate Intelligence Committee on the U.S. Intelligence Community’s Prewar Intelligence Assessments on Iraq is this:

> Overall Conclusions Weapons of Mass Destruction
>
> Conclusion 1. Most of the major key judgments in the Intelligence Community's October 2002 National Intelligence Estimate (NIE), *Iraq’s Continuing Programs for Weapons of Mass Destruction,* either overstated, or were not supported by, the underlying intelligence reporting. A series of failures, particularly in analytical

trade craft, led to the mischaracterization of the intelligence.[1174]

That was the Senate's politically expedient way of expressing that there was no substance to the allegations made by Bush on down about chemical and biological (and nuclear) weapons in Iraq. The Senate Select Intelligence Committee's postwar findings about Iraq's WMD programs included the following summation of its 2004 conclusions regarding biological weapons:

1. SSCI July 2004 Report Conclusion - Biological

> In its July 2004 report, the Committee concluded that the judgment in the NIE that "Baghdad has biological weapons" overstated what was known about Iraq's biological weapons holdings, did not explain the uncertainties underlying the statement, and did not explain that the conclusion that Iraq had a mobile biological weapons program was largely based on the reporting from a single source. The Committee also concluded that the Intelligence Community's judgments that "all key aspects–R&D, production, and weaponization–of Iraq's offensive BW program are active and that most elements are larger and more advanced than they were before the Gulf War" were not supported by the intelligence reporting provided to the Committee.[1175]

The "single source' referred to by the Senate Committee which was used to justify the false statements by Colin Powell and the White House to the American people concerning biological weapons in Iraq was a Iraqi expatriate code named "Curveball."[1176] Curveball's real name is Rafid Ahmed Alwan al-Janabi. Janabi was born on March 12, 1967. His parents had a total of nine other children. In 1990, Curveball graduated from the Bagdad University of Technology with a bachelors degree in chemical engineering. He graduated in the bottom half of his class. Between 1992 and 1995 Curveball worked for a seed purification plant near Bagdad. He was married in 1994 but he left his wife soon thereafter. In 1995, he worked for Babel Media in Iraq but was allegedly fired for stealing equipment from his employer.[1177]

Al-Janabi was thirty one years old when he arrived in Germany in 1999 via a flight from North Africa.[1178] He told German authorities after he landed that he was seeking asylum from the regime of Saddam Hussein in Iraq.[1179] Nothing is known with certainty about why Curveball left Iraq, but investigators eventually obtained evidence that Curveball's brother had worked as a bodyguard for Ahmed Chalabi.[1180] Chalabi was of course a leader in the Iraqi National Congress, (INC) the group funded by the CIA to help topple the regime of Saddam Hussein.[1181] I continue to wonder whether Curveball was a part of the CIA funded INC's campaign of misinformation using phony defectors to feed the Bush Administration's war hungry belly full of the phony evidence of WMD in Iraq that it craved.[1182] Although he had graduated from the Bagdad University of Technology with mediocre grades, Curveball told the German intelligence officers assigned to his case that he had graduated first in his class.[1183] He claimed that he had been hired to work on a germ warfare development team right out of college. His team, Curveball told his BND hosts helped design and build mobile bioweapon labs which could produce WMD containing deadly microbes.[1184]

Curveball provided such detailed, (later known to be fabricated), information about the alleged Iraqi bio weapons program that he convinced the Germans that he should receive both asylum and red-carpet treatment.[1185] Over one hundred intelligence reports were written and passed through the American Intelligence Community with information provided by Curveball.[1186] The Germans provided Curveball with a nice home, and an income in return for his contributions of information about Iraq.[1187] In the early months of 2000 the German intelligence service, which in German is named the Bundesnachrichtendienst or BND, told the American Defense Intelligence Agency (DIA) office in Munich about al-Janabi. Reportedly, it was somebody at the DIA's Munich office, an old and well appointed mansion that housed about thirty DIA staffers, who came up with the codename "Curveball" for al-Janabi.[1188]

Bob Drogin writes in his book about al-Janabi, *Curveball, Spies, Lies And The Con Man Who Caused A War*, that the DIA operative who came up with Curveball's codename did not intend to ridicule al-Janabi's credibility. Drogan bases his belief on the fact that the use of the word "ball' as part of the code name for defectors was a common practice for American intelligence during the cold war. For example the codename "Match Ball" was used for an important cold war era intelligence source, and various others were used according to Drogan.[1189] However, some doubt is raised about Drogan's view concerning the genesis of al-Janabi's codename by the fact that when the Senate investigated Curveball after the war began, and in every investigation which has looked into the matter since that time, the originator of al-Janabi's code name has never been identified.[1190]

Curveball told his German handlers's that German firms had aided Saddam's regime in the construction of bioweapons. It was true that German companies had in the past flaunted export controls on selling goods and services related to prohibited weapons of mass destruction. Dozen's of German companies had illegally aided Saddam's efforts to produce chemical weapons prior to Desert Storm, and German firms had constructed a chemical weapons factory in Libya for Muammar Qaddafi. So the BND did not find Curveball's story that German firms were again helping Saddam unbelievable. The BND did not want the allegation that Germany had again had a hand in helping a tyrant like Saddam make WMD to become known to American intelligence of the public, so they decided to keep Curveball under close wraps.[1191] The Germans told the CIA that Curveball hated Americans and could not speak English. They intimated that Curveball would stop trusting the BND if they let Americans interrogate him.[1192]

From the beginning, the Germans were skeptical about Curveball's veracity.[1193] Defectors and those who seek asylum to escape poverty and misfortune in their home countries frequently lie. They are desperate people and they must establish the grounds for their requests.[1194] In Germany at the time al-Janabi arrived in 1999, immigration officials granted on average only about one in twenty-five requests for asylum.[1195] Defectors that could supply intelligence on WMD in Iraq at the time Saddam was in power in were highly valued, but not automatically trusted.[1196] So when the BND began sending the DIA's "Munich House" reports on Curveball, the Germans never claimed that the information they were sending had been verified.[1197] In March, 2001, nearly two full years before Powell gave his speech packed with Janabi's obvious fabrications, the Germans had informed the CIA that Curveball had changed some of his stories. Also that spring a DIA biological warfare expert warned in a report that al-Janabi's story was "presently compromised by reporting inconsistencies."[1198]

In addition to having told his German handlers inconsistent stories, Curveball had displayed behavioral abnormalities. In early 2001, a top ranking American intelligence agent stationed in Germany, the CIA's chief of station in Berlin, notified the CIA's Counter Proliferation Division (CPD) that the BND had told him that Curveball had disappeared and could not be found, and was "out of control." In addition, in April of 2002, MI6, the famous British spy agency, told CIA that they were having "doubts about Curveball's reliability," and that "elements of his behavior strike us as typical of individuals we would normally assess as fabricators."[1199] Curveball's stories were also found to be inapposite with satellite reconnaissance photos of Djerf al Nadaf, which was the location of a seed purification warehouse. Curveball told a whopper of a lie about Djerf al Nadaf, claiming that it was used as a "docking station" for mobile bioweapons labs. Curveball had described the layout of the building, which he said included an entrance for the mobile labs on one side of the warehouse and an exit on the reverse side. The photos taken of the site showed that an unbroken wall enclosed three sides of the building.[1200] Curveball's story simply did not check out.[1201] Given the number of phony claims the CPD had gotten from Iraqi "defectors," and the obvious fact that Niger documents were fabricated it seems unbelievable that anyone would report Curveball's cockeyed story as proven fact to the world like Bush, Cheney and Colin Powell did.[1202] After all, Curveball's brother was the bodyguard of Chalabi, a fact known to the BND and American Intelligence.[1203]

But there is even more. One of Curveball's most incredible claims was that he had been witness to an accident at a bioweapons facility in 1998 in Bagdad. In Curveball's telling of his WMD fairytale twelve technicians working at the facility were exposed to biological agents and died from their exposure. Consequently it was surmised at the CPD that perhaps Curveball had received a vaccination from his employer as the result of his exposure, and/or had a trace amount of biotoxin in his blood. So in May, 2000 the CPD sent a CIA physician and germ warfare expert named "Les" to Germany with the BND's approval to take a blood sample from Curveball. Curveball (al-Janabi), was told that Les was a German specialist who would take a sample of his blood.[1204] Les returned to CIA HQ at Langley waving a red flag. He told CPD that Curveball did speak English, which should have alerted even the dullest CPD analyst that the BND was hiding something.[1205] Les also reported that when he met Curveball he smelled of alcohol and appeared to have a hangover even though their meeting took place in the morning. Les thought Curveball might be an alcoholic.[1206] Corn and Isikoff wrote in *Hubris* that a CPD "staffer" whose name they do not identify said that "We were watching the whole Curveball thing in horror" "We knew it was bad from the start. We felt powerless ...."[1207]

By late September 2002, there is clear evidence that the head of the CIA's Directorate of Operations, (DO) James L. Pavitt was aware that there was an issue with the trustworthiness of the reports coming across his desk regarding Curveball.[1208] About one month earlier, Vice President Cheney had told a VFW meeting that "the Iraqi regime has in fact been very busy enhancing its capabilities in the field of...biological agents."[1209] Cheney was treating Curveball's unsubstantiated fairy tale as undisputed fact. The down to earth professional analysts of the CPD had wisely leaned toward the conclusion that Curveball's value was "bad from the start"[1210] but a small biological weapons team composed of no more than six analysts in the CIA's Directorate of Intelligence was taking Curveball seriously. The small team of biological warfare analysts worked for WINPAC, the Weapons Intelligence Nonproliferation and Arms Control unit of the Directorate of Intelligence.[1211] Much of the difference in viewpoint between the two CIA units over Curveball resulted from the pressure bearing down on the Intelligence Community from the White House to build a case for invading Iraq, according to authors Corn, Isikoff, Drogin and others.[1212] Washington Post editor Peter Eisner and celebrated investigative journalist Knut Royce tell in their book *The Italian Letter* that Alan A. Foley, Director of WINPAC gave an address to WINPAC staff in December, 2002 in which he stated: "If the president wants to go to war, our job is to find the intelligence to allow him to do so."[1213]

When Pavitt had his biweekly meeting with the head of the European Division within the DO, Tyler Drumheller, in late September 2002, the question of Curveball's reliability was on Pavitt's busy mind. Drumheller mentioned during the meeting that he was having his monthly lunch meeting with the Station Chief of the BND's Washington office the very next day. Pavitt then told Drumheller it would be a good idea for him to ask the BND agent if the CIA could question "that WMD defector the Germans got in Munich" directly. Drumheller had to ask a group chief within the European Division which defector Pavitt was talking about.[1214] The next day Drumheller had his Friday lunch with the German spy, who went by the cover name Gradl.[1215] Gradl told Drumheller that in his opinion Curveball might be a fabricator. He said "you don't want to see him," "the guy's crazy" and that questioning him would be a "waste of time." Grandl also said no to the CIA's request for access to Curveball.[1216]

When Pavitt heard what Gradl had said about Curveball, Pavitt told Drumheller "stay on top of this."[1217] Pavitt also told Drumheller to notify WINPAC about Curveball. Soon after that, Drumheller had his assistant brief Alan Foley, the head of WINPAC, by email about Gradl's comments regarding Curveball.[1218] Drumheller also learned from his group chief, Margaret Henoch that WINPAC was taking Curveball seriously, and that Curveball's intrinsically unreliable reports about mobile bioweapons labs were going to be included in the National Intelligence Estimate (NIE) that had been requested by the Senate Intelligence Committee.[1219] Drumheller was aghast at the thought of such unreliable intelligence being included in an NIE.[1220]

This was the very same NIE that the Senate Intelligence Committee later found had overstated what was known about Iraq's biological weapons holdings, did not explain the uncertainties underlying the statement, and did not explain that the conclusion that Iraq had a mobile biological weapons program was largely based on the reporting from a single source. The Committee also concluded that the Intelligence Community's judgments that "all key aspects–R&D, production, and weaponization–of Iraq's offensive BW program are active and that most elements are larger and more advanced than they were before the Gulf War" were not supported by the intelligence reporting provided to the Committee.[1221]

An intelligence analyst involved in the production of the NIE later told the investigators from the Senate Select Committee on Intelligence

> the going-in assumption was we were going to war, so this NIE was to be written with that in mind... This is about going to war and giving the combatant commander an estimate on which he can properly organize.[1222]

It cannot be said that the deeply flawed NIE was responsible for the Congressional vote that later authorized the President to invade Iraq however. Senate staffers reported that only six members of Congress bothered to even look at the report before they voted in favor of the resolution that permitted Bush to launch the war in Iraq.[1223] Congress was afraid of Bush's popularity, and afraid of a voter backlash because of the misinformation that Bush, Cheney, Rumsfeld, Condolessa Rice, Wolfowitz and others had spread through the media monopoly, with but a hint of criticism and fact checking by reporters.[1224]

British Intelligence was aware at the highest levels that at the CIA "the intelligence and facts were being fixed around the policy."[1225] George Tenet, the CIA Director met with Richard Dearlove, the chief of British intelligence shortly before Dearlove briefed Tony Blair and senior officials of the British government on July 23, 2002 about what was going on behind the scenes in American government: The quote below is from the minutes of Dearlove's secret briefing:

> Military action was now seen as inevitable. Bush wanted to remove Saddam, through military action, justified by the conjunction of terrorism and WMD. But the intelligence and facts were being fixed around the policy. The NSC had no patience with the UN route, and no enthusiasm for publishing material on the Iraq regime's record. There was little discussion in Washington of the aftermath after military action.[1226]

British Foreign Secretary Jack Straw attended the briefing; the minutes from the meeting note his thinking:

> It seemed clear that Bush had made up his mind to take military action, even if the timing was not yet decided. But the case was thin. Saddam was not threatening his neighbors, and his WMD capability was less than that of Libya, North Korea or Iran.[1227]

As for evidence of chemical weapons being produced or stored in Iraq , there was in fact not even a phony witness like Curveball to justify the various false statements made by Bush on down about chemical weapons in Iraq. The Senate Select Intelligence Committee's postwar findings about Iraq's WMD programs included the following summation of its 2004 conclusions regarding chemical weapons:

> 1. SSCI July 2004 Report Conclusion - Chemical
>
> The Committee concluded in its July 2004 report that two of the judgments in the NIE – that "Baghdad has chemical weapons and that Baghdad has covertly procured chemicals and equipment sufficient for limited CW production" – overstated the available intelligence.[1228]
>
> The Committee also noted that several of the Intelligence Community's assessments about Iraq's chemical weapons capabilities and activities were not based directly on intelligence reporting, but were layers of analysis based on a single stream of intelligence reporting. This reporting was that a specific tanker truck, assessed to be a signature for chemical weapons activity, was identified on imagery at a site where transshipment activity was taking place. The Committee concluded that the NIE did not make it clear that if the assessment regarding the tanker truck was incorrect, the additional assessments based on this information would likely be incorrect as well. It was this "layering" effect that gave the reader

of the NIE the impression that Iraq's chemical weapons program was advancing and growing, although the intelligence community had little direct or credible intelligence to indicate that he was.[1229]

Despite Foley's admonition to his WINPAC staffers to find the intelligence that the President needed to go to war, (instead of just finding the truth), WINPAC chemical weapons experts reportedly were, before the preparation of the October, 2002 NIE, "drifting" toward concluding that Saddam had not been rebuilding Iraq's chemical weapons program.[1230] Bob Drogin writes in his book, *Curveball, Spies, Lies And The Con Man Who Caused A War*, that the uncritical acceptance of Curveball's tall tales by the six biowafare experts in WINPAC made the WINPAC chemical weapons analysts uneasy, and drove them to ramp up their conclusions. Drogan quoted an unnamed source within the government who helped investigate how the NIE was prepared; If Saddam was building mobile biological WMD labs, the chemical weapons experts reasoned, so too he must be rebuilding his stock of chemical WMD.[1231] So it was, apparently, that harmless water trucks were morphed into chemical weapons tankers by CIA analysts who were under pressure from higher ups to provide President Bush with a justification for war.[1232]

Assertions regarding: *Iraqi's Alleged Program To Build Nuclear Weapons*

8/26/2002, by Dick Cheney at the National VFW meeting in Nashville

> The Iraqi regime has in fact been very busy enhancing its capabilities.... And they continue to pursue the nuclear program they began so many years ago. On the nuclear question, many of you will recall that Saddam's nuclear ambitions suffered a severe setback in 1981 when the Israelis bombed the Osirak reactor. They suffered another major blow in Desert Storm and its aftermath. But we now know that Saddam has resumed his efforts to acquire nuclear weapons. Among other sources, we've gotten this from the firsthand testimony of defectors -- including Saddam's own son-in-law, who was subsequently murdered at Saddam's direction. Many of us are convinced that Saddam will acquire nuclear weapons fairly soon.[1233]

9/12/2002 stated by George W. Bush at the United Nations:

> Iraq has made several attempts to buy high-strength aluminum tubes used to enrich uranium for a nuclear weapon. Should Iraq acquire fissile material, it would be able to build a nuclear weapon within a year.[1234]

09/18/2002, stated by Donald Rumsfeld, Secretary of Defense before Congress:

> Today, I do want to discuss the task of preventing attacks of even greater magnitude than what was experienced on September 11, attacks that could conceivably kill not just thousands of Americans, but potentially tens of thousands of our fellow citizens. As we meet...nuclear scientists are toiling in weapons labs and underground bunkers, working to give the world's most dangerous dictators weapons of unprecedented power and lethality.
>
> These facts about the Saddam Hussein regime, I think, should be part of this record and our country's considerations.... His regime has an active program to

acquire and develop nuclear weapons....

...Another question that's been asked is, where's the smoking gun? Well, the last thing we want to see is a smoking gun. A gun smokes after it's been fired. And the goal must be to stop such an action before it happens. As the president told the United Nations, "The first time we may be completely certain that a ***terrorist state*** [emphasis added] has nuclear weapons is when, God forbid, they use one. And we owe it to our citizens to do everything in our power to prevent that day from coming.

We do know that the Iraqi regime...we do know they're currently pursuing nuclear weapons...

...Mr. Chairman, my personal view is...he is aggressively pursuing nuclear weapons. The region knows that. The region knows this man very, very well. And they are frightened of him.[1235]

10/5/2002, stated by George W. Bush in a radio address:

The evidence indicates that Iraq is reconstituting its nuclear weapons program. Saddam Hussein has held numerous meetings with Iraqi nuclear scientists, a group he calls his "nuclear mujahideen" - his nuclear holy warriors. Satellite photographs reveal that Iraq is rebuilding facilities at sites that have been part of its nuclear program in the past. Iraq has attempted to purchase high-strength aluminum tubes and other equipment needed for gas centrifuges, which are used to enrich uranium for nuclear weapons.[1236]

10/7/2002, stated by George W. Bush in speech at Cincinnati Union Terminal:

...Before being barred from Iraq in 1998, the International Atomic Energy Agency dismantled extensive nuclear weapons-related facilities, including three uranium enrichment sites. That same year, information from a high-ranking Iraqi nuclear engineer who had defected revealed that despite his public promises, Saddam Hussein had ordered his nuclear program to continue.

The evidence indicates that Iraq is reconstituting its nuclear weapons program. Saddam Hussein has held numerous meetings with Iraqi nuclear scientists, a group he calls his "nuclear mujahideen" -- his nuclear holy warriors. Satellite photographs reveal that Iraq is rebuilding facilities at sites that have been part of its nuclear program in the past. Iraq has attempted to purchase high-strength aluminum tubes and other equipment needed for gas centrifuges, which are used to enrich uranium for nuclear weapons.

If the Iraqi regime is able to produce, buy, or steal an amount of highly enriched uranium a little larger than a single softball, it could have a nuclear weapon in less than a year.[1237]

01/28/2003, stated by George W. Bush during State of the Union Address:

The British government has learned that Saddam Hussein recently sought significant quantities of uranium from Africa. Our intelligence sources tell us that he has attempted to purchase high-strength aluminum tubes suitable for nuclear weapons production. Saddam Hussein has not credibly explained these activities. He clearly has much to hide.[1238]

The Actual Reality regarding: *Iraqi's Alleged Program To Build Nuclear Weapons*

In addition to the obviously forged and quickly discredited Niger - Iraq uranium yellowcake contract documents, written on stolen paper, there was just one other piece of so called, hard evidence, that Saddam was rebuilding Iraq's nuclear WMD program. That was Iraq's attempted purchase in the year 2000 of tubes made of grade 7075-T6 aluminum from an Australian distributer which was partly owned by a Chinese company.[1239] The tubes had been produced in China.[1240] Australian intelligence had tipped off the CIA about the purchase.[1241] The tubes were seized in transit by the government of Jordan at the request of the CIA, whose operatives were present when the seizure took place.[1242]

WINPAC assigned a young CIA agent with a bachelors degree in mechanical engineering named Joe Turner to investigate the tubes and Iraq's reason for wanting them.[1243] WINPAC was concerned about the tubes because they were made of a high strength alloy that can be used to manufacturer rotors for gas centrifuges to separate U-235 from the more prevalent U-238 isotope in naturally occurring uranium. When the concentration of U-235 isotope reaches roughly eighty percent, the uranium mixture is sufficiently enriched to create a nuclear explosion.[1244] WINPAC's interest in the tubes was legitimate - at first. Turner, limited by his lack of scientific knowledge and experience, and operating within the Foley ordained environment of giving the President an excuse to go to war, opined to his superiors that the tubes were meant to be used to enrich uranium.[1245] Turner's analysis ended up in an intelligence report dated April 10, 2001 which was distributed to officials of high rank throughout the national security bureaucracy. President Bush had learned about Turner's finding in his top secret daily briefing even before the April 10, 2001 intelligent report was circulated. Perhaps to Turner's credit, the report contained the caveat that "using aluminum tubes in a centrifuge effort would be inefficient and a step backward from the specialty steel machines Iraq was poised to mass produce at the onset of the Gulf War."[1246]

Needless to say, the White House was delighted to make use of Turner's opinion that the tubes were meant to be used for uranium enrichment. But the good news which came the very next day, on April 11, 2001 in a Department of Energy (DOE) report which challenged Turner's findings, was not something the White House wanted to acknowledge or share with the public. The good news was that a team of Energy Department scientists who were nuclear experts had come out with a report which found that the tubes were not likely to have been purchased for enriching uranium. The tubes had a diameter that was but half that of the tubes that had been used by the Iraqis in a gas centrifuge they tested in 1990, and the tubes were only "marginally large enough for practical centrifuge applications.[1247] News that would have brought smiles and happy faces to the families of our heroic troops; *that war was not necessary,* must have brought only chagrin to Bush and Cheney. So they did not share it with the public or the men and women who do the fighting and the dying.[1248]

On May 9, 2001, the DOE disseminated a report which surmised that the tubes had been purchased to build combustion chambers for launcher fired rockets of a size and type that the Iraqis had previously been known to use. The secret DOE report was published in the *Daily Intelligence Highlight* which is published on a restricted access website for use by the White House and select members of the intelligence community.[1249] Turner had to admit both that tubes did not match the dimensions of any known centrifuge design, and that they did match the tubes the Iraqi's had previously used to make combustion chambers for artillery rockets.[1250]

The DOE's team of scientists was led by the head of the National Security Advanced Technology Division of Oak Ridge National Laboratory, Dr. Jon A. Kreykes. Other members of the team included Dr. Edward Von Halle, a former Oak Ridge nuclear expert, Dr. Duane F. Starr, a leading authority on the threat of nuclear proliferation, and Dr. Houston G. Wood III, a physicist who has the distinction of being one of the world's foremost authorities on nuclear centrifuge devices.[1251] The distinguished American team of crack nuclear experts consulted with Dr. Gernot Zippe, a German scientist who developed a early model centrifuge which Turner claimed was a match for the tubes. Zippe advised the Americans that the Iraqi tubes were not even close to his design. Turner was just plain wrong.[1252] The experience, know-how and scientific knowledge of the DOE team completely dwarfed that of the junior WINPAC analyst Turner.[1253]

On top of that, the DOE was not alone in its findings. As the Department of State's website explains, the federal Bureau of Intelligence and Research (INR) "provides value-added independent analysis of events to U.S. State Department policymakers; ensures that intelligence activities support foreign policy and national security purposes; and serves as the focal point in the State Department for ensuring policy review of sensitive counterintelligence and law enforcement activities around the world."[1254] Towards the end of 2001 the INR investigated Turner's tubes for centrifuges theory, interviewing scientists from national labs that were knowledgeable about the issues involved.[1255] The Director of Proliferation of INR, Greg Thielmann, said of the interviews the INR conducted with government nuclear scientists and experts:

> We were talking to all these experts, and they were telling us No, no, no, this is not the kind of [aluminum tube] you use for centrifuges.[1256]

The INR wrote memorandums to then Secretary of State, Colin Powell during the later part of 2001 and early in 2002 which strongly refuted Turner's theory.[1257] It is difficult to imagine how Powell might have missed both those memos.

That Turner was wrong, and the nation's most prestigious and accomplished nuclear weapons scientists were right, was and remains a "no brainer." Authors Corn and Isikoff tell in their book, *Hubris,* about a confidential interview they conducted with an intelligence analyst employed at Lawrence Livermore National Laboratory. The analyst said that when Department of Energy nuclear scientists "say that an aluminum tube is not for a gas centrifuge, it's like a fish talking about water."[1258]

A good estimate of the financial cost of the Iraq war thus far is $2 trillion, but continuing expenses incurred for veterans from the war could rise to exceed $6 trillion.[1259] Perhaps more than one million human beings lost their lives because of the war.[1260] We lost thousands of our soldiers, and hundreds of thousands of them have been injured or disabled for life.[1261] The war would never have been fought *but for LIES*! We can however do our soldiers, our veterans, the families and friends of our lost and injured soldiers and ourselves justice. We can build a better political system *by building a new kind of political party*. One that is not controlled by financial interests, but by a studied and humane understanding of both the public interest, and private individual rights. As citizens, if ignore our political rights and patriotic obligations, we will have nobody to blame but ourselves when everything comes crashing down around us, and our freedom, happiness and very lives are lost.

If you bring forth what is within you, what you bring forth will save you. If you do not bring forth what is within you, what you do not bring forth will destroy you.

- attributed to *Jesus Christ* in the manuscript commonly known as the Gospel of Thomas

15

Why The Ameritorians Are Needed More Than Ever

The concept of global warming was created by and for the Chinese in order to make U.S. manufacturing non-competitive.

- twitter message from @realDonaldTrump, 11:15 a.m. - Nov. 6, 2012

The scientific evidence is clear: global climate change caused by human activities is occurring now, and it is a growing threat to society....The pace of change and the evidence of harm have increased markedly over the last five years. The time to control greenhouse gas emissions is now.

- Official Statement of The American Association for the Advancement of Science, issued on December 9, 2006

The reality of global warming and the fact that it is clearly resulting in large measure from human activities was previously discussed in chapters 3,6,7 and 13 of this book. If you don't already believe that global warming is a human caused reality *you are part of the climate change problem, not a part of the climate change solution*. Nobody who believes that global warming is really not a problem should become an active member of the Ameritorian Party. There is an overwhelming scientific consensus concerning the existence and cause of climate change, and time is running out for doing what's necessary to combat it.

I spent most of my time writing about the fallacy of free trade in this book, because fixing the economy is job one. The solution to many of our most urgent problems lies in directing substantial financial resources towards solving them. Our national economic policy is in dire need of a major overhaul in order to provide *both* the private and public sectors with the funds they need.

However, the problem of climate change is just as global in scope and effect as our economic problems. It is clear that an integrated strategy is needed for both. In short, we must engage in the serious planning needed to restore prosperity and our military strength, but that alone won't be enough. We must also include in our planning a scientifically valid scheme to convert our energy, manufacturing and transportation infrastructure in ways that will help stop and reverse climate change. Though it represents the greatest challenge ever faced by mankind, we must meet this challenge head on or face eventual widespread catastrophe.

Donald Trump's anti-science view of climate change is of course not the only thing that makes him unsuitable for the office of president. I will not even bother to discuss his disgusting comments about, and treatment of, the fairer sex. The media has already focused enough attention on Trump's "locker room" persona.

Another thing I dislike about Trump are his views on the use of torture. When I was growing up, the message I got from watching TV shows like *Combat* and virtually every one of the dozens and dozens of WWII movies I saw that dealt with the subject of torture was simple: Torture was barbaric, and opposing it was an integral part of the *American Way*. Of course, I grew up and developed a mature understanding of what happens in war, but I have never agreed with the use of torture. Trump seems to have forgotten about, or perhaps he just doesn't care about, the abuses which took place at Abu Ghraib. Trump also fails to understand that torture as used during the Iraqi war, sometimes had the effect of *forcing witnesses to tell lies in order to save themselves from additional torture*.

As discussed in Chapter 14, the Senate Select Intelligence Committee concluded in 2006 that Ibn al-Shaykh al-Libi lied to his debriefers to avoid torture when he claimed that Iraq and al-Qaeda had formed a terrorist alliance. Al - Libi lied for the same reason - to avoid torture - when he told his captors that Iraq had supplied chemical and biological weapons to al-Qaeda. The lesson is clear. Prisoners who are tortured or threatened with torture may make up convincing lies in order to stop being tortured. In addition, torture *can deliberately be used to pry false confessions* from prisoners who are made to be afraid, in some instances, for their very lives. David J. Luban, Ph.D., a professor at Georgetown University who is an expert on human rights and the laws of war, and torture, has said this about torture:

> Torture's rehabilitation by the Bush administration is a regression of democracy, destroyed in the name of protecting it... Today, a slippery slope is leading civilization backwards to barbarism in the name of the struggle against barbarism.[1262]

The quote above from Luban dates to 2008 when George W. Bush was still in office. In March, 2016, questioned about the statements Trump has made about expanding torture Luban had this to say:

> We would be the only country in the world not party to the Geneva Conventions, and the only country ever to quit the Convention Against Torture... It would be one of the biggest foreign policy setbacks the U.S. has ever experienced. It would be a triumph for our international adversaries, a humiliation in the eyes of our allies, and strengthen the hands of every human rights violator on the planet.[1263]

Luban is obviously right. Another problem with the use of torture by the military is that it weakens the barrier to using torture domestically. The sad truth is that American police have in the past used torture to pry false confessions from exhausted and terrified suspects who are under arrest.[1264] Donald Trump is just plain wrong on the subject. The Chicago Tribune recently ran the editorial "The spreading conspiracy of silence." In it, the Tribune editorial board noted that even Chicago's mayor, Rahm Emmanuel, had "acknowledged that an unspoken compact shields rogue police officers from accountability." The Tribune went on to say "that culture extends beyond the rank-and-file, however, to a disciplinary system that can take years to run its course and almost never sustains a complaint against an officer."[1265] It seems like nearly everyone has seen disturbing video evidence of police brutality, and *the simple fact that much of the public wants reform does not mean that the police can no longer do their jobs*. Incredibly, Trump paints police misconduct as something that's almost unheard of. Trump has described the police as having been "absolutely mistreated and misunderstood,"[1266] That is not only untrue. It is positively absurd. Public concern about police misconduct is justified, and reform efforts have a long way to go.[1267]

Trump's plan to cut the highest marginal federal income tax rate to thirty-three percent (he flip flopped it up from twenty five percent late in his campaign) is perhaps the dumbest of his campaign proposals.[1268] Trump is constantly telling us he wants to cut our income taxes and it sounds great to many, but in his next few breaths, Trump warns us about our $20 trillion national debt. Maybe Donald thinks that his "tax on China" will offset the loss of income tax revenue which will result from his income tax cut. However, we have not seen the math on how that will work and we never will because it's surely impossible. First of all, if Trump imposes a tariff on Chinese imports of either 45% (his initial figure), or 35%, (his latest figure), economic disaster will result. Such a high tariff all at once would disrupt the supply chains of domestic corporations, dramatically raise prices to consumers, and throw a monkey wrench into the whole economy. Trump indicated in the March 10, 2016, presidential debate that his proposal to place a 35 percent tax (or some other amount) on Chinese goods was just a threat to be used only in the event China does not cooperate with Trump on trade.

I doubt China will cooperate. China can be counted on to delay and obfuscate during trade negotiations, patiently waiting for the threat posed by term limited upstarts like Trump or Sanders to fade away. It is abundantly clear that a new political party whose membership is not largely wedded to free trade must win the support of the American people or lasting change will never come. We must clean house and stop rewarding failure. The Republican party needs to be whittled down to its insider core of free trade or die climate change contrarians. The Democrats must be whittled down to their insider core of free trade fatalists and moonbeam socialists. The American center must coalesce to form a new political party and a new political order that will bring fairness, justice and prosperity to all Americans.

The Ameritorian Party will follow the example set by Alexander Hamilton and George Washington. Tariffs will be introduced gradually, and start off at a low amount which is affordable for all concerned. America will unilaterally announce and implement its rejection of the current system of illusory free trade. America will work to create a system of international trade that will counter the weaknesses in the current system, weaknesses which have been ably identified by the leading trade theorists whose work is discussed in this book. Friendly, but not weak diplomacy with our trading partners must be the rule. I believe we can work with the

Chinese government and help them learn the benefit of letting their domestic wages rise so as to let wealth spread equitably throughout their economy. Spreading the wealth will increase demand and wean China from its dependence on exports. It's incontrovertible that America grew to become the wealthiest and most powerful country in the world without engaging in foreign trade to any significant extent. Increases in domestic productivity and corresponding increases in wages and employment drove America's economy upward, causing the realization of the American dream for most Americans. American prosperity was not lost until free trade was instituted and transformed America into, (to use a term I coined back in college), the world's largest *undeveloping nation.*

Turning to Bernie Sanders campaign, I will start by applauding his stand on restructuring our trade policy. I love the fact that two of the candidates for President in 2016 (Trump and Sanders) wanted to get tough on trade. I also applaud the Democratic Party for getting a national healthcare bill passed. That may cause many readers of this book to moan and groan, but I believe that our economy should be strong enough for private insurance and public assistance programs to cover all Americans in need. In particular, the thought of any child going without health care is absolutely unacceptable to me. Obamacare seemed to be failing as this book was being written. Quite honestly, the thorny question of how to optimally structure our healthcare system is not one I have an answer to. The merit committee structure of the Ameritorian Party, once it is formed, will have delve into the problems of the healthcare system.

That being said, the truth is that it will almost certainly end up being cheaper if the vast majority of healthcare insurance premiums are paid by private sector employers. If the Ameritorian Party trade policy and other economic reforms are instituted, the American economy will grow rapidly and unemployment will decline to a very low level. Unemployment will be kept low and wages will grow because of smart economic policy. Public expenditures on healthcare will thus fall to much lower levels. Some of the savings on healthcare might be used to reverse and bring an end to the emerging post antibiotic era. MRSA and all the other superbugs are needlessly killing tens of thousands of Americans and millions more in other countries every year, *but not one person should have died! The failure of the republocrats to deal with the failures of the private market pharmaceutical industry is one of their greatest blunders.* It exceeds in its scope and destruction even their mindless military misadventure in Iraq.[1269] No matter where the money comes from, the task of defeating the threat from resistant bacteria must be met with the ferocity of an all out war.

Once you get beyond the good and likeable aspects of Bernie Sanders - his disgust with our bad trade polices and his principled opposition to the excessive influence of *the money power* - it's mostly downhill. You feel like the child who has seen fire for the first time - and reaching into the flame - you get Berned! *You feel your freedom being Berned away.*

I will let Bernie indict himself with his own words:

> "*I believe that, in the long run, major industries in this state and nation should be publicly owned and controlled by the workers themselves.*"
>
> - Bernie Sanders, 1976

"Nobody should earn more than $1 million."

- Bernie Sanders, Statement to the Burlington Free Press in 1974

You can read more about Bernie's formula for instant socialist paradise in the *Politico* article where the above quotes came from.[1270] The election of a quixotic leftist who has said very scary things about people's right to pursue happiness is not what I had in mind for the last four and a half decades as I watched in disgust and anger as America declined. It may however, have been in the minds of a band of leftist insiders who are high up in the Democratic Party. Democrats have trumpeted the benefits of free trade for all those decades with only an occasional whimper from disenchanted Dem pols from rustbelt states. How could Democrats be so blind? Did they wish to foment a socialist revolution? I know this, nobody is going to limit people's incomes to some arbitrary figure or force them to transfer the ownership of their businesses to their employees in America anytime soon. Trade policy needs to be reformed, but the socialist agendas of *freedom does not matter democrats* must never come true. When the day comes that the right to pursue happiness is unfairly infringed by the federal government, the rights to free expression, freedom of the press, and due process under law will also be in danger. I consider Sanders a wolf in sheep's clothing who might try to steal away freedom and liberty from a generation of voters who have been impoverished, not by freedom, but by free trade. In the unlikely event that Sanders someday becomes President, his far left positions will bring more political polarization and gridlock to our country than ever before. He probably won't be able to accomplish anything, unless God forbid, the whole Democratic party signs on to his agenda.

I am totally convinced of the need for a third party to form which unites centrist voters and empowers the political plurality which is not currently being represented. The pathetic choices we have now compel us in every election to choose the lesser of two evils. We walk away from the voting booth holding our noses, knowing that the lesser evil is not that much less evil.

Despite their glaring shortcomings, two political oddballs, Sanders and Trump, deserve great credit for making trade a centerpiece issue in the 2016 election. Thanks to Sanders and Trump, the issue of free trade finally exploded like a ticking time bomb, and it blew up right in Hillary Clinton's face. Because of the tight control *the money power* has over both political parties and the media, it took the Senate's lone socialist and a bombastic *not too deep* billionaire hated by his party's establishment to set off the explosion.

The last candidate from 2016 to discuss is the one polls wrongly predicted would win, Hillary Clinton. If she had won, she would have taken office dripping with present and past scandal. Her pockets would have been stuffed with cash. That's the cash which Hillary collected from her years of giving speeches to corporate elites for a hundred thousand dollars or more a pop.

The moment she took office, Hillary would have returned to her true form when it comes to economic policy. Hillary did not fool the voters of Michigan. Hillary and her husband Bill Clinton have been pushing free trade for years. Hillary did not come out in opposition to the Trans Pacific Trade Agreement until October 7, 2015.[1271] I don't think she can fool anybody about her support for free trade.[1272] The segment quoted below from the presidential debate between Sanders and Clinton in Flint, Michigan provides a revealing look at why Hillary lost the election in Michigan. The bottom line is that not only Michigan but the United States as a whole has been ravaged by free trade, and that's why Clinton lost:

> ANDERSON COOPER, CNN MODERATOR: I want to go to Tanisha Motron, she grew up in Flint and now works in Detroit at the Shinola watch factory which as you know, is often held up as the blueprint for how to save American industry jobs. She says she's leaning towards secretary Clinton and has a question for her.
> QUESTION BY TANISHA: A lot of members work in the auto industry here in Flint. That's ultimately what I wanted to do when I got out of school unfortunately, I was unable to get any one of the big three and that's why I now reside at Shinola. If you are elected president, what are you going to do to [keep jobs] in the United States instead of sending them overseas to other countries?
> COOPER: Secretary Clinton?
> CLINTON: I'm going to do what I think will work which is both carrots and sticks. Let me talk about the carrots. We're going to have a very clear set of proposals and incentives for manufacturing so that we change the way that companies think about making investments again in America. I have a comprehensive manufacturing plan that I will be implementing. We're also going to invest more on infrastructure as we both have said, "it's woefully under resourced." That will put a lot of people to work. I want to do more to help small businesses, they are the source of two thirds of our jobs and we have to help them start and grow, particularly minority and women-owned small businesses. We need to do more to help create clean energy as a source of good jobs but I am also going to go after companies. You know, when a company decides to leave like Nabisco is leaving and they have gotten tax benefits from Chicago and Illinois to stay there, I will claw back the benefits. They will have to pay them back if they are leaving a place that actually invested in them. I am also going to go after companies like Johnson Controls in Wisconsin. They came and got part of the bailout because they were an auto parts supplier and now they want to move headquarters to Europe. They are going to have to pay an exit fee. We are going to stop this kind of job exporting and we are going to start importing and growing jobs again in our country.
> COOPER: Senator Sanders, I will let you...
> SANDERS: I am very glad, Anderson, that Secretary Clinton discovered religion on this issue but it's a little bit too late. Secretary Clinton supported virtually every one of the disastrous trade agreements written by corporate America. NAFTA, supported by the Secretary cost, us 800,000 jobs nationwide, tens of thousands of jobs in the Midwest. Permanent normal trade relations with China cost us millions of jobs. Look, I was on a picket line in early 1990's against NAFTA because you didn't need a PhD in economics to understand that American workers should not be forced to compete against people in Mexico making 25 cents an hour.
> SANDERS: And the reason that I was one of the first, not one of the last to be in

> opposition to the TPP is that American workers…
> … should not be forced to compete against people in Vietnam today making a minimum wage of $0.65 an hour. Look, what we have got to do is tell corporate America that they cannot continue to shut down. We've lost 60,000 factories since 2001. They're going to start having to, if I'm president, invest in this country — not in China, not in Mexico.[1273]

Sanders was not alone in pointing out Clinton's true record on trade issues. Clinton did it herself in her response to Tanisha's question. Instead of talking about changes to trade policy and trade agreements, Clinton instead talked about putting people to work by investing in infrastructure. She never said a word about imposing a tariff on any country, anywhere. She said she was going to "claw back" money that had been previously paid to businesses as an incentive to them to invest in America. She said that she would collect an "exit fee," from companies that close American facilities after having received part of the bailout. Obviously, Clinton's exit fees and claw backs *would never have kept jobs in America to any significant extent, if at all*. Such fees might have generated some money to partially pay for the welfare schemes that states and the federal government have felt forced to create to help people who have lost jobs because of free trade agreements.

As for building infrastructure, that should be done as a matter of course. If America was not in debt $20 trillion because of our horrible trade and tax policies, our infrastructure would not be in horrible condition. I think the facts are clear. Clinton is effectively owned by *the money power*. She is not the solution. She is the problem. It does not seem that I am alone in my assessment of her. An article about Clinton published after her debate with Sanders in Michigan in *Salon* bore the title *Hillary's Cronyism Is Showing: A Closer Look At Her Economic Proposals Reveals A Neoliberal Agenda*. The byline for the article says *Clinton vows to use public funds and policy to promote private-sector gain. Wall Street couldn't be more delighted.* The same article appeared a couple days earlier in *Alternet* as the more negative sounding *Hillary's Economic Agenda Sure Looks Like Payback for Wall St Giving Her Huge Piles of Campaign Cash.*[1274] Another story about Clinton which appeared after the Michigan debate was published at the blog ShadowProof under the sobriquet *Hillary Clinton Runs From Free Trade Record At Debate.*[1275]

Afterword

I had initially planned to include in this book some chapters which discuss and explain at least some of the already famous "Republocrat" failures highlighted on the book's back cover. I wanted to show how everything listed there either directly resulted from, or were materially worsened by the inexcusably bad practices and policies of our two dominant political parties. I also wanted to discuss the need for our new party to create policies to deal with the dangers and take advantage of the opportunities presented by technological advancement in the fields of artificial intelligence and automation. During the writing of the book, it became clear that I would have to narrow the scope of the book to focus almost entirely on the glaring economic policy failure that free trade has been for the United States. It has always been clear to me that the solutions to most of the problems government and the public face rest on the creation and proper administration of sound economic policy by the federal government. It simply was not possible to adequately treat all the other issues and problems I wanted to discuss within the limited pages of a book length manuscript. I decided to place any additional writing related to this book online at the Ameritorian website, *AmeritorianParty.org*. There were some articles there at the time of this writing which discussed the advances China has made in military technology which are mentioned on the back cover of this book.

Having read this book, you personally are now more important than Donald Trump and all the members of the current Congress of The United States. That's because either you will help change the future with me, or politics will go on as before. Nothing is going to change if the people who run the two parties remain in control of our government. *Trump is a divisive, tax cuts for the rich republican with a completely unscientific and wrong view on global warming*. Trump is a selfish, arrogant and insulting man. He is despised worldwide. He is a twit who tweets too much. Sadly, the Democrats won't offer us anything better than Obama, Sanders and Clinton in the next election. What else can we do? There is only one way America can be cured of its problems and a new age of prosperity brought about that will be shared by all Americans. *We the people of the United States must form a more perfect union!* Divided, gridlocked, pay to play government must be brought to a close. My confidence is high that a majority of the people of the United States agree with me. Whether you are one of the greatest scholars in America, or a person who just wants to finish school and get a good job - *please,* do what you can do, what you must do, and do it *today*. Join the Ameritorian movement *today*. In a few short years, a vibrant Ameritorian Party composed of moderate, clear thinking and patriotic American citizens can be established which has been registered and elected officials in every state. A very troubled future awaits each of us if we don't act collectively. Please take action. Go to AmeritorianParty.org (not .com) to register your support and participate to whatever extent you can.

Short Glossary

This glossary is provided for a select few words used in this book related to the subjects of economics or politics which the general reader may have little or no familiarity with.

Comparative Advantage

"Comparative advantage" refers to the ability of a country to produce a particular good at a lower cost as compared to another country. In 1817, David Ricardo wrote the book "On the Principles of Political Economy and Taxation" in which he explained the concept of comparative advantage. Ricardo showed mathematically and in theory, (limited by a list of carefully enumerated conditions), how two countries might best benefit from international trade with each other. The surprising conclusion Riccardo came up with was that a country which could produce both of two different types of goods at a lower cost than a second country, could still benefit by specializing in the production of only the good in which it had the greatest comparative advantage, and importing the other good from the second country.

Dumping

"Dumping" is exportation of goods priced lower than what is charged in the country where the goods are exported from. Such goods may be priced even lower than the cost of producing them. Dumping is a competitive strategy used to eliminate a competing firm or firms by temporarily charging less than the competing firm(s) charge or can afford to charge. National governments sometimes subsidize dumping in order to expand their domestic production, tax revenue and jobs. Dumping is legal under World Trade Organization rules unless it has been proved to have caused an injurious effect by the firm(s) affected by it.

Free Trade

"Free Trade" is a theoretical system under which governments do nothing to restrict imports from, or exports to, other countries. In practice, virtually all governments impose limitations on trade. Some limitations are imposed to protect or to develop sensitive military technology and capabilities. Other limitations are imposed with the intention of developing and nurturing new industries. Still others are imposed to protect industries from being lost to international competition. Economists who favor free trade rely on the theory of comparative advantage in arguing that free trade ultimately benefits all nations. Economists who oppose free trade argue that the logical axioms which upon which the theory of comparative advantage is based are not all true -making the comparative advantage model logically invalid. Economists who oppose free trade also argue that the comparative advantage model is fatally flawed because it ignores economic growth factors that are logically indispensable to measuring the gains and losses from international trade.

Laissez faire, Laissez aller

"Laissez faire, Laissez aller" literally means "let do, let go" in French. It is commonly translated in English as *"hands off* economic policy." It refers to a theoretical economic system where free market transactions take place between individuals and firms without any intrusive banking, pollution control, or consumer protection regulations. In such a system, government would play no active role in helping to create economic prosperity, or in managing economic crises for the general good of society.

Maquiladora plant or factory

"Maquiladora" is a Mexican Spanish word for manufacturing plants set up by American and foreign multinational firms in Mexico. The Mexican government adopted a policy in 1965 of encouraging foreign firms to rent land in special "Maquiladora" districts located close to the Mexican American border. Firms which locate in Mexico can take advantage of extremely low wages, and the extremely low tax and lax regulatory environment which is maintained in the Maquiladora districts by the Mexican government. Since the passage of NAFTA, (the North American Free Trade Agreement), foreign investment in Mexico has mushroomed, and Maquiladora plants are now located all over Mexico, not just near the border with the United States. The word *Maquiladora* is derived from the Spanish word "maquila," which refers to a grain miller's fee. *Maquila* is derived from the old Arabic word makila, which in English means "measured."

Monopoly and Media Monopoly

The word monopoly was not used in this book in the way that economists use it, which is to describe a particular economic market where a single producer or distributer is the sole supplier of a particular good or service. The lack of price competition in a market where a monopoly exists generally results in higher prices to consumers. The word monopoly was used in the political sense in this book, as in the phrase "monopoly on power." When used in a political sense, the word monopoly refers to the total control that an individual or a select group of individuals can have over a group, organization, institution, business or government. The phrase "Media Monopoly" refers to the tiny number of corporations that own and control approximately ninety percent of the press, news media and publishing companies in the United States. Ben Bagdikian made the words "media monopoly" famous with the publication of his 1983 book *The Media Monopoly.*

Bagdikian wrote a second updated version of his book which was published in 2004 and titled *The New Media Monopoly*.

Oligarchy

Oligarchy is a form of national government where a small group or people make the laws and control the military and police forces and the justice system with absolute authority. The word oligarchy is also used to describe any group or organization where a small group of insiders make all of the leadership decisions.

Oligopoly

An oligopoly is a particular economic market where a significantlysmall number of producers or distributers are the sole suppliers of a particular good or service. Because there are so few suppliers in a market where an oligopoly exists, collusion between the small group of suppliers to set prices, thus avoiding *price competition*, can lead to higher prices as happens when there is a monopoly. Ben Bagdikian's famous book *The Media Monopoly* might have been named *The Media Oligopoly* instead, (because a small number of firms own well over ninety percent of America's news and entertainment media), however the word oligopoly is less well known to people.

Service Economy

A service economy is one where service businesses produce more income and employ more people than manufacturing and other industrial firms do. Some examples of service businesses are banks, stock brokerage firms, law firms, business consulting firms, accounting firms and marketing firms. Deindustrialization caused by foreign imports and outsourcing by multinational corporations that originated in or are headquartered in the United States has transformed its economy into a service economy. That transformation has caused the United States to produce fewer patents relative to the rest of the world. It has caused the United States to fall behind China and other countries in various areas of high technology and manufacturing. The consequences are far reaching.

Stagflation

Stagflation, is a portmanteau which combines stagnation and inflation. It was used frequently by economists to describe the economic condition of the United States during the 1970's, when the inflation rate was high, but unemployment was also high.

Index

A

ABC World News Tonight, 15, 22
Adams, John, 28, 29
Adams, John Quincy, 29, 30
Afghanistan, 26, 150, 152, 153, 198, 213, 214, 215, 216
Africa, 124, 130, 211, 227, 234
Al Qaida, 209, 213, 214, 215, 216, 218
al Zarqawi, 213, 214, 215, 217, 218
al-Janabi, Rafid Ahmed Alwan. *See* Curveball
al-Libi, Ibn al-Shaykh, 218, 219, 220, 238
aluminum tubes, 232, 233, 234
American Association For the Advancement of Science, 20
American auto workers, 9, 126
American Chemical Society, 20
American firms, i, 92, 135, 136, 137, 174, 190
American Geophysical Union, 20
American Government, iv
American Medical Association, 20
American Meteorological Society,, 20
American Physical Society, 20
American system, iii, 77
American System, The, 33, 34, 35, 37, 38, 39, 54, 55, 66, 75, 76, 77, 85, 86, 88, 92, 93, 105, 106, 107, 112, 113, 122, 132, 138, 142, 156, 192
American Trade Policy, 11, 161, 162, 164, 165
Americans, iii, iv, v, 1, 2, 3, 5, 6, 7, 8, 19, 28, 29, 31, 34, 38, 48, 54, 59, 64, 65, 68, 73, 74, 75, 76, 80, 84, 88, 93, 95, 97, 101, 102, 103, 104, 107, 108, 109, 110, 111, 113, 115, 117, 119, 120, 121, 122, 125, 126, 127, 130, 131, 134, 135, 136, 137, 138, 144, 145, 156, 158, 159, 160, 161, 169, 174, 175, 177, 178, 179, 180, 184, 185, 186, 187, 190, 191, 192, 195, 196, 198, 199, 204, 205, 212, 228, 232, 235, 239, 240, 244
Ameritorian Party, ii, 112, 159, 179, 185, 186, 192, 193, 194, 195, 196, 237, 239, 240, 244
Ames, Ruth E., 170
Anderson. Allison, 23
anti-miscegenation laws, iii
Asian Financial Crisis, 163
Asian Tigers, 128, 129
Atta, Mohammed, 223

B

Bacevich, Andrew J., 204, 205
Bacevich, Andrew John Jr., 205
Bagdikian, Ben, 13, 78, 246, 247
bailouts, 3, 17, 70, 165
Batra, Ravi, 11, 161
Baumol, William, 60, 188
Bellow, Adam, 181
Bellow, Saul, 181
Bernanke, Ben, 93, 105, 115
big corporations, v, 24, 49, 62, 83, 163, 164
Blodget, Henry, 151
Bosnia, 206
Boykoff, Jules, 20
Boykoff, Maxwell T., 20
Boykoff, Maxwell T., and Boykoff, Jules, 20, 21, 22, 23
Brokaw, Tom, 23
Brookings Institution, 150
Brown, Gordon, 10
Brown, Sherod, 161
Brown, Sherrod, 11, 161, 162, 164
Brunsdale, Anne, 107
Bryen, Stephen, 200, 202
Buchanan, Patrick, 11
Buffet, Warren, 146
Bureau of Labor, 1
Bush, George H. W., 102, 146, 155, 156, 204, 207, 211
Bush, George H.W., 107, 146, 147, 153
Bush, George W., 21, 35, 102, 113, 114, 115, 122, 140, 146, 149, 150, 151, 152, 153, 154, 158, 175, 195, 197, 199, 203, 206, 210, 211, 224, 225, 232, 233, 238
Butler, Smedley, 164

C

CAFTA-DR, 113
Canada, 1, 25, 89, 99, 109, 117, 138
Carter, James Earl Jr., 7, 91, 96, 98, 99, 100, 101, 102, 106, 143, 171, 178, 207
Carter, John R., 171
Cato Institute, 51, 80, 133, 175
CBS Evening News, 15, 22, 25
Census Bureau, 6, 116
Center for Strategic Studies, 10
Chalabi, Ahmad, 208, 218, 227, 229
Chang, Ha Joon, 42, 127
Chang, Ha-Joon, 12, 31, 56, 124, 126, 127, 130, 161, 167, 172, 178
Cheney, Dick, ii, 26, 197, 198, 199, 203, 207, 208, 209, 216, 218, 220, 222, 223, 224, 229, 231, 232, 234
Chimerline, Lawrence, 165
China, i, iii, 2, 3, 4, 5, 8, 9, 35, 37, 40, 41, 43, 45, 46, 51, 52, 53, 56, 59, 86, 88, 92, 94, 112, 116, 117, 118, 119, 125, 126, 130, 131, 132, 134, 135, 137, 138, 139, 141, 156,

157, 158, 159, 161, 162, 164, 173, 174, 177, 184, 186, 189, 192, 234, 239, 240,242, 243, 244, 247
Chinese imports, i, 1, 239
Chinese theft of trade secrets, 3
cigarette manufacturers, 71
Civil War, The, 32, 33, 85
civilian labor participation rate, 1
Clarke, Richard Alan, 203
Clay, Henry, 34, 35, 36, 38, 39, 44, 54, 77, 92
Climate Change, 20, 22, 23, 24, 25, 191
climate contrarians, 19, 23, 123
Climate Contrarians, 112
climate scientists, 19, 23
climate skeptics, 20
Clinton, Bill, 11, 153, 203
Clinton, Hillary, i, iv, 4, 9, 131, 136, 179, 241, 243
Clinton, William, 7, 107, 110, 146, 147, 148, 154, 203, 241
clout, iii, 64, 181
CNN, 3, 15, 19, 242
Cohen, Tyler, 86
Colombia, 116
Committee on Trade Agreements, 87
Comparative Advantage, 38, 39, 40, 42, 43, 44, 45, 46, 47, 55, 57, 59, 60, 61, 68, 88, 90, 108, 120, 121, 124, 129, 136, 161, 170, 245
competitiveness, v, 59, 92, 111, 121, 132, 133
Congress, 3, 4, 22, 29, 30, 35, 54, 64, 83, 84, 85, 87, 89, 91, 95, 96, 99, 115, 116, 117, 118, 135, 143, 144, 145, 147, 149, 152, 157, 165, 178, 187, 192, 208, 209, 220, 224, 226, 227, 231, 232, 244
Congressional Budget Office, 147
Congressional Research Service, 146, 151
Consolidated Omnibus Budget Reconciliation Act of 1985, 143
Constitution of the United States, iii, 169
Consumer Electronics Association, 117
Corn, David, 26, 197
corporations, v, 13, 18, 43, 49, 50, 55, 57, 59, 63, 69, 70, 71, 72, 73, 74, 75, 76, 77, 78, 80, 81, 82, 83, 89, 90, 103, 110, 111, 118, 120, 134, 136, 141, 156, 157, 164, 165, 168, 175, 177, 184, 189, 191, 192, 194, 239, 246, 247
corrupted, v
corruption, iii, v, 70, 121, 124, 169, 171, 181, 182, 183, 185
Costa Rica, 113
Cray, Charles, 72
Cronkite, Walter, 100, 101
cronyism, v
currency manipulation, i, 3, 117, 118, 131, 136
Curveball (Rafid Ahmed Alwan al-Janabi), 197, 227, 228, 229, 230, 231, 232
Czech Republic, 1

D

Debate in the media, v
debtor nation, 31, 61
Decline Of Manufacturing, 8
Defense Policy Board Advisory Committee, 199
Deficit Reduction Act of 1984, 143
democracy, v, 4, 14, 27, 55, 59, 66, 72, 75, 86, 87, 140, 163, 165, 183, 195, 238
Democratic Party, 82, 99, 139, 156, 240, 241
democratization, 10, 163
Democrats, i, iii, iv, v, 8, 25, 31, 49, 54, 61, 83, 95, 100, 107, 108, 110, 113, 123, 136, 137, 138, 139, 140, 153, 157, 159, 180, 184, 186, 191, 194, 195, 239, 241, 244
demopublicans, iv, 112, 198
deregulation, 10, 104, 173
derivatives, 30, 103, 107, 148, 187
Dominican Republic, 113, 164
Dominican Republic-Central America Free Trade Agreement. *See* CAFTA-DR
Drogan, Bob, 197, 228, 232
Drogin, Bob, 228, 230, 232
Drumheller, Tyler, 230
dumping, 30, 126, 165, 166, 245
Dumping, 162, 165, 166, 245

E

echo chamber for the two party debate, v
Eckes, Alfred E., Jr., 85, 87, 88, 90, 99, 105, 106, 107, 108, 122, 125, 160, 166
Economic and Security Review Commission, 132
Economic Growth and Tax Relief Reconciliation Act of 2001, 150
economic history, 12, 57, 111, 158, 160
Economic Policy Institute, 1, 109, 116, 118, 133
economic policymakers, 11
Economic Strategy Institute, 10, 59, 132, 142, 165
economic theory, 9, 57, 87, 111
economics, i, 4, 12, 16, 32, 44, 46, 48, 56, 90, 106, 127, 128, 138, 139, 144, 146, 147, 156, 158, 159, 165, 168, 169, 170, 171, 172, 173, 175, 176, 177, 194, 242, 245
economists, iii, iv, 2, 8, 9, 10, 11, 12, 16, 24, 31, 32, 33, 37, 39, 42, 43, 44, 45, 47, 48, 49, 50, 51, 52, 55, 56, 57, 60, 61, 86, 87, 88, 89, 90, 92, 96, 105, 120, 127, 129, 130, 133, 151, 156, 157, 160, 165, 166, 167, 168, 169, 171, 172, 173, 175, 177, 188, 193, 195, 246, 247
Eichengreen, Barry, 105
Eisenhower, Dwight D., 90, 91, 106, 140, 195
El Salvador, 113
Electoral College, iv, 131
elites, v, 9, 14, 21, 64, 83, 84, 241
Environmental Protection Agency, iv, 50, 112, 136
exchange rates, 10, 93

F

factories, 1, 3, 33, 43, 47, 67, 76, 89, 92, 94, 126, 129, 137, 138, 147, 151, 164, 175, 189, 190, 225, 243
fair trade, 9, 97, 98, 106, 111, 178
Fandz International Law Group, 206
fast track authority, 4, 118
Feith, Dalck, 205
Feith, Douglas, 199, 205, 206, 207, 208, 209
financial crisis, 9, 10, 17, 33, 66, 70, 94, 103, 104, 113, 133, 142, 153, 186
financial crisis of 2008, 9, 10, 17, 70, 133, 142
financial service industries, 3
fiscal discipline, 10
Fletcher, Ian, 12, 42, 56, 57, 59, 127, 130, 135, 136, 161, 173
Foley, Alan A., 230, 232, 234
Ford, Gerald, 206, 207
foreign direct investment, 10, 126
foreign interests, iv, 110, 135
foreign takeovers of iconic American properties, 134
Franklin, Ben, 28
Fraser, Steve, 66
free trade, i, iv, v, 1, 2, 3, 4, 8, 9, 10, 11, 12, 15, 16, 18, 19, 24, 30, 31, 32, 33, 34, 35, 36, 37, 38, 39, 40, 41, 42, 43, 44, 47, 48, 49, 50, 51, 54, 55, 56, 57, 58, 59, 61, 62, 63, 64, 66, 67, 68, 75, 77, 81, 83, 84, 85, 86, 87, 88, 89, 91, 93, 94, 95, 96, 97, 99, 103, 107, 108, 109, 110, 112, 113, 116, 117, 118, 119, 120, 121, 123, 124, 125, 127, 128, 129, 130, 131, 133, 136, 137, 138, 139, 142, 147, 149, 156, 157, 158, 159, 160, 161, 162, 163, 165, 167, 170, 173, 175, 178, 179, 180, 184, 185, 186, 188, 189, 192, 193, 194, 195, 237, 239, 241, 243, 244, 245
Free Trade, i, iv, 1, 4, 11, 12, 31, 38, 46, 48, 57, 83, 108, 113, 118, 124, 135, 149, 158, 160, 161, 162, 164, 167, 243, 245, 246, 254
free trade paradigm, i, 56, 156, 165
Friedman, Milton, 105, 168, 173, 174
Friedman, Thomas, 124

G

Galbraith, John Kenneth, 92, 171
Gephardt, Dick, 178
Germany, 9, 32, 33, 37, 44, 51, 56, 86, 89, 94, 125, 128, 130, 135, 152, 205, 227, 228, 229
Gerstle, Gary, 66
giant sucking sound, 117
global warming, iv, 19, 20, 21, 22, 23, 24, 25, 69, 86, 156, 179, 186, 189, 193, 194, 237, 244
Globalization, 118, 119, 120, 121, 161
Gomory, Ralph, 60, 188
good old days, 1
gospel of free trade, iv
governmental dysfunction, iv
Great Britain, 10, 29, 31, 32, 35, 36, 37, 38, 39, 44, 70, 84, 124, 127, 128, 129, 130
Green, Stephen, 200
Greenhouse Effect, 22
Greenspan, Alan, 107, 157, 158, 168
Gribeauval, Jean Baptiste Vaquette de, 33
Griswold, Daniel, 133, 136
group think, v
growth factors, 9, 246
Guatemala, 113

H

Hamilton, Alexander, 16, 18, 28, 29, 30, 38, 77, 124, 239
Hansen, James, 22
Harley Davidson, 106
Harrison, Benjamin, 122
Heckscher Ohlin Model, 44, 45
Heilbroner, Robert, 172
Hersh, Seymour, 200
high value jobs, iii, 184
Highway Revenue Act of 1982, 143
historians, iv, 66, 113, 114
Honduras, 113
Hong Kong, 128
House of Representatives, 11
Hull, Cordell, 18, 84, 86, 87, 89, 99, 108
Human Development Index, 1
Hussein, Saddam, 26, 113, 196, 197, 198, 199, 203, 204, 205, 207, 209, 211, 212, 213, 214, 215, 216, 217, 218, 219, 220, 224, 225, 226, 227, 228, 231, 232, 233, 234
Huszar, Andrew, 115
Hyundai, 127

I

indicia of national economic health, 1
Indonesia, 44, 163
Indonesia Economic Masterplan 2011-2025, 163
Industrial Economy, 8
industrialization, 19, 86, 128, 173
interchangeable parts, 33, 34
International Monetary Fund, 130, 163
International Trade Commission, 96, 99, 106, 166
International Trade Organization, 110
international trade theory, i, 9, 57
Iraq, ii, iv, 26, 30, 113, 149, 150, 152, 153, 164, 175, 196, 197, 198, 199, 200, 202, 203, 204, 205, 206, 207, 208, 209, 210, 211, 212, 213, 214, 215, 216, 217, 218, 219, 220, 221, 222, 223, 224, 225, 226, 227, 228, 230, 231, 232, 233, 234, 235, 238, 240
Iraqi National Congress, 208
Ireland, 1, 36, 129
Irons, Michael D., 171
Isikoff, Michael, 26, 197, 223, 229, 230, 235

isolationist, i, 112
Israel, 1, 92, 199, 200, 201, 202, 206, 214
Italy, 1, 86, 89, 211

J

Jackson, Henry Martin "Scoop", 200, 203, 206
Japan, 37, 44, 56, 59, 60, 84, 89, 90, 91, 94, 99, 111, 117, 125, 126, 129, 130, 135, 138, 141, 152, 173
Jefferson, Thomas, 28, 29, 30, 33, 34, 75, 166
jet stream, 25
JFK, iii, 91
job losses, 3, 37, 92, 99, 109, 111, 122, 132, 133
jobs, 1, 2, 4, 5, 8, 15, 35, 37, 43, 44, 48, 49, 51, 52, 57, 62, 66, 67, 68, 76, 82, 83, 89, 90, 91, 93, 99, 103, 104, 108, 109, 110, 111, 116, 117, 119, 120, 123, 129, 131, 132, 133, 135, 136, 137, 138, 139, 142, 147, 149, 156, 157, 159, 164, 165, 174, 175, 176, 177, 179, 182, 185, 186, 187, 188, 189, 191, 192, 193, 239, 242, 243, 245
Johnson, Lyndon, 2, 70, 91, 92, 105, 242
journalistic norms
- authority order bias, 20
- balance, 6, 7, 20, 21, 22, 23, 24, 79, 91, 92, 97, 99, 113, 143, 147, 148, 155, 156, 163, 179, 188, 190
- dramatization, 20
- novelty, 20, 21, 22
- personalization, 20, 21, 23

Journalistic Norms, 20
journalists, 9, 20, 21, 22, 26, 30, 83, 160

K

Kemp-Roth Tax Cut, 177
Kennedy Round, The, 91, 92, 105
Kerry, John, 3
Keynes, John Maynard, 105, 171
Keynesianism, 16, 103, 105
Kia, 127
Kintz, Jarod, 172
Kissinger, Henry, 101, 123
Kraev, Egore, 130
Krugman, Paul, 60, 105
Kuntsler, William, 74, 75

L

L.G. Electronics, 127
labor unions, 44, 48, 50, 62, 72, 82, 100, 116, 137, 192
Latin America, 10, 59, 130, 164, 178
Latin American countries, 10, 89, 163
legacy of failures, iv
Libby, Irving Lewis "Scooter", 208, 209, 210, 211, 216, 226
Liebeler, Susan, 107
List, Friedrich, 127, 128
Lodge, George C., 161
Long, Huey, 122
Long, Russell, 122
low wages, 1, 108, 109, 110, 131, 246
Luban, David J., 238
Lynch, Peter, 172

M

Magnus, John, 165
male employment participation rate, 1
Maloof, F. Michael, 207, 208, 209
manufacturing, iii, 1, 2, 3, 4, 5, 8, 29, 30, 31, 32, 33, 34, 35, 39, 40, 43, 44, 47, 48, 49, 51, 52, 54, 55, 59, 61, 62, 66, 67, 68, 73, 76, 77, 84, 88, 90, 93, 95, 103, 104, 107, 111, 112, 117, 118, 124, 125, 127, 128, 132, 133, 135, 137, 138, 166, 174, 175, 176, 177, 178, 179, 180, 184, 186, 187, 189, 192, 193, 237, 238, 242, 246, 247
maquiladoras, 121
market forces, 10, 66
Martino, Rocco, 211, 212, 224
Marwell, Gerald, 170
Massachusetts, 3, 32, 34, 48, 49, 53, 202
Mastel, Greg, 165
McChesney, Robert W., 14, 15, 70, 71, 72, 76, 80, 81, 82
media, iv, v, 1, 2, 4, 8, 9, 12, 13, 14, 15, 16, 18, 19, 20, 21, 22, 23, 24, 25, 26, 27, 30, 31, 40, 49, 50, 57, 59, 61, 63, 66, 70, 71, 73, 76, 77, 78, 79, 80, 81, 82, 83, 104, 106, 110, 111, 117, 120, 126, 129, 131, 134, 135, 136, 138, 146, 147, 160, 176, 178, 179, 188, 189, 190, 194, 196, 197, 207, 208, 213, 226, 231, 238, 241, 246, 247
media monopoly, 178, 246
middle class, v, 46, 57, 62, 81, 84, 86, 93, 96, 104, 109, 112, 116, 132, 138, 139, 142, 143, 146, 147, 156, 157, 159, 163, 164, 165, 186, 188, 191, 192, 195
Ministry of International Trade and Industry, 125
money power, v, 13, 27, 31, 32, 40, 50, 56, 57, 59, 62, 63, 64, 65, 66, 68, 69, 70, 74, 76, 79, 80, 81, 82, 83, 86, 90, 110, 111, 120, 121, 122, 123, 126, 129, 131, 133, 136, 138, 149, 159, 163, 169, 183, 191, 194, 195, 240, 241, 243
monopoly, iv, v, 13, 16, 19, 27, 30, 31, 35, 50, 59, 61, 76, 126, 129, 146, 178, 194, 226, 231, 246, 247
moral, iii, v, 30, 55, 69, 121, 138, 169, 182, 186, 199
Mount Rushmore, i, 28, 29, 30, 32, 33, 66, 75, 76, 77, 83, 85, 99, 107, 113, 156, 166, 174, 185, 192
Myanmar, 163, *See also* Burma
myths about free trade, iv, 161
Myths of Free Trade, iv, v, 14, 16, 18, 19, 30, 31, 52, 61, 81, 105, 106, 129, 135, 136, 158, 160, 161, 162, 165, 186, 196, 216

N

Nader, Ralph, 69, 73, 74, 76

NAFTA, 11, 15, 20, 108, 109, 110, 113, 116, 118, 149, 242, 246
Nankani, Gobind, 11
NASA, 19, 33
Nash-Hoff, Michelle, 160
national debt, i, 1, 4, 7, 8, 40, 61, 64, 102, 103, 107, 110, 113, 122, 133, 139, 140, 142, 143, 145, 146, 147, 148, 149, 150, 152, 153, 154, 155, 156, 158, 160, 174, 178, 184, 193, 239
national interest, iv, 29, 44, 60, 69, 87, 112, 115, 131
National Labor Relations Board, 100
National Network for Manufacturing Innovation, 137
national security, iii, 4, 51, 70, 131, 159, 166, 186, 205, 234, 235
National Security Council, 99, 101, 203
NBC Nightly News, 15, 22, 23, 25
nepotism, v, 181, 182, 183, 184, 194
new political party, iv, v, 9, 12, 28, 50, 54, 75, 112, 129, 131, 139, 156, 169, 178, 179, 180, 184, 239
Nicaragua, 113, 164
Nichols, John, 70
Niger, 211, 212, 223, 229, 234
Nisbet, Robert, 28
Novak, Robert D., 197

O

Obama, Barack, i, iv, 1, 3, 4, 5, 6, 7, 9, 81, 91, 104, 113, 114, 115, 116, 118, 119, 120, 121, 122, 135, 137, 152, 154, 161, 179, 180, 187, 189, 191, 195, 244
Occupy Wall Street, 19, 69
ocean acidification, 22
October Surprise, The, 101, 102
Omnibus Budget Reconciliation Act of 1986, 143
Operation Desert Storm, 147, 204, 211
opinion polls, 2
Organization of Petroleum Exporting Countries, 99
Other Canon Foundation, 56
outsourcing, 1, 2, 3, 33, 44, 66, 107, 118, 131, 136, 138, 247

P

Parry, Robert, 100, 101
Pavitt, James L., 229, 230
Perle, Richard, 199, 200, 201, 202, 203, 206, 207, 208, 211
Perot, Ross, 11, 15, 158, 178, 179, 192
Peter, Laurence J., 172
Phillips, Kevin, 69, 70, 80, 160
Pillar, Paul, 197, 216
Pipes, Richard, 206
plutocrats, 66, 174
police, iii, 62, 185, 223, 238, 247
Policy Counter Terrorism Evaluation Group (PCTEG), 207, 208, 209
political parties, iii, v, 20, 57, 81, 136, 183, 196, 241, 244
politicians, iii, v, 9, 11, 21, 24, 28, 30, 31, 50, 57, 63, 67, 70, 71, 73, 77, 79, 81, 82, 83, 84, 86, 95, 108, 111, 115, 129, 133, 134, 136, 138, 158, 160, 169, 178, 179, 183, 190, 194
polls, 2, 3, 4, 19, 65, 110, 113, 114, 115, 157, 158
pollution, 22, 43, 44, 48, 49, 54, 69, 86, 100, 136, 139, 152, 156, 192, 194, 246
positive externalities, 48, 49, 51, 56, 67, 93, 95, 108, 160, 165, 170
Powell Memo, The, 71, 80
Powell, Colin, 199, 207, 213, 216, 217, 218, 219, 220, 225, 226, 227, 229, 235
Powell, Lewis, 71
Prestowitz, Clyde, 10, 12, 42, 56, 59, 60, 61, 110, 111, 127, 161, 173, 188
privatization, 10, 139
Prochnow, Herbert, 172
production ecosystems, 51, 55, 108, 112, 116, 127, 131, 132, 137, 156, 159, 165, 174, 186
productivity, 9, 34, 39, 41, 48, 49, 55, 58, 61, 66, 84, 86, 92, 93, 97, 122, 127, 160, 176, 240
progress, 4, 17, 19, 28, 31, 32, 33, 34, 37, 40, 49, 55, 57, 75, 95, 106, 117, 147, 163, 185, 189, 208
prosperity, iii, v, 16, 17, 27, 30, 31, 34, 39, 45, 48, 55, 56, 66, 69, 75, 81, 86, 88, 91, 94, 99, 100, 102, 103, 106, 107, 108, 112, 116, 122, 124, 125, 126, 133, 139, 143, 147, 149, 156, 157, 174, 179, 180, 185, 195, 196, 238, 239, 240, 244, 246
Protectionism, 3, 17, 28, 29, 30, 31, 33, 35, 36, 37, 39, 44, 47, 58, 83, 92, 97, 99, 118, 124, 125, 126, 127, 128, 129, 138, 162, 192
protectionist, 9, 16, 18, 29, 31, 32, 33, 34, 35, 37, 38, 40, 42, 43, 47, 77, 84, 88, 91, 94, 98, 105, 107, 110, 112, 125, 126, 128, 131, 135, 136, 163, 165, 166, 173, 195
public sector unions, 62
pundits, 9, 10, 16, 20, 71, 86, 102, 133

Q

quantitative easing, 115, 116, 174

R

Railroad Retirement Revenue Act of 1983, 143
Rand, Ayn, 157, 158, 168, 169
Randbots, 169
Rankin, David M., 15, 16
Reagan, Ronald, 12, 59, 80, 100, 101, 102, 103, 106, 107, 123, 140, 142, 143, 144, 145, 146, 147, 149, 152, 153, 154, 155, 156, 158, 164, 175, 177, 178, 210
Reaganomics, 10, 175, 177
Reich, Charles A., 74
Reinert, Eric S., 11, 12, 56, 57, 124, 127, 130, 161, 173
Reinsch, Bill, 191

Republican Party, 29, 139, 156, 192, 210
Republicans, i, iv, v, 8, 25, 31, 49, 54, 61, 77, 83, 100, 101, 103, 108, 110, 113, 122, 123, 136, 138, 139, 140, 142, 147, 153, 156, 157, 158, 159, 174, 175, 180, 184, 186, 191, 192, 194, 195
republocrats, iv, 240
Ricardo, David, 32, 38, 42, 57, 245
Richelson, Jeff, 210
Ricks, Thomas E., 26, 197
Roberts, Paul Craig, 175, 177
Robinson, Joan Violet, 172
Romney, Mitt, 9, 64, 81
Roosevelt, Franklin Delano, 16, 18, 84, 87, 89, 95
Roosevelt, Theordore, 29, 30, 75, 166
Rosenblum, Jonathan, 100
rule of law, 10
Rumsfeld, Donald, 200, 203, 207, 211, 224, 232
Rust Belt, 1, 47

S

Samsung, 127, 186
Sanders, Bernie, i, 2, 4, 9, 112, 157, 158, 178, 179, 184, 239, 240, 241, 242, 243, 244
Santorum, Rick, 9
Saudia Arabia, 200
Scott, Robert E., 116, 118
Senate Intelligence Committee, 217, 218, 226, 227, 230, 231, 238
Shaw, George Bernard, 172
Singapore, 53, 117, 128
Slovenia, 1
Smiley, Jane, 171
Smith, Adam, 32, 38, 42, 167
Smith, Allen W., 144
Smoot Hawley, 16, 17, 18, 105, 129
Smoot Hawley Myth, 16, 17, 32, 105, 106, 107, 162
Snyder, Michael, 4, 8, 104, 191
Social Security, 104, 142, 143, 144, 145, 146, 147
socialism, i, 76, 77, 86, 112, 157
South Dakota, 29
South Korea, 116, 118, 126, 127, 128, 129, 135, 138, 163, 166, 173
Spain, 1
stagflation, 93, 95, 99, 143
Stahl, Leslie, 101
State Owned Enterprise, 128, 163, 165
Stiglitz, Joseph, 160
Stockman, David, 102, 103, 104, 144, 156
Strauss, Robert, 99
Stumo, Michael, 190
Supreme Court, iii, 71, 72, 74, 81, 90, 149, 201
Sydnor, Eugene, 72
Szamosszegi, Adam, 165

T

Taiwan, 94, 128, 173
Taleb, Nassim Nicholas, 172
tariff, i, 3, 16, 17, 18, 29, 30, 32, 34, 39, 54, 85, 87, 88, 89, 90, 91, 92, 95, 105, 106, 107, 126, 158, 239, 243
tariffs, i, 18, 28, 29, 30, 32, 33, 35, 37, 45, 77, 84, 85, 88, 90, 91, 92, 105, 106, 107, 124, 125, 131, 139, 164, 175, 193
tax cuts, i, iv, 65, 100, 102, 103, 131, 139, 142, 143, 144, 150, 151, 152, 153, 154, 158, 174, 178, 179, 192, 244
Tax Equity and Fiscal Responsibility Act of 1982, 143
technologies, iii, v, 14, 39, 52, 55, 66, 89, 94, 119, 134, 152, 166, 173, 174, 184, 191
technology, iii, 3, 16, 37, 42, 43, 44, 45, 47, 48, 49, 50, 53, 54, 55, 57, 61, 67, 84, 88, 96, 109, 119, 121, 124, 125, 126, 134, 136, 137, 138, 142, 147, 151, 156, 163, 166, 174, 176, 177, 180, 187, 189, 190, 193, 196, 200, 202, 244, 245, 247
Tenet, George, 216, 218, 220, 231
Thaler, Richard, 172
the academic community, v
The Geological Society of America, 20
the great depression, 16, 17, 86, 88, 143
the internet, 4, 13, 14, 72, 119, 184
the media, 2, 13, 14, 15, 16, 19, 20, 23, 24, 26, 27, 50, 66, 70, 73, 83, 111, 129, 135, 178, 194, 198
The Other Canon Foundation, 11
the press, iv, 20, 21, 64, 78, 81, 83, 207, 241, 246
the Tea Party, 19, 159, 179
the two parties, iv, v, 15, 19, 20, 244
The Washington Consensus, i, 10, 11
the World Bank, 11, 130
Tobacco Institute, The, 71, 72, 74
Tobacco Master Settlement Agreement, 71
torture, iii, iv, 198, 218, 219, 238
trade agreements, iv, 2, 4, 8, 89, 91, 116, 118, 120, 185, 187, 195, 242, 243
trade deficit, iii, 1, 3, 40, 54, 56, 61, 91, 92, 93, 96, 97, 99, 109, 113, 116, 132, 133, 138, 140, 142, 149, 176, 187, 188
trade policy, i, 3, 4, 12, 15, 31, 33, 40, 49, 59, 69, 83, 87, 88, 89, 92, 93, 95, 99, 106, 108, 112, 120, 130, 131, 158, 159, 163, 178, 179, 184, 186, 190, 191, 192, 193, 240, 243
trade theory, iv, v, 9, 10, 32, 37, 38, 39, 42, 43, 55, 56, 57, 60, 61, 111, 118, 119, 136, 161, 167, 173, 185
Trans-Pacific Partnership, 4, 9, 118
transparency, 10, 87
trickle down,", 10, 139
Trireme Partners, 200
Truman, Harry, 89, 90, 94, 129
Trump, Donald, i, iv, 2, 3, 4, 9, 49, 50, 61, 112, 123, 131, 136, 139, 146, 156, 157, 158, 178, 179, 180, 184, 192, 195, 196, 238, 239, 240, 241, 244

Turkey, 89, 206
Turner, Stansfield, 200
Tyson, Laura, 60, 151

U

U.S. Chamber of Commerce, 71, 72, 80, 81, 82
U.S. Economy, 4, 8
U.S. Trade Deficit, 3
underemployment, 1, 69, 121, 133
United Arab Emirates, 134
United States, ii, 1, 4, 5, 6, 7, 8, 14, 15, 16, 20, 21, 23, 24, 25, 28, 29, 32, 34, 39, 43, 44, 46, 47, 49, 51, 52, 53, 54, 60, 61, 63, 64, 66, 69, 79, 82, 85, 86, 87, 88, 89, 90, 91, 92, 93, 94, 107, 108, 109, 110, 111, 112, 116, 119, 127, 128, 131, 134, 135, 138, 147, 149, 151, 152, 156, 157, 158, 159, 162, 163, 164, 165, 166, 186, 187, 188, 189, 190, 191, 192, 193, 194, 195, 198, 204, 205, 206, 207, 210, 213, 221, 224, 242, 244, 246, 247
University of Illinois, Champaign, 14
uranium yellow cake, 212
uranium yellowcake, 211, 212, 223, 234
Uruguay Round, 109, 110, 111
US-Colombia Trade Agreement, 116

V

voters, iv, 2, 3, 4, 14, 27, 65, 102, 111, 113, 115, 158, 179, 183, 185, 241

W

Waal, Frans de, 172
wages, 1, 3, 5, 31, 33, 39, 40, 43, 44, 46, 47, 48, 49, 54, 55, 57, 62, 66, 68, 84, 90, 93, 96, 100, 104, 107, 108, 109, 110, 111, 119, 120, 122, 125, 126, 132, 133, 135, 137, 142, 150, 152, 156, 160, 163, 164, 175, 176, 178, 185, 186, 188, 192, 193, 240
Wall Street, v, 2, 3, 4, 12, 13, 17, 18, 19, 22, 49, 56, 63, 66, 68, 69, 70, 81, 82, 83, 103, 104, 107, 108, 111, 115, 123, 129, 131, 136, 143, 148, 149, 156, 157, 164, 168, 169, 174, 175, 177, 179, 186, 188, 189, 195, 243
war in Iraq, iv, 61, 149, 195, 196, 197, 209, 213, 221, 224, 231
War of 1812, 29, 30, 32
Washington Consensus, 8, 9, 10, 11, 12, 16, 59, 125, 129, 165
Washington, George, 7, 16, 18, 28, 29, 34, 38, 75, 77, 107, 122, 138, 166, 196, 239
Washington, Harold, 183
wealth, v, 6, 8, 32, 34, 36, 40, 42, 43, 47, 49, 50, 56, 57, 59, 64, 65, 66, 69, 70, 75, 76, 81, 86, 89, 90, 103, 121, 122, 127, 128, 129, 131, 139, 152, 156, 157, 160, 163, 169, 184, 185, 224, 240
wealthy and powerful, v
wealthy people, iv, 131, 184
Weapons Intelligence Nonproliferation and Arms Control unit of the Directorate of Intelligence, Central Intelligence Agency. *See* WINPAC
weapons of mass destruction, iv, 26, 39, 203, 205, 207, 215, 219, 221, 224, 225, 228
Weapons of Mass Destruction, 113, 135, 149, 196, 198, 199, 203, 205, 208, 211, 213, 216, 217, 218, 220, 221, 225, 226, 227, 228, 229, 230, 231, 232, 234
Weinberger, Caspar, 206
Westwood, Vivienne, 172
Whitney, Eli, 34
Whitworth, Joseph, 34, 39
whorrible politicians, 9, 82, 136
Wildasin, David, 172
Wilkerson, Lawrence, 216, 218, 220, 226
Williamson, John, 10, 11
Wilson, Joe, 212
wind energy, 3
wind energy business, 3
WINPAC (Weapons Intelligence Nonproliferation and Arms Control, a unit of the Central Intelligence Agency), 229, 230, 232, 234, 235
Wolfowitz, Paul, 199, 203, 204, 205, 206, 207, 208, 209, 210, 211, 231
World Trade Organization, 5, 110, 245
World War II, 16, 29, 31, 32, 54, 65, 66, 75, 84, 86, 89, 90, 93, 106, 107, 112, 140, 192, 205, 210
world's largest debtor nation, 9, 59, 137
Wurmser, David, 207, 208, 209

Y

Yoo, John, 198

Z

Zell, Marc, 206
Zidar, Owen, 151

Notes

Chapter 1: The Majority Doesn't Like Free Trade and Why

1. Human Development Index. *Wikipedia The Free Encyclopedia.* (Wikipedia Foundation Inc., Retrieved on July 7, 2015 from https://en.wikipedia.org/wiki/Human_Development_Index
2. Thompson, Laura. February 14, 2011. Intelligence Community Fears U.S. Manufacturing Decline. *Forbes*. Retrieved from http://www.forbes.com/
3. McCormack, Richard. December 21, 2009. The Plight of American Manufacturing. *The American Prospect.* Retrieved from http://prospect.org/
4. Scott, Robert E. May 1, 2000. China and the States - Booming Trade Deficit With China will accelerate job loss in next decade with losses in every state. *Economic Policy Institute*. Retrieved from http://www.epi.org/
5. February 9, 2012. 88 million out of work and not looking for a job. *SFGate.* Retrieved from http://www.sfgate.com/
6. Gongloff, Mark. September 7, 2012. Labor Force Participation Rate Lowest In Three Decades, Though Despair Doesn't Explain It All. *Huff Post Business*. Retrieved from http://www.huffingtonpost.com/mark-gongloff/labor-force-participation-rate_b_1865027.html
7. BLS Database. Data Extracted November 7, 2014. Civilian labor force participation rate 16 years and over. *United States Department of Labor Bureau of Labor Statistics*. Retrieved from http://data.bls.gov/timeseries/LNS11300000; Meyer, Ali. March 3, 2014. Labor Force Participation in 2013 Lowest in 35 Years. *CNS News.* Retrieved from http://cnsnews.com/; Durden, Tyler. October 3, 2014. Labor Participation Rate Drops To 36 Year Low, Record 92.6 Million Americans Not In Labor Force. *Zero Hedge*. Retrieved from http://www.zerohedge.com/; As my copy editor doubted the "not in labor force" number I checked it on December 5, 2016 to convince him. On that date the number stood at over 95 million!
8. BLS Database. Data Extracted January 28, 2016. Civilian labor force participation rate 16 years and over. *United States Department of Labor Bureau of Labor Statistics*. Retrieved from http://data.bls.gov/timeseries/LNS11300000
9. Murray, Sara and Belkin, Douglas. Americans Sour on Trade Majority Say Free-Trade Pacts Have Hurt U.S.; Wedge Issue In Some Races. (Louise Radnofsky and Jim Carlton contributed). *The Wall Street Journal*. Retrieved from http://online.wsj.com/
10. Jones, Jeffrey M. February 10, 2012. Americans Still View China As World's Leading Economic Power. *Gallup*. Retrieved from http://www.gallup.com/
11. Johnson, Dave. February 19, 2014. Poll: Voters Blame Trade Agreements For Job Losses. *Campaign For America's Future*. Retrieved from http://ourfuture.org/; Voters Are Demanding Washington Focus On Job Creation. *Alliance For American Manufacturing*.

Retrieved from http://www.americanmanufacturing.org/2014poll/

12. Johnson, Dave. April 19, 2011. Why Trump Gets Traction From Trade, *Huffington Post*. Retrieved from http://www.huffingtonpost.com/
13. Censky, Annalyn. July 12, 2011. U.S. Trade Deficit Widens in May. *CNN Money*. retrieved from http://money.cnn.com/
14. Murray, Sara and Belkin, Douglas. Americans Sour on Trade Majority Say Free-Trade Pacts Have Hurt U.S.; Wedge Issue In Some Races. (Louise Radnofsky and Jim Carlton contributed). *The Wall Street Journal*. Retrieved from http://online.wsj.com/
15. Weisman, Jonathan. February 14, 2012. U.S. To Share Cautionary Tale of Trade Secret Theft With Chinese Official. *The New York Times*. Retrieved from http://www.nytimes .com/
16. Lee, Don and Person, David. February 14, 2012. Focus Shifts from China's currency to its other trade policies. *Los Angeles Times*. Retrieved from http://articles.latimes.com/
17. Abrams, Jim. February 29, 2012 Trade Official Urges Action In China. *Associated Press*. Retrieved from http://www.foxnews.com/
18. Thompson, Loren. February 14, 2011. Intelligence Community Fears U.S. Manufacturing Decline. *Forbes*. Retrieved from http://www.forbes.com/
19. Blumenthal, Mark. Edwards-Levy, Ariel. and Velencia, Janie. June 12, 2015. Huffpollster: Opinions On Trade Don't Divide Along The Usual Party Lines. *Huffington Post*. Retrieved from http://www.huffingtonpost.com/2015/06/12/free-trade-polls_n_7568724.html
20. Kane, Paul. and Nakamura, David. December 10, 2015. McConnell Warns That Trade Deal Can't Pass Congress Before 2016 Elections. *Washington Post*. Retrieved from https: //www.washingtonpost.com/politics/mcconnell-warns-that-trade-deal-cant-pass-congress -before-2016-elections/2015/12/10/b8151f26-9f66-11e5-8728-1af6af208198_story.html
21. Marans, Daniel. January 27, 2016. How The Presidential Election Could Endanger Obama's Big Trade Deal. *Huffington Post*. Retrieved from http://www.huffingtonpost.co m/
22. Snyder, Michael. February 22, 2012. 55 Interesting Facts about the U.S. Economy in 2012. *The Economic Collapse*. Retrieved from http://theeconomiccollapseblog.com/archives/55-interesting-facts-about-the-u-s-economy-in-2012; I did not read the original sources for the cited article. Mr. Snyder provides hyperlinks to his sources in the body of his work.
23. Snyder, Michael. September 5, 2016. From An Industrial Economy To A Paper Economy – The Stunning Decline Of Manufacturing In America. Retrieved from http://theeconomic collapseblog.com/archives/from-an-industrial-economy-to-a-paper-economy-the-stunning-decline-of-manufacturing-in-america
24. See for eg., Obrien, Matt. January 13, 2016. This May Be The Most Important Chart For Understanding Politics Today. *The Washington Post*. Retrieved from .https://www.washin gtonpost.com/news/wonk/wp/2016/01/13/this-may-be-the-most-important-chart-for-under standing-politics-today/?tid=pm_business_pop_b
25. See, Murray, Sara and Belkin, Douglas. Americans Sour on Trade Majority Say Free-Trade Pacts Have Hurt U.S.; Wedge Issue In Some Races. (Louise Radnofsky and Jim Carlton contributed). *The Wall Street Journal*. Retrieved from http://online.wsj.com/;

Johnson, Dave. February 19, 2014. Poll: Voters Blame Trade Agreements For Job Losses. *Campaign For America's Future*. Retrieved from http://ourfuture.org/; Voters Are Demanding Washington Focus On Job Creation. *Alliance For American Manufacturing*. Retrieved from http://www.americanmanufacturing.org/2014poll/; Blumenthal, Mark. Edwards-Levy, Ariel. and Velencia, Janie. June 12, 2015. Huffpollster: Opinions On Trade Don't Divide Along The Usual Party Lines. *Huffington Post*. Retrieved from http://www.huffingtonpost.com/2015/06/12/free-trade-polls_n_7568724.html and 19.

26. Allen, Frederick E., December 21, 2011. How Germany Builds Twice As Many Cars As The U.S. While Paying Its Workers Twice As Much. *Forbes*. Retrieved from http://www.forbes.com/sites/frederickallen/2011/12/21/germany-builds-twice-as-many-cars-as-the-u-s-while-paying-its-auto-workers-twice-as-much/#739474fd289f
27. It may not seem like it, but both candidates are/were strong supporters of free trade. Santorum is opposed to tariffs in any form. He claims we should "think about the people that free trade effects when we make economic policy." See, Rick Santorum on Free Trade: Republican Jr Senator (PA); 2012 presidential frontrunner *On The Issues*. Retrieved from http://grid.ontheissues.org/2016/Rick_Santorum_Free_Trade.htm; Mitt Romney is a strong advocate for free trade. He argued in the 2012 election that we should "increase our trade," without specifying how our trade balance with low wage countries could ever be improved. See, Mitt Romney on Free Trade. *On The Issues*. Retrieved from http://www.ontheissues.org/Celeb/Mitt_Romney_Free_Trade.htm
28. Flores, Reena. January 7, 2016. Donald Trump wants huge tariffs on Chinese exports to the U.S. *CBS News*. Retrieved from http://www.cbsnews.com/news/donald-trump-wants-huge-tariffs-on-chinese-exports-to-the-u-s/; A single activist President fighting the majority of his own party on the trade issue simply will not be able to recreate America's trade policy in the most effective manner possible. Also, placing a huge tariff on China all at once would work hardship on both America and China. A sophisticated and smart strategy will accomplish change quickly but without causing any pain to the American people. That in fact is how trade policy beginning with President Washington was conducted until the post fifties modern era of free trade policy and the resulting problem of declining wages and general economic disintegration and decline began.
29. See, Marans, Daniel. January 27, 2016. How The Presidential Election Could Endanger Obama's Big Trade Deal. *Huffington Post*. Retrieved from http://www.huffingtonpost.com/
30. Prestowitz, Clyde. *The Betrayal of American Prosperity: Free Market Delusions, America's Decline, and How We Must Compete in the Post-Dollar Era*. (New York: Free Press, 2010), 113.

Chapter 2: The Washington Consensus

31. Ibid.
32. Williamson, John. Did The Washington Consensus Fail? Outline of speech at the Center for Strategic & International Studies, Washington, D.C. November 6, 2002. *Peterson*

Institute for International Economics. https://piie.com/commentary/speeches -papers/did -washington-consensus-fail
33. Weisman, Jonathan and MacDonald, Alistair. April 3, 2009. Obama, Brown Strike Similar Notes on Economy. *The Wall Street Journal*. Retrieved from http://online.wsj.com/
34. Rodrik, Dani. 2006/12. Goodbye Washington Consensus, Hello Washington Confusion? A Review of the World Bank's Economic Growth in the 1990s: Learning from a Decade of Reform. *Journal of Economic Literature*, 44(4): 973-987
35. Lozada, Carlos. April 12, 2009. A Conversation With John Williamson, Economist. *The Washington Post*. Retrieved from http://www.washingtonpost.com/
36. Williamson, John. September 24, 2004. A Short History of the Washington Consensus. *Peterson Institute for International Economics*. 3. Retrieved from http://www.iie.com/ publications/papers/williamson0904-2.pdf
37. Ibid.
38. Batra, Ravi. *The Myth of Free Trade: The Pooring of America*. (New York: Simon & Schustcr, 1993)
39. Brown, Sherrod. *Myths of Free Trade: Why American Trade Policy Has Failed*. (New York: The New Press, 2004)
40. H.R. 3450 (103rd): North American Free Trade Agreement Implementation Act. Passage Date: November 17, 1993. *GovTrak* Retrieved from https://www.govtrack.us/
41. Rodrik, Goodbye Washington Consensus, Hello Washington Confusion? 973-987
42. Ibid.
43. Reinert, Erik S. *How Rich Countries Got Rich ...and Why Poor Countries Stay Poor*. (New York: Carroll & Graf, 2007)
44. Chang, Ha-Joon. *Bad Samaritans: The Myth of Free Trade And The Secret History of Capitalism*. (New York: Bloomsbury Press, 2008)
45. Chang, Ha-Joon. *Kicking Away The Ladder: Development Strategy In Historical Perspective*. (London: Anthem Press, 2002)
46. Prestowitz, Clyde. *The Betrayal of American Prosperity: Free Market Delusions, America's Decline, and How We Must Compete in the Post-Dollar Era*. (New York: Free Press, 2010)
47. Fletcher, Ian. *Free Trade Doesn't Work: What Should Replace It and Why*. (Washington, D.C.: U.S. Business & Industry Council, 2010)

Chapter 3. The Media Oligopoly is a Dysfunctional Echo Chamber for the Two Parties and the Special Interests That Both Parties Serve

48. Bagdikian, Ben H. *The New Media Monopoly* (Boston: Beacon Press, 2004) 27-28.
49. Ibid., 3-10
50. See for eg., Bagdikian, op. cit., 12-16, 103-105, 246
51. McChesney, Robert W. *The Problem of the Media, U.S. Communication Politics in the 21st Century*. (New York: Monthly Review Press, 2004) 7

52. Rankin, David M. Featuring the President as Free Trader: Television News Coverage of U.S. Trade Politics. *Presidential Studies Quarterly* Vol. 36, No. 4. (Dec., 2006) 633-659; McMahon, Kevin., Rankin, David M., Beachler, Donald W., and White, John Kenneth. *Winning the White House, 2008*. (New York: Palgrave Macmillan, 2009)
53. Ibid. p. 649. Rankin quotes the material from Michelson, Melissa R. Explorations In Public Opinion Presidential Power Linkages: Congressional Action On Unpopular Foreign Agreements. *Political Communication* Volume 15, Issue 1. p. 63-82. (1998)
54. For an excellent discussion of the Smoot Hawley Tariff see Eckes, Jr., Alfred E. *Opening America's Market U.S. Foreign Trade Policy since 1776,* (Chapel Hill: The University of North Carolina Press, 1995) 100-139.; See also Fletcher, 139-140.; John Maynard Keynes himself hated the idea that the U.S. would run a trade deficit. See, Geoghegan, Thomas. September 27, 2011. What Would Keynes Do? The GOP declares Keynesianism dead, but it hasn't really been tried. The great economist would have us do much more than "prime the pump" to pull the country out of this morass. *The Nation.* Retrieved from http://www.thenation.com/; Krugman, Paul. *Peddling Prosperity: Economic Sense and Nonsense in an Age of Diminished Expectations.* (New York: W.W. Norton & Company, 1994) 93
55. Fletcher, *Free Trade Doesn't Work: What Should Replace It and Why*, 72-111; Prestowitz, *The Betrayal of American Prosperity: Free Market Delusions, America's Decline, and How We Must Compete in the Post-Dollar Era*, 142-148.
56. Chang, *Bad Samaritans: The Myth of Free Trade And The Secret History of Capitalism*, 48-56.; Fletcher, *Free Trade Doesn't Work: What Should Replace It and Why*, 131-142; Prestowitz, *The Betrayal of American Prosperity: Free Market Delusions, America's Decline, and How We Must Compete in the Post-Dollar Era*, 45-73; An egregious example of misrepresentation by the media about the history of American trade policy is the utterly absurd claim in the following cited *New York Times* article that America's "economic policies...held trade up as a good thing," for two centuries: See, Steinhauer, Jill. Dec. 5, 2016. House G.O.P. Signals Break With Trump Over Tariff Threat. *The New York Times*. Retrieved from http://www.nytimes.com/2016/12/05/us/politics/house-republicans-trade-trump.html?_r=1
57. Prestowitz, op. cit. 72-111; Fletcher, op. cit. 142-148.
58. Opinions vary among economists as to the causes of the Great Depression but a paper produced by the Federal Reserve Bank of St. Louis states that the Great Depression was a result of the Federal Reserve Board "allowing the money stock to collapse as panics engulfed the banking system. If the Fed had stepped up to the plate and ensured that banks had ample reserves to meet their customers' withdrawal demands, the money stock would not have declined, and the economy probably would not have sharply contracted." See, *The Great Depression 1929 - 1939 A Curriculum For High School Students*. (Federal Reserve Bank of St. Louis, 2007) (https://www.stlouisfed.org/education) Retrieved from https://www.stlouisfed.org/great-depression/pdf/the-great-depression-full-curriculum.pdf;
59. John K. Galbraith noted the pronounced effect that buying on margin had in exacerbating the 1929 stock market crash that preceded the Great Depression. After the crash, Congress

passed the Securities Act of 1934 requiring the Federal Reserve Board to set limits on purchases of securities with borrowed funds. See, Galbraith, John Kenneth. *The Great Crash 1929,* (New York: Houghton Mifflin Harcourt, Kindle version, 2009) (Original Publication, 1954)

60. Figures 3.1 and 3.2 were copied from the website known as Exponential Improvement. com. The website contains hyperlinks to the data sources used to construct Figures 3.1 and 3.2. These are in order *U.S. Total Exports and Imports 07/1866-10/1969.* National Bureau of Economic Research. Retrieved from http://www.nber.org/databases/macrohistory/contents/chapter07.html; *Exports.* (data file) National Bureau of Economic Research. Retrieved from http://www.nber.org/databases/macrohistory/rectdata/07/m07023.dat; (export data description file) Retrieved from http://www.nber.org/databases/macrohistory/rectdata/07/docs/m07023.txt; *Imports.* (data file) National Bureau of Economic Research. Retrieved from http://www.nber.org/databases/macrohistory/rectdata/07/m07028.dat; (export data description file) Retrieved from http://www.nber.org/databases/macrohistory/rectdata/07/docs/m07028.txt; *GDP from the National Income (NIPA) and Product Account Historical Tables.* U.S. Department of Commerce Bureau of Economic Analysis. Retrieved from http://www.bea.gov/iTable/iTable.cfm?ReqID=9&step=1#reqid =9&step=1&isuri=1
61. Powell, Bob. February 15, 2009. Smoot-Hawley Fiction. *Exponential Improvement.com.* Retrieved from http://www.exponentialimprovement.com/cms/smoot.shtml#1
62. Famed economist Ha Joon Chang identifies Alexander Hamilton as the first to articulate the infant industry argument. See, Chang, Ha-Joon. September 4, 2002. Kicking Away the Ladder: How the Economic and Intellectual Histories of Capitalism Have Been Re-Written to Justify Neo-Liberal Capitalism. *Post-Autistic Economics Review.* (15) 3. Retrieved from http://www.paecon.net/PAEtexts/Chang1.htm
63. Boehlert, Eric. September 29, 2011. What If The Occupy Movement Had A Cable News Sponsor? *Media Matters For America.* Retrieved from http://mediamatters.org/blog
64. Bunch, Will. November 17, 2011. What If The Occupy Movement Had A Cable News Sponsor? *Media Matters For America.* Retrieved from http://mediamatters.org/blog
65. Boehlert, What If The Occupy Movement Had A Cable News Sponsor?
66. Cooper, Matthew. October 19, 2011. Poll: Most Americans Support Occupy Wall Street. *The Atlantic.* Retrieved from http://www.theatlantic.com/
67. Kroll, Andy. September 28, 2011. Americans Dislike Tea Party More Than Ever Before. *Mother Jones.* Retrieved from http://www.motherjones.com/
68. For another example of unfair coverage of trade issues see, Tucker, Todd. February 1, 2012. The Trade Debate That Wasn't Reported: critics of deals outnumbered more than 4-to-1 in NYT, WSJ. *Fair.* Retrieved from http://fair.org/extra-online-articles/the-trade-debate-that-wasnt-reported/
69. A good primer for on the subject which discusses both the science and politics is Hansen, James. *Storms of My Grandchildren.* (New York: Bloomsbury USA, 2009)
70. Anderegg, W. R. L. June 21, 2010. Expert Credibility in Climate Change, *Proceedings of the National Academy of Sciences* Vol. 107 No. 27, 12107-12109. DOI: 10.1073/pnas.

1003187107; P. T. Doran, P.T. and Zimmerman, M.K. Examining the Scientific Consensus on Climate Change, *Eos Transactions American Geophysical Union* Vol. 90 Issue 3 (2009), 22; DOI: 10.1029/2009EO030002; Oreskes, N. December 3, 2004. Beyond the Ivory Tower: The Scientific Consensus on Climate Change, *Science* Vol. 306 No. 5702,\ p. 1686. DOI: 10.1126/science.1103618

71. According to a website produced by the Earth Science Communications Team at NASA's Jet Propulsion Laboratory, California Institute of Technology. Site Editor, Jenkins, Amber. Consensus 97% of Climate Scientists Agree. *National Aeronautics and Space Administration: Global Climate Change Vital Signs of the Planet.* Retrieved from http://climate.nasa.gov/scientific-consensus/#ft1
72. Ibid.
73. Boykoff, M.T. and J.M. Boykoff. (2007) Climate Change and Journalistic Norms: A Case Study of U.S. Mass-Media Coverage. *Geoforum.* 38(6), 1190-1204. DOI:10.1016/j.geoforum.2007.01.008. Retrieved from http://sciencepolicy.colorado.edu/admin/publication_files/2007.40.pdf (page references in text are to online article)
74. Ibid., 2-4.
75. Ibid., 2
76. Ibid., 3
77. Ibid., 3-4
78. Ibid., 3
79. With respect to NAFTA coverage see Michelson, Melissa R. (1998). Explorations In Public Opinion Presidential Power Linkages: Congressional Action On Unpopular Foreign Agreements. *Political Communication.* Volume 15, Issue 1. 63-82. and Rankin, 649
80. Boykoff, M.T. and J. M. Boykoff, 3.
81. Ibid., 3
82. Ibid., 3
83. Ibid., 3
84. Ibid., 3
85. Ibid., 2-3
86. Ibid., 4
87. Ibid., 4 (quoting from) Stocking, H., and Leonard, J.P. (1990) The Greening Of The Media. *Columbia Journalism Review.* 40.
88. Boykoff, M.T. and J.M. Boykoff, 3-4
89. Ibid., 4
90. Ibid., 4
91. Ibid., 4
92. Ibid., 3
93. Ibid., 4
94. Ibid., 4
95. Ibid., 4
96. Ibid., 4
97. Ibid., 4-5

98. Ibid., 4-5
99. Ibid., 4-5 Note: the words quoted in the text were those of Boykoff and Boykoff, and were not directly quoted from James Hanson.
100. Ibid., 5 (the quote from Thatcher is cited by the authors from) Leggett, J., The Carbon War: Global Warming and the End of the Oil Era. (New York: Routledge, 2001) p. x; Note: For the full text of Thatcher's speech regarding climate change see Thatcher, Margaret. September 27, 1988. Speech to the Royal Society. Speech presented at Fishmongers Hall, London. *Margaret Thatcher Foundation.* Retrieved from http://www.margaretthatcher.org/document/107346
101. Boykoff, M.T. and J.M. Boykoff, 5
102. Ibid., 6-12
103. Ibid., 12
104. Ibid., 6-12
105. Ibid., 7
106. Burns, William C.G. 2008. Ocean Acidification A Greater Threat than Climate Change or Overfishing? *Terrain.Org A Journal of the Built and Natural Environments*. Issue 21
107. Mann, Michael E. *The Hockey Stick And The Climate Wars*. (New York: Columbia University Press, 2012)
108. Hansen, James. *Storms Of My Grandchildren The Truth About The Coming Climate Catastrophe And Our Last Chance to Save Humanity.* (New York: Bloomsbury, 2009)
109. Boykoff, M.T., and J.M. Boykoff, 7, (the quote from Brokaw is cited with the *emphasis added* by the authors) Brokaw, Tom. March 29, 1990. Atmosphere, Global Warming. *NBC Nightly News*
110. See for example, The Associated Press. July 9, 2006. Tom Brokaw Joins the Battle Against Global Warming. *USA Today*. Retrieved from http://usatoday30.usatoday.com/; Walsh, Brian. Mar. 17, 2009. Q&A Tom Brokaw's New Global Warming Documentary. *Time.* Retrieved from http://content.time.com/time/
111. Anderson, Allison. March, 2009. Media, Politics and Climate Change: Towards A New Research Agenda. *Sociology Compass*. Volume 3, Issue 2. 66–182. (Article first published online: 12 Feb. 2009) DOI: 10.1111/j.1751-9020.2008.00188.x
112. Ibid., 170
113. Ibid., 170-171. Anderson cites (Antilla, 2005) as an example of such research. See, Antilla, Lisa. 2005. Climate of Scepticism: US Newspaper Coverage of the Science of Climate Change. *Global Environmental Change* 15: 338–52
114. Gelbspan, Ross. *Boiling Point: How Politicians, Big Oil and Coal, Journalists and Activists Are Fueling the Climate Crisis--And What We Can Do to Avert Disaster*. (New York: Basic Books, 2004
115. Anderson, 171. Anderson cites Gelbspan, *Boiling Point* as the source for her statement.
116. Ibid., 171. Anderson cites Gelbspan, Ross. The Heat is On: The Warming of the World's Climate Sparks a Blaze of Denial. *Harpers Magazine*. December, 1995
117. Ibid., 171. Anderson's source for the information summarized in the text as "Exxon Mobile has paid millions to various groups that work to challenge the science of global

warming and change public opinion on the subject" is Gelbspan, *Boiling Point*

118. Ibid., 171. The research reported about by Anderson is Jacques, Peter., Riley, J., Dunlap, E., and Freeman, Mark. 2008. The Organisation of Denial: Conservative Think Tanks and Environmental Scepticism.' *Environmental Politics* 17: 349–85.
119. Ibid., 171. (quoting from) Jacques, Peter., Riley, J., Dunlap, E., and Freeman, Mark. 2008. The Organisation of Denial: Conservative Think Tanks and Environmental Scepticism. *Environmental Politics* 17: 349–85. 362
120. Ibid. 171. (citing) Sample, Ian. February 2, 2007. Scientists Offered Cash to Dispute Climate Study. *The Guardian*. Retrieved from http://www.guardian.co.uk/environment/2007/feb/02/frontpagenews.climatechange
121. Organization. *Intergovernmental Panel On Climate Change*. Retrieved from https://www.ipcc.ch/organization/organization.shtml
122. Fitzsimmons, Jill. January 8, 2013. Study: Warmest Year On Record Received Cool Climate Coverage. *Media Matters For America*. Retrieved from http://mediamatters.org/
123. About. *Media Matters For America*. Retrieved from http://mediamatters.org/about
124. Fitzsimmons, Study: Warmest Year On Record Received Cool Climate Coverage.
125. Ibid.
126. Naureckas, Jim. January 13, 2013 Ignoring Climate Change When It Stares You in the Face. *FAIR Fairness And Accuracy In Reporting*. Retrieved from http://www.fair.org/blog/
127. Ibid., (the quotes from Holt and Postel are cited by Naureckas from) Holt, Lester. Postel, Greg. January 12, 2013. Comments on the strange winter. *NBC Nightly News*.
128. Naureckas, (quoting from) December 19, 2012. Climate Change And The Jet Stream. *ClimateSight*. Retrieved from http://climatesight.org/ (citing) Francis, Jennifer and Vavrus, Stephen J., March, 2012. Evidence linking Arctic amplification to extreme weather in mid-latitudes. *Geophysical Research Letters*. Volume 39, Issue 6. Wiley Online. DOI: 10.1029/2012GL051000
129. Naureckas, (quoting) Dahlgren, Kristin. January 12, 2013. *NBC Nightly News*.
130. Naureckas, (the word added to the quote from Naureckas)
131. Isikoff, Michael, and Corn, David. *Hubris: The Inside Story of Spin, Scandal, and the Selling of the Iraq War*. (New York: Three Rivers Press, 2007) Note: All citations to Hubris in this book are to the 2007 paperback edition.
132. Ricks, Thomas E., *Fiasco The American Military Adventure in Iraq*. (New York: Penguin Books, 2007)
133. Mitchell, Greg. *So Wrong for So Long, How the Press, The Pundits - And The President - Failed On Iraq*. (New York: Sterling Publishing, 2008)
134. Wheeler, Marcy. *Anatomy of Deceit How the Bush Administration Used the Media to Sell the Iraq War and Out a Spy*. (Berkeley; Vaster Books, 2007)
135. Shear, Micheal D., May 28, 2008. Ex-Press Aid Writes That Bush Mislead U.S. on Iraq. The Washington Post. Retrieved from http://www.washingtonpost.com/
136. Lutz, Ashley. June 14, 2012. These 6 Corporations Control 90% Of The Media In America. *Business Insider*. Retrieved from http://www.businessinsider.com/

137. The commonly used phrase "the media monopoly" appears to have originated with the former Dean of the Graduate School of Journalism at the University of California at Berkeley, Ben Bagdikian. Bagdikian who is a very accomplished journalist as well as a professor wrote the oft cited seminal book *The Media Monopoly,* which is about the consolidation of ownership of the media and its resulting diminution in value as a source of news and public education. See, Bagdikian, Ben. *The Media Monopoly*. (Boston: Beacon Press, 1983)
138. The term "corporate media" is in wide enough use to have earned an article in Wikipedia about it. See, Corporate Media. *Wikipedia The Free Encyclopedia.* (Wikipedia Foundation Inc., page last modified on March 23, 2014 on the date retrieved), Retrieved from http://en.wikipedia.org/wiki/Corporate_media

Chapter 4. The Heritage of the Mount Rushmore Presidents: Prosperity and Strength

139. Only twenty one percent of those surveyed by the U.S. Mint in 2007 could identify the names of the Presidents whose faces have been carved into Mount Rushmore. See, Longley, Robert. August 21, 2007. Mint Survey Shows Most Americans Can't Identify Founding Fathers. *About.Com.* Retrieved from http://usgovinfo.about.com/od/thepresidentandcabinet/a/mintsurvey.htm
140. Nisbet, Robert. Idea of Progress: A Bibliographical Essay by Robert Nisbet. *Literature of Liberty: A Review of Contemporary Liberal Thought.* (vol. II, no. 1, January/March 1979) 23-24 Retrieved from http://lf-oll.s3.amazonaws.com/titles/1290/0353-05_1979v1Bk.pdf (published by the Cato Institute and the Institute for Humane Studies, George Mason University, Fairfax, Virginia) (quoted with permission)
141. Eckes, Jr., Alfred E. *Opening America's Market U.S. Foreign Trade Policy since 1776,* (Chapel Hill: The University of North Carolina Press, 1995) 14-15
142. Ibid., 15
143. Ibid.
144. Ibid., 13-14
145. Ibid., 13-16
146. Chang, *Bad Samaritans: The Myth of Free Trade And The Secret History of Capitalism*, 51
147. Fletcher, *Free Trade Doesn't Work: What Should Replace It and Why*, 141
148. Fletcher, Ian. September 12, 2010. America Was Founded as a Protectionist Nation. *Huff Post Politics*. Retrieved from http://www.huffingtonpost.com/
149. Lind, Michael. February 12, 2009. How Would Lincoln Vote Today? *Salon*. Retrieved from http://www.salon.com/
150. Ibid.
151. Republican Party Platform of 1904. June 21, 1904. Online by Gerhard Peters and John T. Woolley. *The American Presidency Project*. Retrieved from http://www.presidency.ucsb.edu/ws/?pid=29631
152. Eckes, 81 (citing) Morison, Elting E., ed. *The Letters of Theodore Roosevelt*. (Cambridge:

Harvard University Press, 1951) Vol. 4. 932-934

153. Eckes, 30 (citing) Morison, Elting E., ed. *The Letters of Theodore Roosevelt.* (Cambridge: Harvard University Press, 1951) Vol. 4. 934
154. Morison, Elting E., ed. *The Letters of Theodore Roosevelt.* (Cambridge: Harvard University Press, 1951) Vol. 1. 503-504. Retrieved in PDF format from *Internet Archive.* Retrieved from https://archive.org/details/letttersoftheodo006691mbp
155. Eckes, 3-4, 9-19
156. Ibid., 19
157. Ibid.
158. Chang, *Bad Samaritans: The Myth of Free Trade And The Secret History of Capitalism*, 51
159. Ibid., 22
160. Chang, *Bad Samaritans: The Myth of Free Trade And The Secret History of Capitalism*, 51
161. Ibid., 20
162. The Henry George School of Social Science. The Tariff Issue of 1824. *Land and Freedom.* Retrieved from http://www.landandfreedom.org/ushistory/us7.htm
163. Eckes, 23
164. Ibid., 20
165. Fletcher, *Free Trade Doesn't Work: What Should Replace It and Why*, 141;Chang, *Bad Samaritans: The Myth of Free Trade And The Secret History of Capitalism*, 51,
166. Prestowitz, *The Betrayal of American Prosperity: Free Market Delusions, America's Decline, and How We Must Compete in the Post-Dollar Era.* 7-8
167. Amadeo, Kimberly. June 26, 2013. U.S. Trade Deficit By Country. About.com Retrieved from http://useconomy.about.com/od/tradepolicy/p/5_trade_deficit.htm
168. Chang, *Bad Samaritans: The Myth of Free Trade And The Secret History of Capitalism*, 17, 21-26; Fletcher, *Free Trade Doesn't Work: What Should Replace It and Why*, 122-138; Prestowitz, *The Betrayal of American Prosperity: Free Market Delusions, America's Decline, and How We Must Compete in the Post-Dollar Era.* 45-69
169. Chang, *Bad Samaritans: The Myth of Free Trade And The Secret History of Capitalism*, 40-43
170. Ibid.
171. Homepage. *Town of Walpole Massachusetts.* Retrieved from http://www.walpole-ma.gov/
172. Chang, *Bad Samaritans: The Myth of Free Trade And The Secret History of Capitalism*, 43-45
173. *Ibid.,* 45
174. Fletcher, *Free Trade Doesn't Work: What Should Replace It and Why*, 30; Chang, *Bad Samaritans: The Myth of Free Trade And The Secret History of Capitalism*, 43-51
175. Fletcher, Ian. September 12, 2010. America Was Founded as a Protectionist Nation. *Huff Post Politics.* Retrieved from http://www.huffingtonpost.com
176. The direct effect of Smoot-Hawley was in fact expansionary. It did not cause or worsen the Great Depression. See, Eichengreen, Barry. The Political Economy of the Smoot-

Hawley Tariff. *The National Bureau of Economic Research.* Working Paper No. 2001. (Cambridge, Mass.: August, 1986) (DOI: 0.3386/w2001) Retrieved from http://www.nber.org/papers/w2001; Fletcher, *Free Trade Doesn't Work: What Should Replace It and Why* 138-140; Eckes, Jr., Alfred E. *Opening America's Market U.S. Foreign Trade Policy since 1776,* (Chapel Hill: The University of North Carolina Press, 1995) 100-139

177. United States Holocaust Memorial Museum. Introduction to the Holocaust. *Holocaust Encyclopedia.* Retrieved from http://www.ushmm.org/ outreach/en/article.php?ModuleId=10007671
178. See, (incomes figures) Ransom, Rodger. Emeritus Professor. University of California, Riverside. Undated post. The Economics of the Civil War. *EH.Net.* Retrieved from http://eh.net/encyclopedia/the-economics-of-the-civil-war/; (32 times rifles) Arrington, Benjamin T.,Undated post. Industry and Economy during the Civil War. *National Park Service.* Retrieved from https://www.nps.gov/articles/industry-and-economy-during-the-civil-war.htm; (U.S. Navy superiority) Unknown author. Undated post. The Navies of the Civil War. *Civil War Trust.* Retrieved from http://www.civilwar.org/education/history/warfare-and-logistics/warfare/navy.html?; Office of the Historian. Undated post. The Blockade of Confederate Ports, 1861–1865. *Department of State.* United States of America. Retrieved from https://history.state.gov/milestones/1861-1865/blockade
179. This point is made by Edward Luttwak in the forward to Fletcher, *Free Trade Doesn't Work: What Should Replace It and Why*, xiv
180. The Financial Crisis Inquiry Commission. The Financial Crisis Inquiry Report Final Report On The Causes Of The Financial And Economic Crisis In The United States. (Washington D.C.: Government Printing Office, 2011) 5, 85. *GPO U.S. Government Printing Office.* Retrieved from http://www.gpo.gov/
181. Hounshell, David A., *From the American System to Mass Production, 1800-1932: The Development of Manufacturing Technology in the United States*, (Baltimore: Johns Hopkins University Press, 1987) 25-29
182. Burke, James. *Connections* (New York: Little, Brown and Co., 1978) 150
183. Hounshell, 28-31
184. Hounshell, 1-65
185. Roe, Joseph Wickham. *English and American Tool Builders*, (New Haven: Yale University Press, 1916) 102-104
186. Ibid., 104
187. Campbell, Randolph B., The Spanish American Aspect of Henry Clay's American System *The Americas* (Vol. 24, No. 1, July, 1967) 3
188. United States Congress. Clay, Henry, (1777-1852). *Biographical Directory of the United States Congress.* Retrieved from http://bioguide.congress.gov/
189. Eaton, Clement. *Henry Clay and the Art of American Politics.* (Boston: Little, Brown and Company) 20-26.
190. Senate Historical Office. United States Senate. The "Famous Five" Now the "Famous Nine." *Senate.gov Art & History.* Retrieved from http://www.senate.gov/artandhistory/history/common/briefing/Famous_Five_Seven.htm

191. Bird, Robert C., comp. Wendy Wolff. ed. *Senate 1789-1989 Classic Speeches, 1830-1993.* Vol. 3. Bicentennial edition.(Washington: U.S. Government Printing Office, 1995) 91. A copy of Clay's speech may be downloaded in pdf format at Senate.gov Art & History.
192. Elwell, Craig K., October 11, 2007. CRS Report For Congress. The U.S. Trade Deficit: Causes, Consequences, and Cures. (Washington: U.S. Government Printing Office, 2007) 1
193. An excellent compilation of articles which describe the negative consequences of our large trade deficits is available online courtesy of the Economic Policy Institute. See, Trade Deficit. *Economic Policy Institute Research and Ideas for Shared Prosperity.* Retrieved from http://www.epi.org/issues/trade-deficit/
194. Cassiday, John. March 16, 2012. An Inconvenient Truth: It Was George W. Bush Who Bailed Out the Automakers. *The New Yorker.* Retrieved from http://www.newyorker.com/
195. Bird, 91
196. Elwell, 2; Imports to America during the 2001-2006 period Elwell looked at ran close to double the value of American exports.
197. Fletcher, *Free Trade Doesn't Work: What Should Replace It and Why*, 127
198. Bird, 93
199. Ibid., (quoting) Gee, Joshua. *The Trade and Navigation of Great Britain Considered.* (first ed., 1729) 77-78. Retrieved from https://openlibrary.org/; Note: The Senate record indicates Clay cited pages 177,8,9. The quoted text is however found at pages 77-78 of the 1729 edition printed for Sam Buckey. The edition quoted by Clay is unknown to me. No fewer than fifteen editions were published in four languages between 1729 and 1768. Nine were in English, four in French, one in Spanish and one in German. See, Carpenter, Kenneth E., The Economic Bestsellers Before 1850. Bulletin 11. (Boston: Kress Library of Business and Economics, Harvard Business School, May, 1975)
200. Bird., 93
201. Ibid., 100
202. Fletcher, *Free Trade Doesn't Work: What Should Replace It and Why*, 105-106
203. Ibid., 58
204. Ibid., 105-106
205. Ibid., 104-121

Chapter 5. Why the Theory of Free Trade Is Scientifically and Logically Invalid

206. Chetty, Raj. October 20, 2013. Yes, Economics Is a Science. *The New York Times.* Retrieved from http://www.nytimes.com/
207. Batri, Ravi. *The Myth Of Free Trade The Pooring Of America.* (New York: Simon & Schuster, 1993) 1-6; Brown, Sherrod. *Myths of Free Trade.* 2nd. ed. (New York: The New Press, 2006) 175-199; Fletcher, *Free Trade Doesn't Work: What Should Replace It and Why*, 122-126
208. Smith, Adam. *An Inquiry into the Nature and Causes of the Wealth of Nations.* 1 ed.

(London: W. Strahan, 1776)

209. Ricardo, David. *On the Principles of Political Economy and Taxation*. 1 ed. (London: John Murray, 1817),

210. Smith thought that in a system of international free trade countries would sell any and all goods that they manufactured more efficiently than their trading partners. Ricardo argued that a country could profit by importing some goods in which it enjoyed an efficiency advantage over all its trading partner as discussed in the text. Unfortunately, both Smith and Ricardo failed to account for the positive externalities from manufacturing which generate scientific and engineering advances and bring progress and a higher standard of living into their model. The importance of fostering a broad based superiority in engineering, science and production technology in America to generate high value jobs for Americans cannot be overstated. Everybody knows America is in decline but the media monopoly and the Demopublicans will just keep pooring America because they are getting paid to do it. They don't care about the public. We do.

211. Bird, 100

212. Roe, 102-104

213. Nichols, John, and McChesney, Robert. "The Architects of Dollarocracy: Lewis Powell, John Roberts and the Robber Baron Court," in Nichols, John, and McChesney, Robert. *Dollarocracy: How The Money-and-Media Election Complex Is Destroying America.* (New York: Nation Books, 2013) (Ch. 3) 67-95

214. The assumptions listed in the exposition of comparative advantage in the text can be compared by the reader to a description of how comparative advantage works which is used in an actual college economics course. See, College of Business and Economics. University of Idaho. "Absolute and Comparative Advantage." *University of Idaho*. Retrieved from http://db.lib.uidaho.edu/ereserve/courses/b/business/380_01/smith.pdf

215. Dornbusch, R., Fischer, S., Samuelson P. A. "Comparative Advantage, Trade, and Payments in a Ricardian Model with a Continuum of Goods." *The American Economic Review*, Vol. 67, No. 5. (Dec., 1977) 823-839

216. Chang, The double life of Daniel Defoe: How did the rich countries become rich? in *Bad Samaritans: The Myth of Free Trade And The Secret History of Capitalism*, Ch. 2. 40-64

217. This assumption is related to the fallacy that countries operate as though they believe that short term efficiency brings about long term development. See, Fletcher, *Free Trade Doesn't Work: What Should Replace It and Why*, 112-117.

218. With respect to capital mobility see Fletcher, *Free Trade Doesn't Work: What Should Replace It and Why,* 109-112; Schumacher, Reinhard. Deconstructing The Theory of Comparative Advantage. *World Economic Review* Vol. 1 (2013) 88-89. Retrieved from http://www.academia.edu/2555593/Deconstructing the_Theory_of_Comparative_ Advantage; Prasch, Robert. E., Reassessing the Theory of Comparative Advantage. *Review of Political Economy*. Vol. 8, Number 1, (Nov., 1996) 39-42

219. Economists like Ha-Joon Chang, Ian Fletcher, and Clyde Prestowitz have written books in the last decade that rip apart the idea of comparative advantage, exposing the limitations of the theory, the falseness of the underlying assumptions, the potential

benefits of industrial policies and the true history of how rich countries got rich. But back in 1996, establishment economist and media darling Paul Krugman wrote the essay "Ricardo's Difficult Idea" in which he claimed that the reason so many leading intellectuals reject the idea of comparative advantage is that they just don't understand the idea. Krugman was playing the game that free traders have played since Ricardo's time, painting comparative advantage as a law of nature rooted in a sublime mathematical proof that defies all criticism. Today many economists are critical of free trade, and they clearly understand the idea of comparative advantage. Even in 1996, when Krugman wrote his sophist attack on non-economist critics of free trade, it was under attack from within the profession of economics. In 1996, Robert E. Prasch, currently a professor of economics at Middlebury College wrote the article "Reassessing the Theory of Comparative Advantage" in which dubious assumptions central to the model are systematically refuted. See, Prasch, Robert E., Reassessing the Theory of Comparative Advantage. *Review of Political Economy*. Vol. 8, Number 1, (Nov., 1996) 37-55. Early American economists wanted little to do with Riccardo, but it is absurd to say that they were unaware of the arguments being advanced in favor of free trade in their own day.

220. The quote is used with permission but was not made in contemplation of publication and shall remain anonymous.
221. The assumptions listed in the explanation of the HO Model in the text are taken from a description used in an actual college economics course. See, College of Business and Economics. University of Idaho. Heckscher-Ohlin Theorem. *University of Idaho*. Retrieved from http://webpages.uidaho.edu/agecon533/H-OTheory.pdf
222. Prestowitz, 163-165.
223. Irwin, Douglas A., *Free Trade Under Fire*. 3rd. ed. (Princeton, New Jersey: Princeton University Press, 2009)
224. Ibid., 35
225. Ibid.
226. Rustbelt. *Wikipedia The Free Encyclopedia.* (Wikipedia Foundation Inc., Retrieved on August 14, 2014 from http://en.wikipedia.org/wiki/Rust_Belt; Lind, Michael. "Conservative Elites and the Counterrevolution against the New Deal" in Fraser, Steven, and Gerstle, Gary, eds., *Ruling America: A History of Wealth and Power in a Democracy.* (Ch. 8., Section on Globalization and The American Economy) (Cambridge: Harvard University Press, 2005), 280-282
227. See, Ohanian, Lee, and Lagakos, David., Alder, Simeon. January 31, 2013. The Decline of the U.S. Rust Belt: A Macroeconomic Analysis (Working paper presented February 8, 2013 at the NBER program on economic fluctuations and growth at the Federal Reserve Bank in San Francisco). Retrieved from http://conference.nber.org/confer//2013/EFGw13/Alder_Lagakos.pdf
228. Irwin, 104
229. For example, the percentage of Americans in the middle class fell from 61% in 1971 to 49.9% in 2014, according to Pew Research Center. See, Pew Research Center. December 9, 2015. The American Middle Class Is Losing Ground: No longer the majority and

falling behind financially. *Pew Research Center*. Retrieved from http://www.pewsocialtrends.org/2015/12/09/the-american-middle-class-is-losing-ground/

230. McCormack, Richard. ed. Sept. 25, 2013. With Loss of Manufacturing The U.S. Innovation Engine Is No Longer Working. *Manufacturing and Technology News*. (Vol. 20, No. 13). Retrieved from: http://www.manufacturingnews.com/news/PIE0925131.html
231. Regarding positive externalities see Fletcher, *Free Trade Doesn't Work: What Should Replace It and Why*, 105-16, 185-189
232. McCormack, With Loss of Manufacturing The U.S. Innovation Engine Is No Longer Working.
233. Martin Schmidt. *Schmidt Research Group*. Retrieved on August 15, 2014 from http://web.mit.edu/maschmid/martin-a-schmidt.html
234. Schmidt, Martin. Interview by Manufacturing and Technology News, in McCormack, Richard. ed. Sept. 25, 2013. With Loss of Manufacturing The U.S. Innovation Engine Is No Longer Working. *Manufacturing and Technology News*. (Vol. 20, No. 13). Retrieved from: http://www.manufacturingnews.com/news/PIE0925131.html
235. Chang, Ha Joon. December 30, 2013. Kicking Away The Ladder The "Real" History of Free Trade. Edited by John Gershman. *Foreign Policy In Focus*. 5-6. Retrieved on August 15, 2014 from http://www.ilocarib.org.tt/trade/documents/economic_policies/SRtrade2003.pdf
236. Bird, 100
237. Fletcher, *Free Trade Doesn't Work: What Should Replace It and Why*, 183
238. Ibid., 184
239. Ibid.
240. Founding Members of The Other Canon: Erik S. Reinert. *The Other Cannon*. Retrieved on August 15, 2014 from http://www.othercanon.org/board/about-Reinert.html
241. Reinert. Erik S., *How Rich Countries got Rich and Why Poor Countries Stay Poor*. (New York: Carroll & Graf, 2007) xi
242. Ibid., xxiii
243. Ibid.
244. Externalities "occur when the profits of an industry do not reflect its full economic value." See, Fletcher, *Free Trade Doesn't Work: What Should Replace It and Why*, 185. When such externalities help "upgrade" the economy of the country in which they occur they help it climb the "ladder," thus the term "ladder externalities." See, Fletcher, Comparative Advantage vs. Ladder Externalities in *Free Trade Doesn't Work: What Should Replace It and Why*, 185-189.
245. Fletcher, *Free Trade Doesn't Work: What Should Replace It and Why*, 185.
246. Ibid., 186
247. Ibid., 187
248. Ibid., 191
249. Ibid.
250. Ibid.
251. Hope, Yen. Associated Press. July 28, 2013. 80 Percent of U.S. Adults Face Near-

Poverty, Unemployment, Survey Finds. *Huff Post Business*. Retrieved from http://www.huffingtonpost.com/
252. Vitali, Stefania., Glattfelder, James B., Battiston, Stefano. October 26, 2011. The Network of Global Corporate Control. *Plos One*. DOI: 10.1371/journal.pone.0025995 Retrieved from http://www.plosone.org/
253. Staff Bios. Clyde V. Prestowitz, Jr., *Economic Strategy Institute*. http://www.econstrat.org /about-us/staff-bios/20-clyde-v-prestowitz-jr-president
254. Prestowitz, 165
255. Ibid., 166-168
256. Ibid., 168
257. Ibid.
258. Ibid.

Chapter 6. Who and What The Money Power is.

259. Walter, Karla, and Madland, David. January 20, 2011. Report: As Union Membership Rates Decrease, Middle Class Incomes Shrink. *Think Progress*. Retrieved from http://thinkprogress.org/
260. Labor Unions In The United States. *Wikipedia The Free Encyclopedia*. (Wikipedia Foundation Inc.), Retrieved on August 20, 2014 from http://en.wikipedia.org/wiki/ Labor_unions_in_the_United_States
261. Ibid.
262. Union Members Summary. Economic News Release. January 24, 2014. *Bureau of Labor Statistics, United States Department of Labor*. Retrieved from http://www.bls.gov/ news.release/union2.nr0.htm
263. Dayen, David. December 9, 2013. Robbing Illinois Public Employees. *The American Prospect*. Retrieved from http://prospect.org/
264. Rosenfeld, Jake. Little Labor: How Union Decline is Changing the American Landscape in Grusky, David, ed. and Szelenyi, Szonja. ed. *The Inequality Reader: Contemporary and Foundational Readings in Race, Class, and Gender*, 2nd Ed. (Boulder, Colorado: Westview Press, 2011)
265. For a look into Koch brother *money power* you can google up a storm of articles in seconds. A book came out this year which has a self-explanatory title; See, Schulman, David. *Sons of Wichita: How the Koch Brothers Became America's Most Powerful Private Dynasty*. (New York: Grand Central Publishing, 2014)
266. On the subject of foreign influence little seems to be known. See, Foreign Money? Really? FactCheck.Org. (October 15, 2010). Retrieved from http://www.factcheck.org/2010/10/foreign-money-really/
267. Gilens, Martin, and Page, Benjamin I., March 7, 2014. Testing Theories of American Politics: Elites, Interest Groups, and Average Citizens. (working paper, final version for publication in *Perspectives on Politics*). Retrieved from http://www.polisci.northwestern.edu/

268. Hayes, Rutherford B. (diary entry quoted in) Williams, Charles Richard, ed. *The Diary and Letters of Rutherford B. Hayes, Nineteenth President of the United States*. Vol. 4. (Columbus, Ohio: Ohio State Archeological and Historical Society, 1922). 354
269. Mother Jones News Team. September 19, 2012. Full Transcript of the Mitt Romney Secret Video. *Mother Jones*. Retrieved from http://www.motherjones.com/
270. Jones, Jeffrey M. October 11, 2013. In U.S., Perceived Need for Third Party Reaches New High: Twenty-Six Percent Believe Democratic and Republican Parties Do Adequate Job. Gallup Politics. Retrieved from http://www.gallup.com/poll/165392/perceived-need-third-party-reaches-new-high.aspx
271. Fraser, Steven, and Gerstle, Gary, Introduction to Steve Fraser and Gary Gerstle, eds., *Ruling America: A History of Wealth and Power in a Democracy.* (Cambridge: Harvard University Press, 2005), 4-5
272. Morici, Peter. February 7, 2013. Our Terrible Trade Deficit Is Slowing Our Recovery.Fox News. Retrieved from http://www.foxnews.com/
273. Scott, Robert E., September 30, 2013. Trading Away The Manufacturing Advantage: China Trade Drives Down U.S. Wages and Benefits and Eliminates Good Jobs for U.S. Workers. *Economic Policy Institute.* http://www.epi.org/publication/trading-manufacturing-advantage-china-trade/
274. Houseman, Susan., and Baker, Dean. April 2, 2014. Full Employment Requires Job Growth in Manufacturing, Reduction in Trade Deficit. *Roll Call.* Retrieved from http://www.rollcall.com/news/full_employment_requires_job_growth_in_manufacturing_reduction_in_trade-231882-1.html
275. Ensinger, Dustin. July 14, 2010. Service Economy Taking Over U.S. *Economy In Crisis: America's Economic Report Daily*. Retrieved from http://economyincrisis.org/
276. Ibid.
277. Ibid.
278. Goodman, Amy., and Mate, Aaron. June 3, 2014. Interview with Ralph Nader. American Fascism: Ralph Nader Decries How Big Business Has Taken Control of the U.S. Government. *Democracy Now Global News Hour*. Retrieved from http://www.democracynow.org/2013/6/4/american_fascism_ralph_nader_decries_how
279. Phillips, Kevin *Wealth and Democracy.* (New York: Broadway Books, 2002) (quote from the publisher's summary of the book's contents on the dust jacket)
280. Ibid.
281. For a discussion of the transformation of the banking system from one that was properly regulated to one which obtained political hegemony in Washington and brought about the deregulation that resulted in the financial collapse of 2007-2008, See, Johnson, Simon., and Kwak, James. *13 Bankers: The Wall Street Takeover And The Next Financial Meltdown.* (New York, Pantheon Books, 2010)
282. Johnson, Simon., and Kwak, James. *13 Bankers: The Wall Street Takeover And The Next Financial Meltdown.* (New York, Pantheon Books, 2010) (quote from the publisher's synopsis on the dust jacket.)
283. Nichols, John, and McChesney, Robert. *Dollarocracy: How The Money-and-Media*

Election Complex Is Destroying America. (New York: Nation Books, 2013) (quote from the publisher's synopsis on the dust jacket.)

284. Ibid., p. 4
285. See for example, Moyers, Bill and Company, September 14, 2012, The Powell Memo: A Call-To-Arms For Corporations. *Moyers & Company*. Retrieved from http://billmoyers.com/; The exact extent of the Powell Memo's influence on the development of right wing think tanks is not certain. Powell's memo may have served more to inspire a new approach by right wing organizations than to have served as a complete blueprint for them. This idea is developed in a 2016 book which posits the theory that William Baroody Sr., (President of the American Enterprise Institute between 1962 and 1978), had a pre-existing plan for developing a network of aggressive right wing think tanks which he put into action after he was sent a copy of the Powell memo. See, Schmidt, Mark. The myth of the Powell memo. Washington Monthly. (September/October 2016) Retrieved from http://washingtonmonthly.com/magazine/septemberoctober-2016/the-myth-of-the-powell-memo/ (book review of) Stahl, Jason. Right Moves: The Conservative Think Tank in American Political Culture Since 1945. (Chapel Hill: The University of North Carolina Press, 2016.)
286. Lewis F. Powell, Jr. *Wikipedia The Free Encyclopedia.* (Wikipedia Foundation Inc.), Retrieved on August 26, 2014 from http://en.wikipedia.org/wiki/Lewis_F._Powell,_Jr.#Legal_career
287. Nichols, John, and McChesney, Robert., op. cit. 72
288. Tobacco Institute. *Wikipedia The Free Encyclopedia.* (Wikipedia Foundation Inc.), Retrieved on August 26, 2014 from http://en.wikipedia.org/wiki/Tobacco_Institute
289. Ibid.
290. Ibid.
291. Tobacco Master Settlement Agreement. *Wikipedia The Free Encyclopedia.* (Wikipedia Foundation Inc.), Retrieved on August 26, 2014 from http://en.wikipedia.org/wiki/Tobacco_Master_Settlement_Agreement
292. Nichols, John, and McChesney, Robert., 72
293. Ibid., 73
294. Ibid., 72-73
295. Home page. *Center For Corporate Policy*. Retrieved from http://www.corporatepolicy.org/
296. Drutman, Lee., and Cray, Charlie. *The People's Business: Controlling Corporations and Restoring Democracy.* (St. Paul: MHS Press, 2004)
297. Cray, Charlie. August 23, 2011. The Lewis Powell Memo - Corporate Blueprint to Dominate Democracy. *Greenpeace USA*. Retrieved from http://www.greenpeace.org/
298. Nichols, John, and McChesney, Robert., 73
299. Powell, Lewis August 23, 1971. Confidential Memorandum: Attack On American Free Enterprise System. *Washington and Lee University School of Law Powell Archives.* Retrieved from http://law.wlu.edu/powellarchives/
300. Unsafe At Any Speed. *Wikipedia The Free Encyclopedia.* (Wikipedia Foundation Inc.),

Retrieved on August 27, 2014 from http://en.wikipedia.org/wiki/Unsafe_at_Any_Speed

301. Hirschhorn Norbert. The Tobacco Industry documents. What They Are, What They Tell Us, And How To Search Them: A Practical Manual. 2nd ed. *World Health Organization.* 2005. Retrieved from http://www.who.int/tobacco/surveillance/ti_monitoring/publications /en/index.html
302. Powell, Confidential Memorandum: Attack On American Free Enterprise System.
303. Charles A. Reich. *Wikipedia The Free Encyclopedia.* (Wikipedia Foundation Inc.), Retrieved on August 26, 2014 from http://en.wikipedia.org/wiki/Charles_A._Reich
304. William Kuntsler. *Wikipedia The Free Encyclopedia.* (Wikipedia Foundation Inc.), Retrieved on August 26, 2014 from http://en.wikipedia.org/wiki/William_Kunstler
305. The phrase in quotes is found in may critiques of the Powell memo, including Dollarocracy, whose authors attribute it to Charlie Cray. See, Nichols, John, and McChesney, Robert., *Dollarocracy: How The Money-and-Media Election Complex Is Destroying America.* (New York: Nation Books, 2013) 73
306. Powell, Confidential Memorandum: Attack On American Free Enterprise System.
307. Ibid.
308. Ibid.
309. Prestowitz, 11; American System (economic plan). *Wikipedia The Free Encyclopedia.* (Wikipedia Foundation Inc.), Retrieved on August 26, 2014 from http://en.wikipedia.org/ wiki/American_System_(economic_plan)
310. Powell, Confidential Memorandum: Attack On American Free Enterprise System.
311. Prestowitz, 11; American System (economic plan). *Wikipedia The Free Encyclopedia.* (Wikipedia Foundation Inc.), Retrieved on August 26, 2014 from http://en.wikipedia.org/ wiki/American_System_(economic_plan)
312. The Demopublicans spread the myths of free trade and a false history of America's economic rise. See, Chang, *Bad Samaritans The Myth of Free Trade And The Secret History of Capitalism*; Brown, *Why American Trade Policy Has Failed; Myths of Free Trade*; Prestowitz, *The Betrayal of American Prosperity: Free Market Delusions; America's Decline, and How We Must Compete in the Post-Dollar Era;* Fletcher, *Free Trade Doesn't Work What Should Replace It and Why*; Batri, *The Myth of Free Trade The Pooring of America;* Navarro, Peter., and Autry, Gene., *Death by China Confronting the Dragon - A Global Call To Action*; Navarro, Peter., and Autry, Gene., *Death by China: Confronting the Dragon - A Global Call To Action.* (Upper Saddle River, NJ: Prentice Hall, 2011)
313. Powell, Confidential Memorandum: Attack On American Free Enterprise System.
314. Bagdikian, *The New Media Monopoly*, 15
315. Powell, Confidential Memorandum: Attack On American Free Enterprise System.
316. Ibid.
317. Nichols, John, and McChesney, Robert., 78
318. Ibid.
319. Phillips-Fein, Kim. *Invisible Hands: The Making of the Conservative Movement From The New Deal to Reagan.* (New York: W.W. Norton & Company, Inc., 2009)

320. Cray, The Lewis Powell Memo - Corporate Blueprint to Dominate Democracy
321. Powell, Confidential Memorandum: Attack On American Free Enterprise System.
322. Phillips-Fein, 161-162
323. Nichols, John, and McChesney, Robert., 73
324. Nichols, John, and McChesney, Robert., The Architects of Dollarocracy: Lewis Powell, John Roberts, and the Robber Baron Court, in *Dollarocracy: How The Money-and-Media Election Complex Is Destroying America.* 67-95
325. Moyers, Bill. October 20, 2011. Speech to Public Citizen's 40th Anniversary Gala. Speech presented at Omni Shoreham Hotel in Washington D.C., *Citizen Vox: Standing Up To Corporate Power*. Retrieved from http://www.citizenvox.org/2011/11/01/bill-moyers-public-citizen-40th-anniversary-gala-occupy-wall-street-citizens-united-democracy-we-the-people/
326. See, Wagner, Bridget G., *Policy Experts: The Insider Guide to Public Policy Experts and Organizations* 2008-2009. (Washington D.C.: Heritage Foundation, 2008); The Heritage Foundation. Insider Online: Policy Ideas For Advancing Liberty. *Policy Experts.Org.* Retrieved from http://www.policyexperts.org/
327. United States Chamber of Commerce. *Wikipedia The Free Encyclopedia.* (Wikipedia Foundation Inc.), Retrieved on August 29, 2014 from http://en.wikipedia.org/wiki/United_States_Chamber_of_Commerce#Lobbying_expenditures2014
328. Ibid.
329. Gibson, Carl. July 15, 2013. A Bagful of Cash: How The U.S. Chamber of Commerce Orchestrated a Takeover of Government. *Shut The Chamber.* Retrieved from *http://shutthechamber.org/*
330. Ibid.
331. Ibid.
332. Nichols, John, and McChesney, Robert., 79
333. Stoller, Matt. May 22. 2012. Bill Clinton's $80 Million Payday, or Why Politicians Don't Care That Much About Reelection. Naked Capitalism. Retrieved from http://www.nakedcapitalism.com/
334. About Fair. *FAIR: Fairness and Accuracy in Reporting.* Retrieved from http://fair.org/about-fair/
335. Ibid.
336. Ibid.
337. Croteau, David. June 1, 1998. Examining the 'Liberal Media' Claim Journalists' Views on Politics, Economic Policy and Media Coverage. *FAIR: Fairness and Accuracy in Reporting*. Retrieved from http://fair.org/press-release/examining-the-quotliberal-mediaquot-claim/

Chapter 7. The Descent of America: A Story of Weak Presidents and Misguided Priorities

338. Eckes, Jr., 141
339. Carter Jerome, March 24, 2013. An Introduction To Mercantilism. *Humanities 360.*

Retrieved from http://www.humanities360.com/index.php/an-introduction-to-mercantilism-1821/

340. Eckes, Jr., 14-17

341. Eckes, Jr., 36. For a short discussion of differences in regional perspectives about the role *American System* tariffs played in bringing about the Civil War see, Loewen, James W., February 26, 2011. Five Myths About Why The South Seceded. *The Washington Post*. Retrieved from http://www.washingtonpost.com/; The genius of the American System, and the reluctance of Southern plantation *money power* to take advantage of the protective tariff and industrialize like the North lead to a massive imbalance in wealth and productive power between the two regions. This difference explains the northern victory in the war between the states almost entirely. See generally, Arrington, Benjamin T., Industry and Economy During The Civil War. National Park Service. Retrieved from http://www.nps.gov/resources/story.htm?id=251

342. New South. *Wikipedia The Free Encyclopedia.* (Wikipedia Foundation Inc., Retrieved on August 14, 2014 from http://en.wikipedia.org/wiki/New_South; Rustbelt. *Wikipedia The Free Encyclopedia.* Wikipedia Foundation Inc., Retrieved on August 14, 2014 from http://en.wikipedia.org/wiki/Rust_Belt

343. Dam, Kenneth W., Significance of the Reciprocal Trade Agreements Act. *Cordell Hull Institute Trade Policy Analyses*. Vol. 6., No. 4, June, 2004. (quoting from) Cordell Hull, *The Memoirs of Cordell Hull.* (New York: Macmillan Company, 1948), Vol. I, 356

344. Hull, Cordell. *The Memoirs of Cordell Hull.* (New York: Macmillan Company, 1948), Vol. I, 82

345. Ibid., 84

346. Hull, Cordell. May 18, 1941. Aid To Britain Will Be Delivered: We Will Not Permit Our Purpose to Be Frustrated. Speech delivered over the radio from Washington, D. C., published by *Vital Speeches of the Day*. Vol II, 484-485. Published online by *Ibiblio*. Retrieved from http://www.ibiblio.org/pha/policy/1941/1941-05-18a.html

347. Eckes, 142.

348. Ibid., (quoting) Hull, Cordell. Testimony before the U.S. Senate Finance Committee, April 26, 1934 Hearings on H.R. 8687, p. 7. Used by permission of publisher.

349. Eckes, 142 (quoting FDR transmittal message from) Nixon, Edgar B., ed. *Franklin D. Roosevelt and Foreign Affairs*. (Cambridge, Mass.: Belknap Press of Harvard University Press, 1969). 2:1-3. Used by permission of publisher.

350. Eckes, 142-143 Used by permission of publisher.

351. See generally, Fletcher, Free Trade As Foreign Policy in *Free Trade Doesn't Work What Should Replace It and Why*. 27-28

352. See for eg., Kelly, Tim., Macfie, Nick. ed. April 5, 2014. U.S. Backs Militarization of Japan In Response To China. *Business Insider*. Retrieved from http://www.businessinside r.com/; Blanchard, Ben., Fernandez, Clarence., ed. China's President Xi Urges Greater Military Use Of Space. *Reuters Uk*. Retrieved from http://uk.reuters.com/

353. See for eg., Chang, Kicking Away The Ladder The "Real" History of Free Trade; Reinert, Globalization and Primitivization in *How Rich Countries Got Rich ...and Why*

Poor Countries Stay Poor. 165-201

354. See generally, Batri, *The Myth of Free Trade The Pooring of America;* Navarro, Peter., and Autry, Gene., *Death by China: Confronting the Dragon - A Global Call To Action.* (Upper Saddle River, NJ: Prentice Hall, 2011)
355. See generally, Chang., Gordon G., January 1, 2012. China is 175.6% Dependent on The U.S., *Forbes*. Retrieved from http://www.forbes.com/; Smith, Charles Hugh., September 14, 2010. Here's Why China Can Never Escape Export Dependency. Business Insider. Retrieved from http://www.businessinsider.com/
356. Even free trade loving economist Paul Krugman seems willing to admit that global warming is much worse overall because of China's explosive export-driven growth. See, Kavoussi, Bonnie. December 12, 2012. "Paul Krugman: 'Chinese Growth Is A Wonderful Human Success Story That Could Kill Us All." *Huff Post Business*. Retrieved from http://www.huffingtonpost.com; For robust evidence in support of the *pollution haven hypothesis* in the chemical industry, See, Timmons, Christopher D. and Wagner, Ulrich J., Agglomeration Effects In Foreign Direct Investment and the Pollution Haven Hypothesis. *Environmental and Resource Economics*. Vol. 43, Issue 2., June, 2009. 231-236; It has been shown that pollution in the western United States is worse because of pollution carried there from smog thick China. See, Wong, Edward. January 20, 2014. China Exports Pollution to U.S., Study Finds. *New York Times*. Retrieved from http://www.nytimes.com/
357. See generally, Fascism. *Wikipedia The Free Encyclopedia.* Wikipedia Foundation Inc., Retrieved from http://en.wikipedia.org/wiki/Fascism
358. De Bromhead, Alan., Eichengreen, Barry. and O'Rourke, Kevin H., February 27, 2012. Right-wing political extremism in the Great Depression. *Vox.* Retrieved from http://www.voxeu.org/article/right-wing-political-extremism-great-depression
359. Cohen, Tyler. *The Great Stagnation: How America Ate All The Fruit of Modern History, Got Sick and Will Eventually Feel Better*. (New York: Dutton Books, 2011); Cohen, Tyler. *Average is Over: Powering America Beyond The Age of the Great Stagnation.* (New York: Dutton Books, 2013). See also, Cohen, Tyler. October 28, 2013. Why Texas Is Our Future. *Time.* Retrieved from: http://time.com/80005/why-texas-is-our-future/
360. See for eg., Westneat, Danny. November 10, 2012. Republicans Blew This Election With Insults, Immature Behavior. *The Seattle Times*. Retrieved from http://seattletimes.com/
361. Eckes, 143
362. Ibid., 142-143
363. Ibid., 143
364. See for eg., McCormack, Richard. ed. Sept. 9, 2014. Growing Trade Deficit Negates The Budding Manufacturing 'Renaissance' And Will Cost The U.S. 400,000 Manufacturing Jobs This Year Alone. *Manufacturing and Technology News.* (Vol. 21, No. 13). Retrieved from: http://www.manufacturingnews.com/; McCormack, Richard. ed. Sept. 9, 2014. U.S. Drops A Rank In Global Innovation Index; How Is It Possible For The U.S. To Be Less Innovative Than Great Britain? *Manufacturing and Technology News.* (Vol. 21, No. 13). Retrieved from: http://www.manufacturingnews.com/;

365. Eckes, 143 (quoting) Henry Fowler and Harry Hawkins Memo of February 13, 1935. Henry Fowler Papers. Lyndon B. Johnson Library. Austin, Texas. Used by permission of publisher.
366. Ibid., 144. Used by permission of publisher.
367. Eckes, 59-61; Fletcher, *Free Trade Doesn't Work What Should Replace It and Why*. 126-131, Prestowitz, 59-72
368. Eckes, 145 (quoting) Henry J. Feis Memoranda, February 15, 26, 1935. Herbert Feis Papers. Manuscript Division. Library of Congress.; (citing) Phillips, William. Ventures In Diplomacy. (Boston: Beacon Press, 1952) 161. Used by permission of publisher.
369. Ibid.
370. Ibid., 147-148
371. See for eg., Fletcher, *Free Trade Doesn't Work What Should Replace It and Why*. 127-131
372. Eckes, 148., Eckes provides the following sources and explanation for the quotes: Statement of President Franklin D. Roosevelt to Chairman Doughton. January 17, 1937. U.S. House of Representatives Ways and Means Committee. Report To Accompany House Joint Resolution 96, 75th Congress, 1st Session, 1937 p. 1-2; Eckes also cites a statement made by Hull on February 21, 1937 to British negotiators in which described their talks as "in the direction of world economic appeasement."
373. Eckes, 153-156
374. Ibid., 149-152
375. Ibid., 154-156
376. Ibid., 158, (quoting) Letter from Vice President Truman to C.E. Garner. May 5, 1941. Harry S. Truman Papers. Senate Papers. Harry S. Truman Library, Independence, MO. Used by permission of publisher.
377. All quotations in the paragraph are from Powell, Confidential Memorandum: Attack On American Free Enterprise System.
378. Eckes, 167
379. Eckes, 157-158.
380. Eckes, 158 (quoting) A Trade and Tariff Policy in the National Interest. U.S. Public Advisory Board for Mutual Security (Government Printing Office, 1953) pp.1, 18-21. Used by permission of publisher.
381. Eckes, 164. (quoting) British Foreign Office document 'United States Economic Policy., January, 1954.' Foreign Office 371-110148, Public Record Office. Kew, England. Used by permission of publisher.
382. Eckes, 178-179
383. Ibid., 179
384. Ibid., 181. Used by permission of publisher. (quoting) President Dwight Eisenhower. December 7, 1960. Memorandum to Secretary of State Herter. *Foreign Relations of the United States. 1958-1960.* Vol. IV, Foreign Economic Policy. Document 141. Online by *U.S. Department of State. Office of the Historian* Retrieved from https://history.state.gov/historicaldocuments/frus1958-60v04/d141

385. Eckes, 189 Used by permission of publisher. (quoting) Harry Hawkins and Janet Norwood. Kelly, William B., ed. *Studies in United States Commercial Policy*. (Chapel Hill: University of North Carolina Press, 1963) 122-123
386. Ibid., 179
387. Ibid., 201
388. Ibid., 201-202
389. Ibid., 202-203
390. Ibid., 202
391. Ibid., 203
392. Bird, 100
393. Prestowitz, 11; American System (economic plan). *Wikipedia The Free Encyclopedia.* (Wikipedia Foundation Inc.), Retrieved on August 26, 2014 from http://en.wikipedia.org/wiki/American_System_(economic_plan)
394. McCormack, Richard. July 31, 2013. America's Biggest Companies Continue To Move Factories Offshore And Eliminate Thousands of American Jobs. *Manufacturing and Technology News*. Vol. 20. No. 10. Retrieved from http://www.manufacturingnews.com/news/TAA0731131.html; Kahn, Joseph. and Landler, Mark. December 21, 2007. China Grabs West's Smoke-Spewing Factories. *The New York Times Asia Pacific.* Retrieved from http://www.nytimes.com/; Harris, Paul. August 10, 2012. I'm Sick to My Stomach, Anger Grows in Illinois at Bain's Latest Outsourcing Plan. *The Guardian.* Retrieved from http://www.theguardian.com/
395. Eckes, 203
396. Eckes, 211
397. 1973 Oil Crisis. *Wikipedia The Free Encyclopedia.* (Wikipedia Foundation Inc.) Retrieved on August 26, 2014 from http://en.wikipedia.org/wiki/1973_oil_crisis
398. Eckes, 210-215
399. Ibid., 206-208
400. Nixon Shock. *Wikipedia The Free Encyclopedia.* (Wikipedia Foundation Inc.) Retrieved on August 26, 2014 from http://en.wikipedia.org/wiki/Nixon_Shock
401. See generally, Eckes, 216-218.
402. D'Arista, Jane. The Evolving International Monetary System. *Cambridge Journal of Economics*. Vol. 33. Issue 4. 633-652. (2009, doi: 10.1093/cje/bep027) Retrieved from http://cje.oxfordjournals.org/; Boughton, J.M., American In The Shadows: Henry Dexter White and The Design of The International Monetary Fund. *International Monetary Fund*. Working Paper 06/6. Retrieved from http://www.imf.org/external/pubs/ft/wp/2006/wp0606.pdf; White believed in free trade in part because of Hulls' idea of peace through trade. He was accused of idealistically inspired spying for the Soviet Union and subsequently investigated by the FBI and Congress. See, Henry Dexter White. *Wikipedia The Free Encyclopedia.* (Wikipedia Foundation Inc.) Retrieved from *Wikipedia The Free Encyclopedia.* (Wikipedia Foundation Inc.) Retrieved from *http://en.wikipedia.org/wiki/Harry_Dexter_White*; Haynes, John Earl., and Vassiliev, Alexander. *Spies: The Rise and Fall of the KGB in America*. (New Haven, CT: Yale University Press, 2009)

259–60. See generally, Steil Benn. *The Battle of Bretton Woods: John Maynard Keynes, Harry Dexter White, and the Making of a New World Order*. (Princeton, NJ: Princeton University Press, 2013)

403. Bernanke, Ben S., and Carey Kevin. "Nominal Wage Stickiness and Aggregate Supply in The Great Depression." in Bernanke, Ben. *Essays On The Great Depression*. (Princeton, NJ: Princeton University Press, 2000) (Ch. 9, kindle version)
404. See generally, Bretton Woods System. *Wikipedia The Free Encyclopedia.* (Wikipedia Foundation Inc.) Retrieved from http://en.wikipedia.org/wiki/Bretton_Woods_system
405. I recall Nixon's famous platitudes quite well, but for those of you who don't you might see Peace with Honor. *Wikipedia The Free Encyclopedia.* (Wikipedia Foundation Inc.) Retrieved from http://en.wikipedia.org/wiki/Peace_with_Honor; Richard Nixon Presidential Campaign, 1968. *Wikipedia The Free Encyclopedia.* (Wikipedia Foundation Inc.) Retrieved from http://en.wikipedia.org/wiki/Richard_Nixon_presidential_campaign,_1968
406. Lowenstein, Roger. August 4, 2011. The Nixon Shock. *Bloomberg Business Week Magazine*. Retrieved from http://www.businessweek.com/
407. Eckes, 179
408. Eckes, 202-210
409. Garber, Peter M., "The Collapse of the Bretton Woods Fixed Exchange Rate System." in Bordo, Michael D. and Eichengreen, Barry. eds. *A Retrospective on the Bretton Woods System: Lessons for International Monetary Reform*. (Chicago: University of Chicago Press, 1993) 464
410. Bretton Woods System. *Wikipedia The Free Encyclopedia.* (Wikipedia Foundation Inc.) Retrieved from http://en.wikipedia.org/wiki/Bretton_Woods_system
411. See generally, Lind, Michael. *Vietnam the Necessary War: A Reinterpretation of America's Most Disastrous Military Conflict*. (New York: Simon and Schuster, 1999) 135-139; 1972 Nixon visit to China. *Wikipedia The Free Encyclopedia.* (Wikipedia Foundation Inc.) Retrieved from http://en.wikipedia.org/wiki/1972_Nixon_visit_to_China
412. Navarro, Peter.,and Autry, Gene., "Death to America's Manufacturing Base: Why We Don't Play (or Work) in Peoria Anymore." in *Death by China: Confronting the Dragon - A Global Call To Action*. (Upper Saddle River, NJ: Prentice Hall, 2011) Ch. 4. 49-66
413. China Balance of Trade 1983-2014. Trading Economics Scott trade Official Site. Retrieved from http://www.tradingeconomics.com/china/balance-of-trade
414. Monaghan, Angela. January 10, 2014. China Surpasses US as World's Largest Trading Nation. *The Guardian*. Retrieved from http://www.theguardian.com/
415. Navarro, Peter.,and Autry, Gene., "Death By Blue Water Navy: Why China's Military Rise Should Raise Red Flags." in *Death by China: Confronting the Dragon - A Global Call To Action*. Ch. 8. 111-126; Bodeen, Christopher. April 24, 2014. China's Military Is On A Spending Spree While U.S. Holds Back. *The World Post*. Retrieved from http://www.huffingtonpost.com/; Brook, Tom Vanden. December 2, 2013. Pentagon Builds Forces In Pacific, Eyes China. *USA Today*. Retrieved from http://www.usatoday.com/

416. Obe, Mitsuru., and Mandhana, Niharika. September 1, 2014. India and Japan Pursue Closer Ties to Counter China: Prime Ministers for Asia's Two Biggest Democracies Emphasize Security Cooperation. *The Wall Street Journal*. Retrieved from http://online.wsj.com/
417. Eckes, 210-212, 242-245
418. Ibid., 242-245
419. McCormack, Richard. ed. Sept. 25, 2013. With Loss of Manufacturing The U.S. Innovation Engine Is No Longer Working. *Manufacturing and Technology News*. (Vol. 20, No. 13). Retrieved from: http://www.manufacturingnews.com/news/PIE0925131.html
420. Lind, Michael. "Conservative Elites and the Counterrevolution against the New Deal" in Fraser, Steven, and Gerstle, Gary, eds., *Ruling America: A History of Wealth and Power in a Democracy*. (Ch. 8., Section on Globalization and The American Economy) 280-282
421. Spiro Agnew. *Wikipedia The Free Encyclopedia.* (Wikipedia Foundation Inc.) Retrieved from http://en.wikipedia.org/wiki/Spiro_Agnew
422. Greene, John Robert. ed. "Impact and legacy" in Essays on Gerald Ford and His Administration. *Miller Center, University of Virginia*. Retrieved from http://millercenter.org/president/ford/essays/biography/9
423. Eckes, 249
424. Fletcher, *Free Trade Doesn't Work What Should Replace It and Why*. 143
425. The Second Carter-Ford Presidential Debate. October 6, 1976. *Commission On Presidential Debates*. Retrieved from http://www.debates.org/
426. James Earl Carter. *Wikipedia The Free Encyclopedia.* (Wikipedia Foundation Inc.) Retrieved from http:/en.wikipedia.org/wiki/Jimmy_Carter
427. Carter, James Earl. January 19, 1978. The State of the Union Address. Delivered Before a Joint Session of the Congress in Washington, D.C., Online by Gerhard Peters and John T. Woolley. *The American Presidency Project*. Retrieved from http://www.presidency.ucsb.edu/
428. Eckes, 249. Used by permission of publisher.
429. Ibid.
430. Arizona Copper Mine Strike of 1983. *Wikipedia The Free Encyclopedia.* (Wikipedia Foundation Inc.) Retrieved from http://en.wikipedia.org/wiki/Arizona_Copper_Mine_Strike_of_1983#cite_ref-1
431. Rosenblum, Jonathan D. *Copper Crucible: How the Arizona Miners' Strike of 1983 Recast Labor-Management Relations in America*. (Ithaca, N.Y.: ILR Press, 1995)
432. Iranian Hostage Crisis. *Wikipedia The Free Encyclopedia.* (Wikipedia Foundation Inc.) Retrieved from http://en.wikipedia.org/wiki/Iran_hostage_crisis
433. Bivens, W. Carl. Jimmy Carter's Economy: Policy in an Age of Limits. (Chapel Hill: University of North Carolina Press, 2002) 1-41
434. Parry, Robert. November 13, 2009. The October Surprise: Crystal Balls. *Consortium News*. Retrieved from https://consortiumnews.com/2009/111309.html
435. Ibid.
436. October Surprise conspiracy theory. *Wikipedia The Free Encyclopedia.* (Wikipedia

Foundation Inc.) Retrieved from http://en.wikipedia.org/wiki/October_Surprise_conspiracy_theory#Kevin_Phillips
437. Robert Parry (journalist). *Wikipedia The Free Encyclopedia.* (Wikipedia Foundation Inc.) Retrieved from http://en.wikipedia.org/wiki/Robert_Parry_(journalist)
438. October Surprise conspiracy theory. *Wikipedia The Free Encyclopedia.* (Wikipedia Foundation Inc.) Retrieved from http://en.wikipedia.org/wiki/October_Surprise_conspiracy_theory#Kevin_Phillips
439. Parry, Robert. May 6, 2010. Key October Surprise Evidence Hidden. *Consortium News.* Retrieved from http://www.consortiumnews.com/
440. Text of Russian Govt. Communication to Lee G. Hamilton, Chairman of the Working Group of the House Foreign Relations Committee of the U.S. Congress. January 22, 1993. *Consortium News.* Retrieved from http://www.consortiumnews.com/2005/russianreport1980.html
441. October Surprise. *Wikipedia The Free Encyclopedia.* (Wikipedia Foundation Inc.) Retrieved from http://en.wikipedia.org/wiki/October_surprise
442. Sick, Gary. *October Surprise: America's Hostages in Iran and the Election of Ronald Reagan.* (New York: Times Books, 1991)
443. See for eg., Emerson, Steven. Gary Sick's Bald-Faced Lies: The October Surprise Hoax Is Laid To Rest -- At Least Outside The Clinton Administration. *The America Spectator.* March, 1993 Issue. Retrieved from http://spectator.org/
444. By "January Surprise," I refer to the shocking announcement made within minutes of Reagan's inauguration on January 20, 1981, that the Iranian government was releasing all 52 Americans taken hostage in Iran during the Iranian revolution of 1979.
445. Regarding the Iran Contra affair, See generally, Walsh, Lawrence E., *Firewall: The Iran-Contra Conspiracy and Cover Up.* (New York: W.W. Norton & Company, 1997); Iran–Contra Affair. *Wikipedia The Free Encyclopedia.* (Wikipedia Foundation Inc.) Retrieved from http://en.wikipedia.org/wiki/Iran%E2%80%93Contra_affair
446. One example of a Republican who croons over Reagan's economic record is Senator Ted Cruz. See, Jackson, Brooks. March 19, 2013. Ted's Twisted History. *Fact Check.Org: A Project of the Annenberg Public Policy Center.* Retrieved from http://www.factcheck.org/2013/03/teds-twisted-history/
447. Bode, K. (Reporter), & Chancellor, J. (Anchor). February 10, 1982. Voodoo Economics. NBC Nightly News. *NBC Learn K*-12. Retrieved from https://archives.nbclearn.com/portal/site/k-12/browse/?cuecard=33292; To watch a very revealing video from the NBC Archive on youtube of George H.W. Bush using the term voodoo economics go to https://www.youtube.com/watch?v=o8hnM6xNjeU
448. Shafer, Jack. April 2, 2007. The Stockman "Woodshed" Myth How a calculated lie became a man's most personal truth. *Slate.* Retrieved from http://www.slate.com/
449. Stockman, David A., *The Triumph of Politics Why the Reagan Revolution Failed.* (New York: Harper & Row, 1986)
450. The evolution of our national debt is covered in chapter 10. How the Republocrats made America the World's Largest Debtor Nation: The Eighteen Trillion Dollar National Debt.

451. Stockman, David, op. ed. July 31, 2010. *Four Deformations of the Apocalypse*. The New York Times. Retrieved from http://www.nytimes.com/2010/08/01/opinion/01stockman.html?_r=0
452. Ibid.
453. Ibid.
454. Ibid.
455. Ibid.
456. For an excellent discussion of the transformation of the banking system from one of many banks professionally focused on financing the expansion of America's industrial capacity to one run by an oligarchy of too big too fail banks greedily focused on speculative gain, see Johnson, Simon., and Kwak, James. *13 Bankers: The Wall Street Takeover And The Next Financial Meltdown*. (New York, Pantheon Books, 2010) 61-87
457. Ibid.
458. Snyder, Michael. November 11, 2013. Meet One Of The Victims Of Obama's "Economic Recovery." *The Economic Collapse*. Retrieved from http://theeconomiccollapseblog.com/
459. Snyder, Michael. November 10, 2013. 10 Facts About The Growing Unemployment Crisis In America That Will Blow Your Mind. *The Economic Collapse*. Retrieved from http://theeconomiccollapseblog.com/archives/10-facts-about-the-growing-unemployment-crisis-in-america-that-will-blow-your-mind
460. Eckes, 202-209
461. Ibid., 102. Used by permission of publisher.
462. The direct effect of Smoot-Hawley was in fact expansionary. It did not cause or worsen the Great Depression. See, Eichengreen, Barry. The Political Economy of the Smoot-Hawley Tariff. *The National Bureau of Economic Research.* Working Paper No. 2001. (Cambridge, Mass.: August, 1986) (DOI: 0.3386/w2001) Retrieved from http://www.nber.org/papers/w2001; Fletcher, *Free Trade Doesn't Work: What Should Replace It and Why* 138-140; Eckes, Jr., Alfred E. *Opening America's Market U.S. Foreign Trade Policy since 1776,* (Chapel Hill: The University of North Carolina Press, 1995) 100-139; John Maynard Keynes himself hated the idea that the U.S. would run a trade deficit. See, Geoghegan, Thomas September 27, 2011. What Would Keynes Do? The GOP declares Keynesianism dead, but it hasn't really been tried. The great economist would have us do much more than "prime the pump" to pull the country out of this morass. *The Nation.* Retrieved from http://www.thenation.com/; Krugman, Paul. *Peddling Prosperity: Economic Sense and Nonsense in an Age of Diminished Expectations.* (New York: W.W. Norton & Company, 1994) 93; John K. Galbraith noted the pronounced effect that buying on margin had in exacerbating the crash of the stock market in 1929 that preceded the Great Depression. See, Galbraith, John Kenneth. *The Great Crash 1929,* (New York: Houghton Mifflin Harcourt, Kindle version, 2009) (Original Publication, 1954); Milton Friedman never mentioned tariffs or Smoot Hawley in his famous book which devotes an entire chapter to the cause of the Great Depression. See, Friedman, Milton., and Jacobson Schwartz, Anna. *A Monetary History of the United States, 1867–1960* (Princeton, NJ: Princeton University Press, 1963) (reissued 1993); For an instructive description of how

Friedman, an ardent free trader, avoided soiling himself by not arguing on behalf of the Smoot-Hawley myth - while he did help others to propagate it, See Streitz, Paul. March 20, 2010. Milton Friedman's Smoot-Hawley Lie. *Magic City Morning Star*. http://www.magic-city-news.com/Paul_Streitz_67/Milton_Friedman_s_Smoot-Hawley_Lie 13239.shtml; Finally, Bernanke's very clear rejection of the idea that Smoot-Hawley was a material factor in the causing or lengthening the Great Depression is being undermined by Smoot-Hawley Myth propagators, including possibly Bernanke himself. Bernanke made the comment "Economists still agree that Smoot-Hawley and the ensuing tariff wars were highly counterproductive and contributed to the depth and length of the global Depression." during a speech he gave in 2013. But the rest of his speech reveals that Bernanke was ascribing the belief that Smoot-Hawley caused, worsened, or lengthened the Great Depression to "economists" in general, and not to himself in particular. We might call that type of behavior *Milting the Myth*. See, Bernanke, Ben. March 25, 2013. Speech to invited guests on"Monetary Policy and the Global Economy" at a conference hosted by the Bank of England. Speech presented at the London School of Economics, London, England. *Board of Governors of the Federal Reserve System.* Retrieved from http://www.federalreserve.gov/newsevents/speech/bernanke20130325a.htm; For an example of how free traders have used Bernanke as spokesperson for the Smoot Hawley myth, even though Bernanke specifically ruled out tariffs as a material causative factor in the Great Depression in his famous *Essays on the Great Depression,* See, Smoot-Hawley Tariff Act. *Wikipedia The Free Encyclopedia.* (Wikipedia Foundation Inc.) Retrieved from http://en.wikipedia.org/wiki/Smoot%E2%80%93Hawley_Tariff_Act

463. Bernanke, Ben S. *Essays on the Great Depression*. (Princeton: Princeton University Press, Kindle version, 2004,) Ch. 8. Section V.
464. Domitrovic, Brian. March 27, 2012. Ben Bernanke's Views on Gold Are Rather Passé. *Forbes*. Retrieved from http://www.forbes.com/
465. Eichengreen, Barry J. The Political Economy of the Smoot-Hawley Tariff. Working Paper No. 2001. *National Bureau of Economic Research*. August, 1986. 62
466. Eckes, 139. Used by permission of publisher.
467. Ibid., 100-139
468. Reagan, Ronald. August 31, 1985. Radio Address to the Nation on Free and Fair Trade. Speech given at Rancho Del Cielo. Online by Gerhard Peters and John T. Woolley *The American Presidency Project*. Retrieved from http://www.presidency.ucsb.edu/ws/index.php?pid=39044
469. Eckes, 102-103. Used by permission of publisher.
470. Kurtz, Howard. June 7, 2004. 15 Years Later, the Remaking of a President. *Washington Post*. Retrieved from http://www.washingtonpost.com/
471. Eckes, 245-256
472. Ibid., 253
473. Ibid., 252-253
474. Trickle-down economics. *Wikipedia The Free Encyclopedia.* (Wikipedia Foundation Inc.) Retrieved from http://en.wikipedia.org/wiki/Trickle-down_economics

475. Eckes, 254
476. Susan Liebler. *Wikipedia The Free Encyclopedia.* (Wikipedia Foundation Inc.) Retrieved from http://en.wikipedia.org/wiki/Susan_Liebeler
477. Andersen, Claudia. February 13, 2006. Anne Brunsdale. 1923-2006. *The Weekly Standard.* Retrieved from http://www.weeklystandard.com/
478. Eckes, 254
479. Ibid. Used by permission of publisher.
480. Eckes, 279
481. Fletcher, Ian. September 12, 2010. America Was Founded as a Protectionist Nation. *Huff Post Politics.* Retrieved from http://www.huffingtonpost.com/
482. Ibid., 255-256
483. Ibid., 254-257
484. Ibid., 280
485. Economic policy of Bill Clinton. *Wikipedia The Free Encyclopedia.* (Wikipedia Foundation Inc.) Retrieved from http://en.wikipedia.org/wiki/Economic_policy_of_Bill _Clinton; It's the economy, stupid. *Wikipedia The Free Encyclopedia.* (Wikipedia Foundation Inc.) Retrieved from http://en.wikipedia.org/wiki/It's_the_economy,_stupid
486. Irrational exuberance. *Wikipedia The Free Encyclopedia.* (Wikipedia Foundation Inc.) Retrieved from http://en.wikipedia.org/wiki/Irrational_exuberance;
487. Johnson, Simon., and Kwak, James. *13 Bankers: The Wall Street Takeover And The Next Financial Meltdown.* (New York, Pantheon Books, 2010) 135-136
488. Reagan got the top marginal federal income tax reduced for the richest 1.2% of Americans from 70 percent to 28 percent while raising taxes on the poor and middle class. Clinton got the highest marginal rate increased to 39.6 percent, thus preserving over 83 percent of Reagan's tax cut for the rich. See, Center for Federal Tax Policy. October 17, 2013. U.S. Federal Individual Income Tax Rates History, 1862-2013 (Nominal and Inflation-Adjusted Brackets). *Tax Foundation.* Retrieved from http://taxfoundation.org/; Economic policy of Bill Clinton. *Wikipedia The Free Encyclopedia.* (Wikipedia Foundation Inc.) Retrieved from http://en.wikipedia.org/wiki/Economic_policy_of_Bill Clinton; Domestic policy of the Ronald Reagan administration. *Wikipedia The Free Encyclopedia.* (Wikipedia Foundation Inc.) Retrieved from http://en.wikipedia.org/wiki /Domestic_policy of_the_Ronald_Reagan_administration
489. Harris, Evan. April 17, 2010. Clinton: I Was Wrong to Listen to Wrong Advice Against Regulating Derivatives. *ABC News.* Retrieved from http://abcnews.go.com/blogs/politics/
490. Levine, Richard M. I Feel Your Pain: How To Host The Presidency in 12 Steps. Mother Jones. July/August, 1993. Retrieved from http://www.motherjones.com/; Ambinder, Mark. October 5, 2012. Feeling your pain. *The Week.* Retrieved from http://theweek.com/ article/index/234413/feeling-your-pain; The phrase "I feel your pain" became a Clinton trademark following his verbal exchange with activist Bob Rafsky during Clinton's campaign speech on March 26, 1992 at Laura Belle supper club in New York City. See, The 1992 Campaign Verbatim. March 28, 1992. Heckler Stirs Clinton Anger: Excerpts From the Exchange. *New York Times.* Retrieved from http://www.nytimes.com/

491. See for eg. Dreyfuss, Bob., and Dreyfuss, Mary. July 9, 2014. The Hillary Clinton Juggernaut Courts Wall Street and Neocons. *The Nation*. Retrieved from http://www.thenation.com/
492. See for eg. Irwin, 58-68, 212-214.
493. Eckes, 283
494. Ibid., 284
495. Ibid., 284
496. One such democrat is Ohio Senator Sherrod Brown, author of *Why American Trade Policy Has Failed; Myths of Free Trade.* (New York: The New Press, 2004, 2006), but see Smith, Yves. June 20, 2013. Sherrod Brown Wimps Out on Secret Trade Negotiations In USTR Vote; Elizabeth Warren Takes Risk in Bucking Obama. *naked capitalism.* Retrieved from http://www.nakedcapitalism.com
497. Eckes, 282
498. Lewis, Charles R. E., December 26, 1993. The NAFTA-Math; Clinton Got His Trade Deal, but How Many Millions Did It Cost the Nation? *Washington Post.*
499. William J. Clinton. September 14, 1993. Speech at the Signing Ceremony for the Supplemental Agreements to NAFTA. Online by Gerhard Peters and John T. Woolley *The American Presidency Project*. Retrieved from http://www.presidency.ucsb.edu/ws/?pi d =47070; See also, Clinton, Bill. September 19, 1993. Clinton Makes His Case For Nafta "Nafta Will Create 200,000 American Jobs In Two Years." *Philly.Com.* Retrieved from http://articles.philly.com/1993-09-19/news/25987801 1global-trade-nafta-american-jobs
500. NAFTA's Broken Promises 1994-2013: Outcomes of the North American Free Trade Agreement. *Public Citizen*. Retrieved from http://www.citizen.org/documents/NAFTAs -Broken-Promises.pdf
501. Eckes, 285, 347, note 21 (quoting and citing) *Fortune*, December 14, 1992. pp. 6, 52
502. Ibid., 285, 347, note 21 (quoting and citing) *Business Week*, August 10, 1992. p. 1, August 15, 1994, p. 78
503. Ibid., 285, 347, note 21 (quoting and citing) *The Economist*, October 1, 1994 p. 70
504. Ibid., 284-285
505. See generally, Ch. 3. "Settling Disputes" in *Understanding the WTO*. 5th ed. (Geneva, Switzerland: WTO Information Division, 2011) *WTO.* Retrieved from http://www.wto .org/
506. Prestowitz, 114
507. Ibid., 109
508. There is a glut of opinion in agreement with the statements in the text about the influence of money over policy, policymakers and the public. See for eg., Parramore, Lynn. August 11, 2016. New Evidence On How Money Shapes America's Elections. *The Huffington Post*. Retrieved from http://www.huffingtonpost.com/lynn-parramore/new-evidence-on-how-money_b_11450952.html; T.N. from Los Angeles. April 4, 2014. Money in politics: Cash rules everything around us. *The Economist.* blogs: Democracy In America. Retrieved from http://www.economist.com/blogs/democracyinamerica/2014/04/money-politics-0; Shaw, Jonathan, A Radical Fix for the Republic: Lawrence Lessig thinks

American democracy requires a constitutional overhaul to counter the "economy of influence." *Harvard Magazine*. July-August 2012. 21-23; O'Connor, William. June 9, 2014. Speed Read: Kenneth Vogel's 'Big Money' Shows How PACs Control Politics. *The Daily Beast*. Retrieved from http://www.thedailybeast.com/; Worstall, Tim. April 18, 2014. New shocking research proves that rich people control American politics. *Pando*. Retrieved from http://pando.com/; Funny Money Quotes. *Made of Money*. Retrieved from http://itsamoneything.com/money/in-politics/#.VCs7OitALGw

509. Ibid.; The media's slant concerning free trade is discussed in Chapter 3.
510. The media's slant concerning free trade is discussed in Chapter 3 under the subtitle "Slanted Coverage of Trade Issues." Regarding the MIT study, see note 234 and the accompanying text in Chapter 5.
511. Chapter 7 discusses how other nations have traditionally sought to improve their economies by trading away tacit support of American foreign policy objectives in return for trade concessions from America. A look at America's leading exports confirms the hypothesis that foreigners are interested in selling not buying American. They buy in the main energy, raw materials, specialized industrial machines and electrical apparatus they can't produce at home, commercial aircraft, which few countries produce, and pharmaceuticals. America clearly has some remaining advantage in creating new drugs over smaller and less developed countries. See, Perry, Mark. August 16, 2013. Chemicals are America's second largest export category this year, but 'Big Chemical' wants to restrict natural gas exports? *AEI-Ideas*. Retrieved from http://www.aei.org/publication/chemicals-are-americas-second-largest-export-category-this-year-but-big-chemical-wants-to-restrict-natural-gas-exports/; It does not seem likely that citizens of Asian countries, are any less disdainful of products they associate with the United States than Europeans are known to be. It seems that the citizens of most countries wisely associate their personal economic well being with a national trade surplus with America. See generally, Gross, Daniel. January 13, 2005. Don't Buy American: Why Europeans hate American Express and Wal-Mart, but like MasterCard and Colgate. *Slate*. Retrieved from http://www.slate.com/articles/business/moneybox/2005/01/dont_buy_american.html
512. Amadeo, Kimberly. April 21. 2014. U.S. Imports and Exports Components What Does the U.S. Import and Export? *About.com*. Retrieved from http://useconomy.about.com/od/tradepolicy/p/Imports-Exports-Components.htm
513. Fletcher, *Free Trade Doesn't Work: What Should Replace It and Why*, 40; Prestowitz, *The Betrayal of American Prosperity: Free Market Delusions; America's Decline, and How We Must Compete in the Post-Dollar Era*, 7-8; Prestowitz, Clyde. August 15, 2011. Find The Jobs Where They Are. *Foreign Policy*. Retrieved from http://prestowitz.foreignpolicy.com/
514. See generally, Snyder, Michael. April 28, 2014. The Real Unemployment Rate: In 20% Of American Families, EVERYONE Is Unemployed. *End Of The American Dream*. Retrieved from http://endoftheamericandream.com/
515. See generally, Johnson, Dave. February 19, 2014. Poll: Voters Blame Trade Agreements For Job Losses. *Campaign For America's Future*. Retrieved from http://ourfuture.org/;

Voters Are Demanding Washington Focus On Job Creation. *Alliance For American Manufacturing*. Retrieved from http://www.americanmanufacturing.org/2014poll/; Murray, Sara and Belkin Douglas. Americans Sour on Trade Majority Say Free-Trade Pacts Have Hurt U.S.; Wedge Issue In Some Races. (Louise Radnofsky and Jim Carlton contributed). *The Wall Street Journal*. Retrieved from http://online.wsj.com/

516. See generally, Dominican Republic–Central America Free Trade Agreement. *Wikipedia The Free Encyclopedia.* (Wikipedia Foundation Inc.) Retrieved from http://en.wikipedia.org/wiki/Dominican_Republic%E2%80%93Central_America_Free_Trade_Agreement
517. Trade In Goods with CAFTA-DR. 2005-2014. United States Census Bureau. Retrieved from https://www.census.gov/foreign-trade/balance/c0017.html#2013
518. Ibid.
519. Dominican Republic–Central America Free Trade Agreement. *Wikipedia The Free Encyclopedia.* (Wikipedia Foundation Inc.) Retrieved from http://en.wikipedia.org/wiki/Dominican_Republic%E2%80%93Central_America_Free_Trade_Agreement; Hansen-Kuhn, Karen. Central Americans Speak Out Against CAFTA: Major Issues and Mobilizations. *Global Exchange*. (March, 2005) Retrieved from http://www.globalexchange.org/resources/cafta/speak; Meyerson, Harold. March 30, 2005. CAFTA's Profit Motive. *The Washington Post*. Retrieved from http://www./washingtonpost.com/; Avirgan, Tony. September 23, 2009. Trade agreement favors pharmaceutical companies over sick. *Economic Policy Institute*. Retrieved from http://www.epi.org/
520. Stop CAFTA Coalition. December 8. 2008. DR-CAFTA: Effects and Alternatives. *Stop CAFTA*. Retrieved from http://www.stopcafta.org/
521. DiNovella, Elizabeth. March 24, 2011. Obama Didn't Get the Memo on CAFTA. *The Progressive*. Retrieved from http://www.progressive.org/
522. The New York Times Editorial Board. February 21, 2008. Bush's Popularity: A (Really) New Low? *International New York Times*. Retrieved from http://theboard.blogs.nytimes.com/
523. McElvaine, Robert S. December5, 2005. Historians vs. George W. Bush. History News Network. Retrieved from http://historynewsnetwork.org/
524. Horton, Scott. April 5, 2008. "Worst. President. Ever." *Harper's*. Retrieved from http://http://harpers.org/blog/
525. Backus, Fred., Dutton, Sarah., De Pinto, Jennifer., Salvanto, Anthony. November 20, 2013. Poll: Obamacare support, Obama approval sink to new lows. *CBS News.* Retrieved from http://www.cbsnews.com/
526. Backus, Fred., Dutton, Sarah., De Pinto, Jennifer., Salvanto, Anthony. June 23, 2014. Poll: Lagging approval for Obama overall and on Iraq. *CBS News.* Retrieved from http://www.cbsnews.com/
527. Rasmussen Archive. October 1, 2014. 25% Say U.S. Heading in Right Direction. *Rasmussen Reports*. Retrieved from http://www.rasmussenreports.com/public_content/archive/mood_of_america_archive/right_direction_or_wrong_track/october_2014/25_sa

y_u_s_heading_in_right_direction
528. Dugan, Andrew. July 15, 2014. Congressional Approval Rating Languishes at Low Level: More than one in five say replacing all members is best way to fix it. *Gallup*. Retrieved from http://www.gallup.com/poll/172859/congressional-approval-rating-languishes-low-level.aspx
529. Montanaro, Domenico. October 10, 2013. NBC/WSJ poll: 60 percent say fire every member of Congress. *NBC News*. Retrieved from http://www.nbcnews.com/
530. Ibid.
531. See for eg., Weil, Dan. September 21, 2012. CNNMoney: Fed Easing Favors Rich Over Poor. *NewsMax Money News*. Retrieved from http://www.moneynews.com/; Kurtzleben, Danielle. May 1, 2013. Why The Fed's QE3 Is Great for the Rich: Bernanke & Co. may be helping the rich accumulate more wealth even more now than with QE1 or QE2. U.S. News & World Report. Retrieved from http://www.usnews.com/news/
532. For a general overview see, Quantitative easing. *Wikipedia The Free Encyclopedia.* (Wikipedia Foundation Inc.) Retrieved from http://en.wikipedia.org/wiki/Quantitative_easing
533. Huszar, Andrew. November 13, 2013. Confessions of a Quantitative Easer. Wall Street Journal. Retrieved from http://online.wsj.com/
534. Ibid.
535. Obama defended the Transpacific Partnership Agreement (TPP) during an April, 2014 meeting in Tokyo stating it would bring "a greater good for all people." See, Superville, Darlene. Associated Press. April 24, 2014. Obama rejects notion that Asia-Pacific trade deal is in danger. *PBS Newshour*. Retrieved from http://www.pbs.org/
536. Scott, Robert E., July 18, 2013. No Jobs from Trade Pacts: The Trans-Pacific Partnership Could Be Much Worse than the Over-Hyped Korea Deal. *Economic Policy Institute*. Retrieved from http://www.epi.org/
537. Scott, Robert E., March 14, 2014. U.S.-South Korea Trade Deal Resulted in Growing Trade Deficits and Nearly 60,000 Lost Jobs. *Economic Policy Institute*. Retrieved from http://www.epi.org/
538. Scott, Robert E., April 7, 2011. Colombia shouldn't be rewarded with a Free Trade Agreement. *Economic Policy Institute*. Retrieved from http://www.epi.org/
539. Ibid.
540. Norby, Micheal., Fitzpartrick, Brian. May 31, 2013. The Horrific Costs of the US-Colombia Trade Agreement. *The Nation*. Retrieved from http://www.thenation.com/
541. Ibid.
542. 2013 : U.S. trade in goods with Colombia. *United States Census Bureau*. Retrieved from https://www.census.gov/foreign-trade/balance/c3010.html
543. 2014 : U.S. trade in goods with Colombia. *United States Census Bureau*. Retrieved from https://www.census.gov/foreign-trade/balance/c3010.html
544. Tomaselli, Wesley. Aug 28, 2013. As peso weakens, Colombia's manufacturers still hurting over US trade deal. *Columbia Reports*. Retrieved from http://colombiareports.co/colombia-manufacturing-edge/

545. Munoz, Sara Schaefer., February 27, 2014. Colombian Finance Minister Sees Strong Growth Prospects. *Wall Street Journal.* Retrieved from http://online.wsj.com/
546. Tomaselli, Wesley. Aug 28, 2013. As peso weakens, Colombia's manufacturers still hurting over US trade deal. *Columbia Reports.* Retrieved from http://colombiareports.co /colombia-manufacturing-edge/
547. Ibid.
548. Ross Perot coined the term "giant sucking sound" during his 1992 campaign to become president. See, Giant Sucking Sound. *Wikipedia The Free Encyclopedia.* (Wikipedia Foundation Inc.) Retrieved from https://en.wikipedia.org/wiki/Giant_sucking_sound; Regarding the TPP, See, Trans-Pacific Partnership. *Wikipedia The Free Encyclopedia.* (Wikipedia Foundation Inc.) Retrieved from http://en.wikipedia.org/wiki/Trans-Pacific Partnership
549. Shapiro, Gary. March 28, 2009. President Obama Sounds Like a Free Trader, So Why Are His Actions Contradicting His Words. *Huff Post Politics.* Retrieved from http://www.huffingtonpost.com/gary-shapiro/president-obama-sounds-li_b_170000.html
550. Fletcher, *Free Trade Doesn't Work: What Should Replace It and Why*, 142-143, 206
551. Sauter, Michael B., Frohlich, Thomas C., Hess, Alexander E. M., November 15, 2013. Ten Companies Paying Americans the Least. *24/7 Wall Street.* Retrieved from http://247wallst.com/special-report/2013/11/15/ten-companies-paying-americans-the-least/; Democratic Staff of The United States Congress House of Representatives Committee On Education and the Work Force. The Low Wage Drag On Our Economy: Wal-Mart's Low Wages and Their Effect on Taxpayers and Economic growth. *Committee on Education & The Workforce Democrats.* (May, 2013) Retrieved from http://democrats.edworkforce.house.gov/
552. Carter, Zach. June 18, 2013. Alan Grayson On Trans-Pacific Partnership: Obama Secrecy Hides 'Assault On Democratic Government.' *Huffington Post.* Retrieved from http://www.huffingtonpost.com/
553. Carter, Zach. April 24, 2014. Why Corporations Are Freaking Out About Obama's Big Trade Deal. *Huffington Post.* Retrieved from http://www.huffingtonpost.com/
554. Kellen, Patrick. July 5, 2014. SOPA and PIPA Are Coming back Unless We Stop the Trans-Pacific Partnership. *Economy In Crisis.* Retrieved from http://economyincrisis.org/
555. Lee, Don. September 26, 2013. Currency Manipulation At Issue in Pacific Free-Trade Talks. Senators press the Obama administration to address foreign currency manipulation in talks with Japan and 10 other nations in the so-called Trans-Pacific Partnership. *Los Angeles Times.* Retrieved from http://articles.latimes.com/
556. Weisbrot, Mark. November 19, 2013. The Trans-Pacific Partnership Treaty Is The Complete Opposite of 'Free Trade:' The TPP would strip our constitutional rights, while offering no gains for the majority of Americans. It's a win for corporations. *The Guardian.* Retrieved from http://www.theguardian.com/
557. Hern, Alex., Rushe, Dominic. November 13, 2013. WikiLeaks publishes secret draft chapter of Trans-Pacific Partnership Treaty negotiated in secret between 12 nations 'would trample over individual rights and free expression', says Julian Assange. *The*

Guardian. Retrieved from http://www.theguardian.com/

558. Carter, Zach. June 18, 2013. Alan Grayson On Trans-Pacific Partnership: Obama Secrecy Hides 'Assault On Democratic Government.' *Huffington Post*. Retrieved from http://www.huffingtonpost.com/
559. Hern, Alex., Rushe, Dominic. November 13, 2013. WikiLeaks publishes secret draft chapter of Trans-Pacific Partnership Treaty negotiated in secret between 12 nations 'would trample over individual rights and free expression', says Julian Assange. *The Guardian*. Retrieved from http://www.theguardian.com/
560. Scott, Robert E., July 18, 2013. No Jobs from Trade Pacts: The Trans-Pacific Partnership Could Be Much Worse than the Over-Hyped Korea Deal. *Economic Policy Institute*. Retrieved from http://www.epi.org/
561. Ibid.
562. Experts page: Robert E. Scott. *Economic Policy Institute*. Retrieved from http://www.epi.org/people/robert-e-scott/
563. Ibid.
564. Obama, Barack Hussein. June 30, 2005. Why I oppose CAFTA: The proposed accord does less to protect U.S. labor than previous trade agreements, and does little to address environmental standards in the Central American countries. *Chicago Tribune*. Retrieved from http://articles.chicagotribune.com/
565. McCormack, Richard. ed. Sept. 25, 2013. With Loss of Manufacturing The U.S. Innovation Engine Is No Longer Working. *Manufacturing and Technology News*. (Vol. 20, No. 13). Retrieved from: http://www.manufacturingnews.com/news/PIE0925131.html
566. If you do an internet search for the phrase "Globalization and Technology" or the phrase "The Technology Revolution" you will produce search results that contain either phrase depending on which phrase you searched with. If you do an internet search for the phrase "Globalization is a Technological Revolution" you won't find any results that contain that phrase. If you do find such a result it will have a publication date later than this book.
567. Obama, Barack Hussein. June 30, 2005. Why I oppose CAFTA: The proposed accord does less to protect U.S. labor than previous trade agreements, and does little to address environmental standards in the Central American countries. *Chicago Tribune*. Retrieved from http://articles.chicagotribune.com/2005-06-30/news/0506300212_1_cafta-central-american-countries-trade-agreements
568. Ibid.
569. Ibid.
570. Shakespeare, William. Macbeth. Act 5, Scene 5, 19-23. *Enotes*. Retrieved from http://www.enotes.com/shakespeare-quotes/tomorrow-tomorrow-tomorrow
571. See for eg., Irwin, Douglas A., *Free Trade Under Fire*. 3rd. ed. (Princeton, New Jersey: Princeton University Press, 2009)
572. Muroyama, Janet H., Stever, H. Guyford., eds. *Globalization of Technology: International Perspectives*. Proceedings of the Sixth Convocation of The Council of Academies of Engineering and Technological Sciences. (Washington, D.C.: National

Academy Press, 1988)
573. Ibid., 30
574. Ibid., 1
575. Johnson, Tim. June 17, 2012. Mexico's 'Maquiladora' Labor System Keeps Workers In Poverty. *McClatchy D.C.* Retrieved from http://www.mcclatchydc.com/2012/06/17/152220_mexicos-maquiladora-labor-system.html?rh=1
576. Eckes, 279
577. Ibid. Used by permission of publisher.
578. Obama, Barack Hussein. June 30, 2005. Why I oppose CAFTA: The proposed accord does less to protect U.S. labor than previous trade agreements, and does little to address environmental standards in the Central American countries. *Chicago Tribune*. Retrieved from http://articles.chicagotribune.com/2005-06-30/news/0506300212_1_cafta-central-american-countries-trade-agreements
579. Huey Long. *Wikipedia The Free Encyclopedia.* (Wikipedia Foundation Inc.) Retrieved from http://en.wikipedia.org/wiki/Huey_Long
580. Russell B. Long. *Wikipedia The Free Encyclopedia.* (Wikipedia Foundation Inc.) Retrieved from http://en.wikipedia.org/wiki/Russell_B._Long; Reagan, Ronald. October 16, 1985. Speech Honoring Senator Russell B. Long held at the Madison Hotel in Washington D.C., *Ronald Reagan Presidential Library and Museum Archive at the University of Texas*. Retrieved from http://www.reagan.utexas.edu/archives/speeches/1985/101685d.htm
581. Russell B. Long. op. cit.; Cushman, John H. May 11, 2003. Russell B. Long, 84, Senator Who Influenced Tax Laws. *The New York Times*. Retrieved from http://www.nytimes.com
582. Eckes, 283

Chapter 8. Free Trade is a Bunch of Bananas, Protectionism is a Bushel of Apples.

583. Reinert, Erik S. *How Rich Countries Got Rich ...and Why Poor Countries Stay Poor.* (New York: Carroll & Graf, 2007)
584. Chang, Ha-Joon. *Bad Samaritans: The Myth of Free Trade And The Secret History of Capitalism.* (New York: Bloomsbury Press, 2008)
585. Ibid., 15; Reinert, *How Rich Countries Got Rich ...and Why Poor Countries Stay Poor*, xxviii
586. Chang, *Bad Samaritans: The Myth of Free Trade And The Secret History of Capitalism.*, 25
587. Fletcher, *Free Trade Doesn't Work: What Should Replace It and Why*, 131-138
588. Both books should be read in their entirety but see for eg., Chang, *Bad Samaritans: The Myth of Free Trade And The Secret History of Capitalism*, 16-18, 67-80; Reinert, *How Rich Countries Got Rich ...and Why Poor Countries Stay Poor.* xxiii-xxix
589. See for eg., Bradford, Harry. January 24, 2013. 12 Iconic American Products That Are No Longer Made In The U.S. *Huffington Post*. Retrieved from http://www.huffingtonpost.

com/; La Botz, Dan. July 24, 2009. The Decline of Manufacturing and Machine Tools, and the Future of American Industry and the Working Class. *MR Zine.* Retrieved from http://mrzine.monthlyreview.org/; Bettis, Richard A., Bradley, Stephen P., Hamel, Gary. Outsourcing and Industrial Decline, *The Executive.* Vol. 6, No. 1 (Feb., 1992), 7-22

590. Chang, *Bad Samaritans: The Myth of Free Trade And The Secret History of Capitalism,* 19
591. Freidman, Thomas L., *The Lexus and the Olive Tree.* (New York: Anchor Books, 2000) 2. ed.
592. Chang, *Bad Samaritans: The Myth of Free Trade And The Secret History of Capitalism, 20*
593. Freidman, Thomas L., Freidman, Thomas L., *The Lexus and the Olive Tree.* 105
594. Chang, *Bad Samaritans: The Myth of Free Trade And The Secret History of Capitalism, 20*
595. Ibid.
596. Eckes, 200. Used by permission of publisher.
597. Fletcher, *Free Trade Doesn't Work: What Should Replace It and Why*, 71
598. Ibid.
599. Ibid.
600. Florida, Richard. January 9, 2012. Which Countries Pay Blue Collar Workers the Most? *The Atlantic Citylab.* Retrieved from http://www.citylab.com/
601. Allen, Frederick E., December 12, 2011. How Germany Builds Twice As Many Cars As The U.S. While Paying Its Workers Twice As Much. *Forbes.* Retrieved from http://www.forbes.com/s
602. Florida, Which Countries Pay Blue Collar Workers the Most?
603. Fletcher, *Free Trade Doesn't Work: What Should Replace It and Why*, 71, 176
604. Ibid., 74-77
605. Butrica, Barbara A., Iams, Howard M., Smith, Karen E., Toder Eric J., The Disappearing Defined Benefit Pension and Its Potential Impact on the Retirement Incomes of Baby Boomers. Social Security Bulletin, Vol. 69 No. 3, 2009. *U.S. Social Security Administration.* Retrieved from http://www.ssa.gov/policy/docs/ssb/v69n3/v69n3p1.html; Griswold, Doug. October 5, 2014. Fretting the Decline of the Traditional Pension Plan. *Philly.Com.* Retrieved from http://www.philly.com/philly/; Silverman, Dan., Mitchell, Olivia S., Crime and Early Retirement Among Older Americans. (Philadelphia: Boettner Center for Pensions and Retirement Research, 2004). *University of Pennsylvania Population Aging Research Center.* Retrieved from http://parc.pop.upenn.edu/sites/parc.pop.upenn.edu/files/parc/PARCwps04-01.pdf
606. Siedle, Edward. March 20, 2013. The Greatest Retirement Crisis In American History. *Forbes.* Retrieved from http://www.forbes.com/
607. Chang, *Bad Samaritans: The Myth of Free Trade And The Secret History of Capitalism,* 3
608. South Korea. *Wikipedia The Free Encyclopedia.* (Wikipedia Foundation Inc.) Retrieved from http://en.wikipedia.org/wiki/South_Korea
609. Chang, *Bad Samaritans: The Myth of Free Trade And The Secret History of Capitalism,* 3

610. Ibid., 3-15
611. Ibid., 4
612. Garrett, Jay. November 1, 2013. Android owns 81% of smartphone market with Samsung outselling everyone. *Gadget News*. Retrieved from http://gadgetynews.com/
613. Chang, *Bad Samaritans: The Myth of Free Trade And The Secret History of Capitalism*. 3
614. Ibid., 3-4
615. For a quick overview see, Chang, *Bad Samaritans: The Myth of Free Trade And The Secret History of Capitalism*. 3-15
616. Chang, *Bad Samaritans: The Myth of Free Trade And The Secret History of Capitalism,* 14
617. Ibid., 14, 109, 112-113, 120-121
618. Ibid., 14-15, Reinert, *How Rich Countries Got Rich ...and Why Poor Countries Stay Poor,* xxviii, 77-83; Fletcher, *Free Trade Doesn't Work: What Should Replace It and Why*, 122-123, 126-135, 144-145; Prestowitz, *The Betrayal of American Prosperity: Free Market Delusions; America's Decline, and How We Must Compete in the Post-Dollar Era*, 45-58, 73-74.
619. See for eg., Fletcher, *Free Trade Doesn't Work: What Should Replace It and Why*, 127-129
620. Chang, *Bad Samaritans: The Myth of Free Trade And The Secret History of Capitalism,* 15-17;
621. Chang, *Bad Samaritans: The Myth of Free Trade And The Secret History of Capitalism,* 16, 224; Chang's quote from List in note 8 on page 224 of *Bad Samaritans* omits the phrase "by means of protective duties and restrictions on navigation" after "Any nation which" from List's original writing. Chang cites an "1885 translation by Samuel S. Lloyd of List, Friedrich. *The National System of Political Economy*. published by London: Longmans, Green and Co. pp.295-6;" I quoted List, Friedrich. *The National System of Political Economy*. trans. Sampson S. Lloyd, Introduction by J. Shield Nicholson. (London: Longmans, Green and Co., 1909) 295 - 296. Online by *Online Library of Liberty*. pdf version retrieved from http://oll.libertyfund.org/titles/315
622. South Korea. *Wikipedia The Free Encyclopedia.* (Wikipedia Foundation Inc.) Retrieved from http://en.wikipedia.org/wiki/South_Korea; Taiwan. *Wikipedia The Free Encyclopedia.* (Wikipedia Foundation Inc.) Retrieved from http://en.wikipedia.org/wiki/Taiwan; Hong Kong. *Wikipedia The Free Encyclopedia.* (Wikipedia Foundation Inc.) Retrieved from http://en.wikipedia.org/wiki/Hong_Kong; Singapore. *Wikipedia The Free Encyclopedia.* (Wikipedia Foundation Inc.) Retrieved from http://en.wikipedia.org/wiki/Singapore
623. Chang, *Bad Samaritans: The Myth of Free Trade And The Secret History of Capitalism,* 29
624. Ibid.
625. Ibid.
626. List, Friedrich. *The National System of Political Economy*. trans. Sampson S. Lloyd, Introduction by J. Shield Nicholson. (London: Longmans, Green and Co., 1909) 20

Online by *Online Library of Liberty*. pdf version retrieved from http://oll.libertyfund.org /titles/315

627. Hendersen, William Otto., *Freidrich List, Economist and Visionary, 1789 - 1846.* (New York: Frank Cass and Co. Ltd., 1983) 2
628. Friedrich List. *Wikipedia The Free Encyclopedia.* (Wikipedia Foundation Inc.) Retrieved from http://en.wikipedia.org/wiki/Friedrich_List
629. Ibid.
630. List, *The National System of Political Economy.*
631. Historical School of Economics. *Wikipedia The Free Encyclopedia.* (Wikipedia Foundation Inc.) Retrieved from http://en.wikipedia.org/wiki/Historical_school_of _economics; Tribe, Keith. Historical Schools of Economics: German and English. *Keele Economics Research Papers*. (February, 2002) Retrieved from http://128.118.178.162/ eps/mhet/papers/0211/0211002.pdf
632. Schools Of Economic Thought. *Wikipedia The Free Encyclopedia.* (Wikipedia Foundation Inc.) Retrieved from http://en.wikipedia.org/wiki/Schools_of_economic _thought
633. List's influence goes well beyond economists such as Ha Joon Chang and Erik Reinert who are critical of neoliberal trade theory. Political scientists and economists who study comparative political economy, regulatory governance, economic growth and globalization are also influenced by and interested in List's ideas about economic development and economic nationalism. For example see, Levi-Faur, David. Friedrich List And The Political Economy Of The Nation-State. *Review of International Political Economy*, Vol. 4, No. 1 (Spring, 1997), pp. 154-178.
634. Friedrich List. *Wikipedia The Free Encyclopedia.* (Wikipedia Foundation Inc.) Retrieved from http://en.wikipedia.org/wiki/Friedrich_List; Reinert, *How Rich Countries Got Rich ...and Why Poor Countries Stay Poor*, 82-83
635. Eckes, xvi, xviii-xix, 157-159, 200-201,
636. Weissmann, Jordan. March 5, 2013. "How Wall Street Devoured Corporate America. *The Atlantic.* Retrieved from http://www.theatlantic.com; Roberts, Paul Craig., Kranzler, Dave., Titus, John. August 11, 2014. The De-industrialization of America. *Institute for Political Economy*. Retrieved from http://www.paulcraigroberts.org/; Pierce, Justin., Schott, Peter. The Surprisingly Swift Decline of U.S. Manufacturing Employment. (November, 2013) *Board of Governors of The Federal Reserve System*. Retrieved from http://www.federalreserve.gov/pubs/feds/2014/201404/201404pap.pdf; Eckes, 216-218, 259
637. For an example of a Wall Street CEO who mixed God with his self interest in free trade see Lagan, Alfred. October 22, 2008. Free Trade and the Common Good. *Crisis Magazine: A Voice For The Faithful Catholic Laity*. Retrieved from http://www.crisis magazine.com/2008/free-trade-and-the-common-good; See generally, Moreton, Bethany., *To Serve God and Wal-Mart: The Making of Christian Free Enterprise.* (Boston: Harvard University Press, 2010)
638. Bookman, Jay. August 6, 2014. For Corporations Patriotism A Foreign Concept.

AJC.com. Retrieved from http://www.ajc.com/; McIntyre, Robert. May 15, 2015 American Companies Put Profit Over Patriotism. *Newsday*. Retrieved from http:// www.newsday.com/; Prestowitz, Clyde. "Companies Without A Country" in Prestowitz, Clyde. *The Betrayal of American Prosperity: Free Market Delusions, America's Decline, and How We Must Compete in the Post-Dollar Era.* (New York: Free Press, 2010) 193-222

639. Fineman, Howard. January 23, 2014. A New Gilded Age Threatens The State Of Our Union. *Huff Post Politics*. Retrieved from http://www.huffingtonpost.com/; Krugman, Paul. May 8, 2014. Why We're in a New Gilded Age. *The New York Review of Books.* Retrieved from http://www.nybooks.com/; O'Hehir, Andrew. April 26, 2014. The New Gilded Age: A Bigger Con Job Than The First One. *Salon.* Retrieved from http://www.salon.com/
640. Gettys, Travis. April 17, 2014. Paul Krugman: We Live In The Most Unequal Society Ever, And It's Only Getting Worse. *RawStory*. Retrieved from http://www.rawstory.com/
641. Berman, Jillian. December 19, 2011. U.S. Income Inequality Higher Than Roman Empire's Levels: Study. *Huff Post Business.* Retrieved from http://www.huffington post.com/; De Chant, Tim. December 16, 2011. Income inequality in the Roman Empire. *Per Square Mile*. Retrieved from http://persquaremile.com/
642. Regarding cherry picked and juggled statistics, See, Fletcher, *Free Trade Doesn't Work: What Should Replace It and Why*, 58, 162-164; Regarding the Smoot-Hawley myth see the pertinent discussion in chapters 3 and 7 of this book and the references provided in note 462.
643. Melamed, Claire. The Economics of Failure: The Real Cost of 'Free' Trade for Poor Countries. Christian Aid. (June, 2005) Retrieved from http://www.christianaid.org.uk/ Images/economics_of_failure.pdf
644. Kraev,Egore. June 21, 2005. Estimating GDP Effects Of Trade Liberalisation On Developing Countries. *Christian Aid.* Retrieved from http://egor.ch/FinalVersion.pdf
645. Melamed, 1
646. Murshed, Syed Mansoob. The Conflict-Growth Nexus and the Poverty of Nations. *Institute of Social Studies*. (2007)
647. Fletcher, *Free Trade Doesn't Work: What Should Replace It and Why*, 156-157
648. Murshed, 2
649. Fletcher, *Free Trade Doesn't Work: What Should Replace It and Why*, 156-162

Chapter 9. Don't Be Fooled: Those Trade Deficits Are Killing Us.

650. The current rule of thumb on job losses from imports is from 9000 to 15,000 lost jobs per billion dollars of imports. See, Fletcher, *Free Trade Doesn't Work: What Should Replace It and Why*, 40; Prestowitz, *The Betrayal of American Prosperity: Free Market Delusions; America's Decline, and How We Must Compete in the Post-Dollar Era*, 7-8; Prestowitz, Clyde. August 15, 2011. Find The Jobs Where They Are. *Foreign Policy*. Retrieved from http://prestowitz.foreign policy.com/

651. United States Congress. U.S. - China Economic and Security Review Commission. Hearing held on August 22, 2006: China's Financial System and Monetary Policies - The Impact on U.S. Exchange Rates, Capital Markets, and Interest Rates. (109th Cong.) 93-94 (Prepared Statement of Dr. Peter Morici, Professor Robert H. Smith School of Business, University of Maryland, College Park, MD) (GPO, October, 2006) Retrieved from http://www.uscc.gov/hearings_2006
652. Mutikani, Lucia . (Via Reuters) August 21, 2013. 75 Percent Of Jobs Created This Year Were Part-Time Due To Weak Economy, Obamacare Concerns. *Huff Post Business.* Retrieved from http://www.huffingtonpost.com/
653. See, U.S. Financial Crisis Inquiry Commission. The Financial Crisis Inquiry Report. (GPO, 2011) xx -xxiiii. Retrieved from http://www.gpo.gov/fdsys/pkg/GPO-FCIC/pdf/GPO-FCIC.pdf; The Financial Crisis Inquiry Commission was established to "examine the causes, domestic and global, of the current financial and economic crisis in the United States." The Commission was created with the passage of the Fraud Enforcement and Recovery Act, which became law in May, 2009. For a good overview of how the government has failed to regulate the financial system effectively see Johnson, Simon., and Kwak, James. *13 Bankers: The Wall Street Takeover And The Next Financial Meltdown.* (New York, Pantheon Books, 2010)
654. The fact that free trade makes the American dream of home ownership less and less accessible to more and more workers is obviously part of the explanation as to why so many junk mortgages were created and securitized prior to the financial crash of 2007/2008. Highly regarded economist and financial analyst Michael Pettis argues that our huge trade imbalances were clearly the primary cause of the financial crisis and that there is no mystery about it. See, Pettis, Michael. "Trade Imbalances and the Global Financial Crisis." in Pettis, Michael. *The Great Rebalancing: Trade, Conflict, and the Perilous Road Ahead for the World Economy.* (Princeton, New Jersey: Princeton University Press, 2013) (Ch. 1) 1-22
655. Griswold, Daniel. June 14, 2011. Truth about Trade Deficits and Jobs. *Washington Times.* Retrieved from http://www.cato.org/publications/commentary/truth-about-trade-deficits-jobs
656. Ibid.
657. Ibid.
658. Ibid.
659. Ibid.
660. Ibid.
661. Ibid.
662. Claremont, Robin. April 14, 2014. The Surprising Truth Behind Tax Day: Where Your Taxes Go. *Moyers and Company.* Retrieved from http://billmoyers.com/
663. Durden, Tyler, April 3, 2014. The Chinese Are Buying Large Chunks Of Land Across America (And Zillow Is Now Enabling It). Zero Hedge. Retrieved from http://www.zerohedge.com/news/; Agence France-Presse. September 16, 2014. China Tells Domestic Companies -- Go Make Overseas Acquisitions. *Industry Week.* Retrieved from http://ww

w.industryweek.com/; Putzier, Konrad. October 01, 2016. Meet the Chinese moguls pouring money into NYC: From marrying into the political elite to soldiering in the deserts of Mongolia, a look at the rise of China's biggest property tycoons. *The Real Deal: New York Real Estate News*. Retrieved from http://therealdeal.com/issues_articles/meet-the-chinese-moguls-pouring-money-into-nyc

664. Maduri, Frank J., October 25, 2013. China's Ownership of an Iconic American Food Company. *UPI*. Retrieved from http://www.upi.com/; Bittman, Mark. November 5, 2103. On Becoming China's Farm Team. *New York Times*. Retrieved from http://www.nytimes .com/
665. Duggan, Jennifer. April 17, 2014. Dead Pigs Floating In Chinese River. *The Guardian*. Retrieved from http://www.theguardian.com/
666. Cole, Robert J., October 31, 1989. Japanese Buy New York Cachet With Deal for\ Rockefeller Center. *New York Times*. Retrieved from http://www.nytimes.com/
667. Fingleton, Eamonn. June 23, 2013. Will Sony's Columbia Pictures Ever Revert To U.S. Control? No Way, Jose!
668. Marco, Meg. July 14, 2008. Budweiser Sold To The Maker Of Stella Artois, Becks. *Consumerist*. Retrieved from http://consumerist.com/
669. Bagli, Charles V., July 10, 2008. Abu Dhabi Buys 90% Stake in Chrysler Building. *New York Times*. Retrieved from http://www.nytimes.com/
670. This Day In History. May 7, 1998. Daimler-Benz announces purchase of Chrysler Corp. *History*. Retrieved from http://www.history.com/this-day-in-history/
671. Sauter Michael B., Stockdale, Charles B., McIntyre, Douglas A., October 8, 2010. The Most Famous American Brands In Foreign Hands. *Huff Post Business*. (first online at 24/7 Wall St.) Retrieved from http://www.huffingtonpost.com/; Olen, John. March 30, 2014. Many American-Made Companies Are Now Under Foreign Control! *Economy In Crisis*. Retrieved from http://economyincrisis.org/
672. Helm, Leslie. July 18, 1995. TV Maker Fades to Black : Zenith to Sell Majority Stake to S. Korean Conglomerate. *Los Angeles Times*. Retrieved from http://articles.latimes.com/
673. Rapoza, Kenneth. July 30, 2014. For Rich Chinese, U.S. Becoming Giant Monopoly Game. *Forbes*. Retrieved from http://www.forbes.com/; Gittelsohn, John. July 9, 2014. Chinese Cash-Bearing Buyers Drive U.S. Foreign Sales Jump. *Bloomberg*. Retrieved from http://www.bloomberg.com/news/; Logan, Tim. July 8, 2014. Chinese Drive Surge In Foreign Home-Buying in U.S., Southern California. *Los Angeles Times*. Retrieved from http://www.latimes.com/
674. Dubai Ports World Controversy. *Wikipedia The Free Encyclopedia*. (Wikipedia Foundation Inc.) Retrieved from http://en.wikipedia.org/wiki/Dubai_Ports_World_controversy
675. Kirchgaessner, Stephanie. February 28, 2006. US Coast Guard Warned on Dubai Ports Deal. Financial Times. Retrieved from http://www.ft.com/; Beisecker, Randall. March 1, 2006. DP World and U.S. Port Security. *NTI*. Retrieved from http://www.nti.org/
676. Sanger, David E., Lipton, Eric. February 22, 2006. Bush Would Veto Any Bill Halting Dubai Port Deal. *New York Times*. Retrieved from http://www.nytimes.com/

677. Dubai Ports World Controversy. *Wikipedia The Free Encyclopedia.* (Wikipedia Foundation Inc.) Retrieved from http://en.wikipedia.org/wiki/Dubai_Ports_World_controversy

678. World Net Daily. February 24, 2006. 22 ports in Arab deal, not just 6 as reported World Net Daily. *WND*. Retrieved from http://www.wnd.com/2006/02/34981/

679. Sanger, David E. March 10, 2006. Under Pressure, Dubai Company Drops Port Deal. *New York Times*. Retrieved from http://www.nytimes.com/; Weisman, Jonathan., Graham, Bradley. March 10, 2006. Dubai Firm to Sell U.S. Port Operations. *Washington Post*. Retrieved from http://www.washingtonpost.com/

680. Hamilton, James D., March 28, 2006. Homeland Security's Curious "Fact Sheet." *Econbrowser*. Retrieved from http://econbrowser.com/; Hamilton, James D., March 8, 2006. Still no correction from Homeland Security. *Econbrowser*. Retrieved from http://econbrowser.com/;

681. Carey, Nick., Grenon, Andre. August 27, 2008. Foreign Ownership of U.S. Companies Jumps. *Reuters*. Retrieved from http://www.reuters.com/

682. Feinberg, Alan. March 10, 2011. Foreign Ownership of U.S. Companies 51% by 2033 with Skyrocketing U.S. Unemployment Projected due to the Trojan Horse Trade Deficit. *Economy In Crisis*. Retrieved from http://economyincrisis.org/

683. Fletcher, *Free Trade Doesn't Work: What Should Replace It and Why*, 2

684. Byrne, John Aidan. October 5, 2013. IBM Now Employs More Workers In India Than US. *New York Post*. Retrieved from http://nypost.com/

685. Fletcher, *Free Trade Doesn't Work: What Should Replace It and Why*, 32-44

686. There is not even data that proves that the savings to consumers from buying imports is greater than the wages lost from not making goods domestically. See, Fletcher, *Free Trade Doesn't Work: What Should Replace It and Why*, 33.

687. Ibid.; See, Rodrick, Dani. April 28, 2007. Can the wrong answer in the classroom be the right answer in public debate? *Dani Rodrik's weblog*. Retrieved from http://rodrik.typepad.com/dani_rodriks_weblog/2007/04/can_the_wrong_a.html; Obviously the wages lost because of imports are only one of the losses incurred. Far more valuable than the lost wages are the positive externalities associated with presence of the lost production. These later losses are of such inestimably high value that they gave the arguments of Henry Clay and the other architects of the American System sufficient force to overcome all opposition. It was only after America had developed into the world's preeminent economic and military power that it fell into the age old trap of free trade: the enticing vision dominant powers see of great gains and strategic advantages from opening their markets to foreign powers thought to be too far behind technologically to ever catch up.

688. Here is a homework helper for beginning econ students that explains why trade deficits can be expected to cause currency devaluation. See, Dr. Econ. Why does a trade deficit weaken the currency? *Federal Reserve Bank of San Francisco*. (October, 1999) Retrieved from http://www.frbsf.org/education/publications/

689. Regarding the significance of trade deficits see generally Fletcher, *Free Trade Doesn't*

Work: What Should Replace It and Why, 37-55

690. McCormack, Richard. ed. Sept. 25, 2013. With Loss of Manufacturing The U.S. Innovation Engine Is No Longer Working. *Manufacturing and Technology News*. (Vol. 20, No. 13). Retrieved from: http://www.manufacturingnews.com/news/PIE0925131.html

691. Pierce, Justin., Schott, Peter. The Surprisingly Swift Decline of U.S. Manufacturing Employment. (November, 2013) *Board of Governors of The Federal Reserve System*. Retrieved from http://www.federalreserve.gov/pubs/feds/2014/201404/201404pap.pdf; Eckes, 216-218; Roberts, Paul Craig., Kranzler, Dave., Titus, John. August 11, 2014. The De-industrialization of America. *Institute for Political Economy*. Retrieved from http://www.paulcraigroberts.org/2014/08/11/de-industrialization-america/; McCormack, Richard. July 31, 2013. America's Biggest Companies Continue To Move Factories Offshore And Eliminate Thousands of American Jobs. *Manufacturing and Technology News*. Vol. 20. No. 10. Retrieved from http://www.manufacturingnews.com/news/TAA0731131.html; McCormack, Richard. December 21, 2009. The Plight of American Manufacturing. *The American Prospect*. Retrieved from http://prospect.org/

692. Bartash, Jeffry. June 10, 2014. Fewer good jobs in the new economy. *MarketWatch*. Retrieved from http://www.marketwatch.com/; White, Martha C., November 6, 2014. Unemployment Is Down, But Good Jobs Are Scarce. *NBCNews*. Retrieved from http://www.nbcnews.com/; Blake, Aaron. September 5, 2014. The jobs report isn't great. But, at this point, Americans have really low expectations. *The Washington Post*. Retrieved from http://www.washingtonpost.com/blogs/the-fix/

693. Associated Press. June 24, 1986. U.S. Becomes the World's Largest Debtor Country. *Los Angeles Times*. Retrieved from http://articles.latimes.com/; Robinson, Jerry. October 18, 2013. U.S. National Debt Hits $17 Trillion: How Did We Get Here? *FTM Daily*. Retrieved from http://ftmdaily.com/daily-briefing/how-did-we-get-here/

694. Gongloff, Mark. September 7, 2012. Labor Force Participation Rate Lowest In Three Decades, Though Despair Doesn't Explain It All. *Huff Post Business*. Retrieved from http://www.huffingtonpost.com/mark-gongloff/labor-force-participation-rate_b_1865027.html; FRED Economic Data. Data updated January 1, 2015. Civilian Labor Force Participation Rate - Men. *Federal Reserve Bank of St. Louis*. (2015-1: 68.7 Percent) Retrieved from http://research.stlouisfed.org/fred2/series/LNU01300001

695. Hess, Amanda. August 13, 2013. Marriage Is the New Middle-Class Luxury Item. *Slate*. Retrieved from http://www.slate.com/; Keene, Meg. February 23, 2012. Is Marriage An Economic Privilege? *A Practical Wedding*. Retrieved from http://apracticalwedding.com/2012/02/is-marriage-an-economic-privilege/; Daum, Meghan. October 20, 2011. Inside the mating economy. *Los Angeles Times*. Retrieved from http://articles.latimes.com/; Barber, Nigel. June 13, 2013. Can Young People Afford to Marry? Even if they want to marry, young people face financial hurdles. *Psychology Today*. Retrieved from http://www.psychologytoday.com/

696. Beachy, Ben. February 11, 2013. Obama's Export Promise Falls 18 Years Behind Schedule as Exports Decline under FTAs. Public Citizen. Retrieved from http://citizen.typepad.com/eyesontrade/

697. Margolis, Jason. August 12, 2013. Regional Manufacturing Hubs, to Compete with Foreign Competition, Begin in Youngstown, Ohio. *PRI.* Retrieved from http://www.pri.org/stories/
698. Jarrett, Kenneth, Wendholt, Amy. March 1, 2010. Transferring Technology to Transform China—Is It Worth It? *China Business Review*. Retrieved from http://www.chinabusinesreview.com/; Navarro and Autry, *Death by China: Confronting the Dragon - A Global Call To Action* 86-87; Millward, Steven. August 24, 2012. The China R&D Dilemma for Foreign Tech Companies. *Tech In Asia*. Retrieved from https://www.techinasia.com/china-indigenous-innovation-and-foreign-companies/; On the subject of technology transfer generally see Prestowitz, *The Betrayal of American Prosperity: Free Market Delusions; America's Decline, and How We Must Compete in the Post-Dollar Era*, 77, 93, 97, 183, 273-274, 288.
699. Ibid.
700. 2012 : Trade in Goods with World, Not Seasonally Adjusted. *United States Census Bureau*. retrieved from https://www.census.gov/foreign-trade/balance/c0015.html#2012
701. A Bureau of Labor spokesperson confirmed the number of closed and closing factories to Politifact. See, Eaton, Sabrina. November 7th, 2011. Betty Sutton says that on average, 15 U.S. factories close each day. *Poltifact*. Retrieved from http://www.politifact.com/
702. Clifford, Stephanie. September 19, 2013. U.S. Textile Plants Return, With Floors Largely Empty of People. *International New Your Times*. Retrieved from http://www.nytimes.com
703. Scott, Robert E., September 30, 2013. Trading away the manufacturing advantage: China trade drives down U.S. wages and benefits and eliminates good jobs for U.S. workers. *Economic Policy Institute*. Retrieved from http://www.epi.org/
704. Ibid.; Snyder, Michael. October 28, 2013. 29 Incredible Facts Which Prove That Poverty In America Is Absolutely Exploding. *Infowars.* Retrieved from http://www.infowars.com/; Scott, Robert E., Weller, Christian E., Hersh, Adam S., October 1, 2001. The unremarkable record of liberalized trade After 20 years of global economic deregulation, poverty and inequality are as pervasive as ever. *Economic Policy Institute*. Retrieved from http://www.epi.org/; Olen, John. October 17, 2014. There Is No Path Out of Poverty for Americans. *Economy In Crisis*. Retrieved from http://economyincrisis.org/
705. The slanted coverage given to trade issues is discussed in Chapter 3.
706. For an example of the viewpoint that transfer payments can help spread the benefits of free trade see Madrick, Jeff. October 3, 2014. Our Misplaced Faith in Free Trade. *International New York Times*. Retrieved from http://www.nytimes.com/
707. Leonard, David. December 1, 2013. China's 1st Moon Rover Launches On Lunar Journey. *Space.com*. Retrieved from http://www.space.com/
708. The Week Staff. April 27, 2012. NASA's dwindling budget: Why has America stopped reaching for the stars? *The Week*. Retrieved from http://theweek.com/

Chapter 10. How the Republocrats Made America the World's Largest Debtor Nation: The Eighteen Trillion Dollar National Debt.

709. Apple Ipad Application. *Uncle Sam's Debt Clock.* Vers.2.6. igibe Accessed December 12, 2013
710. The figure of $13 trillion was arrived at by adding trade balance figures obtained from the U.S. Census Bureau with historical trade balance figures compiled by Andrew Reamer & Associates and available at Econdata.net. See, U.S. Imports, Exports, and Trade Balance: 1940-2005. *EconoData.Net.* Retrieved from http://www.econdataus.com/trade05.html; U.S. Trade In Goods By Country. *United States Census Bureau.* Retrieved from https://www.census.gov/foreign-trade/balance/
711. U.S. Department of the Treasury. The Daily History of the Debt Results, Historical Returns for December 31, 2013. *Treasury Direct.* Retrieved from http://www.treasury direct.gov/govt/reports/pd/pd_debttothepenny.htm
712. Congressional Research Service. Foreign Holdings of Federal Debt. By Marc Labonte and Jared C. Nagel. Report No. RS22331. June 16. 2014. *Federation of American Scientists.* Retrieved from https://www.fas.org/sgp/crs/misc/RS22331.pdf
713. See for eg., Rapoza, Kenneth. June 27, 2013. The Foreign Companies That Are Buying Up America. Forbes. Retrieved from http://www.forbes.com/
714. For an intelligent discussion of the linkage between America's trade deficits and its national debt, See, Blecker, Robert. A. May, 2011 revision. Global Imbalances and the U.S. Trade Deficit. Retrieved from http://nw08.american.edu/~blecker/research/Blecker_Imbalances_May2011.pdf; The obvious linkage between the size of our national debt and the size of trade deficits is sometimes described as a hypothesis. See for eg., Twin Deficits Hypothesis. *Wikipedia The Free Encyclopedia.* (Wikipedia Foundation Inc.) Retrieved from http://en.wikipedia.org/wiki/Twin_deficits_hypothesis
715. United States Congress. U.S. - China Economic and Security Review Commission. Hearing held on August 22, 2006: China's Financial System and Monetary Policies - The Impact on U.S. Exchange Rates, Capital Markets, and Interest Rates. (109th Cong.) 93-94 (Prepared Statement of Dr. Peter Morici, Professor Robert H. Smith School of Business, University of Maryland, College Park, MD) (GPO, October, 2006) Retrieved from http://www.uscc.gov/hearings_2006
716. Reaganomics. *Wikipedia The Free Encyclopedia.* (Wikipedia Foundation Inc.) Retrieved from http://en.wikipedia.org/wiki/Reaganomics
717. Ronald Reagan`s Military Buildup. *United States History.* Retrieved from http://www.u-s-history.com/pages/h1957.html
718. As you know, I am not enamored with the state of the field of economics. Thus I refer you to the incomplete, imperfect and consistently inconsistent viewpoints found in wikipedia with caution. That being said, See generally, 1973-1975 recession. *Wikipedia The Free Encyclopedia.* (Wikipedia Foundation Inc.) Retrieved from http://en.wikipedia.org/wiki/1973%E2/%80%9375_recession; Stagflation. *Wikipedia The Free Encyclopedia.* (Wikipedia Foundation Inc.) Retrieved from http://en.wikipedia.org/wiki/Stagflation
719. See generally, Post–World War II economic expansion. *Wikipedia The Free Encyclopedia.* (Wikipedia Foundation Inc.) Retrieved from http://en.wikipedia.org/

wiki/Post%E2%80%93World_War_II_economic_expansion
720. Reaganomics. *Wikipedia The Free Encyclopedia.* (Wikipedia Foundation Inc.) Retrieved from http://en.wikipedia.org/wiki/Reaganomics
721. Reagan, Ronald. February 5, 1981. Radio and television address on the economy. Speech made in the Oval Office at the White House. Online by Gerhard Peters and John T. Woolley. *The American Presidency Project*. Retrieved from: http://www.presidency.ucsb.edu/ws/?pid=43132
722. Bartlett, Bruce. "Starve the Beast": Origins and Development of a Budgetary Metaphor. The Independent Review, v. XII, n. 1, Summer 2007, 5–26. Published online in pdf format by *The Independent Institute*. Retrieved from http://www.independent.org/publications/tir/article.asp?a=641; See generally, May 7, 2010. Bartlett, Bruce. Tax Cuts And 'Starving The Beast.' *Forbes*. Retrieved from http://www.forbes.com/
723. Bartlett. "Starve the Beast": Origins and Development of a Budgetary Metaphor.13
724. Stephen Herrington, May 27, 2011. Conservative Myth Busting: Lowering Taxes Raises Government Revenue. *Huff Post Politics*. Retrieved from http://www.huffingtonpost.com/
725. Smith, Allen W. *Ronald Reagan and the Great Social Security Heist*: *How Reagan Gave Birth to The Looting of Social Security*. (Winter Haven, Florida: Ironwood Publications, 2013)
726. Smith, Allen W. October 11, 2013. Ronald Reagan and The Great Social Security Heist. *FedSmith*. Retrieved from http://www.fedsmith.com/ (quoting) Reagan, Ronald. April 20, 1983. Remarks on Signing the Social Security Amendments of 1983. Online by Gerhard Peters and John T. Woolley, *The American Presidency Project*. Retrieved from http://www.presidency.ucsb.edu/ws/?pid=41211.
727. Smith, op. cit., (quoting) Reagan, Ronald. May 21, 1981. Letter To Congressional Leaders On The Social Security System. Online by *U.S. Social Security Administration.* Retrieved from http://www.ssa.gov/history/reaganstmts.html#letter
728. Smith, op. cit., (quoting) Reagan, Ronald. July 18, 1981. Letter To Congressional Leaders About The Social Security System. Online by *U.S. Social Security Administration.* Retrieved from http://www.ssa.gov/history/reaganstmts.html#letter2
729. Smith, op. cit., (quoting but not citing) Ronald Reagan.'a prepaid vacation plan for freeloaders.' first quoted on April 28, 1966. *San Francisco Bee*., I was unable to determine the original source for "a brainchild of Karl Marx," but see, Jeffrey, Terry. December 5, 2012. Ronald Reagan: Progressive Taxation Came Direct From Karl Marx. *Townhall*. Retrieved from http://townhall.com/; 'welfare program' can reportedly be found in Reagan, Ronald. Address to the Orange County Press Club. July 28, 1961. See, Jeffrey, (cited within this note).
730. Smith, Ronald Reagan and The Great Social Security Heist.
731. Isidore, Chris March 4, 2013. Buffett says he's still paying lower tax rate than his secretary. *CNN Money*. Retrieved from http://money.cnn.com/; Harwell, Drew. May 21, 2016. "Trump once revealed his income tax returns. They showed he didn't pay a cent." *The Washington Post*. Retrieved from https://www.washingtonpost.com/politics/trumps-income-tax-returns-once-became-public-they-showed-he-didnt-pay-a-cent/2016/05/20/f

fa2f63c-1b7c-11e6-b6e0-c53b7ef63b45_story.html?utm_term=.4b410952a443
732. Congressional Research Service. An Analysis of the "Buffett Rule." By Thomas L. Hungerford. Report No. R42043. March 28, 2012. *Federation of American Scientists.* Retrieved from *http://w.,ww.fas.org/sgp/crs/misc/R42043.pdf*
733. Fry, Richard., Kochhar, Rakesh. December 17, 2014. America's wealth gap between middle-income and upper-income families is widest on record. *Pew Research Center.* Retrieved from http://www.pewresearch.org/fact-tank/
734. Desilver, Drew. December 5, 2013. U.S. income inequality, on rise for decades, is now highest since 1928. *Pew Research Center.* Retrieved from http://www.pewresearch.org/fact-tank/
735. Amadeo, Kimberly. U.S. Debt by President: By Dollar and Percent Why the Winner Is...Barack Obama. *About.com.* (Undated and subject to revision) Retrieved on January 20, 2015, from http://useconomy.about.com/od/usdebtanddeficit/p/US-Debt-by-President.htm
736. It's The Economy, Stupid. *Wikipedia The Free Encyclopedia.* (Wikipedia Foundation Inc.) Retrieved from http://en.wikipedia.org/wiki/It'stheeconomy,stupid
737. See generally, American Experience History Series. General Article: The Election of 1992. (text and video) *PBS.* Retrieved from http://www.pbs.org/wgbh/american experience/features/general-article/bush-election92/
738. Bush, George. August 18, 1988. Address Accepting the Presidential Nomination at the Republican National Convention in New Orleans. Online by Gerhard Peters and John T. Woolley *The American Presidency Project.* Retrieved from: http://www.presidency.ucsb.edu/ws/?pid=25955
739. Bush, George. Video of Bush carried on NBC Nightly News. Voodoo Economics. Ken Bode, correspondent. NBC Nightly News. February 10, 1982. (online in pdf and video). *NBC Learn K-12.* Retrieved from http://archives.nbclearn.com/portal/site/k-12/flatview?cuecard=33292
740. Amadeo, Kimberly. Deficit by President What Budget Deficits Don't Tell You About the Debt. *About.com.* (Undated and subject to revision). Retrieved on January 20, 2015, from http://useconomy.about.com/od/people/fl/Deficit-by-President.htm
741. US Department of Defense. (DoD), Final Report to Congress: Conduct of the Persian Gulf War. (Washington, D.C.: DoD, 1992), 24.
742. Congressional Budget Office. (CBO) CBO Paper: Projecting Federal Tax Revenues and The Effect Of Changes In Tax Law. December, 1998. *Congressional Budget Office.* Retrieved from http://www.cbo.gov/sites/default/files/taxrev.pdf
743. Amadeo, U.S. Debt by President: By Dollar and Percent Why the Winner Is...Barack Obama
744. Ibid.
745. Clinton, Bill. September 19, 2010. Statement made by Clinton on Meet The Press that "the debt was quadrupled in the 12 years before I became president and then we paid down the debt for four years, paid down $600 billion on the national debt, and then my budget was abandoned and they doubled the debt again." David Gregory, Moderator.

Meet The Press. (video and transcript online). *NBC News*. Retrieved from http://www.nbcnews.com/id/39235412/ns/meet_the_press-transcripts/#.VMv3xStALGw

746. Congressional Budget Office. (CBO) The Budget and Economic Outlook: 2014 to 2014. February 2014. Appendix H. Historical Budget Data. 156. *Congressional Budget Office*. Retrieved from https://www.cbo.gov/sites/default/files/45010-Outlook2014_Feb_0.pdf

747. Amadeo, Kimberly. President Bill Clinton's Economic Policies. *About.com*. (Undated and subject to revision). Retrieved on January 20, 2015, from http://useconomy.about.com/od/Politics/fl/President-Bill-Clintons-Economic-Policies.htm

748. Amadeo, U.S. Debt by President: By Dollar and Percent Why the Winner Is...Barack Obama.

749. Amadeo, President Bill Clinton's Economic Policies.; With regard to Clinton's cuts in defense spending, See. Gharib, Ali.July 14, 2011. Chart: Past Presidents' Cuts In Military Spending To Reduce The Deficit. *Think Progress*. Retrieved from http://thinkprogress.org/security/2011/07/14/269154/chart-military-spending-deficit/.

750. I don't know if anybody has proven mathematically that Clinton's efforts to reduce budget deficits (including his claims of budget surpluses) contributed to the rise in the stock market during his presidency, but I am quite certain they did. See, Ask Factcheck. December 7, 2007. Clinton and Economic Growth in the '90s. *FactCheck.Org*. Retrieved from http://www.factcheck.org/; Johnson and Kwak, *98*

751. Johnson and Kwak, 134 -137.

752. Ibid., 126-137

753. See generally, Johnson and Kwak, 90-137; There is evidence that Clinton, a Rhodes scholar known for his intelligence, may nonetheless not really have understood the danger of removing regulatory barriers on Wall Street to any significant degree. He was pressured by his key financial advisors to deregulate Wall Street and the (then) highly influential head of the federal reserve, Alan Greenspan, backed deregulation as well. Clinton may simply have been rushed to his very unwise choices and he simply lacked sufficient knowledge to make better decisions. See, Roberts, Dan. April 19, 2014. Wall Street Deregulation Pushed By Clinton Advisors. *The Guardian*. Retrieved from http://www.theguardian.com/; Johnson and Kwak, 103-104. President Clinton in fact admitted that he was "wrong to listen to wrong advice" about derivatives. See, Harris, Evan. April 17, 2010. Clinton: I Was Wrong to Listen to Wrong Advice Against Regulating Derivatives* *ABC News Blog Political Punch*. Retrieved from http://abcnews.go.com/blogs/politics/

754. See for eg., Baker, Dean. December 25, 2012. There Is No Santa Claus and Bill Clinton Was Not an Economic Savior. *Huff Post Business*. Retrieved from http://www.huffingtonpost.com/

755. An excellent discussion of how the money power has controlled the media and political agenda on free trade, and has exerted influence on the Clintons, Obama and the other Demopublicans can be seen and read here: Moyers, Bill. Interview of MacArthur, John R., December 12, 2014. Full Show: Democrats Bow Down to Wall Street. *Moyers & Company*. Retrieved from http://billmoyers.com/

756. United States Congress. U.S. - China Economic and Security Review Commission. Hearing held on August 22, 2006: China's Financial System and Monetary Policies - The Impact on U.S. Exchange Rates, Capital Markets, and Interest Rates. (109th Cong.) 93-94 (Prepared Statement of Dr. Peter Morici, Professor Robert H. Smith School of Business, University of Maryland, College Park, MD) (GPO, October, 2006) Retrieved from http://www.uscc.gov/hearings_2006
757. Lewis, The NAFTA-Math; Clinton Got His Trade Deal, but How Many Millions Did It Cost the Nation?
758. Beachy, Ben. February, 2014. NAFTA's 20 -Year Legacy and the Fate of the Trans-Pacific Partnership. *Public Citizen*. Retrieved from http://www.citizen.org/documents/NAFTA-at-20.pdf
759. 2000 Presidential Popular Vote Summary For All Candidates Listed On At Least One State Ballot. Updated December, 2001. *U.S. Federal Election Commission*. Retrieved from http://www.fec.gov/pubrec/fe2000/prespop.htm
760. Supreme Court Case Study: Bush v. Gore. Undated. *For Dummies*. Retrieved on February 11, 2015 from http://www.dummies.com/how-to/content/supreme-court-case-study-bush-v-gore.html
761. Barstow, David., Van Natta., Don Jr. July 15, 2001. Examining The Vote; How Bush Took Florida: Mining the Overseas Absentee Vote. *New York Times*. Retrieved from http://www.nytimes.com/
762. See for eg., Bushism. *Wikipedia The Free Encyclopedia.* (Wikipedia Foundation Inc.) Retrieved from http:/en.wikipedia.org/wiki/Bushism; Weisberg, Jacob. March 20, 2009. The Complete Bushisms. *Slate*. Retrieved from http://www.slate.com/
763. Bush, George W., June 6, 2008. Bush made the statement during interview by Gianni Riotta of Italy's Rai TV at the White House. Online by Gerhard Peters and John T. Woolley. *The American Presidency Project*. Retrieved from http://www.presidency.ucsb.edu/ws/index.php?pid=77497&st=true+history&st1=
764. In this Bushism, the President mispronounces "plan pays' as "pan plays." The audio can be found here: Finn, Andy. Top Bushisms in the Category of: Mispronunciation. #3 "My pan plays down an unprecedented amount of our national debt." - George W. Bush, in his budget address to Congress, Feb. 27, 2001 (Audio Recording). Retrieved from http://andyfinn.us/bush_league/bushisms1_mispronunciation.htm; The full text of Bush's budget address which does not reprint his mispronounciation can be found here: Bush, George W., February 27, 2001. Address Before a Joint Session of the Congress on Administration Goals. Online by Gerhard Peters and John T. Woolley. *The American Presidency Project*. Retrieved from http://www.presidency.ucsb.edu/ws/index.php?pid=29643&st=&st1=
765. Center on Budget and Policy Priorities. March 5, 2009. Policy Basics: The 2001 and 2003 Tax Cuts. *Center on Budget and Policy Priorities*. Retrieved from http://www.cbpp.org/cms/?fa=view&id=2705; Holan, Angie Drobnic., June 24, 2009. Bush tax cuts greater than health care? Probably. Politifact.com. Retrieved from http://www.politifact.com/
766. Infoplease. 2012. Estimated War-Related Costs, Iraq and Afghanistan. *Infoplease*.

Retrieved from http://www.infoplease.com/ipa/A0933935.html
767. Potter, Samara R., and Gale, William G., June, 2002. The Bush Tax Cut: One Year Later. *Brookings*. Retrieved from http://www.brookings.edu/research/papers/2002/06/useconomics-gale
768. Bush, George W., January 12, 2009. Presidential News Conference at the White House. Online by Gerhard Peters and John T. Wooll.*The American Presidency Project*. Retrieved from http://www.presidency.ucsb.edu/ws/index.php?pid=85430&st=&st1=
769. Blodget, Henry. September 21, 2012. Bombshell: New Study Destroys Theory That Tax Cuts Spur Growth. *Business Insider*. Retrieved from http://www.businessinsider.com/study-tax-cuts-dont-lead-to-growth-2012-9
770. Hungerford, Thomas L., December 12, 2012. Taxes and the Economy: An Economic Analysis of the Top Tax Rates Since 1945. *Federation of American Scientists.* Retrieved from https://www.fas.org/sgp/crs/misc/R42729.pdf
771. Tyson, Laura D'Andrea., and Zidar, Owen. October 19, 2012. Tax Cuts for Job Creators. *New York Times Economix Blog*. Retrieved from http://economix.blogs.nytimes.com/2012/10/19/tax-cuts-for-job-creators/
772. Alvaredo, Facundo., Atkinson, Anthony B., Piketty, Thomas., Saez, Emmanuel. February 17, 2013. The Top 1 Percent in International and Historical Perspective *The National Bureau of Economic Research.* Working Paper No. 19075. (DOI: 10.3386/w19075) Retrieved from http://www.nber.org/papers/w19075; Facundo Alvaredo & Anthony B. Atkinson & Thomas Piketty & Emmanuel Saez, 2013. "The Top 1 Percent in International and Historical Perspective," Journal of Economic Perspectives, American Economic Association, vol. 27(3), Summer, 2013. pp. 3-20 DOI: 10.1257/jep.27.3.3
773. U.S. Department of the Treasury. The Daily History of the Debt Results, Historical Returns for fiscal years 2001 - 2009. *Treasury Direct*. Retrieved from http://www.treasurydirect.gov/govt/reports/pd/pd_debttothepenny.htm
774. Amadeo, Kimberly. U.S. Debt by President: By Dollar and Percent Why the Winner Is...Barack Obama. *About.com*. (Undated and subject to revision) Retrieved on January 20, 2015, from http://useconomy.about.com/od/usdebtanddeficit/p/US-Debt-by-President.htm
775. U.S. Department of the Treasury. The Daily History of the Debt Results, Historical Return for September 30, 2009. *Treasury Direct*. Retrieved from http://www.treasurydirect.gov/govt/reports/pd/pd_debttothepenny.htm
776. Ibid., Returns for fiscal years 2010 -2014.
777. Amadeo, Kimberly. National Debt Under Obama How Much Did Obama Really Add to the Nation's Debt? *About.com*. (Undated and subject to revision) Retrieved on February 18, 2015, from http://useconomy.about.com/od/usdebtanddeficit/p/National-Debt-Under-Obama.htm
778. U.S. Department of the Treasury. The Daily History of the Debt Results, Historical Return for February 16, 2015. *Treasury Direct*. Retrieved from http://www.treasurydirect.gov/govt/reports/pd/pd_debttothepenny.htm
779. The creator of figures 10.3 and 10.4, Dr. Steven Stoft, Ph.D., who runs the Zfacts website

where I found the charts , estimates that if Reagan and Bush I & II had balanced their budgets the national debt would be $13.5 trillion less. However Dr. Stoft assigned the continuing and ever growing cost of the Reagan and Bush II tax cuts that accrued during the Clinton and Obama presidencies to those two men. I would not compute it that way. Federal revenues have been out of wack with federal spending ever since Reagan slashed taxes on the rich and raised them on the poor. All Bush II did was to restore a small portion of the Reagan tax cut after Clinton cut a slightly larger portion out of it. Thus the national debt attributable to Reagan - Bush II tax cuts for the rich is significantly larger than $13.5 trillion. The lions share of the national debt is attributable to Ronald Reagan and his plan to eliminate social security, the rest of the new deal programs and government regulation in general. For Stoft's estimate, See, Stoft, Steven. October 24, 2014. National Debt Graph by President. ZFacts. (subject to revision) Retrieved from http://zfacts.com/p/318.html

780. Johnson, and Kwak, *13 Bankers: The Wall Street Takeover And The Next Financial Meltdown*. 135-136, 156-157, 92 - 131; The Financial Crisis Inquiry Commission. The Financial Crisis Inquiry Report Final Report On The Causes Of The Financial And Economic Crisis In The United States. (Washington D.C.: Government Printing Office, 2011) *GPO U.S. Government Printing Office*. Retrieved from http://www.gpo.gov/; Heffner, Thomas. May 31, 2012 Why "Free Trade" Devastates America. *Economy In Crisis*. Retrieved from http://economyincrisis.org/content/why-free-trade-hurts-america
781. Domestic policy of the Ronald Reagan administration. *Wikipedia The Free Encyclopedia.* (Wikipedia Foundation Inc.) Retrieved from http://en.wikipedia.org/wiki/Domestic_polic yof_the_Ronald_Reagan_administration
782. Economic policy of Bill Clinton. *Wikipedia The Free Encyclopedia.* (Wikipedia Foundation Inc.) Retrieved from http://en.wikipedia.org/wiki/EconomicpolicyofBill Clinton
783. Bush tax cuts. *Wikipedia The Free Encyclopedia.* (Wikipedia Foundation Inc.) Retrieved from http://en.wikipedia.org/wiki/Bush tax cuts
784. Smith, Allen W. October 11, 2013. Ronald Reagan and The Great Social Security Heist. *FedSmith*. Retrieved from http://www.fedsmith.com/ (quoting) Reagan, Ronald.
785. Ibid.
786. Ibid.
787. Ibid.
788. Ibid; Stockman, *The Triumph of Politics Why the Reagan Revolution Failed.*
789. Bush, George H. W., Video of Bush using the term "Voodoo Economics." Broadcast on NBC Nightly News. Ken Bode, correspondent forNBC Nightly News. February 10, 1982. (online in pdf and video). *NBC Learn K-12*. Retrieved from http://archives.nbc learn.com/portal/site/k-12/flatview?cuecard=33292
790. FRED Economic Data. Data updated January 1, 2015. Civilian Labor Force Participation Rate - Men. *Federal Reserve Bank of St. Louis*. (2015-1: 68.7 Percent) Retrieved from http://research.stlouisfed.org/fred2/series/LNU01300001
791. Clifton, Jim February 3, 2015. The Big Lie: 5.6% Unemployment. *Gallup*. Retrieved from

http://www.gallup.com/opinion/chairman/181469/big-lie-unemployment.aspx

792. Feinberg, Alec. March 10, 2011. Foreign Ownership of U.S. Companies Rising: Foreign Ownership of U.S. Companies 51% by 2033 with Skyrocketing U.S. Unemployment Projected due to the Trojan Horse Trade Deficit. *Economy In Crisis.* Retrieved from http://economyincrisis.org/content/foreign-ownership-us-companies-rising
793. Ibid.
794. Rugaber, Christopher S. December 17, 2013. Income Inequality Is Hurting The Economy, 3 Dozen Economists Say. *Huffington Post.* Retrieved from http://www.huffingtonpost.com/
795. Gardiner, Nile. November 30, 2012. 45 percent of US Democrats favour socialism. Fortunately most Americans still believe in capitalism. *The Telegraph.* Retrieved from http://blogs.telegraph.co.uk/
796. Newport, Frank. February 4, 2010. Socialism Viewed Positively by 36% of Americans. *Gallup.* Retrieved from http://www.gallup.com/.
797. Eichler, Alexander. December 29, 2011. Young People More Likely To Favor Socialism Than Capitalism: Pew. *Huffington Post.* Retrieved from http://www.huffingtonpost.com/
798. Obama used the phrase "new jobs of tomorrow" in a letter to Chicago Tribune. See, Obama, Barack Hussein. June 30, 2005. Why I oppose CAFTA: The proposed accord does less to protect U.S. labor than previous trade agreements, and does little to address environmental standards in the Central American countries. *Chicago Tribune.* Retrieved from http://articles.chicagotribune.com/2005-06-30/news/0506300212_1_cafta-central-american-countries-trade-agreements
799. Topaz, Jonathan. and Schreckinger, Ben. July 6, 2015. The Socialist Surge: The rise of Bernie Sanders is proving awkward for the Democratic Party. Politico. Retrieved from http://www.politico.com/story/2015/07/bernie-sanders-socialist-surge-119785#ixzz3fKDyp0Me
800. Bush not only believes in Jesus, he also believes that God wanted him to run for President. See, Harris, Paul. November 2, 2003. Bush says God chose him to lead his nation. *The Guardian.* Retrieved from http://www.theguardian.com/world/2003/nov/02/usa.religion
801. Compassionate conservatism. *Wikipedia The Free Encyclopedia.* (Wikipedia Foundation Inc.) Retrieved from http://en.wikipedia.org/wiki/Compassionate_conservatism
802. Miller, Steven P., May 18, 2014. The evangelical presidency: Reagan's dangerous love affair with the Christian right: How Reagan's landslide victory in 1980 made the Moral Majority a force to be reckoned with in American politics. *Salon.* Retrieved from http://www.salon.com/
803. Objectivist movement. *Wikipedia The Free Encyclopedia.* (Wikipedia Foundation Inc.) Retrieved from http://en.wikipedia.org/wiki/Objectivist_movement
804. Wolf, Tobias Barrington, August 14, 2012. The Virtue of Selfishness: Romney, Ryan and Rand. *Huff Post Politics.* Retrieved from http://www.huffingtonpost.com/
805. Smith, George H., October 23, 2012. Ayn Rand and Altruism, Part 1. *Libertarianism.org.* Retrieved from http://www.libertarianism.org/publications/essays/excursions/ayn-rand

-altruism-part-1
806. Objectivist movement. *Wikipedia The Free Encyclopedia.* (Wikipedia Foundation Inc.) Retrieved from http://en.wikipedia.org/wiki/Objectivist_movement
807. Greenspan, Alan. *The Age of Turbulence: Adventures In A New World.* (New York: The Penguin Press, 2007) 52
808. Ferguson, David. April 26, 2012. Under Catholic pressure Paul Ryan backs away from Rand, Objectivism. *Rawstory.* Retrieved from http://www.rawstory.com/rs/2012/04/under-catholic-pressure-paul-ryan-backs-away-from-rand-objectivism/; Weinger, Mackenzie. April 26, 2012. 7 politicians who praised Ayn Rand. Politico. Retrieved from http://www.politico.com/news/stories/0412/75667.html
809. Weinger, op. cit.
810. For a concise easy to digest summary of Lincoln's views on protectionism not otherwise cited in this book, See, The Lincoln Institute. Abraham Lincoln and the Tariff. *Abraham Lincoln's Classroom.* Retrieved from http://abrahamlincolnsclassroom.org/abraham-lincoln-in-depth/abraham-lincoln-and-the-tariff/
811. Monthly crude steel production archive. 1/1/13-12/31/14. *World Steel Association.* Retrieved from http://www.worldsteel.org/statistics/statistics-archive/monthly-steel-archive.html
812. Bird, Mike. October 8, 2014. China Just Overtook The US As The World's Largest Economy. *Business Insider.* Retrieved from http://www.businessinsider.com/
813. China's military rise and its increasing militarism is of great concern. My guess is you never heard of China's hypersonic missiles that fly ten times the speed of sound. See, Tarantola, Andrew. January 15, 2014. China's New Hypersonic Missile Can Scream Past US Air Defenses. *Gizmodo.* Retrieved from http://gizmodo.com/chinas-new-hypersonic-missile-can-scream-past-us-air-d-1501458331; Hoffman, Mike. January 14, 2014. Congress Reacts to Chinese Hypersonic Missile Test. *Defense Tech.* Retrieved from http://defensetech.org/2014/01/14/congress-reacts-to-chinese-hypersonic-missile-test/; Alexander, David. and Shalal, Andrea. Aug 25, 2014. Experimental U.S. Hypersonic Weapon Destroyed Seconds After Launch. *Reuters.* Retrieved from http://www.reuters.com/article/us-usa-military-hypersonic-idUSKBN0GP1ED20140825

Chapter 11. Recounting The Myths Of Free Trade.

814. Gottinger, Hans W., and Goosen, Mattheus F. A., Editors. *Strategies of Economic Growth and Catch Up: Industrial Policies and Management.* (New York: Nova Science Publishers, 2012); Cimoli, Mario., Dosi, Giovanni., and Stiglitz, Joseph. *Industrial Policy and Development: The Political Economy of Capabilities Accumulation.* (New York, Oxford University Press, 2009); Nash-Hoff, Michelle. *Can Manufacturing Be Saved? Why We Should and How We Can.* (La Mesa, California: MM Bernard Publications, 2009)
815. Brown, Sherrod. *Why American Trade Policy Has Failed; Myths of Free Trade.* (New York: The New Press, 2004, 2006)

816. Lodge's comment can be found on the back cover of Ian Fletcher's book, *Free Trade Doesn't Work: What Should Replace It and Why*. (Washington, D.C.: U.S. Business & Industry Council, 2010)

817. Chang, Ha-Joon. *Bad Samaritans: The Myth of Free Trade And The Secret History of Capitalism*. (New York: Bloomsbury Press, 2008); Brown, Sherrod. *Why American Trade Policy Has Failed; Myths of Free Trade*. (New York: The New Press, 2004, 2006); Prestowitz, Clyde. *The Betrayal of American Prosperity: Free Market Delusions, America's Decline, and How We Must Compete in the Post-Dollar Era*. (New York: Free Press, 2010); Fletcher, Ian. *Free Trade Doesn't Work: What Should Replace It and Why*. (Washington, D.C.: U.S. Business & Industry Council, 2010); Batra, Ravi. *The Myth of Free Trade: The Pooring of America*. (New York: Simon & Schuster, 1993); one of the cases mentioned above, involves past and continuing instances of the dumping and subsidization of semiconductor imports. In this case, there is clear evidence ; Reinert, Erik S. *How Rich Countries Got Rich ...and Why Poor Countries Stay Poor*. (New York: Carroll & Graf, 2007)

818. Senator Brown did not provide the source for his quote from Wei Jingsheng. See, Brown, op. cit. 97

819. Ibid., 98

820. Ibid., 97-109

821. Economy of Indonesia. *Wikipedia The Free Encyclopedia*. (Wikipedia Foundation Inc.) Retrieved from http://en.wikipedia.org/wiki/Economy_of_Indonesia; Chang, *Bad Samaritans: The Myth of Free Trade And The Secret History of Capitalism*. 156-157, 178;

822. For an excellent history and analysis of the development of functional democracy in Indonesia, See. Horowitz. Donald. *Constitutional Change and Democracy in Indonesia*. (New York: Cambridge University Press, 2013)

823. Economy of Indonesia. *Wikipedia The Free Encyclopedia*. (Wikipedia Foundation Inc.) Retrieved from http://en.wikipedia.org/wiki/Economy_of_Indonesia;

824. IFC Advisory Services In Indonesia. *The Indonesia Corporate Governance Manual*. (Jakarta: International Finance Corporation, 2014) 512, retrieved from http://www.ifc.org/wps/wcm/connect/64185f0042cc3ab0b145fd384c61d9f7/Indonesia_CG_Manual_Feb2014.pdf?MOD=AJPERES

825. Van der Schaar Investments B.V., Indonesian Masterplan for Acceleration and Expansion of Indonesia's Economic Development. *Indonesia Investments*. (unofficial summary). Retrieved from http://www.indonesia-investments.com/projects/government-development-plans/masterplan-for-acceleration-and-expansion-of-indonesias-economic-development-mp3ei/item306; Indonesia. March 6, 2013. Trade Policy Review Report. *World Trade Organization*. Retrieved from https://www.wto.org/english/tratop_e/tpr_e/g278_e.pdf

826. An obvious example of a country where a surplus of exports to the United States obtained by following a protectionist industrial policy helped to bring about and strengthen democracy is South Korea. See generally, Chang, *Bad Samaritans: The Myth of Free Trade And The Secret History of Capitalism*, 171-181

827. Ibid., 179

828. Ibid., 171-181
829. Johnson, Tim. June 17, 2012. Mexico's 'Maquiladora' Labor System Keeps Workers In Poverty. *McClatchy D.C.* Retrieved from http://www.mcclatchydc.com/2012/06/17/152220_mexicos-maquiladora-labor-system.html?rh=1
830. Economic history of Mexico. *Wikipedia The Free Encyclopedia.* (Wikipedia Foundation Inc.) Retrieved from http://en.wikipedia.org/wiki/Economic_history_of_Mexico
831. NAFTA's Broken Promises 1994-2013: Outcomes of the North American Free Trade Agreement. *Public Citizen.* Retrieved from http://www.citizen.org/documents/NAFTAs-Broken-Promises.pdf
832. Johnson, Tim. June 17, 2012. Mexico's 'Maquiladora' Labor System Keeps Workers In Poverty. *McClatchy D.C.* Retrieved from http://www.mcclatchydc.com/2012/06/17/152220_mexicos-maquiladora-labor-system.html?rh
833. Brown, *Why American Trade Policy Has Failed; Myths of Free Trade.* 99
834. Butler, Smedley D., America's Armed Forces: In Time of Peace: The Army. *Common Sense Magazine.* Volume 4, No. 11 (November, 1935) 8-12; (Excerpt online and downloadable in pdf by Furr, Grover) Retrieved at https://msuweb.montclair.edu/~furrg/Vietnam/butler.pdf
835. Brown, *Why American Trade Policy Has Failed; Myths of Free Trade.* 100-101
836. 1964 Brazilian coup d'état. *Wikipedia The Free Encyclopedia.* (Wikipedia Foundation Inc.) Retrieved from http://en.wikipedia.org/wiki/1964_Brazilian_coup_d'%C3%A9tat
837. 1973 Chilean coup d'état. *Wikipedia The Free Encyclopedia.* (Wikipedia Foundation Inc.) Retrieved from http://en.wikipedia.org/wiki/1973_Chilean_coup_d'%C3%A9tat
838. Contras. *Wikipedia The Free Encyclopedia.* (Wikipedia Foundation Inc.) Retrieved from http://en.wikipedia.org/wiki/Contras
839. Nobody does a better job of arguing that allowing other countries to dump products in America is a good idea than Professor Douglas Irwin at Dartmouth. But Professor Irwin does not take technological externalities, productivity losses, the destruction of our production ecosystem, wage inequities, and violations of Ricardo's limiting assumptions into account in evaluating the benefits of allowing dumping in particular, and free trade in general, even when our trading partners are also using currency manipulation and other protectionist measures in addition to dumping to take out entire high value industries. Professor Irwin's mind is so cocooned withing the comforting false assumptions of comparative advantage theory, he cannot see that the U.S. is literally transferring its comparative advantage to its protectionist trading partners like China by allowing them to systematic buy up American based companies and impose technology disclosure agreements on foreign companies that do business in China. See, Irwin, Douglas A., "Ch. 5. Relief from Foreign Competition: Antidumping and the Escape Clause." in Irwin, *Free Trade Under Fire.* 3rd. ed. (Princeton, New Jersey: Princeton University Press, 2009)
840. Ibid.; For a view contrary to Irwin's, See, Prestowitz, Clyde. *The Betrayal of American Prosperity: Free Market Delusions, America's Decline, and How We Must Compete in the Post-Dollar Era.* (New York: Free Press, 2010) 1-12, 96-102, 107, 171, 269, 288

841. Irwin, op. cit; For a view contrary to Irwin's, See, Prestowitz, op. cit.
842. Irwin, op. cit; For a view contrary to Irwin's, See, Prestowitz, op. cit.
843. Irwin, op. cit; For a view contrary to Irwin's, See, Prestowitz, op. cit.
844. Eckes, 257-278
845. Chimerline, Lawrence, Mastel, Greg, Szamosszegi, Andrew. and Magnus, John. *Strong Trade Laws As The Foundation of a Sound American Trade Policy Enforcing the Rules.* (Washington, DC.: American Alliance For Manufacturing, 2007) z
846. Ibid., 20
847. Eckes, 178-289
848. Navarro and Autry, *Death by China: Confronting the Dragon - A Global Call To Action* 5-6, 63-66; Talent, Jim. August 26, 2014. The U.S. Giant Slumbers: The U.S. could check China, but our leaders need to wake up to the threat. *National Review.* Retrieved from http://www.nationalreview.com/article/386272/us-giant-slumbers-jim-talent; Ensinger, Dustin. December 11, 2010. China Is World's Top Dumping Offender. Economy In Crisis. Retrieved from http://economyincrisis.org/

Chapter 12. So, Now What?

849. Chang, Ha-Joon. *Bad Samaritans: The Myth of Free Trade And The Secret History of Capitalism.* (New York: Bloomsbury Press, 2008)
850. Chang, Ha-Joon. *23 Things They Don't Tell You About Capitalism.* (New York: Bloomsbury Press, 2010)
851. Ibid., 242.
852. Unknown Author. "Ebenezer Lennox Scroggie (1792-1836)." *The Literary Cemetery.* Retrieved on April 1, 2015 from http://theliterarycemetery.blogspot.com/2013/05/ebenezer-lennox-scroggie-1792-1836.html; I would not put too much stock in the first description of the inspiration for Scrooge's name in the text if I were you, but similar claims can be found at several other websites. See for eg., Geer, Samuel. "Ebenezer Lennox Scroggie." (Burial Record) *Find a Grave Memorial.* Retrieved on July 18, 2016 from http://www.findagrave.com/cgi-bin/fg.cgi?page=gr&GRid=102003197; I found the word scrouge in an old dictionary. See, "Scrouge" *Websters New College Dictionary.* (Springfield, Massachusetts: G. & C. Merriam Company, 1981); See, Ebenezer Scrooge. *Wikipedia The Free Encyclopedia.* (Wikipedia Foundation Inc.) Retrieved from https://en.m.wikipedia.org/wiki/Ebenezer_Scrooge
853. *It's a Wonderful Life.* Dir. Frank Capra. Perf. James Stewart, Donna Reed, Lionel Barrymore, and Thomas Mitchell. RKO. 1946. Film.
854. *Wall Street.* Dir. Oliver Stone. Perf. Michael Douglas, Martin Sheen, Charlie Sheen, and Daryl Hannah. Twentieth Century Fox. 1987. Film.; *Wall Street: Money Never Sleeps.* Dir. Oliver Stone. Perf. Michael Douglas, Shia LaBeouf, Josh Brolin, Carey Mulligan, Frank Langella, and Eli Wallach, Twentieth Century Fox. 2010. Film.
855. *The Wolf of Wall Street.* Dir. Martin Scorsese. Perf. Leonardo DiCaprio, Jonah Hill,

Margot Robbie, Kyle Chandler, Rob Reiner, Jon Bernthal, Jon Favreau, Jean Dujardin, Joanna Lumley, and Matthew McConaughey. Paramount Pictures. 2013. Film.

856. Roose, Kevin. May 29, 2013. Why Are College Students Flocking to Economics? *New York Magazine*. Retrieved from http://nymag.com/; Rampell, Catherine. December 21, 2011.Out of Harvard, and Into Finance. *The New York Times Economix Blog*. Retrieved from http://economix.blogs.nytimes.com/

857. Camerer, Colin F., and Fehr, Ernst. January 6, 2006. When Does "Economic Man" Dominate Social Behavior? *Science*. Vol. 311. (DOI:10.1126/science.1110600) p.47

858. For an excellent look at Ayn Rand's selfist philosophy which mentions Greenspan's involvement with Rand and Rand's effect on society, See, Weiss, Gary. *Ayn Rand Nation: The Hidden Struggle For America's Soul*. 1st. ed. (New York: St. Martin's Press, 2012); See additionally, Monbiot, George. March 5, 2012. How Ayn Rand became the new right's version of Marx. *The Guardian*. Retrieved from http://www.theguardian.com/

859. See, Think Again: Alterman, Eric. August 2, 2012. Thoughts on Milton Friedman and Gore Vidal. *Center For American Progress*. Retrieved from https://www.american progress.org/

860. Friedman, M. Introduction to Capitalism and Freedom in Friedman, M. *Capitalism and Freedom*. (Chicago: University of Chicago Press, 1962)

861. *Star Trek II: The Wrath of Khan*. Dir. Nicholas Meyer. Perf. William Shatner, Ricardo Montalbán, Leonard Nimoy, DeForest Kelley, James Doohan, George Takei, Nichelle Nichols, Ike Eisenmann, Walter Koenig, Kirstie Alley, Bibi Besch and Merritt Butrick. Paramount Pictures Corporation. 1982. Film.

862. *Randbot*: A soulless individual who, following the philosophy of Ayn Rand, places their self interest at the center of the universe. To them, their self interest is above God (who they deny) and country. Synonym: Randroid. For an example of usage, See, Scheer, Peter Z., November 13, 2011. Ayn Rand Fans Mortified by DVD Slander. *Truthdig*. Retrieved from http://www.truthdig.com/arts_culture/item/ayn_rand_fans_mortified_by_dvd_slander_20111113

863. Armstrong, Ari. September 12, 2013. Spock's Illogic: 'The Needs of the Many Outweigh the Needs of the Few.' *The Objective Standard*. Retrieved from https://www.the objectivestandard.com/2013/09/spocks-illogic-the-needs-of-the-many-outweigh-the-needs-of-the-few/

864. Ibid.

865. *Lost In Space*. Produced and Directed by Irwin Allen. Perf. Guy Williams, June Lockhart, Mark Goddard, Marta Kristen, Angela Cartwright, Billy Mumy, Jonathan Harris, (as Dr. Zachary Smith). CBS. September 15, 1965 - March 6, 1968. TV Series.

866. Rubinstein, Ariel. A Sceptics Comment On The Study Of Economics. *The Economic Journal*, 116. March, 2006. C1–C9

867. Ibid.

868. For an excellent discussion about the role of positive "ladder" externalities in bringing economic growth and prosperity, See, Fletcher, Ian. (Chapter 9) "Where Does Growth Really Come From" in Fletcher, Ian. *Free Trade Doesn't Work: What Should Replace It*

and Why. (Washington, D.C.: U.S. Business & Industry Council, 2010) 183-211

869. Marwell, Gerald and Ames, Ruth E., Economists Free Ride, Does Anyone Else? Experiments on The Provision of Public Goods, IV. *Journal of Public Economics*. Vol. 15, Issue 3, June, 1981. 295-310

870. Carter, John R., and Irons, Michael D., Are Economists Different, and If So, Why? *Journal of Economic Perspectives*. Vol 5. No. 2. Spring, 1991. DOI: 10.1257/jep.5.2.171. p. 171-177

871. Frank, Robert H., Gilovich, Thomas and Regan, Dennis T., Does Studying Economics Inhibit Cooperation? *Journal of Economic Perspectives*. Vol. 7. No. 2. Spring, 1993. 159-171

872. Franka, Björn and Schulzeb, Günther G., Does Economics Make Citizens Corrupt. *Journal of Economic Behavior & Organization*. Volume 43. Issue 1. September, 2000. 101-113; See additionally, Mortimer, Josiah. September 24, 2014. Confirmed: Economists Are Liars. *Huff Post*. Retrieved from http://www.huffingtonpost.co.uk/josiah-mortimer/economics-research_b_5619894.html; Weissmann, Jordan. December 18, 2012. Research Says: Studying Economics Turns You Into a Liar. The Atlantic. Retrieved from https://www.theatlantic.com/business/archive/2012/12/research-says-studying-economics-turns-you-into-a-liar/266423/

873. "Attributed to Richard Thaler." Economics Quotes. *Quotes Archive*. Retrieved from http://quotes.cat-v.org/economics

874. Chang, Ha-Joon. *Bad Samaritans: The Myth of Free Trade And The Secret History of Capitalism*. 217

875. Chang, Ha-Joon. *23 Things They Don't Tell You About Capitalism*. (New York: Bloomsbury Press, 2010) 247-248

876. Durono, Ben. July 31, 2012. 9 Unforgettable Quotes From Milton Friedman. *Business Insider*. Retrieved on April 17, 2015 from http://www.businessinsider.com/milton-friedman-quotes-2012-7; (quote cited to) Hawkins, John. February 25, 2012. An Interview With Milton Friedman. *Right Wing News*. Retrieved on April 17, 2015 from http://right wingnews.com/interviews/an-interview-with-milton-friedman-2/; Wikiquote, The Free Quote Compendium. Retrieved on April 17, 2015 from http://en.wikiquote.org/wiki/Milton_Friedman (quote cited to) Viguerie, Richard A., *Conservatives Betrayed : How George W. Bush And Other Big Government Republicans Hijacked The Conservative Cause* (Los Angeles: Bonus Books, 2006) 46; Prante, Gerald. July 31, 2006. Happy 94th Birthday Milton Friedman. *Tax Foundation*. Retrieved on April 17, 2015 from http://taxfoundation.org/blog/happy-94th-birthday-milton-friedman; Posted by unknown person. November 9, 2012. Milton Friedman in His Own Words. *Becker Friedman Institute For Research In Economics The University of Chicago*. Retrieved on April 17, 2015 from https://bfi.uchicago.edu/post/milton-friedman-his-own-words

877. See for eg., Sreenivasan, Hari. Interview of Sudeep Reddy. September 6, 2014. U.S. Unemployment Decrease Reflects More Workforce Dropouts. (transcript and video) *PBS NewsHour*. Retrieved from http://www.pbs.org/newshour/bb/reddy/

878. See generally, Testimony of the Honorable Dennis C. Shea. December 5, 2012. Hearing

on The Impact of International Technology Transfer on American Research and Development. United States House of Representatives. *Committee on Science, Space, and Technology Subcommittee on Investigations and Oversight*. Retrieved from https://science.house.gov /sites/republicans.science.house.gov/files/documents/HHRG -112-SY21-WState-DShea-20121205.pdf; See generally, Testimony of the Honorable Robert D. Atkinson. December 5, 2012. Hearing on The Impact of International Technology Transfer on American Research and Development. United States House of Representatives. *Committee on Science, Space, and Technology Subcommittee on Investigations and Oversight*. Retrieved from https://science.house.gov/sites/republicans.science.house.gov/files/documents/HHRG-112-SY21-WState-RAtkinson-20121205.pdf

879. Ibid.; Prestowitz, Clyde. *The Betrayal of American Prosperity: Free Market Delusions, America's Decline, and How We Must Compete in the Post-Dollar Era*, 273-274. The quoted phrase is found at p. 274.
880. Duhigg, Charles. and Bradsher, Keith. January 21, 2012. How the U.S. Lost Out On iPhone Work. *The New York Times*. Retrieved from http://www.nytimes.com/
881. About Paul Craig Roberts. *Institute For Political Economy*. Retrieved on April 25, 2015 from http://www.paulcraigroberts.org/pages/about-paul-craig-roberts/; Paul Craig Roberts. *Wikipedia The Free Encyclopedia.* (Wikipedia Foundation Inc.) Retrieved from http://en.wikipedia.org/wiki/Paul_Craig_Roberts
882. Roberts, Paul Craig. May 24 2005. A Reputation in Tatters. *Center For Research In Globalisation*. (Previously published May 17, 2005 by LewRockwell.com) Retrieved from http://globalresearch.ca/articles/ROB505A.html; Paul Craig Roberts. *Wikipedia The Free Encyclopedia.* (Wikipedia Foundation Inc.) Retrieved from http://en.wikipedia.org/wiki/Paul_Craig_Roberts
883. Roberts, Paul Craig. *The Failure of Laissez-Faire Capitalism and the Economic Erosion of the West*, (Atlanta: Clarity Press, 2013)
884. Roberts, Paul Craig. January 28, 2014. How Junk Economists Help The Rich Impoverish The Working Class. *Institute For Political Economy*. Retrieved from http://www.paul craig roberts.org/2014/01/28/junk-economists-help-rich-impoverish-working-class-paul-craig-roberts/
885. About Paul Craig Roberts. *Institute For Political Economy*. Retrieved on April 25, 2015 from http://www.paulcraigroberts.org/pages/about-paul-craig-roberts/; Paul Craig Roberts. *Wikipedia The Free Encyclopedia.* (Wikipedia Foundation Inc.) Retrieved from http://en.wikipedia.org/wiki/Paul_Craig_Roberts
886. Paul Craig Roberts. *Wikipedia The Free Encyclopedia.* (Wikipedia Foundation Inc.) Retrieved from http://en.wikipedia.org/wiki/Paul_Craig_Roberts
887. Ibid.
888. Ibid.; *The Supply-Side Revolution: An Insider's Account of Policymaking in Washington* (Cambridge: Harvard University Press, 1984)
889. Chang, *23 Things They Don't Tell You About Capitalism*. 252
890. See for eg., Dick Gephardt on Free Trade. *On The Issues: Every Political Leader on Every Issue*. Retrieved on April 25, 2015 from http://www.ontheissues.org/house/Dick_

Gephardt_Free_Trade.htm

891. Jones, Sebastian. September 30, 2009. Dick Gephardt's Spectacular Sellout / As a politician he was a champion of progressive reform. Now he lobbies for its enemies. (also published in The Nation on October 19, 2009) *The Nation*. Retrieved from http://www.thenation.com/article/dick-gephardts-spectacular-sellout

892. See for eg., DelReal, Jose A., October 13, 2014. Elizabeth Warren: Obama 'protected Wall Street' over middle class families. *The Washington Post*. Retrieved from http://www.washingtonpost.com/blogs/post-politics; Kelly, Jack. November 24, 2013. Obama's Policies Have Helped Wall St. Fat Cats. *Real Clear Politics*. Retrieved from http://www.realclearpolitics.com/articles/2013/11/24/obamas_policies_have_helped_wall_st_fat _cats _120768.html; Sirota, David. January 29, 2013. Barack Obama, Wall Street co-conspirator: From appointments of Lanny Breuer to Mary Jo White, the president has let big banks off the hook at every turn. *Salon*. Retrieved from http://www.salon.com/; Curry, Bill. July 27, 2014. My party has lost its soul: Bill Clinton, Barack Obama and the victory of Wall Street Democrats: A former Clinton aide on how Democrats lost their way chasing Wall Street cash, and new populism the party needs. *Salon*. Retrieved from http://www.salon.com/

893. Jones, Jeffrey M., October 11, 2013. In U.S., Perceived Need for Third Party Reaches New High: Twenty-Six Percent Believe Democratic and Republican Parties Do Adequate Job. *Gallup Politics*. Retrieved from http://www.gallup.com/poll/165392/perceived-need -third-party-reaches-new-high.aspx; Jones, Jeffrey M., September 24, 2014. Americans Continue to Say a Third Political Party Is Needed. *Gallup Politics*. Retrieved from http://www.gallup.com/poll/177284/americans-continue-say-third-political-party-needed.aspx

894. Jones, Jeffrey M., September 10, 2010. Americans OK Allowing Tax Cuts for Wealthy to Expire: One in three favor keeping tax cuts for all taxpayers. *Gallup Politics*. Retrieved from http://www.gallup.com/poll/142940/americans-allowing-tax-cuts-wealthy-expire.aspx

895. Republicans and Democrats pay the deserved price of political death when they argue that social security benefits should be cut, or the program privatized. Consequently, many politicians lie about their view of social security. That's what Ronald Reagan did when he claimed to be saving social security when he raised social security taxes to defray the cost of huge income tax cuts for the rich, as discussed in Chapter Ten. For an informative article which discusses how the Republocrats will deal with the Social Security "third rail" issue in the 2016, See, Eskow, Richard J., April 22, 2015. The Surprise Issue of the 2016 Election? *Huff Post Politics*. Retrieved from http://www.huffingtonpost.com/

896. Sargent, Greg. February 9, 2015. Republicans planning stealth attack on Social Security, Democrats fear. *The Washington Post*. Retrieved from http://www.washingtonpost.com/; Garofalo, Pat. April 1, 2014. Ryan's Kabuki Social Security Dance: Republicans would love it if President Obama had some ideas for cutting Social Security. *U.S. News & World Report*. Retrieved from http://www.usnews.com/opinion/blogs/; Waldman, Paul. January 26, 2015. Why is GOP going after Social Security? *CNN*. Retrieved from http://www.cnn.com/2015/01/26/opinion/waldman-social-security/

897. Recognizing that the majority of Americans disapprove of widening income inequality, joblessness, low wages and humongous trade deficits, the Republicans came up with the Tea Party scam to make Americans believe there are true "populist' reformers within the GOP. That's how I see the Tea Party. Its followers appear to deny that global warming is human caused, back tax cuts, back repealing Obamacare, want to scale back social security benefits as much as possible, and believe in laissez faire capitalism. For a good article which discusses their phony claims of wanting to fix trade policy, See, Carter, Zach and Siddiqui, Sabrina. December 3, 2014. Strange Bedfellows Are Blocking The McConnell-Obama Trade Deal. *Huff Post Politics*. Retrieved from http://www.huffington post.com/2014/12/03/mitch-mcconnell-tpp-tea-party_n_6182126.html; See also, Lester, Simon. November 18, 2013. (Commentary) The Tea Party and Trade. *International Economic Law and Policy Blog*. Retrieved from http://worldtradelaw.typepad.com/ielp blog/2013/11/the-tea-party-and-trade.html

898. Jilani, Zaid. September 30, 2010. Most Tea Partiers Think Free Trade Agreements That Tea Party Candidates Support Are Bad For The Country. *Think Progress*. Retrieved from http://thinkprogress.org/politics/2010/09/30/121808/tea-partiers-trade-bad/; Harwood, John. September 28, 2010 53% in US Say Free Trade Hurts Nation: NBC/WSJ Poll. *CNBC*. Retrieved from http://www.cnbc.com/id/39407846;

899. Obama Approval Index History. *Rasmussen Reports*. Retrieved on April 27, 2015 from http://www.rasmussenreports.com/public_content/politics/obama_administration/obama_approval_index_history

900. For two years running Gallop polls have found upwards of 60% of Americans feel a third political party is needed to govern the nation. See, Jones, Jeffrey M., October 11, 2013. In U.S., Perceived Need for Third Party Reaches New High: Twenty-Six Percent Believe Democratic and Republican Parties Do Adequate Job. *Gallup Politics*. Retrieved from http://www.gallup.com/poll/165392/perceived-need-third-party-reaches-new-high.aspx; Jones, Jeffrey M., September 24, 2014. Americans Continue to Say a Third Political Party Is Needed. *Gallup Politics*. Retrieved from http://www.gallup.com/poll/177284/americans -continue-say-third-political-party-needed.aspx

Chapter 13. The Who, What, When, Where, and How of Restoring American - and A Bit More On Why We Must Do It.

901. Bellow, Adam. *In Praise of Nepotism: A Natural History*, (New York: Doubleday, 2003)
902. Ibid., 486.
903. Ibid., 508
904. Ibid., 23
905. Ibid., 23
906. See for eg., Bellow, op. cit., 410-413
907. Ibid., 24-25
908. Definition of Nepotism. *Merriam Webster*. Retrieved on March 6, 2015 from http://www.merriam-webster.com/dictionary/nepotism

909. See for eg., VandenDolder, Tess. March 11, 2014. All in the Family: 7 Examples of Nepotism in the Political Class. *DCInno*. Retrieved from http://dcinno.streetwise.co/2014/03/11/examples-of-nepotism-in-washington-dc/#; Malone, Claire. February 27, 2014. New Nepotism: Get Elected, Get Your Kids Rich: Washington Is Spoiled Rotten. *The Daily Beast*. Retrieved from http://www.thedailybeast.com/; Stephens-Davidowitz, Seth., March 21, 2015. Just How Nepotistic Are We? *The New York Times*. Retrieved from http://www.nytimes.com/; Pareene, Alex. August 21, 2013. The rich, summed up: Nepotism, cronyism, narcissism: The New York Times' Andrew Ross Sorkin defends corrupt hiring practices. *Salon*. Retrieved from http://www.salon.com/; Bloom, Trystyn. November 11, 2014. Government Report Finds Rampant Nepotism At The DOJ. *The Daily Caller*. Retrieved from http://dailycaller.com/2014/11/11/government-report-finds-rampant-nepotism-at-justice-department/; For a quick look at my home state of Illinois, check this out: Editorial. March 9, 2015. The stench at IDOT: Wrongdoing in the Illinois Department of Transportation deserves attention from law enforcement. *The News Gazette*. Retrieved from http://www.news-gazette.com/opinion/editorials/2015-03-09/stench-idot.html; Schouten, Fredreka., and Schnaars, Christopher. March 18, 2013. Lawmakers Add Relatives To Campaign Payrolls. *USA Today*. Retrieved from http://www.usatoday.com/

910. Kreisler, Harry. April 12, 1999. Abner Mikva Interview: Conversations with History. *Institute of International Studies, UC Berkeley*. Retrieved from http://globetrotter.berkeley.edu/people/Mikva/mikva-con2.html

911. Davey, Monica. December 7, 2011. Blagojevich Sentenced to 14 Years in Prison. *The New York Times*. Retrieved from http://www.nytimes.com/

912. Sirota, David. April 11, 2014. In Chicago, You Have to Pay to Play With Public Money. *TruthDig*. Retrieved from http://www.truthdig.com/

913. Washington, Harold. February 6, 1986. Speech to students at Loop College, now known as Harold Washington College, 30 E. Lake Street, Chicago, Illinois. Audio mp3 file was obtained courtesy of John Dempsey, News Anchor, WLS AM 890 Radio in Chicago, IL and Cumulus Media. Additional information regarding Mayor Washington's speech was provided through the courtesy of Bill Cameron, Reporter for WLS AM 890.

914. See for eg., Ylisela Jr., James. November 20, 2013. Michael Madigan Is the King of Illinois The Democrat has ruled the statehouse for decades. At age 71, he's as powerful as ever. But his latest moves make you wonder: What does Madigan really want? Chicago Magazine. Retrieved from http://www.chicagomag.com/; Chase, Brett., Schroedter, Andrew., Herguth Robert., and Rehkamp., Patrick. February 1, 2015. Suburban Chicago Nepotism Is An Entrenched Family Business. *Chicago Sun Times*. Retrieved from http://chicago.suntimes.com/; Simpson, Dick., Nowlan, James., Gradel, Thomas J., Mouritsen Zmuda, Melissa., Sterrett, David., and Cantor, Douglas. April 18, 2012. Chicago and Illinois, Leading the Pack in Corruption: Anti-Corruption Report Number 5. *University of Illinois at Chicago Department of Political Science*. Retrieved fromhttp://pols.uic.edu/docs/default-source/chicago_politics/anti-corruption_reports/leadingthepack.pdf?sfvrsn=2; Koeneman, Keith. July 17, 2013. Is Nepotism Dying in Illinois?

Huffington Post. Retrieved from http://www.huffingtonpost.com/; In answer to the question by Keith Koeneman in the foregoing article the answer is *apparently not*. See, Spielman, Fran. February 4, 2015. Mell's Office Space Gift To Daughter Sparks Demand For Probe. *Chicago Sun Times*. Retrieved from http://chicago.suntimes.com/; Kreisler, Harry. April 12, 1999. Abner Mikva Interview: Conversations with History. *Institute of International Studies, UC Berkeley*. Retrieved from http://globetrotter.berkeley.edu/people/Mikva/mikva-con2.html

915. Powerless Stooge. November 10, 2008. Definition of Nepocracy. *Urban Dictionary*. Retrieved from http://www.urbandictionary.com/define.php?term=Nepocracy; See also, Nepocracy. *DefiniThing*. Retrieved on August 17, 2016 from http://definithing.com/nepocracy/

916. See for eg., Bellow Adam. In Praise of Nepotism (July/August print ed.) *The Atlantic*. Retrieved from http://www.theatlantic.com/magazine/archive/2003/07/in-praise-of-nepotism/302753/

917. At the start of 2015, 43 percent of Americans polled identified themselves as political independents, 36 percent of Americans saw themselves as democrats, and 26 percent of Americans saw themselves as republicans. See, Jones, Jeffrey M., January 7, 2015. In U.S., New Record 43% Are Political Independents. *Gallup Politics*. Retrieved from http://www.gallup.com/poll/180440/new-record-political-independents.aspx; For two years running Gallop polls have found upwards of 60% of Americans feel a third political party is needed to govern the nation. See, Jones, Jeffrey M., October 11, 2013. In U.S., Perceived Need for Third Party Reaches New High: Twenty-Six Percent Believe Democratic and Republican Parties Do Adequate Job. *Gallup Politics*. Retrieved from http://www.gallup.com/poll/165392/perceived-need-third-party-reaches-new-high.aspx; Jones, Jeffrey M., September 24, 2014. Americans Continue to Say a Third Political Party Is Needed. *Gallup Politics*. Retrieved from http://www.gallup.com/poll/177284/americans-continue-say-third-political-party-needed.aspx; A majority view free trade agreements as harmful to America. See, Murray, Sara and Belkin Douglas. Americans Sour on Trade Majority Say Free-Trade Pacts Have Hurt U.S.; Wedge Issue In Some Races. (Louise Radnofsky and Jim Carlton contributed). *The Wall Street Journal*. Retrieved from http://online.wsj.com/; NAFTA's Broken Promises 1994 -2013: Outcomes of the North American Free Trade Agreement. *Public Citizen*. Retrieved from http://www.citizen.org/documents/NAFTAs-Broken-Promises.pdf

918. See generally, Subramanian, Arvind. *Eclipse: Living in the Shadow of China's Economic Dominance*. (Washington, DC: Peterson Institute for International Economics, 2011); Navarro, Peter., and Autry, Gene., *Death by China: Confronting the Dragon - A Global Call To Action*. (Upper Saddle River, NJ: Prentice Hall, 2011); Mosher, Steven W. *Hegemon: China's Plan to Dominate Asia and the World*. (San Francisco: Encounter Books, 2000); Buckley, Chris. February 28, 2010. China PLA Officer Urges Challenging U.S. Dominance. *Reuters U.S. Ed.* Retrieved from http://www.reuters.com/article/; Mearsheimer, John. September 17, 2004 Why China's Rise Will Not Be Peaceful.

University of Chicago. Retrieved on May 17, 2015 from http://mearsheimer.uchicago.edu/

pdfs/A0034b.pdf; Oualaalou, David. February 8, 2015. US Era of Dominance Is Dwindling as China Takes Over the World Economy. *Huff Post Politics*. Retrieved from http://www.huffingtonpost.com/

919. Articles about another economic collapse are easy to find. Even Alan Greenspan has predicted that a "significant correction" is on the way. See, Wile, Rob. July 30, 2014. Greenspan: A 'Significant' Market Correction Has To Come. *Business Insider*. Retrieved from http://www.businessinsider.com/
920. Min, Qin. February 24, 2014. Seeking a Hit, Lenovo Buys Motorola Mobility and 2,000 Patents. *Caixin*. Retrieved from http://english.caixin.com/2014-02-24/100642427.html
921. Ibid.
922. For the last fifty years the wages of most U.S,. workers have either fallen or failed to budge in real terms. See, Desilver, Drew. October 9, 2014. For most workers, real wages have barely budged for decades. *Pew Research Center*. Retrieved from http://www.pew research.org/fact-tank/2014/10/09/for-most-workers-real-wages-have-barely-budged-for-decades/; Chinese wages however have been rising. See, Bradsher, Keith. January 9, 2014. Even as Wages Rise, China Exports Grow. *New York Times*. Retrieved from http://www.nytimes.com/
923. See, Denning, Steve. January 8, 2013. Big Banks and Derivatives: Why Another Financial Crisis Is Inevitable. *Forbes*. Retrieved from http://www.forbes.com/; U.S. banks own about $280 trillion worth of derivatives. See, Eavis, Peter. September 3, 2014. Regulators Propose Rule to Reduce Risk of Derivatives. *The New York Times*. Retrieved from http://dealbook.nytimes.com/
924. Prestowitz, Clyde. January 30, 2014. The All-Too-Real Costs Of Free Trade To Average Americans. Los Angeles Times. Retrieved from http://www.latimes.com/
925. See discussion and authorities cited in Chapter 3 of this book.
926. Duhigg, Charles and Bradsher, Keith. January 21, 2012. How the U.S. Lost Out On iPhone Work. *The New York Times*. Retrieved from http://www.nytimes.com/
927. Mutikani, Lucia . (Via Reuters) August 21, 2013. 75 Percent Of Jobs Created This Year Were Part-Time Due To Weak Economy, Obamacare Concerns. *Huff Post Business*. Retrieved from http://www.huffingtonpost.com/; Diamond, Dan. September 4, 2014. Part-Time Jobs Are Increasing. But Don't Blame Obamacare - Yet. *Forbes*. Retrieved from http://www.forbes.com/
928. Kurtzleben, Danielle. May 4, 2012. When An Unemployment Rate Decline is Bad News: The decline in the jobless rate is not the positive news it may seem to be. *U.S. News & World Report*. Retrieved from http://www.usnews.com/news/; Kurtzleben, Danielle. May 2, 2012. Long-Term Unemployment a Problem That Won't Go Away: Long-term joblessness does not spare older or well-educated workers. *U.S. News & World Report*. Retrieved from http://www.usnews.com/news/; Durden, Tyler. April 3, 2015. Americans Not In The Labor Force Soar To Record 93.2 Million As Participation Rate Drops To February 1978 Levels. *Zero Hedge*. Retrieved from http://www.zerohedge.com/news/; Spence, Michael. Globalization and Unemployment: The Downside of Integrating Markets. *Foreign Affairs*. July/August 2011 Issue. Retrieved from https://www.foreign

affairs.com/

929. Bergen, Kathy. February 2, 2014. After 2 decades in Illinois, Chinese trailblazer looks to new challenge: Head of Elgin-based Wanxiang America boosts outreach to developing markets overseas. *Chicago Tribune*. Retrieved from http://articles.chicagotribune.com/

930. Bergen, op. cit.; Bergen reports that Wanxiang America has long sought inroads into the electric vehicle market, recently purchasing leading American high tech battery maker, A123 Systems towards that end. Using technology acquired from A123 will help Wanxiang to enter the EV market, most probably according to Bergen in China first. It is therefore inconceivable that Wanxiang America will build electric vehicles in America. Wanxiang will undoubtedly put its production plant(s) in China to take advantage of cheap labor, lax environmental laws and closeness to its market. Bergen nonetheless tries to spin the disastrous loss of auto manufacturing in America into a win for America workers, cities and states. It is instead a loss for our workers, cities and states and a threat to our military forces as China's economic power continues to grow relative to the U.S. and the military threat China poses continues to escalate.

931. Ghosn, Carlos. February 17, 2013. China's Green Drivers. Business Today. Retrieved from http://businesstoday.intoday.in/story/carlos-ghosn-on-china-green-drivers/1/191975.html

932. See generally, Subramanian, Arvind. *Eclipse: Living in the Shadow of China's Economic Dominance*. (Washington, DC: Peterson Institute for International Economics, 2011); Navarro, Peter., and Autry, Gene., *Death by China: Confronting the Dragon - A Global Call To Action*. (Upper Saddle River, NJ: Prentice Hall, 2011); Mosher, Steven W. *Hegemon: China's Plan to Dominate Asia and the World*. (San Francisco: Encounter Books, 2000); Buckley, Chris. February 28, 2010. China PLA Officer Urges Challenging U.S. Dominance. *Reuters U.S. Ed.* Retrieved from http://www.reuters.com/article/; Mearsheimer, John. September 17, 2004 Why China's Rise Will Not Be Peaceful. University of Chicago. Retrieved on May 17, 2015 from http://mearsheimer.uchicago.edu/pdfs/A0034b.pdf; Oualaalou, David. February 8, 2015. US Era of Dominance Is Dwindling as China Takes Over the World Economy. *Huff Post Politics*. Retrieved from http://www.huffingtonpost.com/

933. Rapoza, Kenneth. June 27, 2013. The Foreign Companies That Are Buying Up America. *Forbes*. Retrieved from http://www.forbes.com/

934. See generally, Prestowitz, *The Betrayal of American Prosperity: Free Market Delusions, America's Decline, and How We Must Compete in the Post-Dollar Era*, 256-279; Fletcher, *Free Trade Doesn't Work: What Should Replace It and Why*, 71; Navarro and Autry, *Death by China: Confronting the Dragon - A Global Call To Action*. 49-76; Chang, *Bad Samaritans: The Myth of Free Trade And The Secret History of Capitalism*, 26-31

935. Stumo, Michael. May 18, 2014. USTR Dangerously Ignores Balance of Trade. *Economy In Crisis*. Retrieved from http://economyincrisis.org/content/ustr-dangerously-ignores-balance-of-trade

936. Bolton, Alexander. Needham, Vicky. January 29, 2014. Reid shunts TPA onto slow

track. *The Hill*. Retrieved from http://thehill.com/homenews/senate/196853-reid-rejects-obamas-plea-for-trade-power
937. Zagorsky, Jay. January 3, 2017. Column: I'm predicting an economic recession in 2017. Are you ready? *WTTW PBS Newshour*. Retrieved from http://www.pbs.org/newshour/making-sense/get-ready-economic-recession-coming-2017/; Hans, Peter. December 27, 2016. Recession in 2017? *Forbes*. Retrieved from http://www.forbes.com/sites/peterhans/2016/12/27/recession-in-2017/#57bec5439b6f; Long, Heather. June 19, 2016. The Next President Will Likely Face a Recession. *CNN Money*. Retrieved from http://money.cnn.com/2016/06/19/news/economy/donald-trump-hillary-clinton-recession/index.html; Gurdus, Elizabeth. January 25, 2017. Here's why the Trump Rally won't last, says former US Labor Secretary Robert Reich. *CNBC*. Retrieved from http://www.cnbc.com/2017/01/25/heres-why-the-trump-rally-wont-last-says-former-us-labor-secretary.html; Tencer, Daniel. January 20, 2017.Trump Setting Up Repeat Of '29 Market Crash: Nobel-Winning Economist. *Huffington Post Canada*. Retrieved from http://www.huffington post.ca/2017/01/19/robert-shiller-donald-trump-stock-market-crash_n_14268676.html
938. Snyder, Michael. February 2, 2014. You Can Buy A House For One Dollar Or Less In Economically Depressed Cities All Over America. *The Economic Collapse*. Retrieved from http://theeconomiccollapseblog.com/archives/you-can-buy-a-house-for-one-dollar-or-less-in-economically-depressed-cities-all-over-america
939. Ibid.
940. Ibid.
941. Searcey, Dionne and Gebeloff, Robert. January 25, 2015. Middle Class Shrinks Further as More Fall Out Instead of Climbing Up. *The New York Times*. Retrieved from http://www.nytimes.com/
942. Murray, Sara and Belkin Douglas. Americans Sour on Trade Majority Say Free-Trade Pacts Have Hurt U.S.; Wedge Issue In Some Races. (Louise Radnofsky and Jim Carlton contributed). *The Wall Street Journal*. Retrieved from http://online.wsj.com/
943. For two years running Gallop polls have found upwards of 60% of Americans feel a third political party is needed to govern the nation. See, Jones, Jeffrey M., October 11, 2013. In U.S., Perceived Need for Third Party Reaches New High: Twenty-Six Percent Believe Democratic and Republican Parties Do Adequate Job. *Gallup Politics*. Retrieved from http://www.gallup.com/poll/165392/perceived-need-third-party-reaches-new-high.aspx; Jones, Jeffrey M., September 24, 2014. Americans Continue to Say a Third Political Party Is Needed. *Gallup Politics*. Retrieved from http://www.gallup.com/poll/177284/americans-continue-say-third-political-party-needed.aspx;
944. See, Daily Presidential Tracking Poll. May 26, 2015. *Rasmussen Reports*. Retrieved from http://www.rasmussenreports.com/public_content/politics/obama_administration/daily_presidential_tracking_poll

Chapter 14. How Bush and Cheney Untruthed us into Iraq.

945. See Isikoff, Michael, and Corn, David. *Hubris: The Inside Story of Spin, Scandal, and the*

Selling of the Iraq War. (New York: Three Rivers Press, 2007)

946. Ricks, Thomas E., *Fiasco The American Military Adventure in Iraq*. (New York: Penguin Books, 2007).

947. Mitchell, Greg. *So Wrong for So Long, How the Press, The Pundits - And The President - Failed On Iraq*. (New York: Sterling Publishing, 2008)

948. Drogan, *Bob. Curveball: Spies, Lies, And The Con Man Who Caused A War* (New York: Random House, 2007)

949. Wheeler, Marcy. *Anatomy of Deceit How the Bush Administration Used the Media to Sell the Iraq War and Out a Spy*. (Berkeley; Vaster Books, 2007)

950. No effort can be made to summarize in one endnote the large volume of evidence and arguments put forth in the books about the Iraq War mentioned in the text which support the conclusions that Saddam Hussein was not working with al qaeda and not responsible for 9/11, or that Iraq's WMD had been largely eliminated and posed no the threat to America before start of the War In Iraq.

951. By early 1996 thc Intcrnational Atomic Energy Commission had reported to the UN Security Council member states that Iraq had never succeeded in making a nuclear weapon, that its secret program to build a nuclear weapon had been eliminated, and that all enriched uranium needed to make a bomb had been removed from the country. See, Clemson, Frank Ronald. September 1, 2013. What Happened to Saddam's Weapons of Mass Destruction? *Arms Control Today Online Edition*. Retrieved from https://www.armscontrol.org/act/2003_09/Cleminson_09

952. See for eg., Eggen, Dan. June 16, 2004. No Evidence Connecting Iraq to Al Qaeda, 9/11 Panel Says. *The Washington Post*. Retrieved from http://www.washingtonpost.com/; Mount, Mike. March 13, 2008. *CNN*. Hussein's Iraq and al Qaeda not linked, Pentagon says. Retrieved from http://www.cnn.com/2008/US/03/13/alqaeda.saddam/

953. See for eg., Pallister David., September 18, 2002. 'Even if Iraq managed to hide these weapons, what they are now hiding is harmless goo' *The Guardian*. Retrieved from http://www.theguardian.com/world/2002/sep/19/iraq.features11; Landay, Jonathan S., September 12, 2002. Iraq has been unable to get materials needed for nuclear bomb, experts say. (Published originally in Knight Ridder Newspapers) *McClatchDC*. Retrieved from http://www.mcclatchydc.com/; Landay, Jonathan S., September 6, 2002. Lack of Hard Evidence of Iraqi Weapons Worries Top U.S. Officials. (Published originally in Knight Ridder Newspapers) *McClatchDC*. Retrieved from http://www.mcclatchydc.com/; FAIR. February 27, 2003. Star Witness on Iraq Said Weapons Were Destroyed: Bombshell Revelation From A Defector Cited by White House and Press. *Fair*. Retrieved from http://fair.org/; Barry, John. March 2, 2003. Exclusive: The Defector's Secrets. *Newsweek*. Retrieved from http://www.newsweek.com/; Sadler, Brent. September 21, 1995. Transcript of part one of Correspondent Brent Sadler's exclusive interview with Hussein Kamel. *CNN*. Retrieved from http://www.cnn.com/WORLD/9509/iraq_defector/kamel_transcript/index.html

954. See for eg., Schurmann, Frank. January 20, 1992. Islamic Fundamentalism: A Force To Be Reckoned With. *The Chicago Tribune*. Retrieved from http://articles.chicagotribune.

com/1992-01-20/news/9201060434_1_arab-islamic-islamic-fundamentalism-saddam-hussein; Benjamin, Daniel. September 30, 2002. Saddam Hussein and Al Qaeda Are Not Allies. *Time*. Retrieved from http://www.nytimes.com/; Strobel, Warren P., and Landay, Jonathan S., October 24, 2002. Infighting Among U.S. Intelligence Agencies Fuels Dispute Over Iraq. (Published originally in Knight Ridder Newspapers) *McClatchDC*. Retrieved from http://www.mcclatchydc.com/; Strobel, Warren P., October 7, 2002. Some In Bush Administration Have Misgivings About Iraq Policy. (Published originally in Knight Ridder Newspapers) *McClatchDC*. Retrieved from http://www.mcclatchydc.com/

955. Iraqi no-fly zones. *Wikipedia The Free Encyclopedia.* (Wikipedia Foundation Inc.) Retrieved from https://en.wikipedia.org/wiki/Iraqi_no-fly_zones

956. Iraq's longest range missile, the Al-Hussein, had a range of only 400 miles. It could not have reached the Atlantic Ocean let alone the United States. All the Al Hussein missiles Iraq possessed were destroyed following Operation Desert Storm, by July, 1991, under UN supervision. See, Al Hussein (missile). *Wikipedia The Free Encyclopedia.* (Wikipedia Foundation Inc.) Retrieved from https://en.wikipedia.org/wiki/Al_Hussein_(missile); In 2003, prior to the start of the Iraq war, Iraq did not have military branch known as the "Iraq Navy." Iraq had instead a "coastal defense force." The Iraqi coastal defense force was nearly obliterated during the 1991 Gulf War. About 100 Iraqi ships, the vast majority of which were small patrol boats, were destroyed. The ships were not replaced and the Iraqi coastal defense force played no role in the War in Iraq. The idea that tiny Iraqi naval force posed a WMD threat to the United States in the months before Bush ordered his war is utterly absurd. See, Iraqi Navy. *Wikipedia The Free Encyclopedia.* (Wikipedia Foundation Inc.) Retrieved from https://en.wikipedia.org/wiki Iraqi_Navy; If Saddam had wanted to attack America with WMD via an attack by terrorists he could have done so at any time before Bush attacked Iraq, or thereafter, but Saddam and his government denied any desire to attack America. There simply was no strategic or tactical benefit Saddam would have gained in attacking America.

957. See for eg., Al-Azzawi, Saif. September 15, 2014. I Despised Saddam's Police State, But The Islamic State Would Not Exist Under His Rule: The U.S. Wars Set The Stage For The Islamic State. *The Washington Post*. Retrieved from http://www.washingtonpost.com/; Hadar, Leon T., August 27, 1992. The "Green Peril": Creating the Islamic Fundamentalist Threat. Cato Policy Analysis No. 107. *Cato Institute*. Retrieved from http://www.cato.org/pubs/pas/pa-177.html; Zakaria, Fareed. September 4, 2014. Why they still hate us, 13 years later. *The Washington Post*. Retrieved from http://www.washingtonpost.com/

958. Hubris: The Inside Story of Spin, Scandal, and the Selling of the Iraq War. February 18, 2013. Maddow, Rachel. Host and Narrator. *MSNBC*. Documentary based on the book by the same name: Isikoff, Michael, and Corn, David. *Hubris: The Inside Story of Spin, Scandal, and the Selling of the Iraq War*. (New York: Three Rivers Press, 2007) ; Why We Did It. March 6, 2014. Maddow, Rachel. Host and Narrator. Documentary which examines the reasons for the Iraq War. Produced in conjunction with NBC News Peacock

Productions. *MSNBC.*

959. "Great Moments in Presidential Speeches" was a regular segment shown on the CBS Late Show hosted by David Letterman, who retired on May 20, 2015. See, List of David Letterman sketches. *Wikipedia The Free Encyclopedia.* (Wikipedia Foundation Inc.) Retrieved from https://en.wikipedia.org/wiki/List_of_David_Letterman_sketches#Great_Moments_in_Presidential_Speeches

960. Regarding violations of the Geneva Convention, See, Soltz, Jon. June 29, 2009. Petraeus Says U.S. Violated Geneva Conventions - What Will Cheney and Rush Say? *Huff Post Politics.* Retrieved from http://www.huffingtonpost.com/; Babington, Charles and Abramowitz, Michael., July 12, 2006. U.S. Shifts Policy on Geneva Conventions. *The Washington Post.* Retrieved from http://www.washingtonpost.com/; Regarding lawyer John Yoo, See, A Guide to the Memos on Torture by the New York Times. (2005) Contributed to by Neil A. Lewis. Compiled with memos obtained by the New York Times, Newsweek, The Washington Post and The Wall Street Journal. The New York Times. Retrieved from http://www.nytimes.com/ref/international/24MEMO-GUIDE.html

961. The phrase "Axis of Evil" is an obvious take off from the phrase "Axis Powers" which refers to the World War II alliance between Germany, Japan and Italy. The word "axis" as was used by President Bush seemed a poor choice given that Iran and Iraq had fought a bloody war and remained enemies. President Bush's effort to elevate the potential threat posed by Iraq, Iran and North Korea to the equivalent of the threat posed to America during WWII was seen by many as laughable. See generally, Axis of Evil. *Wikipedia The Free Encyclopedia.* (Wikipedia Foundation Inc.) Retrieved from https://en.wikipedia.org/wiki/Axis_of_evil; Ferrell, Will. Axis of Evil Cold Opening. Saturday Night Live. Season 27. Episode 13 Original broadcast March 2, 2002 on NBC. *SNL On Yahoo.* Retrieved from https://screen.yahoo.com/will-ferrell-snl-skits/celebrity-jeopardy-sean-connery-burt-000000211.html; Jill Dougherty July 1, 2007. 'Axis of Evil' Inspires Laughs. *CNN.* Retrieved from http://www.cnn.com/; Will Ferrell also performed an act paroding President Bush on stage to great acclaim, See, You're Welcome America. *Wikipedia The Free Encyclopedia.* (Wikipedia Foundation Inc.) Retrieved from https://en.wikipedia.org/wiki/You%27re_Welcome_America; See additionally, Weisberg, Jacob. October 11, 2006. That Axis of Evil: It's here now. Thank you, Mr. President. *Slate.* Retrieved from http://www.slate.com/

962. My linkage of Wolfowitz, Perle and Feith is based largely on my reading of the book *Hubris.* See, Isikoff, Michael, and Corn, David. *Hubris: The Inside Story of Spin, Scandal, and the Selling of the Iraq War.* (New York: Three Rivers Press, 2007). There are too many references to those three men in the aforesaid book to list them all here. The three men have been noted as being among the architects or leading proponents of the Iraq War by other sources as well. See for eg., Special Report. March 22, 2006. The Architects of the War Where Are They Now. *Think Progress.* Retrieved from http://thinkprogress.org/report/the-architects-where-are-they-now/; Roth, Zachary., March 18, 2013. 10 years later: The Architects of the Iraq War. *MSNBC.* Retrieved from http://www.msnbc.com/msnbc/; See additionally, Kaiser, Robert G., February 9, 2003. Bush

and Sharon Nearly Identical on Mideast Policy. *The Washington Post*. Retrievable online at the Washington Post paid archive; Green, Stephen. February 28, 2004. Neo-Cons, Israel and the Bush Administration. *Counterpunch*. Retrieved from http://www.counter punch.org/2004/02/28/neo-cons-israel-and-the-bush-administration/

963. See, Goodstein, Laurie. March 15, 2003. Divide Among Jews Leads to Silence on Iraq War. *The New York Times*. Retrieved from http://www.nytimes.com/2003/03/15/national /15JEWS.html

964. See, Jones, Jeffrey. February 23, 2007. Among Religious Groups, Jewish Americans Most Strongly Oppose War: Opposition Goes Beyond Jewish Americans' Political Affiliations. *Gallop News Service*. Retrieved from http://www.gallup.com/poll/26677/ among-religious-groups-jewish-americans-most-strongly-oppose-war.aspx

965. See for eg., Hitchens, Christopher. March 27, 2006. Overstating Jewish Power: Mearsheimer and Walt give too much credit to the Israeli lobby. *Slate*. Retrieved from http://www.slate.com/articles/news_and_politics/fighting_words/2006/03/overstating _jewish_power.html; Mearsheimer, John and Walt, Stephen. March 23, 2006. The Israel Lobby. *London Review of Books*. Vol. 28 No. 6 · 23 March 2006, pages 3-12. Retrieved from http://www.lrb.co.uk/v28/n06/john-mearsheimer/the-israel-lobby; For a commentary about the dangers of anti-Semitic references by journalists, See, Black, Edwin. September 27, 2004. The Pentagon Insider Who Spread Rumors that Sounded Anti-Semitic. *HNN.* Retrieved from http://historynewsnetwork.org/article/7582; See also, Stein, Jeff. May 6, 2014. Israel Won't Stop Spying on the U.S. *Newsweek*. Retrieved from http://www.newsweek.com/; Sherwood, Harriet. November 26, 2013. Arnon Milchan Reveals Past As Israeli Spy. The Guardian. Retrieved from http://www.theguardian.com/; Weiss, Phillip. October 27, 2013. Pro-Israel organization sought to survey US Jews on dual loyalty. *Mondoweiss*. Retrieved from http://mondoweiss.net/2013/10/organization-sought-loyalty#sthash.MBxYDnnN.dpuf; Gelb, Leslie H., September 23, 2007. Dual Loyalties. *The New York Times*. Retrieved from http://www.nytimes.com/2007/09/ 23/books/review/Gelb-t.html?pagewanted=all&_r=0; Christison, Kathleen and Christison, Bill. September 6, 2004. The Bush Neocons and Israel. *Counterpunch*. Retrieved from http://www.counterpunch.org/2004/09/06/the-bush-neocons-and-israel/

966. See, Notable Names Database. Profile of Richard Perle. *NNDB*. Last retrieved on August 2, 2015 from http://www.nndb.com/people/354/000022288/

967. See, Defense Policy Board Advisory Committee. *Wikipedia The Free Encyclopedia.* (Wikipedia Foundation Inc.) Retrieved from https://en.wikipedia.org/wiki/Defense Policy_Board_Advisory_Committee

968. See, Federal Advisory Committee Act. *Wikipedia The Free Encyclopedia.* (Wikipedia Foundation Inc.) Retrieved from https://en.wikipedia.org/wiki/Federal_Advisory_ Committee_Act

969. Hersh, Seymour M., March 17, 2003. Lunch With the Chairman. *The New Yorker*. Retrieved from http://www.newyorker.com/; Shafer, Jack. March 13, 2003. Put Up or Shut Up, Richard Perle I double-dare him to sue Seymour Hersh. *Slate*. Retrieved from http://www.slate.com/

970. Ibid.; See generally, Trireme Partners. *Wikipedia The Free Encyclopedia.* (Wikipedia Foundation Inc.) Retrieved from https://en.wikipedia.org/wiki/Trireme_Partners
971. Hersh, Seymour M., March 17, 2003. Lunch With the Chairman. *The New Yorker.* Retrieved from http://www.newyorker.com/
972. Gerth, Jeff. April 17, 1983. Aide Urged Pentagon to Consider Weapons Made by Former Client. *New York Times.* Retrieved from http://www.nytimes.com/1983/04/17/us/aide-urged-pentagon-to-consider-weapons-made-by-former-client.html
973. See, Green. Stephen. February 28, 2004. Neo-Cons, Israel and the Bush Administration. *Counterpunch.* Retrieved from http://www.counterpunch.org/2004/02/28/neo-cons-israel-and-the-bush-administration/
974. Hersh, Seymour M., March 17, 2003. Lunch With the Chairman. *The New Yorker.* Retrieved from http://www.newyorker.com/
975. See, Print Guide to Senator Henry M. Jackson, 1912 -1983. Guide Index topic: Staff. Richard Perle. *University of Washington Libraries.* July 8, 2015 update. Retrieved on September 2, 2015 from http://guides.lib.washington.edu/content.php?pid=228100&sid=1888525; Green, op. cit.
976. Wedel, Janine R., *Shadow Elite: How The World's New Power Brokers Undermine Democracy, Government, And The Free Market.* (New York, Basic Books, 2009) 148 (citing) Hersh, Seymour M., Kissinger and Nixon in the White House. *The Atlantic.* May, 1982 ed. Retrieved from http://www.theatlantic.com/magazine/archive/1982/05/kissinger-and-nixon-in-the-white-house/308778/; Green, op. cit.
977. Ibid.
978. Green. Stephen. February 28, 2004. Neo-Cons, Israel and the Bush Administration. *Counterpunch.* Retrieved from http://www.counterpunch.org/2004/02/28/neo-cons-israel-and-the-bush-administration/
979. Wedel, 169-170; Isikoff and Corn, 77-78; Bamford, James. *A Pretext For War.* (New York: Doubleday, 2004) 265
980. Wedel, 170; Isikoff and Corn, 78
981. Paul Wolfowitz. *Wikipedia The Free Encyclopedia.* (Wikipedia Foundation Inc.) Retrieved from https://en.wikipedia.org/wiki/Paul_Wolfowitz (citing) Cassidy, John. April 9, 2007. The Next Crusade: Paul Wolfowitz at the World Bank. *The New Yorker.* Retrieved from http://www.newyorker.com/
982. For an interesting report about a "bizarre conspiracy theory" "promoted" by Wolfowitz, See, Corn. David. May 13, 2015. The Jeb Bush Adviser Who Should Scare You: Paul Wolfowitz not only championed the Iraq War—he obsessively promoted a bizarre conspiracy theory. *Mother Jones.* Retrieved from http://www.motherjones.com/; Wolfowitz was also accused of what might be called unbalanced thinking in his role as the President of the World Bank, which he resigned from in 2007, under fire for allegedly showing favoritism to his girl friend. Weisman, Steven R., May 18, 2007. Wolfowitz Resigns, Ending Long Fight at World Bank. *The New York Times.* Retrieved from http://www.nytimes.com/
983. Unger, Craig. House of Bush, House of Saud The Secret Relationship between the

World's Two Most Powerful Dynasties. (New York: Scribner, 2004) 44; Drew, Elizabeth. June 12, 2003. The Neocons In Power. *The New York Review of Books*. Retrieved from http://www.nybooks.com/articles/archives/2003/jun/12/the-neocons-in-power/; Curtiss, Richard H., The Pentagon's Dynamic Duo: Richard Perle and Paul Wolfowitz. *Washington Report on Middle East Affairs*. April, 2003 Issue. 14-15

984. Wedel, 170; Isikoff and Corn, 78
985. Wolfowitz was one of a group of foreign policy advisors to George W. Bush before he officially launched his first campaign for President who were later appointed to office by President Bush. Among the others were Donald Rumsfeld, Colin Powell and Condoleezza Rice. See, Frontline. The War Behind Closed Doors. February 20, 2003. PBS Documentary Television Series produced by WGBH, Boston. Kirk. Michael, Episode Producer, Writer and Dir. Audette, Steve. Episode Ed. The full program is available online at http://www.pbs.org/wgbh/pages/frontline/shows/iraq/view/; An online timeline "Chronology: The Evolution Of The Bush Doctrine" contains information relevant to the statement in the text at date March, 1999. *PBS*. Retrieved from http://www.pbs.org/wgbh/pages/frontline/shows/iraq/etc/cron.html
986. Office of the Assistant Secretary of Defense for Public Affairs. United States Department of Defense. News Transcript of Interview of Paul Wolfowitz by Robert Collier for the San Francisco Chronicle. February 23, 2002. Available online by *Leading To War*. Retrieved from http://www.leadingtowar.com/PDFsources_claims_atta/2002_02_23_dept_defense.pdf
987. Kampfner, John. *Blair's Wars*. (New York: Simon and Schuster, 2003) 156;
988. Ibid.
989. Isikoff and Corn, 78
990. Ibid., See the footnote to the cited text. Though not a signatory to the 1998 letter to Clinton, Cheney did sign the founding statement of the Project for a New American Century.
991. Isikoff and Corn, 78
992. Clarke, Richard A. *Against All Enemies: Inside America's War on Terrorism*. (New York: Free Press, 2004) 30
993. See in addition to other cited works in this chapter relating to the opinion expressed in the text, Lewis, Charles, Smith, Mark Reading. January 23, 2008. Updated June 30, 2014. Iraq The War Card: False Pretenses, Following 9/11, President Bush and seven top officials of his administration waged a carefully orchestrated campaign of misinformation about Saddam Hussein's Iraq. *The Center For Public Integrity*. Retrieved from http://www.publicintegrity.org/2008/01/23/5641/false-pretenses; Associated Press. January 23, 2008. Study: Bush Lead The U.S. To War On False Pretenses. *NBC News*. Retrieved from http://www.nbcnews.com/; Tyler, Taylor. August 31, 2015. Donald Trump Wanted George Bush Impeached For 'Lying' The U.S. Into War With Iraq. *Headlines & Global News*. Retrieved from http://www.hngn.com/; Horton, Scott. January 34, 2008. 935 Lies on the Way to a War. Harper's Browsings Blog. Retrieved from http://harpers.org/blog/2008/01/935-lies-on-the-way-to-a-war/

994. See, Tyler, Patrick E. March 8, 1992. U.S. Strategy Plan Calls for Insuring No Rivals Develop: A One Superpower World. *New York Times*. Retrieved from http://www.nytimes.com/

995. An online timeline "Chronology: The Evolution Of The Bush Doctrine" contains a hyperlink to an excerpt quoted in part in the text from the 1992 Defense Planning Guidance document at date "1999." *PBS*. Retrieved from http://www.pbs.org/wgbh/pages/frontline/shows/iraq/etc/wolf.html; The online materials are part of the website for the PBS program Frontline. See, Frontline. The War Behind Closed Doors. February 20, 2003. PBS Documentary Television Series produced by WGBH, Boston. Kirk. Michael, Episode Producer, Writer and Dir. Audette, Steve. Episode Ed. The full program is available online at http://www.pbs.org/wgbh/pages/frontline/shows/iraq/view/

996. Bacevich, Andrew J., A Letter To Paul Wolfowitz Occasioned by The Tenth Anniversary of The Iraq War. *Harpers Magazine*. March, 2013. Retrieved online in pdf courtesy of Harpers Magazine from http://harpers.org/archive/2013/03/a-letter-to-paul-wolfowitz/

997. See, Andrew Bacevich. *Wikipedia The Free Encyclopedia.* (Wikipedia Foundation Inc.) Retrieved from https://en.wikipedia.org/wiki/Andrew_Bacevich

998. See, Faculty Profile of Andrew J. Bacevich. *Boston University Pardee School of Global Studies*. Retrieved on September 11, 2015 from http://www.bu.edu/pardeeschool/profile/andrew-j-bacevich/; Bacevich, Andrew J. Curriculum Vitae. *Boston University*. Retrieved on September 11, 2015 from http://www.bu.edu/history/files/2011/01/Bacevich-CV.pdf

999. *Breach of Trust: How Americans Failed Their Soldiers and Their Country* (New York: Metropolitan Books, 2013). *Washington Rules: America's Path to Permanent War* (New York: Metropolitan Books, 2010); *The Limits of Power: The End of American Exceptionalism* (New York: Metropolitan Books, 2008); *The Long War: A New History of US National Security Policy since World War II* (New York: Columbia University Press, 2007) (editor); *The New American Militarism: How Americans Are Seduced by War* (New York: Oxford University Press, 2005); and *American Empire: The Realities and Consequences of U. S. Diplomacy* (Cambridge, Massachusetts: Harvard University Press, 2002) A more complete list of Professor Bacevich's books, monographs and other major works with full citations is contained in his online Curriculum Vitae; See, Faculty Profile of Andrew J. Bacevich. *Boston University Pardee School of Global Studies*. Retrieved on September 11, 2015 from http://www.bu.edu/pardeeschool/profile/andrew-j-bacevich/; Bacevich, Andrew J. Curriculum Vitae. *Boston University*. Retrieved on September 11, 2015 from http://www.bu.edu/history/files/2011/01/Bacevich-CV.pdf

1000. See generally, Wolfowitz Doctrine. *Wikipedia The Free Encyclopedia.* (Wikipedia Foundation Inc.) Retrieved from https://en.wikipedia.org/wiki/Wolfowitz_Doctrine; For an excellent short essay about the Wolfowitz Doctrine, See, The Spectre of Wolfowitz: A Controversial 1992 Defense Strategy Has Helped Shape the US Foreign Policy Mindset of Containing Russia In Its Own Backyard. *American Review*. March, 2015. Retrieved from http://americanreviewmag.com/opinions/The-spectre-of-Wolfowitz

1001. Dalck Feith. *Wikipedia The Free Encyclopedia.* (Wikipedia Foundation Inc.) Retrieved from https://en.wikipedia.org/wiki/Dalck_Feith; Myers, Zara. October 27, 2005. Dalck

Feith, Electronics Chief and Community Leader, Dies at 91. *Jewish Exponent.* http://www. jewishexponent.com/dalck-feith,-electronics-chief-and-community-leader,-dies-at-91-0; Douglas J. Feith. *Wikipedia The Free Encyclopedia.* (Wikipedia Foundation Inc.) Retrieved from https://en.wikipedia.org/wiki/Douglas_J._Feith; Betar. *Wikipedia The Free Encyclopedia.* (Wikipedia Foundation Inc.) Retrieved from https://en.wikipedia org/wiki/Betar; Institute For Policy Studies. Douglas Feith. November 21, 2014. *Right Web.* Retrieved from http://www.rightweb.irc-online.org/profile/feith_douglas; Notable Names Data Base. Douglas Feith. *NNDB.* Retrieved from http://www.nndb.com/people/100/000047956/

1002. Douglas J. Feith. *Wikipedia The Free Encyclopedia.* (Wikipedia Foundation Inc.) Retrieved from https://en.wikipedia.org/wiki/Douglas_J._Feith

1003. Ibid; See additionally, Feith, Douglas J. Defense, April 22, 2004. Democracy, and the War on Terrorism. Speech to John F. Kennedy School of Government, Harvard University, April 22, 2004, *Douglas J. Feith Website.* Retrieved from http://www. dougfeith.com/docs/2004_04_22_Harvard_GWOT.pdf; Profile of Douglas J. Feith. November 14, 2014. *Right Web.* Retrieved from http://www.rightweb.irc-online.org/profile/Feith_Douglas

1004. Pipes is thought of as one of the intellectual fathers of the "Bush Doctrine." See, Tanenhaus, Sam. November 2, 2003. The Hard-Liner: Harvard historian Richard Pipes shaped the Reagan administration's aggressive approach to the Soviet Union. His support for confrontation over containment prefigured the Bush foreign policy of today. *Boston.com.* Retrieved from http://www.boston.com/news/globe/ideas/articles/2003/11/02/the_hard_liner/; Pipes wrote an autobiography first published in 2003 by the title: "Vixi: Memoirs of a Non-Belonger." (USA, R. R. Donnelley & Sons, 2003). See generally, Richard Pipes. *Wikipedia The Free Encyclopedia.* (Wikipedia Foundation Inc.) Retrieved from https://en.wikipedia.org/wiki/Richard_Pipes

1005. See, Douglas J. Feith. *Wikipedia The Free Encyclopedia.* (Wikipedia Foundation Inc.) Retrieved from https://en.wikipedia.org/wiki/Douglas_J._Feith; Feith, Douglas J. Defense, April 22, 2004. Democracy, and the War on Terrorism. Speech to John F. Kennedy School of Government, Harvard University, April 22, 2004, *Douglas J. Feith Website.* Retrieved from http://www.dougfeith.com/docs/2004_04_22_Harvard_GWOT.pdf; Profile of Douglas J. Feith. November 14, 2014. *Right Web.* Retrieved from http://www.rightweb.irc-online.org/profile/Feith_Douglas; Borger, Julian. December 5, 2002. Democrat Hawk Whose Ghost Guides Bush: Scoop Jackson's body is 20 years in the grave but his spirit goes marching on. *The Guardian.* Retrieved from http://www.theguardian.com/world/2002/dec/06/usa.julianborger; Profile: Douglas Feith. *History Commons.* Retrieved from http://www.historycommons.org/entity.jsp?entity=douglas_feith

1006. Ibid. In 1981, Feith began work under Pipes at the NSA. In 1976, Pipes worked on project "Team B." for the NSA See generally, Team B. *Wikipedia The Free Encyclopedia.* (Wikipedia Foundation Inc.) Retrieved from https://en.wikipedia.org/wiki/Team_B; Profile: Team B. *History Commons.* Retrieved from http://www.historycommons.org/entity.jsp?entity=_team_b__1; Profile: Douglas Feith. *History Commons.*

Retrieved from http://www.historycommons.org/entity.jsp?entity=douglas_feith

1007. Douglas J. Feith. *Wikipedia The Free Encyclopedia.* (Wikipedia Foundation Inc.) Retrieved from https://en.wikipedia.org/wiki/Douglas_J._Feith; Feith, Douglas J. Defense, April 22, 2004. Democracy, and the War on Terrorism. Speech to John F. Kennedy School of Government, Harvard University, April 22, 2004, *Douglas J. Feith Website*. Retrieved from http://www. dougfeith.com/docs/2004_04_22_Harvard_GWOT .pdf; Profile of Douglas J. Feith. November 14, 2014. *Right Web*. Retrieved from http://www.rightweb.irc-online.org/profile/Feith_Douglas; Profile of Douglas J. Feith. November 14, 2014. *Right Web*. Retrieved from http://www.rightweb.irc-online.org/profi le/Feith_Douglas

1008. See, Feith and Zell, P.C., *Sourcewatch.* (Center For Media and Democracy) Retrieved from http://www.sourcewatch.org/index.php/Feith_and_Zell,_P.C. ; Barry, Tom. September 16, 2004. Douglas Feith: Portrait of a Neoconservative. *Antiwar.com.* Retrieved from http://original.antiwar.com/tom-barry/2004/09/15/douglas-feith-portrait-of-a-neoconservative/

1009. Marc Zell. *Wikipedia The Free Encyclopedia.* (Wikipedia Foundation Inc.) Retrieved from https://en.wikipedia.org/wiki/Marc_Zell; Alon Shvut. *Wikipedia The Free Encyclopedia.* (Wikipedia Foundation Inc.) Retrieved from https://en.wikipedia.org/wiki/ Alon_Shvut; See additionally, Whitaker. Brian. October 6, 2003. Zionist settler joins Iraqi to promote trade. *The Guardian*. Retrieved from http://www.theguardian.com/ world/2003/oct/07/iraq.israel

1010. Douglas Jay Feith. *Sourcewatch.* (Center For Media and Democracy) Retrieved from http://www.sourcewatch.org/index.php/Douglas_Jay_Feith; Regarding the derivation of the name "Fandz," See, Whitaker, Brian. September 24, 2003. Friends Of The Family: Companies wishing to make money in post-Saddam Iraq need look no further than an Iraqi uncle and nephew, and their hawkish friends in Washington. *The Guardian*. Retrieved from http://www.theguardian.com/world/2003/sep/24/worlddispatch.usa

1011. Ibid; Green. Stephen. February 28, 2004. Neo-Cons, Israel and the Bush Administration. *Counterpunch*. Retrieved from http://www.counterpunch.org/2004/02/28/neo-cons-israel-and-the-bush-administration/

1012. See, Feith and Zell, P.C., *Sourcewatch.* (Center For Media and Democracy) Retrieved from http://www.sourcewatch.org/index.php/Feith_and_Zell,_P.C. ; Barry, Tom. September 16, 2004. Douglas Feith: Portrait of a Neoconservative. *Antiwar.com.* Retrieved from http://original.antiwar.com/tom-barry/2004/09/15/douglas-feith-portrait-of-a-neoconservative/; Marc Zell. *Wikipedia The Free Encyclopedia.* (Wikipedia Foundation Inc.) Retrieved from https://en.wikipedia.org/wiki/Marc_Zell; Alon Shvut. *Wikipedia The Free Encyclopedia.* (Wikipedia Foundation Inc.) Retrieved from https://en.wikipedia.org/wiki/Alon_Shvut; Whitaker. Brian. October 6, 2003. Zionist settler joins Iraqi to promote trade. *The Guardian*. Retrieved from http://www.theguardia n.com/world/2003/oct/07/iraq.israel; Douglas Jay Feith. *Sourcewatch.* (Center For Media and Democracy) Retrieved from http://www.sourcewatch.org/index.php/Douglas_Jay_ Feith; Regarding the derivation of the name "Fandz," See, Whitaker, Brian. September

24, 2003. Friends Of The Family: Companies wishing to make money in post-Saddam Iraq need look no further than an Iraqi uncle and nephew, and their hawkish friends in Washington. *The Guardian*. Retrieved from http://www.theguardian.com/world/2003/sep/24/worlddispatch.usa ; Stephen. February 28, 2004. Neo-Cons, Israel and the Bush Administration. *Counterpunch*. Retrieved from http://www.counterpunch.org/2004/02/28/neo-cons-israel-and-the-bush-administration/; See additionally, Kamen, Al. September 10, 2003. Feith-Based Initiative. *Washington Post*. Sec. A 17. Retrieved from https://secure.pqarchiver.com/washingtonpost/doc/409504313.html?FMT=FT&pf=1

1013. Ibid. See for eg. Rein, Lisa. November 17, 2003. Bill Moyers On The Insider Business Deals Between Bush Administration Officials And Iraqi Reconstruction Companies. *On Lisa Rein's Radar*. Retrieved from http://www.onlisareinsradar.com/archives/002015.php; Cash and Carry. November 14, 2003. First segment of "Now" News program on PBS. Pitra, Katie. Prod., Amron, Allison. Ed., Baskin, Roverta. Corr. *PBS*. Full Transcript online at http://www.pbs.org/now/transcript/transcript242_full.html

1014. Pipes is thought of as one of the intellectual fathers of the "Bush Doctrine." See, Tanenhaus, Sam. November 2, 2003. The Hard-Liner: Harvard historian Richard Pipes shaped the Reagan administration's aggressive approach to the Soviet Union. His support for confrontation over containment prefigured the Bush foreign policy of today. *Boston.com*. Retrieved from http://www.boston.com/news/globe/ideas/articles/2003/11/02/the_hard_liner/; Pipes wrote an autobiography first published in 2003 by the title: "Vixi: Memoirs of a Non-Belonger." (USA, R. R. Donnelley & Sons, 2003). See generally, Richard Pipes. *Wikipedia The Free Encyclopedia.* (Wikipedia Foundation Inc.) Retrieved from https://en.wikipedia.org/wiki/Richard_Pipes; See additionally, Richard Pipes. *Sourcewatch*. (Center For Media and Democracy) Retrieved from http://www.sourcewatch.org/index.php/Richard_Pipes; Profile of Richard Pipes. July 10, 2013. *Right Web*. Retrieved from http://www.rightweb.irc-online.org/profile/Pipes_Richard; Profile: Richard Pipes. *History Commons*. Retrieved from http://www.historycommons.org/entity.jsp?entity=richard_pipes

1015. Ibid., See, Douglas J. Feith. *Wikipedia The Free Encyclopedia.* (Wikipedia Foundation Inc.) Retrieved from https://en.wikipedia.org/wiki/Douglas_J._Feith; Feith, Douglas J. Defense, April 22, 2004. Democracy, and the War on Terrorism. Speech to John F. Kennedy School of Government, Harvard University, April 22, 2004, *Douglas J. Feith Website*. Retrieved from http://www.dougfeith.com/docs/2004_04_22_Harvard_GWOT.pdf; Profile of Douglas J. Feith. November 14, 2014. *Right Web*. Retrieved from http://www.rightweb.irc-online.org/profile/Feith_Douglas; Borger, Julian. December 5, 2002. Democrat Hawk Whose Ghost Guides Bush: Scoop Jackson's body is 20 years in the grave but his spirit goes marching on. *The Guardian*. Retrieved from http://www.theguardian.com/world/2002/dec/06/usa.julianborger; Profile: Douglas Feith. *History Commons*. Retrieved from http://www.historycommons.org/entity.jsp?entity=douglas_feith; See additionally, Unger, Craig. (Chapter Four) "The ForeShadowing." in *The Fall Of The House Of Bush: The Untold Story Of How A Band Of True Believers Seized The Executive Branch, Started The Iraq War, And Still Imperils America's Future*. (New

York: Scribner, 2007); Shankbone, David. November 12, 2007. Interview with Craig Unger: Vanity Fair contributing editor Craig Unger on the Bush family feud, neoconservatives and the Christian right. *Wikinews*. Retrieved from https://en.wikinews.org/wiki/Vanity_Fair_contributing_editor_Craig_Unger_on_the_Bush_family_feud,_neoconservatives_and_the_Christian_right

1016. Ibid.
1017. Ibid.
1018. Ibid., See additionally, Korb, Lawrence J., August 18, 2004. It's Time to Bench "Team B" Second-Guessing The CIA Has Led The U.S. Astray. *Los Angeles Times*. Retrieved from http://articles.latimes.com/2004/aug/08/opinion/oe-korb8
1019. Ibid.
1020. Matthias, Willard C. *America's Strategic Blunders*. (University Park, Penn.: Pennsylvania State University Press, 2001), 305-06
1021. Goodman, Melvin A., November 19, 2004. Righting the CIA (About Team B). *The Baltimore Sun*. Retrieved from http://bailey83221.livejournal.com/51190.html
1022. See generally, Context of 'November 26, 2001: Defense Official Asks for 'Team B'-Like Assessment of Terrorist Intelligence.' *History Commons*. Retrieved from http://www.historycommons.org/context.jsp?item=a112601rodhamteamb#a112601rodhamteamb;For an academic review of problems inherent to the Team B approach, See, Mitchell. Gordon R., Team B Intelligence Coups. *Quarterly Journal of Speech*. Vol. 92, No. 2, May 2006, 144-173
1023. See, Reuters. February 19, 2004. Pentagon Offices Face Probe On Iraq Claim. *ABC News Online.* Online by Internet Archive Wayback Machine. Retrieved from http://web.archive.org/web/20040222151945/http://www.abc.net.au/news/newsitems/s1048656.htm; Context of 'Shortly After September 11, 2001: Pentagon Officials Wolfowitz and Feith Set Up Counter Terrorism Evaluation Group.' *History Commons*. Retrieved from http://www.historycommons.org/context.jsp?item=complete_timeline_of_the_2003_invasion_of_iraq_82#complete_timeline_of_the_2003_invasion_of_iraq_82; Context of 'September 2002: 'Office of Special Plans' Created; 'Stovepipes' Questionable Intelligence Reports to Office of Vice President.' *History Commons*. Retrieved from http://www.historycommons.org/context.jsp?item=complete_timeline_of_the_2003_invasion of_iraq_78#complete_timeline_of_the_2003_invasion_of_iraq_78; Isikoff, Michael, and Corn, David. (Chapter Six) "The Secret Diggers" in *Hubris: The Inside Story of Spin, Scandal, and the Selling of the Iraq War*. (New York: Three Rivers Press, 2007) 101-114; Counter Terrorism Evaluation Group. *Sourcewatch*. Retrieved from http://www.sourcewatch.org/index.php/Counter_Terrorism_Evaluation_Group
1024. Ibid; Context of 'July 8, 1996: Neoconservative Think Tank Advocates Aggressive Israeli Foreign Policy.' *History Commons*. Retrieved from http://www.historycommons.org/context.jsp?item=complete_timeline_of_the_2003_invasion_of_iraq_74&scale=1#completetimeline_of_the_2003_invasion_of_iraq_74
1025. Risen, James. April 28, 2004. How Pair's Finding on Terror Led To Clash on Shaping Intelligence. *The New York Times*. Retrieved from http://www.nytimes.com/

1026. The statement in the text is my opinion. It's based on my research. For instance, in *Hubris*, a high level CIA officer named Paul Pillar is reported to have viewed the work of the Feith "Iraq intelligence cell" as a "fraud," by authors Isikoff and Corn. Pillar was reportedly "stunned" by one intelligence presentation made by Feith in which the work of his unit was reported. Pillar reportedly said that "It was a deliberate effort to try to stitch things together to try to make a case. It had nothing to do with intelligence analysis as I understood it - which is ultimately to try to get at the truth." See, Isikoff and Corn, *Hubris*, 114, 109-113.

1027. That is my opinion, and it seems to be widely shared. See for eg., Walls, Seth Colter. June 13, 2008. Senate Report: Bush Used Iraq Intel He Knew Was False. *Huff Post Politics*. Retrieved from http://www.huffingtonpost.com/2008/06/05/divided-senate-committee_n_105374.html; Stein, Jonathan. and Dickinson, Tim. Lie by Lie: A Timeline of How We Got Into Iraq. (September/October, 2006). *Mother Jones*. Retrieved from http ://www.motherjones.com/politics/2011/12/leadup-iraq-war-timeline; Dreyfuss, Robert. and Vest, Jason. The Lie Factory. A Mother Jones Special Investigation: The inside story of how the Bush administration pushed disinformation and bogus intelligence and led the nation to war. (January/February, 2004) *Mother Jones*. Retrieved from http://www. motherjones.com/politics/2004/01/lie-factory; Leopold, Jason. November 23, 2005. How Pre-War Iraq Intel Was Cooked. *Truthout*. Retrieved from http://truth-out.org/archive/ component/k2/item/58808:jason-leopold-how-prewar-iraq-intel-was-cooked

1028. Ibid.

1029. Ibid., Isikoff and Corn, *Hubris*, 49-56, 109-111

1030. See, Iraqi National Congress. *Wikipedia The Free Encyclopedia.* (Wikipedia Foundation Inc.) Retrieved from https://en.wikipedia.org/wiki/Iraqi_National_Congress; Iraqi National Congress. *Sourcewatch*. Retrieved from http://www.sourcewatch.org/index.php/ Iraqi_National_Congress; Profile: Iraqi National Congress (INC) *History Commons*. Retrieved from http://www.historycommons.org/entity.jsp?entity=iraqi_national_ congress

1031. Walls, Seth Colter. June 13, 2008. Senate Report: Bush Used Iraq Intel He Knew Was False. *Huff Post Politics*. Retrieved from http://www.huffingtonpost.com/2008/06/05/ divided-senate-committee_n_105374.html; Stein, Jonathan. and Dickinson, Tim. Lie by Lie: A Timeline of How We Got Into Iraq. (September/October, 2006). *Mother Jones*. Retrieved from http://www.motherjones.com/politics/2011/12/leadup-iraq-war-timeline; Dreyfuss, Robert. and Vest, Jason. The Lie Factory. A Mother Jones Special Investigation: The inside story of how the Bush administration pushed disinformation and bogus intelligence and led the nation to war. (January/February, 2004) *Mother Jones*. Retrieved from http://www.motherjones.com/politics/2004/01/lie-factory; Leopold, Jason. November 23, 2005. How Pre-War Iraq Intel Was Cooked. *Truthout*. Retrieved from http://truth-out.org/archive/component/k2/item/58808:jason-leopold-how-prewar -iraq-intel-was-cooked

1032. Ibid. See also notes 1023, 1027, 1029, 1033, 1034, and 1035; See additionally, Ahmed Chalabi. *Wikipedia The Free Encyclopedia.* (Wikipedia Foundation Inc.) Retrieved from https://en.wikipedia.org/wiki/Ahmed_Chalabi; Mayer, Jane. June 7, 2004. The Manipulator: Ahmad Chalabi pushed a tainted case for war. Can he survive the occupation? *The New Yorker*. Retrieved from http://www.newyorker.com/magazine/2004/06/07/the-manipulator; See generally, Roston, Aram. *The Man Who Pushed America To War: The Extraordinary Life, Adventures and Obsessions of Ahmed Chalabi*. (New York: Nation Books, 2008); Gelb, Leslie H., April 27, 2008. Neoconner. *The New York Times*. Retrieved from http://www.nytimes.com/2008/04/27/books/review/Gelb-t.html?_r=0

1033. See, Lang, Patrick W., Drinking the Kool-Aid. *Middle East Policy*. (Vol. XI, Summer 2004, Number 2) 39-60; Counter Terrorism Evaluation Group. *Sourcewatch*. Retrieved from http://www.sourcewatch.org/index.php/Counter_Terrorism_Evaluation_Group; Risen, James. April 28, 2004. How Pair's Finding on Terror Led to Clash on Shaping Intelligence. *The New York Times*. Retrieved from http://www.nytimes.com/2004/04/28/politics/28INTE.html?position=&hp=&pagewanted=print&position=; United States Senate. Select Committee On Intelligence. 110th Congress. June 5, 2008. Report on Intelligence Activities Relating To Iraq Conducted By The Policy Counterterrorism Evaluation Group And The Office Of Special Plans Within The Office Of The Under Secretary Of Defense For Policy. *U.S. Senate Select Committee On Intelligence*. Report for the 110th Congress. 2d Session. S. Report 110-346. Retrieved from http://www.intelligence.senate.gov/sites/default/files/publications/110346.pdf; Office of Special Plans. *Wikipedia The Free Encyclopedia.* (Wikipedia Foundation Inc.) Retrieved from https://en.wikipedia.org/wiki/Office_of_Special_Plans

1034. Isikoff, Michael, and Corn, David. (Chapter Six) "The Secret Diggers" in *Hubris: The Inside Story of Spin, Scandal, and the Selling of the Iraq War*. (New York: Three Rivers Press, 2007) 109-114

1035. Richelson, Jeffrey T., ed. Posted online February 20, 2014. Deception, Intelligence, and Policy Counterterrorism. National Security Archive Briefing Book No. 456. *The National Security Archive*. Retrieved from http://nsarchive.gwu.edu/NSAEBB/NSAEBB456/

1036. Isikoff and Corn, op. cit. 111

1037. Richelson, op. cit.

1038. Ibid; Isikoff and Corn, op. cit. 26-28, 101-107, 109-114; Alfano, Sean. April 6, 2007. Pentagon: No Saddam-Al Qaeda Link. *CBS News*. Retrieved from http://www.cbsnews.com/news/pentagon-no-saddam-al-qaeda-link/; Giraldi, Phillip. March 12, 2007. Saving Feith: A new report gives the Pentagon intelligence peddler a pass. *The American Conservative*. Retrieved from http://www.theamericanconservative.com/articles/saving-feith/; Lang, Patrick W., Drinking the Kool-Aid. *Middle East Policy*. (Vol. XI, Summer 2004, Number 2) 39-60; Counter Terrorism Evaluation Group. *Sourcewatch*. Retrieved from http://www.sourcewatch.org/index.php/Counter_Terrorism_Evaluation_Group; Risen, James. April 28, 2004. How Pair's Finding on Terror Led to Clash on Shaping Intelligence. *The New York Times*. Retrieved from http://www.nytimes.com/2004/04/28/politics/28INTE.html?position=&hp=&pagewanted =print&position=; United States Senate. Select Committee On Intelligence. 110th Congress. June 5, 2008. Report on

Intelligence Activities Relating To Iraq Conducted By The Policy Counterterrorism Evaluation Group And The Office Of Special Plans Within The Office Of The Under Secretary Of Defense For Policy. *U.S. Senate Select Committee On Intelligence*. Report for the 110th Congress. 2d Session. S. Report 110-346. Retrieved from http://www.intelligence.senate.gov/sites/default/files/publications/110346.pdf; Office of Special Plans. *Wikipedia The Free Encyclopedia.* (Wikipedia Foundation Inc.) Retrieved from https://en.wikipedia.org/wiki/Office_of_Special_Plans ;

1039. Isikoff and Corn, 113
1040. Isikoff and Corn, 110 -114
1041. Isikoff and Corn, 101-103, 110-114, 139-140; Smith, Jeffrey. April 6, 2007. Hussein's Prewar Ties To Al-Qaeda Discounted. *Washington Post*. Retrieved from http://www.washingtonpost.com/; Weisman, Jonathan. September 10, 2006. Saddam Had No Links To al-Qaeda. *The Age*. Retrieved from http://www.theage.com.au/news/world/saddam-had-no-links-to-alqaeda/2006/09/09/1157222383981.html
1042. Editorial. February 10, 2007. The Build-a-War Workshop. *International New York Times*. Retrieved from http://www.nytimes.com/2007/02/10/opinion/10sat1.html?_r=0; Cloud, David., and Mazzetti, Mark. February 9, 2007. Prewar Intelligence Unit at Pentagon Is Criticized. *International New York Times*. Retrieved from http://www.nytimes.com/2007/02/09/washington/09feith.html; Saving Feith: A new report gives the Pentagon intelligence peddler a pass. *The American Conservative*. Retrieved from http://www.theamericanconservative.com/articles/saving-feith/; Press Release From The Office of U.S. Senator Carl Levin. April 5, 2007. Levin Releases Newly Declassified Pentagon Inspector General Report on Intelligence Assessment Activities of the Office of Under Secretary of Defense Doug Feith. Online by the Federation of American Scientists. *FAS*. Retrieved from http://fas.org/irp/news/2007/04/levin040507.html
1043. Ibid.
1044. Richelson, op. cit.
1045. There is confusion in media reports about what connection existed between the intelligence analysis done by PCTEG and the later work done by the Office of Special Plans (OSP) which operated under Douglas Feith as Under Secretary Of Defense For Policy. See, Office of Special Plans and Other Pentagon Offices under Douglas Feith. *History Commons*. Retrieved from http://www.historycommons.org/searchResults.jsp?search text=Office+of+Special+Plans+and+Other+Pentagon+Offices+under+Douglas+Feith&events=on&entities=on&articles=on&topics=on&timelines=on&projects=on&titles=on&descriptions=on&dosearch=on&search=Go; Richelson, op. cit.; Office of Special Plans. *Wikipedia The Free Encyclopedia.* (Wikipedia Foundation Inc.) Retrieved from https://en.wikipedia.org/wiki/Office_of_Special_Plans
1046. Richelson, op. cit.
1047. See, Profile of Dr. Jeffrey T. Richelson. National Security Archive Staff and Fellows. *The National Security Archive*. Retrieved from http://nsarchive.gwu.edu/nsa/arc_staff.html; Dr. Jeffrey T. Richelson. *Wikipedia The Free Encyclopedia.* (Wikipedia Foundation Inc.) Retrieved from https://en.wikipedia.org/wiki/Jeffrey_T._Richelson

1048. Richelson, Jeffrey T., ed. Posted online February 20, 2014. Deception, Intelligence, and Policy Counterterrorism. National Security Archive Briefing Book No. 456. *The National Security Archive*. Retrieved from http://nsarchive.gwu.edu/NSAEBB/NSAEBB456/
1049. Ibid.
1050. See, Operation Bodyguard. *Wikipedia The Free Encyclopedia.* (Wikipedia Foundation Inc.) Retrieved from https://en.wikipedia.org/wiki/Operation_Bodyguard
1051. Richelson, op. cit.
1052. Isikoff and Corn, *Hubris*, 5
1053. Scooter Libby. *Wikipedia The Free Encyclopedia.* (Wikipedia Foundation Inc.) Retrieved from https://en.wikipedia.org/wiki/Scooter_Libby (citing) Mirkinson, Jack. October 5, 2005. Libby Leaned Left Before Serving As Cheney's Chief Of Staff. Yale Daily News.
1054. Ibid; Isikoff and Corn, *Hubris*, 5; Paul Wolfowitz. *Wikipedia The Free Encyclopedia.* (Wikipedia Foundation Inc.) Retrieved from https://en.wikipedia.org/wiki/Paul_Wolfo witz; Unger, Craig. *The Fall Of The House Of Bush: The Untold Story Of How A Band Of True Believers Seized The Executive Branch, Started The Iraq War, And Still Imperils America's Future*. (New York: Scribner, 2007) (Kindle version for iPad, 130-133) ; Wolfowitz Doctrine. *Wikipedia The Free Encyclopedia.* (Wikipedia Foundation Inc.) Retrieved from https://en.wikipedia.org/wiki/Wolfowitz_Doctrine. See additionally, David, Anthony. May 19, 2007. The Apprentice. *The American Prospect*. Retrieved from http://prospect.org/article/apprentice
1055. Isikoff and Corn, *Hubris*, 78; Project for the New American Century. *Wikipedia The Free Encyclopedia.* (Wikipedia Foundation Inc.) Retrieved from https://en.wikipedia.org/wiki/ Project_for_the_New_American_Century
1056. Mayer, Jane. June 7, 2004. The Manipulator: Ahmad Chalabi pushed a tainted case for war. Can he survive the occupation? *The New Yorker*. Retrieved from http://www.new yorker.com/magazine/2004/06/07/the-manipulator; Context of 'May 1991: President Bush Authorizes CIA to Create Conditions for Removal of Saddam Hussein; CIA Hires PR Firm.' *History Commons*. Retrieved from http://www.historycommons.org/context.jsp ?item=complete_timeline_of_the_2003_invasion_of_iraq_3217#complete_timeline_of _the_2003_invasion_of_iraq_3217
1057. Why We Did It. March 6, 2014. Maddow, Rachel. Host and Narrator. Documentary which examines the reasons for the Iraq War. Produced in conjunction with NBC News Peacock Productions. *MSNBC.*
1058. Wheeler, Marcy. (Chapter 1) "Sixteen Words." in *Anatomy of Deceit How the Bush Administration Used the Media to Sell the Iraq War and Out a Spy*. (Berkeley; Vaster Books, 2007) 18; Isikoff and Corn, *Hubris*. 86-87, 144, 169-171
1059. Bush. George W. January 28, 2003. State of the Union Address made at U.S. Capitol. Online by Gerhard Peters and John T. Woolley. *The American Presidency Project*. Retrieved from: http://www.presidency.ucsb.edu/ws/index.php?pid=29645
1060. Isikoff and Corn, *Hubris*, 85-100, 133-152
1061. See, Duelfer, Charles September 30, 2004. Investigation Into Uranium Pursuits and Indigenous Production Capabilities in Foreign Pursuits in "A Comprehensive Report of

the Special Advisor to the Director Central Intelligence on Iraq's WMD." *Central Intelligence Agency*. Retrieved from https://www.cia.gov/library/reports/general-reports-1/iraq_wmd_2004/chap4.html#sect4; Isikoff, Michael, and Corn, David. (Chapter Five) "The Niger Caper" in *Hubris: The Inside Story of Spin, Scandal, and the Selling of the Iraq War*. (New York: Three Rivers Press, 2007) 85-100

1062. See, Pilger, John. March 3, 2000. Squeezed To Death. *The Guardian*. Retrieved from http://www.theguardian.com/theguardian/2000/mar/04/weekend7.weekend9; Crossette, Barbara. December 1, 1995. Iraq Sanctions Kill Children, U.N. Reports. *The New York Times*. Retrieved from http://www.nytimes.com

1063. Ibid; See, Duelfer, Charles September 30, 2004. Investigation Into Uranium Pursuits and Indigenous Production Capabilities in Foreign Pursuits in "A Comprehensive Report of the Special Advisor to the Director Central Intelligence on Iraq's WMD." *Central Intelligence Agency*. Retrieved from https://www.cia.gov/library/reports/general-reports-1/iraq_wmd_2004/chap4.html#sect4; Isikoff, Michael, and Corn, David. (Chapter Five) "The Niger Caper" in *Hubris: The Inside Story of Spin, Scandal, and the Selling of the Iraq War*. (New York: Three Rivers Press, 2007) 85-100; See generally, Oil-for-Food Programme. *Wikipedia The Free Encyclopedia.* (Wikipedia Foundation Inc.) Retrieved from https://en.wikipedia.org/wiki/Oil-for-Food_Programme; Rieff, David. July 27, 2003. Were Sanctions Right? The New York Times. Retrieved from http://www.nytimes.com/2003/07/27/magazine/27SANCTIONS.html?pagewanted=all

1064. See generally, Oil-for-Food Programme. *Wikipedia The Free Encyclopedia.* (Wikipedia Foundation Inc.) Retrieved from https://en.wikipedia.org/wiki/Oil-for-Food_Programme; Rieff, David. July 27, 2003. Were Sanctions Right? The New York Times. Retrieved from http://www.nytimes.com/2003/07/27/magazine/27SANCTIONS.html?pagewanted=all

1065. See, Isikoff, Michael, and Corn, David. (Chapter Five) "The Niger Caper" in *Hubris: The Inside Story of Spin, Scandal, and the Selling of the Iraq War*. (New York: Three Rivers Press, 2007) 85-100; For another article which touches upon some but not all of the material covered in the text See, Unger, Craig. The War They Wanted, The Lies They Needed. *Vanity Fair*. (July, 2006) Retrieved from http://wwwvanityfair.com/news/2006/07/yellowcake200607

1066. Ibid.

1067. Ibid.

1068. Isikoff and Corn, *Hubris*, 162-164

1069. Isikoff and Corn, *Hubris,* 92-98

1070. Isikoff and Corn, *Hubris,* 201-205

1071. Bush. George W., January 28, 2003. State of the Union Address made at U.S. Capitol. Online by Gerhard Peters and John T. Woolley. *The American Presidency Project.* Retrieved from: http://www.presidency.ucsb.edu/ws/index.php?pid=29645

1072. Isikoff and Corn, *Hubris*, 174.

1073. Bush. George W., January 28, 2003. State of the Union Address made at U.S. Capitol. Online by Gerhard Peters and John T. Woolley. *The American Presidency Project.*

Retrieved from: http://www.presidency.ucsb.edu/ws/index.php?pid=29645

1074. Leung, Rebecca. January 9, 2004. Bush Sought 'Way' To Invade Iraq? O'Neill Tells "60 Minutes" Iraq Was 'Topic A" 8 Months Before 9-11. *CBS News*. Retrieved from http://www.cbsnews.com/news/bush-sought-way-to-invade-iraq/; Lie by Lie: A Timeline of How We Got Into Iraq. (September/October, 2006). *Mother Jones*. Retrieved from http://www.motherjones.com/politics/2011/12/leadup-iraq-war-timeline; Borger, Julian. January 11, 2004. Bush decided to remove Saddam 'on day one.' *The Guardian*. Retrieved from http://www.theguardian.com/world/2004/jan/12/usa.books

1075. Powell, Colin L., February 5, 2003. Speech made as U.S. Secretary of State to the U.N. Security Council. New York City. (Transcript, video clips and slides included) *U.S. Department of State Archive*. Retrieved from http://2001-2009.state.gov/p/nea/disarm/

1076. Ibid.

1077. Depending on the source, Zarqawi's birth is reported as having occurred on either October 20 or October 30, 1966 . See generally, Abu Musab al-Zarqawi. *Wikipedia The Free Encyclopedia.* (Wikipedia Foundation Inc.) Retrieved from https://en.wikipedia.org/wiki/Abu_Musab_al-Zarqawi; Whitlock, Craig. Hernandez, Nelson. Boustany, Nora. contrib. "Al-Zarqawi's Biography." June 8, 2006. (updated from Sept. 27, 2004) *The Washington Post.* Retrieved from http://www.washingtonpost.com/; Abu Mussab al-Zarqawi Biography. *Encyclopedia of World Biography*. Retrieved from http://www.notablebiographies.com; Abu Musab al-Zarqawi. *Encyclopaedia Britannica*. Retrieved from http://www.britannica.com/biography/Abu-Musab-al-Zarqawi

1078. Meaning of Musab. *Quranic Names*. Retrieved from http://quranicnames.com/musab/

1079. Ibid; See additionally, Weaver, Mary Anne. The Short, Violent Life of Abu Musab al-Zarqawi: How a video-store clerk and small-time crook reinvented himself as America's nemesis in Iraq. (July - August, 2006). *The Atlantic*. Retrieved from http://www.theatlantic.com/magazine/archive/2006/07/the-short-violent-life-of-abu-musab-al-zarqawi/304983/?single_page=true; Teslik, Lee Hudson. June 8, 2006. Profile: Abu Musab al-Zarqawi. *Council on Foreign Relations*. Retrieved from http://www.cfr.org/iraq/profile-abu-musab-al-zarqawi/p9866; Mapping Militant Organizations Team of Stanford University. Profile of "The Islamic State." *Stanford University*. Retrieved from http://web.stanford.edu/group/mappingmilitants/cgi-bin/groups/view/1

1080. See, Abu Musab al-Zarqawi. *Wikipedia The Free Encyclopedia.* (Wikipedia Foundation Inc.) Retrieved from https://en.wikipedia.org/wiki/Abu_Musab_al-Zarqawi; Whitlock, Craig. Hernandez, Nelson. Boustany, Nora. contrib. "Al-Zarqawi's Biography." June 8, 2006. (updated from Sept. 27, 2004) *The Washington Post.* Retrieved from http://www.washingtonpost.com/; Abu Mussabal-Zarqawi Biography. *Encyclopedia of World Biography*. Retrieved from http://www.notablebiographies.com; Abu Musab al-Zarqawi. *Encyclopaedia Britannica*. Retrieved from http://www.britannica.com/biography/Abu-Musab-al-Zarqawi

1081. See, Weaver, Mary Anne. The Short, Violent Life of Abu Musab al-Zarqawi: How a video-store clerk and small-time crook reinvented himself as America's nemesis in Iraq. (July - August, 2006). *The Atlantic*. Retrieved from http://www.theatlantic.com/magazine

/archive/2006/07/the-short-violent-life-of-abu-musab-al-zarqawi/304983/?single_page=true; Teslik, Lee Hudson. June 8, 2006. Profile: Abu Musab al-Zarqawi. *Council on Foreign Relations*. Retrieved from http://www.cfr.org/iraq/profile-abu-musab-al-zarqawi/p9866; Mapping Militant Organizations Team of Stanford University. Profile of "The Islamic State." *Stanford University*. Retrieved from http://web.stanford.edu/group/mappingmilitants/cgi-bin/groups/view/1; See additionally, Jund al-Sham. *Wikipedia The Free Encyclopedia.* (Wikipedia Foundation Inc.) Retrieved from https://en.wikipedia.org/wiki/Jund_al-Sham; Roggio, Bill. March 30, 2005. Exodus and Ascent. *The Long War Journal*. Retrieved from http://www.longwarjournal.org/archives/2005/03/exodus_and_asce.php

1082. Ibid; See additionally, Zelin, Aaron Y., The War between ISIS and al-Qaeda for Supremacy of the Global Jihadist Movement. (Number 20, June 2014). *The Washington Institute For Near East Policy*. Retrieved from http://www.washingtoninstitute.org/uploads/Documents/pubs/ResearchNote_20_Zelin.pdf; Jama'at al-Tawhid wal-Jihad. *Wikipedia The Free Encyclopedia.* (Wikipedia Foundation Inc.) Retrieved from https://en.wikipedia.org/wiki/Jama%27at_al-Tawhid_wal-Jihad

1083. Timeline: Key Events in the Life of al-Zarqawi. June 8, 2006. The New York Times. Retrieved from http://www.nytimes.com/2006/06/08/world/08timeline-zarqawi.html?_r=0; Ansar al-Islam. *Wikipedia The Free Encyclopedia.* (Wikipedia Foundation Inc.) Retrieved from https://en.wikipedia.org/wiki/Ansar_al-Islam; Mapping Militant Organizations Team of Stanford University. Narrative summary of Ansar al-Islam. October 2, 2015 update. *Stanford University*. Retrieved from http://web.stanford.edu/group/mappingmilitants/cgi-bin/groups/view/13; October 20 or October 30, 1966 . See generally, Abu Musab al-Zarqawi. *Wikipedia The Free Encyclopedia.* (Wikipedia Foundation Inc.) Retrieved from https://en.wikipedia.org/wiki/Abu_Musab_al-Zarqawi; Whitlock, Craig. Hernandez, Nelson. Boustany, Nora. contrib. "Al-Zarqawi's Biography." June 8, 2006. (updated from Sept. 27, 2004) *The Washington Post*. Retrieved from http://www.washingtonpost.com/; Abu Mussabal-Zarqawi Biography. *Encyclopedia of World Biography*. Retrieved from http://www.notablebiographies.com; Abu Musab al-Zarqawi. *Encyclopaedia Britannica*. Retrieved from http://www.britannica.com/biography/Abu-Musab-al-Zarqawi

1084. Ibid. See also, Jama'at al-Tawhid wal-Jihad. *Wikipedia The Free Encyclopedia.* (Wikipedia Foundation Inc.) Retrieved from https://en.wikipedia.org/wiki/Jama%27at_al-Tawhid_wal-Jihad; Narrative summary of The Islamic State. May 15, 2015 update. *Stanford University*. Retrieved from http://web.stanford.edu/group/mappingmilitants/cgi-bin/groups/view/1

1085. See, Schanzer, Jonathan. Ansar al-Islam: Back in Iraq . *Middle East Quarterly*. (Winter, 2004) 41-50. Retrieved from https://www.washingtoninstitute.org/uploads/Documents/opeds/4224e31e5fa37.pdf

1086. Jonathan Weisman. September 10, 2006. Saddam had no links to al-Qaeda. *The Washington Post*. Online by *The Age*. Retrieved from http://www.theage.com.au/news/world/saddam-had-no-links-to-alqaeda/2006/09/09/1157222383981.html?page=2; United

States Senate. Select Committee On Intelligence.109th Congress. September 8, 2006. Report of the Select Committee On Intelligence on Postwar Findings About Iraq's WMD Programs And Links To Terrorism And How They Compare With Pre War Assessments. pp. 109 -111. Retrieved from http://www.gpo.gov/fdsys/pkg/CRPT-109srpt331/pdf/CRPT-109srpt331.pdf

1087. See generally, Abu Musab al-Zarqawi. *Wikipedia The Free Encyclopedia.* (Wikipedia Foundation Inc.) Retrieved from https://en.wikipedia.org/wiki/Abu_Musab_al-Zarqawi; Whitlock, Craig. Hernandez, Nelson. Boustany, Nora. contrib. "Al-Zarqawi's Biography."June 8, 2006. (updated from Sept. 27, 2004) *The Washington Post.* Retrieved from http://www.washingtonpost.com/; Abu Mussab al-Zarqawi Biography. *Encyclopedia of World Biography.* Retrieved from http://www.notablebiographies.com; Abu Musab al-Zarqawi.*Encyclopaedia Britannica.* Retrieved from http://www.britannica.com/biography/Abu-Musab-al-Zarqawi; Weaver, Mary Anne. The Short, Violent Life of Abu Musab al-Zarqawi: How a video-store clerk and small-time crook reinvented himself as America's nemesis in Iraq. (July - August, 2006). *The Atlantic.* Retrieved from http://www.the atlantic.com/magazine/archive/2006/07/the-short-violent-life-of-abu-musab-al-zarqawi/304983/?single_page=true; Teslik, Lee Hudson. June 8, 2006. Profile: Abu Musab al-Zarqawi. *Council on Foreign Relations.* Retrieved from http://www.cfr.org/iraq/profile-abu-musab-al-zarqawi/p9866; Mapping Militant Organizations Team of Stanford University. Profile of "The Islamic State." *Stanford University.* Retrieved from http://web.stanford.edu/group/mappingmilitants/cgi-bin/groups/view/1; Timeline: Key Events in the Life of al-Zarqawi. June 8, 2006. The New York Times. Retrieved from http://www.nytimes.com/2006/06/08/world/08timeline-zarqawi.html?_r=0; Ansar al-Islam. *Wikipedia The Free Encyclopedia.* (Wikipedia Foundation Inc.) Retrieved from https://en.wikipedia.org/wiki/Ansar_al-Islam; Mapping Militant Organizations Team of Stanford University. Narrative summary of Ansar al-Islam. October 2, 2015 update. *Stanford University.* Retrieved from http://web.stanford.edu/ group/mappingmilitants/cgi-bin/groups/view/13; October 20 or October 30, 1966 . See generally, Abu Musab al-Zarqawi. *Wikipedia The Free Encyclopedia.* (Wikipedia Foundation Inc.) Retrieved from https://en.wikipedia.org/wiki/Abu_Musab_al-Zarqawi; Whitlock, Craig. Hernandez, Nelson. Boustany, Nora. contrib. "Al-Zarqawi's Biography." June 8, 2006. (updated from Sept. 27, 2004) *The Washington Post.* Retrieved from http://www.washingtonpost.com/; Abu Mussabal-Zarqawi Biography. *Encyclopedia of World Biography.* Retrieved from http://www.notablebiographies.com; Abu Musab al-Zarqawi. *Encyclopaedia Britannica.* Retrieved from http://www.britannica.com/biography/Abu-Musab-al-Zarqawi

1088. Powell, Colin L., February 5, 2003. Speech made as U.S. Secretary of State to the U.N. Security Council. New York City. (Transcript, video clips and slides included) *U.S. Department of State Archive.* Retrieved from http://2001-2009.state.gov/p/nea/disarm/

1089. Ibid.

1090. Ibid.

1091. Ibid.

1092. Ibid.
1093. Ibid.
1094. See, Schwartz, Johnathan. February 5, 2013. (updated April 7, 2013) Lie After Lie After Lie: What Colin Powell Knew Ten Years Ago Today and What He Said. *Huff Post Politics*. Retrieved from http://www.huffingtonpost.com/jonathan-schwarz/colin-powell-wmd-iraq-war_b_2624620.html; Swanson, David. February 18, 2011. Colin Powell's Disgraceful Lies. *ConsortiumNews.com*. Retrieved from https://consortiumnews.com/2011/021811a.html; Isikoff and Corn, *Hubris*, 174 - 190
1095. Ibid.
1096. Ibid; See, Jonathan Weisman. September 10, 2006. Saddam had no links to al-Qaeda. *The Washington Post*. Online by *The Age*. Retrieved from http://www.theage.com.au/news/world/saddam-had-no-links-to-alqaeda/2006/09/09/1157222383981.html?page=2; United States Senate. Select Committee On Intelligence.109th Congress. September 8, 2006. Report of the Select Committee On Intelligence on Postwar Findings About Iraq's WMD Programs And Links To Terrorism And How They Compare With Pre War Assessments. pp. 109 -111. Retrieved from http://www.gpo.gov/fdsys/pkg/CRPT-109srpt331/pdf/CRPT-109srpt331.pdf See generally, Saddam Hussein and al-Qaeda link allegations. *Wikipedia The Free Encyclopedia.* (Wikipedia Foundation Inc.) Retrieved from https://en.wikipedia.org/wiki/Saddam_Hussein_and_al-Qaeda_link_allegations
1097. Isikoff and Corn, *Hubris*, 176-177
1098. Ibid. Weisman, op. cit.
1099. Isikoff and Corn, *Hubris*, 177
1100. Isikoff and Corn, *Hubris*, 177-178, 31-32, 133-139
1101. Isikoff and Corn, *Hubris*, 179
1102. Isikoff and Corn, *Hubris*, 136
1103. Isikoff and Corn, *Hubris*, 133-140, 174-190; Weisman, op. cit.; United States Senate. Select Committee On Intelligence.109th Congress. September 8, 2006. Report of the Select Committee On Intelligence on Postwar Findings About Iraq's WMD Programs And Links To Terrorism And How They Compare With Pre War Assessments. pp. 109 - 111. Retrieved from http://www.gpo.gov/fdsys/pkg/CRPT-109srpt331/pdf/CRPT-109srpt331.pdf See generally, Saddam Hussein and al-Qaeda link allegations. *Wikipedia The Free Encyclopedia.* (Wikipedia Foundation Inc.) Retrieved from https://en.wikipedia.org/wiki/Saddam_Hussein_and_al-Qaeda_link_allegations; Schwartz, Johnathan. February 5, 2013. (updated April 7, 2013) Lie After Lie After Lie: What Colin Powell Knew Ten Years Ago Today and What He Said. *Huff Post Politics*. Retrieved from http://www.huffingtonpost.com/jonathan-schwarz/colin-powell-wmd-iraq-war_b_2624620.html; Swanson, David. February 18, 2011. Colin Powell's Disgraceful Lies. *ConsortiumNews.com*. Retrieved from https://consortiumnews.com/2011/021811a.html;
1104. Ibid.
1105. United States Senate. Select Committee On Intelligence.109th Congress. September 8, 2006. Report of the Select Committee On Intelligence on Postwar Findings About Iraq's WMD Programs And Links To Terrorism And How They Compare With Prewar

Assessments. Retrieved from http://www.gpo.gov/fdsys/pkg/CRPT-109srpt331/pdf/CRPT-109srpt331.pdf;

1106. Ibid., 105
1107. Ibid., 105-106
1108. Ibid., 71 (citing) United States Senate. Select Committee On Intelligence.108th Congress. July 9, 2004. Report of the Senate Intelligence Committee on the U.S. Intelligence Community's Prewar Intelligence Assessments on Iraq. S. Rept. 108-301. p. 337
1109. Ibid., 70-71
1110. McGovern, Ray. May 19, 2009. How Colin Powell Got Duped by the CIA. *Counterpunch*. Retrieved from http://www.counterpunch.org/2009/05/19/how-colin-powell-got-duped-by-the-cia/; McGovern, Ray. February 4, 2013. Colin Powell: Conned or Con-Man? ConsortiumNews.com. Retrieved from https://consortiumnews.com/2013/02/04/colin-powell-conned-or-con-man/; Isikoff and Corn, *Hubris*, 119-124, 180-181, 187-188, 363
1111. Ibid; 1030
1112. McGovern, Ray. May 19, 2009. How Colin Powell Got Duped by the CIA. *Counterpunch*. Retrieved from http://www.counterpunch.org/2009/05/19/how-colin-powell-got-duped-by-the-cia/; McGovern, Ray. February 4, 2013. Colin Powell: Conned or Con-Man? ConsortiumNews.com. Retrieved from https://consortiumnews.com/2013/02/04/colin-powell-conned-or-con-man/; Isikoff and Corn, *Hubris*, 119-124, 180-181, 187-188, 363
1113. United States Senate. Select Committee On Intelligence.109th Congress. September 8, 2006. Report of the Select Committee On Intelligence on Postwar Findings About Iraq's WMD Programs And Links To Terrorism And How They Compare With Pre War Assessments. 106-108 Retrieved from http://www.gpo.gov/fdsys/pkg/CRPT-109srpt331/pdf/CRPT-109srpt331.pdf.
1114. Report of the Select Committee On Intelligence on Postwar Findings About Iraq's WMD Programs And Links To Terrorism And How They Compare With Pre War Assessments op. cit. p. 77. The quoted language was first by made public in a press release by the office of Senator Carl Levin. See, Office of U.S. Senator Carl Levin. November 18. 2005. Levin and Reed Compare Bush Administration Statements with Intelligence Community Statements on Pre-War Iraq Intelligence. Press Release. (quoting) Defense Intelligence Agency's Defense Intelligence Terrorism Summary (DITSUM No. 044-02), issued February 22, 2002. Online by Modulus Studios in conjunction with the 2008 film and related website *Leading to War*. (Dir. Barry J. Hershey, Prod. Lewis D. Wheeler, Ellie Lee, Beth Sternheimer) Retrieved from http://wwwleadingtowar.com/PDFsourcesclaims_training/2002_02_22_LevinPreWarIntelligence.pdf; Modulus Studios. Timeline of Bush Administration Facts Versus Claims. *Leading To War*. Retrieved from http://www.leadingtowar.com/claims_facts_training.php; See generally, Jehl, Douglas. November 6, 2005. Report Warned Bush Team About Intelligence Doubts. *The New York Times*. Retrieved from http://www.nytimes.com/2005/11/06/politics/report-warned-bush-team-about-intelligence-doubts.html

1115. Report of the Select Committee On Intelligence on Postwar Findings About Iraq's WMD Programs And Links To Terrorism And How They Compare With Pre War Assessments op. cit.

1116. Ibid. p. 77-78; See generally, Ibn al-Shaykh al-Libi. *Wikipedia The Free Encyclopedia.* (Wikipedia Foundation Inc.) Retrieved from https://en.wikipedia.org/wiki/Ibn_al-Shaykh_al-Libi#cite; For more background on al-Libi, See, Isikoff and Corn, *Hubris*, 119-124

1117. Isikoff and Corn, *Hubris*, 180-181; McGovern, Ray. May 19, 2009. How Colin Powell Got Duped by the CIA. *Counterpunch*. Retrieved from http://www.counterpunch.org/2009/05/19/how-colin-powell-got-duped-by-the-cia/; McGovern, Ray. February 4, 2013. Colin Powell: Conned or Con-Man? ConsortiumNews.com. Retrieved from https://consortiumnews.com/2013/02/04/colin-powell-conned-or-con-man/; See additionally, Isikoff and Corn, *Hubris*, 119-124, 187-188, 363

1118. Isikoff and Corn, *Hubris*, 133-140, 174-190; Weisman, op. cit.; United States Senate. Select Committee On Intelligence.109th Congress. September 8, 2006. Report of the Select Committee On Intelligence on Postwar Findings About Iraq's WMD Programs And Links To Terrorism And How They Compare With Pre War Assessments. pp. 109 - 111. Retrieved from http://www.gpo.gov/fdsys/pkg/CRPT-109srpt331/pdf/CRPT-109srpt331.pdf See generally, Saddam Hussein and al-Qaeda link allegations. *Wikipedia The Free Encyclopedia.* (Wikipedia Foundation Inc.) Retrieved from https://en.wikipedia.org/wiki/Saddam_Hussein_and_al-Qaeda_link_allegations; Schwartz, Johnathan. February 5, 2013. (updated April 7, 2013) Lie After Lie After Lie: What Colin Powell Knew Ten Years Ago Today and What He Said. *Huff Post Politics*. Retrieved from http://www.huffingtonpost.com/jonathan-schwarz/colin-powell-wmd-iraq-war_b_2624620.html; Swanson, David. February 18, 2011. Colin Powell's Disgraceful Lies. *ConsortiumNews.com*. Retrieved from https://consortiumnews.com/2011/021811a.html; McGovern, Ray. May 19, 2009. How Colin Powell Got Duped by the CIA. *Counterpunch*. Retrieved from http://www.counterpunch.org/2009/05/19/how-colin-powell-got-duped-by-the-cia/; McGovern, Ray. February 4, 2013. Colin Powell: Conned or Con-Man? ConsortiumNews.com. Retrieved from https://consortiumnews.com/2013/02/04/colin-powell-conned-or-con-man/

1119. Isikoff and Corn, *Hubris*, 181

1120. Isikoff and Corn, *Hubris*, 101-105

1121. Corn. David. February 16, 2003. "Hubris": New Documentary Reexamines the Iraq War "Hoax." Mother Jones. Retrieved from http://www.motherjones.com/politics/2013/02/hubris-rachel-maddow-documentary-iraq-war-david-corn

1122. Ibid.

1123. Schwarz, Jonathan. February 5, 2013. Lie After Lie After Lie: What Colin Powell Knew Ten Years Ago Today and What He Said. *Huff Post Politics*. Retrieved from http://www.huffingtonpost.com/jonathan-schwarz/colin-powell-wmd-iraq-war_b_2624620.html

1124. Woodward, Bob. *Plan of Attack.* (New York: Simon and Schuster, 2004)

1125. Schwartz, op. cit.

1126. Ibid.

1127. Ibid; Schwartz points out that the original transcript of the Iraqi conversation was removed by the State Department from its website, but not before a copy of it was safely placed by a third party at the website archive.org. See, U.S. Dept. of State. Iraq: Failing to Disarm: Transcript of Iraqi Conversation -- Ammunition. *Internet Archive WayBack Machine*. Retrieved fromhttp://web.archive.org/web/20030404073844/http://www.state.gov/r/pa/ei/pix/events/secretary/2003/17399.htm; The transcripts and recording of Powell's UN speech, which contain the evidence fabricated by Powell of statements made by the Iraqi's that cannot be heard on the audio recording are available online. See, Secretary Colin Powell. February 5, 2003. Remarks to the United Nations Security Council. *U.S. Department of State Archive January 20, 2001 to January 20, 2009*. Retrieved from http://2001-2009.state.gov/secretary/former/powell/remarks/2003/17300.htm

1128. Ibid.

1129. Schwartz, op. cit. Schwartz cites Woodward's book *Plan of Attack* for the quotes from Powell; The pages of my Kindle copy of Woodward's "*Plan of Attack*" are not numbered, but I found the quoted portion in Chapter 29 of the book; See Woodward, op. cit.

1130. Borger, Julian. October 7, 2004. There were no weapons of mass destruction in Iraq. *The Guardian*. Retrieved from http://www.theguardian.com/world/2004/oct/07/usa.iraq1; Drum, Kevin. October 15, 2014. No, There's Still No Evidence There Was an Active WMD Program in Iraq. *Mother Jones*. Retrieved from http://www.motherjones.com/; Benen, Steve. October 15, 2014. Conservatives continue to get Iraqi WMD story wrong. *MSNBC The Rachel Maddow Show / The Maddow Blog*. Retrieved from http://www.msnbc.com/rachel-maddow-show/conservatives-continue-get-iraqi-wmd-story-wrong; Miller, Joe. February 19, 2008. There were no WMDs in Iraq. *FactCheck,Org*. Retrieved from http://www.factcheck.org/2008/02/no-wmds-in-iraq/; The foregoing articles rebut the absurd claim that the dangerous WMD Bush had warned the world about was actually found in Iraq. What was found were some very old chemical weapons left over from the Iran - Iraq War. These included approximately five thousand old artillery shells, warheads and aviation bombs. The Bush administration kept the discovery of those weapons during the Iraq War secret because the weapons were made with the help of western nations including the United States, starting around 1981. The U.S. has been at loggerheads with Iran since the Iranian revolution in 1979, and the resultant Iranian Hostage Crisis. See, Chivers, C.J., October 14, 2014. The Secret Casualties of Iraq's Abandoned Chemical Weapons. *The New York Times*. Retrieved from http://www.nytimes.com/interactive/2014/10/14/world/middleeast/us-casualties-of-iraq-chemical-weapons.html?_r=0;

1131. Ibid; Nichols, Bill. March 22, 2004 U.N.: Iraq had no WMD after 1994. USA Today. Retrieved from http://usatoday30.usatoday.com/news/world/iraq/2004-03-02-un-wmd_x.htm; UN Security Council Press Release. United Nation's Weapons Inspectors Report To Security Council On Progress In Disarmament Of Iraq. March 7, 2003. *United Nations*. Retrieved from http://www.un.org/press/en/2003/sc7682.doc.htm; Rothkopf. Joanna.

May 20, 2015. George W. Bush's CIA briefer admits Iraq WMD "intelligence" was a lie. *Salon*. Retrieved from http://www.salon.com/

1132. Ibid; See, Douglas J. Feith. *Wikipedia The Free Encyclopedia.* (Wikipedia Foundation Inc.) Retrieved from https://en.wikipedia.org/wiki/Douglas_J._Feith; Feith, Douglas J. Defense, April 22, 2004. Democracy, and the War on Terrorism. Speech to John F. Kennedy School of Government, Harvard University, April 22, 2004, *Douglas J. Feith Website*. Retrieved from http://www.dougfeith.com/docs/2004_04_22_Harvard_GWOT .pdf; Profile of Douglas J. Feith. November 14, 2014. *Right Web*. Retrieved from http:// www.rightweb.irc-online.org/profile/Feith_Douglas; Borger, Julian. December 5, 2002. Democrat Hawk Whose Ghost Guides Bush: Scoop Jackson's body is 20 years in the grave but his spirit goes marching on. *The Guardian*. Retrieved from http://www.theguar dian.com/world/2002/dec/06/usa.julianborger; Profile: Douglas Feith. *History Commons*. Retrieved from http://www.historycommons.org/entity.jsp?entity=douglas_feith; See additionally, Unger, Craig. (Chapter Four) "The ForeShadowing." in *The Fall Of The House Of Bush: The Untold Story Of How A Band Of True Believers Seized The Executive Branch, Started The Iraq War, And Still Imperils America's Future*. (New York: Scribner, 2007); Shankbone, David. November 12, 2007. Interview with Craig Unger: Vanity Fair contributing editor Craig Unger on the Bush family feud, neoconservatives and the Christian right. *Wikinews*. Retrieved from https://en.wikinews. org/wiki/Vanity_Fair_contributing_editor_Craig_Unger_on_the_Bush_family_feud,_neo conservatives_and_the_Christian_right

1133. Schwarz, Jonathan. February 5, 2013. Lie After Lie After Lie: What Colin Powell Knew Ten Years Ago Today and What He Said. *Huff Post Politics*. Retrieved from http://www. huffingtonpost.com/jonathan-schwarz/colin-powell-wmd-iraq-war_b_2624620.html

1134. See, Cranberg, Gilbert, June 29, 2003. Bring Back the Skeptical Press. *The Washington Post*. Retrieved from http://pqasb.pqarchiver.com/washingtonpost/doc/409581054.html? FMT=ABS&FMTS=ABS:FT &date=Jun+29%2C+2003&author=Cranberg%2C+Gilbert &desc=.+.+.+Bring+Back+the+Skeptical+Press; See additionally Parry, Robert. April 8, 2003. Bush's Alderaan: "F--- Saddam," Bush said. "We're taking him out." March 2002. *Information Clearing House*. Retrieved from http://www.informationclearinghouse.info/ article2835.htm; Editorial. July 18, 2003. Bush Uranium Lie Is Tip of the Iceberg. *FAIR. Fairness and Accuracy In Reporting*. Retrieved from http://fair.org/press-release/bush-uranium-lie-is-tip-of-the-iceberg/

1135. Ibid; See generally, Schwarz, Jonathan. February 5, 2013. Lie After Lie After Lie: What Colin Powell Knew Ten Years Ago Today and What He Said. *Huff Post Politics*. Retrieved from http://www.huffingtonpost.com/jonathan-schwarz/colin-powell-wmd-iraq -war_b_2624620.html

1136. See, U.S. Dept. of State. Iraq: Failing to Disarm: Transcript of Iraqi Conversation -- Ammunition. *Internet Archive WayBack Machine*. Retrieved from http://web.archive.org/ web/20030404073844/http://www.state.gov/r/pa/ei/pix/events/secretary/2003/17399.htm; The transcripts and recording of Powell's UN speech, which contain the evidence fabricated by Powell of statements made by the Iraqi's that cannot be heard on the audio recording are available online. See, Secretary Colin Powell. February 5, 2003. Remarks to the United Nations Security Council. *U.S. Department of State Archive January 20, 2001 to January 20, 2009.* Retrieved from http://2001-2009.state.gov/secretary/former/powell/remarks/2003/17300.htm

1137. NBC News' Meet The Press. December 9, 2001. Transcript of Interview with Vice-President Dick Cheney on Meet the Press. Tim Russert, Moderator. Online by eMediaMillWorks. *Washington Post.* Retrieved from http://www.washingtonpost.com/wp-srv/nation/specials/attacked/transcripts/cheneytext_120901.html

1138. NBC News' Meet The Press. September 8, 2002. Transcript of Interview with Vice-President Dick Cheney on Meet the Press. Tim Russert, Moderator. Online by Modulus Studios in conjunction with the 2008 film and related website *Leading to War.* (Dir. Barry J. Hershey, Prod. Lewis D. Wheeler, Ellie Lee, Beth Sternheimer) Retrieved from http://www.leadingtowar.com/PDFsources_claims_aluminum/2002_09_08_NBC.pdf

1139. NBC News' Meet The Press. September 7, 2002. Transcript for September 14, 2002. Vice-President Dick Cheney on Meet the Press. Guest: Dick Cheney, Vice President, Tim Russert, Moderator. NBC News. Retrieved from http://www.nbcnews.com/id/3080244/ns/meet_the_press/t/transcript-sept/#.VoRKrN5Z3lt

1140. Isikoff and Corn, *Hubris*, 101-105; MSNBC Documentaries. March 22, 2013 (Updated October 14, 2013) How The Bush Administration Sold The Iraq War. March 22, 2013 (Updated October 14, 2013) *MSNBC*. Retrieved from http://www.msnbc.com/msnbc/how-the-bush-administration-sold-the-iraq-war

1141. Isikoff and Corn, *Hubris*, 103-104

1142. Isikoff and Corn, *Hubris*, 101-105; MSNBC Documentaries. March 22, 2013 (Updated October 14, 2013) How The Bush Administration Sold The Iraq War. March 22, 2013 (Updated October 14, 2013) *MSNBC*. Retrieved from http://www.msnbc.com/msnbc/how-the-bush-administration-sold-the-iraq-war

1143. U.S. National Commission on Terrorist Attacks upon the United States. 9/11 Commission Report: The Official Report of the 9/11 Commission (Washington, D.C: GPO, 2004) 228-229 *Government Printing Office*. Retrieved from https://www.gpo.gov/fdsys/pkg/GPO-911REPORT/content-detail.html

1144. NBC News' Meet The Press. December 9, 2001. Transcript of Interview with Vice-President Dick Cheney on Meet the Press. Tim Russert, Moderator. Online by eMediaMillWorks. *Washington Post.* Retrieved from http://www.washingtonpost.com/wp-srv/nation/specials/attacked/transcripts/cheneytext_120901.html

1145. How The Bush Administration Sold The Iraq War. March 22, 2013 (Updated October 14, 2013) *MSNBC*. Retrieved from http://www.msnbc.com/msnbc/how-the-bush-administration-sold-the-iraq-war (quoting) Hubris: The Inside Story of Spin, Scandal, and the Selling of the Iraq War. Interview of FBI Agent Mark Rossini. First broadcast on February 18, 2013. Rachel Maddow, Host and Narrator. *MSNBC*. Documentary based on the book by the same name written by Michael Isikoff and David Corn

1146. Hubris: The Inside Story of Spin, Scandal, and the Selling of the Iraq War. Interview of

FBI Agent Mark Rossini. First broadcast on February 18, 2013. Rachel Maddow, Host and Narrator. *MSNBC*. Documentary based on the book by the same name written by Michael Isikoff and David Corn; The quote by Rossini can be read online. See for eg., Washingtonsblog post. March 20,2013. CIA and FBI Counter-Terrorism Officials: Cheney Lied About 9/11 Hijacker. *WashingtonsBlog*. Retrieved from http://www.washingtonsblog.com/2013/03/cia-and-fbi-counter-terrorism-officials-cheney-lied-about-911-hijacker.html

1147. Full text of Vice President Dick Cheney's speech delivered to the Veterans of Foreign Wars (VFW) national convention in Nashville, Tennessee on August 26, 2002. Online on August 27, 2002 by *The Guardian*. Retrieved from http://www.theguardian.com/world/2002/aug/27/usa.iraq
1148. President Bush's Address to the United Nations. September 12, 2002. Transcript posted online. *CNN*. Retrieved from http://edition.cnn.com/2002/US/09/12/bush.transcript/
1149. Secretary of Defense Donald H. Rumsfeld. Testimony to the House Armed Services Committee regarding Iraq given at the Rayburn House Office Building, Washington, D.C., September 18, 2002. Transcript online by the Political Science Department of *UCLA*. Retrieved from http://www.sscnet.ucla.edu/polisci/faculty/trachtenberg/useur/rumsfeld180902.html
1150. Bush, George W., October 5, 2002. The President's Radio Address. Audio online by Gerhard Peters and John T. Woolley. *The American Presidency Project*. Retrieved from: http://www.presidency.ucsb.edu/mediaplay.php?id=25047&admin=43
1151. Bush, George W., Address to the Nation on Iraq made from the Grand Rotunda at the Cincinnati Museum Center at Union Terminal. October 7, 2002. Transcript online by Gerhard Peters and John T. Woolley, *The American Presidency Project*. Retrieved from http://www.presidency.ucsb.edu/ws/?pid=73139.
1152. Bush, George W., January 28, 2003. Address Before a Joint Session of the Congress on the State of the Union, Online by Gerhard Peters and John T. Woolley, *The American Presidency Project*. http://www.presidency.ucsb.edu/ws/?pid=29645.
1153. See, Secretary Colin Powell. February 5, 2003. Remarks to the United Nations Security Council. *U.S. Department of State Archive January 20, 2001 to January 20, 2009.* Retrieved from http://2001-2009.state.gov/secretary/former/powell/remarks/2003/17300.htm
1154. Ibid.
1155. Ibid.
1156. Ibid.
1157. Bush, George W., March 17, 2003. Address to the Nation on Iraq, Online by Gerhard Peters and John T. Woolley, The American Presidency Project. http://www.presidency.ucsb.edu/ws/?pid=63713.
1158. Isikoff and Corn, *Hubris*, 12, 15
1159. Ibid., 12
1160. Ibid., 13

1161. Ibid., 12-15
1162. Ibid., 13-15
1163. Ibid., 14, 52-53
1164. Isikoff and Corn, *Hubris*, 49-56, 109-111 See additionally, Ahmed Chalabi. *Wikipedia The Free Encyclopedia.* (Wikipedia Foundation Inc.) Retrieved from https://en.wikipedia.org/wiki/Ahmed_Chalabi; See generally, Roston, Aram. *The Man Who Pushed America To War: The Extraordinary Life, Adventures and Obsessions of Ahmed Chalabi*. (New York: Nation Books, 2008); Gelb, Leslie H., April 27, 2008. Neoconner. *The New York Times*. Retrieved from http://www.nytimes.com/2008/04/27/books/review/Gelb-t.html?_r=0; Mayer, Jane. June 7, 2004. The Manipulator: Ahmad Chalabi pushed a tainted case for war. Can he survive the occupation? *The New Yorker*. Retrieved from http://www.newyorker.com/magazine/2004/06/07/the-manipulator; Context of 'May 1991: President Bush Authorizes CIA to Create Conditions for Removal of Saddam Hussein; CIA Hires PR Firm.' *History Commons*. Retrieved from http://www.historycommons.org/context.jsp?item=complete_timeline_of_the_2003_invasion_of_iraq_3217#complete_timeline_of_the_2003_invasion_of_iraq_3217
1165. See notes 1032 - 1035, 1037.
1166. Isikoff and Corn, *Hubris*, 180-185; Corn. David. February 16, 2003. "Hubris": New Documentary Reexamines the Iraq War "Hoax." Mother Jones. Retrieved from http://www.motherjones.com/politics/2013/02/hubris-rachel-maddow-documentary-iraq-war-david-corn; Leung, Rebecca. October 14, 2013. The Man Who Knew: Ex-Powell Aide Says Saddam-Weapons Threat Was Overstated. *CBS News*. Retrieved from http://www.cbsnews.com/news/the-man-who-knew-14-10-2003/
1167. Ibid.; Powell's knowledge has been attested to not only by his own statements and actions, but by his own high ranking aides, Greg Thielmann and Lawrence Wilkerson. Theilmann was formerly the acting director of the Office of Strategic Proliferation and Military Affairs at the Department of State. As such he had access to essentially all important intelligence data about Iraqi WMD. His job included communicating intelligence reports to then Secretary of State Powell. Wilkerson was Powell's Chief of Staff; See additionally, Isikoff and Corn, *Hubris,* 40; I don't know why General Powell doesn't just go public and tell us "why," as he told Senator Joe Biden he would do someday over a cup of coffee. See, Isikoff and Corn, *Hubris*, 185
1168. See, Isikoff and Corn, *Hubris*, 176-178
1169. See, Isikoff and Corn, *Hubris*, 180-181
1170. The State Department's Bureau of Intelligence and Research, (INR) sent Powell a report during the drafting of his speech which indicated that thirty-eight claims made in a preliminary draft were "unsubstantiated," "weak," or from "questionable sources." Ultimately four such allegations remained in the final draft. Powell should have been aware that he was ignoring the advice of his own intelligence experts. See, Isikoff and Corn, *Hubris*, 179
1171. United States Senate. Select Committee On Intelligence.108th Congress. July 9, 2004. Report of the Senate Intelligence Committee on the U.S. Intelligence Community's

Prewar Intelligence Assessments on Iraq. S. Rept. 108-301. p. 14. *GPO*. Retrieved from https://www.gpo.gov/fdsys/search/pagedetails.action?granuleId=CRPT-108srpt301&packageId=CRPT-108srpt301

1172. I don't see how a person could reasonably conclude that Bush was deceived by the intelligence community. The NIE was clearly filled with false conclusions based on weak evidence and faulty analysis. Senator Bob Graham, who served as a Chair of the Senate Intelligence Committee in 2002, while discussing the NIE, said that "the intelligence community was being used as almost a public relations operation to validate the war against Saddam Hussein." John Brennan, Deputy Director of the CIA at the time said "I think there was a feeling within the agency that intelligence was increasingly becoming the meat in the sandwich on this one; that we were being asked to do things and to make sure that justification was out there." and "...there was concern that intelligence was being pushed forward as the justification for war." Former CIA analyst Melvin Goodman said [The NIE] "was so weak that if you go back now to all of the key judgments -- and I saw this estimate in a classified form as well as an unclassified form -- every key judgment was wrong." "...This was comparable to sort of judge shopping in the courthouse: If you want a certain verdict on a decision, you usually know which judge you can go to. ... George Tenet and John McLaughlin picked the very people in the National Intelligence Council ... who had a very hard line on all of these issues. So three or four key people were picked to write this estimate that was a fraud; I don't know how else to describe that National Intelligence Estimate. It should be fully released. I don't know why they're protecting sources and methods because the sources were obviously specious or flawed in one way or another. The methodology, obviously, was a disgrace. And it should be studied; it should be part of the national understanding of how we went to war." You can read the transcripts of the interviews of Brennan, Graham and Goodman, which contain the aforesaid quotes, and those of other knowledgeable experts by PBS. See, Frontline. The Dark Side Analysis: The October '02 National Intelligence Estimate: Excerpts from Frontline's Interviews with John Brennan, Vincent Cannistraro, Tyler Drumheller, Carl W. Ford Jr., Melvin Goodman, Senator Bob Graham, David Kay, Richard J Kerr, W Patrick Lang, John Mcgloughlin, Paul Pillar, and Lawrence Wilkerson. *PBS*. Retrieved from http://www.pbs.org/wgbh/pages/frontline/darkside/themes/nie.html; Pulitzer prize winning journalist and author Ron Suskind claims that President George W. Bush ordered the CIA to fabricate evidence of a connection between Iraq and al Qaeda. The claim is found in in his book, *The Way of the World: A Story of Truth and Hope in an Age of Extremism* (New York: Simon and Schuster, 2008). The CIA and the witnesses that Suskind reportedly quotes in his book have denied Suskind's charge. However, questions remain. I myself wonder where the phony Niger documents came from if not from the people who pushed the Iraq war on America. Suskind's book was discussed in a Wikipedia article, which described the allegations by Suskind and the denials at the time of this writing. See, The Way of the World (book). *Wikipedia The Free Encyclopedia.* (Wikipedia Foundation Inc.) Retrieved on January 5, 2015 from https://en.wikipedia.org/wiki/The_Way_of_the_World_(book); The text of

Chapter 14 discusses the positions of some leading intelligence and weapons experts within the Bush administration who were at odds with conclusions presented in the October 2002, NIE. Their arguments were highly persuasive, and yet Bush and Cheney and their White House staff, plus Tenet at the CIA, rejected their counsel. How can Bush and Cheney plausibly claim to have been so ignorant? In the interview excerpt cited previously in this note, John Brennan, Deputy Director of the CIA at the time, said this: "It was a document that contained, in my judgment, more grist for debate than people understand. If you added up the number of pages in it that contained alternative views or dissenting opinions, it would probably come to at least 10, some say 15, depending on who you count as a dissenter. While it was clear in its conclusions about Saddam possessing chemical and biological weapons, there were dissents clearly expressed on the nuclear program. The State Department dissented in a major way, and the Department of Energy, it is not often realized, had three full pages of dissents on the role of aluminum tubes, expressing the skepticism that they were intended for centrifuge and therefore for uranium enrichment. There were dissents also on things like the potential for unmanned aerial vehicles [UAVs] to be used for disseminating biological weapons. The Air Force expressed that dissent and dissents on other issues. So there was a lot of grist in that NIE for a serious debate."

1173. See, Iraq and the Media: A Critical Timeline. March 19, 2007. *Fair*. Retrieved from http://fair.org/take-action/media-advisories/iraq-and-the-media/; Moyers, Bill. Mod. Karen Hughs. Prod. and Dir. Allison Amron. Ed. April 24, 2007. (first broadcast on PBS) Buying The War: How did The Mainstream Press Get It So Wrong? Online PBS web site with link to the film transcript. The video link is disabled. *Bill Moyers Journal*. Retrieved from http://www.pbs.org/moyers/journal/btw/watch.html. A link to the video was online by cinvox as of May 28, 2014. Retrieved from https://www.youtube.com/watch?v=0KzYL6e3sV0; Mitchell, Greg. *So Wrong for So Long, How the Press, The Pundits - And The President - Failed On Iraq*. (New York: Sterling Publishing, 2008); My personal view of the matter is that it was overwhelming obvious *to me* at the time, from day one, that Bush and Cheney were lying whenever they attempted to connect al Qaeda with 911, and whenever they claimed Iraq had a WMD program that was a credible threat to America. The media was *in my opinion, all along, for the most part,* helping the administration lie to the American people. Our nation will continue to decline and it may not even survive if we continue under the rule of the Demopublicans. We must build a new political party as quickly as possible.

1174. United States Senate. Select Committee On Intelligence.108th Congress. July 9, 2004. Report of the Senate Intelligence Committee on the U.S. Intelligence Community's Prewar Intelligence Assessments on Iraq. S. Rept. 108-301. p. 14. *GPO*. Retrieved from https://www.gpo.gov/fdsys/search/pagedetails.action?granuleId=CRPT-108srpt301&packageId=CRPT-108srpt301

1175. United States Senate. Select Committee On Intelligence.109th Congress. September 8, 2006. Report of the Senate Intelligence Committee on Postwar Findings About Iraq's WMD Programs And Links To Terrorism And How They Compare With Prewar

Assessments. S. Rept. 109-331. p. 28. *GPO*. Retrieved from http://www.gpo.gov/fdsys/pkg/CRPT-109srpt331/pdf/CRPT-109srpt331.pdf

1176. Ibid., 30-32

1177. Allen, Paddy., Blason, Jo., Pidd, Helen and Chulov, Martin. February 15, 2011. Life and times of Rafid Ahmed Alwan al-Janabi, AKA Curveball. The Guardian. Retrieved from http://www.theguardian.com/world/interactive/2011/feb/15/curveball-cia-iraq-interactive-timeline

1178. Drogan, Bob. *Curveball: Spies, Lies, And The Con Man Who Caused A War* (New York: Random House, 2007) 3

1179. Drogan, Bob and Goetz, John. November 20, 2005. How U.S. Fell Under the Spell of 'Curveball.' *The Los Angeles Times*. Retrieved from http://www.latimes.com/world/middleeast/la-na-curveball20nov20-story.html#axzz2zMtXfKO9

1180. Ibid.

1181. Isikoff and Corn, *Hubris*, 49-56, 109-111 See additionally, Ahmed Chalabi. *Wikipedia The Free Encyclopedia.* (Wikipedia Foundation Inc.) Retrieved from https://en.wikipedia.org/wiki/Ahmed_Chalabi; See generally, Roston, Aram. *The Man Who Pushed America To War: The Extraordinary Life, Adventures and Obsessions of Ahmed Chalabi*. (New York: Nation Books, 2008); Gelb, Leslie H., April 27, 2008. Neoconner. *The New York Times*. Retrieved from http://www.nytimes.com/2008/04/27/books/review/Gelb-t.html?_r=0; Mayer, Jane. June 7, 2004. The Manipulator: Ahmad Chalabi pushed a tainted case for war. Can he survive the occupation? *The New Yorker*. Retrieved from http://www.newyorker.com/magazine/2004/06/07/the-manipulator; Context of 'May 1991: President Bush Authorizes CIA to Create Conditions for Removal of Saddam Hussein; CIA Hires PR Firm.' *History Commons*. Retrieved from http://www.historycommons.org/context.jsp?item=complete_timeline_of_the_2003_invasion_of_iraq_3217#complete_timeline_of_the_2003_invasion_of_iraq_3217

1182. Bob Drogan writes in both his book and the article he wrote with John Goetz that the CIA suspected Curveball was working for Chalabi and INC, but no proof was ever found. Curveball's phony evidence was nevertheless used as center stage material in the now debunked NIE that formed the basis Colin Powell's UN speech. See, Drogan and Goetz, op. cit.; Drogan, *Curveball: Spies, Lies, And The Con Man Who Caused A War,* 232

1183. Drogan and Goetz report that Curveball's personnel file was found by a CIA unit in an Iraqi government storeroom. The file indicated that Curveball graduated last in his class, not first as he had told the BND. See, Drogan, Bob and Goetz, John. November 20, 2005. How U.S. Fell Under the Spell of 'Curveball.' *The Los Angeles Times*. Retrieved from http://www.latimes.com/world/middleeast/la-na-curveball20nov20-story.html#axzz2zMtXfKO9 An article in the Guardian states that on his second effort, Curveball placed 33rd out of 45 classmates on test modules that were required either for his degree or to work as a chemical engineer in Iraq. See, Allen, Paddy., Blason, Jo., Pidd, Helen and Chulov, Martin. February 15, 2011. Life and times of Rafid Ahmed Alwan al-Janabi, AKA Curveball. The Guardian. Retrieved from http://www.theguardian.com/world/interactive/2011/feb/15/curveball-cia-iraq-interactive-timeline

1184. Drogan, *Curveball: Spies, Lies, And The Con Man Who Caused A War,* 50-59
1185. Ibid., 12-13, 21, 95-97
1186. Drogan and Goetz, op. cit.
1187. Drogan, *Curveball: Spies, Lies, And The Con Man Who Caused A War,* 12-13, 21, 95-97
1188. Ibid, 34
1189. Ibid., 34-35
1190. Ibid., 35
1191. Ibid., 28-31
1192. Ibid., 36
1193. Gibson, Martin. March 20, 2013. The Spies Who Fooled the World – BBC. *War and Security*. Retrieved from http://warandsecurity.com/tag/rafid-ahmed-alwan-al-janabi/; Prados, John. ed. November 5, 2007. National Security Archive Electronic Briefing Book No. 234: The Record On Curveball. *The National Security Archive at George Washington University*. Retrieved from http://nsarchive.gwu.edu/NSAEBB/NSAEBB234 /index.htm; Harding, Luke. April 1, 2004. Germans Accuse US Over Iraq Weapons Claim. The Guardian. Retrieved from http://www.theguardian.com/world/2004/apr/02/ iraq.germany; Drogan. 98-99, 113-114, 131; Pidd, Helen. February 17, 2011. Curveball Doubts Were Shared With CIA, Says Ex-German Foreign Minister: Joschka Fischer accuses former CIA chief George Tenet over his knowledge of Iraqi defector's sketchy background. *The Guardian*. Retrieved from http://www.theguardian.com/world/2011/feb/ 17/curveball-doubts-cia-german-foreign
1194. Drogan, 11-12, 23-24
1195. Ibid., 10-11
1196. Ibid., 12
1197. Drogan; 180-181; See note 1193
1198. Drogan, 131
1199. Ibid.
1200. Drogan, 55-73, 131
1201. Curveball was described as having provided "98 percent of the assessment as to whether or not the Iraqis had a biological weapon," by Senator Pat Roberts, who chaired the Senate Intelligence Committee in 2004. See, Starr, Barbara. July 11, 2004. Pentagon's Prewar Intelligence Role Questioned: Roberts Criticizes Reliance On Single, 'troubled' Source. *CNN Politics*. Retrieved from http://www.cnn.com/2004/ALLPOLITICS/07/11/ senate.pentagon/; Ensor, David. July 9, 2004. Report Slams CIA For Iraq Intelligence Failures Analysts' 'group think' Blamed For False Assumptions On Weapons. *CNN Politics*. Retrieved from http://www.cnn.com/2004/ALLPOLITICS/07/09/senate.intellige nce/index.html; Tyler Drumheller, then Chief of the European division for clandestine operations in the CIA's Directorate of Operations, reportedly stated in an interview that he had personally looked for errors in a classified draft of Powell's UN speech and had crossed out the portion of Powell's speech which was about mobile bioweapon labs because it was based on Curveball's reports. Drumheller knew that Curveball was suspected of being "mentally unstable and a liar." Drumheller was

"completely surprised" when he watched Colin Powell use Curveball's discredited claims in his UN speech anyway. See, Warrick, Joby. June 25, 2006. Warnings on WMD 'Fabricator' Were Ignored, Ex-CIA Aide Says. *The Washington Post*. Retrieved from http://www.washingtonpost.com/wp-dyn/content/article/2006/06/24/AR200606240108 1.html; Drumheller confirms in his book *On The Brink* that he and his assistant Ava did review a draft of Powell's speech and highlight the parts based on Curveball's reports for removal for Powell's speech. Drumheller states as well that he warned higher ups repeatedly about Curveball's credibility. Drumheller also charged in his book that the intelligence gathering and reporting process was "politicized" during the Bush administrations "rush to war." See, Drumheller, Tyler, and Monaghan, Elaine. *On The Brink: An Insider's Account Of How The White House Compromised America's Intelligence*. (New York: Carroll & Graf, 1st. ed., 2006) 78-82, 83-87, 89-98, 99-103

1202. See for eg., BBC News. July 9, 2003. White House 'warned over Iraq claim.' BBC. Retrieved from http://news.bbc.co.uk/2/hi/americas/3056626.stm; Colter, Seth. June 13, 2008. Senate Report: Bush Used Iraq Intel He Knew Was False. *Huff Post Politics*. Retrieved from http://www.huffingtonpost.com/2008/06/05/divided-senate-committee_n_105374.html; Wilson, Valerie Plame. and Wilson, Joe. February 27, 2013. How The Bush Administration Sold The War – And We Bought It. *The Guardian*. Retrieved from http://www.theguardian.com/commentisfree/2013/feb/27/bush-administration-sold-iraq-war; DeYoung, Karen. April 28, 2007. Tenet Details Efforts to Justify Invading Iraq. *The Washington Post*. Retrieved from http://www.washingtonpost.com/wp-dyn/content/article/2007/04/27/AR2007042700550.html?nav=most_emailed; Anonymous Contributors. February 20, 2013. Newly-Released Memo by Donald Rumsfeld Proves Iraq War Started On False Pretenses. *Washington's Blog*. Retrieved from http://www.washingtonsblog.com/2013/02/newly-released-memos-of-donald-rumsfeld-prove-knowing-iraq-war.html; Begala, Paul. July 18, 2014. Does Dick Cheney believe his lies? CNN. Retrieved from http://www.cnn.com/2014/07/17/opinion/begala-dick-cheney-lies/index.html; Matthews, Dylan. July 19, 2014. 17 Reasons Not To Trust Dick Cheney On Iraq. *Vox*. Retrieved from http://www.vox.com/2014/6/19/5822482/17-reasons-not-to-trust-dick-cheney-on-iraq; Specifically on the subject of phony claims by Iraqi "defectors," See, Isikoff and Corn, *Hubris*, 14, 52-53, 182, 209; Drumheller and Monaghan, op. cit. 78-87, 89-98, 99-103; Only one of the three defector's mentioned by Colin Powell in his UN speech who alleged facts about biological WMD in Iraq similar to the false claims made by Curveball has been identified publicly. That defector, whose name is Mohammad al-Harith, is a former Iraqi major who defected in 2001. He was planted by the Iraqi National Congress and guided into the intelligence community by former CIA Director James Woolsey. Major al-Harith was determined to be a fabricator by the Defense Intelligence Agency one year before Powell presented his UN address. See, Isikoff and Corn, *Hubris*, 182

1203. Drogan, Bob and Goetz, John. November 20, 2005. How U.S. Fell Under the Spell of 'Curveball.' *The Los Angeles Times*. Retrieved from http://www.latimes.com/world/middleeast/la-na-curveball20nov20

1204. Isikoff and Corn, *Hubris*, 131

1205. Ibid., The BND had denied American intelligence agency requests to question Curveball, telling the Americans that Curveball hated Americans and that he did not even speak English. When American intelligence learned that Curveball did speak English it should have tipped them off that the BND had something to hide.
1206. Ibid.
1207. Ibid., 131-132
1208. For what the CIA Director of Operations James Pavitt learned about Curveball by September, 2002, see, Isikoff and Corn, *Hubris*, 130-132; See additionally, Drogan, Bob and Miller, Greg. April 2, 2005. 'Curveball' Debacle Reignites CIA Feud. Los Angeles Times. Retrieved from http://articles.latimes.com/2005/apr/02/nation/na-intel2
1209. Full text of Vice President Dick Cheney's speech delivered to the Veterans of Foreign Wars (VFW) national convention in Nashville, Tennessee on August 26, 2002. Online on August 27, 2002 by *The Guardian*. Retrieved from http://www.theguardian.com/world /2002/aug/27/usa.iraq
1210. Isikoff and Corn, *Hubris*, 131-132
1211. Ibid., 130, 167-168, Drogan, *Curveball: Spies, Lies, And The Con Man Who Caused A War,* 64-65
1212. Isikoff and Corn, *Hubris*, 4-5, 15, 18, 91, 135-140, 163-168, 170; Drogan, 106-107, 117-118, 127, 129-146; Unger, Craig. *The Fall Of The House Of Bush: The Untold Story Of How A Band Of True Believers Seized The Executive Branch, Started The Iraq War, And Still Imperils America's Future.* (New York: Scribner, 2007) (Kindle version for iPad) p. 296, note I
1213. Eisner, Peter and Knut Royce. *The Italian Letter: How the Bush Administration Used a Fake Letter to Build the Case for War in Iraq.* (New York: Rodale, 2007) 118-119; Melvin A. Goodman, an adjunct professor at Johns Hopkins University and a former division chief at the CIA has written extensively about the politicization of intelligence gathering and analysis at the CIA. See for eg., Goodman, Melvin. March 17, 2008. The CIA and the Perils of Politicization. *Center for International Policy*. Retrieved from http: //www.ciponline.org/research/entry/cia-perils-politicization
1214. Drogan, *Curveball: Spies, Lies, And The Con Man Who Caused A War,* 107-111
1215. Ibid., 112-113
1216. Ibid., 114
1217. Isikoff and Corn, *Hubris* 132
1218. Drogan, *Curveball: Spies, Lies, And The Con Man Who Caused A War,* 117
1219. Ibid., 110, 129-132; Isikoff and Corn, *Hubris*, 132
1220. Isikoff and Corn, *Hubris*, 132
1221. United States Senate. Select Committee On Intelligence.109th Congress. September 8, 2006. Report of the Senate Intelligence Committee on Postwar Findings About Iraq's WMD Programs And Links To Terrorism And How They Compare With Prewar Assessments. S. Rept. 109-331. p. 28. *GPO*. Retrieved from http://www.gpo.gov/fdsys /pkg/CRPT-109srpt331/pdf/CRPT-109srpt331.pdf
1222. United States Senate. Select Committee On Intelligence.108th Congress. July 9, 2004.

Report of the Senate Intelligence Committee on the U.S. Intelligence Community's Prewar Intelligence Assessments on Iraq. S. Rept. 108-301. p. 505. *GPO*. Retrieved from https://www.gpo.gov/fdsys/search/pagedetails.action?granuleId=CRPT-108srpt301&packageId=CRPT-108srpt301

1223. Isikoff and Corn, *Hubris*, 137

1224. Ibid., 137-138. Iraq: Kamiya, Gary. April 10, 2007. Why the media failed. *Salon*. Retrieved from http://www.salon.com/2007/04/10/media_failure/

1225. Isikoff and Corn, *Hubris*, 82; The minutes of the July 23, 2002 meeting are part of a collection of records known as the "Downing Street Memos." The original memo was printed in the Sunday Times on May 1, 2005. A copy of the memo can be found here: Text of the original Downing Street "Memo." *The Downing Street Memos*. Retrieved from http://downingstreetmemo.com/memos.html

1226. Ibid.

1227. Ibid.

1228. United States Senate. Select Committee On Intelligence.109th Congress. September 8, 2006. Report of the Select Committee On Intelligence on Postwar Findings About Iraq's WMD Programs And Links To Terrorism And How They Compare With Prewar Assessments. p. 40. Retrieved from http://www.gpo.gov/fdsys/pkg/CRPT-109srpt331/pdf/CRPT-109srpt331.pdf; (citing) United States Senate. Select Committee On Intelligence.108th Congress. July 9, 2004. Report of the Senate Intelligence Committee on the U.S. Intelligence Community's Prewar Intelligence Assessments on Iraq. S. Rept. 108-301. p. 211, 214

1229. United States Senate. Select Committee On Intelligence.109th Congress. September 8, 2006. Report of the Select Committee On Intelligence on Postwar Findings About Iraq's WMD Programs And Links To Terrorism And How They Compare With Prewar Assessments. p. 40-41 Retrieved from http://www.gpo.gov/fdsys/pkg/CRPT-109srpt331/pdf/CRPT-109srpt331.pdf; (citing) United States Senate. Select Committee On Intelligence.108th Congress. July 9, 2004. Report of the Senate Intelligence Committee on the U.S. Intelligence Community's Prewar Intelligence Assessments on Iraq. S. Rept. 108-301. p. 212, 213

1230. Drogan, *Curveball: Spies, Lies, And The Con Man Who Caused A War,* 127 (citing) Report To The President. March 31, 2005. Intelligence Capabilities of the United States Regarding Weapons of Mass Destruction. p. 173 (Co-Chaired by Laurence H. Silberman and Charles S. Robb) *CyberCemetary*. Retrieved from http://govinfo.library.unt.edu/wmd/report/wmd_report.pdf

1231. Ibid.

1232. See generally, Diamond, John. February 4, 2004. A desert mirage: How U.S. misjudged Iraq's arsenal. *USA Today*.

1233. Full text of Vice President Dick Cheney's speech delivered to the Veterans of Foreign Wars (VFW) national convention in Nashville, Tennessee on August 26, 2002. Online on August 27, 2002 by *The Guardian*. Retrieved from http://www.theguardian.com/world/2002/aug/27/usa.iraq

1234. President Bush's Address to the United Nations. September 12, 2002. Transcript posted online. *CNN*. Retrieved from http://edition.cnn.com/2002/US/09/12/bush.transcript/
1235. Secretary of Defense Donald H. Rumsfeld. Testimony to the House Armed Services Committee regarding Iraq given at the Rayburn House Office Building, Washington, D.C., September 18, 2002. Transcript online by the Political Science Department of *UCLA*. Retrieved from http://www.sscnet.ucla.edu/polisci/faculty/trachtenberg/useur/rumsfeld180902.html
1236. Bush, George W., Address to the Nation on Iraq made from the Grand Rotunda at the Cincinnati Museum Center at Union Terminal. October 7, 2002. Transcript online by Gerhard Peters and John T. Woolley, *The American Presidency Project*. Retrieved from http://www.presidency.ucsb.edu/ws/?pid=73139.
1237. Bush, George W., Address to the Nation on Iraq made from the Grand Rotunda at the Cincinnati Museum Center at Union Terminal. October 7, 2002. Transcript online by Gerhard Peters and John T. Woolley, *The American Presidency Project*. Retrieved from http://www.presidency.ucsb.edu/ws/?pid=73139.
1238. Bush, George W., January 28, 2003. Address Before a Joint Session of the Congress on the State of the Union, Online by Gerhard Peters and John T. Woolley, *The American Presidency Project*. http://www.presidency.ucsb.edu/ws/?pid=29645.
1239. With regard to the phony Niger documents, see notes 1066-1070 and the appurtenant text. The story of how the CIA cooked their analysis of the aluminum tubes to help Bush and Cheney is discussed by Drogan and at greater length by Isikoff and Corn. See, Isikoff and Corn, *Hubris*, 34-42, 60-62, 118-119, 163-165, 306-307; Drogan, *Curveball: Spies, Lies, And The Con Man Who Caused A War,* 107, 153-154, 264; See additionally, Bush Administration Claims vs. The Facts: The Aluminum Tubes Were Not Suitable For Nuclear Weapons Development. (report and time line of relevant facts) Online by Modulus Studios in conjunction with the 2008 film and related website *Leading to War*. (Dir. Barry J. Hershey, Prod. Lewis D. Wheeler, Ellie Lee, Beth Sternheimer) Retrieved from http://www.leadingtowar.com/claims_facts_aluminum.php; Albright, David. December 5, 2003. Iraq's Aluminum Tubes: Separating Fact from Fiction. ISIS Institute For Science and International Security. Retrieved from http://www.isis-online.org/publications/iraq/IraqAluminumTubes12-5-03.pdf
1240. Albright, Iraq's Aluminum Tubes: Separating Fact from Fiction, op. cit
1241. Ibid.
1242. Ibid; Isikoff and Corn, *Hubris*, 39
1243. Isikoff and Corn, *Hubris*, 40, 46
1244. Ibid., 37-38; Albright, Iraq's Aluminum Tubes: Separating Fact from Fiction, op. cit; Uranium-235 *Wikipedia The Free Encyclopedia.* (Wikipedia Foundation Inc.) Retrieved from https://en.wikipedia.org/wiki/Uranium-235
1245. Isikoff and Corn, *Hubris*, 38
1246. The idea that Joe Turner is probably responsible for the caveat "using aluminum tubes in a centrifuge effort..." was gleaned from the following sources: Report of the Senate

Intelligence Committee on the U.S. Intelligence Community's Prewar Intelligence Assessments on Iraq. S. Rept. 108-301. p. 88. (see note 1173); Barstow, David., Broad William J., and Gerth, Jeff. October 3, 2004. How the White House Embraced Disputed Arms Intelligence. *The New York Times*; Gellman, Barton and Pincus, Walter. August 10, 2003. Depiction of Threat Outgrew Supporting Evidence. *The Washington Post*. Retrieved from http://www.washingtonpost.com/wp-dyn/content/article/2006/06/12/AR2006061200932.html; Isikoff and Corn, *Hubris*, 34-42, 60-62, 118-119, 163-165, 306-307; In the aforesaid newspaper articles, Joe Turner was identified only as "Joe T." The government reportedly wanted to keep his last name classified because he remained a CIA operative. However, in *Hubris* and other books, the last name of Turner is given.
I was unable to determine how Turner's last name became public knowledge.
It's quite a coincidence that the character Robert Redford played in the hit spy movie *Three Days of the Condor* was also a CIA operative named Joe Turner. The existence of a fictional CIA agent named Joe Turner casts some doubt on the authenticity of the name given to the nonfictional one.

1247. Isikoff and Corn, *Hubris*, 38-39

1248. In the fall of 2001, the office of the President's national security adviser, Condoleezza Rice, was advised that the Department of Energy's most accomplished nuclear weapons experts were of the opinion that the aluminum tubes were not purchased by Iraq for use in uranium enrichment. The war did not begin until March 20, 2003. CIA Director George Tenet later stated that the alternative view held by the DOE scientists was shared by the CIA with the administration after a revised National Intelligence Estimate was prepared in late September 2002. See, Barstow, David., Broad William J., and Gerth, Jeff. October 3, 2004. How the White House Embraced Disputed Arms Intelligence. *The New York Times*; On September 19, 2002, United Press International reported that David Albright, President of the Institute for Science and International Security, and a former UN weapons inspector in Iraq, said that nuclear weapons experts at the Department of Energy who disagreed with what the administration was telling the public about the tubes felt too intimidated to speak out. See, Otterman, Sharon. September 19, 2002. Experts question key Iraq nuke evidence. *UPI*. Retrieved from http://www.upi.com/Top_News/2002/09/19/Experts-question-key-Iraq-nuke-evidence/59401032479700/; See also, Albright, David. December 5, 2003. Iraq's Aluminum Tubes: Separating Fact from Fiction. *Institute For Science and International Security*. Retrieved from http://www.isis-online.org/publications/iraq/IraqAluminumTubes12-5-03.pdf; See additionally, Maloy, Simon. February 10, 2015. Yes, Bush lied about Iraq: Why are we still arguing about this? Sorry, WSJ: Reminding everyone that George W. Bush lied about Iraq is good and necessary -- because man, did he lie. *Salon*. Retrieved from http://www.salon.com/2015/02/10/yes_bush_lied_about_iraq_why_are_we_still_arguing_about_this/

1249. See, Barstow, Broad , and Gerth, How the White House Embraced Disputed Arms Intelligence op. cit.; See additionally, Isikoff and Corn, *Hubris*, 39

1250. Ibid.

1251. Barstow, Broad , and Gerth, How the White House Embraced Disputed Arms

Intelligence, op. cit; Albright, Iraq's Aluminum Tubes: Separating Fact from Fiction, op. cit.

1252. See, Isikoff and Corn, *Hubris*, 39; Accord, Barstow, Broad, and Gerth, op. cit.

1253. See, Isikoff and Corn, *Hubris*, 40-41

1254. About the Bureau of Intelligence and Research. *U.S. Department of State*. Retrieved from http://www.state.gov/s/inr/

1255. See, Isikoff and Corn, *Hubris*, 40

1256. Ibid.

1257. Ibid.

1258. Ibid.

1259. Trotta, Daniel. March 14, 2013. Iraq war costs U.S. more than $2 trillion: study. *Reuters*. Retrieved from http://www.reuters.com/article/us-iraq-war-anniversary-idUSBRE92D0PG20130314; The aforesaid figures do not include any of the expenses incurred by our efforts to destroy the Islamic State.

1260. Baker, Luke. Jan 30, 2008. Iraq conflict has killed a million Iraqis: survey. Reuters. http://www.reuters.com/article/us-iraq-deaths-survey-idUSL3048857920080130; See additionally, Tirman John. Pub. Contrib. *Iraq: the Human Cost*. A website hosted by *MIT*. Retrieved from http://web.mit.edu/humancostiraq/contact.html

1261. In 2008, President George W. Bush signed the U.S.- Iraq Status of Forces Agreement. President Obama honored the agreement, which set a deadline of December 31, 2011 for the withdrawal of all US soldiers from Iraq. On December 18, 2011, the last American forces officially left Iraq. See, Jaffe, Greg. December 18, 2011. Last US troops cross Iraqi border into Kuwait. *Washington Post*. Retrieved from https://www.washingtonpost.com/; Allison Tom, June 17, 2010. Memo To Media: Bush Set A Timetable For Withdrawal From Iraq. *Media Matters for America*. Retrieved from http://mediamatters.org/; As of December 31, 2011, the official withdrawal date agreed to by President Bush, 4,485 American soldiers had been killed in the war. See, Iraq Coalition Military Fatalities By Year. *iCasualties - Iraq*. Retrieved from http://icasualties.org/; As of April, 2015, 3,481 U.S. civilians working in Iraq have also died. See, Chart. Allied Combatants Killed In Iraq. March 2003 - April, 2015. *Costs of War*. A website hosted by the *Watson Institute of International and Public Affairs* at *Brown University*. Retrieved from http://watson.brown.edu/costsofwar/costs/human/military; There are also over 130,000 U.S. service men and women, and veterans since 2001 who have been diagnosed (most cases are never diagnosed), with post traumatic stress disorder. An additional 253,300 of our soldiers sustained traumatic brain injuries between the 2000 and 2012. See, Ackerman, Spencer. February 8, 2013. The Cost of War Includes at Least 253,330 Brain Injuries and 1,700 Amputations. *Wired*. Retrieved from http://www.wired.com/2013/02/cost-of-war/

Chapter 15. Why The Ameritorians Are Needed Now More Than Ever.

1262. The quote from Luban was found at a website for the book On Torture, Hilde, John C. Ed. (Baltimore: Johns Hopkins University Press, 2008), *Johns Hopkins University Press*.

Retrieved from https://jhupbooks.press.jhu.edu/content/torture

1263. Armbruster, Ben. March 7, 2016. Experts Blast Trump, Cruz On Legalizing Torture: It Would 'Humiliate' America. *BNR Blue Nation Review*. Retrieved from http://bluenation review.com/legalizing-torture-would-humiliate-the-u-s/

1264. See generally, Bellware, Kim. October 6, 2014. This Cop Oversaw The Torture Of More Than 100 Black Men. Now He's Out After Less Than 4 Years In Jail. *HuffPost Crime*. Retrieved from http://www.huffingtonpost.com/2014/10/02/jon-burge-released_n_5923 784.html; Schweitzer, Jeff. May 4, 2015. A Troubling Response to Brutality. *HuffPost Politics*. Retrieved from http://www.huffingtonpost.com/jeff-schweitzer/a-troubling-resp onse-to-b_b_7204398.html; Coakley, Michael. April 28, 1985. New York Shaken By Charges Of Stun-Gun Torture By Police. *Chicago Tribune*. Retrieved from http://articles .chicagotribune.com/1985-04-28/news/8501250716_1_106th-precinct-police-officers-stun-gun; Ackerman, Spencer. February 18, 2015. Bad lieutenant: American police brutality, exported from Chicago to Guantánamo. *The Guardian*. Retrieved from http://w ww.theguardian.com/; Torture and the United States. *Wikipedia The Free Encyclopedia.* (Wikipedia Foundation Inc.) Retrieved from https://en.wikipedia.org/wiki/Torture_and_ the_United_States; Associated Press. February 5, 2016. Police Officials Slam Proposal to Rein in Cops' Use of Force. *CBS News*. Retrieved from http://www.cbsnews.com/news/ police-officials-slam-proposal-to-rein-in-cops-use-of-force/

1265. Chicago Tribune Editorial Board. January 4, 2016. The Spreading Conspiracy of Silence. *Chicago Tribune*. Retrieved from http://www.chicagotribune.com/

1266. Democracy Now News Hour. Goodman, Amy. Host. February 8, 2016. "Trump Calls Police "Absolutely Mistreated"; Kasich Backs Collaboration Between Communities & Cops." (includes video segment of February 6, 2016 presidential debate, with accompanying rush transcript and news article). *Democracy Now* . Retrieved from http:// www.democracynow.org/2016/2/8/trump_calls_police_absolutely_mistreated_kasich

1267. See for eg., Chicago Tribune Editorial Board. January 4, 2016. The Spreading Conspiracy of Silence. op. cit.

1268. See, Pozen, Robert. March 8, 2016. Donald Trump's Tax Plan Could Tack $10 Trillion onto America's Debt. *Fortune*. Retrieved fromhttp://fortune.com/2016/03/08/donald-trumps-tax-plan-primary/; See additionally, Gleckman Howard. December 22, 2015. Trump Would Slash Taxes for the Top 0.1 Percent By An Average of $1.3 Million, Add Nearly $10 Trillion to the Debt. *Tax Policy Center Taxvox*. Retrieved from http://taxvox. taxpolicycenter.org/2015/12/22/trump-would-slash-taxes-for-the-top-0-1-percent-by-an-average-of-1-3-million-add-nearly-10-trillion-to-the-debt/

1269. An excellent discussion of how big pharma and government dropped the ball on antibiotic development can be found here: Childress, Sarah. October 22, 2013. Dr. Brad Spellberg: Antibiotic Resistance Is Everyone's Fault. *PBS*. Retrieved from http://www. pbs.org/wgbh/frontline/article/dr-brad-spellberg-antibiotic-resistance-is-everyones-fault/; See generally, Walsh, Fergus. December 11, 2016. Superbugs to kill 'more than cancer' by 2050. *BBC News*. Retrieved from http://www.bbc.com/news/health-30416844; Stobbe, Mike., and Tanner, Lindsey. September 16, 2013. Updated November 16, 2013.

Drug-Resistant Bacteria Deaths Are Common, Report Finds. *Huffpost*. Retrieved from http://www.huffingtonpost.com/2013/09/16/drug-resistant-bacteria-deaths-_n_3936820.html

1270. Topaz, Jonathan., and Schreckinger, Ben., July 6, 2015. 2016 The Socialist Surge: The Rise of Bernie Sanders is Proving Awkward for the Democratic Party. *Politico*. Retrieved from http://www.politico.com/story/2015/07/bernie-sanders-socialist-surge-119785#ixzz3fKDyp0Me

1271. Merica, Dan., and Bradner, Eric. October 7, 2015. Hillary Clinton Comes Out Against TPP Trade Deal. *CNN politics*. Retrieved from http://www.cnn.com/2015/10/07/politics/hillary-clinton-opposes-tpp/index.html/

1272. Wright, Dan. March 9, 2016. Hillary Clinton Runs From Free Trade Record At Debate. *ShadowProof*. Retrieved from https://shadowproof.com/2016/03/07/hillary-clinton-runs-from-free-trade-record-at-debate

1273. Time Staff. March 6, 2016. Read the Full Text of the Seventh Democratic Debate in Flint. *Time*. Retrieved from http://time.com/4249183/democratic-debate-flint-full-text-transcript-seventh/

1274. Leopold, Les. March 8, 2016. Hillary's Cronyism Is Showing: A Closer Look At Her Economic Proposals Reveals A Neoliberal Agenda: Clinton Vows To Use Public Funds And Policy To Promote Private-Sector Gain. Wall Street Couldn't Be More Delighted. *Salon*. Retrieved from http://www.salon.com/2016/03/08/hillarys_cronyism_is_showing_a_closer_look_at_her_economic_proposals_reveals_her_neoliberal_agenda_partner/; Leopold, Les. March 6, 2016. Hillary's Economic Agenda Sure Looks Like Payback for Wall St Giving Her Huge Piles of Campaign Cash. *Alternet*. Retrieved from http://www.alternet.org/election-2016/hillarys-economic-agenda-sure-looks-payback-wall-st-giving-her-huge-piles-campaign

1275. Wright, Dan. March 9, 2016. Hillary Clinton Runs From Free Trade Record At Debate. *ShadowProof*. Retrieved from https://shadowproof.com/2016/03/07/hillary-clinton-runs-from-free-trade-record-at-debate

Made in the USA
Monee, IL
04 November 2026

67387308R00215